About the Author

Peter D. Hipson is a developer, consultant, and author. His work is mostly in the Microsoft Windows arena, both at the programming and user levels. Peter is a member of the Microsoft beta-test team for QuickC for Windows; Visual C++ 1.0, 1.5, 2.0, and 4.0; Windows 3.0 and 3.1; Windows for Workgroups 3.1 and 3.11; Windows 95; and Windows NT 3.5, 3.51, and 4.0 Workgroup and Server.

Peter is the author of *Advanced C, What Every Visual C++ 2 Programmer Should Know, Database Developer's Guide With Visual C++, Visual C++ Developer's Guide*, and *Using QuickC for Windows*. He has also contributed to *Programming Windows 95 Unleashed*, and other titles as an uncredited contract author. His latest book, *Database Developer's Guide With Visual C++ 4*, Second Edition, was published early in 1996.

Peter often speaks at conferences and user groups including Boston University's WinDev windows developer's conference held each year in Boston, Massachusetts and in Santa Clara, California. When not banging on the keyboard or doing other difficult work, Peter can usually be found on his road bicycle, or perhaps sailing his catamaran.

THE Windows NT 4 Server BOOK

The Definitive Resource for Building & Maintaining Your Network

THE Windows NT 4 Server BOOK

The Definitive Resource for Building & Maintaining Your Network

PETER HIPSON

VENTANA

The Windows NT 4 Server Book

Library of Congress Cataloging-in-Publication Data

Hipson, Peter.
The Windows NT 4 server book: the definitive resource for building & maintaining your network / Peter D. Hipson.
p. cm.
Includes index.
ISBN 1-56604-495-2
1. Microsoft Windows NT. 2. Client/server computing. 3. Internet (Computer network) I. Title.
QA76.76.063H573 1996
005.7'1369—dc20 96-27464
CIP

First Edition 9 8 7 6 5 4 3 2 1

Printed in the United States of America

Ventana Communications Group, Inc.
P.O. Box 13964
Research Triangle Park, NC 27709-3964
919.544.9404
FAX 919.544.9472
http://www.vmedia.com

Limits of Liability and Disclaimer of Warranty

The author and publisher of this book have used their best efforts in preparing the book and the programs contained in it. These efforts include the development, research, and testing of the theories and programs to determine their effectiveness. The author and publisher make no warranty of any kind, expressed or implied, with regard to these programs or the documentation contained in this book.

The author and publisher shall not be liable in the event of incidental or consequential damages in connection with, or arising out of, the furnishing, performance or use of the programs, associated instructions and/or claims of productivity gains.

Trademarks

Trademarked names appear throughout this book. Rather than list the names and entities that own the trademarks or insert a trademark symbol with each mention of the trademarked name, the publisher states that it is using the names only for editorial purposes and to the benefit of the trademark owner with no intention of infringing upon that trademark.

Chief Executive Officer
Josef Woodman

Vice President of Content Development
Karen A. Bluestein

Managing Editor
Lois J. Principe

Production Manager
John Cotterman

Technology Operations Manager
Kerry L. B. Foster

Product Marketing Manager
Jamie Jaeger Fiocco

Creative Services Manager
Diane Lennox

Art Director
Marcia Webb

Acquisitions Editor
Neweleen A. Trebnik

Developmental Editors
Michelle Corbin Nichols
Lisa A. Bucki

Project Editor
Jennifer R. Huntley

Copy Editor
Marie Dobson

Assistant Editor
Patrick Bragg

Technical Director
Dan Brown

Technical Reviewer
Russ Mullen

Desktop Publisher
Jaimie Livingston

Proofreader
Christopher Riffer

Indexer
Sherry Massey

Cover Designer
Laura Stalzer

Acknowledgments

This book is not just my product. Far from it! A fine team effort on the part of many individuals is what made this book possible.

First, thanks go to Ventana, which has one of the world's best editing and management teams. Neweleen Trebnik (who worked with me on my very first book, some years back) did wonderfully as our Acquisitions Editor. Jennifer Huntley, our Project Editor, kept me on track through a trying time while writing the book. Without Jennifer's understanding, I doubt I'd have been able to finish this book.

Michelle Nichols' work as Developmental Editor was invaluable in making this book a quality product. Never one to give up, Michelle would keep after me to make sure that everything was just right.

Marie Dobson served well as the Copy Editor. Marie's work made this book readable. Russ Mullen made sure the book was accurate. Not much escapes his sharp eyes!

A special thanks to Lisa Bucki, who worked very hard with Michelle Nichols on the development of this book. Lisa's work was greatly appreciated—more than she realizes.

Away from Ventana, many friends helped. Some of these people don't even realize their assistance. If nothing else, they are leaders in the field, and their assistance, no matter what the circumstances, is greatly appreciated!

Pedro P. Pokaloff III's assistance in the use of Windows NT 4 Server as an ISP made Appendix B, "Windows NT 4 Server as an ISP," a reality. Felix Kasza provided a lot of valuable general information and advice. Some day I hope to be able to better repay each and every one of these people for their help and encouragement.

Special thanks to Lisa Swayne, my agent. Without Lisa I would never have written this book.

Last and certainly not least, my thanks to Nang, my wife, for forgiving me for a four-month absence. Although I never left home, Nang certainly didn't see much of me for these past four months!

Thank you all!

Dedication

This book is dedicated to Marie Theplama, my newest—and also oldest—granddaughter!

Contents

Introduction .... **xxi**

Section I: Introduction to Windows NT 4

1 Introduction to Windows NT 4 Server **1**

The History of Windows NT 2

Why Windows NT 4 Server? 3

Windows NT 4 Server Unwrapped 6

Accessories & Optional Hardware ◆ Network Protocols Support ◆ Network Interface Card Support ◆ Inter-Process Calls ◆ Performance ◆ File Systems ◆ Directory Support ◆ Fault Tolerance & Redundancy ◆ Backup & Restore ◆ Security ◆ Security Auditing ◆ User Access ◆ Print Services ◆ Administration ◆ Companion Products

2 What's New in Windows NT 4 Server **23**

What's New 23

The Windows 95 User Interface ◆ Internet Explorer ◆ Microsoft Windows Messaging System ◆ Hardware Profiles ◆ Microsoft WordPad ◆ Microsoft Paint ◆ File Find & Search ◆ Enhanced Control Panel ◆ The Windows NT 4 Server Wizard ◆ DHCP Relay Agent ◆ Domain Name Service (DNS) ◆ DNS & WINS Integration ◆ DNS Support in UNC Names ◆ Microsoft Internet Information Server (IIS) ◆ Multi-Protocol Routing (MPR) ◆ Remote Administration ◆ Remote Booting of Windows 95 Clients ◆ User-Defined Internet Special Groups ◆ Changes in the Driver Structure ◆ Common Groups ◆ Dial-Up Networking and Remote Access Server ◆ Differences Between the Server & Workstation Products ◆ The Hardware Compatibility List

3 Installing Windows NT 4 Server 49

Getting Started 50

Installation Options 52

The Windows NT 4 Server Setup Program 54

A Clean Windows NT 4 Server Installation 57

Upgrading MS-DOS or Windows 95 ◆ Upgrading Windows NT 3.5x Server ◆ Upgrading Windows NT 4 Server Beta Versions

Creating Boot Diskettes 62

Getting Down to Business: Installing Windows NT 4 Server 62

Before You Begin... ◆ Beginning the Installation ◆ Additional System Administrator Installation Tasks ◆ Moving On to Networking

4 Windows NT 4 Server Components 107

Configuring the Server 109

Optimizing Memory & Performance ◆ LAN Manager 2.x Option

Configuring Workstation 110

Configuring Remote Boot Service 110

Automatic Configuration of Workstations ◆ Manual Configuration of Workstations ◆ Other Remote Boot Manager Functions ◆ The RPLCMD Utility

Configuring RPC 127

Configuring the NetBIOS Interface 129

5 Configuring TCP/IP Services 131

Configuring TCP/IP Services 133

Assigning IP Addresses ◆ Configuring TCP/IP

Configuring RIP for Internet Protocol 153

Configuring Simple TCP/IP Services 156

Configuring Microsoft DHCP Server 158

Working With IP Addresses ◆ Setting Options

Configuring DHCP Relay Agent 165

Configuring Microsoft DNS Server 167
The BOOT File ◆ The CACHE File ◆ The PLACE.DOM File ◆ The ARPA-192.REV File ◆ The Domain Name Service Manager

Configuring Windows Internet Name Service (WINS) 175
Setting WINS Options

6 Interacting With Other LANs 185

Configuring NetWare Services 187
Configuring Gateway Services ◆ Configuring RIP Services ◆ Configuring SAP Agent ◆ Configuring SNMP Service

Configuring Macintosh File Servers & Print Servers 197
Configuring Connections to Macintosh Clients

Configuring Services for Banyan 199

7 Configuring Dial-Up Networking 201

Configuring Dial-Up Networking (DUN) 202
Creating a DUN Configuration

Configuring Remote Access Service (RAS) 210
Configuring a RAS Port ◆ Configuring Network Protocols for the Port

Managing RAS/DUN 218
The RASDIAL Program ◆ The RASADMIN Program

8 Configuring Hardware 223

Hardware Tuning 223
RAM & CPU Upgrades ◆ System Buses ◆ Disk I/O ◆ High-Performance NICs ◆ Video Cards ◆ CD-ROM Drives ◆ Modems & ISDN Lines ◆ Hard Disks

Using the Disk Administrator 228
Working With Partitions ◆ Working With Fault Tolerance ◆ Using the Disk Administrator's Tools

File Formats 240
Benefits of NTFS ◆ Comparing NTFS to Other Formats ◆ Converting From FAT to NTFS ◆ Compressing Files Using Windows Explorer

9 Monitoring Windows NT 4 Server Performance...... 251

The Network Monitor 252

Installing the Network Monitor Agent and Tools ◆ Using the Network Monitor Program ◆ Configuring the Network Monitor Agent ◆ Monitoring Performance With the Network Monitor

The Performance Monitor 265

Starting Performance Monitor ◆ Viewing the Data ◆ Saving Chart Settings ◆ Counters and Objects ◆ Objects and Counters in Performance Monitor

The Windows NT Task Manager 294

Section II: Optional at Extra Cost

10 Microsoft BackOffice 301

Microsoft SNA Server 303

Installing SNA Server ◆ Using the Microsoft SNA Server Admin Program ◆ Other Microsoft SNA Server Program Items

Microsoft Systems Management Server 312

Installing Microsoft Systems Management Server ◆ Installing Microsoft Systems Management Server Clients ◆ Using the Microsoft Systems Management Server Administrator

11 Microsoft Exchange Server & Client 335

Installation Requirements 336

Installing Microsoft Exchange 337

Optimizing Performance 343

Components of the Microsoft Exchange Server & Client 347

Microsoft Exchange Server Books Online ◆ Microsoft Exchange Administrator ◆ Microsoft Exchange Migration Wizard ◆ Microsoft Exchange Optimizer ◆ Monitoring Microsoft Exchange Server ◆ Internet Mail Connector Monitoring ◆ Microsoft Exchange Setup Editor

12 **Microsoft SQL Server 6.5 .... 367**

Installing SQL Server 6.5 368
Starting the Setup ◆ Setup Options ◆ Setting the Licensing Mode ◆ The SQL Master Database ◆ Microsoft SQL Documentation—Books Online ◆ The Administrator's User ID

ISQL/w 374

Microsoft ODBC SQL Server Driver Help File 376

MS Query 376

The Readme File 379

SQL Client Configuration Utility 379
The DBLibrary Tab ◆ The Net Library Tab ◆ The Advanced Tab

SQL Distributed Management Objects Help 384

SQL Enterprise Manager 388
Database Devices ◆ Backup Devices ◆ Databases ◆ Logins

SQL Performance Monitor 395

SQL Security Manager 398

SQL Server Books Online 401

SQL Server Web Assistant 401

SQL Service Manager 408

SQL Setup 410

SQL Trace 410

Section III: Windows NT 4 and the Internet

13 **The Microsoft Internet Information Server 415**

Installing Microsoft IIS 417
Installing IIS From the Desktop ◆ Installing IIS From the Control Panel ◆ Installing IIS From the Windows NT 4 Server CD-ROM ◆ The IIS Setup Program ◆ Setting Up & Configuring IIS

The Microsoft Internet Information Server Manager 421

Configuring the FTP, Gopher & Web Servers 423
Setting Up the Services ◆ Setting Up FTP Messages ◆ Setting Up Directories ◆ Setting Up Logging ◆ Setting Up Access

Reliability 450

Performance 451

14 The Microsoft IIS Gopher & FTP Services 453

The IIS Gopher Service 453
Setting Up the Gopher Service

The IIS FTP Server 464
Setting Up an FTP Site

15 The Microsoft IIS WWW Server 467

The IIS WWW Server 468
Setting Up a Web Site ◆ IIS WWW Server Samples ◆ Sample IIS WWW Server Pages

Creating Initial WWW HTML Pages 475
Using Microsoft Internet Assistant ◆ Using Microsoft FrontPage

The Secure Sockets Layer (SSL) 479
Enabling SSL Security ◆ Obtaining an SSL Certificate ◆ Installing the SSL Certificate ◆ SETKEY Reference ◆ KEYGEN Reference

Reliability 489

Section IV: Advanced Windows NT 4

16 Sharing 495

Sharing Files 496
Using Explorer ◆ Using the Server Manager or, Who's Using the Share?

Sharing Printers 514
Adding Printers ◆ Specifying Printer Properties

Other Sharing 534

17 Security & Users 535

System Security 535
Network Security ◆ Internet and Intranets ◆ Securing RAS

Groups 547

Users 549
Defining Users ◆ Defining Profiles

Working With Users & Groups 556
Rights & Privileges ◆ Printing a List of Users ◆ Backing Up the User List ◆ Account Policy ◆ Audit Policy ◆ Trust Relationships

Physical Security 570
Server Locations ◆ Power Security—the UPS ◆ Environmental Security

18 Backing Up the System 577

Backup Strategies 578
Frequency & Aging of Backups ◆ Physical Security of Backups ◆ What Do I Back Up? ◆ Incremental Backups ◆ Complete Backups

Backup Hardware 584
Tape Technologies ◆ Optical Media ◆ Diskettes ◆ Hard Drive Backups

Windows NT Backup 588
Installing Hardware ◆ Backing Up ◆ Restoring Backups

A Final Note About Erasing Tapes 600

19 The Registry 603

The Windows NT 4 Server Registry 603
The Registry and .INI Files ◆ Files in the Registry ◆ Hives = Folders ◆ Changing the Registry ◆ Registry Data Types ◆ Major Keys in the Registry

BOOT.INI 624
Adding More Operating Systems ◆ Windows NT Boot Options ◆ Troubleshooting Hints & Tricks

Other Windows NT Customization 631

20 Accessories, Toys, Fun & Games 633

Accessories 633

Calculator ◆ Character Map ◆ Chat ◆ Clipboard Viewer ◆ Clock ◆ HyperTerminal ◆ Imaging ◆ Notepad ◆ Object Packager ◆ Paint ◆ Phone Dialer ◆ Telnet ◆ WordPad

System Tool: Inbox Repair Tool 647

Multimedia 648

CD Player ◆ Media Player ◆ Sound Recorder ◆ Volume Control

Games 652

FreeCell ◆ Minesweeper ◆ Pinball ◆ Solitaire

Section V: Appendices

Appendix A Windows NT 4 Server Resources....... 659

Appendix B Windows NT 4 Server as an ISP........ 669

Index 687

Introduction

Windows NT 4 Server is becoming the de facto standard for network servers. This popularity has been earned, in part, by the fact that Windows NT 4 Server is a solid, high-performance network operating system that many corporations find very cost effective.

Windows NT 4 Server is Microsoft's newest release of Windows NT Server. The inclusion of the Windows 95 user interface makes Windows NT 4 Server easy to use. The Explorer program (which replaces the File Manager and Program Manager found on earlier versions of Windows NT Server) makes Windows NT 4 Server fun.

New "wizards" take you, the user, through many of the more complex configuration tasks. Microsoft's wizards are more than just guideposts, however—they are automated programs capable of performing many of the preliminary tasks that you were required to do in the past. The addition of considerable Internet support in the form of the Internet Information Service (which provides Web, Gopher, and FTP servers), FrontPage, and support for using Windows NT 4 Server as an ISP all make Windows NT 4 Server and the Internet a winning combination.

What's Inside

This book shows you how easy it is to use Windows NT 4 Server. *The Windows NT 4 Server Book* has four parts. Part I, "Introduction to Windows NT 4," introduces you to Windows NT 4 Server. Use Part I of the book as a tutorial for installing the Windows NT 4 Server components you need. Part II, "Optional at Extra Cost," gets you acquainted with optional products you can purchase. Use Part II to familiarize yourself with the desktop and server products that Microsoft has on the market that you can use with Windows NT 4 Server. The applications in Microsoft BackOffice, such as Microsoft Exchange Server and Microsoft SQL Server, allow you to take advantage of Internet functionality more fully. Part III, "Windows NT 4 & the Internet," describes the Internet functionality built into Windows NT 4 Server including Web servers. Part IV, "Advanced Windows NT 4," provides you with instructions for using the advanced Windows NT 4 Server features including sharing, security, and the registry.

This book is further organized into the following chapters:

Chapter 1, "Introduction to Windows NT 4 Server," introduces Windows NT 4 Server. It describes some of the history and functionality of Windows NT 4 Server.

Chapter 2, "What's New in Windows NT 4 Server," describes what has changed in this new version of Windows NT Server. So much of the user interface is new that many users (who are not familiar with Windows 95) won't even recognize Windows NT 4 Server as Windows!

Chapter 3, "Installing Windows NT 4 Server," walks you through the installation process. Installation, while not difficult, is time consuming. Clean installations as well as upgrades over earlier versions of Windows NT Server are covered in this chapter.

Chapter 4, "Windows NT 4 Server Components," describes a number of components that are part of Windows NT 4 Server. Included with this chapter are configuring the server, configuring the workstation, and the remote boot service.

Chapter 5, "Configuring TCP/IP Services," covers TCP/IP, which is the protocol used with the Internet. TCP/IP is becoming more and more popular with smaller networks as well. Some of the items covered in this chapter include WINS, DNS, DHCP, and routing.

Chapter 6, "Interacting With Other LANs," covers gateway and client services for NetWare, and services for Macintosh. RPC support for Banyan, and SAP agents are also covered in this chapter.

Chapter 7, "Configuring Dial-Up Networking," describes dial-up networking, remote access server, and the NetBIOS interface.

Chapter 8, "Configuring Hardware," covers how to get the maximum amount of performance from Windows NT 4 Server. Topics include hardware tuning, the Disk Administrator program, and tips on how to choose the best file format for a Windows NT 4 Server installation.

Chapter 9, "Monitoring Windows NT 4 Server Performance," covers system performance monitoring. The performance monitoring programs, Performance Monitor and Network Monitor, are described. Many of the specific items that Performance Monitor monitors are covered in this chapter.

Chapter 10, "Microsoft BackOffice," describes the add-on Microsoft product BackOffice. BackOffice is a collection of server products including Microsoft SQL Server, SNA Server, IIS, Exchange Server, and other products.

Chapter 11, "Microsoft Exchange Server & Client," covers the Microsoft Exchange Server, an e-mail product that replaces Microsoft Mail. Exchange Server is available either as part of Microsoft BackOffice or as a stand-alone product.

Chapter 12, "Microsoft SQL Server 6.5," describes Microsoft's entry into the client/server database market. Probably the most commonly used server component run under Windows NT 4 Server, Microsoft SQL Server is critical in providing access to database resources to large numbers of client users.

Chapter 13, "The Microsoft Internet Information Server," describes the Microsoft Internet Information Server, which provides Web, Gopher, and FTP services to the Internet.

Chapter 14, "The Microsoft IIS Gopher & FTP Services," describes the Gopher and FTP server components of IIS.

Chapter 15, "The Microsoft IIS WWW Service," describes the World Wide Web server component of IIS.

Chapter 16, "Sharing," covers issues you encounter when sharing resources such as folders, files, and printers.

Chapter 17, "Security & Users," describes some of the issues facing administrators responsible for maintaining Windows NT 4 Server security.

Chapter 18, "Backing Up the System," describes backup techniques, technologies, and the Windows NT 4 Server backup program.

Chapter 19, "The Registry," covers some of the issues you need to consider when making changes to the Windows NT 4 Server registry. The registry, which contains critical system information, and the two registry editing programs (RegEdit and RegEDT32) are described in this chapter.

Chapter 20, "Accessories, Toys, Fun & Games," covers all the accessories, such as WordPad, Paint, and the games (like the very popular Windows 95 game, Pinball) that are part of Windows NT 4 Server.

Appendix A contains sources of information, and products that may be used with Windows NT 4 Server.

Appendix B, "Windows NT as an ISP," covers some of the issues you may confront when using Windows NT 4 Server as an Internet Service Provider. Both in-house and external clients are supported by Windows NT 4 Server, and options for dial-in connections are covered in this chapter.

Online Updates

As we all know, the Internet changes constantly. So though I might try to make this book up to date, new products and technology are being developed even as this book goes to press. Ventana provides an excellent way to combat this problem and keep the information

in this book constantly current—the Windows NT 4 Server Online Updates. Access this resource at Ventana's World Wide Web site, and you'll find updated material relevant to this book. To get to the Online Updates, aim your browser at http://www.vmedia.com/updates.html.

Before You Go On

If possible, find a spare computer on which to install a test copy of Windows NT 4 Server. By creating a test installation of Windows NT 4 Server, you can test your processing and security requirements, experiment with the new features and functionality of Windows NT 4 Server, and start designing and building your intranet or Internet infrastructures.

SECTION I

Introduction to Windows NT 4

1 Introduction to Windows NT 4 Server

Microsoft Corporation's announcement on July 31 confirmed the future of Windows NT as the server technology of choice among Fortune 1,000 organizations. In a special issue of *Reseller Management*, VAR Workbook Series, titled "Selling Windows NT," a study predicts that by 1999, Windows NT will have captured over 80% of the server/host operating system market share. This increase in market share will come at the expense of all other server/host operating systems. As an example, the study predicts that Novell's NetWare, the leader in 1994 with a 43% market share, will drop to a 7% market share by 1999.

In this chapter, we take a precursory look at Windows NT 4 Server. Windows NT 4 Server, as the newest member in the Windows NT Server line, replaces Windows NT 3.51 Server.

Windows NT 4 Server offers a number of very valuable enhancements for users of Windows NT Server. This chapter introduces those enhancements and some of the features of Windows NT 4 Server which, though not new, are important to those who are now implementing Windows NT 4 Server for the first time.

The History of Windows NT

Windows NT was Microsoft's first 32-bit operating system. Windows NT 4 Server is the third major release of the Windows NT operating system.

At introduction, Windows NT required more resources than most users could (or would) pay for in a desktop system. Windows NT 3.x required substantial memory and CPU resources. Today, users of high-end operating systems have no problem with Windows NT 4 Server's system requirements.

When introduced, Windows NT's requirement of 16MB of RAM exceeded the typical computer's 2 to 4MB of RAM. RAM prices were very high at that time (in the order of $100 per MB), and as a result, the adoption of Windows NT was very slow at the initial stages. By the time Windows NT 3.51 was introduced, the memory requirement was substantially reduced, and constantly dropping RAM prices make it quite feasible to have servers (and workstations) with 16 to 128MB of RAM.

Microsoft has produced a number of versions of Windows NT. While Windows NT 3.1 gained some success, Windows NT 3.51 was the first commercially successful version of Windows NT produced. Windows NT 3.51's sales, both in the server and workstation versions, has been exceptional, perhaps even exceeding Microsoft's expectations.

A Question

Microsoft markets two types of Windows NT: Server and Workstation. Differences exist between the two, but basically they are the same operating system. For example, Windows NT 4 Workstation may share both drives and printers; Windows NT 4 Workstation also does many (but perhaps not all) of the things that Windows NT 4 Server does.

If Windows NT 4 Workstation is not intended to be a server, then why can it share devices such as drives? Simple answers include the ability to remotely back up the workstation, and to allow a limited few in a workgroup access to common files without sharing those files on the main network.

There is little in Windows NT 4 Workstation's performance which precludes it from performing as a limited server. Windows NT Workstation is basically identical to Windows NT 4 Server—it is just that the server version of Windows NT has functionality and performance enhancements more appropriate to a server.

Why Windows NT 4 Server?

There are three reasons to consider Windows NT 4 Server:

- You are upgrading an existing Windows NT Server.
- You are upgrading an existing non-Windows NT server.
- You are creating a new network or network server.

In the first case, you are probably familiar with the basics of Windows NT Server. In the second case, you should know the basics about networks and servers, but you may not be familiar with Windows NT 4 Server. In the third case, networks and servers may be a new subject for you, though perhaps you have used Windows.

Users upgrading an existing Windows NT Server installation will find that though the details may be different, and the user interface is better, Windows NT 4 Server is similar to previous versions of Windows NT. Once you're past these details, then move into Windows NT 4 Server's new features such as the Internet Information Server.

Those of us converting from another server platform have our work cut out for us. First, this is not a trivial task! Recommendations (like you didn't know?) include parallel servers (get Windows NT 4 Server running as a second server, then move the existing server's information to the Windows NT 4 Server installation) and trial runs. Windows NT 4 Server works well in a multiserver environment, so running both Windows NT 4 Server and your existing server should be possible.

Users new to servers, networks, and Windows NT have their work cut out. First, set up a Windows NT 4 Server installation. Get the server running, then toss on a workstation (or two). Finally, start at the first chapter in this book, and work your way through the first part of the book, using it as a tutorial. Install only those components that you will need. Next, jump to Part IV, Advanced Windows NT, and learn about sharing, security, and the registry. Setting up a basic network isn't difficult. Make sure the workstations and the server are running the same protocol, and are correctly connected—you should be (almost) up and running. Anyone without networking experience will find both training courses and consultants to be a valuable investment.

In this book you will find information that will assist you in learning Windows NT 4 Server. Emphasized are topics such as Windows NT 4 Server's new features and the new user interface. Topics also include third-party products (such as Web servers and database client/server products), and products from Microsoft which work with Windows NT 4 Server (such as Microsoft Back Office, Microsoft Exchange Server, and Microsoft SQL Server).

First, let's consider what a network is. In the past, we had a Local Area Network (LAN), which connected computers at a single site, a Wide Area Network (WAN), which connected computers (and LANs) at multiple sites, and the Internet, which is a general WAN connecting computers at many, diverse sites.

Today, we have two buzz words: *intranet* and *Internet*. Intranet is the newer of the two words and describes a corporate or organizational network (which could be either LAN or WAN) that uses TCP/IP. An intranet works just like the Internet, except that it is private and offers e-mail and content sharing only between computers within the organization, while the Internet is public and allows users to exchange e-mail and share information with computers all over the world. Often there are links between an intranet and the Internet, using gateways or firewalls.

In this book, we are going to assume that you know the basics about networking, you know what a protocol is, and you understand the relationship between a server and a client. If you feel a refresher course in networks is in order, then you might also consider reading *Windows NT Web Server Book* by Larry Budnick or *Microsoft Windows NT 4 Workstation Desktop Companion* by Richard Mansfield and Charles Brannon. Both of these books are published by Ventana.

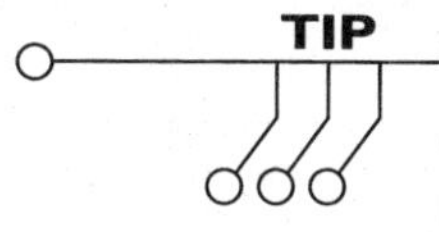

You should be familiar with the following terms used in this book:

- ***Internet**: a public network that connects many computers around the world. Typically, academic, business, commercial, and home computers can connect to the Internet. There is only one Internet.*
- ***Intranet**: a private network that connects the computers of an organization using TCP/IP protocol. Works much like the Internet except that intranets are private. There are many intranets.*
- ***NOS**: Network Operating System. Windows NT 4 Server is an NOS, as is Novell's NetWare and IBM's OS/2 Warp Server Advanced.*
- ***LAN**: Local Area Network, which connects computers at a single site or location together.*
- ***Server**: A computer or a program that provides a particular service on a network or on the Internet. Typical services include file access, printing, e-mail, FTP, and so on. The computers and software that access servers are called clients.*
- ***WAN**: Wide Area Network, which connects computers and LANs together. A WAN networks geographically separated facilities together.*

Windows NT 4 Server Unwrapped

Microsoft positioned Windows NT 4 Server as a direct competitor to network operating systems made by Novell, Sun Microsystems, and IBM. Since there is a great demand and interest in new Microsoft products, many computer manufacturers have already pledged to include Windows NT 4 Server on their machines. This news pleases Microsoft's chief executive, Bill Gates, I'm sure!

This book will show you that the Windows NT 4 Server is an excellent choice for a network server. Additionally, the features described below make Windows NT 4 Server the "leading contender" for a network server.

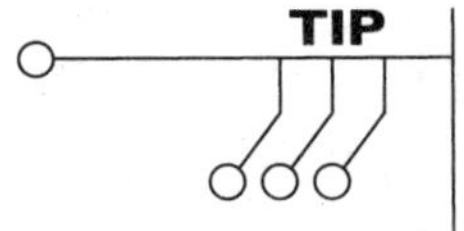

Things change. In the computer industry, things change quickly. Features, hardware, prices, and functionality are all in a constant state of flux. Therefore, features shown in this chapter should not be taken as absolute fact, but simply as guidelines.

Windows NT 4 Server is a powerful, preemptive, multiuser NOS. It runs on Intel (486 or better), MIPS, DEC Alpha, and Motorola PowerPC platforms. Microsoft recommends that Windows NT 4 Server be run on a minimum of 16MB of RAM; however, I would say that a minimum of 32MB of RAM (for a serious server) is more realistic.

Some of Windows NT 4 Server's major architecture features are:

- Windows NT 4 Server offers symmetric multiprocessing, allowing up to four processors from Microsoft, and supporting up to 32 processors using special Original Equipment Manufacturer (OEM) builds. The support for various hardware designs is done using a feature called a Hardware Abstraction Layer (HAL).
- Windows NT 4 Server offers full support for Installable File Systems (IFS), and comes with support for both FAT (File Allocation Table) and NTFS (NT File System). Microsoft plans to offer support for FAT-32 as soon as possible, perhaps as early as late 1996.

- Paged virtual memory and a dynamic memory cache make Windows NT 4 Server an efficient server, capable of supporting an almost unlimited number of user connections.
- Powerful memory protection for applications helps Windows NT 4 Server avoid the problems that plague Windows 95—errant applications which may cause the entire operating system to fail.
- Management features such as audit alerts (which can be as simple as telling you that a drive is full) assist the system administrator in managing the Windows NT 4 Server installation.
- Windows NT 4 Server supports Unicode. Virtually out of the box, Windows NT 4 Server eases entry into multi-language environments and supports languages easily and quickly.

Accessories & Optional Hardware

Windows NT 4 Server supports a vast array of accessories from tape drives to sound cards. Though Windows NT 4 Server does not support as wide a variety of hardware as does Windows 95, nearly all users will find the hardware support for Windows NT 4 Server quite adequate for their needs.

Hardware (specific cards and devices that are supported by Windows NT 4 Server) may be determined by looking at the Windows NT 4 Server Hardware Compatibility List (HCL). The HCL is packaged with the Windows NT 4 Server product.

Microsoft updates the HCL on a regular basis, and you should make an effort to view the most recent version of the HCL, preferably online. Microsoft maintains the HCL at their support Web site: http://198.105.232.4/support/.

Realize that Windows NT 4 Server does not support PnP (Plug-and-Play). There are various bits and pieces of PnP support included with Windows NT 4 Server, but these bits and pieces do not constitute support for PnP. Any device that is exclusively PnP may not work correctly with Windows NT 4 Server.

Windows NT 4 Server offers support for CD-ROM drives (IDE, SCSI, and proprietary interfaces are all supported), SCSI adapters, plotters, and scanners. Though Windows NT 4's hardware support is not as extensive as Windows 95's, for example, there is support for most hardware.

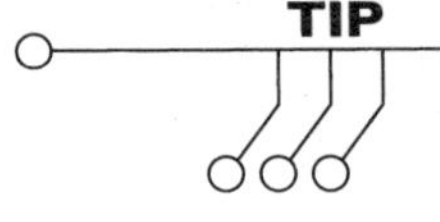

Before purchasing new hardware (other than common items), it would be wise to make sure the hardware is compatible with Windows NT 4 Server. Most device drivers for earlier versions of Windows NT will not work with Windows NT 4. Make absolutely certain that Windows NT 4 drivers are included if they are needed.

Any hardware device that uses a DOS-based initialization file (such as Diamond's TeleCommander series sound card or modem board) will not work with Windows NT 4 unless there is a Windows NT device driver (to initialize the device)—even if no device driver is required to use the hardware under DOS or Windows 95.

Network Protocols Support

Windows NT 4 Server supports network protocols to allow interaction with essentially any network available: TCP/IP to interact with both the Internet and intranets, IPX/SPX to work with NetWare, NetBEUI for IBM, and Microsoft networks, to name a few. There is even optional (perhaps limited) support for Banyan networks.

This network protocols support makes placing a Windows NT 4 Server on an existing network easy and safe. The Windows NT 4 Server will be able to work with nearly all client-side systems, providing maximum interoperability from the beginning.

Some of the network protocols that Windows NT 4 Server supports are listed below. Supporting multiple protocols is important when you have a network with clients of different types. For example, your network could have Windows 95, Apple Macintosh, UNIX, and OS/2 clients, all of which will need to access your Windows NT 4 Server!

- AppleTalk
- DHCP
- DLC
- IPX/SPX
- NetBEUI
- NetBIOS
- TCP/IP (PPTP)
- TCP/IP

Chapter 5, "Configuring TCP/IP Services," and Chapter 6, "Interacting With Other LANs," both contain information about protocols.

Network Interface Card Support

Windows NT 4 Server supports most common Network Interface Cards (NICs). As well, Windows NT 4 Server works very well with state-of-the-art PCI bus NICs such as 3Com's 3c590 NIC, providing impressive performance for a desktop server.

Inter-Process Calls

Inter-Process Calls (IPCs) are an important feature of any operating system. They allow the operating system to work with the user's applications to perform complex tasks, such as communicating with other applications and systems.

Some of the IPCs supported by Windows NT 4 Server include:

- Named Pipes (client and server)
- Sockets
- Transport Library Interface
- DCE-compatible RPC
- LU 6.2, LU1, LU0, LU2, LU3 using SNA Server
- HLLAPI with third-party software
- Local Procedure Call (LPC)

- Semaphores
- Mutexes
- Timers
- Asynchronous Procedure Calls

Performance

Performance is a critical feature of any network operating system. If the server's performance lags, client users will quickly become dissatisfied and will let you, the network administrator, know there is a problem.

Virtually all operating systems can function as rudimentary servers (for example, Windows for Workgroups is technically a server). For a server to process more than a trivial number of client requests, performance must be optimal. It would make no sense to connect 50 or 100 clients to a Windows for Workgroups server—performance would be practically nonexistent in that configuration, if it worked at all. Note: Windows 95 and Windows NT 4 Workstation both limit the number of client connections so that performance is less impacted with these non-server operating systems.

Some performance features offered by Windows NT 4 Server include:

- Dynamic cache of 1GB per process
- Read-ahead caching
- Background writes
- Overlapped seeks
- Split seeks
- Directory hashing
- Directory caching
- File caching
- Virtual memory
- Returnable memory

Chapter 8, "Configuring Hardware," and Chapter 9, "Monitoring Windows NT 4 Server Performance," both deal with performance issues.

File Systems

A server's file system must be efficient. When the File Allocation Table (FAT) file system was developed, a 20MB hard drive with a 40-millisecond seek time was considered large and fast; anything over 100MB was unheard of. Now personal computer users consider a 100MB hard drive a toy (or probably a paperweight or a door stop), and multi-gigabyte drives are common. Within a few more years, nine-gigabyte drives will be the minimum usable (today we consider a one-gigabyte drive the real minimum for a workstation).

Most servers are configured with SCSI drives, with 10 or more gigabytes of hard drive space being a minimum. The server on which this book was written has over 10 gigabytes of hard drive space—and I am constantly running out of free space!

The file system, as drives grow larger, is critical. FAT is fine if the drive has a few hundred MB of space, and perhaps a few thousand files. When drives are 2, 4, or more MB in size, and contain tens of thousands of files, FAT fails to deliver needed performance. It is necessary to move to an advanced file system such as NTFS to support larger drives with large numbers of files.

The Windows and OS/2 desktop servers and workstations support one (or more) of the different types of FAT. All support FAT-16; Windows 95 will support FAT-32 (according to a recent Microsoft announcement), and Windows NT 4 Server may support FAT-32, at a later date.

Windows NT 4 Server supports NTFS (NT File System), which is a high-performance network file system. NTFS supports compression (at the file, directory, and drive level). There is also support for extensive security in NTFS, which is considered a secure file system.

OS/2 supports HPFS (High Performance File System), which is IBM's replacement for the FAT file system. Though HPFS has been supported in the past by Windows NT Server, support for HPFS is no longer provided with Windows NT 4 Server; to use HPFS drives with Windows NT 4 Server, you must convert the HPFS drives to NTFS (or FAT).

Some features of the Windows NT 4 Server file system are shown in Table 1-1, below.

Feature	Description
File System Maximum number of file locks	Unlimited
File System Maximum number of file opens	Unlimited
File System Maximum file size	17 billion GB
File System Efficient sub-block allocation	Yes, 512 bytes
File System File compression	Yes
File System Transaction-based file system	Yes
File System Support for DOS files	Yes
File System Support for Mac files	Yes
File System Support for OS/2 files	Yes
File System Support for NFS	Yes, using third-party support
Volumes/files span drives	Yes
Total disk storage	708 million TB
Maximum volumes/server	25
Maximum physical drives/server	Limited by hardware
Maximum partition size	17,000 TB
Maximum volume size	17,000 TB
Disk quotas	Yes, using third-party support
High-performance asynchronous I/O	Yes
Memory-mapped File I/O	Yes
Maximum length of file name	255
Long file names made visible to MS-DOS programs	Yes, FAT-16 and NTFS

Table 1-1: NT File System features for Windows NT 4 Server.

Directory Support

Directory support is closely linked to the file system used. Fortunately, with Windows NT 4 Server, most of the functionality supported by NTFS is also supported by FAT, such as long file names. However, FAT does not support individual right to directories and files, which NTFS does. Nor does FAT support compression at the file or folder level, which NTFS does.

Some directory and file features require support at the client side, also. For example, long file names are only significant when the client supports them also.

With the NTFS file system, you can assign a number of rights to file system objects (files, folders, and drives), including:

- Right to read
- Right to write
- Right to execute
- Right to delete
- Right to change permissions (Grant)
- Right to take ownership
- Right to list Directory
- Right to create files in Directory

Chapter 16, "Sharing," and Chapter 17, "Security & Users," both deal with issues of directory support.

Fault Tolerance & Redundancy

Failure doesn't always have to mean disaster. Fault tolerance and redundancy can help to minimize the impact of hardware (and software) failures.

Typical fault tolerance technologies include: uninterruptable power supplies (UPS), Redundant Arrays of Inexpensive Drives (RAID), duplexing, and disk mirroring. You can find additional information about fault tolerance and redundancy in Chapter 17, "Security & Users."

Fault Tolerance features found in Windows NT 4 Server include:

- File system recovery log
- Redundant directory structures
- Directory verification during power-up
- Read-after-write verification
- Recover files/undelete (for FAT file systems only)
- UPS support
- Disk duplexing
- Disk mirroring
- Software RAID levels 0, 1, and 5 support
- Server mirroring using third-party products
- Dynamic volume sets

Backup & Restore

Backup and restore functions are critical operations on any computer system. When the system is a server, backup and restore functions are paramount; any failure can lead to disaster of unmitigated proportions.

Windows NT 4 Server has a competent tape backup facility built-in. Features include support for SCSI devices including DAT drives, the ability to back up client systems, and other backup/restore task management. Windows NT 4 Server backup support includes:

- Backup/restore of server disk with security
- On-line backup of account files
- A backup utility
- Workstation backup (Windows for Workgroups, Windows 95, Windows NT Workstation)
- Automatic file replication service
- Server job scheduling

- DOS 3.x Client support
- Macintosh System 7.5 Client support
- Windows 3.1 Client support
- Windows 95 Client support
- Windows NT Workstation Client support
- Windows for Workgroups Client support

Chapter 18, "Backing Up the System," deals with Windows NT 4 Server backup.

Security

Windows NT 4 Server is a secure server. While most servers are secure, the degree of security offered varies depending on the design of the server. The United States government produced a set of documents that sets the standards for security and defines the tests a computer system must pass in order to be considered secure.

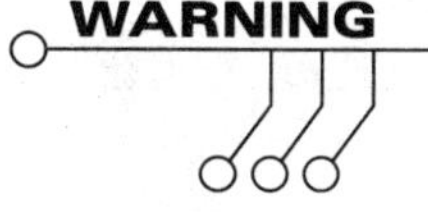

Windows NT 4 Server (and any other server) qualifies as a secure operating system only if the server is physically secure. If the server can be physically tampered with, then Windows NT 4 Server's security can be circumvented, especially if the FAT file system is used. It is virtually impossible for a server to be considered secure if the hardware itself is not physically secure as well.

Security is of paramount concern for servers. The ability to protect the confidentiality of shared data, users' accounts, and other resources is critical. For systems connected to either the Internet or to a broad WAN, security must always be considered.

When security is ignored, you will find that servers connected to the Internet are quickly breached, and their contents are compromised. In-house security is also critical in any larger organization: if employees are able to gain access to sensitive or mission-critical data, it can spell disaster for the organization.

Most weaknesses in security are created by users and system administrators. Poor password choices, lax standards, and failure to maintain physical security are all warning signs that unacceptable security risks are present. It is usually a wise investment to work with a security consultant to find and repair any security weaknesses in your system.

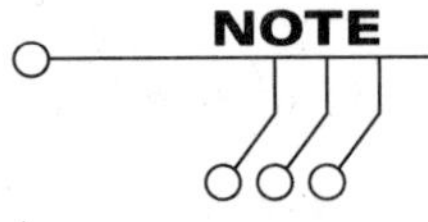

A company once hired me to "break into" their mainframe computer as a test of the system's security. The administrators thought the system was totally secure.... However, it took me only about ten minutes to defeat the system's security, promote a normal user's account into a super user, and then use the account to access the entire system.

When I was working as a security consultant, I would often tell customers that I would not charge them if I could not find any weaknesses in their systems.... No one was ever able to take me up on that offer.

Windows NT 4 Server offers both C2 level security and B2 security (when used with additional third-party support). The use of domains allows the Windows NT 4 Server to manage security for entire organizations—even Windows 95 clients (notorious for their general lack of security).

Windows NT 4 Server offers the following security features:

- Minimum password length restrictions
- Password encryption, aging, and history
- Set account expiration date
- Minimum time until password can be changed
- Account lockout
- Restrict login to specific workstation, or by time and day
- Replaceable client login
- Disconnect when access time expires
- Re-key password verify
- Configurable administrative rights

- Centralized security event auditing
- Security event alerts
- File system auditing

Chapter 17, "Security & Users," deals with security and user access.

Security Auditing

Security is meaningless if you cannot trust it. To trust your system's security, you must be able to show that security has not been breached or compromised. To monitor security, the server must perform checking and reporting of certain critical events, referred to as auditing.

Simple auditing might be a log of user login failures and user file accesses. More complex tasks include monitoring specific users or events and automatic reporting of specific events (such as multiple password failures—indicative of attempts to "guess" a password).

Windows NT 4 Server offers a number of auditing features, including those listed below. Use these audit log filter capabilities to find problem areas and security breaches quickly.

- Audit user security transactions
- Audit user file transactions
- Audit administrator transactions
- Audit file-creation statistics
- Audit volume statistics
- Audit security policy changes
- Audit restart or shutdown of system

User Access

Users are what a server is all about. Without client users, a server has no purpose in life.

With Windows NT 4 Server, users may have a broad range of rights and privileges. As well, in a well-designed system, the server may also express some control over client users.

Some features offered by Windows NT 4 Server include: the ability to access workstations from the network, extensive client backup capabilities, and even support for remote booting of client workstations including remote booting of Windows 95 clients.

Chapter 16, "Sharing," deals with user access.

Print Services

Servers, such as Windows NT 4 Server, typically serve more than disk files. Though most servers provide access to disk resources (files), many also provide access to shared printers. Shared printers allow many users to use the same printer, thereby minimizing the number of printers that must be obtained.

On larger networks, a dedicated printer server would be implemented. However, on mid-sized and smaller networks, the same server may provide both disk and printer sharing. Typically, print servers do not require a great deal of resources; however, laser printer spool files can be rather large, so plan accordingly. Printer support provided by Windows NT 4 Server includes:

- Remote printer port on Workstations, and Peer print services
- Multiple queues to a single printer, with priorities
- Multiple printers on one queue, to allow faster printing of time-critical items
- Cross-platform printing for OS/2, UNIX, NetWare, and SNA
- Remote queue management
- Network attached printer support
- User notification of job completion and print problems
- Operator notification of print problem
- Printer alert for out of paper, job deletion, job completion, printer offline, and paper jams

Administration

Windows NT 4 Server requires a certain amount of administration. You, or the system administrator, must interact with the Windows NT 4 Server to ensure that the system performs as well as possible.

As well, Windows NT 4 Server provides a number of important services to the system and network, such as Domain Name Servers (DNS). The system administrator also maintains these services.

Administration Operators

In larger networks, the duties of the system administrator may be split among several different people. This permits the organization to have a number of different administrators (such as an administrator whose sole task may be to administrate users).

Windows NT 4 Server has, in addition to the server operator, six different classes of administrators. These administrators are usually referred to as operators, much as in the mainframe world.

An operator may be assigned to one or more classes, while the default system operator (administrator) is assigned all of the classes. The following is a list of Windows NT 4 Server's classes of administrators:

- Account operator
- Backup operator
- Directory administrator
- Enterprise administrator
- Print operator
- Replication operator

Administration Messages

Whenever an event of significance (such as a drive becoming full) occurs, the operating system should be able to notify the administrator so that corrective action may be taken. Which events have alerts associated with them varies greatly between network operating systems.

Some of the alert messages Windows NT 4 Server supports include:

- Volume is getting full, or is full
- Error log is full
- Disk utilization above threshold

Performance Monitoring

To ensure that your Windows NT 4 Server is performing as well as possible, it is necessary to monitor events such as disk I/O, memory utilization, network I/O, and so on, on a recurring basis. Typically, a graphical monitor program, such as PERFMON.EXE, is used to monitor the system. In later chapters, we will examine PERFMON and how it is used.

Some of the items Windows NT 4 Server Performance Monitor is capable of viewing include:

- View CPU usage, including total, privileged, user, and idle times
- View disk use performance, for both virtual and physical volumes
- View cache utilization
- View network usage and performance
- View physical and virtual memory usage
- Log performance statistics

Companion Products

Windows NT 4 Server has a large number of features that make it an excellent choice for your network server. In addition to the built-in features of Windows NT 4 Server, Microsoft offers a number of companion products, including:

- SQL Server
- SNA Server
- Microsoft BackOffice
- Exchange Server

Each of these additional companion products provides a powerful set of enhancements to Windows NT 4 Server. In Part II, "Optional at Extra Cost," we describe each of the above products.

Part III, "Windows NT 4 & the Internet," describes the Microsoft Internet Information Server, which includes servers for Gopher, FTP, and WWW (World Wide Web).

Other chapters in this book include information about products from third-party sources.

The Windows NT 4 Server distribution CD-ROM contains a program, which if run will seriously damage your installation of Windows NT 4 Server. This program, intended to configure OEM copies of Windows NT, is called ROLLBACK.EXE. ROLLBACK will not prompt for parameters, has no help mode, cannot be stopped, and the effects of running ROLLBACK cannot be reversed without reinstalling Windows NT 4 Server. Do not run this program!

Moving On

In this chapter we introduced Windows NT 4 Server, its history, and functions. This easy-to-use and easy-to-manage server operating system comes with built-in Web services.

In Chapter 2, we will talk about the new features that come with Windows NT 4 Server. Windows NT 4 Server represents a major change in the Windows NT operating system.

2

What's New in Windows NT 4 Server

Windows NT 4 Server moves the Windows NT user into a world resembling Windows 95. A new user interface and new ways of doing things make utilizing Windows NT 4 Server an easy and pleasant task!

When Microsoft first planned Windows NT 4 Server, they wanted to do more than simply graft on the Windows 95 user interface. Microsoft also wanted to make Windows NT 4 Server more user-friendly, more functional, and bring Windows NT 4 Server into the '90s. Now, I may be biased, but I think that Microsoft has done an excellent job with Windows NT 4 Server. You can decide for yourself as you use it.

What's New

Windows NT 4 Server offers a number of new and improved features. This is not to say that Windows NT 3.51 Server was lacking, rather, it is indicative that Microsoft can make an outstanding product even better.

This section reviews the following new and improved features: the Windows 95 user interface, Internet Explorer Version 3, Microsoft Windows messaging system, Hardware Profiles, Microsoft WordPad, Microsoft Paint, a File Find & Search utility, an enhanced Control Panel, the DHCP relay agent, Domain Name Service, Microsoft Internet Information Server (IIS), multi-protocol routing, remote administration, remote booting of Windows 95 clients, user-defined Internet special groups, changes in the driver structure, differences between the Server & Workstation products, and a hardware compatibility list.

The Windows 95 User Interface

Network system administrators commonly ask, "What is the Windows 95 user interface?" The main reason for this unfamiliarity with Windows 95 is the fact that Microsoft has primarily promoted Windows 95 to the home market and not to corporate users. Microsoft has continued to promote Windows NT 4 Workstation as the client of choice for corporate users.

Ask any seasoned Windows 95 user about the Windows 95 user interface and they will tell you that the user interface is one of the most important enhancements made to Windows by Microsoft.

Microsoft gave Windows NT a total desktop workout. The result is that Windows NT *looks* great with its updated graphical user interface. This new user interface is integral to Windows, and as such, presents a much better appearance to the user. In earlier versions of Windows NT, the main user interface components were the Program Manager and File Manager. These components were separate applications with only modest interaction with the Windows operating system.

In Windows NT 4, Microsoft tossed aside the boxed-in look of the Program Manager and removed many of the constraints of the File Manager program. Microsoft conditioned and toned the Windows desktop by significantly reducing the limitations on Windows that were really limitations of the disk operating system (DOS) that ran behind Windows. For example, in Windows NT, you are no longer bound by the filenaming convention "filename.ext" that exists for DOS. You still think a filename can contain no more than eight characters? Think again. In Windows 95, you can have up to 255 characters, and the filename extensions of up to three characters are now optional. Come on now, stretch; name your next file "MY FILE FOR MY IMPORTANT STUFF"—Windows NT will let you!

If you're having a tough day or are simply too busy to get creative with your filenames, Windows NT has another feature that may interest you. This one is basically a navigational tool, but the difference can be compared to driving your own car home during rush hour versus having the corporate helicopter fly you directly to your pad. Windows NT keeps track of the last 15 files or programs you used. To quickly return to any of these, just click the saved option from Start | Documents on the Windows desktop—Wow! You're there already!

The Windows 95 user interface is much more usable when your computer is equipped with a Windows 95 compatible keyboard. The Windows 95 compatible keyboards have two new keys, the Windows key, which displays the start menu, and the Context (sometimes referred to as the application) key, which has a pop-up menu as a keycap symbol.

The Windows 95 user interface main components are:

- Windows Explorer, which replaces the original File Manager in older versions of Windows and Windows NT. Windows Explorer offers a great deal of performance and usability. With Windows Explorer, you can browse (using an extensible set of viewers) and manage files, network connections, and drives. Figure 2-1 illustrates one way (a hierarchical view by drive) the Windows Explorer can present these objects.

  Users of Windows 95 will find that the Windows NT user interface and Windows Explorer are almost exactly the same as their Windows 95 counterparts. The minor differences (which reflect the differences in architecture of the two operating systems) are difficult to find.

  If you are fortunate enough to have Microsoft's new Natural Keyboard, then the Window-E key will launch Windows Explorer.

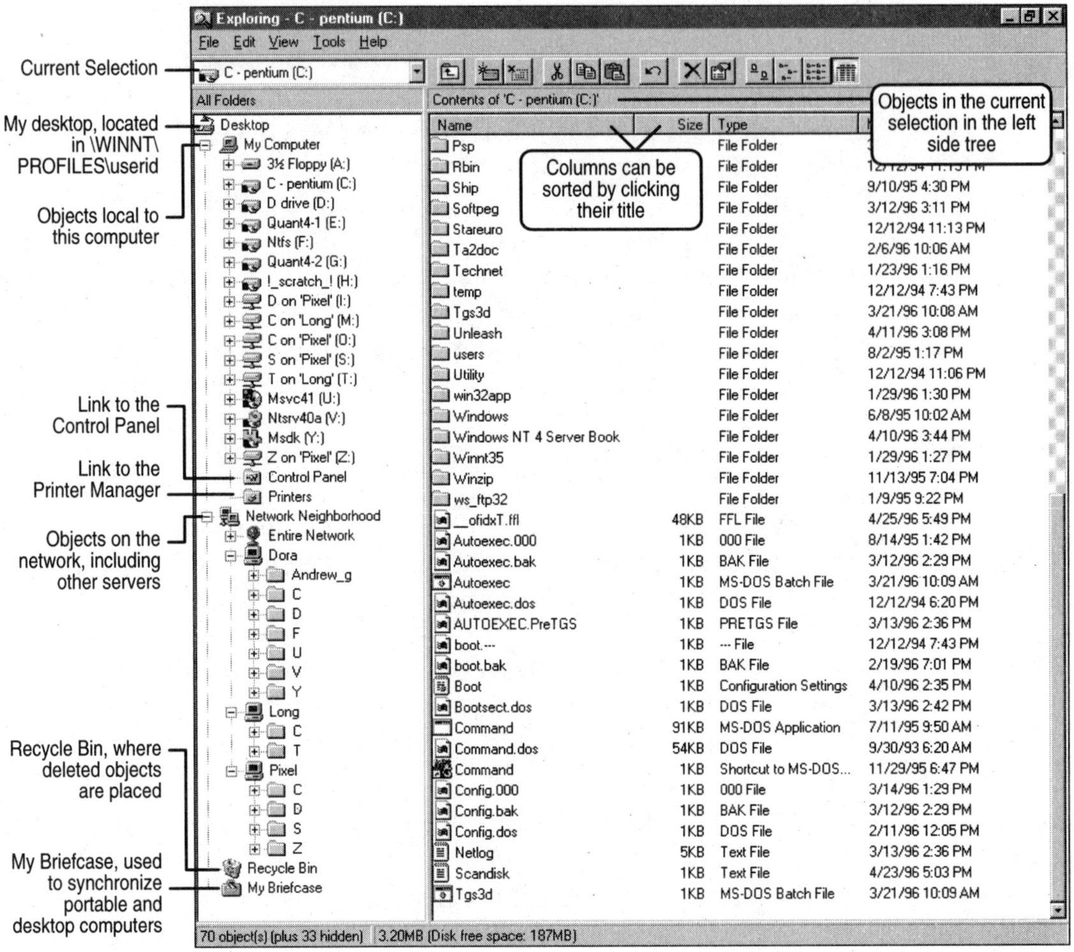
Exploring - C - pentium (C:)
Current Selection
My desktop, located in \WINNT\PROFILES\userid
Objects local to this computer
Link to the Control Panel
Link to the Printer Manager
Objects on the network, including other servers
Recycle Bin, where deleted objects are placed
My Briefcase, used to synchronize portable and desktop computers
Columns can be sorted by clicking their title
Objects in the current selection in the left side tree
70 object(s) (plus 33 hidden) 3.20MB (Disk free space: 187MB)

Figure 2-1: The Windows Explorer.

- The Taskbar, which consists of the Start button menu, the task buttons, and the tray area. The tray area may have a clock and other helper tools, such as a volume control. Figure 2-2 shows the Taskbar.
- The Start menu, which is slightly different from Windows 95. The difference stems from the fact that Windows 95 is primarily a single user operating system, whereas multiple users

utilize Windows NT 4 Server. Under Windows NT 4 Server, the Programs component of the Start menu is divided into two parts: the upper part is specific to the currently logged on user; the lower part is visible to *all users*.

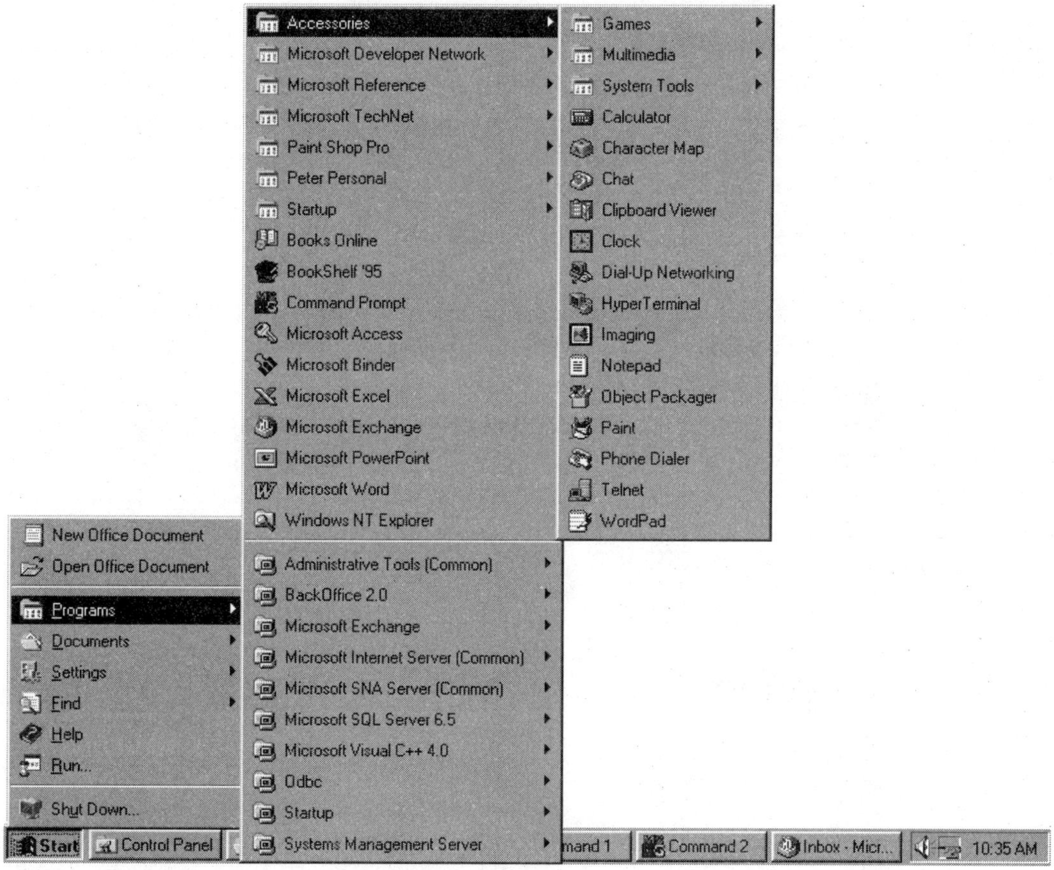

Figure 2-2: The Windows NT 4 Taskbar and Start menu.

- The Desktop, which expands on the original Windows desktop, allows the user to place applications, folders (directories), files, and other objects within easy reach.

Along with the change in the basic user interface, Windows NT 4 Server also adopted the object/folder paradigm from Windows 95. As such, what we referred to as directories (or subdirectories) in the past are now called folders. A folder typically contains files (which are objects), but may contain other objects as well.

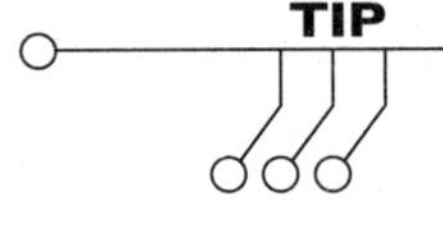

Microsoft, with the introduction of Windows NT 4, has changed the terminology for directories. The new term for a directory (any directory) is a folder. In some instances, some components of Windows NT 4 Server still refer to directories and sub-directories; rest assured—a folder is the same as either a directory or a sub-directory.

We expect that the next release of Windows NT (perhaps as soon as 1998, or 1999) will be fully object oriented. As it is now, there is support for some object concepts, but Windows NT 4 Server is not yet the fully object-oriented operating system of the future. We will have to take small steps on our way there.

Internet Explorer

Included with Windows NT 4 Server is Microsoft Internet Explorer. Microsoft Internet Explorer is a powerful Internet Web browser that has gained a great deal of acceptance from Windows 95 users.

Microsoft Windows Messaging System

The Microsoft Windows Messaging System is the component of Windows NT 4 Server that allows you, as a user, to send and receive e-mail, which can now include other objects.

A major part of the Microsoft Windows Messaging System is the Microsoft Exchange. Microsoft Exchange *Client* is an integral part of Windows NT 4 Server (and Windows NT 4 Workstation), while Microsoft Exchange *Server* is Microsoft's new, heavy-duty, e-mail server, which is a separate add-on product.

Using Microsoft Exchange, the user is able to send e-mail (including *internal* e-mail within the network, Internet e-mail, and

e-mail to online information services to which the user subscribes, such as CompuServe).

Features found in Microsoft Exchange include an integrated (and sharable) Address Book and a message storage database (also sharable, if desired).

Look for more information about Microsoft Exchange Server, an additional component you can add to Windows NT 4 Server, in Chapter 11, "Microsoft Exchange Server."

Hardware Profiles

You can use Hardware Profiles to create a set of different hardware configurations. Typically you use this when working on a portable or laptop computer which can be plugged into a docking station. Admittedly, Windows NT 4 Server is not often installed on this type of hardware (though Windows NT 4 Workstation would be). However, when it is necessary to install Windows NT 4 Server on systems where the hardware configuration does change frequently, you will find the Hardware Profiles feature very valuable.

You create and manage Hardware Profiles using the Control Panel's System applet; you manage devices in the Hardware Profiles using the Control Panel's Devices applet.

Windows NT 4 Server does not support Plug-n-Play (PnP). Although Windows 95 does support Plug-n-Play, Microsoft was unable to include the Plug-n-Play features in Windows NT 4 Server.

There is a Plug and Play service in Windows NT 4. However, this service does not implement many of the features of PnP, so be very cautious of purchasing PnP devices for use with Windows NT 4 Server.

Microsoft WordPad

Microsoft WordPad is a simple word processing program that replaces the Microsoft Write program included with Windows NT 3.51. WordPad offers a number of new capabilities, including the ability to read and write Microsoft Word .DOC files and the ability to edit Rich Text Format (RTF) files.

WordPad is a surprisingly full-featured word processor—various fonts, formatting, and other features all combine to make WordPad an excellent part of Windows NT 4 Server.

Microsoft Paint

Microsoft Paint is the replacement product for PaintBrush, which was included with Windows NT 3.51. Many users may feel that Microsoft Paint is not as good a product as PaintBrush because Microsoft Paint can not manipulate the .PCX file format, which is a graphics file format widely supported by personal computers.

If you need to edit .PCX files, you have two choices: either attempt to use the original Microsoft PaintBrush program, or use one of the commercially available programs, such as Paint Shop Pro.

Figure 2-3 shows Microsoft Paint and its tools.

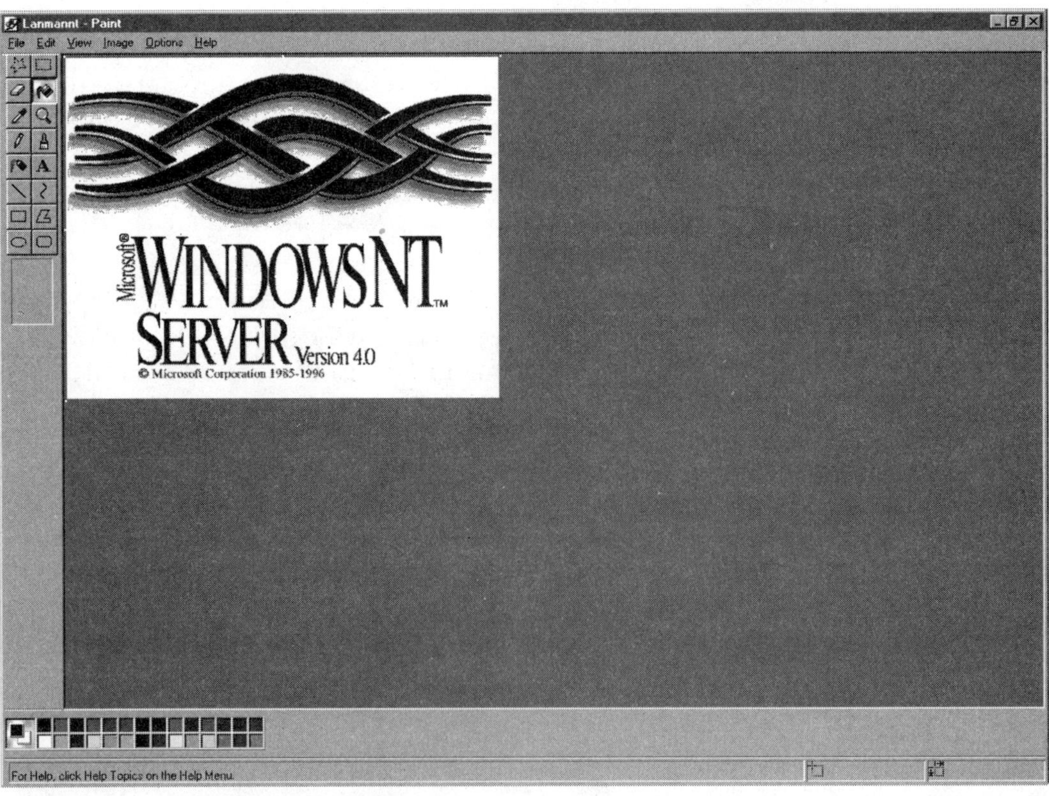

Figure 2-3: Microsoft Paint in operation.

File Find & Search

Since Windows was first introduced, the issue of finding files, or specific strings in a file has been a problem. Several sets of utilities have been introduced to solve this problem, such as Norton's File Find and several UNIX-like GREP utilities.

Many of the add-in search programs, not designed for Windows NT, fail when searching for text in files made with the Unicode character set. Unicode characters are not formatted the same way as Windows 95 and Windows 3.x characters.

Windows 95 introduced a new File Find and Search utility into the Windows NT 4 Server. You use this utility to search for names or text. A timesaving feature of this utility is that you can use a date, file size, location, and/or text string to further qualify your search. An example of a search for the text string (or word) "prompt" in all files on the C drive is shown in Figure 2-4.

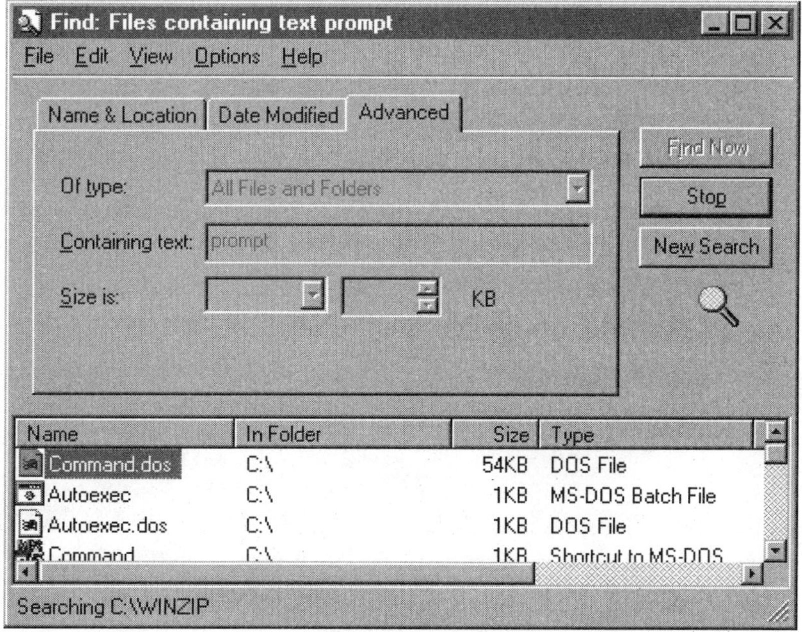

Figure 2-4: The Windows NT 4 File Find feature.

This search located over 1,000 files which contained the string "prompt" and searched a 2GB hard drive in only a few minutes.

Enhanced Control Panel

Microsoft has enhanced the functionality of the Windows Control Panel for Windows NT 4. New objects added to the Control Panel include:

- PC Card (PCMCIA), which provides support for portable computers and the interface and expansion cards they use.
- Telephone support, which allows configuration of TAPI (modem/telephone) devices.
- Add/Remove Programs, which allows the user to add or remove applications and subsystems in Windows NT 4. Also allows the user to re-install or re-configure Windows NT 4.
- Multimedia, which allows for support of multimedia devices and services, such as video, MIDI, sound, and CD music.
- Tape Devices, which configures tape backup devices.
- Modems, which installs and configures modems.
- SCSI, which installs and configures SCSI (including IDE) devices.
- Display, which allows the user to configure the video display mode. Resolution, color depth, appearance, and screen saver—all are configured in the Display applet.

Along with the above additions to Control Panel, the following *existing* applets have been enhanced or otherwise changed:

- Mouse, which includes user interface enhancements, and a re-designed Mouse Properties dialog.
- Sounds, which replaces Sound Mapper found in earlier versions of Windows NT. The use of Schemes is new to Windows NT 4 Server, being adopted from Windows 95. My favorite is the Utopia scheme.
- Network, which supports a new, easier to use applet. Managing Services, Protocols, Adapters, and Bindings is much easier in Windows NT 4 Server.

- Fonts, another Windows 95 adoptee, brings a more powerful management tool for fonts to Windows NT 4 Server. You may add fonts, delete fonts, list fonts by similarity, even open a font and see (and print) an example of the font in a number of different sizes.
- Regional Settings, which replaces International found in earlier versions of Windows NT. You may set time zones and choose a preferred style of date, time, number, and currency formatting.
- Keyboard, which allows you to set parameters for the keyboard, such as locales, speed, and general settings, which allows you to change the type of keyboard selected.

Figure 2-5 shows the new Windows NT 4 Server Control Panel. Realize that each user's Control Panel may be different, as items are added (and removed) depending on the user's specific configuration and installation.

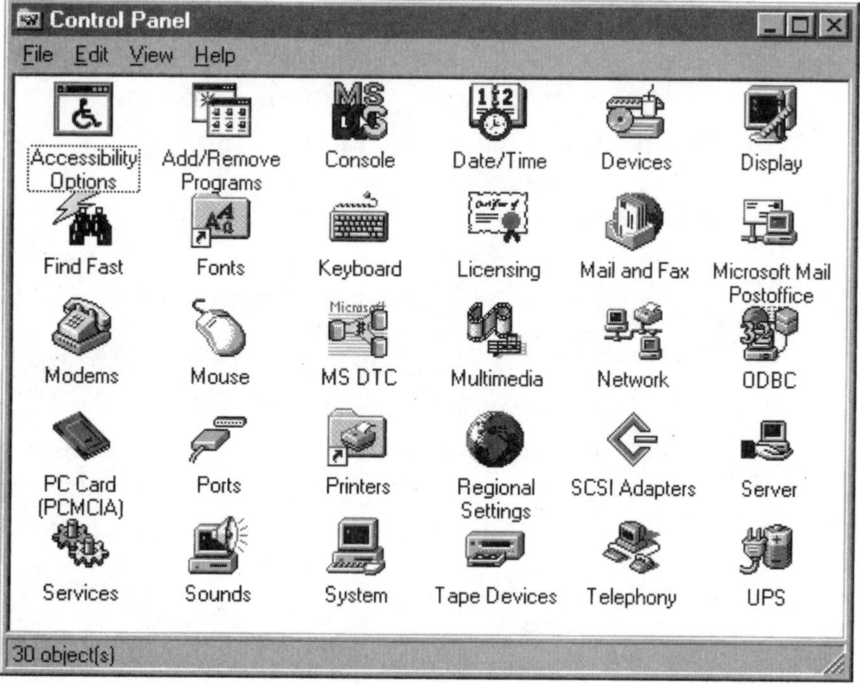

Figure 2-5: A typical Control Panel display.

The Windows NT 4 Server Wizard

New with Windows NT 4 Server is the Administrative Wizards program. This program calls up a number of "wizards," which make administration of Windows NT 4 Server a snap!

Within Administrative Wizards are eight wizards for the administrator:

- Add User Accounts—runs the Add User Account Wizard, which allows you to add a user to the user list easily.
- Group Management—runs the Group Management Wizard, which allows you to add a group or modify an existing group.
- Managing File and Folder Access—runs the Managing File and Folder Access wizard, which allows you to manage file and folder access both on the current and any other domain.
- Add Printer—runs the Add Printer Wizard, which allows you to install either a local or network printer.
- Add/Remove Programs—adds (and removes) applications to Windows NT 4 Server. This wizard is a shortcut to the Control Panel's Add/Remove Programs applet.
- Install New Modem—adds, removes, or modifies modems. This wizard is a shortcut to the Control Panel's Modems applet.
- Network Client Administrator—manages client configuration, allowing the administrator to make installation startup disks, installation disk sets, copy client-based network administration tools, and view remote boot client information.
- License Compliance—the License Compliance Wizard allows you to search for license compliance on both the current domain and other domains.

DHCP Relay Agent

The Dynamic Host Configuration Protocol (DHCP) was designed as an extension to the already existing bootstrap protocol (BOOTP). BOOTP currently boots and configures diskless workstations across the network.

Windows NT 4 Server now serves as a BOOTP relay agent. This allows a client to boot from a DHCP server that is located on a different subnet. A BOOTP relay agent means that you need have only one DHCP server on a large TCP/IP network, rather than having two or more DHCP servers.

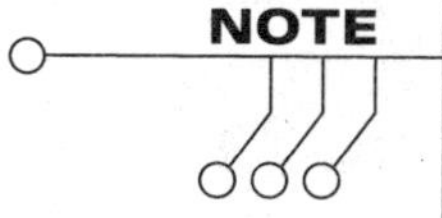

BOOTP was originally defined in RFC 951. (An RFC (Request For Comments) establishes a standard for Internet and TCP/IP. RFCs never change; if changes are needed, then the entire RFC is replaced.) As well, the latest definition of BOOTP is contained in RFC 1542. This RFC includes support for DHCP.

Domain Name Service (DNS)

Windows NT 4 Server includes a built-in DNS to facilitate network connections using TCP/IP protocol. The Windows NT 4 Server DNS is fully RFC compliant.

DNS works by providing a distributed database of names and Internet addresses. When a client system requires the Internet address for a given name (for example, a client knows my Internet name is darkstar.mv.com), the DNS tells the client that my Internet address is 199.125.78.23. Now that might be viewed as magic, but it is simpler than that. The client resolves the lowest part of my name, "mv.com," and then requests, from mv.com, the Internet address for the darkstar domain.

RFC 1034 and RFC 1035 contain a hierarchical naming system for identifying hosts on the Internet.

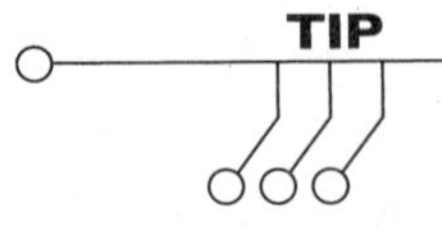

For a copy of an RFC, try http://michael.nii.ncb.gov.sg:4242/ietf/rfc for a complete list of RFCs. This site is an FTP site with the RFCs in text format. See the file http://michael.nii.ncb.gov.sg:4242/ietf/rfc/rfc-retrieval.txt for more information about retrieving a specific RFC.

Windows NT 4 Server also supports WINS (Windows Internet Names Service). WINS is similar to DNS; however, there are some differences. WINS is specific to Windows and doesn't exist on the Internet the way that DNS servers do. DNS uses a static Internet address to resolve a node or network name. WINS, on the other hand, resolves this mapping in a dynamic manner, and requires somewhat less effort to administer.

The main DNS database is managed by InterNIC (Internet Network Information Center).

InterNIC

The InterNIC is a fundamental part of the Internet. InterNIC's own description is:

"In January of 1993 the InterNIC was established as a collaborative project between AT&T, General Atomics, and Network Solutions, Inc. and supported by three five-year cooperative agreements with the National Science Foundation. AT&T was to manage the InterNIC Directory and Database Services project, NSI was to manage the Registration Services project, and General Atomics was to manage the Information Services project."

You can reach InterNIC on the Web at http://ds2.internic.net/ds/dspg01.html. Starting at this page you can do searches, obtain documentation, and interact with InterNIC as needed.

DNS is configured as a client-server database system. The DNS servers contain information about a part of the DNS database that is unique to the domain, and make this information available to the client resolver. DNS resolvers are clients that attempt to determine

an Internet address based on the name information provided by the client. The necessary software for the resolver is installed with the Microsoft TCP/IP protocol.

DNS is typically important when you are running a TCP/IP network, or when you have an Internet or intranet address with sub-domains that must be resolved. If you are connected to the Internet as a single node (typically through an independent ISP), then the need for your own DNS is non-existent; your ISP will configure their DNS to include information about your node or sub-domain.

DNS & WINS Integration

As mentioned above, DNS and WINS are very similar. Both are used to resolve names to Internet (TCP/IP) addresses. WINS works with dynamic Internet addresses, while DNS works with fixed addresses.

Windows NT 4 Server now integrates WINS and DNS into a single unified structure, which makes management of both WINS and DNS easier. For more information about WINS and DNS, see Chapter 5, "Configuring TCP/IP Services."

DNS Support in UNC Names

The Windows Unified Naming Convention (UNC) is, in Windows NT 4 Server, able to support DNS names. A UNC name is expressed as \\server\share.

This support allows clients to connect to a Windows NT 4 Server shared folder (share). The server DORA has the DNS (Internet) name of darkstar.mv.com. With DNS names support in Windows NT 4 Server, a user can use either the DNS name or the Windows networking name to connect to a share. For example, with Windows networking, a user might connect to the share "andrew_g" on the server DORA using the following name: \\DORA\andrew_g.

The same share expressed as a UNC share is \\darkstar.mv.com\andrew_g.

Normally the client would connect to andrew_g on the server named DORA, if the DNS did not support UNC names.

Microsoft Internet Information Server (IIS)

The Microsoft Internet Information Server is a complete family of servers for Internet and intranets. In keeping with Microsoft's goal to move fully into the world of the Internet, the Microsoft Internet Information Server (IIS) was provided as an optional feature for Windows NT 3.51 Server. IIS is now included in the Windows NT 4 Server base product; Microsoft is offering a limited-feature version of IIS for use with Windows NT 4 Workstation and plans to offer the same with future versions of Windows 95.

Intranets

In the section "Why Windows NT 4 Server?" of Chapter 1, we began a discussion about networks and introduced you to the term intranet. Are you still confusing an intranet with the Internet?

We have become, in the last few years, used to living with the Internet. Now, we keep hearing the term intranet! An intranet (note: Internet, a proper noun, is capitalized, while intranet, a common noun, is not) is a private network that works just like the Internet: you can have Web pages, FTP sites, Gopher sites, Telnet, and all the other goodies that the Internet supports on an intranet. There is one, and only one, Internet. There are many, many intranets throughout the world.

What's the difference? An intranet is private, being self contained within an organization. Some intranets are interconnected to the Internet, but such connections are typically limited, usually not allowing outside Internet users access to the resources found on the intranet.

Take an intranet, connect it to the Internet with no restrictions for access, and the intranet ceases to exist: it becomes a part of the Internet.

Microsoft Internet Information Server consists of three separate servers:

- Gopher
- FTP
- World Wide Web (WWW)

Of these three servers, the WWW server will be extensively customized by the user, to provide a great deal of individuality to the Web site. In addition, the administrator of the IIS may set a number of options to configure the other IIS services.

Part III, "Windows NT 4 & the Internet," covers IIS and the IIS servers.

Figure 2-6 shows the IIS Internet Service Manager program running with servers for WWW, FTP, and Gopher active.

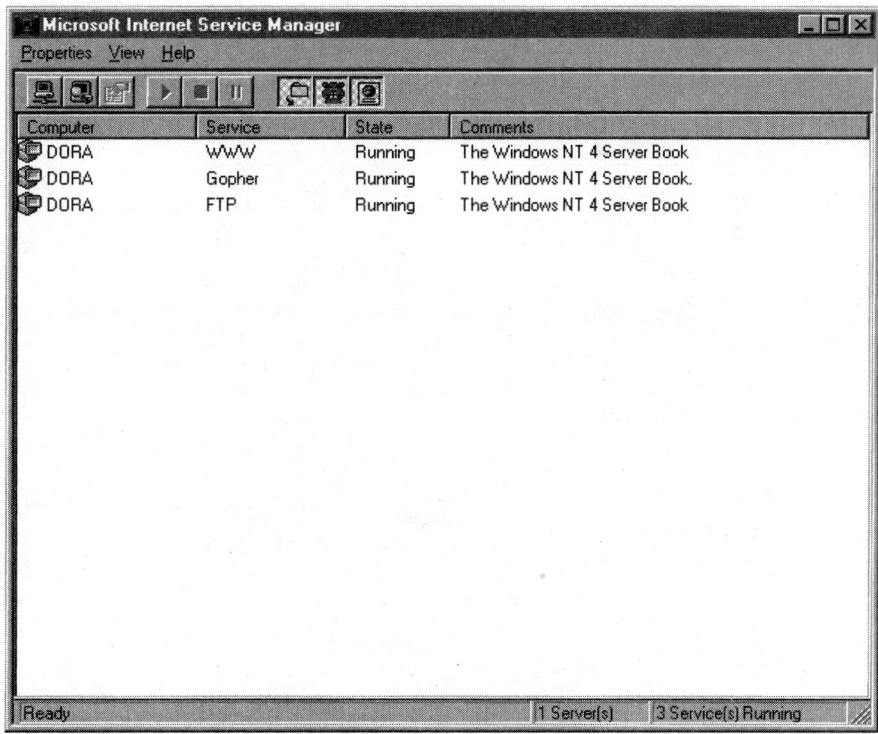

Figure 2-6: The IIS Internet Service Manager.

Multi-Protocol Routing (MPR)

Windows NT 4 Server is able to work fully as a router. A router is a computer that transfers messages or other information from one network to another. For example, you may take Windows NT 4 Server and connect it to the Internet, as a first network. Then from the Windows NT 4 Server you may create a second network that connects all the other systems in your facility. In this configuration, the other computers, on the second network, are able to access resources on the first (Internet) network.

Multi-protocol routing allows the first and second networks to support different protocols. A classic example of this is when there are Novell NetWare servers mixed with Windows NT 4 Servers. Figure 2-7 shows a typical example, where the clients connected to the Windows NT 4 Server are able to access resources found on the NetWare server. Also shown in Figure 2-7 is the connection of a Macintosh client to the network.

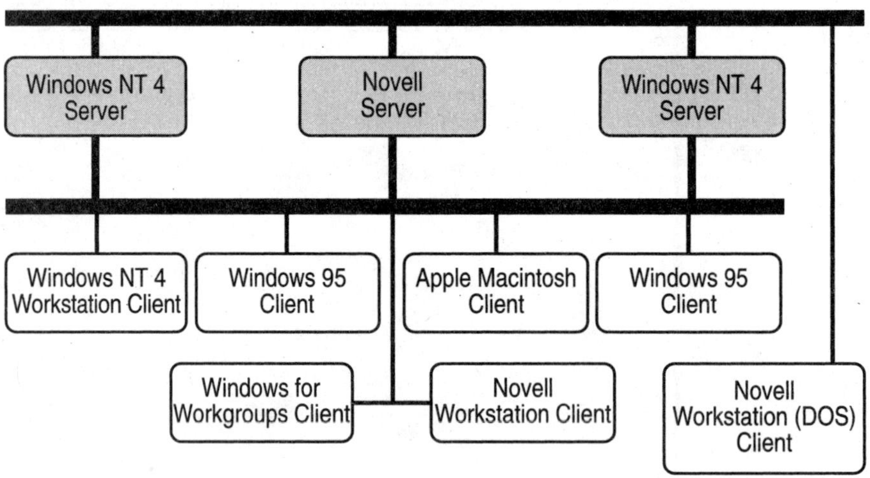

Figure 2-7: A mixed server/client network.

Routing multi-protocols is often a difficult task. It is beyond the scope of this book to provide detailed steps to configuring a multi-protocol router.

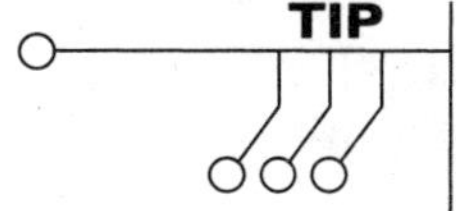

You will need to have two (or more) NICs (Network Interface Cards) installed in your Windows NT 4 Server to utilize routing. In some cases, it is possible that one NIC can be your RAS (Remote Access Server, the facility where client users may dial into the Windows NT 4 Server) configuration, which uses a modem as one NIC.

Remote Administration

Remote administration allows the system administrator to perform Windows NT 4 Server administration tasks from either Windows 95 or Windows for Workgroups computers. The tools, and their administration tasks, are covered below.

Using remote administration allows the system administrator to be physically situated in a different location than the server: this is useful when the server's location is based on performance requirements, while the administrator's location is based on other criteria! A remotely administered Windows NT 4 Server may be located any distance from the administrator, though typically the administrator can, if need be, gain physical access to the server.

A second use for remote administration is for organizations that have more than one Windows NT 4 Server. These organizations benefit from the ability to manage all servers from a central location (which may be one of the servers).

Remote Server Management

The server manager program (SRVMGR.EXE) allows a remote system administrator to:

- Select a domain, workgroup, or computer to be administered.
- Manage the computer by viewing connected users, view shared and open resources, manage services and shared directories, and send messages to connected users.

- Manage a domain, including promoting a Backup Domain Controller (BDC) to a Primary Domain Controller (PDC), synchronize servers with the PDC, and add/remove computers from the domain.

The server manager is a flexible program for remote administration.

Remote User Management

The user manager program (USRMGR.EXE) allows a remote system administrator to manage:

- User accounts
- Groups
- Windows NT 4 Server security policies

Remote Event Viewing

The event view program (EVENTVWR.EXE) is very useful in allowing the remote system administrator to view the server's event logs. The event log is the log of all exception conditions that have occurred on the server. Not all entries in the event log are errors—there will be information as well as error entries in the typical event log.

Using the event log may point you toward a problem that will require you to locally interact with the server. Such is life—the event log may well inform the administrator of hardware failures, software problems, or other issues requiring local intervention at the server.

Remote Booting of Windows 95 Clients

At first glance, this feature doesn't make sense. The feature implies that the system administrator can, perhaps with a push of a button, cause a client to "reboot." Alas, this is not so (though sometimes you may wish for such a feature).

Remote booting is for organizations with "diskless" workstations. A diskless workstation does not have a local hard drive (though it usually has a floppy drive) to boot from. Rather, booting is done from a PROM (Programmable Read-Only Memory) chip on the NIC.

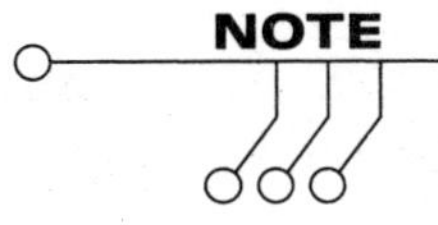

The remote booting service does not support either Windows 3.0 or Windows for Workgroups clients. Remote booted clients may be MS-DOS (version 3.3 or higher), Windows 3.1, or Windows 95 clients only.

Configuring a remote booting system is a rather complex process. It requires that the administrator (re)install Windows 95 on the client machine and make other changes in the installation procedure.

For more information on the remote booting features, see the file \clients\rpl\readme.txt found on the Windows NT 4 Server CD.

User-Defined Internet Special Groups

With Windows NT 4 Server it is possible to create a special group. Special groups are useful when you wish to group resources (for example, printers) for easier reference or browsing.

You would use either the LMHOSTS or WINS to create your special groups. The WINS service is covered in Chapter 5, "Configuring TCP/IP Services."

The LMHOSTS file (located in the Windows NT 4 Server base folder) can map a name to an IP address. This enables Windows to match the name to the IP address without consulting a DNS server. For example, you could create an LMHOSTS file with the following entry:

```
199.125.78.23  dora
```

The above LMHOSTS entry would tell Windows that whenever the name dora was specified, the IP address 199.125.78.23 should be used. You could, if you knew the correct passwords, then establish links to my shared resources by specifying a NET USE command:

```
NET USE q: \\dora\c password
```

The LMHOSTS file is read and parsed each time it is used, so the file's size should be limited—do not add extraneous comments to the LMHOSTS file; rather, create a documentation file (perhaps call the documentation file LMHOSTS.TXT).

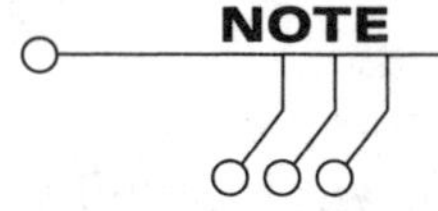

Special groups are limited to a maximum of 25 members.

Changes in the Driver Structure

Windows NT 4 Server (and Windows NT 4 Workstation) have had internal changes to their hardware drivers. This change improved Windows NT 4 Server's performance, which now rivals Windows 95's more streamlined system.

A downside of this change is that drivers for Windows NT 3.51 will not function with Windows NT 4. Any special video drivers will have to be replaced with updated versions. If your video card is not listed on the HCL (Hardware Compatibility List, which is supplied with Windows NT 4 Server), then you should (prior to installing Windows NT 4 Server) contact the hardware manufacturer to obtain updated drivers, or suffer with the generic VGA mode drivers.

Printer drivers have also been changed somewhat. As printers don't change as quickly as video drivers, this should present few problems to most Windows NT 4 Server users.

Common Groups

Common groups allow multiple users to work with a single Windows NT 4 Server system. For example, you may have two, three, or more operators (for example, backup, user, and system administrator) who are logging onto the same machine.

With common groups, you can have a single set of Start menu items shared between all users. For example, on my DORA server, I have common groups for:

Administrative Tools (Common)

Microsoft Internet Server (Common)

Network Administration (Common)

Startup

The common groups are stored in the folder C:\WINNT\profiles\ All Users\Start Menu\programs (where C:\WINNT is the folder in which Windows NT 4 Server is installed). In the above list of folders, most are suffixed with "(Common)," which is used to indicate to the user that the folder is shared between all users.

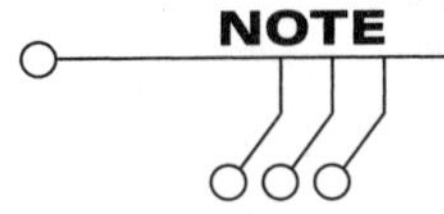

It is not possible to limit the sharing of the common groups. Any folder in "All Users\Start Menu\programs" will be accessible to any user who is able to log onto your Windows NT 4 Server. This does not mean that any user will have the privileges to run the program or application. For example, most of the tools in Administrative Tools (Common) require the user have Administrator privileges before they will run.

Notice that there is a second "Startup" group. This startup folder functions in exactly the same manner as the user's startup folder. Any applications or other tasks that must be initiated on startup (regardless of the user) should be placed in the "All Users\Start menu\programs\Startup" folder, and not in each individual's startup folder.

Dial-Up Networking and Remote Access Server

Dial-Up Networking (DUN) has been a standard feature on Windows 95. With Windows NT 4, the Windows NT Remote Access Server (RAS) functionality has been revamped to work like the Windows 95 DUN.

Additionally, Microsoft has renamed the Remote Access Server client facilities to Dial-Up Networking to make the terminology consistent across platforms.

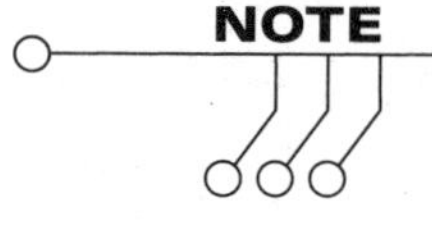

DUN, on future versions of Windows 95, will also be slightly redesigned to match that which is found on Windows NT 4. These changes will first be seen in the OEM releases of Windows 95, and as part of an enhancement package that should be available online to existing Windows 95 users.

DUN and RAS will be covered in Chapter 7, "Configuring Dial-Up Networking."

Differences Between the Server & Workstation Products

There are a number of differences between Windows NT 4 Server and Windows NT 4 Workstation. For example, both products function as a server; however, Windows NT 4 Workstation does have limitations in how many users may connect to devices shared by Windows NT 4 Workstation.

Table 2-1 lists the main differences between Windows NT 4 Server and Windows NT 4 Workstation. We use the term "limited" to indicate a feature that is present with limited functionality.

Feature	Server	Workstation
Hardware Profiles	Yes	Yes
Internet Explorer	Yes	Yes
Messaging Subsystem	Yes	Yes
Paint	Yes	Yes
Windows 95 User Interface	Yes	Yes
Windows Explorer	Yes	Yes

Feature	Server	Workstation
WordPad	Yes	Yes
Device Sharing	Yes	Limited
Internet Information Server (IIS)	Yes	Limited
DHCP Relay Agent	Yes	No
DNS and WINS	Yes	No
DNS Name Service	Yes	No
Multi-Protocol Routing (MPR)	Yes	No
Remote Administration	Yes	No
Remote Boot for Clients	Yes	No
User-defined Special Interest Groups	Yes	No

Table 2-1: Windows NT 4 Server and Windows NT 4 Workstation compared.

The Hardware Compatibility List

As we stated in the "Accessories & Optional Hardware" section of Chapter 1, Microsoft publishes a complete Hardware Compatibility List (HCL) for Windows NT 4 Server and Windows NT 4 Workstation. For most users, any recent version of the HCL will be adequate. For users who are contemplating (or committed to) new, state-of-the-art hardware, the most recent HCL is necessary.

To obtain the most recent HCL, you should contact Microsoft's Web site at http://198.105.232.4/support/ or FTP a copy at ftp://ftp.microsoft.com in bussys/winnt/winnt-docs/hcl/hcl400.

Moving On

In this chapter we introduced Windows NT 4 Server. We referred to Windows 95 many times, since Windows NT 4 Server *looks* so much like Windows 95. Basically, Microsoft has given us a new way to use our computers. There's less pointing and clicking involved to find files and start programs. We've discussed the Microsoft Windows Explorer, the Start button menu, and the taskbar. We've also seen how Microsoft has enhanced the Windows Control Panel to reduce system administration tasks. Windows NT 4 Server has built-in intranet and Internet support and is packaged with the fastest Web server on the market today, the Microsoft Internet Information Server (IIS). So what are you waiting for? Get ready to install!

In the next chapter, "Installing Windows NT 4 Server," we will cover issues that the system administrator will face when installing Windows NT 4 Server. Both installations as upgrades over Windows NT 3.51 Server and clean installations will be discussed.

3

Installing Windows NT 4 Server

This chapter provides an overview of the installation process for Windows NT 4 Server. Due to the complexity of Windows NT 4 Server and the different configurations you can install, the information in this chapter is, perhaps, a bit general. Typical installation situations are covered, but each installation is unique! If your first installation doesn't work as expected, don't be afraid—simply try again.

Some of the questions covered in this chapter include:

- How is Windows NT 4 Server installed?
- Do I install Windows NT 4 Server as a clean, new, installation, or can Windows NT 4 Server upgrade Windows NT 3.5x Server?
- Is this a good time to change our networking model or configuration?
- How can I minimize the impact of installing Windows NT 4 Server?

You need to address each of these critical questions (and many more which are unvoiced!) when installing a new network operating system. In this chapter we will find the answers to these questions, and much more.

Getting Started

Installation of Windows NT 4 Server can be either a new installation, an upgrade of an existing Windows NT Server installation, or an installation over another operating system such as NetWare, OS/2, Windows 95, or even MS-DOS.

Generally, conversions between disparate operating systems present the most difficult problems. Neither Novell's NetWare disk format nor OS/2's HPFS are compatible with Windows NT 4 Server. Upgrading these systems can be a daunting task and may require considerable work: creating a compatible backup, reformatting the drive, and restoring the user files.

In this section of the chapter we take a quick look at what you need to do before you begin a typical new installation. The minimum system hardware requirements are found in the "System Requirements" section of Chapter 2, "What's New in Windows NT 4 Server."

Installing Windows NT 4 Server can be as simple as placing the Windows NT 4 Server distribution CD in the drive and running the installation program. A few preliminary steps are in order before doing this, however:

1. Check the hardware compatibility list (HCL) to make sure that your hardware is compatible. Though Windows NT 4 Server may well install on hardware that is not on the HCL (which is supplied with the Windows NT 4 Server documentation), there is no guarantee that it will work correctly.
2. Make sure you have sufficient resources to install Windows NT 4 Server. Check RAM (though 12MB is the listed minimum, a working Windows NT 4 Server installation needs an absolute minimum of 16MB and will work better on a 32MB machine). Check the hard drive free space—to do the installation a few hundred MB of free space is needed. Check your video card to make sure you have drivers for it, otherwise you may end up using that new user interface in 640/480 16-color mode—ugh.

3. Check to make absolutely sure you have a current backup. Better yet, make sure you have two current backups, if there is any critical data on the system. A flawed backup pretty much guarantees that you will have serious problems with your installation of the operating system. Do make sure that your backup is complete and current. Make sure that applications and systems (such as BackOffice, Office 95, compilers, and the like) disks are available to allow reinstallation with a minimum of problems.
4. Make sure you have enough time to do the installation. Anticipate problems and exceptions. Getting halfway through the installation doesn't give you half of the server! Plan ahead… Consider what may go wrong, and know that these items probably won't be a problem. Things you don't take into consideration are the things that will go wrong and halt the installation. Murphy's Law understands installations and strikes constantly at this stage!

Throughout this chapter, I refer to a person called the system administrator. This is typically you, the reader, the person who is responsible for the Windows NT Server and its administration. Throughout the documentation and help files, Microsoft tells you "if you don't know this item, ask your system administrator." This can be a difficult task! When the system administrator logs onto Windows NT 4 Server, the "administrator" login (or user) ID is used. The Windows NT 4 Server's installation program only creates one login ID automatically, the "administrator" login ID.

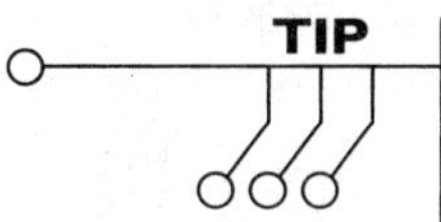

There is nothing to prevent you from having multiple installations of Windows NT Server. For example, you can have a working copy of Windows NT 4 Server, a working copy of Windows NT 3.51 Server, and a test version of Windows NT 4 Server on the same machine. In fact, you can have as many "versions" of Windows NT Server as disk space and licensing allow.

Having a working copy of Windows NT 3.51 Server provides a "fallback" system in the event that unexpected problems make the new installation of Windows NT 4 Server unstable.

Installation Options

An important question is: How is Windows NT 4 Server installed? There are a number of installation situations, depending on whether the installation is an upgrade of an existing system, a new server being placed online, or perhaps, a new network or organization. The types of installations arising from these situations include:

- Clean installation. Starting from scratch with nothing on the hard drive you want to keep.
- Upgrading from another operating system. In this situation, you have several options. First, Windows NT 4 Server won't upgrade Windows 3.x or Windows 95. You can either replace the existing version of Windows, or create a dual-boot installation. When creating a dual-boot machine, you must not convert the boot drive's file system to NTFS (NT File System): DOS and Windows 95 cannot be booted from an NTFS partition. Generally, there is no advantage to replacing an existing copy of Windows 95—simply create a dual-boot system, and delete the Windows 95 installation at a convenient time in the future.
- Upgrading from a previous version of Windows NT. Typically this will be Windows NT 3.5x, though you may be upgrading over Windows NT 3.x. You can upgrade over Windows NT 3.5x successfully. However, you may find it advantageous to do a clean installation rather than upgrading an existing installation—a clean installation creates a known starting point for debugging when problems develop.
- Upgrading from a previous beta version of Windows NT Server. In this case, I strongly recommend that you make a clean installation. It may be acceptable to create a dual-boot system to allow items to be transferred to the new version of Windows NT 4 Server, but upgrading a beta version of Windows is not even recommended by Microsoft!
- Upgrading either OS/2 (with HPFS partitions) or Novell NetWare servers. This can be problematic. The safest method to upgrade either of the above is to:

1. Install a second server, using a different computer (you could rent, for a short period of time, a computer to host the new server if you do not have hardware available).
2. Install Windows NT 4 Server on the second computer.
3. Get the Windows NT 4 Server (the new server) system running correctly. Make sure client users are able to access the second Windows NT 4 Server.
4. Migrate the data from your OS/2 or NetWare server to the new Windows NT 4 server.
5. Once all data has been migrated, ensure that all client user needs are being met, then shut down the original OS/2 or NetWare server.
6. If all hell doesn't break loose after a few days, back up the original server, low-level format the drive, and install a second copy of Windows NT 4 Server.
7. A restore of your server's data from the temporary server completes the installation. If you have only one license for Windows NT 4 Server, don't leave both servers installed.

You can install Windows NT 4 Server on Intel (486, Pentium, or Pentium Pro), PPC, MIPS, or Alpha platforms. Regardless of the platform, the basic installation steps are identical.

Throughout this chapter, the installation examples are for the Intel platform (the most commonly used platform). Whenever the CD folder I386 is referred to in this book, and you are using a non-Intel platform, substitute PPC, MIPS, or ALPHA for the folder on the CD where the Windows NT 4 Server installation files are found.

Regardless of which installation option you choose, you can install Windows NT 4 Server either by booting the Windows NT 4 Server distribution CD-ROM, booting the boot diskettes, or by running the WINNT32.EXE (or WINNT.EXE for Windows 95 users) setup program. When running the setup program you can choose to:

- Install without using boot diskettes (the easiest and fastest option).

- Create, then install, using boot diskettes (the safest but slower option).
- Install using a previously created set of boot diskettes (which is safer and faster than creating the boot diskettes).

Whenever possible, install without using boot diskettes; the installation will be faster and easier.

The Windows NT 4 Server Setup Program

Existing Windows NT users install Windows NT 4 Server using the setup program—WINNT32.EXE. Existing Windows 95 (or Windows 3.x) system users install Windows NT 4 Server using the WINNT.EXE program. There is no difference between these two programs, other than the fact that WINNT.EXE is a 16-bit version of WINNT32.EXE. Both setup programs install the same version of Windows NT 4 Server; the difference is that the 16-bit version is designed to run under Windows 95 and Windows 3.x.

The options and functionality of WINNT32.EXE and WINNT.EXE are identical, therefore I refer to both of these programs generically as the "setup program." Simply use the correct version for whichever operating system you are using to install Windows NT 4 Server.

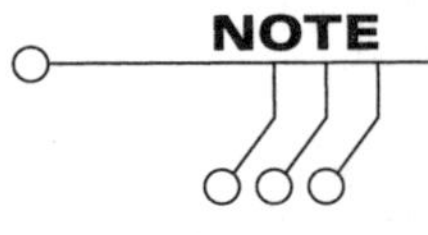

The installation program's output and flow may change with each option, selection, and feature you select. Generally, things may be added, or missing from your installation as compared to the installation described in this chapter. However, the general flow of installation will be similar.

(There is a murmuring out there... and questions... Do I hear questions?)

Q: Why doesn't Windows 95, a 32-bit operating system, use the 32-bit version of the setup program?

A: I don't know. For reasons that only Microsoft knows, the 32-bit version of the setup program works only under Windows NT. To install from Windows 95, you must use the 16-bit version. Since the results of the installation are identical in either case, this is not a problem.

Q: *Can I upgrade my Windows 95 installation to Windows NT 4 Server?*

A: *No, there is no upgrade path between Windows 95 and Windows NT 4 Server. You probably will want to install Windows NT 4 Server as a second operating system and use the dual boot feature.*

Q: *If I do a clean installation of Windows NT 4 Server, do I have to reinstall all my applications?*

A: *Generally speaking, yes. Some applications are able to repair their own installations (Visual C++ is one example) so that they run correctly even if not installed under the current operating system.*

Q: *If I have Microsoft Office installed under Windows 95, and install dual boot Windows NT 4 Server, do I have to have two copies of Microsoft Office installed?*

A: *No, install Microsoft Office under Windows 95, into the MSOffice folder, then in Windows NT 4 Server install Microsoft Office into the same folder a second time. This works for Microsoft Office and most other applications.*

Q: *Do I need to use the bootable diskettes if I am upgrading from an earlier version of Windows NT or installing a dual boot system from Windows 95?*

A: *No, probably not. Use the WINNT32.EXE's /B option to disable the creation and use of boot diskettes.*

Q: *I want to install Windows NT 4 Server with dual boot to retain my Windows 95 installation. Later if I want to delete both Windows 95 and dual boot, can I do this?*

A: *Sure. Use DELTREE (or Explorer) to delete the Windows 95 folder, then edit the BOOT.INI file (see Chapter 19, "The Registry," for more information on the BOOT.INI file) in the root folder to remove the reference to the other operating system. Finally, in the Control Panel's System applet, set the time delay on boot to one second.*

Q: *Will my Windows 95 (and Windows 3.x) applications work under Windows NT 4 Server?*

A: *Generally. The great majority do, though from time to time, we see applications (mostly older ones) that don't behave the way we expected.*

(No more questions? Okay, then.)

Options for the setup program are shown below in Table 3-1. You can enter these options when starting the setup program, as well as modify some after you have begun the installation.

Option	Description
/?	Tells the setup program to display the options screen.
/S:*sourcefile*	Specifies the source path to the Windows NT 4 Server setup files. The default is the current path. You can run the setup program from a folder other than the one on the distribution CD.
/I:*inffile*	Specifies the file name and/or path to the Windows NT 4 Server setup .INF file. The default is the current path, DOSNET.INF. Some installations may use customized setup .INF files.
/T:*tempDrive*	Specifies the drive to which the Windows NT 4 Server installation temporary files are written. The default is the C drive. This option is very useful when your C drive has limited free space.
/X	Tells the setup program to not create installation boot diskettes. You must have a set of the boot diskettes (either from the distribution package or a set that you create using the /O option).
/B	Tells the setup program to not use installation boot diskettes. The installation is done by reading the necessary files from the CD directly to the temporary file location. Typically this is the fastest way to install Windows NT 4 Server, but requires that you have an operating system already installed that supports your CD-ROM drive.
/O	Tells the setup program to create the boot diskettes only. Diskettes created with the /O option are used only when installing Windows NT 4 Server using the setup program. These diskettes should not be booted except when prompted by the setup program. Windows NT 4 Server is not installed with this option. You use this option to create boot diskettes for a system unable to create the boot diskettes (perhaps because the target system does not yet have any operating system installed). Note: the diskettes you supply must be formatted and blank.

Option	Description
/OX	Tells the setup program to create the boot diskettes for a CD-ROM or diskette-based installation. Windows NT 4 Server is not installed with this option. You use this option to create boot diskettes for a system that is unable to create the boot diskettes (perhaps because the target system does not yet have any operating system installed). Note: the diskettes you supply must be formatted and blank. You use boot diskettes created with the /OX option to boot from power-up to install Windows NT 4 Server.

Table 3-1: Setup program options.

You modify options, such as whether to create boot diskettes and specifying the name and location of the .INF setup file, using the first dialog box of the setup program.

A Clean Windows NT 4 Server Installation

A clean Windows NT 4 Server installation, on a computer which does not already have an operating system, can be the easiest installation to do. However you must have properly planned your server and network, and have all the necessary information about your system and network at hand (including user names, network topography, and so on).

With systems that have bootable CD-ROM drives, an installation of Windows NT 4 Server can be as simple as placing the Windows NT 4 Server distribution CD into the CD-ROM drive and booting the computer. Only some newer Intel-based systems (equipped with SCSI CD-ROM drives) and most non-Intel platforms have bootable CD-ROM drives.

For systems that do not allow booting from the CD-ROM, it is necessary to boot the diskettes that accompany the Windows NT 4 Server distribution package. If you do not have the distribution boot diskettes, you can create boot diskettes using a computer with the same architecture (Intel, MIPS, Alpha, or PPC) and a CD-ROM drive. (Creating boot diskettes is described later in this chapter.)

To begin the installation it is necessary to boot the system. Regardless of which method you use (diskette or CD-ROM booting), the setup program runs, tests the hardware, and installs the necessary drivers to access the CD-ROM drive and drivers for other necessary system hardware (such as your mouse). Once this part of the setup program is complete, the installation is virtually identical to an installation that is done as an upgrade from an earlier version of Windows NT.

Upgrading MS-DOS or Windows 95

Doing an installation over either MS-DOS or Windows 95 is a simple task. As neither of these operating systems may be upgraded to Windows NT 4 Server, you can treat each situation as a new installation.

One nice aspect of Windows NT 4 Server is that it automatically supports dual-booting. This allows you to retain your existing MS-DOS or Windows 95 installation if necessary.

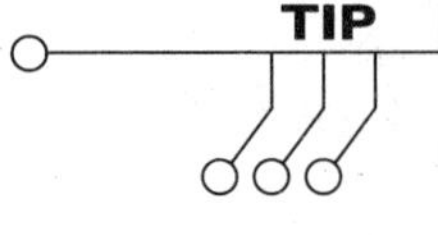

If you're doing an installation over MS-DOS or Windows 95 and you wish to retain your existing DOS or Windows 95 installation, do not change the drive's format to NTFS. Neither DOS nor Windows 95 can directly read an NTFS-formatted drive.

If you are a Windows 95 user with a FAT-32 file system installed, convert back to FAT-16 prior to installing Windows NT 4 Server. As Microsoft plans to support FAT-32 in later releases of Windows NT 4 Server, check the release notes for more on FAT-32 support.

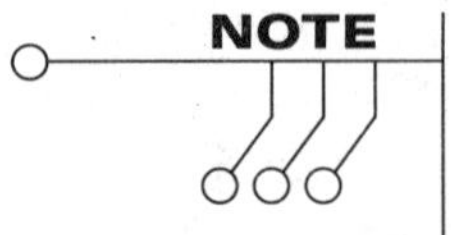

When this book was written, there was no support for FAT-32, Microsoft's new high-capacity FAT file system. Microsoft has made it clear that they are working on a FAT-32 enhancement for Windows NT 4 Server that should be released shortly after the initial release of Windows NT 4 Server.

You are not prompted to create a dual-boot system: the Windows NT 4 Server setup program automatically creates a dual-boot system for you. If you later delete the MS-DOS or Windows 95 system from your computer, you can manually edit the BOOT.INI file (found in the boot drive's root folder, as a system, read-only file) to remove the DOS or Windows 95 boot option.

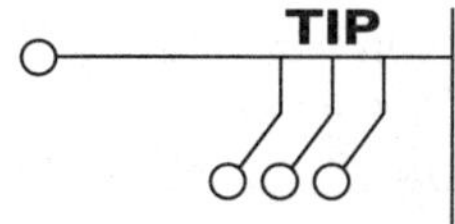

To add a MS-DOS/Windows 95 dual boot option after doing a clean installation of Windows NT 4 Server, simply install DOS or Windows 95. Then, use the Emergency Repair Disk (ERD) to restore the Windows NT 4 Server boot. The ERD fixes the boot options for the system.

Plug-and-Play

For those of us who are using PCI bus machines, with PnP active, it is important to realize that Plug-and-Play (PnP) and PCI create situations that are not what most system administrators expect—Windows NT 4 Server does not support PnP.

PCI, when used with PnP, is slot dependent. For example, let's say you have three PCI slots, numbered one through three. In slot one you have your video card, in slot two you have your network card, and in slot three you have your SCSI controller card. PnP assigns each card an IRQ. You install Windows 95, and it checks each time it is booted to see what PCI PnP cards are installed and what resources these cards are using.

Fine, and next you install Windows NT 4 Server. During installation, Windows NT 4 Server looks at the PCI cards, determines the resources used by each card, and never checks again. All would be fine, but you later find that for some reason (perhaps a cable is too short) you must move your PCI cards to different slots. When the PCI cards are moved, Windows 95 and PnP reassign resources to the cards. Windows 95 automatically detects changes each time it is booted, notes these changes, and works correctly. Windows NT 4 Server, however, is not PnP compatible, and cannot detect when resources have changed; thus Windows NT 4 Server fails the next time it is restarted.

To solve this problem, if you receive a message that a device (or service) cannot be started, check the system error log. Note which device failed. Then make sure the correct resources are assigned to that device.

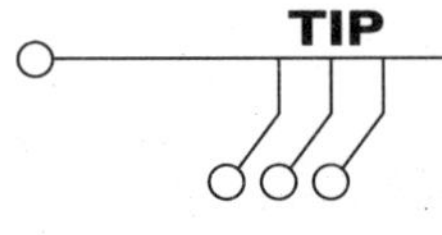

Unlike Windows 95, Windows NT 4 Server does not have a single unified location for reviewing and setting device resources. For Windows NT 4 Server you must use the Control Panel, and select the applet for the device in question. For example, to set the resources for your sound card, you would select the Multimedia applet, Devices tab, and select properties for the Audio device that matches your sound card.

Upgrading Windows NT 3.5x Server

Upgrading to Windows NT 4 Server from Windows NT 3.5x Server is a relatively simple process. The installation can be done from a Windows NT 3.51 Server command prompt, the File Manager's Run menu selection, or by booting the bootable Windows NT 4 Server installation disks.

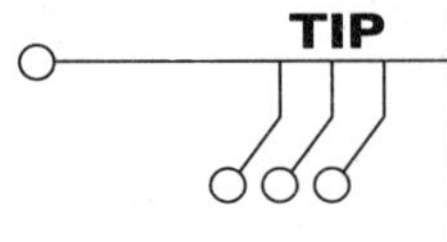

It is not an option to upgrade a Windows NT Workstation installation to Windows NT Server. You must create a clean installation of Windows NT 4 Server if you are currently using Windows NT Workstation on the target computer.

If the target machine has a local CD-ROM drive, and you wish to perform the simplest installation, then from a command prompt, or File Manager, simply execute the WINNT32.EXE program with the /B option. This installs Windows NT 4 Server in a multiple-step process, copying the necessary files from the CD-ROM to a local drive, and then performing the installation.

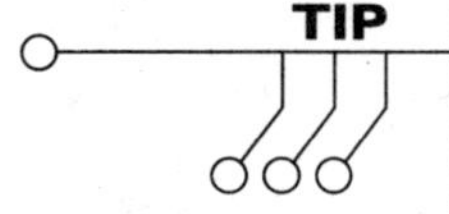

There are good reasons to install Windows NT 4 Server as a new installation:

- *Any components that are not fully compatible are excluded from the installation.*
- *You can preserve your existing Windows NT Server installation and use it to keep the server running if difficulties are encountered.*
- *The size of the installation is smaller—the Windows NT 4 Server installation program doesn't remove old, no longer used files from the Windows NT system directories when upgrading.*

Upgrading Windows NT 4 Server Beta Versions

Neither Microsoft nor I myself recommend that a final release version of a product be installed as an upgrade over a previous beta version of the product. If you have already installed one of the beta versions of Windows NT 4 Server, then I most strongly recommend that you make your final installation clean and delete the beta installation folder.

The best method for removing an existing Windows NT installation is to back up your data and reformat the drive. Although a clean installation requires that you reinstall your applications, this task is not quite as radical as it seems!

A second method which is almost as good, for drives using the FAT file system, is to reinstall the system boot files to the drive using the SYS command (using an MS-DOS or Windows 95 boot diskette). This action disables the Windows NT 4 Server boot code. Then you can boot to DOS (or Windows 95), use DELTREE to remove the Windows NT directory, and reinstall Windows NT 4 Server.

Creating Boot Diskettes

You create boot diskettes by running the Windows NT 4 Server setup program. You would use the option /O, which tells the setup program to create the boot diskettes and not do an installation. Specifying /OX creates boot diskettes for either a CD-ROM or diskette installation.

Whenever you create boot diskettes (as a separate step) no files are written to the system that creates the boot diskettes. This way you don't make any changes, nor require any resources (such as disk space) on the machine that creates the boot diskettes.

Getting Down to Business: Installing Windows NT 4 Server

All installations of Windows NT 4 Server are unique. You may encounter other steps than the ones that are documented below. Don't panic, follow the prompts, and use common sense, use the help features whenever in doubt.

In the following installation example, a primary domain controller (PDC) Windows NT 4 Server is created. Note that the computer system in the example consists of the following components:

- An Intel Pentium 90 (PCI bus) with 32MB of RAM.
- An Adaptec 2940 SCSI adapter (PCI bus) with four hard drives (a 2GB Quantum, a 1GB Micropolis, a 1GB Toshiba, and a 4GB Quantum), and a Toshiba CD-ROM drive.
- A Matrox Millennium adapter (PCI bus) with 4MB of video RAM.
- A 3Com 3c590 combo network adapter (PCI bus).
- Two Panasonic IDE CD-ROM drives, connected to an internal PCI bus IDE adapter. Yes, I have three CD-ROM drives on this server—the next CD-ROM drive will probably be a changer, however.

All the other hardware on this system is common: Microsoft mouse, standard SVGA monitor, 3.5" diskette drive, etc. The installation CD drive is one of the IDE CD-ROM drives.

The computer system in this example has several versions of Windows NT Server already installed: since I wanted to keep these earlier versions of Windows NT Server, I decided to do a clean install of Windows NT 4 Server, with dual-boot capabilities.

Now, on to our installation!

Before You Begin...

Here are a few details that require our attention before we begin:

- Make sure your hardware is operating correctly. If the system has been unstable lately, don't install a new operating system hoping things will get better. A new operating system will not correct hardware flaws or failures.
- Ensure that you have enough space on your target drive to hold Windows NT 4 Server. The setup program tests to make sure that there is enough space to install, but why put up with a failed installation? If installing on your C drive, 120 to 200MB of free space is sufficient.
- Make sure that you have a current and complete backup of the drives! Mr. Murphy has personally assured me that he is watching and will take the necessary steps if your backup is lacking.
- Make sure you have the user list with names, groups, passwords, and such to allow restoring, from scratch, the user database.
- Make sure that you have all the necessary hardware configuration information. If you have Windows 95 installed on the target machine, print the equipment summary report (Control Panel, System applet) and save this. If necessary, write down the cards, drives, IRQs, DMA channels, and I/O addresses used on your system. Understand the implications of installing Windows NT 4 Server on a PCI machine that is dual-booted with Windows 95.

- Make sure you have a hard copy of any other significant information that you may need. Computer names, domain names, passwords, and telephone numbers may all be critical to a successful installation. You probably won't be able to stop your installation to look up a name or number!

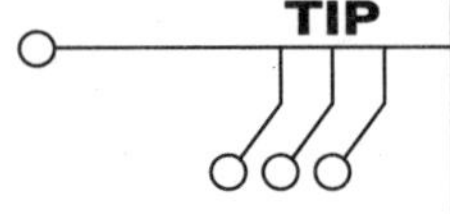

If you have Windows 95 installed, you can use the Windows 95 Control Panel's System applet to print an extensive report on the system: select the Device Manager tab, click "Computer" at the top of the tree view, and then click the Print button.

Now let's do a "typical" installation. We'll try making a clean installation on a machine that already has Windows NT 3.51 Server installed. In this situation, I used File Manager's File | Run option to execute the startup command.

Prior to installing, advise your client users the system will be down, or that performance (if you have multiple servers) may be degraded, as the operating system is being upgraded. If you have backup servers—great, they can take the load while you are installing Windows NT 4 Server. If no backup server is available, then you probably will have to upgrade either at night or on a weekend so as to minimize the impact on users.

Beginning the Installation

Put the Windows NT 4 Server CD in the CD-ROM drive. More than one CD-ROM drive? (I have three on my server.) Use the fastest CD-ROM drive you have—the installation process moves a large number of files from the CD to the hard drive.

Start a command window running. Change to the CD-ROM drive with the CHDIR command. Do a DIR /s command to make sure that the Windows NT 4 Server distribution CD can be read properly. It can be painful to get partway through the installation and find there is a read error on the CD. If there is a read error on the CD, the setup program aborts the installation—you do not risk losing anything if this happens.

TIP

It's not the end of the world if there is a read error on the CD. The Windows NT 4 Server setup program reads all required files from the CD and copies them to a temporary folder, prior to performing the actual installation. You may abort an installation at virtually any step!

You need to change to the folder that matches your system's architecture (for example, the folder I386 if you are using an Intel 486, Pentium, or Pentium Pro). In this chapter we are installing Windows NT 4 Server on a Pentium-based system.

To install, start the setup program (WINNT32.EXE or WINNT.EXE). Generally, you don't need to use boot diskettes to install Windows NT 4 Server as an upgrade, so try installing with the /B option.

Once the program starts, it checks the hard drive free space on all local drives.

After the drives have been checked for free space, a dialog box prompts you for the location of the Windows NT 4 Server files. The default is the path that the setup program was started from, which for most installations is the correct location. Additionally, the dialog box, as shown in Figure 3-1, has an Options button that displays the Options dialog (see Figure 3-2).

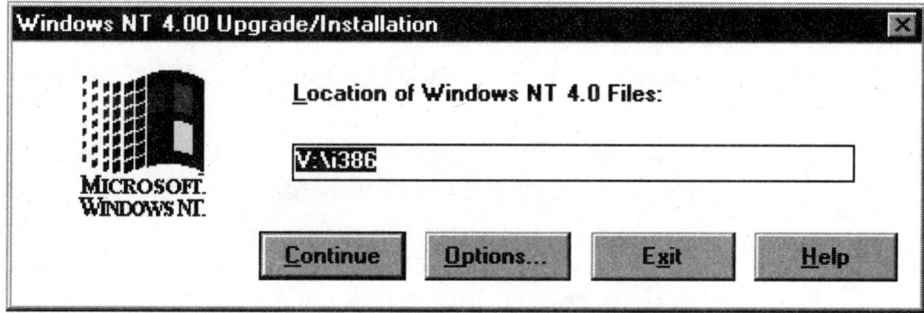

Figure 3-1: The Windows NT 4.0 Upgrade/Installation dialog box.

With the Options dialog, you may change several options, including the creation of boot diskettes, creation of local source, and the name of the installation script file.

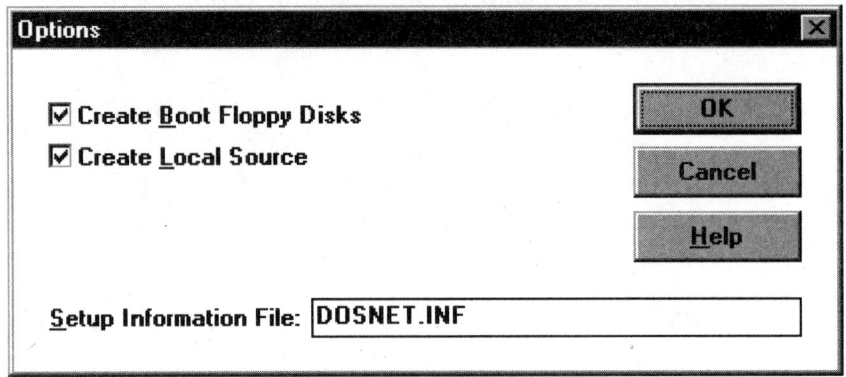

Figure 3-2: The Options dialog box for installation.

After setting any options desired, click OK on the Options dialog box.

Copying Files to the Temporary Directory

The next stage of the installation is copying files from the CD-ROM to the local temporary directory. The file copy process can be lengthy: it may be best if you spend the time checking that you have all the information needed to install Windows NT 4 Server at this time. A double-speed CD-ROM drive gives you enough time to grab a quick lunch.

When the setup program has completed copying the installation files from the CD to the local hard drive, the system prompts you to restart the computer and continue the installation.

Starting the Installation

When the system is rebooted by the setup program, the boot manager starts the Windows NT 4 Server installation procedure. After the computer has booted, the text screen shown in Figure 3-3 displays.

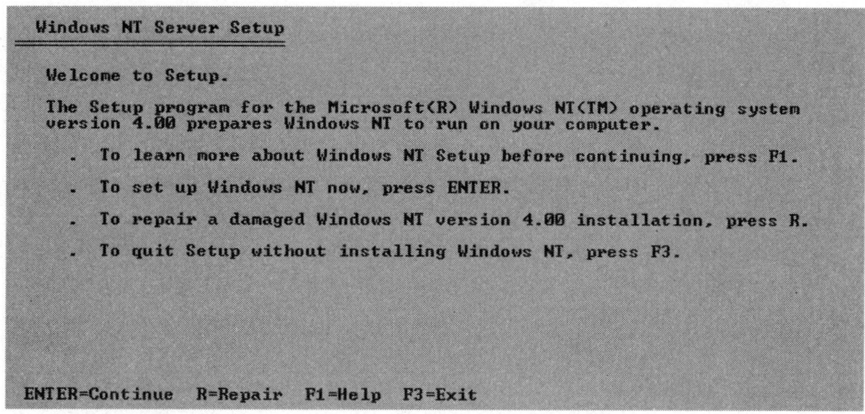

Figure 3-3: The Windows NT Server Setup welcome screen.

Using the setup program you can continue with the installation, repair an existing installation, get help, or exit the installation process. For a clean installation, press Enter to continue.

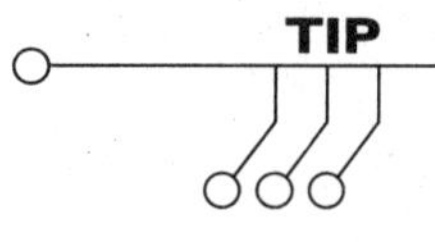

If you had already installed Windows NT 4 Server, but are having problems (perhaps system files were either damaged or deleted in error) you could choose to repair the existing installation. Repair is useful as a complete reinstallation of supporting applications, and systems are not needed.

Scanning for Mass Storage

The next stage of the installation process is to scan for mass storage (hard disks and CD-ROM drives) installed on the computer. Generally, the setup program automatically detects both SCSI and IDE drives.

For some devices you may need to specify the adapter. Figure 3-4 shows the results of the scan for mass storage devices on my computer; your devices will be different, though the screen will be similar. If for some reason the setup program does not find a mass storage device to install Windows NT 4 Server to, the installation cannot continue.

```
Windows NT Server Setup

  Setup has recognized the following mass sotrage devices in your computer:

  IDE CD-ROM (ATAPI  1.2)/Dual-channel PCI IDE Controller
  Adaptec AHA-294X/AHA-394X or AIC-78XX PCI SCSI Controller


  * To Specify additional SCSI Adapters, CD-ROM drivers, or special
    disk controllers for use with Windows NT, including those for which
    you have a device support disk from a mass storage device
    manufacturer, press S.

  * If you do not have any device support disks from a mass storage
    device manufacturer, or do not want to specify additional
    mass storage devices for use with Windows NT, Press ENTER

S=Specify Additional Device ENTER=Continue  F3=Exit
```

Figure 3-4: The Windows NT Server Setup mass storage detection screen lists the storage (disk) devices.

Generally, if most of your mass storage (including your CD-ROM, boot, and installation drives) are detected, you can perform a successful installation. At this stage, you can add to the list of devices any devices that were installed but not detected. Table 3-2 lists some of the supported adapters that are detected or that you can add manually.

Adaptec AHA-151X/AHA-152X or AIC-6260/AIC-6360 SCSI Host Adapter
Adaptec AHA-154X/AHA-164X SCSI Host Adapter
Adaptec AHA-174X EISA SCSI Host Adapter
Adaptec AHA-274X/AHA-284X/AIC-777X SCSI Host Adapter
Adaptec AHA-294X/AHA-394X or AIC-78XX PCI SCSI Controller
AMD PCI SCSI Controller/Ethernet Adapter
AMIscsi SCSI Host Adapter
BusLogic SCSI Host Adapter
Compaq Drive Array
Dell Drive Array
DPT SCSI Host Adapter

Future Domain TMC-7000EX EISA SCSI Host Adapter
Future Domain 8XX SCSI Host Adapter
Adaptec AHA-2920 or Future Domain 16XX/PCI/SCSI2Go SCSI Host Adapter
IBM MCA SCSI Host Adapter
IDE CD-ROM (ATAPI 1.2)/Dual-channel PCI IDE Controller
Mitsumi CD-ROM Controller
Mylex DAC960/Digital SWXCR-Ex RAID Controller
NCR 53C9X SCSI Host Adapter
NCR C700 MCA SCSI Host Adapter
NCR 53C710 MCA SCSI Host Adapter
Symbios Logic C810 PCI SCSI Host Adapter
Olivetti ESC-1/ESC-2 SCSI Host Adapter
QLogic PCI SCSI Host Adapter
MKEPanasonic CD-ROM Controller
Sony Proprietary CD-ROM Controller
UltraStor 14F/14FB/34F/34FA/34FB SCSI Host Adapter
UltraStor 24F/24FA SCSI Host Adapter

Table 3-2: Mass storage adapters supported by the Windows NT 4 Server Setup program.

Once the mass storage adapters have been detected, the setup program will then check to see if there is an existing copy of Windows NT Server already installed on the system. If setup finds an existing copy of Windows NT, the existing copy of Windows NT may be upgraded, or left untouched.

Choosing the Type of Installation

This is the first critical point in your installation: you must choose to either upgrade your existing Windows NT installation (you lose the existing installation and have nothing to go back to if there are problems) or install a clean copy of Windows NT 4 Server (you have to reinstall all existing systems, applications, and networking information fresh). Figure 3-5 shows the list of previous installations. In my example, there were previous installations for both Windows NT 3.51 Server and Windows NT 3.5 Server.

Generally, a clean installation is more reliable in most situations. There is nothing inherent to Windows NT 4 Server that prevents you from having more than one copy of Windows NT 4 Server installed on the same computer: the DORA server that was the example for this chapter has several copies of Windows NT 3.5x Server and Windows 95 installed and managed with Windows NT 4 Server's dual-boot manager.

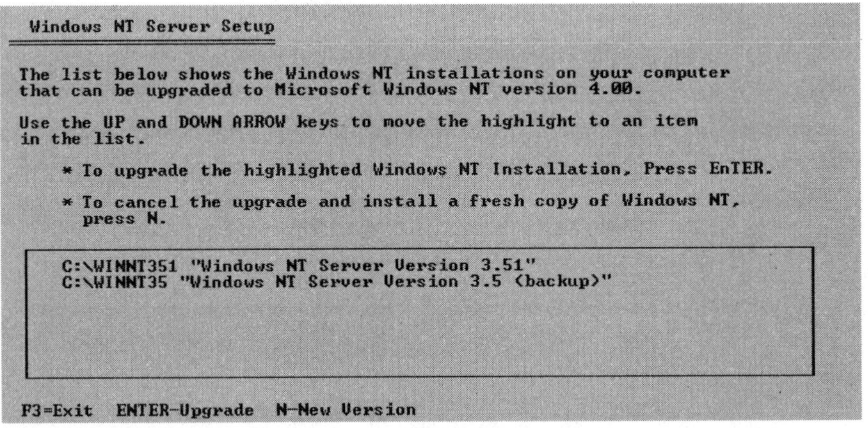

Figure 3-5: The Windows NT Server Setup screen lists the current Windows NT installations.

For this installation, I pressed the N key (for New Version) to do a new installation.

Updating the List of Standard Devices

When doing a clean installation, the setup program lists the "standard devices" for the target system. For these devices (video, system, keyboard, mouse, and so on) the default selections (as shown in Figure 3-6) are generally satisfactory.

```
Windows NT Server Setup
═══════════════════════════

Setup has determined that your computer contains the following hardware
and software components.

         Computer: Standard PC
          Display: VGA or Compatible
         Keyboard: XT, AT, or Enhanced Keyboard (83-104 keys)
  Keyboard Layout: US
  Pointing Device: Microsoft Serial Mouse

       No Chanters: The above list matches my computer

If you want to change any item in the list, prese the UP or DOWN ARROW
key to move the highlight to the item you want ot change. Then press
ENTER to see alternatives for that item.

When all items in the list are correct, move the highlight to
"The above list matches my computer" and press ENTER


ENTER=Select  F3=Exit
```

Figure 3-6: The Windows NT Server Setup default selections screen shows video, keyboard, and system types.

If you have a higher performance video adapter (such as DORA's Matrox Millennium) use the "standard VGA" selection for video adapter on this screen. Later, Windows NT 4 Server will detect the correct video adapter and install the correct drivers. It is important to check the list of non-standard computers to make sure that you are not installing Windows NT 4 Server on one of these systems. If you are installing Windows NT 4 Server on one of the non-standard systems, you must tell the setup program. The non-standard systems are listed in Table 3-3.

AST Manhattan SMP
Compaq SystemPro Multiprocessor or 100% Compatible
Corollary C-bus Architecture
Corollary C-bus Micro Channel Architecture
IBM PS/2 or other Micro Channel-based PC
MPS Uniprocessor PC
MPS Multiprocessor PC
MPS Multiprocessor Micro Channel PC

➡

NCR System 3000 Model 3360/3450/3550
Olivetti LSX5030/40
Standard PC
Standard PC with C-Step i486
Wyse Series 7000i Model 740MP/760MP

Table 3-3: System types supported by the Windows NT 4 Server Setup program.

Selecting an Installation Drive

The Windows NT 4 Server setup program lists the drives available on which you can install the Windows NT 4 Server. You do not have to install Windows NT 4 Server on the C drive—any drive with sufficient free space can be used for installation. Figure 3-7 shows the D drive selected, which is an NTFS-formatted drive.

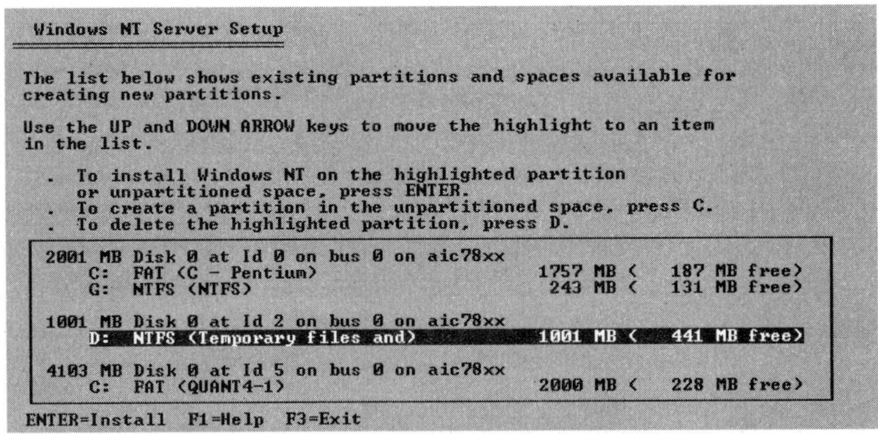

Figure 3-7: The Windows NT Server Setup screen shows the D drive selected as the drive on which we want to install Windows NT 4 Server.

If the partition to which you are installing Windows NT 4 Server is currently FAT-based, the setup program prompts you, with a message similar to the one shown in Figure 3-8, to convert the partition to the NTFS file system. The drive selected for our installation example was already formatted with the NTFS file system; therefore, the setup program allows only one choice: leave the current file system intact.

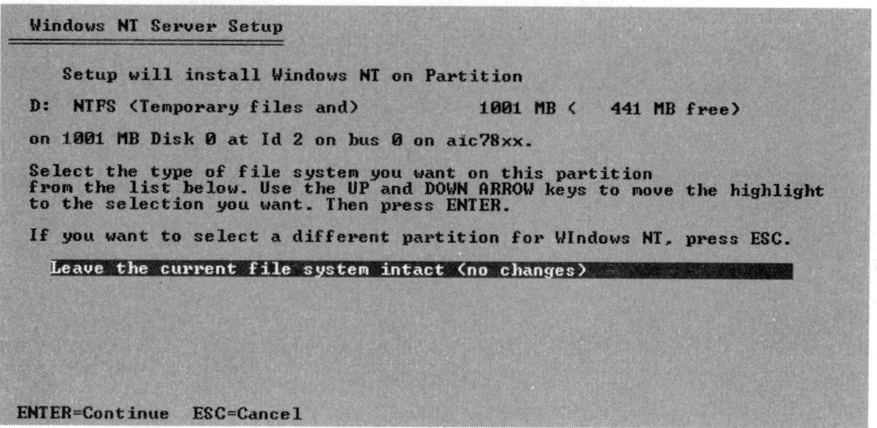

Figure 3-8: The Windows NT Server Setup screen is where you select the type of file system you want on the installation drive/partition.

Do not convert the C partition to NTFS if the computer is being dual-booted to an operating system other than Windows NT (for example, Windows 95 or MS-DOS), as the other operating system is unable to access the NTFS partition(s). If you install only Windows NT 4 Server on the target machine, then converting to NTFS can be advantageous for either security, compression, or performance reasons.

Chapter 8, "Configuring Hardware," discusses the issues of conversion to NTFS.

Selecting an Installation Directory

Once you have selected your installation drive, you must select the directory into which you're going to install Windows NT 4 Server. If you are upgrading an existing Windows NT Server installation, then the directory is the one where Windows NT Server is already installed. Figure 3-9 shows the screen where you can change the installation directory's name.

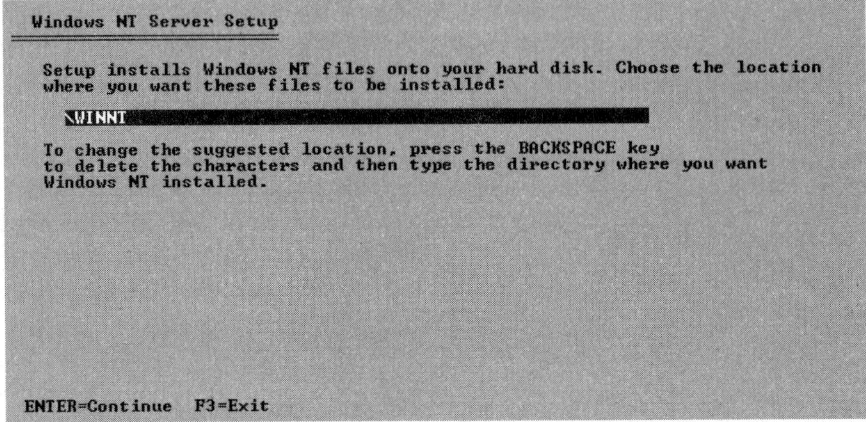

Figure 3-9: Use the Windows NT Server Setup screen to specify the installation directory name.

If you are creating a new, clean, installation of Windows NT 4 Server, then you must specify a directory name. The suggested name for this directory is \WINNT; however, you can override this default if the directory exists already or if you wish to place this installation of Windows NT 4 Server into a different directory.

Examining Hard Disks

The next step in the installation of Windows NT 4 Server is for the install program to prompt you to do a thorough inspection of your drive, as shown in Figure 3-10. It is highly recommended that you allow the setup program to perform this inspection—it is possible that your drive has defects, errors, or problems of which you are unaware.

```
Windows NT Server Setup

Setup will now examine your hard disk(s) for corruption.

In addition to basic examination, Setup can perform a more exhaustive
secondary examination on some drives. This can be a time consuming
operation, especially on large or very full drives.

  * To allow Setup to perform an exhaustive secondary examination of
    your hard disk(s), press ENTER.

  * To skip the exhaustive examiniation, press ESC.

ENTER=Continue   ESC=Skip Operation
```

Figure 3-10: The Windows NT Server Setup hard disk examination screen allows you to examine the drive prior to installation.

If you skip this test, the setup program does a simple test of the drive. However, this simple test is not exhaustive enough to detect any serious problems. Skip this inspection *only* if you are absolutely certain that your drive has no problems or errors.

Copying Files

After checking the drive for errors, the setup program copies files from the temporary directory created above. This file copy process doesn't take as much time as did copying the files from the CD-ROM—this is a hard drive to hard drive copy operation. Once all the files are copied to their final location, the setup program displays a reboot screen, as shown in Figure 3-11.

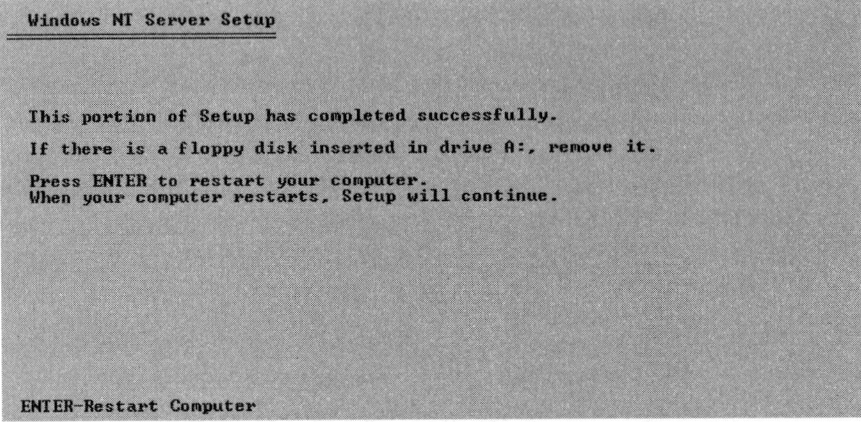

Figure 3-11: The Windows NT Server Setup screen with the reboot message.

A reboot starts the third phase of the installation process. A special version of Windows NT is started, which does the main installation of the Windows NT 4 Server components.

The Windows NT 4 Server license agreement displays. You must agree to this license agreement (please read it) before you complete the installation. If for some reason you cannot agree to the license agreement, you must not install Windows NT 4 Server.

Additional System Administrator Installation Tasks

Most of the Windows NT 4 Server installation is performed by the Setup Wizard. Using the standard wizard user interface, two buttons are presented in most of the screens: Next and Back. Click the Next button to proceed to the next stage of the installation. Click the Back button to return to the previous screen. There are certain points where there is no Back button—any changes prior to this point have already been committed. The commitment points are revealed when the Next button is replaced with a button called Finish.

After agreeing to the license agreement, the welcome window for the installation appears as shown in Figure 3-12. Read the message describing the next three parts of the setup program and click the Next button.

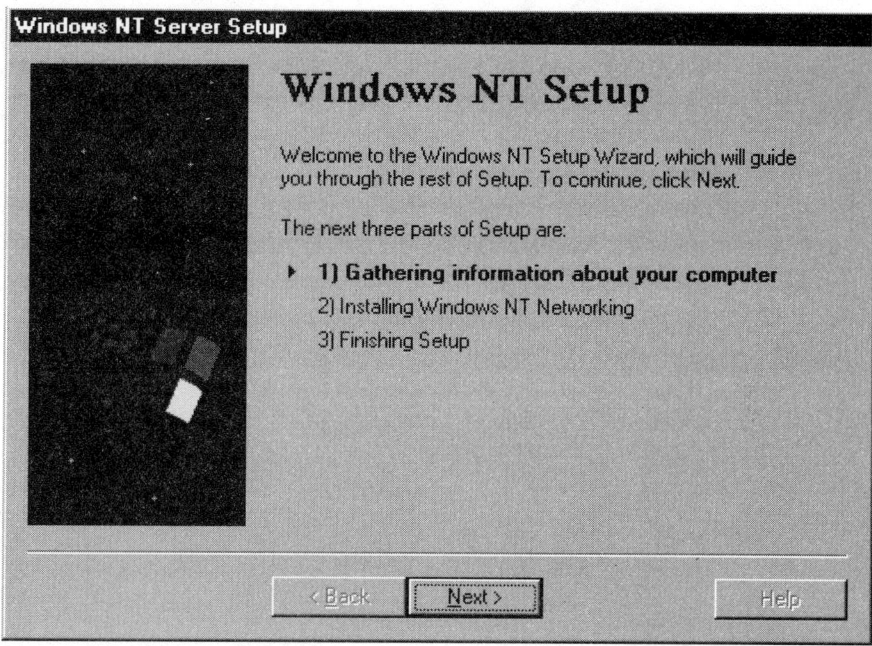

Figure 3-12: The Windows NT Server Setup Wizard welcome window.

Giving Background Information

The next information required by the setup program is your name and organization. This information is placed in the Windows NT 4 Server registry for registration purposes. Figure 3-13 shows the Name and Organization window. To complete this window, enter your name and organization in the text boxes and then click the Next button.

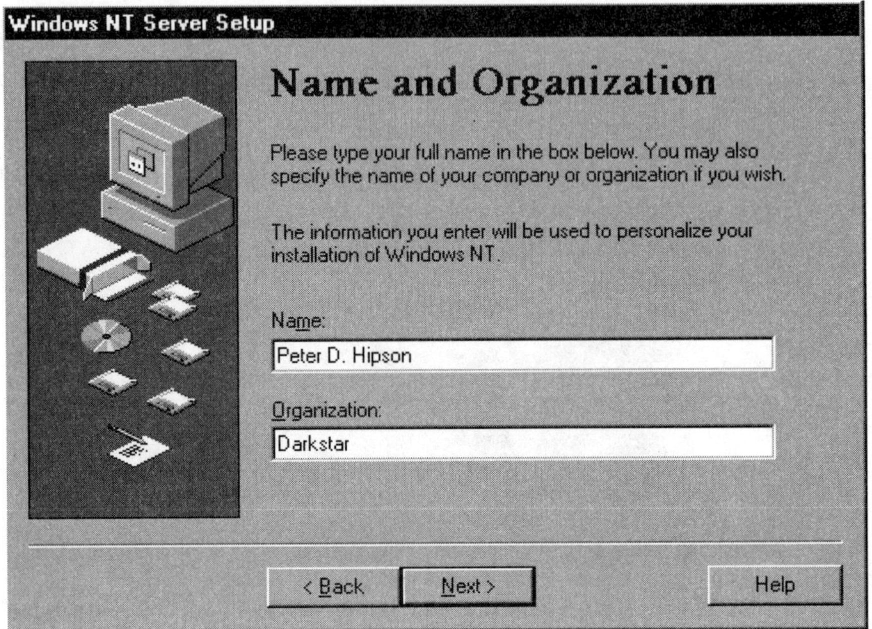

Figure 3-13: Use the Windows NT Server Setup window to enter your name and organization.

Most installations of Windows NT 4 Server prompt for a product ID code, which is found on the back of the Windows NT 4 Server CD case. Enter this number when prompted, and click the Next button.

The Windows NT 4 Server licensing mode must be determined by the user. The window shown in Figure 3-14 allows you to choose either Per Server or Per Seat licensing modes.

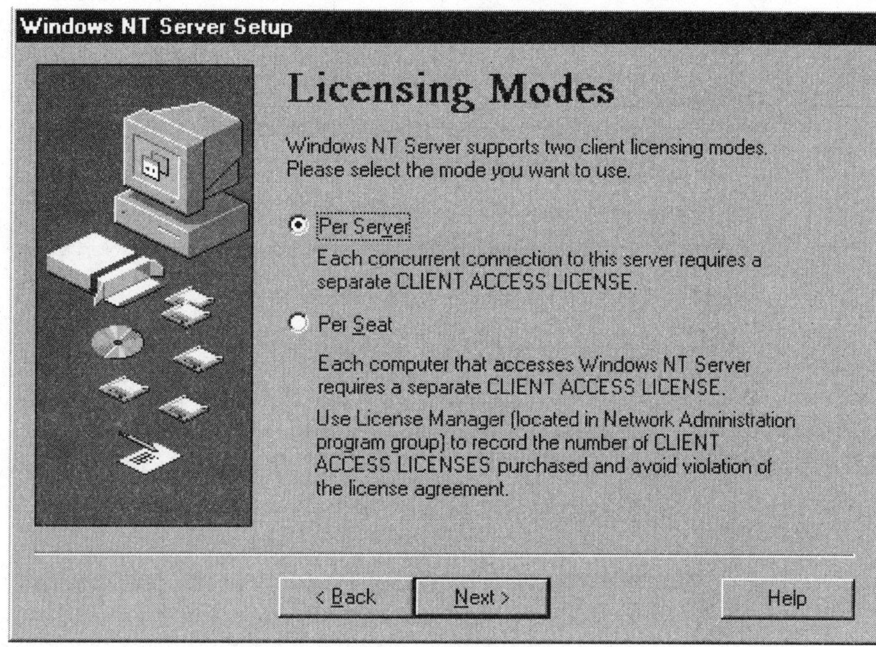

Figure 3-14: Use the Windows NT Server Setup Licensing Modes window to select one of the two licensing modes supported: Per Server or Per Seat.

Windows NT Server supports two client licensing modes: Per Server, or Per Seat. Some simple hints for selecting your licensing mode are:

- If you have only one server, Microsoft recommends that you choose the Per Server option. With the Per Server mode, Microsoft allows you to change **once** to the Per Seat mode. You can make this change any time after selecting the Per Server option.
- However, if you have more than one server and the total number of Client Access Licenses for all servers to support the Per Server mode is equal to or greater than the number of computers or workstations, you should choose (or later convert) to the Per Seat license option.

After selecting your licensing mode, click the Next button.

The Setup Wizard prompts you for a computer name, as shown in Figure 3-15. In my case, the computer name is DORA, so that other client computers will access shares on DORA, in the format of \\DORA\share name. After entering the computer name, click the Next button.

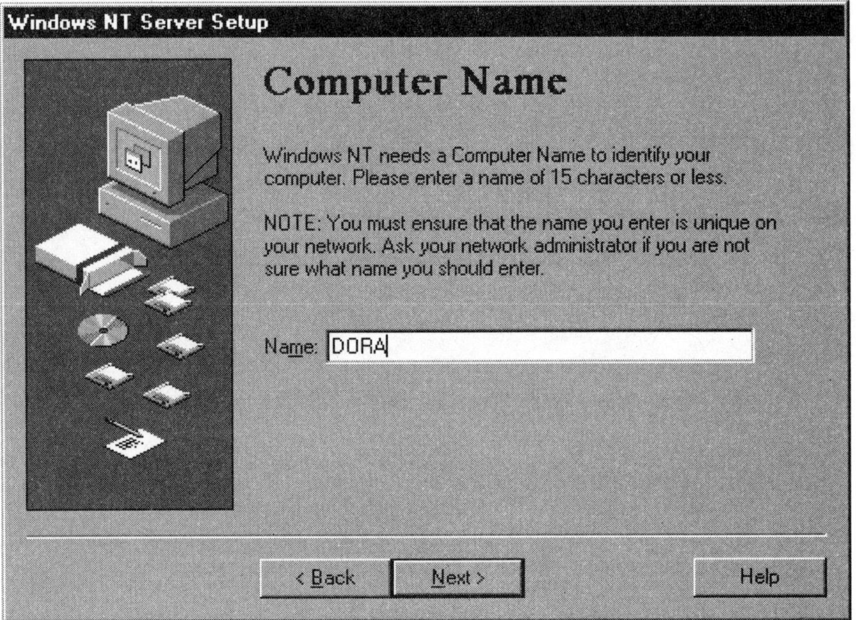

Figure 3-15: The Windows NT Server Setup window is where you give your computer a name.

Selecting the Type of Server

Things have looked easy up till now. There have been no hard choices, no difficult decisions. All of a sudden, Microsoft prompts you to select your server type. System administrators who are not experienced with Microsoft networks (Windows NT Server in particular) may find this prompt confusing, or at the very least, thought provoking.

As Figure 3-16 shows, you must decide whether you are setting up a Primary Domain Controller (PDC), a Backup Domain Controller (BDC), or a stand-alone server. What's the difference?

A stand-alone server is the only server on the network, and the network model is called a workgroup. There can be other servers (such as a NetWare server) but this server is the only Windows NT 4 Server on the network. User information is entered at the server one time and is not shared between servers—this is the only server which has user information.

A domain is a network that (usually) has more than one server. With a domain, one server is designated as the PDC, which manages security for the entire domain. There are usually one or more BDC servers too: each of these servers has a backup copy of the security information (which is automatically updated by the PDC). If anything happens to the PDC, a BDC is able to "take over" as a new PDC. If you only have one server, it can still be a domain controller (it is always a PDC).

With a domain, you can use a domain controller as a way to share login authorizations so that user identification information doesn't have to be updated manually on each server.

If you are unsure of which selection to take, configure your server as a domain and set the server as the PDC. Later you may "demote" the server to a BDC if needed.

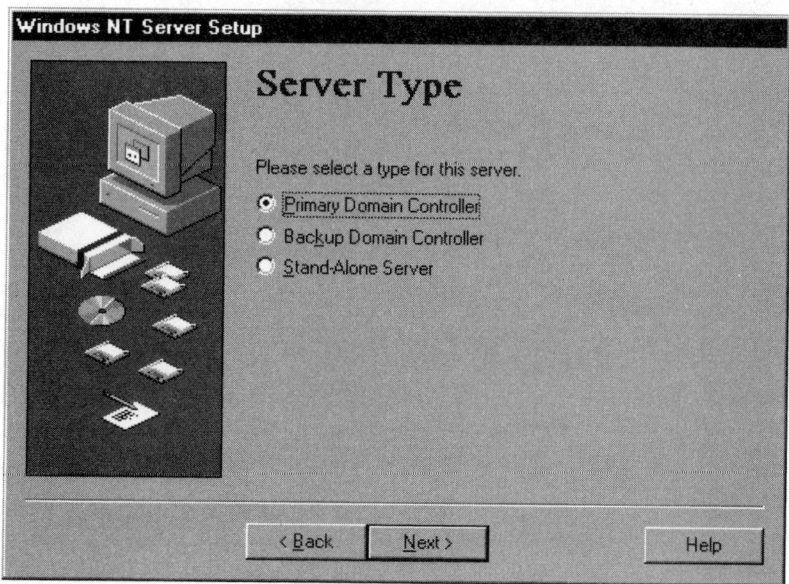

Figure 3-16: The Windows NT Server Setup Server Type window is where you select whether this is a domain or not.

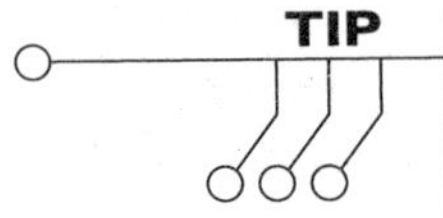

TIP

If you are unsure, set your system up as a Primary Domain Controller (PDC)—you cannot convert from a stand-alone server to a PDC at a later date: you would have to reinstall Windows NT 4 Server. Having a stand-alone server configured to run as a PDC doesn't add too much to the overhead of the system.

After selecting your server type, click the Next button.

Setting Up the Administrator's Account

Next, the only user ID that is created by the Setup Wizard is the administrator account. This account is the main account that the system administrator uses to manage Windows NT 4 Server. A password must be specified for the administrator account, as shown in Figure 3-17.

Figure 3-17: The Windows NT Server Setup Administrator Account window is where you supply the administrator's password.

Select this password carefully—the administrator account is powerful, and if abused, could cause substantial problems. Also, forgetting the administrator account's password may well result in having to reinstall Windows NT 4 Server! After entering the administrator's password, click the Next button.

Specifying You Want an ERD

You use a Windows NT emergency repair disk (ERD) to fix the system when serious corruption or other problems prevent Windows NT from being booted. The Setup Wizard prompts you, as shown in Figure 3-18, to create this emergency repair disk. Respond YES! Even if you already have an emergency repair disk, create a new one for each installation.

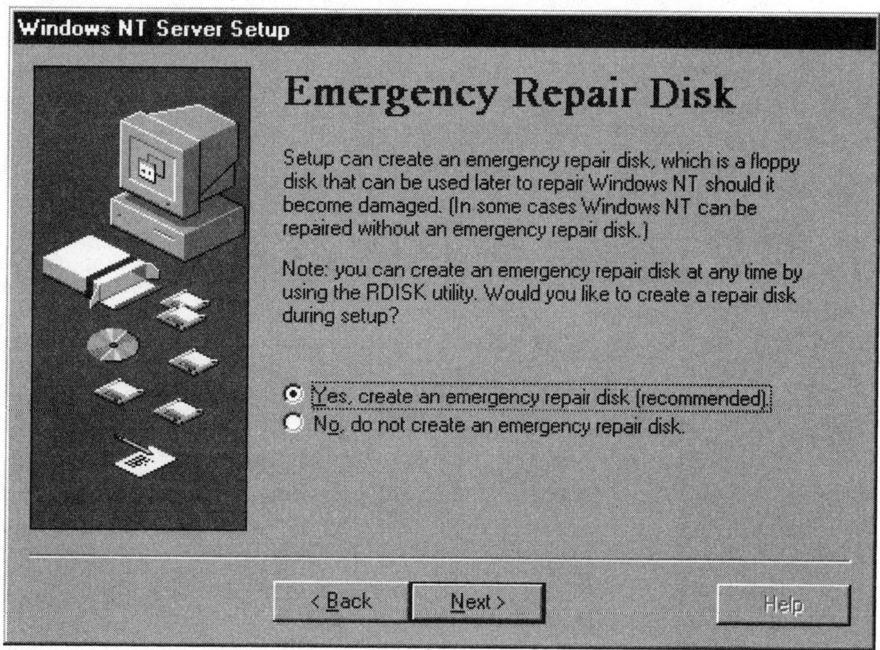

Figure 3-18: Use the Windows NT Server Setup Emergency Repair Disk window to create an emergency repair disk.

When this disk is created, make sure you mark it with a notation that describes which computer the disk is for. Without an emergency repair disk there are a number of simple problems that require reinstallation of Windows NT 4 Server to correct. After selecting whether you wish to create an ERD or not, click the Next button.

Selecting Which Components to Install

The Setup Wizard next prompts you to select the Windows NT 4 Server components. Figure 3-19 shows the six main categories of components that were selected for this installation example. If you have sufficient space on your installation drive, you can select all components; this saves you from having to reinstall components at a later time.

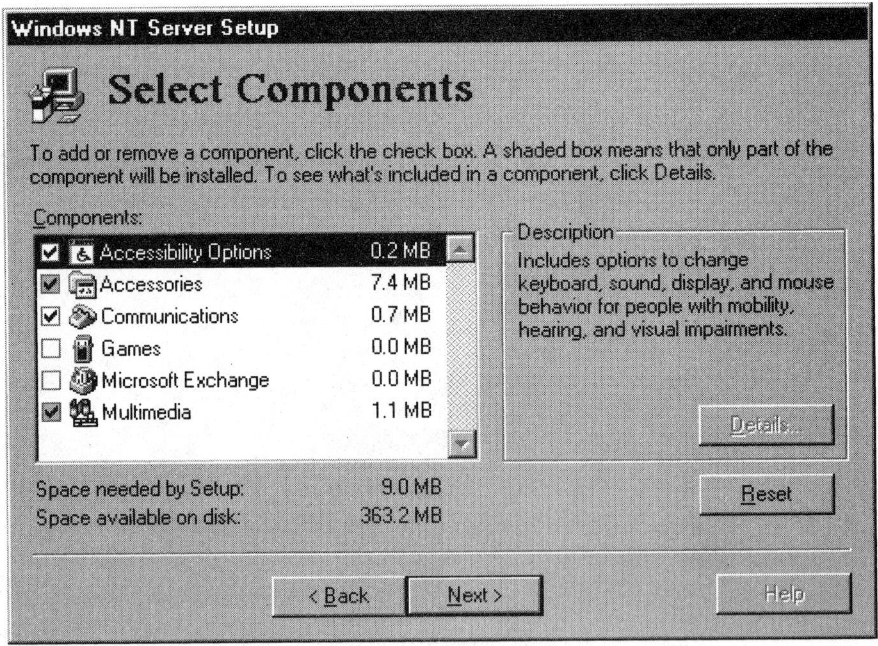

Figure 3-19: The Windows NT Server Setup Select Components window is where you select options to install.

- Accessibility Options—Options that assist users who have an impairment or disability. Items in this category include keyboard, mouse, and sound support. An applet, called Accessibility Options, is added to the Control Panel, allowing customization of the Accessibility Options.
- Accessories—Items that include a number of other useful utilities. Selecting all accessories at installation time may make the installation easier.
- Communications—Options in the communications area include the HyperTerminal program for communications.
- Games—We all play games sometimes. The Games group includes a number of games including Pinball, FreeCell, Solitaire, and Minesweeper. These games serve a very valid purpose, in that you can use them to test the functionality of your installation. Install Games, unless they are not allowed by your organization.
- Exchange—Microsoft Exchange includes the Exchange client (not server). Exchange is a very competent e-mail client that can be used with Microsoft Mail, Internet mail, Fax, and MSN mail.
- Multimedia—The Multimedia group includes the CD Player, Media player, and a number of other useful utilities. If you have a CD-ROM drive and a sound card, it is recommended that you select the Multimedia option.

After selecting options and setting details as necessary, click the Next button.

Moving On to Networking

The next stage of the setup program is perhaps the most important part of your Windows NT 4 Server installation. Figure 3-20 shows step two, installing the network functionality. This stage of the installation is critical, as this is a server! Click the Next button to begin installing network components.

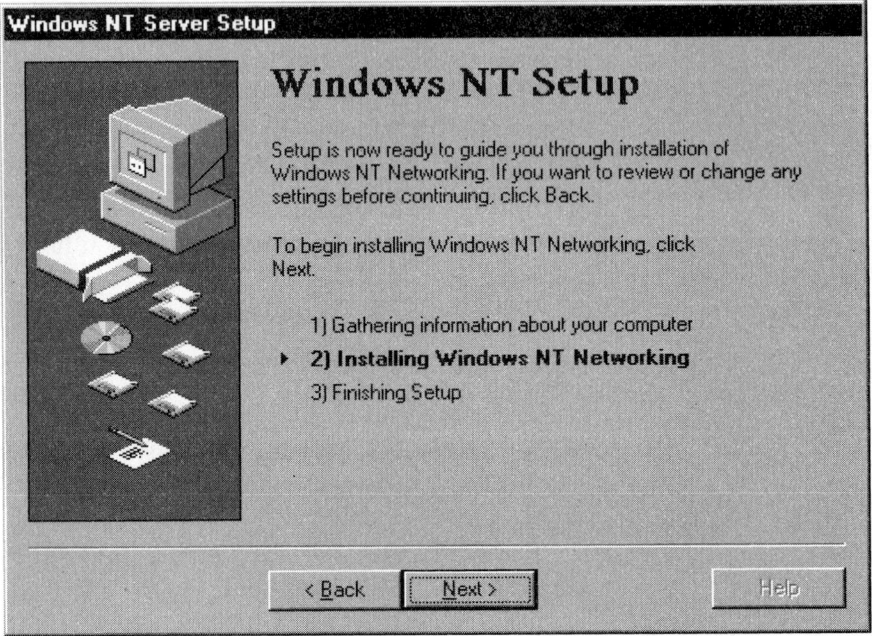

Figure 3-20: Use the Windows NT Server Setup Networking window to begin installing Windows NT Networking.

At this stage, your knowledge of both the system and the network is critical: notes and other information should be on hand at this stage.

Selecting Network Options

The first networking choice is how the server is connected to a network, as Figure 3-21 shows. You have two, nonexclusive choices on this window.

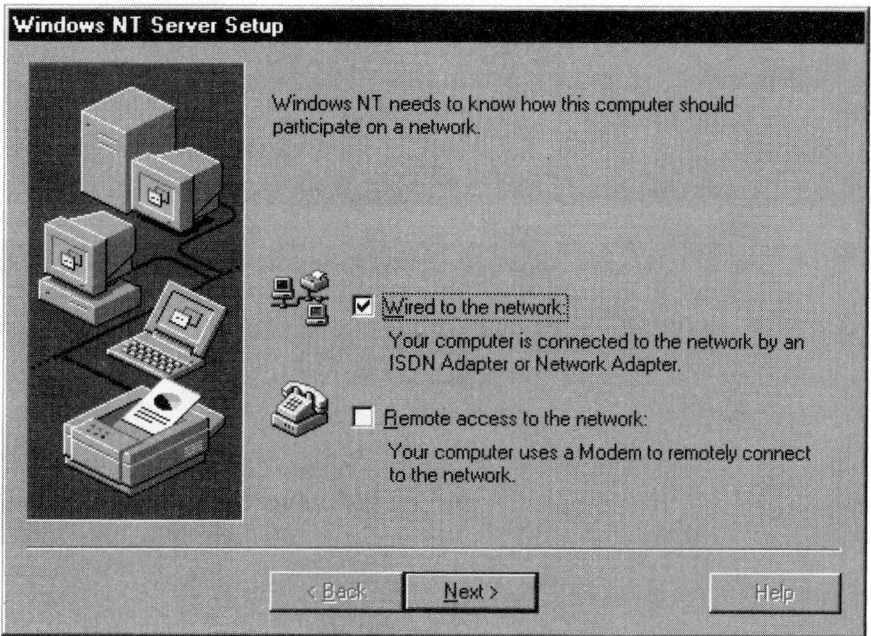

Figure 3-21: The Windows NT Server Setup network access window is where you select what network types to use.

- Wired to the Network—Where the system is permanently connected to the network, using either a Network Interface Card (NIC) or via ISDN.
- Remote Access to the Network (Modem)—Usually called Remote Access Server (RAS). This is where clients dial into the system using one (or more) modems connected to the system's serial ports.

Remember: if need be, you can select both choices. After selecting the network types, click the Next button.

You are next prompted, by Setup Wizard, to install Microsoft's Internet Information Server (IIS) (see Figure 3-22). This is optional: if this server will not be used on either the Internet or an intranet, then there is no purpose in installing IIS. However, if at a later date you determine that you do need to install IIS, there is an icon on the desktop called "Install Internet Information Server," which automatically installs IIS for you. After selecting whether to install IIS or not, click the Next button.

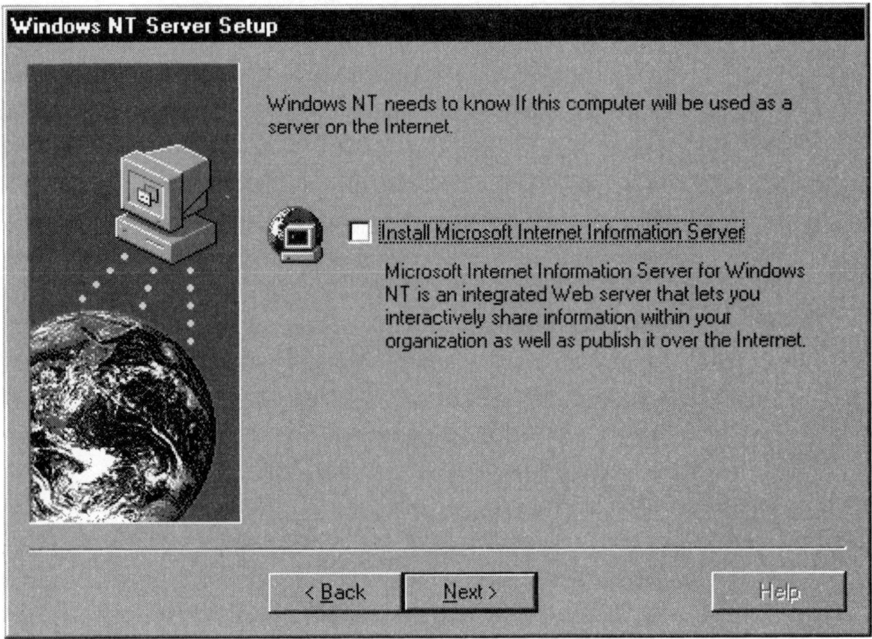

Figure 3-22: The Windows NT Server Setup Internet connection window is where you specify if you want to install the Microsoft Internet Information Server.

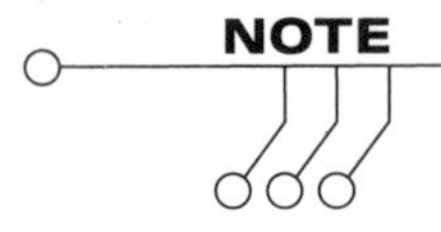

The version of IIS that is shipped with Windows NT 4 Server installs under both Windows NT 4 Workstation and Windows 95. These versions (Windows NT 4 Workstation and Windows 95) have a more limited capability than the version that installs under Windows NT 4 Server.

The server's NIC is the next stage in the setup program. Generally, the Setup Wizard can detect the correct NIC when you select the Detect (or Find Next) button. The button's title changes from Detect to Find Next once the first NIC has been found. Figure 3-23 shows the Network Adapters after I clicked the Find Next button. You may have more than one NIC. If so, select all the installed NICs you want to use. It is not necessary to select modems for RAS at this time. You can configure RAS at a later time. If, by chance, your NIC is not detected, you can manually add it to the list of NICs available.

After detecting and selecting your NIC, click the Next button.

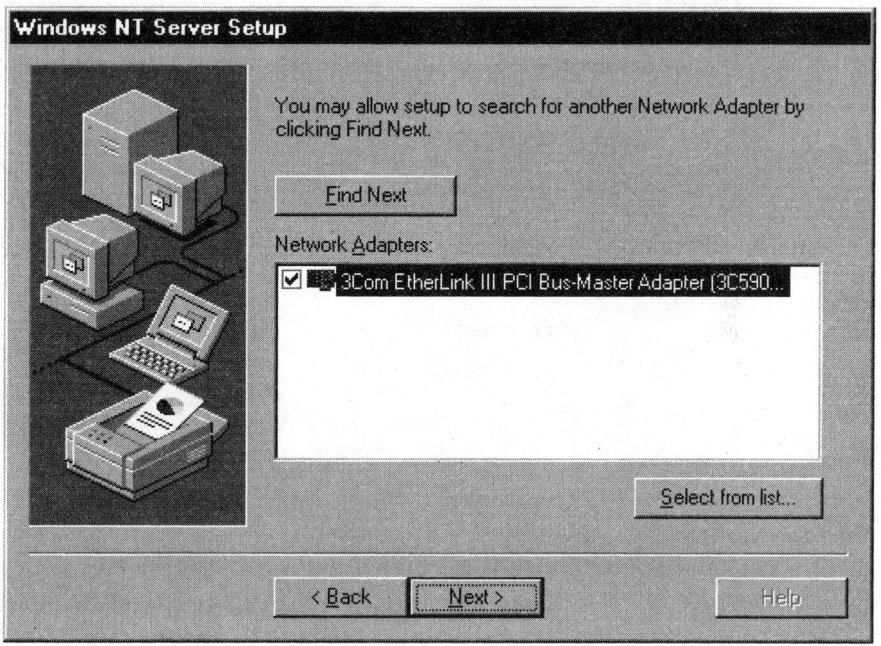

Figure 3-23: The Windows NT Server Setup Network Adapter selection window is where you select the correct network adapter.

Selecting Network Protocols & Services

You must also select the network protocol you want to use. After installing Windows NT 4 Server, you can choose to add protocols. Realize, however, that the TCP/IP protocol is difficult to remove once installed. Figure 3-24 shows the network protocols selection window. After selecting the network protocols you want to install, click the Next button.

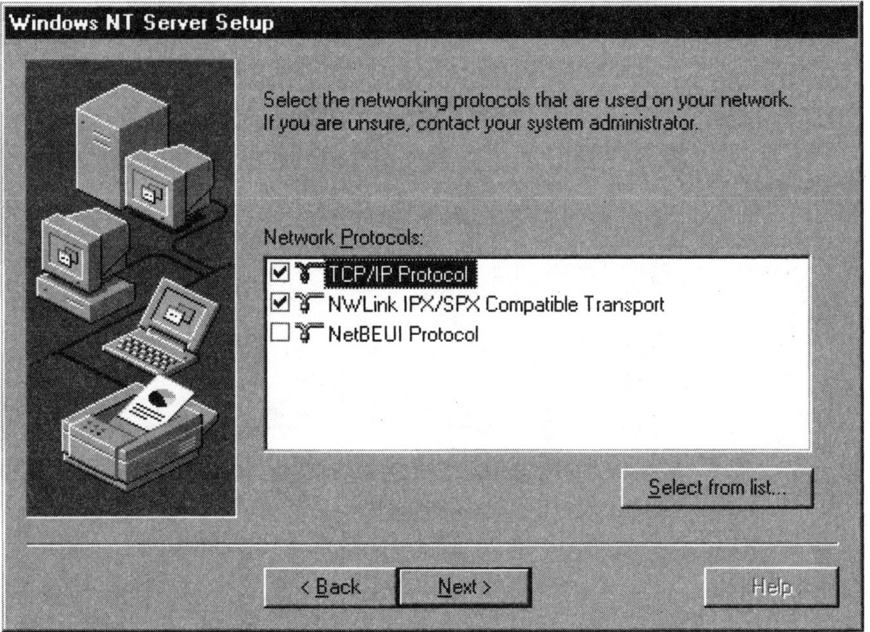

Figure 3-24: Use the Windows NT Server Setup network protocols selection window to select the network protocols.

The Selecting Services portion of the setup program may prove to be the most difficult portion of the network installation. There are a number of services to select from, and if you are not familiar with the correct services to select from, you may have an unsuccessful Windows NT 4 Server installation.

Figure 3-25 shows the Network Services selection list. Clicking the Select from list... button allows you to select from all services listed in Table 3-4. After selecting the services to install, click the Next button.

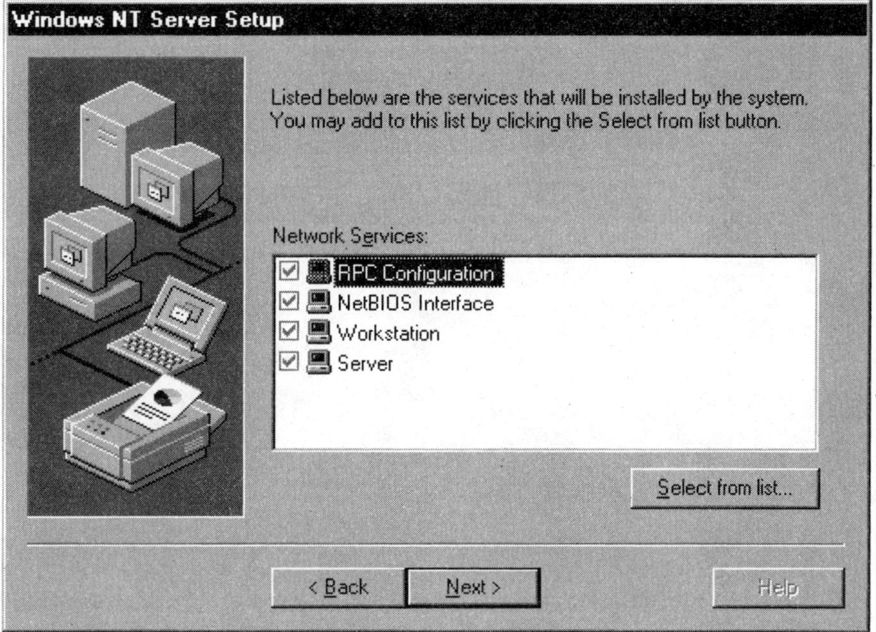

Figure 3-25: Use the Windows NT Server Setup network services window to select which services to install.

Table 3-4 lists the different services Setup Wizard makes available to you. These services are grouped into two categories: those available by default (you select them using the main Select Services page), and services you choose by selecting optional services.

Generally, it is a good idea to install the services that Microsoft selects as defaults. Usually, installing a service that you later do not use will not cause problems.

Service	Default	Description
Remote Access Server	Yes	The Remote Access Server allows you to dial into other servers and allows clients to dial into your server.
RPC Configuration	Yes	The Remote Procedure Call configuration allows clients to execute procedures on the server.
NetBIOS Interface	Yes	Installs the NetBIOS network interface.
Workstation	Yes	Installs the workstation interface.
Server	Yes	Installs the server interface.
DHCP Relay Agent	No	The Dynamic Host Configuration Protocol agent. For more information about the DHCP Relay Agent, see the public specification RFC 1542, which you can retrieve using FTP, at ds.internic.net in the RFC sub-folder.
Gateway (and client)	No	Used to support Novell NetWare. services for NetWare
Microsoft DHCP Server	No	The Dynamic Host Configuration Protocol server. For more information about the DHCP Relay Agent, see the public specification RFC 1542, which you can retrieve using FTP, at ds.internic.net in the RFC sub-folder.
Microsoft DNS Server	No	The Microsoft DNS server allows an Internet/ intranet TCP/IP network to resolve names at a local level.
NS IIS 2.0	No	The Microsoft Internet Information Server. This option allows you to install IIS.
Microsoft TCP/IP	No	Printers, connected directly to a TCP/IP protocol network, are supported by Windows NT 4 Server.
Network Monitor Agent	No	Included with Microsoft Systems Management Server (SMS) is a utility called Network Monitor. This utility is a network analyzer with the ability to capture real-time network data. Windows NT 4 Server includes Network Monitoring Agent Service, which can be used with the Systems Management Server (SMS) Network Monitor utility.

Service	Default	Description
Network Monitor Tools and Agent	No	Both the Network Monitor Agent and additional monitoring tools.
Remote Boot Service	No	Allows you to boot "diskless" workstations connected to the Windows NT 4 Server from the network.
RIP for Internet Protocol	No	Routing Information Protocol routes network packets between two or more network adapters. This implementation is used for the Internet Protocol (IP).
RIP for NwLink IPX/SPX Compatible Transport	No	Routing Information Protocol routes network packets between two or more network adapters. This implementation is used for the IPX/SPX transport.
RPC support for Banyan		The Remote Procedure Call configuration allows clients to execute procedures on the server. This implementation is for the Banyan VINES network.
SAP Agent	No	NetWare clients use the Service Advertising Protocol (SAP) to perform name resolution on NetWare networks. NetWare servers advertise their services through periodic SAP broadcasts.
Services for Macintosh	No	The Services for Macintosh features allow the Windows NT 4 Server to be connected to, and function with, an Apple Macintosh network.
Simple TCP/IP Services	No	Additional support for the TCP/IP protocol.
SNMP Service	No	Windows NT 4 Server administrators use Simple Network Management Protocol (SNMP) to monitor and control remote hosts and gateways.
Windows Internet Name Service	No	The Windows Internet Name Service, or WINS, resolves names for the TCP/IP protocol. Works much like a DNS server.

Table 3-4: Services you can select at installation time.

Once you provide the necessary network information and click the Next button, the Windows NT 4 Server setup program installs the components selected. See Figure 3-26.

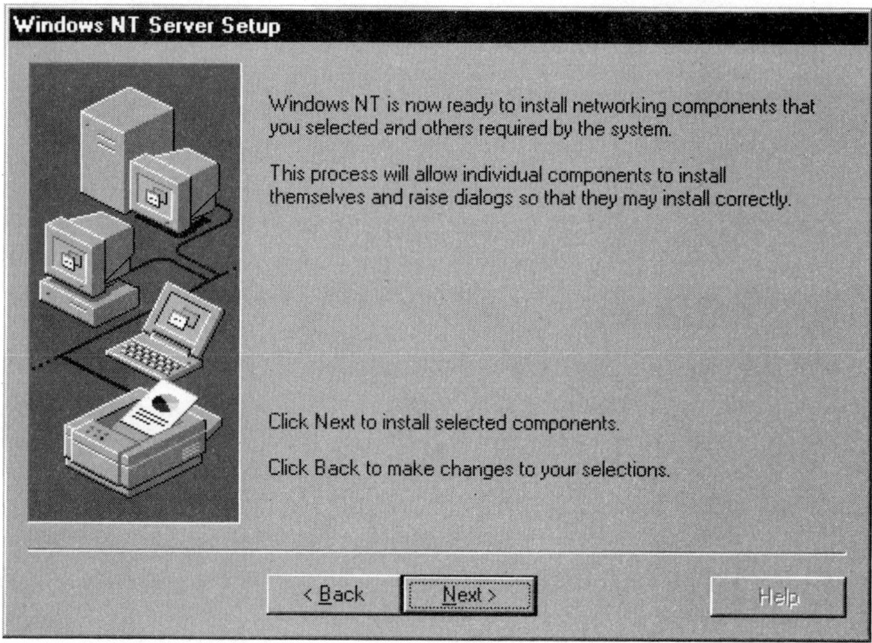

Figure 3-26: Click Next to install selected components.

Configuring Server Pieces

The next step in the setup program is to configure the server portion of Windows NT 4 Server. The Setup Wizard prompts you to supply all the information the setup program needs. Respond to prompts as appropriate.

Earlier, if you chose to allow remote clients using a modem to access your computer (see Figure 3-21), then the RAS modem (if you selected RAS) is now detected and configured. If you do not yet have your RAS modem installed, you can postpone this step

till after the installation is complete. If your modem is not correctly detected, you may be able to select a compatible modem from the list. Knowing which other modems are similar to your modem is beneficial.

RAS is configured (if you have selected RAS) after the modem is detected and installed. Make sure you configure whether this server can make calls (a client), receive calls (a server), or both.

TCP/IP configuration is the next step. You need to know the IP address of your server, the IP address of the Domain Name Server (DNS), and you may configure other parts of TCP/IP if necessary. If you selected TCP/IP you will be prompted (see Figure 3-27) to use a DHCP server. If you have a DHCP server installed (on a different server) then you may wish to select Yes, otherwise select the default button, No.

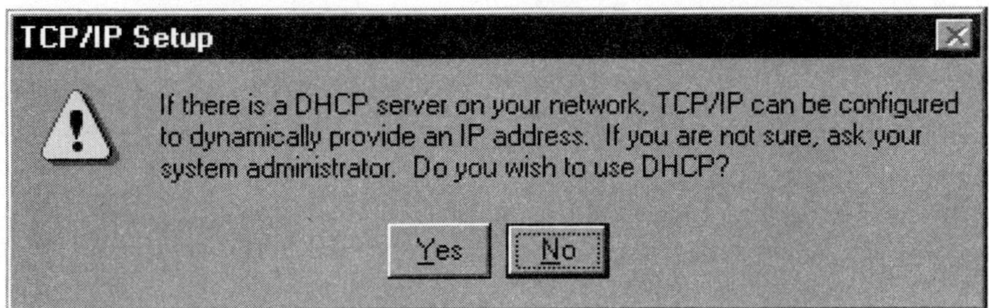

Figure 3-27: Do you wish to use a DHCP server to obtain an IP address?

The Microsoft TCP/IP Properties window is shown in Figure 3-28. You can display this window using the Control Panel's Network applet any time after installation.

After configuring the TCP/IP properties, click the OK button to continue.

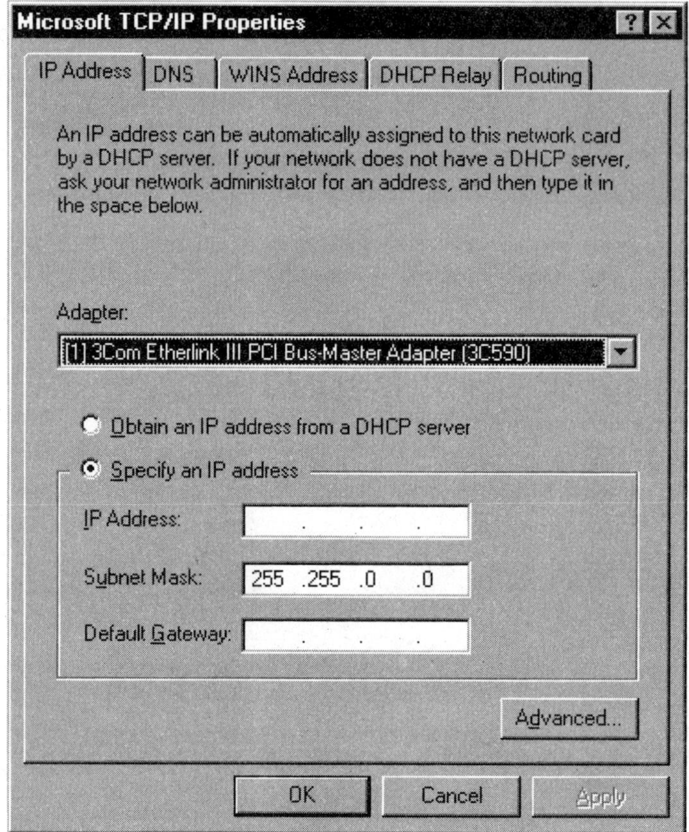

Figure 3-28: Microsoft TCP/IP Properties window.

The Setup Wizard reviews the current network configuration and allows you to make any modifications that are necessary. One caution: though you can make most any changes to the networking components to Windows NT 4 Server that you may need, be very careful not to delete the TCP/IP protocol, as it may not be possible to reinstall it later without reinstalling Windows NT 4 Server.

The bindings (which "connect" the network components together) display, as shown in Figure 3-29. You can modify bindings as needed. After configuring the bindings, click the Next button.

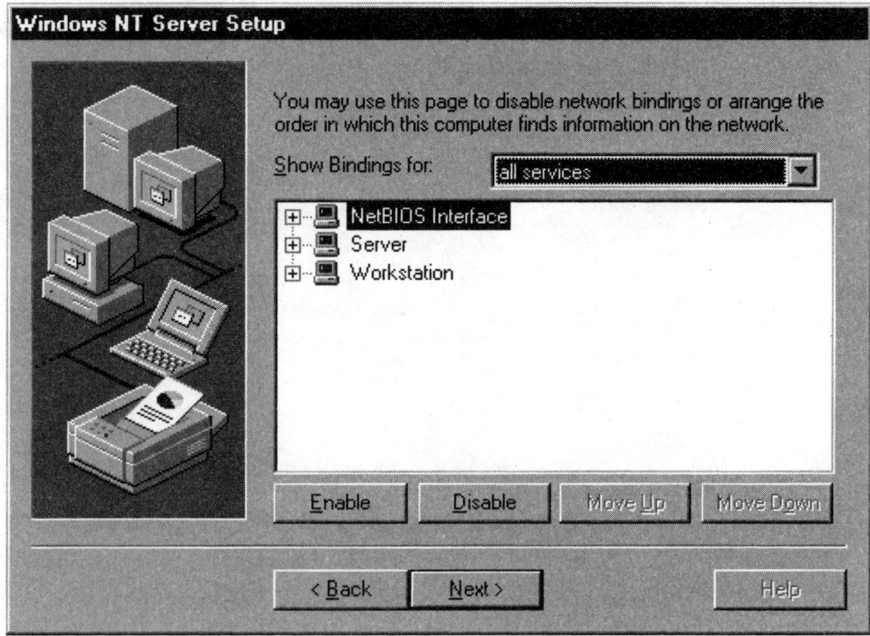

Figure 3-29: Use the Windows NT Server Setup Show Bindings window to review network bindings.

Starting the Network

Once you accept the network configuration, Setup Wizard starts networking (see Figure 3-30) and finishes the installation of Windows NT 4 Server. Click the Next button to start the network and continue with the installation.

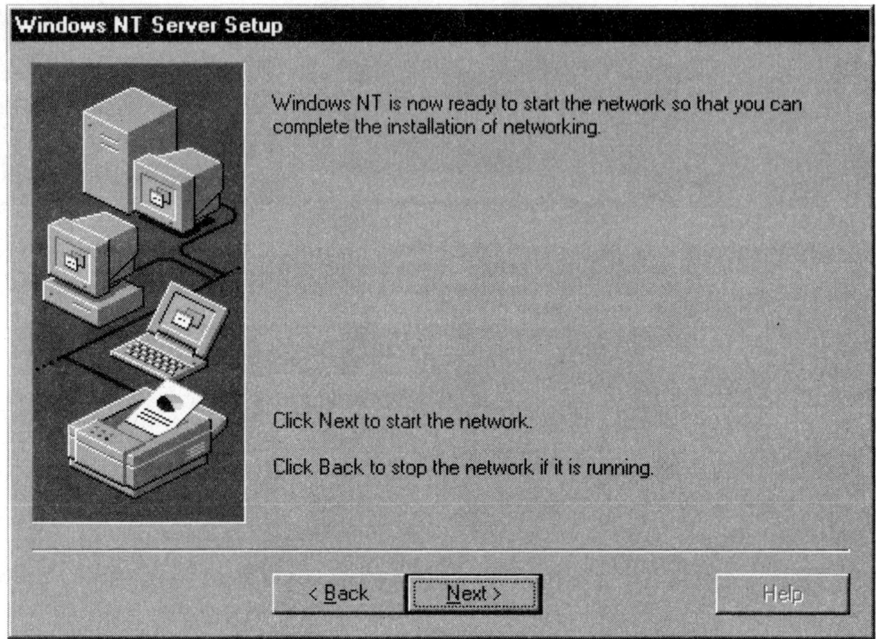

Figure 3-30: Use this window to start the network for the first time.

You will need to provide the computer name and domain name when the network is started for the first time, as shown in Figure 3-31. If you selected a stand-alone server, then this prompt is for a Computer Name and a Workgroup instead of a Computer Name and a Domain. After entering your Computer Name and Domain, click the Next button.

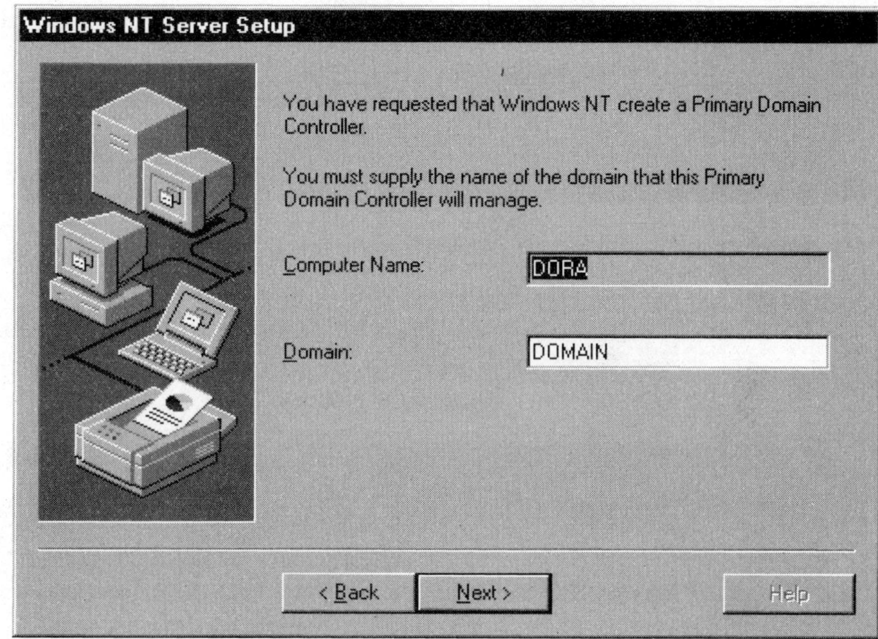

Figure 3-31: Use this window to supply the computer name and domain.

The Setup Wizard completes the configuration of the installation and notifies you using the status window as shown in Figure 3-32. Click the Finish button to complete this stage of the installation.

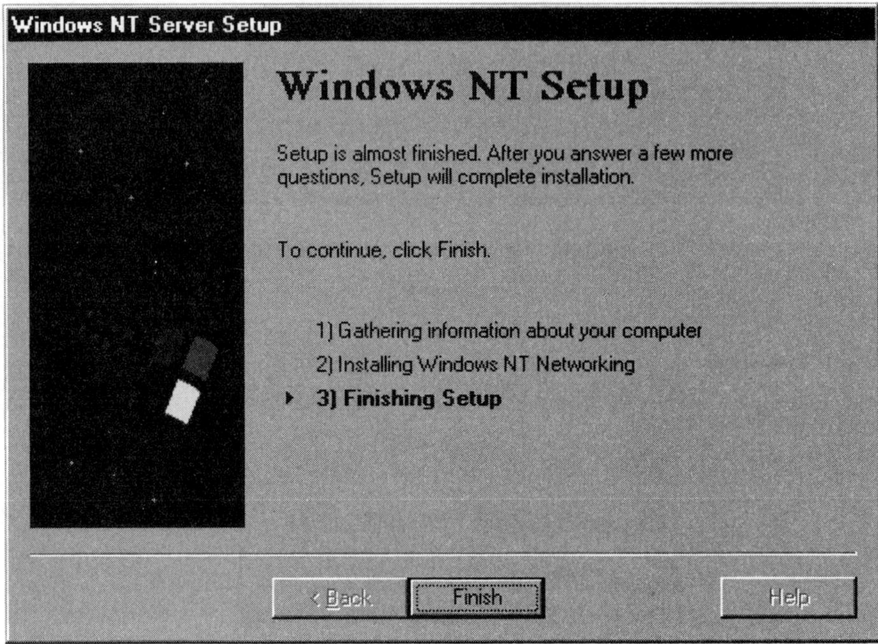

Figure 3-32: We are almost finished with the setup!

The Final Configuration

The final stages of installation are to configure some basic features such as time, date, and video display.

Time zone (and setting the correct time and date) is one of the final tasks that the Setup Wizard handles; see Figure 3-33. Find your time zone, and if in your time zone you use daylight savings time (DST), you can instruct Windows NT 4 Server to allow for DST. Click the Close button after you set the date and time information.

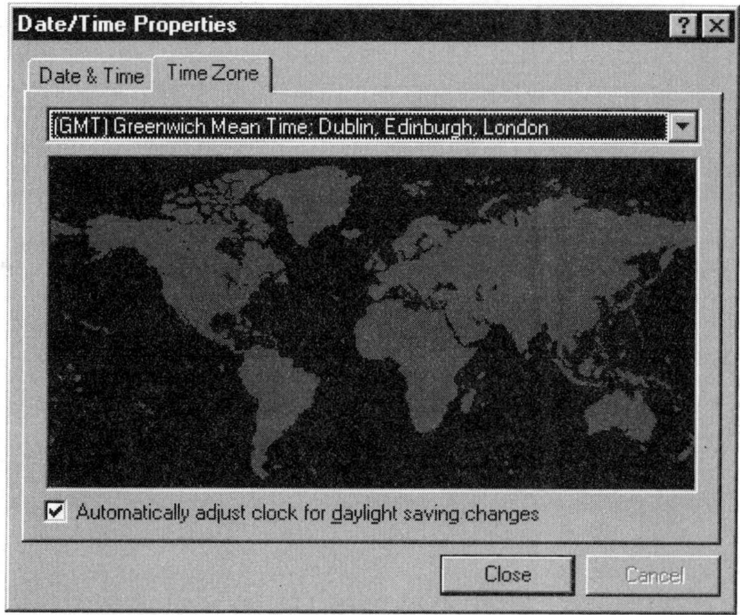

Figure 3-33: The Date/Time Properties dialog box.

If you have a video adapter that is more than a standard VGA adapter, Setup Wizard will detect it, and prompt you to determine whether you wish to configure the adapter. For my Matrox Millennium, the Detected Display dialog appears in Figure 3-34. Click the OK button to continue with the display configuration part of the installation.

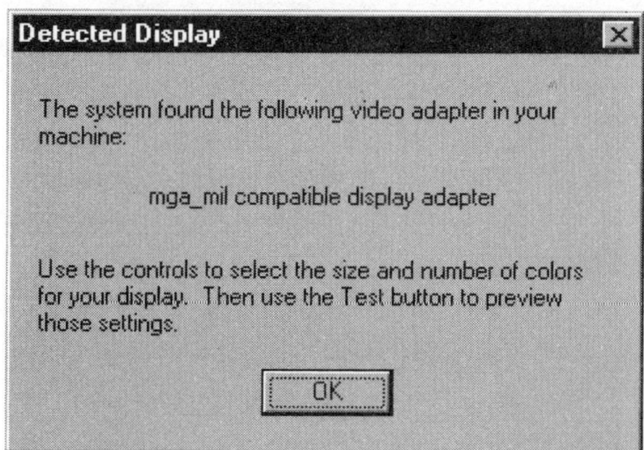

Figure 3-34: The Setup Wizard has detected a display.

The Video configuration involves setting the resolution and color depth (the setup program prompts you to test the settings). Each video adapter has slightly different settings and parameters, some allow setting refresh rates also. Figure 3-35 shows the Display Properties dialog box.

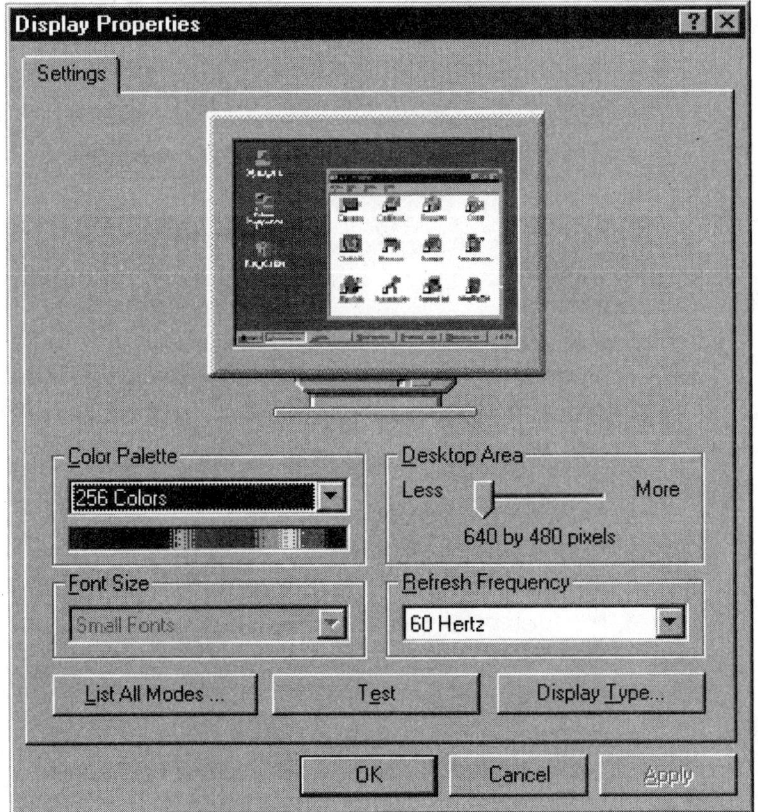

Figure 3-35: The Display Properties dialog box.

When you are finished setting your display options, click the OK button.

Creating the ERD

The final step in the setup program is to create the Emergency Repair Disk (ERD), if you specified an ERD as shown in Figure 3-18 above. An ERD is vital to restoring a damaged installation of Windows NT 4 Server that no longer boots correctly. If by chance you chose not to create an ERD, when Windows NT 4 Server restarts you can select the RDISK.EXE utility (found in the Windows NT 4 Server folder) to create a new repair disk. Figure 3-36 shows the prompt to insert the disk you want to use for the ERD. Insert a diskette in the A drive, and click the OK button to create the ERD disk.

Figure 3-36: Insert your ERD disk into the diskette drive.

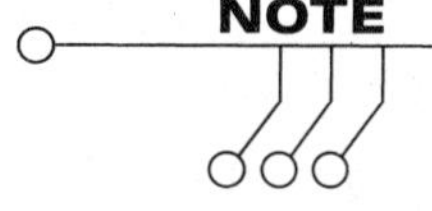

If you inadvertently leave one of your Windows NT 4 Server installation diskettes in the drive, the program is smart enough to tell you that the disk cannot be used for the ERD!

When the Emergency Repair Disk creation process is completed, the Setup Wizard reboots the computer for a final time. Once the reboot is completed, you can logon as the system administrator and configure your shares, users, and other devices specific to your installation.

One Final Reboot & a Test or Two!

The installation process end is marked with a dialog (Figure 3-37) that prompts you to reboot the system. You must reboot to implement the features and components you have installed. Click the Restart Computer button to restart the computer.

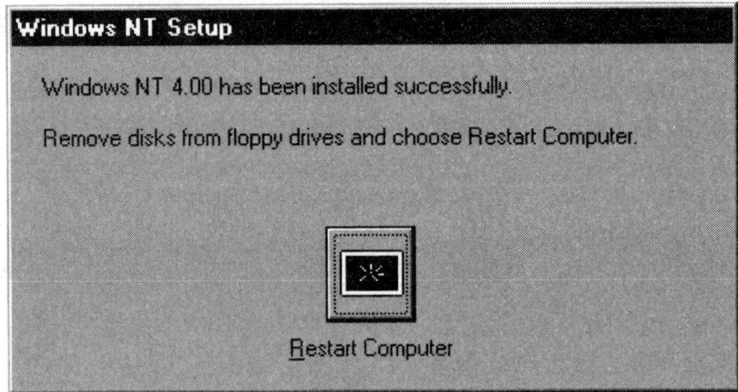

Figure 3-37: We are finished! A successful installation.

When installing Windows NT 4 Server, it is important to completely test the installation. From a workstation, make sure that users can access shared devices such as drives and printers. Also test RAS (if installed) and other special features as needed.

Reinstall any applications you want to run from the server if this was a clean installation. Examples of this are Microsoft BackOffice, Microsoft SQL Server, Microsoft Office, and other products that would normally run on this computer.

The above steps are typical for a simple, single-server system. Your installation may be quite different; however, the general flow of any installation will be similar to the above description.

Moving On

In this chapter we showed a typical (yet simple) installation of Windows NT 4 Server. Although there were quite a few setup windows to step through, the Setup Wizard has greatly reduced the number of tasks performed by the system administrator.

Next, in Chapter 4, "Windows NT 4 Server Components," we cover configuration of both the server and workstation components of Windows NT 4 Server, configuration of the Remote Boot Service, and configuration of RPC (Remote Procedure Call).

In Chapter 8, "Configuring Hardware," we cover issues that confront the system administrator when configuring and tuning Windows NT 4 Server. Other chapters in the first part of the book expand on the configuration of many of the installation choices and describe how to install additional components.

4

Windows NT 4 Server Components

This chapter covers configuration and tuning for a number of optional components of Windows NT 4 Server. These include:

- Server—The Windows NT 4 Server manager.
- Workstation—The Windows NT 4 Server workstation functionality, which allows Windows NT 4 Server to function as a workstation on the network.
- Remote Boot Service—A service that allows *diskless* workstations, running a number of operating systems such as Windows 95 and MS-DOS, to boot from the network. This functionality allows easier management of workstations, since all storage is located on the server, making backup and other management tasks easier.
- RPC—Remote Procedure Calls are a method of executing procedures on the Windows NT 4 Server.

Unless mentioned otherwise, you can install each component of Windows NT 4 Server using the Control Panel's Network applet. To select components to install, follow the steps below:

1. Start the Control Panel's Network applet.
2. Select the Services tab.
3. Click the Add button. The Select Network Service dialog box appears.
4. Select the component you wish to install from the Network Service list.

If you are not using a particular service, then there is no need to consider installing, configuring, or tuning that particular service.

Configuration is often a part of installation; here it is a critical step in getting Windows NT 4 Server up and running effectively. Windows NT 4 Server usually performs much better if you, the system administrator, ensure that the system is optimally configured. An optimally configured system not only performs better but is more reliable as well. First you install, then you configure the installation. Finally you tune the configuration for optimal performance.

Configuration and tuning are interrelated to a certain extent. For example, it is common for changes in the configuration to affect system performance. If and when you make changes in the configuration, especially when adding new services (and servers, such as IIS), you should also consider the impact on system performance.

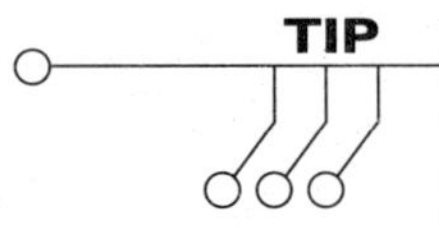

There is nothing to prevent you from having multiple installations of Windows NT Server on a single computer. You can have one installation that you keep relatively simple, and another system that you are tuning and customizing. That way, if you make a change that adversely affects the server's reliability or performance, you can fall back on your other system.

There are a number of ancillary parts of Windows NT 4 Server that you must install and configure. Some of these parts you configure when you initially install Windows NT 4 Server. Other parts you can configure later, when you add additional components, services, or servers. The following sections describe each component and include information on configuring the component.

Configuring the Server

To configure the server portion of Windows NT 4 Server, follow the steps below:

1. Start the Control Panel's Network applet.
2. Select the Services tab.
3. Select Server in the Services tab's Network Services listbox, and click the Properties button. The Server configuration dialog box appears as shown in Figure 4-1.

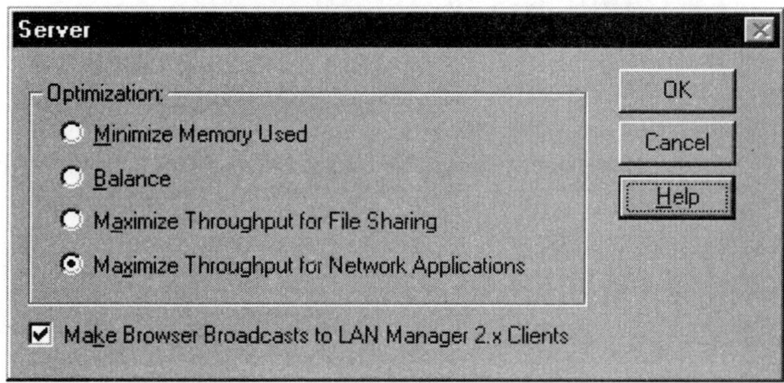

Figure 4-1: The Server dialog box.

Optimizing Memory & Performance

You may choose one of four server models to optimize your server. The four optimization models are:

- Minimize Memory Used—Minimizes the amount of memory used, while probably adversely affecting performance. This optimization is suitable only for a server that has less than a few, non-demanding, clients attached.
- Balance—Tries to find a happy medium between memory used and performance.

- Maximize Throughput for File Sharing—Optimizes the file-sharing capabilities at the expense of memory used.
- Maximize Throughput for Network Applications—The default server optimization model. Optimizes the performance of network applications (such as client/server applications) at the expense of memory used.

Many simpler networks perform well with the Balance optimization model. If your system does not have sufficient RAM and has minimal network server duties, you can try specifying the Minimize Memory Used optimization model.

LAN Manager 2.x Option

A second option for Server is Make Browser Broadcasts to LAN Manager 2.x Clients. You use this option to make the Windows NT 4 Server visible to LAN Manager 2.x clients. If you have no LAN Manager 2.x clients, then you can clear this option.

Configuring Workstation

The Microsoft Windows Workstation Service allows your Windows NT 4 Server to function as a workstation on the network (allowing the Windows NT 4 Server to access shared resources). The Workstation Service is not configurable and there are no options to set for the Workstation Service.

Configuring Remote Boot Service

The Remote Boot Service allows you to boot diskless workstations on your network from your Windows NT 4 Server. Remote Boot Service uses the boot PROM (Programmable Read-Only Memory) found on many popular NICs (Network Interface Cards).

Windows for Workgroups & Windows 3.1x Not Supported?

Remote Boot Service is not supported for Windows NT 4 Workstation clients. Remote Boot Service also does not support Windows 3.1x, or Windows for Workgroups.

Why? Because each of these two operating systems expects to run its network software in protected mode and were not written to remotely access the operating system from a network connection. Neither Windows for Workgroups nor Windows 3.1x can load a real mode network (needed to remote boot) and then load the protected mode network drivers after the real mode drivers are loaded.

Best fix? Convert the remote boot workstation to Windows 95, which is compatible with Remote Boot Service.

You must install the DLC protocol for a successful installation of the Remote Boot Service (sometimes called the Remoteboot Service). (Data Link Control protocol is typically used when communicating with mainframe computers.) To check to see if you have installed the DLC protocol, follow the steps below:

1. Start the Control Panel's Network applet.
2. Select the Protocol tab.
3. Visually scan the Network Protocols list for the DLC Protocol. If it appears, continue to step 4. If it doesn't, see the procedure that follows Figure 4-2.
4. Highlight the network protocol DLC Protocol as shown in Figure 4-2.

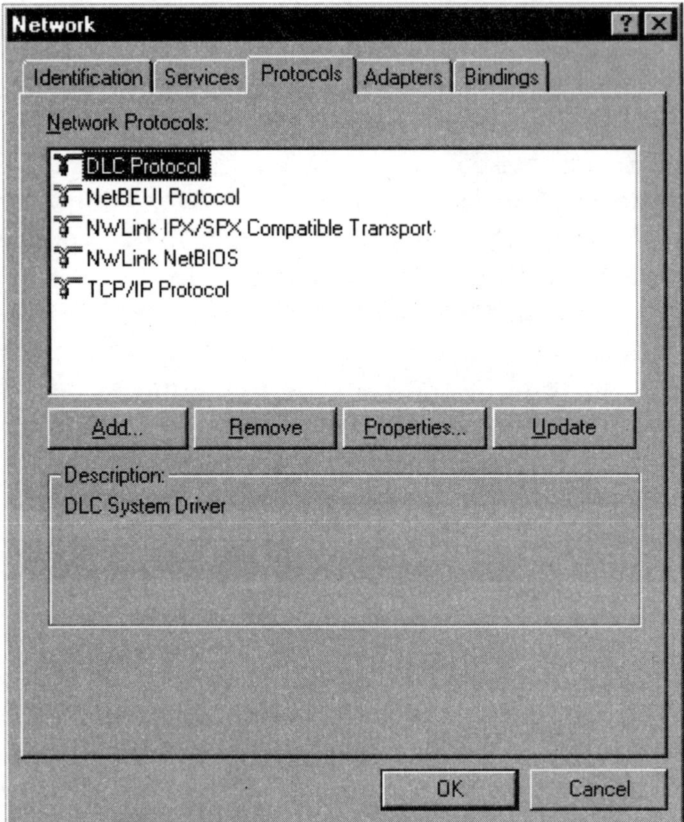

Figure 4-2: The Control Panel's Network applet, Protocols tab.

To select the DLC Protocol if you do not already have the DLC Protocol installed, follow the steps below:

1. Start the Control Panel's Network applet.
2. Select the Protocol tab.
3. Click the Add button.
4. Select DLC Protocol from the Network Protocols list.

The Remote Boot Service installation is just a bit more complex than most other services. Before you begin, consider the following:

- What is the drive and directory of the Windows NT 4 Server installation source?

- Where are your client files located?

The Remote Boot Service installation program prompts you to specify two directories during the installation:

- The Windows NT 4 Server installation source directory.
- The location of the client files (which are found in the V:\clients\rpl folder—where V is the drive in which the Windows NT 4 Server CD-ROM is located).

If you specify the wrong directory for the client files, the program issues a number of "file not found" error messages—abort the installation of Remote Boot Service and restart, specifying the correct location for the client files.

To configure Remote Boot Service once it has been installed, follow the steps below:

1. Start Remote Boot Service using the Control Panel's Services applet.
2. Select the Services tab.
3. Highlight Remoteboot Service in the Service list box.
4. Click the Start button (see Figure 4-3).

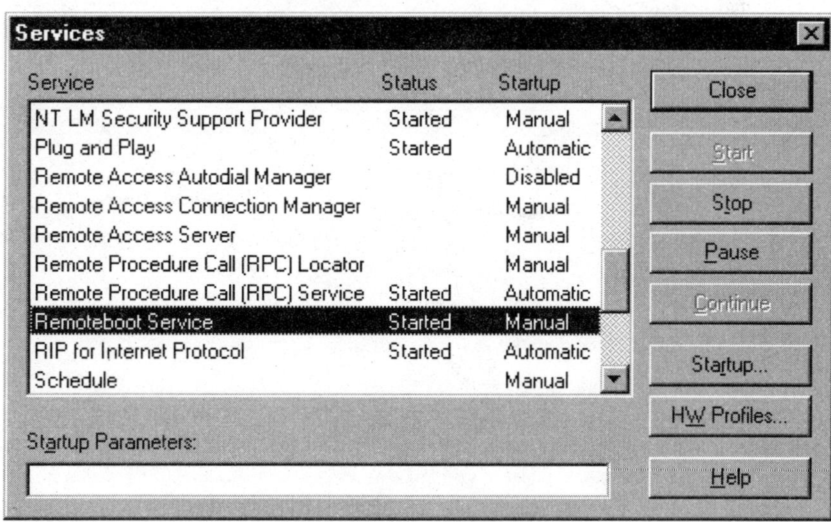

Figure 4-3: The Service list box.

Note: You can choose to have Remote Boot Service started automatically if you anticipate using Remote Boot Service on this server frequently. To set up automatic Remote Boot Service, follow the steps below:

1. Start the Control Panel's Network applet.
2. Select the Services tab.
3. Click the Startup button.
4. Change the Startup Type to Automatic.

When Remote Boot Service is running, you can use the Remoteboot Manager program to administer the Remote Boot Service. To start the Remote Boot Service program, follow the steps below:

1. Click the Start menu button. The Start menu appears.
2. Point at the word Programs. A list of programs or folders appears.
3. Point at Administrative Tools (Common).
4. Select Remoteboot Manager from the list of Administrative Tools.

The Remoteboot Manager is the main application you use to create and manage your Remote Boot Service. The main screen for Remoteboot Manager is shown in Figure 4-4.

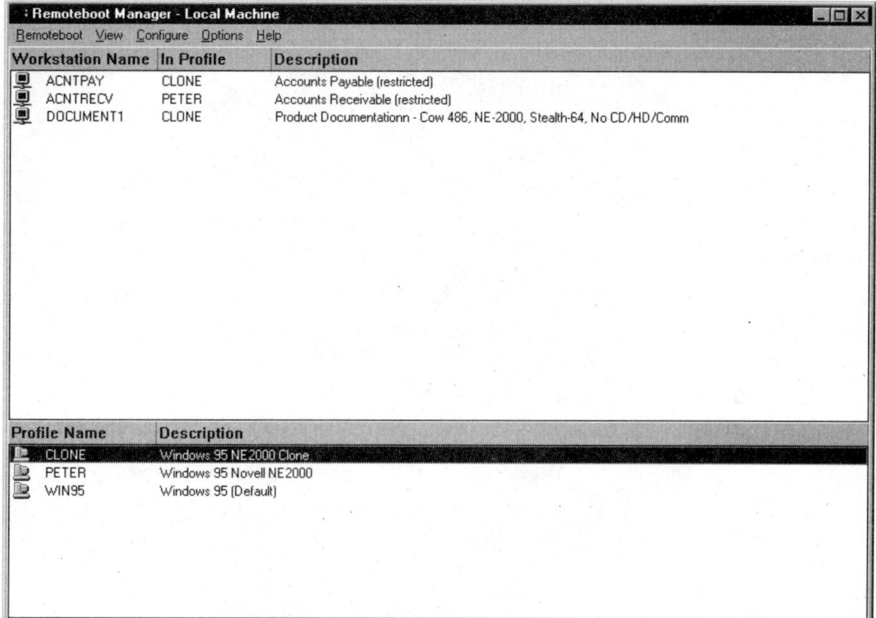

Figure 4-4: The Remoteboot Manager.

To configure Remoteboot Service, you must first create a profile. The profile describes its configuration. Windows NT 4 Server provides you with a list from which you can choose appropriate configurations. See Figure 4-5.

In the New Profile dialog box, you must supply the profile name ("WIN95-ELNK" in the example shown) and a description (something that is meaningful). You must also select the configuration type from the drop-down list box. Configuration types are combinations of NICs and operating systems.

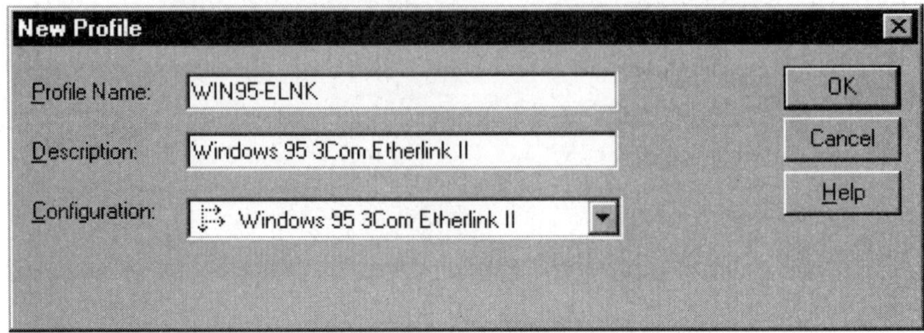

Figure 4-5: Remoteboot Manager profile creation.

Once one or more profiles have been created, you can then begin the task of creating your workstation configurations. Microsoft has provided two ways to create the necessary workstation configurations: manually or automatically. Using the automatic method may prove to be the least difficult as you do not need to know the NIC's ID number.

Automatic Configuration of Workstations

To automatically create a workstation configuration, it is necessary to boot the workstation. You need do nothing other than start Remote Boot Service on the Windows NT 4 Server.

When a workstation is booted, it attempts to boot from the NIC. This attempt creates an adapter record on the server. Once this adapter record has been created, you can convert it to a workstation configuration by adding a workstation name and setting the profile.

The automatic configuration is much easier to use than the manual method as you do not have to know the NIC's ID. To find the NIC's ID, you must either run a special utility (supplied with the NIC) or open the computer and find the NIC's ID, which is typically placed on a sticker found on the NIC.

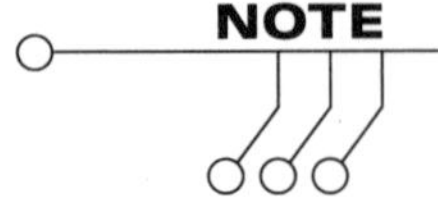

NICs have a singular identifier so that they are unique on a network. This number is typically placed in a PROM (Programmable Read-Only Memory) chip by the manufacturer of the NIC.

To automatically create a remote boot client record, follow the steps below. The client can be any configuration for which you wish to have a new record created.

1. Log on to the Windows NT 4 Server as the administrator, and start Remoteboot Manager.
2. Boot the workstation you want to use as the Remote Boot Service client.
3. The workstation should not boot. If it does, you have a problem. Remove the floppy disk from the A drive if there is one and disable the hard disk if there is a hard disk installed. These actions force the workstation to boot from the NIC.
4. When the workstation attempts to boot using the NIC, a boot request is sent to the Windows NT 4 Server.
5. Remote Boot Service doesn't respond to the boot request as there is no workstation record for this workstation yet in existence.
6. Remote Boot Service creates a boot record that contains the workstation NIC's ID.
7. Refresh the screen from Remoteboot Manager. Press F5 to force Remoteboot Manager to update.
8. Select the adapter record that now appears in Remoteboot Manager. The new record has a NIC ID in the Workstation Name column (see Figure 4-6). This new record also has the network adapter ID number in place of the workstation name.
9. From the Remoteboot menu, select Convert Adapters. If you have more than one workstation to add using this technique, you can boot all the workstations, select all the boot records, and then select Convert Adapters. Remoteboot Manager prompts you for each boot record you want to convert.

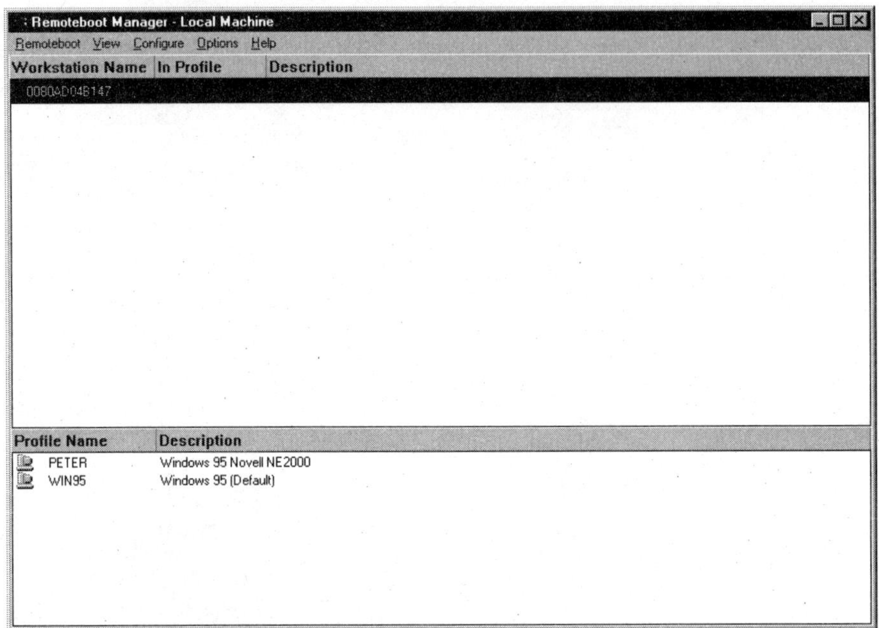

Figure 4-6: A boot record in Remoteboot Manager.

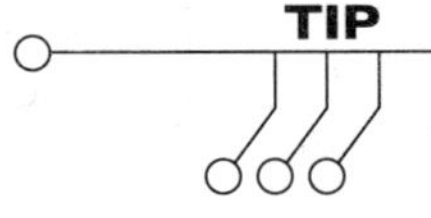

It is not possible to create a boot record manually. A boot record is created only when Remoteboot Manager detects a workstation that does not have a workstation record making a boot request.

10. Choose a workstation from the list by selecting Remoteboot | Properties (or press Enter, the shortcut key, or double-click the workstation name in the list) from the menu.
11. The Remoteboot Workstation Properties dialog box (which is identical to the New Remoteboot Workstation dialog box) appears as shown in Figure 4-7.

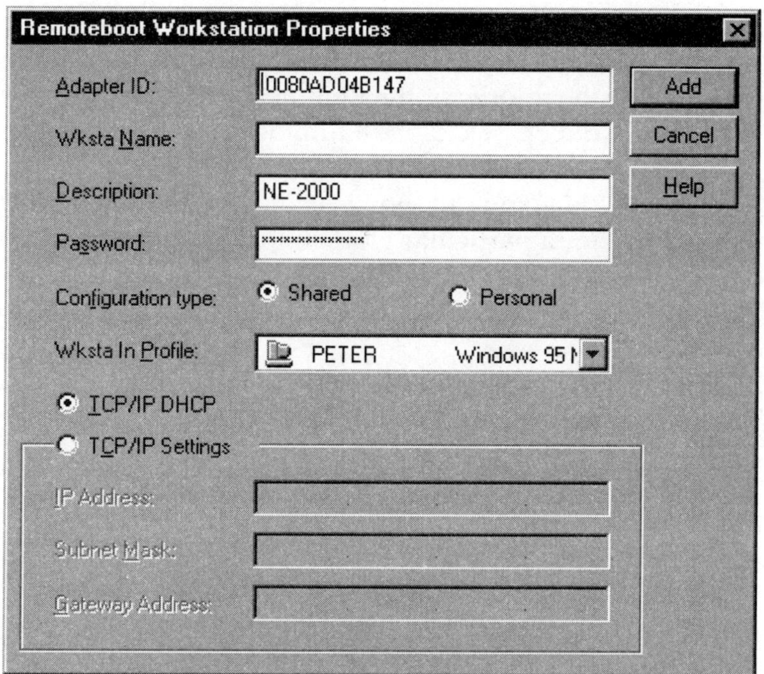

Figure 4-7: The Remoteboot Workstation Properties dialog box.

12. Enter the workstation name in the Wksta Name field. The Wksta Name field is a required field and is 1 to 15 characters long. For those Remote Boot Service installations where the RPL folder is located on a FAT file system drive, the workstation name is limited to an 8.3 format (eight characters, an optional period, and three optional, trailing characters).
13. Next enter a meaningful description for the workstation. The Description field is an optional field. Remoteboot Manager also creates a Windows NT 4 Server user account for the workstation. This allows the workstation to boot, but this account is not used by the user. Users must have their own account to use the server. Finally, provide a password for this workstation.

14. Choose the type of configuration required for this workstation. The Configuration type radio buttons are located in the middle of the Remoteboot Workstation Properties dialog box. Since a number of workstations can share the same configuration, do not customize a shared configuration. You can, however, customize a personal configuration for a particular workstation. (For example, you can designate special device drivers for a particular user.)
15. Choose a profile for the workstation from the Wksta In Profile drop-down list box in the Remoteboot Workstation Properties dialog box. The profile must match the NIC contained in the workstation (the NIC's type is identified by the first six digits in the NIC ID). All profiles not suitable for the NIC are marked with a red X. You must create a *new* profile to match the NIC type if no suitable profiles are listed.
16. If you are not using DHCP to assign TCP/IP addresses, then you must fill in the TCP/IP settings. You must know the IP address, subnet address, and the Gateway address for the workstation.

If you are unable to use the automatic configuration of workstations (for example, you are not able to gain access to the workstation for a test boot), then you must configure the workstation manually, as shown in the following section.

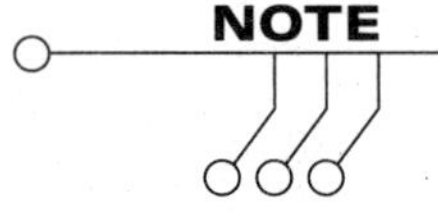

If you do not select any boot records, and then select Convert Adapters, Remoteboot Manager converts all existing boot records.

Manual Configuration of Workstations

To create a new workstation configuration, it is necessary to know the ID for the NIC that is installed with the PC. Usually, in order to find the NIC's ID, you must either run a special utility (supplied with the NIC) or open the computer's case, visually inspect the NIC, and find the NIC's ID. The NIC's ID is typically placed on a sticker attached to the NIC.

NIC manufacturers install a unique NIC product ID on all NICs. The ID is a two-part, 12-digit hexadecimal number such as 00 80 AD 04 B1 47. The first six digits identify the NIC type (an NE-2000 clone's identifier typically is 00 80 AD, while a 3Com 3C501 is 02 60 8C); the last six digits uniquely identify the specific adapter. The two parts are shown in different places on some NICs, such as a sticker on the card for the first six digits and a sticker on the PROM (where the unique card identifier is stored) with the last six digits.

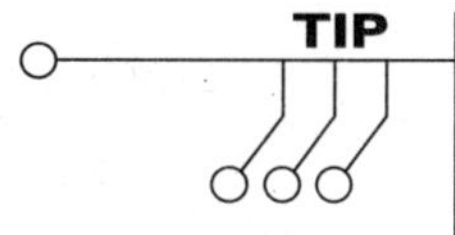

If you receive the error "Chosen profile is incompatible with this workstation," the Adapter ID value doesn't match the Adapter ID value defined for the profile you chose for this workstation. Choose the profile that matches the workstation's NIC.

See the section below titled, "The RPLCMD Utility," for information on how to add a new NIC or operating system to the Remote Boot Service database.

Once you know the NIC ID number, you can proceed with creating the workstation configuration. You must be logged on as an administrator to administer Remote Boot Service.

1. Start Remoteboot Manager. Then manually create a blank new workstation record (select Remoteboot | New Workstation from the menu). Alternatively, you can select an existing record with similar attributes (if there are any) and copy the record to create your new record.
2. Enter the workstation's NIC ID number, which you have already determined, in the Adapter ID edit box.
3. Enter the workstation name in the Wksta Name field. The Wksta Name field is a required field and is 1 to 15 characters long. For those Remote Boot Service installations where the RPL folder is located on a FAT file system drive, then the workstation name is limited to 8.3 format (eight characters, an optional period, and three trailing characters).

4. Next enter a meaningful description for the workstation. The Description field is an optional field. Remoteboot Manager also creates a Windows NT 4 Server user account for the workstation. This allows the workstation to boot, but this account is not used by the user. Users must have their own account to use the server. Finally, provide a password for this workstation.
5. Choose the type of configuration required for this workstation. The Configuration type radio buttons are located in the middle of the New Remoteboot Workstation dialog box. Since a number of workstations can share the same configuration, do not customize a shared configuration. You can, however, customize a personal configuration for a particular workstation. (For example, you can designate special device drivers for a particular user.)
6. Choose a profile for the workstation from the Wksta In Profile drop-down list box in the New Remoteboot Workstation dialog box. The profile must match the NIC contained in the workstation (the NIC's type is identified by the first six digits in the NIC ID). All profiles not suitable for the NIC are marked with a red X. You must create a *new* profile to match the NIC type if no suitable profiles are listed.
7. If you are not using DHCP to assign TCP/IP addresses, then you must fill in the TCP/IP settings. You must know the IP address, subnet address, and the Gateway address for the workstation.
8. Select Add to save the workstation configuration.

An example of a new workstation configuration is shown in Figure 4-8.

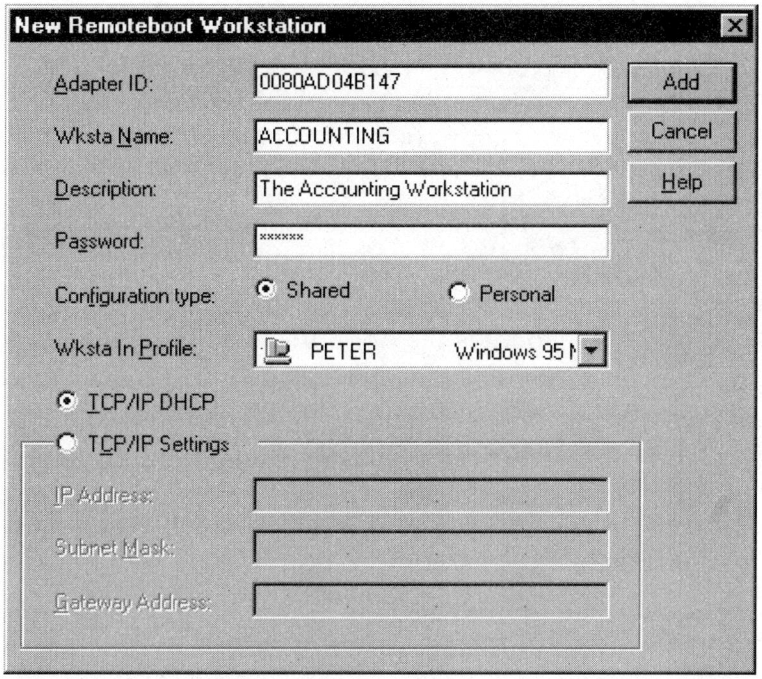

Figure 4-8: The Remoteboot Manager New Remoteboot Workstation dialog.

Either method for creating workstation configurations is acceptable. If you have many remote booting workstations, then the first method may be the easiest—you will not have to make a substantial effort determining the NIC IDs.

Other Remote Boot Manager Functions

In Remote Boot Manager there are three additional significant functions. These functions are found under the Configure menu selection:

- Fix Security—Allows Remoteboot Manager to modify the various security settings to allow proper access for remoteboot workstations. Use the Fix Security option when you install Remote Boot Service and after you add or remove a remote boot operating system.

The Fix Security option does the following:

- Overwrites permissions throughout the \%systemroot%\rpl folder. (The identifier %systemroot% contains the location of Windows NT 4 Server, which is typically C:\WINNT.)
- Creates accounts for remoteboot workstations and the RPLUSER local account, when these accounts have not already been created.
- Updates the domain entry in the LANMAN.INI files (there is a LANMAN.INI file for each bootable configuration).

- Check Configurations—Builds configurations (configurations are the combinations of operating systems and network adapter types) which you can assign to profiles. Select the Check Configurations option each time you change operating system or network adapter support.
- Backup Database—Creates backup copies of the Remoteboot Manager database files. These files are not in standard Microsoft Access format despite the .MDB extension. Backup copies of j5000001.log, rplsvc.mdb, and rplsvc.pat are created in a folder located in \%systemroot%\rpl\backup\.

The Remote Boot Service is a complex system that can take some effort to make functional. As well, you must consider the issues of server resources (including network loading) that remoteboot clients require.

The RPLCMD Utility

The RPLCMD utility is a command line driven program you use to modify the RPL database. The RPL database is where information about client configurations is stored.

This program views and updates the Remote Boot Service database and has functionality that the Remote Boot Service Manager program does not have.

You can issue the RPLCMD from a command window or from a response file, which is a file containing commands that a program runs automatically. (There are a number of example response files in the Windows NT 4 Server distribution CD-ROM.) The example response files for RPLCMD have an extension of .RPL. For example, the RPLCMD response file MADGE.RPL to add the MADGE NIC adapter is:

```
b
a
DOS
0000F6
BBLOCK\NETBEUI\MADGE\DOSBB.CNF
Madge Smart 16/4 Ringnode
0
v
a
0000F6
Madge Smart 16/4 Ringnode
q
```

When you enter these commands by hand, the command "b" selects the Boot option, "a" selects add, "DOS" is the BootName, 0000F6 is the NIC product identifying number, "BBLOCK\NETBEUI\MADGE\DOSBB.CNF" is the MADGE configuration file, and so on. You do not need to add additional NICs (in an ideal world); however, it is possible, or even probable, that you do have a NIC not listed in Remoteboot Manager, which you need to install manually if remote boot support is necessary.

Why Do I Have to Add a NIC?

The main reason that all NICs are not already configured is that a manufacturer may choose to create a new NIC product. The new NIC, although 100% hardware-compatible with an existing NIC, has its own identifier!

For example, there are probably 20 or more NE-2000–compatible NICs produced by as many hardware producers. As well, outside the United States, there are probably just as many different, yet compatible cards available!

If the NIC configuration you want is not present, you must install the files for the appropriate operating system (see the Windows NT Server Installation Guide) and check the configuration (from the Configure menu, choose Check Configurations).

An example of an RPLCMD session (RPLCMD was run in a CMD window) is shown below. In this session a clone NE-2000 NIC is added to the RPL database. The clone NE-2000 NIC has a different NIC product-identifying number than a *real* NE-2000. Items that were entered by the system administrator in this session are shown in boldface type.

```
Windows NT Version 4.0 C:\winnt\rpl
rplcmd
Adapter Boot Config Profile Service Vendor Wksta [Quit]: b
Add Del Enum: a
BootName=W95Gen
VendorName=0080AD
BbcFile=bblock\netbeui\ne2000\w95bb.cnf
        All other parameters are optional
BootComment=Windows 95 NE2000 Clone
WindowSize=0
Adapter Boot Config Profile Service Vendor Wksta [Quit]: c
Add Del Enum: a
ConfigName=W95gen
BootName=W95gen
DirName=DOS
DirName2=WIN95
FitShared=fits\win95.fit
FitPersonal=fits\win95p.fit
        All other parameters are optional
ConfigComment=Windows 95 NE2000 Clone
DirName3=
DirName4=
Adapter Boot Config Profile Service Vendor Wksta [Quit]: q

Windows NT Version 4.0 C:\winnt\rpl
```

In the above example, I added a new entry for an almost standard NE-2000 clone NIC. This clone card carried a different NIC product-identifying code (0080AD) than a *real* NE-2000 NIC (00001B).

The input script file win95.rpl in the folder V:\clients\rpl\update\win95 (where V is the drive letter for your Windows NT 4 Server installation CD-ROM) demonstrates how adapters and operating systems are added. A convenient method for adding one or more adapters and operating systems is to read and edit the input script file.

Configuring RPC

RPCs—Remote Procedure Calls—are an important part of Windows NT 4 Server and are relatively easy to configure. To configure RPC, you must have the RPC Service running. To start the RPC Service, follow the steps below:

1. Start the Control Panel's Services applet.
2. Select Remote Procedure Call in the Service list.
3. Click the Start button.

Many components, systems, and applications use RPC to function. Examples of RPC users include both Exchange Server and DNS Server.

To display the RPC Configuration dialog, follow the steps below:

1. Start the Control Panel's Network applet.
2. Select the Services tab.
3. Select the entry for RPC Configuration from the Network Services list.
4. Click the Properties button to display the RPC Configuration dialog box. The RPC Configuration dialog appears as shown in Figure 4-9.
5. Fill in the Name Service Provider, Network Address, and Security Service Provider fields.

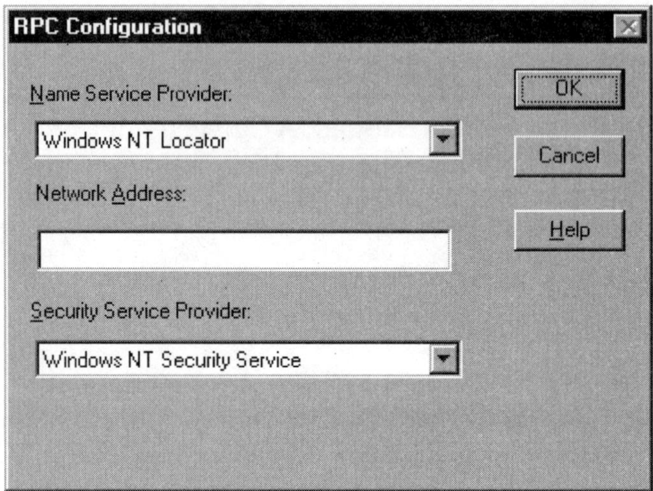

Figure 4-9: The RPC Configuration dialog.

For a Name Service Provider, you have a choice between Windows NT Locator (the default) and DCE (Distributed Computing Environment) Cell Directory Service. Typically, the Windows NT Locator will suffice; however, some configurations (those using Cell Directory Service to allow clients to locate resources on the network) may need to select the DCE Cell Directory Service. The DCE Cell Directory Service is accessed through the DCE NSID.

When you select the DCE Cell Directory Service, you must also provide the Network Address (the Windows NT Locator doesn't use the Network Address field). A Network Address is a string of no more than 80 characters. For example, a TCP/IP address, such as 199.125.78.23, is a valid entry in the Network Address Field.

The final field in the RPC Configuration dialog is the Security Service Provider. At the time of this writing, the only Security Service Provider is the Windows NT Security Service. It is possible that Microsoft, or other parties, will provide other Security Service Providers in the future.

Configuring the NetBIOS Interface

The NetBIOS Interface is the software component that provides a NetBIOS mapping layer between NetBIOS applications and the TID (Tree ID) compliant transport protocols.

To configure the NetBIOS Interface, select the Services tab from the Control Panel's Network applet. In the Network Services list, select "NetBIOS Interface," and then click the Properties button. The NetBIOS configuration dialog box displays.

Figure 4-10 shows the NetBIOS configuration dialog box. This dialog box allows the administrator to configure the LANA (LAN adapter) number that specifies a network adapter routing.

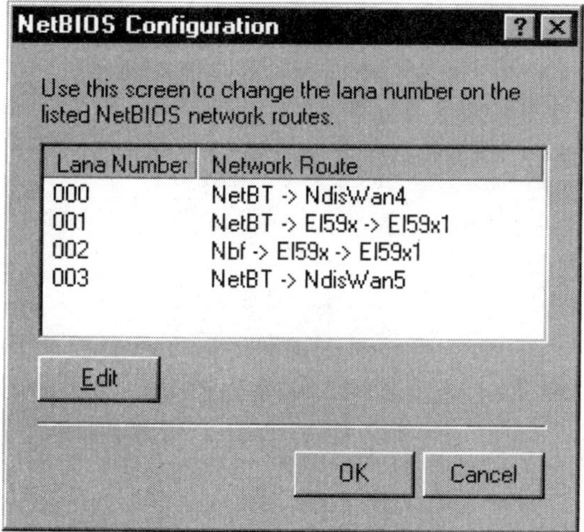

Figure 4-10: The NetBIOS Configuration dialog.

When using the NetBIOS Configuration dialog box, you are able to set the LANA number for any of the routes listed. LANA numbers are assigned by the LAN manager automatically. A LANA number is an identifier used by the LAN manager's redirector to identify a NIC and the NIC's protocol driver.

Generally, you should not need to change the LANA numbers for the NetBIOS Interface—Windows NT 4 Server automatically assigns the LANA numbers for you. The only time you might need to change a LANA number would be if there were a conflict in LANA numbers.

Moving On

What do you think? After reading this chapter can you configure your server, workstation, Remote Boot Service, Remote Procedure Calls, and NetBIOS Interface yourself? I hope the answer is Yes! This chapter also provided valuable information to help you optimize memory and performance and to make you more knowledgeable about the LAN Manager 2.x option and Remote Boot Manager functions. If you're thirsting for more, read on to see what you can look forward to in Chapter 5, "Configuring TCP/IP Services."

The next chapter covers configuring TCP/IP services, including the DNS, DHCP, WINS, and the Simple TCP/IP Services. Since the next chapter is rather long, right now may be a good time to get up and stretch!

5

Configuring TCP/IP Services

This chapter covers configuration and tuning of TCP/IP (Transmission Control Protocol/Internet Protocol) Services of Windows NT 4 Server. These services include:

- TCP/IP Services—The basic TCP/IP protocol used with local area networks (LANs), wide area networks (WANs), the Internet, and intranets. Unlike most other network protocols, TCP/IP does require configuration.
- RIP for Internet Protocol—RIP (Routing Information Protocol) has no user configurations. RIP for Internet Protocol exists because all hosts on the Internet need to talk to routers. (Routers connect two or more Internet Protocol networks.) The Windows NT 4 Server exchanges routing information with other Internet servers.
- Simple TCP/IP Services—TCP/IP clients use Simple TCP/IP Services. Windows NT 4 Server offers these services to allow your Windows NT 4 Server to compete with other TCP/IP-based servers.

- Microsoft DHCP Server and the Microsoft DHCP Agent—Dynamically assign IP addresses to TCP/IP clients who connect on a part-time basis, usually using dial-up networking connections.
- Microsoft DNS (Domain Name Server)—A service that resolves names on a TCP/IP address. The Microsoft DNS provides the actual IP address for each name.
- Microsoft WINS (Windows Internet Name Service)—A system that resolves names on a TCP/IP address and provides the actual IP address for each name. Only Windows clients use this service (which works like DNS).

Unless otherwise specified, you can install the services components of Windows NT 4 Server using the Control Panel's Network applet. To select services to install, follow the steps below:

1. Start the Control Panel's Network applet.
2. Select the Services tab.
3. Click the Add button. The Select Network Service dialog box appears.
4. Select the services component you wish to install from the Network Service list.

If you are not using any of the TCP/IP services, then there is no need to consider installing, configuring, or tuning that particular service. Installing unneeded network protocols can create problems, as each protocol consumes system resources, including network bandwidth.

As well, don't forget to consider using TCP/IP for basic LANs. Many system administrators shy away from TCP/IP because of the configuration issues. Actually, private TCP/IP-based networks are as easy to configure as any other protocol. If you are not connecting to any external network, then you have full control over allocation of IP addresses. Assigning IP addresses is as simple as deciding which numbers to use (most system administrators do use some sort of plan for assigning IP addresses).

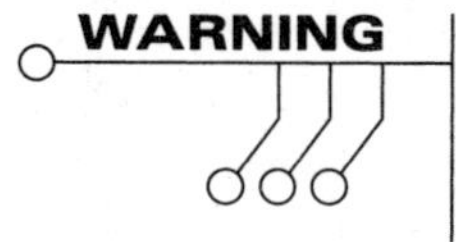

If your LAN provides an internal Web server for local use and an external server for the Internet, you must provide each server with a different IP address. Additionally, be aware that on the Internet, an IP address-assigning organization assigns the IP addresses.

Configuration is often a part of installation; here it is a critical step in getting Windows NT 4 Server up and running effectively. Windows NT 4 Server usually performs much better if you, the system administrator, optimally configure the system. First you install, then you configure the installation, and finally you tune the configuration for optimal performance.

Configuration and tuning are interrelated to a certain extent. For example, it is common for changes in the configuration to affect system performance. If, and when, you make changes in the configuration, especially when adding new services (and servers, such as IIS) consider the impact on system performance.

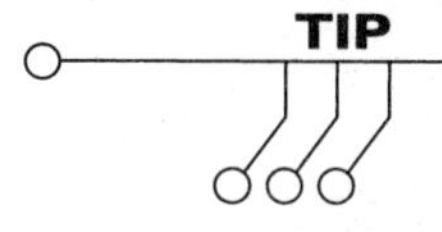

Nothing prevents you from having multiple installations of Windows NT Server on a single computer. You could have one relatively simple installation and another installation for tuning and customizing your TCP/IP. That way you have a system to fall back on, in case a change made while tuning adversely affects the server's reliability or performance.

Configuring TCP/IP Services

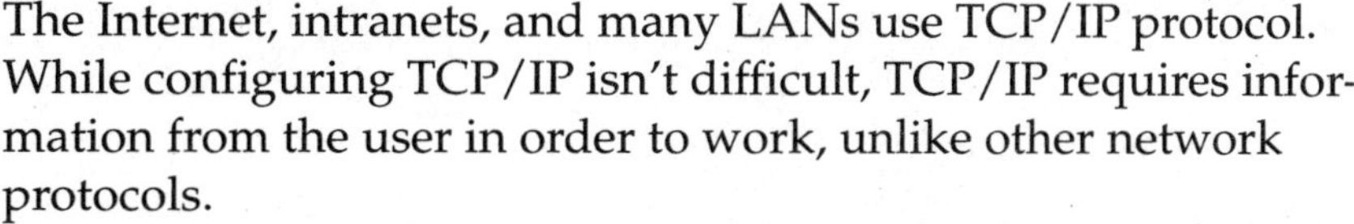

The Internet, intranets, and many LANs use TCP/IP protocol. While configuring TCP/IP isn't difficult, TCP/IP requires information from the user in order to work, unlike other network protocols.

TCP/IP configuration includes the IP addresses of the server and clients, the DNS address, and sometimes, a gateway. All of this information is usually available from the system administrator for your network, if you're not the administrator. If your TCP/IP network is not connected to any external network (which you don't administer) then you can create your own IP addresses.

Information required to connect your network to the Internet varies somewhat depending on the connection. Common connection techniques include dial-up (using Remote Access Service/ Dial-Up Networking (RAS/DUN)), ISDN dial-up, and dedicated connections. In virtually all cases, however, the required information is the same. Only the source of the information can vary.

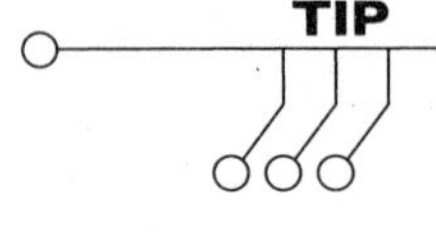

Throughout this book we refer to RAS/DUN. Readers familiar with Windows NT 3.5x Server are familiar with the term RAS (Remote Access Service). Users who know about Windows NT 4 Server (and who are familiar with Dial-Up Networking for Windows 95) know the term DUN. To avoid confusion, I use the term RAS/DUN to refer to the Windows NT 4 Server ability to connect remotely to a network such as the Internet, as either a client (DUN) or as a server (RAS).

To obtain the necessary information for configuring TCP/IP (if you do not already know it) start with the site to which you are connected. Talk to that site's system administrator to obtain TCP/ IP configuration and address information.

For example, if you are configuring a dial-up system (either analog or digital (ISDN)) then you probably connect with an ISP (Internet Service Provider). The ISP's system administrator will provide you with the necessary information to configure your TCP/IP.

To configure TCP/IP you must set options in several places.

For a network that is *hard wired*, (not using RAS/DUN and modems, but connected using a NIC), follow the steps below:

1. Start the Control Panel's Network applet.
2. In the Protocols tab, add TCP/IP Protocol if it is not installed.
3. In the Protocols tab, select TCP/IP Protocol, and click the Properties button.
4. Provide the IP Address, DNS, WINS Address, DHCP Relay, and Routing information as necessary, then click OK. Only IP Address and DNS information is mandatory—WINS Address, DHCP Relay, and Routing can be left at their defaults.

To configure a RAS/DUN TCP/IP connection, you must start the RAS manager and then update the configuration. Configuration tasks are described later. To start the RAS manager, follow the steps below:

1. Select Start Menu | Programs | Accessories | Dial-Up Networking.
2. Either create a new Phonebook entry (click the New button) or select an existing entry. From the More button's menu, select Edit Entry and Modem Properties.
3. Select the Server tab.
4. In Network protocols, ensure that TCP/IP is selected, then click the TCP/IP Settings button.
5. In the PPP TCP/IP Settings, provide the IP address, DNS Server, WINS server (if WINS is being used), and select Use IP header compression and Use default gateway on remote network as applicable. Generally, both compression and default gateway are selected for most dial-up connections.

Assigning IP Addresses

You can create your own IP addresses for TCP/IP networks not connected to an external network.

IP addresses consist of a set of four numbers (referred to as an octet) that range in value from 1 to 256, each number separated from the other with a period. For example, my computer's IP address is 199.125.78.23. IP addresses are categorized into *classes*:

- **Class A**. An IP address with the first octet fixed (or assigned by the Internet IP address-assigning body). The system administrator then assigns the remaining three octets as needed. Only the largest organizations qualify for a Class A IP address: there are only 256 possible Class A addresses for the entire Internet. A Class A IP address can have 16,777,216 nodes (clients) arranged as a block of 256 Class B addresses.

- **Class B**. An IP address with the first two octets fixed (or assigned by the Internet IP address-assigning body). The system administrator then assigns the remaining two octets as needed. Large companies and organizations use Class B IP addresses: each Class A IP address is composed of 256 Class B IP addresses. A Class B IP address can have 65,535 nodes (clients), arranged as a block of 256 Class C addresses.
- **Class C**. An address with the first three octets fixed (or assigned by the Internet IP address-assigning body). The system administrator then assigns the remaining octet as needed. Many companies and organizations use Class C IP addresses: each Class C IP address is composed of 256 node (client) IP addresses.
- **Class D**. These addresses (usually referred to as simply an IP address) have all four octets fixed by the assigning body. An IP address is assigned to one, and only one, node (client) on the network.

Just How Big Is the Internet?

The Internet has a problem.

There can be, by design, a maximum of only 4,294,967,296 nodes (clients) on the Internet. However, due to inefficiencies in assigning hierarchical addresses (a company or organization may "own" a Class B IP address, but only have assigned a small percentage of the individual IP addresses), not all of these addresses are really available for assignment to new users!

This is creating a problem. We will soon run out of IP addresses (at the current rate of IP address assignments, this may happen as soon as mid-1998). Running out of IP addresses would be a major disaster—much the same way that running out of telephone numbers would be a major problem to the telephone company.

The Internet governing body plans to increase the size of an IP address from 32 bits to 48 bits to give us a total of 2.814749767107e+14 possible IP addresses. This change is scheduled to happen in the next few years, and the change will affect all Internet users! Now, what is the population of the world? Will we have enough IP addresses for everyone (assuming we each have two, one for home and one for work)? I'll leave the math up to you!

Typically, for a Class C IP address, the server's (the *domain*) IP address ending octet is one. The remaining 254 IP addresses (the address xxx.xxx.xxx.0 is not used) are assigned to nodes (clients) connected to the server. All computers in a domain must be physically connected to the server. This is because TCP packets are routed based on the hierarchy, and the network does not know how to route information.

If you have a group with more than 255 clients, then you must allocate the next higher class of addresses (Class B), which would allow the domain to service 65,535 nodes (clients).

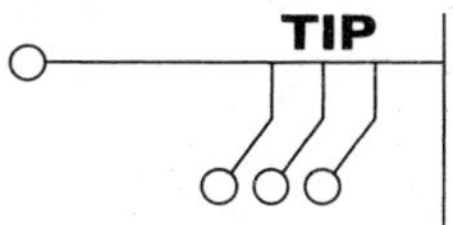

Microsoft's Catapult product, due to be released after Windows NT 4 Server, will make assigning IP addresses easier. Check both Microsoft's Web pages, and Appendix B, "Windows NT as an ISP," for more information about Catapult.

IP addresses are assigned by organization on a hierarchical basis. To map your IP addresses, you first create a hierarchy for your organization. Then break the organization down into groups. For example, R&D, Accounting, Sales, Marketing, and Administration.

Follow these guidelines when assigning IP addresses:

- Be logical with numbers. Start at a point and assign IP addresses sequentially. For clients, start with a low number. You need to reserve the first ten (or more, if you have a large organization) IP addresses in your Class B or Class C address space to your domain servers, DNS servers, and the mail servers.

- Remember that all client IP addresses in a Class C IP address must be physically connected to the server. The network looks at the IP address, beginning at the leftmost octet, and routes the packet to the computer at that address. That computer then looks at the second octet, and again routes the packet, and so forth. OK, it's not that simple. There are routing tables (which tell you the "best" path between two nodes), and other factors, which are beyond the scope of this discussion.

What Is a Gateway, Why Do We Have Routers & What Do Firewalls Do?

We often hear of a computer called a *gateway*. A gateway is a server that connects a group of computers to the entire network.

A router is a computer (often a dedicated system) that simply passes TCP/IP information between two networks. For example, your company connects to the Internet (perhaps with an ISDN line) using a single Windows NT 4 Server, and then the client computers in your company connect to the Windows NT 4 Server using Ethernet. The Windows NT 4 Server then functions both as a router and as a gateway.

A *firewall* is a system (again usually a dedicated system) that isolates your network from the Internet. Microsoft's Catapult works very well as a firewall. Using a firewall makes it much more difficult for anyone outside your organization to gain access to computers and information on your network. The firewall blocks all IP traffic except for those IP addresses that the administrator specifically authorizes.

For more information about routers, gateways, and firewalls, see Appendix B, "Windows NT as an ISP."

Configuring TCP/IP

To configure TCP/IP for networks that are connected using a Network Interface Card (NIC), follow the steps below:

1. Start the Control Panel's Network applet.
2. Select the Protocols tab as shown in Figure 5-1.

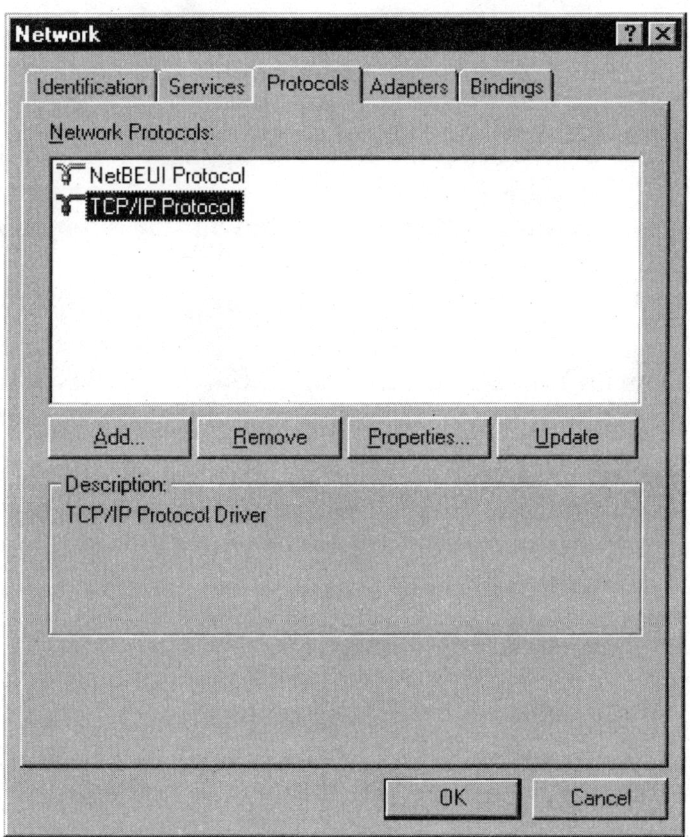

Figure 5-1: The Control Panel's Network applet Protocols tab.

3. Select the TCP/IP Protocol from the Network Protocols list box. When TCP/IP is not listed it has not been installed. You must install TCP/IP.

To configure TCP/IP for networks connected using RAS (Remote Access Server), follow the steps below:

1. Start the Control Panel's Network applet.
2. Select the Services tab.
3. Select Remote Access Service.
4. Click Properties. The Remote Access Setup dialog box appears.
5. Click the Network button. The Network Configuration dialog box appears.
6. Click the Configure button next to TCP/IP. The TCP/IP Configuration dialog box appears. Refer to the "Configuring Remote Access Service (RAS)" section of Chapter 7, "Configuring Dial-Up Networking," for configuration information.

DUN (Dial-Up Networking) requires that either you or the host computer specify an IP address indicating the location of the DNS (Domain Name Server) and an optional WINS Server. Note that at logon time, the host server may automatically provide these IP addresses.

To install TCP/IP, follow the steps below:

1. Start the Control Panel's Network applet.
2. Select the Protocols tab.
3. Click the Add button. The Select Network Protocol dialog box appears.
4. Highlight the TCP/IP Protocol.
5. Select OK. TCP/IP is installed from the distribution CD.

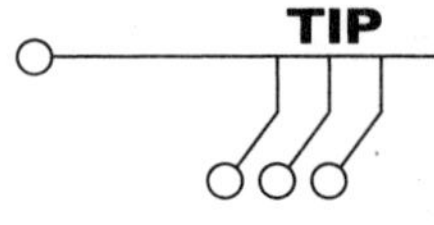

Installing a new protocol requires that you restart the system. Before starting with this type of configuration, make sure that client users will not be inconvenienced when the server is shut down.

TCP/IP & Windows NT

Previous versions of Windows NT have not reacted well to deleting the TCP/IP protocol and then attempting to reinstall it. Experience with Windows NT 4 Server shows that this same problem still exists. The problem is more serious than having to refresh the copy of Windows NT 4 Server: you must do a clean reinstall of Windows NT 4 Server if you inadvertently delete TCP/IP and need to reinstall it.

If you are feeling adventurous, you can try to reinstall TCP/IP. Delete the registry key HKEY_LOCAL_MACHINE\SYSTEM\CurrentControlSet\Services\Tcpip and the registry key HKEY_LOCAL_MACHINE\SYSTEM\CurrentControlSet\Services\Netbt. As well, remove any services that use TCP/IP, such as RAS, WINS, DHCP, and DNS. As always, when modifying the registry, make absolutely sure you have a valid, current backup of the registry.

Do not, under any circumstances, delete all networking under the Control Panel's Network applet's Services tab. You will not be able to logon to Windows NT 4 Server. Networking controls local logons!

Once you have TCP/IP installed, you can configure the protocol. To configure TCP/IP, follow the steps below:

1. Start the Control Panel's Network applet.
2. Select the Protocols tab.
3. Highlight the TCP/IP protocol in the Protocols list box.
4. Select the Properties button (see Figure 5-1). The Microsoft TCP/IP Properties dialog box appears as shown in Figure 5-2. The Microsoft TCP/IP Properties dialog box has five tabs: IP Address, DNS, WINS, DHCP Relay, and Routing. The most important tabs are the IP Address and the DNS entries.
5. Fill out the IP Address and the DNS tabs to enable the TCP/IP protocol to work correctly.

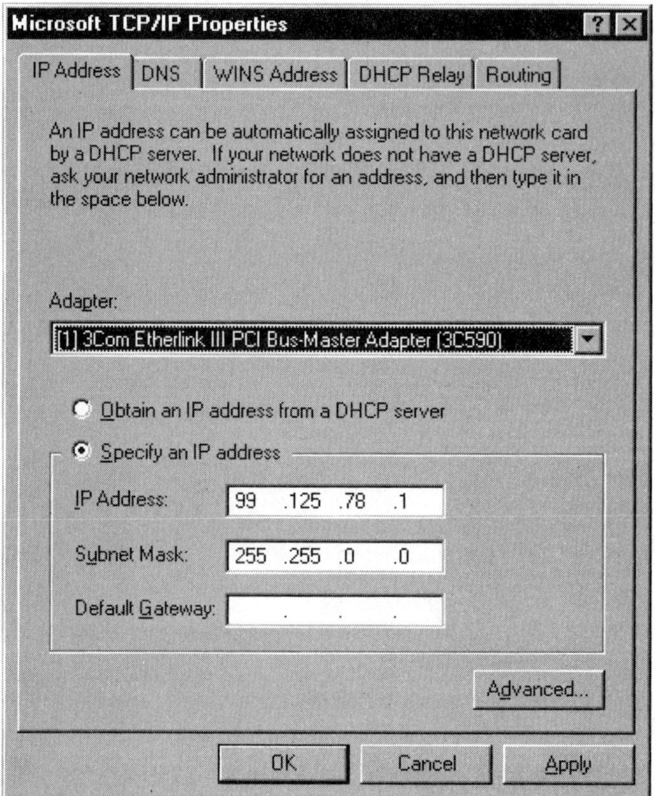

Figure 5-2: Microsoft TCP/IP Properties IP Address tab.

Setting IP Addresses

From the Microsoft TCP/IP Properties dialog box, follow the steps below to specify IP addresses.

1. Select the first tab, IP Address, as shown in Figure 5-2.
2. Select the network Adapter (NIC) you want to configure from the Adapter drop-down list. If your server has only one NIC, you have only one configuration. If your server has multiple NICs, you have to configure each NIC in turn.

You can configure each NIC as a separate step. This enables you to configure and test the operation of each leg of the network. This procedure is described in a moment. For each NIC you must either supply an IP address, or specify that a DHCP server provides the IP address. If you want to specify that the DHCP server provides the IP address, check the appropriate check box. If you are providing a fixed IP address, you must enter both the IP address and the Subnet Mask (which is 255.0.0.0 for a Class A address, 255.255.0.0 for a Class B address, and 255.255.255.0 for a Class C address).

You might need to fill in the default gateway. Your computer is connected to the gateway. Many Internet configurations do not require that the default gateway be set.

Advanced Addressing

To perform advanced addressing, follow the steps below:

1. Highlight the Adapter you want to configure in the drop-down list located on the IP Address tab on the Microsoft TCP/IP Properties dialog box.
2. Click the Advanced button. The Advanced IP Addressing dialog box appears as shown in Figure 5-3.

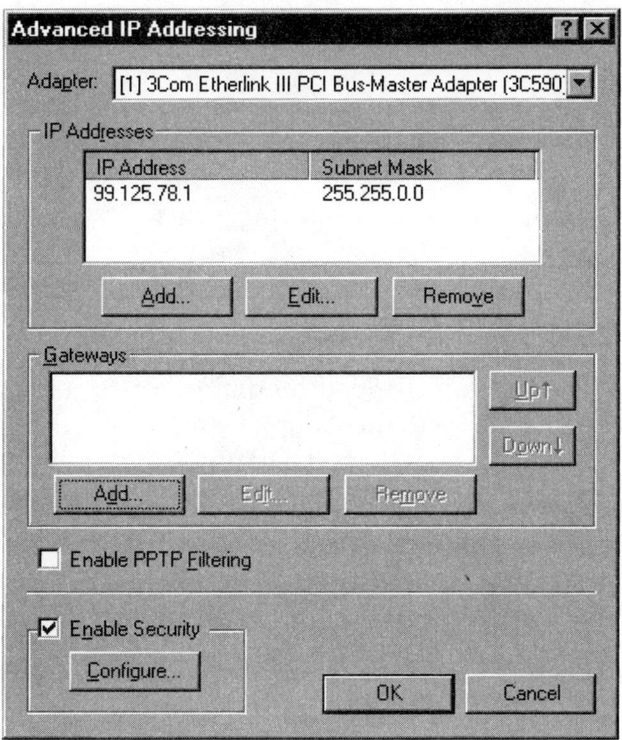

Figure 5-3: The Advanced IP Addressing dialog.

The Advanced IP Addressing page allows you to set your IP address for each NIC that you have installed in your Windows NT 4 Server system. This duplicates similar functionality found in the Microsoft TCP/IP Properties dialog. You can define and configure up to five alternate gateway addresses. The local IP router connects your computer to a specific destination located outside the local network.

The Advanced IP Addressing page also allows you to set PPTP filtering. Use PPTP (Point to Point Tunneling Protocol) when you have more than one LAN that is not using TCP/IP protocol and you want to link these networks securely across the Internet. Click to place a check beside the Enable PPTP Filtering check box. You can set the Enable PPTP Filtering option for each NIC in the system.

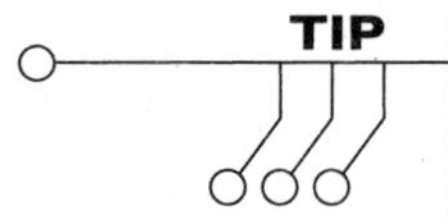

PPTP protocol is exclusive—with PPTP protocol, only PPTP packets are visible to the NIC. Do not select PPTP if the NIC must handle traffic that is not PPTP.

Setting Security

To enable and manage IP Security (for all NICs), follow the steps below:

1. Check the Enable Security check box on the Advanced IP Addressing dialog box.
2. Click the Configure button. The TCP/IP Security dialog box appears as shown in Figure 5-4.
3. Use the TCP/IP Security dialog box to configure the NIC that appears in the Adapter drop-down list. You can configure TCP Ports, UDP ports, and IP Protocols.
    - For TCP Ports, you can choose to either allow all ports to reach the server, or to permit only those TCP Ports that you specify to reach the server.
    - For UDP Ports, you can choose to either allow all ports to reach the server, or to permit only those UDP Ports that you specify to reach the server.

- For IP Protocols, you can choose to allow all protocols to reach the server, or to permit only those IP Protocols that you specify to reach the server.

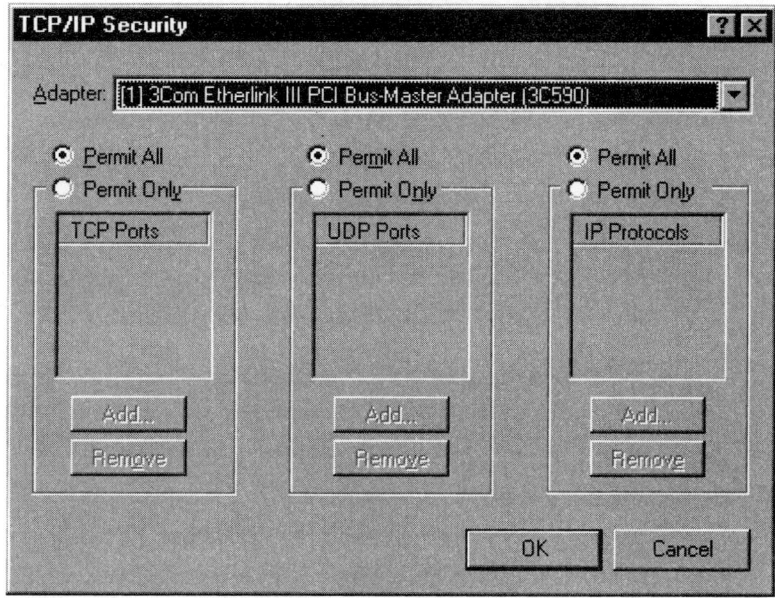

Figure 5-4: The TCP/IP Security dialog box.

4. Click OK (or Cancel to discard your changes) to accept the changes you made on the TCP/IP Security dialog box. The Advanced IP Addressing dialog box appears.
5. Close this dialog box with either the OK or Cancel buttons.

Specifying DNS Entries

To specify DNS entries, follow the steps below:

1. Start the Control Panel's Network applet.
2. Select the Protocols tab.
3. Highlight the TCP/IP protocol in the Protocols list box.
4. Select the Properties button. The Microsoft TCP/IP Properties dialog box appears.

5. Select the second tab, DNS. The Domain Name System tab moves to the front of the Microsoft TCP/IP Properties dialog box as shown in Figure 5-5.
6. Enter the host name. The host name is typically the same as your server's name.
7. Enter the domain name. Your Internet network administrator assigns your network domain name.

The host name is then combined with the domain name to form the fully qualified name for the computer on the TCP/IP network. For example, my host name is "darkstar," and the domain name is "mv.com." These two names form the correct Internet address for my computer: "darkstar.mv.com."

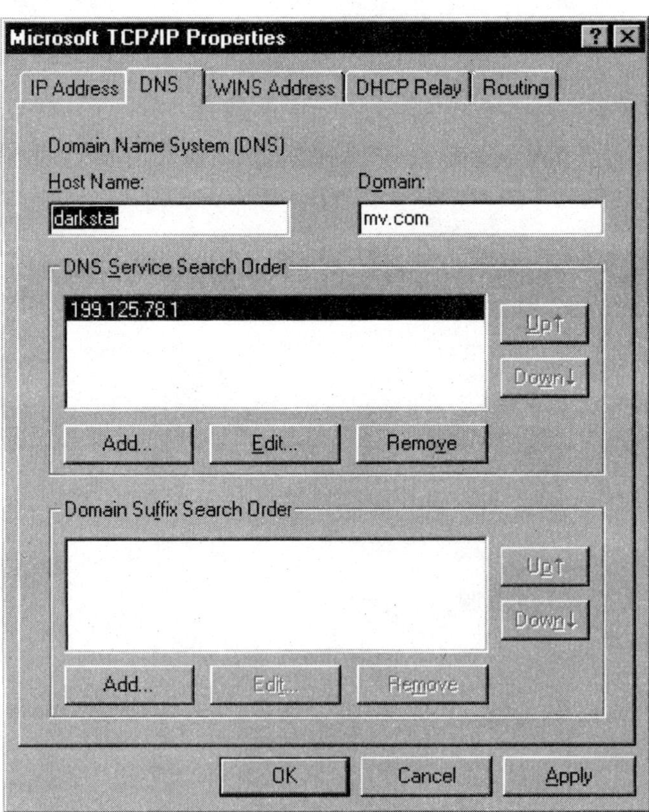

Figure 5-5: The Microsoft TCP/IP Properties DNS tab.

Also found on the DNS tab is the DNS Service Search Order, which is a list of the network DNS servers.

8. Add each DNS's IP address to the DNS Service Search Order list (you cannot enter a name here as there isn't a DNS server to resolve the name to an IP address). You can enter one or more DNS servers here. If the first DNS server isn't reachable to resolve a name, then the second DNS server (if specified) resolves the name.
9. Add (as needed) zero to six domain suffixes to the Domain Suffix Search Order list. DNS appends these suffixes to the DNS host name entries when resolving a name.

For both DNS servers and DNS Suffix Search Order, you can add, edit, and remove entries. You can also choose to reorder entries by moving entries either up or down in the list. This allows you to set a preferred DNS server, or a commonly used suffix for example.

Setting Up WINS

To set up the WINS servers, follow the steps below:

1. Start the Control Panel's Network applet.
2. Select the Protocols tab.
3. Highlight the TCP/IP protocol in the Protocols list box.
4. Select the Properties button. The Microsoft TCP/IP Properties dialog box appears.
5. Select the third tab, WINS Address. The WINS Address tab moves to the front of the Microsoft TCP/IP Properties dialog box as shown in Figure 5-6.
6. Enter the primary and secondary WINS servers. A WINS server (Windows Internet Name Service) resolves Internet names to the IP address, in the same manner that a DNS resolves Internet names.

The primary WINS server is the first WINS server to check when resolving names, while the secondary WINS server checks whenever the primary WINS server is unavailable.

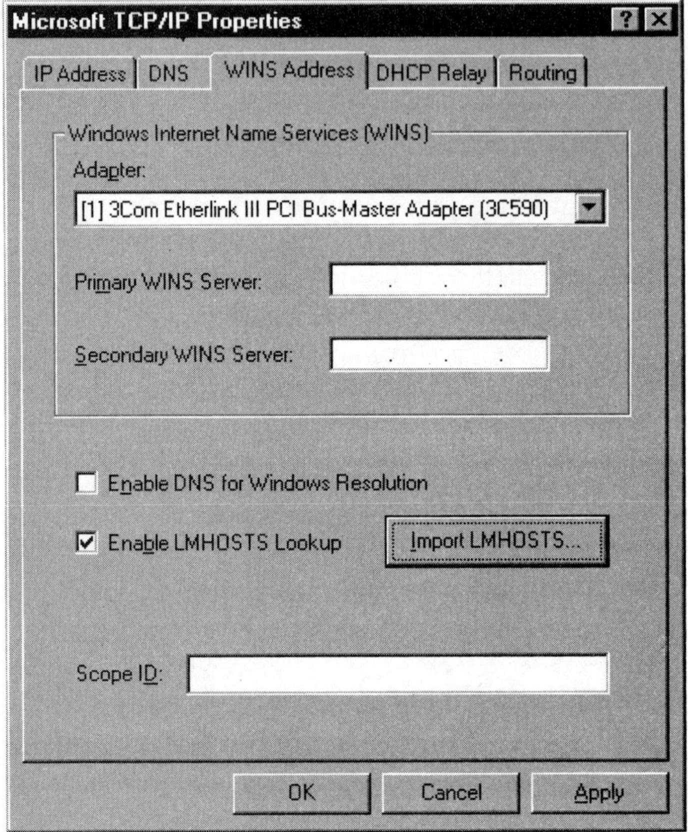

Figure 5-6: The Microsoft TCP/IP Properties WINS Address tab.

7. Click the Enable DNS for Windows Resolution check box if you want to enable this option. When DNS for Windows Resolution is selected, then DNS is used to resolve names on Windows networks.
8. Click the Enable LMHOSTS Lookup check box if you want to enable this option. LMHOSTS is a file that contains a table of names and TCP/IP addresses.
9. Click the Import LMHOSTS button (see the file LMHOSTS.SAM in the C:\winnt\system32\drivers\etc folder), if you want to use the LMHOSTS feature.

10. Enter a scope ID in the edit box provided, if your network uses scope IDs. All computers on a network must use the same scope ID when using scope IDs; however, most networks don't use the scope ID feature.

Setting Up DHCP Relay

To set up the DHCP Relay service, follow the steps below:

1. Start the Control Panel's Network applet.
2. Select the Protocols tab.
3. Highlight the TCP/IP protocol in the Protocols list box.
4. Select the Properties button. The Microsoft TCP/IP Properties dialog box appears.
5. Select the fourth tab, DHCP Relay. The DHCP Relay tab moves to the front of the Microsoft TCP/IP Properties dialog box as shown in Figure 5-7.
6. Enter the Seconds threshold using the spin control provided. The Seconds threshold limits Discover broadcast messages. The default value is 4.
7. Enter the Maximum hops using the spin control provided. Maximum hops limits the scope of Discover broadcast messages. The default value is 4.

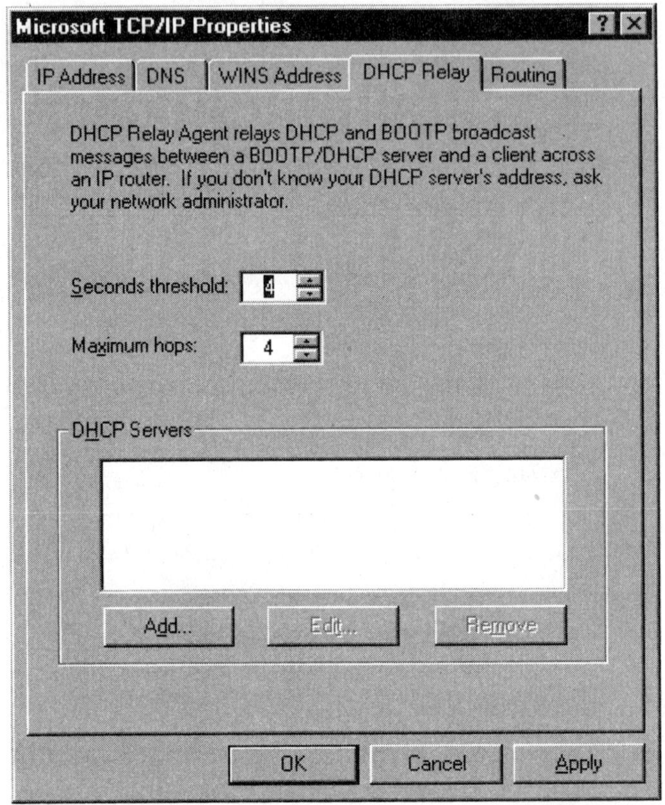

Figure 5-7: The Microsoft TCP/IP Properties DHCP Relay tab.

8. Click the Add button to add one or more DHCP (Dynamic Host Configuration Protocol) servers that issue IP addresses dynamically. You specify the DHCP server using an IP address. DHCP servers are not required. You can choose to statically assign IP addresses or decide to use a WINS server to allocate IP addresses.

Setting Up Routing

To set up the routing for TCP/IP, follow the steps below:

1. Start the Control Panel's Network applet.
2. Select the Protocols tab.

3. Highlight the TCP/IP protocol in the Protocols list box.
4. Select the Properties button. The Microsoft TCP/IP Properties dialog box appears.
5. Select the fifth tab, Routing. The Routing tab moves to the front of the Microsoft TCP/IP Properties dialog box as shown in Figure 5-8.
6. Click the Enable IP Forwarding check box if you want to enable this option. IP Forwarding enables IP packet forwarding on a multi-homed system. RIP for Internet Protocol is discussed in the next section, "Configuring RIP for Internet Protocol."

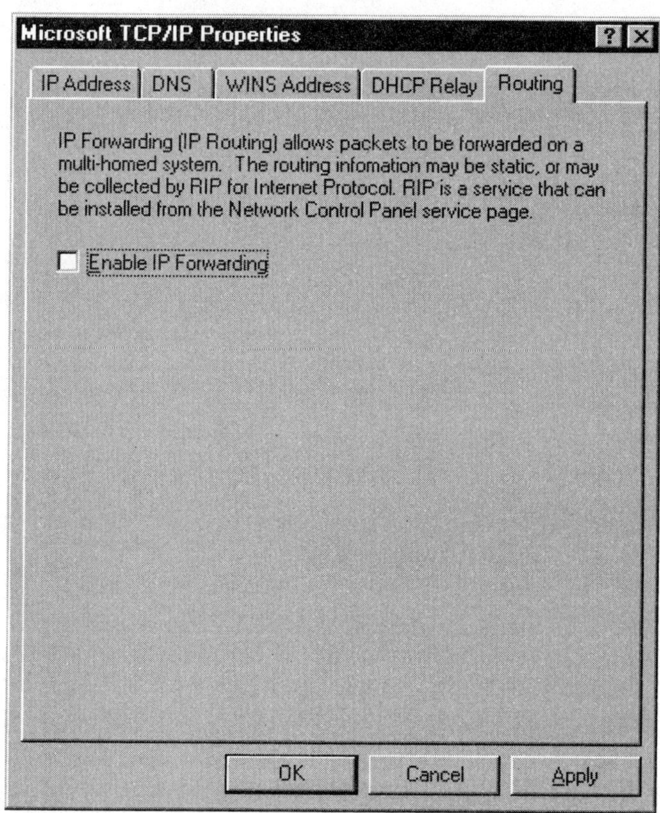

Figure 5-8: The Microsoft TCP/IP Properties Routing tab.

Use the ROUTE command, from a command prompt, to manage routing. For example, you can display a list of the current routing table's entries using the route command with the print option. Figure 5-9 below is an example of the output from the ROUTE command:

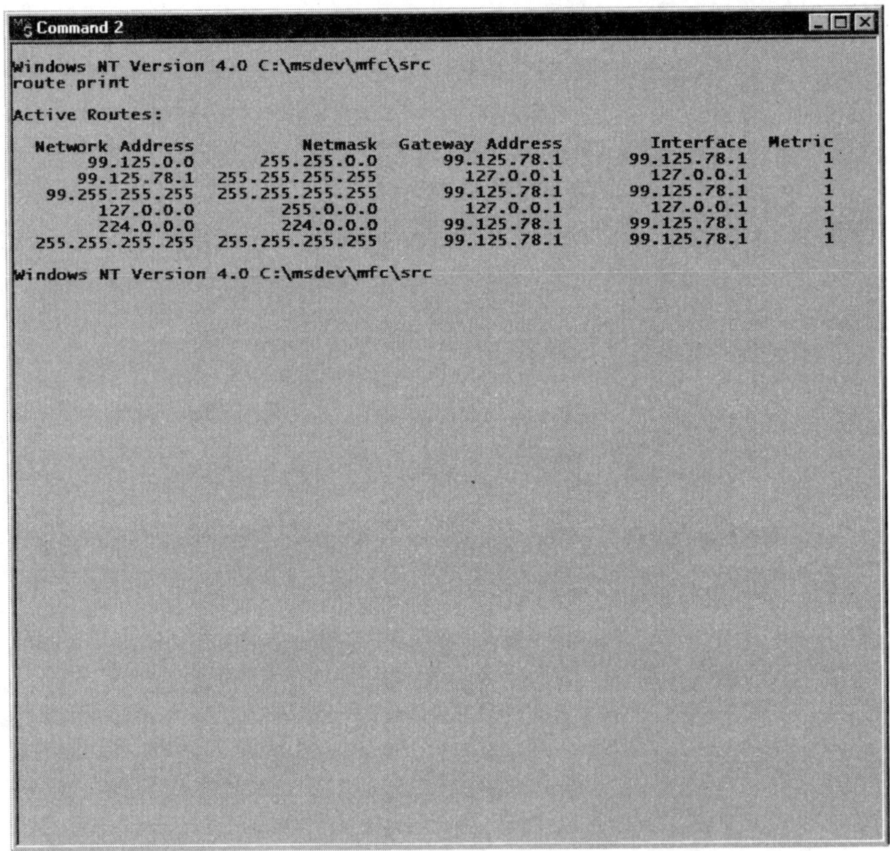

Figure 5-9: Sample output received having issued the route print command.

Routing is basically automatic—the RIP service listens for routing information and saves this information. You can also add a route manually if desired. RIP and the ROUTE command are discussed below, in "Configuring RIP for Internet Protocol."

Configuring RIP for Internet Protocol

The RIP (Routing Information Protocol) for Internet really has no user configurations. RIP for Internet is configured automatically; however, you can, if you desire, inspect the configuration of RIP for Internet using the Registration database editor, RegEdt32.

To install RIP for Internet protocol, follow the steps below:

1. Start the Control Panel's Network applet.
2. Select the Services tab.
3. Click the Add button. The Select Network Service dialog box appears.
4. Select the RIP for Internet Protocol from the Network Service list.
5. Start REGEDT32.
6. Go to the key HKEY_LOCAL_MACHINE\System\CurrentControlSet\Services\IpRip for the RIP for Internet configuration. One specific registry key is worthy of mention.

   The key HKEY_LOCAL_MACHINE\System\CurrentControlSet\Services\IpRip\Parameters\SilentRip controls how RIP for Internet works. SilentRip is either 0 (RIP for Internet listens for RIP packets and sends RIP packets), or 1 (RIP for Internet only listens for RIP packets). Chapter 19, "The Registry," goes into detail about the registry. Check there for more information.

When you install RIP for Internet, the Windows NT 4 Server exchanges routing information with other Internet servers. If you make an error in the specification of any IP addresses, network performance can be seriously impacted. Microsoft recommends not installing RIP for Internet unless you understand TCP/IP, routing, and the configuration of your network.

After you install RIP for Internet, the Enable IP Forwarding check box is checked (automatically), in the Microsoft TCP/IP Properties Routing tab as shown in Figure 5-10.

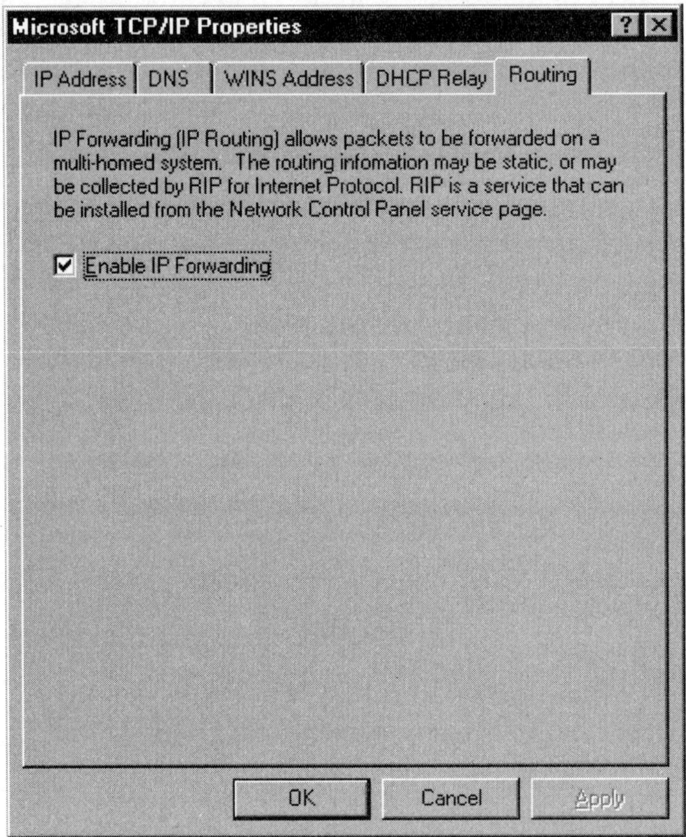

Figure 5-10: The Microsoft TCP/IP Properties Routing tab with Enable IP Forwarding activated.

To start and stop RIP for Internet, follow the steps below:

1. Start the Control Panel's Services applet. The Services dialog box appears.
2. Select RIP for Internet Protocol from the Service list.
3. Start, stop, or modify the startup options for RIP for Internet, as shown in Figure 5-11.

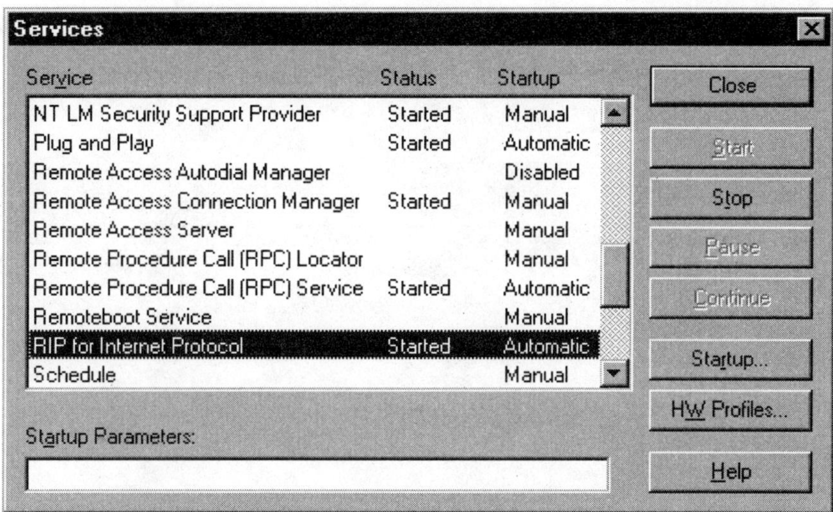

Figure 5-11: The Control Panel's Services applet dialog box.

4. Close the Control Panel's Network dialog box after installing RIP for Internet Protocol.
5. Reboot, if Windows NT 4 Server prompts you to do so.
6. Determine your Internet routing, using the command ROUTE PRINT once RIP for Internet Protocol is running. The ROUTE PRINT command displays a list of all active routes, as shown in Figure 5-12. As this figure shows, there is a column marked "Metric." This column contains a numeric value, either a one, or a value greater than one. The Metric being greater than one signifies routes learned using RIP.

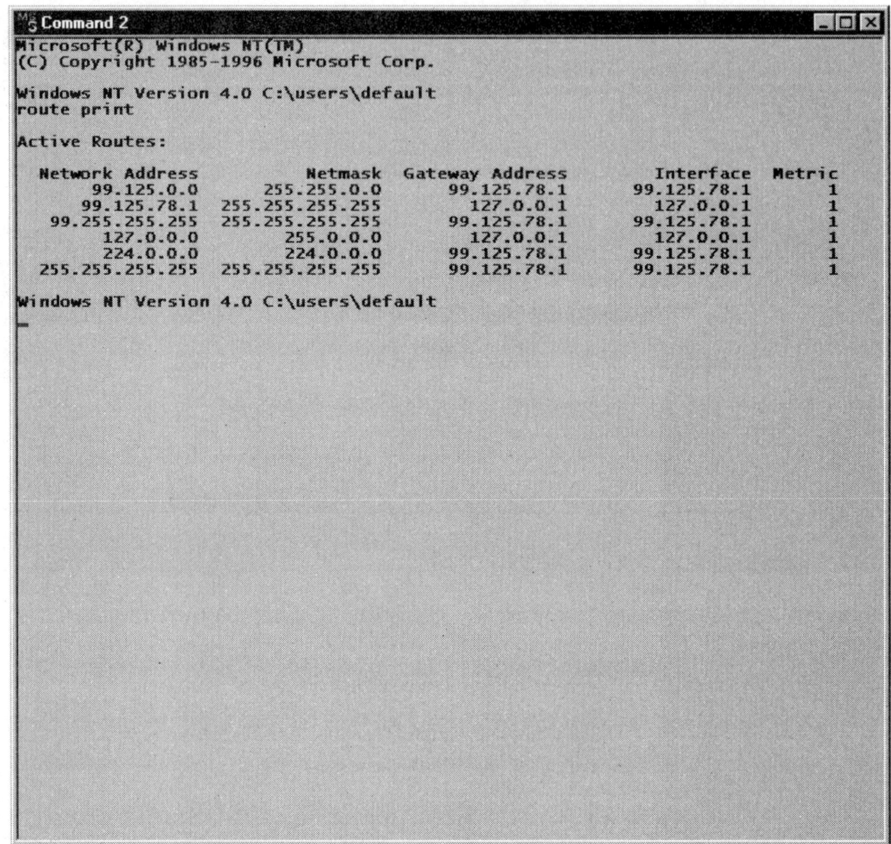

Figure 5-12: The ROUTE PRINT command.

Configuring Simple TCP/IP Services

Windows NT 4 Server configures Simple TCP/IP Services during installation. There are a number of services under Simple TCP/IP Services, and while most (except for Quotes) of the Simple TCP/IP Services cannot be configured, there is a quick description of each service below. The Simple TCP/IP Services provides the following TCP/IP services: CHARGEN, DAYTIME, DISCARD, ECHO, and QUOTE.

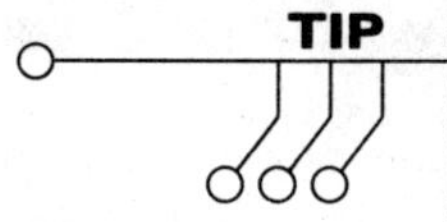

Don't confuse Simple TCP/IP Services with the TCP/IP protocol, earlier in this chapter. Simple TCP/IP Services are a group of specialized services that the server offers to TCP/IP clients, such as ECHO, DAYTIME, and QUOTE. You don't need to install Simple TCP/IP Services to use TCP/IP.

Simple TCP/IP Services is server-based. You will notice no changes in how your Windows NT 4 Server functions. Simple TCP/IP Services supports client users, who have support for CHARGEN, DAYTIME, DISCARD, ECHO, or QUOTE.

- CHARGEN—The CHARGEN service sends predetermined data to the client regardless of the client's input. The client can send any data to the CHARGEN service; however, Microsoft recommends that you use a recognizable pattern. The CHARGEN service is defined in RFC 864.
- DAYTIME—The DAYTIME service sends the current date and time to the client upon request. The text in the client's request is ignored. The DAYTIME service is defined in RFC 867.
- DISCARD—The DISCARD service discards or throws away any data received. The DISCARD service is defined in RFC 863.
- ECHO—The ECHO service returns received data, verbatim. The ECHO service is defined in RFC 862.
- QUOTE—The QUOTE service sends a "quote of the day" to the client upon request. QUOTE ignores all text in the client's request. Quotes are defined in the file C:\winnt\system32\drivers\etc\quotes, where C:winnt is the folder in which Windows NT 4 Server is installed. Figure 5-13 shows a text file that you can customize as desired. You can add a quote having one or more lines with a maximum length of 512 characters (about six 80-character lines). The QUOTE service is defined in RFC 865.

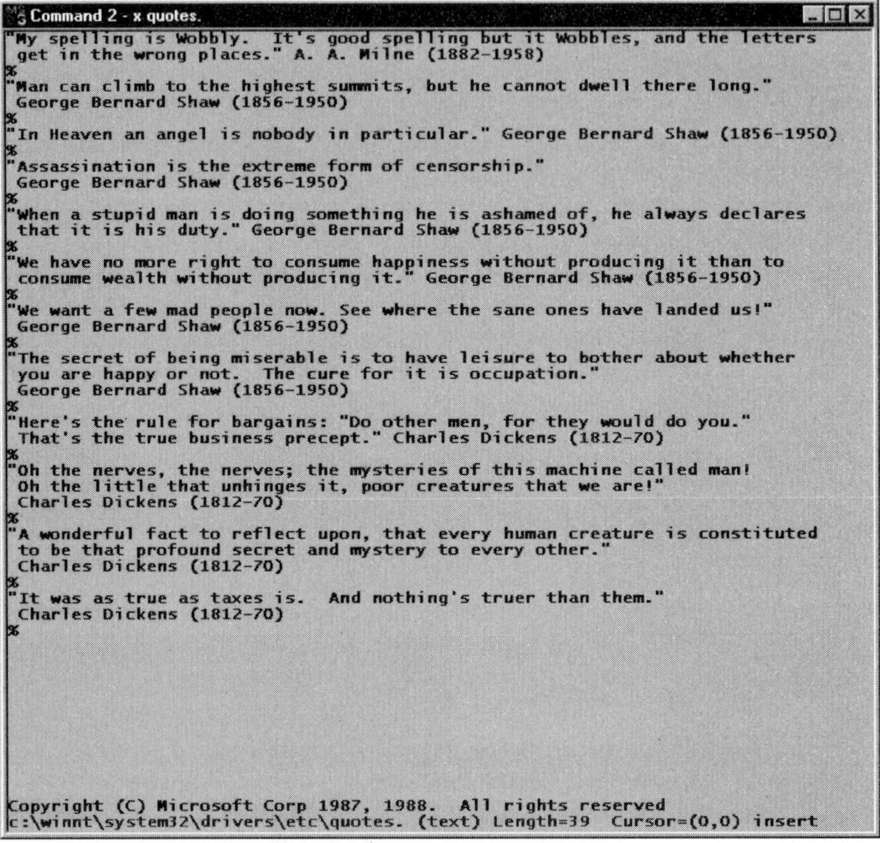

Figure 5-13: The default QUOTE file.

Configuring Microsoft DHCP Server

The Microsoft DHCP (Dynamic Host Configuration Protocol) Server issues IP addresses dynamically and is managed using the DHCP Manager. To start the DHCP Manager, click Start Menu | Programs | Administrative Tools (Common) | DHCP Manager.

In addition to the DHCP Server, there is the DHCP Relay Agent. You can find more information about the latter in the section "Configuring DHCP Relay Agent."

The DHCP Manager, shown in Figure 5-14, allows you to manage both local and remote DHCP Servers. The main window shows the current DHCP servers and the address blocks that each server manages.

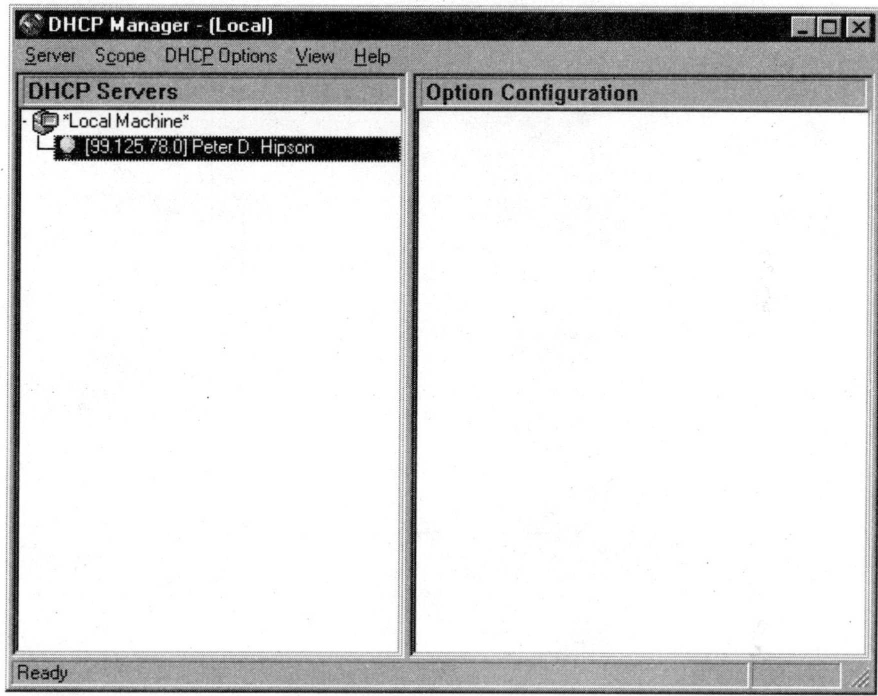

Figure 5-14: The DHCP Manager's main window.

Because you do not manipulate and save data with the DHCP Manager, there is no File menu. Using the Server menu, you can add and remove DHCP servers, which are running on servers other than the user's local machine.

Working With IP Addresses

Using the Scope menu, you can create, modify, activate, delete, and reserve IP addresses for a specific DHCP server. To specify IP address ranges, follow the steps below:

1. Select the Scope | Create menu. The Create Scope dialog box appears as shown in Figure 5-15.

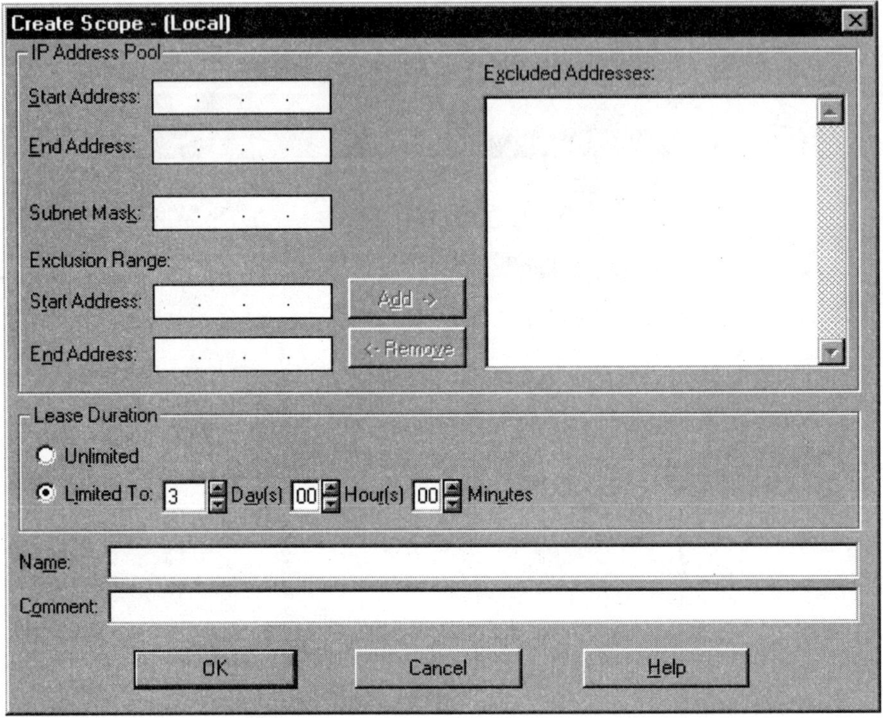

Figure 5-15: The DHCP Manager's Create Scope dialog box.

2. Enter a starting IP address (in the Start Address field).
3. Enter an ending IP address (in the End Address field).
4. Enter a Subnet Mask (subnet masks vary depending on the range of the IP addresses being assigned, but are typically either 255.255.255.0, 255.255.0.0, or 255.0.0.0).
5. Use the Exclusion Range edit control boxes to exclude one or more ranges of addresses (the excluded addresses may be dedicated to other nodes in the network, or may be unavailable for other reasons).
6. Use the Lease Duration radio buttons to indicate if you want to limit the lifetime of an assigned IP address to a specific interval (the default is three days), or make the lifetime unlimited. When the DHCP server assigns an IP address to a client, the client has a lease on that IP address. This configuration option gives you control over the duration of the lease.

To modify an existing scope, follow the steps below:

1. Select the Scope | Properties menu. The Scope Properties dialog box appears (identical to the Create Scope dialog box shown in Figure 5-15).
2. Modify the IP Address Pool and/or Lease Duration edit controls for the scope.
3. Click OK (or Cancel to discard your changes) to accept the changes you made on the Scope Properties dialog box.

Once you create a scope, you must activate it. When a scope is created, DHCP Manager will prompt to determine if the scope is to be made active. To activate a scope, select the Scope | Activate menu.

To delete a scope, select the Scope | Delete menu.

Sometimes you must reserve an IP address for a certain client machine, or other purpose (such as a networked printer). To reserve a scope for a client machine, follow the steps below:

1. Select the Scope | Add Reservations menu. The Add Reserved Clients dialog appears as shown in Figure 5-16.

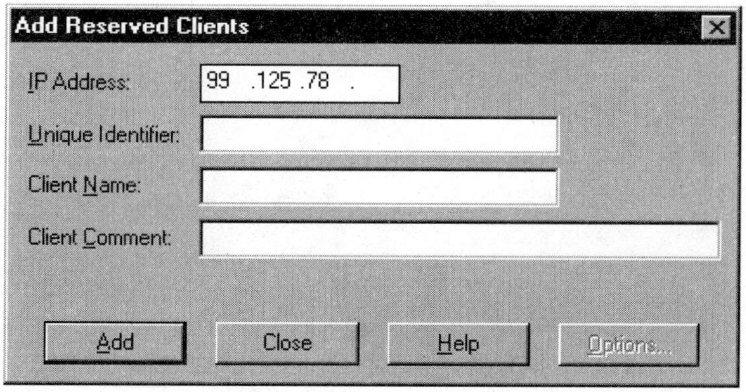

Figure 5-16: The DHCP Manager's Add Reserved Clients dialog box.

2. Enter the IP Address (required). The initial part of the IP address will be supplied.
3. Enter a Unique Identifier (required). The MAC (Media Access Control) identifier: use the Net Config Wksta command to determine this value.

4. Enter a Client Name (required). Used only to describe this entry, and does not affect the client user.
5. Enter a Client Comment (optional, though it is recommended that you fill in the Client Comment also).
6. The Options button (active only when viewing Client Properties, and not when adding reservations) allows setting of various DHCP options.

When the DHCP Server is running, it assigns IP addresses to clients who request IP addresses. To display addresses assigned to active clients, follow the steps below:

1. Select the Scope | Active Leases menu. The Active Leases dialog box appears as shown in Figure 5-17.

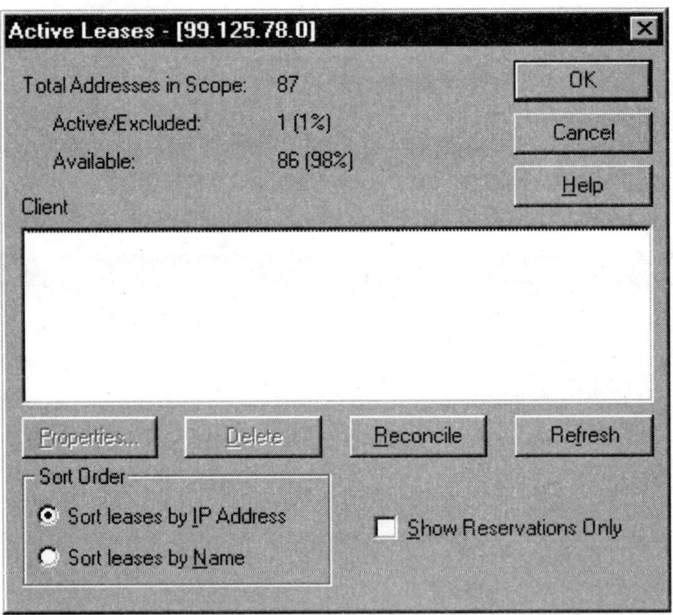

Figure 5-17: The DHCP Manager's Active Leases dialog box.

2. In the Active Leases dialog box, you can click the Properties button to display the properties of any active clients.
3. You can sort the leases by IP Address or Name, using the Sort Order radio buttons on the Active Leases dialog box.

4. You can choose to show only those IP addresses that have reservations, using the check box on the Active Leases dialog box.

Setting Options

To specify various DHCP options, follow the steps below:

1. Select the Options | Scope menu. The DHCP Options: Scope dialog box appears as shown in Figure 5-18.

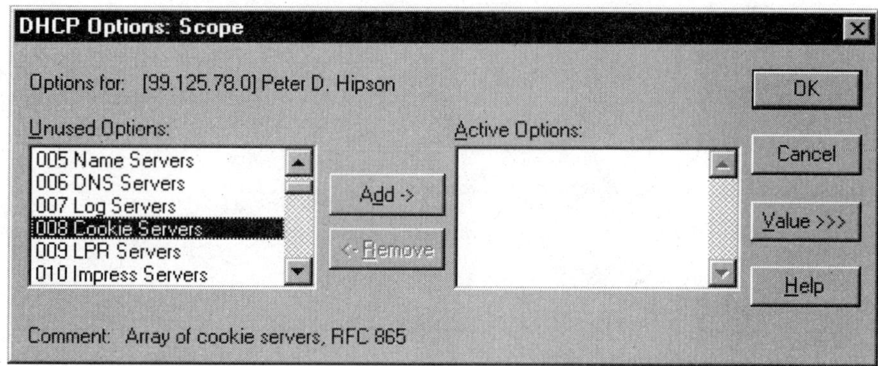

Figure 5-18: The DHCP Manager's DHCP Options: Scope dialog box.

2. To select an option from the Unused Options list box, click the Add button. The options you choose show up in the Active Options list box.
3. Click OK (or Cancel to discard your changes) to accept the changes you made on the DHCP Options: Scope dialog box.

To access *all* of the DHCP options, follow the steps below:

1. Select the Options | Global menu, which displays a dialog box like the one shown in Figure 5-19. Global options affect all IP addresses assigned by DHCP, while Scope options affect only the IP address specified.

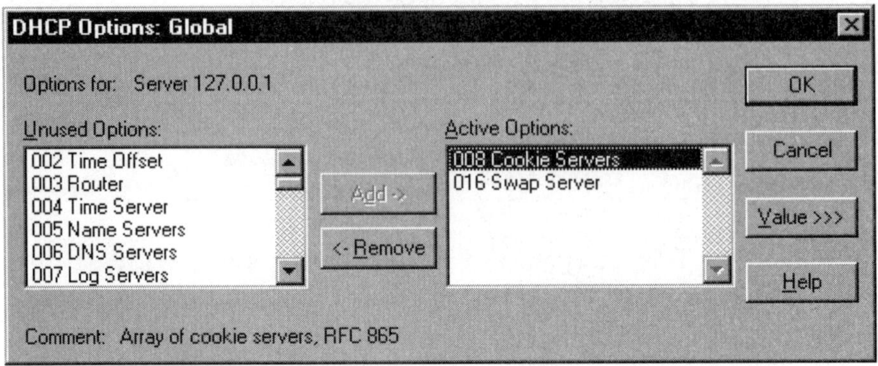

Figure 5-19: The DHCP Manager's DHCP Options: Global dialog box.

2. To select an option from the Unused Options list box, click the Add button. The options you choose show up in the Active Options list box.
3. Click OK (or Cancel to discard your changes) to accept the changes you made on the DHCP Options: Global dialog box.

To specify default values for DHCP server options, follow the steps below:

1. Select the Option | Default menu. The Options: Default Values dialog box appears as shown in Figure 5-20. You are prompted for the correct type of values.

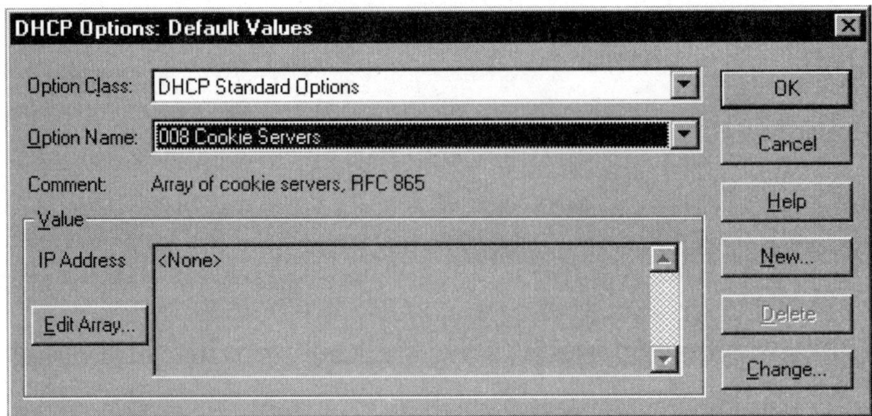

Figure 5-20: The DHCP Manager's DHCP Options: Default Values dialog box.

2. When specifying options for DHCP servers, you need to know the IP address(es) that the DHCP server is allocating, any reserved client addresses, reserved IP address ranges, and any options that your installation requires.

Configuring DHCP Relay Agent

Use the DHCP (Dynamic Host Configuration Protocol) Relay Agent to permit the server to relay DHCP messages across a TCP/IP LAN. As an example, DHCP Relay Agent is useful when there is more than one LAN in the network, there is a router between the two LANs, and there is only a single DHCP Server on one of the LANs. The DHCP Relay Agent works to provide configuration information for the clients who are on the LAN that do not have the DHCP server. Creating two DHCP servers can be costly and requires additional maintenance. We discussed configuring DHCP servers in the previous section.

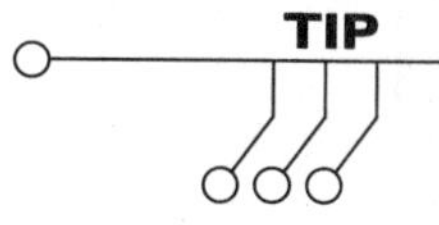

To obtain additional information about DHCP Relay Agents, see the public specification RFC1542. Retrieve the specification through anonymous FTP to ds.internic.net in the rfc subdirectory.

To configure the DHCP agent, follow the steps below:

1. Start the Control Panel's Network applet.
2. Select the Protocols tab.
3. Select the TCP/IP Protocol from the Network Protocols list box.
4. Click the Properties button to display the TCP/IP Properties dialog box.
5. Select the DHCP Relay tab as shown in Figure 5-21.
6. Set the Seconds threshold (threshold prevents relay agent from forwarding DHCP packets where the seconds field is less than the threshold value).

7. Set the Maximum hops (specifies the maximum number of routers that can be traversed).
8. Enter the IP Address for each DHCP Server. DHCP Relay Agent can manage more than one DHCP Server. Both Seconds threshold and Maximum hops are optional—you can use the default values as a starting point.

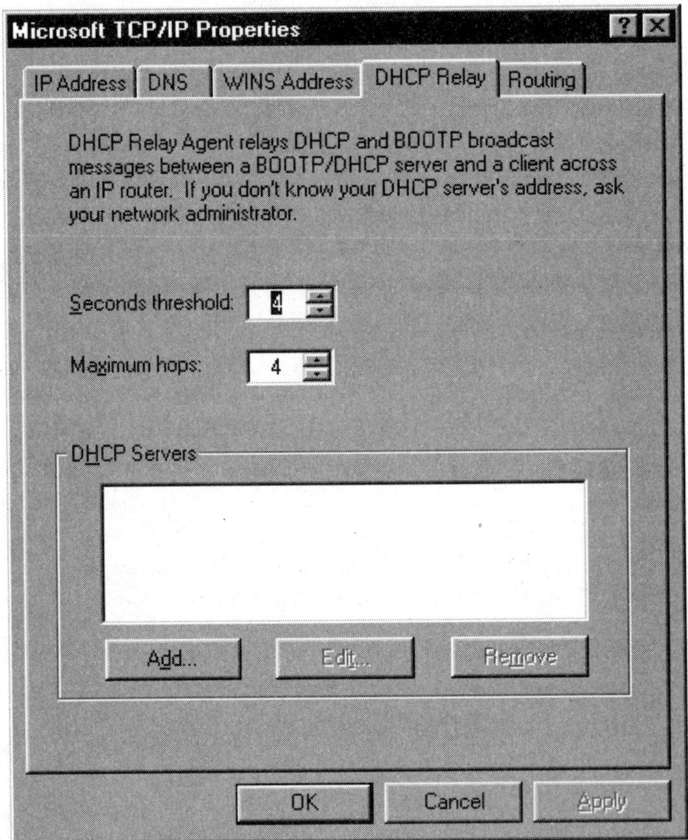

Figure 5-21: Microsoft TCP/IP Properties dialog box.

Configuring Microsoft DNS Server

The Microsoft Domain Name Server (DNS) resolves names to IP addresses, and typically you use DNS with intranets and other internal TCP/IP-based networks. You can configure the Microsoft DNS server with a set of files provided for this purpose.

Microsoft provides default files for DNS in the \winnt\system32\dns folder. Modify these default files to customize your DNS server.

By modifying the DNS configuration files, you create a working DNS server. The file names in Table 5-1, given in the text, assume that you have installed Windows NT 4 Server in the C directory winnt.

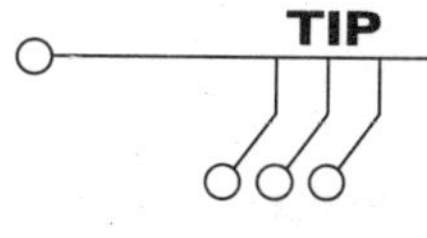

In the DNS server control files, anything on a line following a semicolon (;) is a comment and is ignored by the system. Use comments to document your changes whenever you modify the DNS server control files.

C:\winnt\system32\dns\BOOT	The BOOT file is the master configuration file for the DNS server. The instructions in the BOOT file tell the DNS server what is done when DNS is first started. Anything on a line following a semicolon ';' is a comment, and is ignored.
C:\winnt\system32\dns\CACHE	The CACHE file is an initial cache for a root domain server. An external CACHE file is not required when your DNS is a root domain server, and your network is a private intranet. If that is the case, you can remove references to the CACHE file from the BOOT file.

C:\winnt\system32\dns\SAMPLES\ARPA-192.REV	The .REV file(s) provide reverse name lookups. Given an IP address, the DNS can look up the actual name for the given IP address. The example given is for the 192.5.29 class C IP address.
C:\winnt\system32\dns\SAMPLES\BOOT	A second copy of the BOOT file.
C:\winnt\system32\dns\SAMPLES\CACHE	A second copy of the CACHE file.
C:\winnt\system32\dns\SAMPLES\PLACE.DOM	Lookup file for place.dom domain, this file is (basically) the opposite of the ARPA-192.REV file mentioned above. Names in the 192.5.29 domain are placed in this file.

Table 5-1: DNS Server files.

The files found in the system32\dns\SAMPLES folder are examples and are useful when problems develop.

In all the example files provided by Microsoft, the domain, place.dom, and the IP address, 192.5.29.xxx, are fictitious.

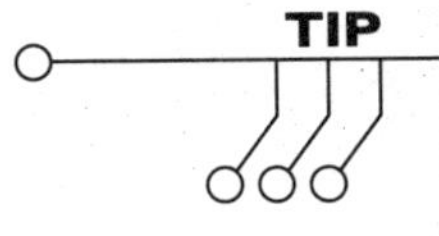

The IP address 192.5.29.xxx is a fictional address *that Microsoft uses to show you where to place your IP addresses. In your installation, make sure to use your real names and IP addresses, not the examples provided by Microsoft.*

You use the Domain Name Service Manager (DNS Manager) to modify the DNS configuration files. These configuration files include BOOT, CACHE, PLACE.DOM, and ARPA-192.REV.

The BOOT File

The BOOT file is the master configuration file for the DNS server. The BOOT file refers to all the other files that DNS uses (PLACE.DOM, ARPA-192.REV, and CACHE). If you decide to rename any of those BOOT files, you must make sure that the BOOT file's reference to the file is also changed to the new name.

The BOOT file tells the DNS server what is done when DNS is first started. There are liberal comments in each of the DNS configuration files to allow you to edit these files manually if desired.

The BOOT file (which has no extension) initializes the DNS server. You modify the BOOT file to include information relevant to your system. For example, your network's address ranges would be specified in the BOOT file. (For a Class C address, this address takes the form of 192.5.29.xxx, where xxx is a hexadecimal number expressed in decimal. However, the IP address in this example, 192.5.29.xxx, is fictitious.)

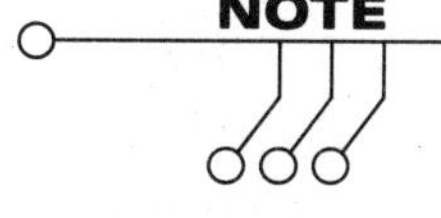

The BOOT file contains a minor typographical error in one of the comments. This may lead to confusion:

```
;
;PRIMARY DOMAINS
;
;"Primary" domains are listed below.  The second column
;is the name of the domain for which this name server
;is authoritative.  The third column is the name if the
;database file which contains the authoritative data.
;
```

This comment should read as follows (note the bold "of"):

```
;
;PRIMARY DOMAINS
;
;"Primary" domains are listed below.  The second column
;is the name of the domain for which this name server
;is authoritative.  The third column is the name of the
;database file which contains the authoritative data.
;
```

The CACHE File

The CACHE file (there is no extension) is an initial cache for a root domain server. When your DNS is a root domain server, and your network is a private intranet, then it is not necessary to use an external CACHE file. If that is the case, you can remove references to the CACHE file from the BOOT file.

Generally, you do not have to make changes to the CACHE file when using the DNS server on the Internet. When there is an updated root name list issued, you may have to make changes to the CACHE file.

When connected to an intranet, you replace the contents of the CACHE file and add NS (Name Server) and A (Address) records for the DNS server authoritative for the root domain at your site, to allow DNS to function correctly.

The PLACE.DOM File

The file PLACE.DOM is the domain management file that looks up names in the place.dom domain. As with all the DNS files, liberal comments in the PLACE.DOM file guide you in creating your own domain management file. In this file are names in Microsoft's example 192.5.29 domain.

There is nothing to prevent you from renaming the PLACE.DOM file to a new name. However, if you rename PLACE.DOM, then you must update the BOOT file to refer to the new name.

When you install your DNS, a new file called your_domain.DOM (where your_domain is the name for your domain) is created. In the BOOT file, create an entry pointing to the new .DOM file.

All domain names that are specified in the .DOM file and not terminated using a single period (".") are automatically appended with the domain name you created. In the example files, the example default domain name is "place.dom." To illustrate, if your default domain name is *place.dom*, the name "darkstar" becomes "darkstar.place.dom." The name "darkstar.mv.com." would remain unchanged and would not have place.dom appended, as it ends in a period.

The ARPA-192.REV File

The .REV file(s) provide reverse name lookups. Given an IP address, the DNS can look up the actual name for the given IP address. The example given is for the fictitious 192.5.29 Class C IP address.

Create a .REV file to match your site. The comments contained in the ARPA-192.REV file guide you in creating your own .REV file to match your site.

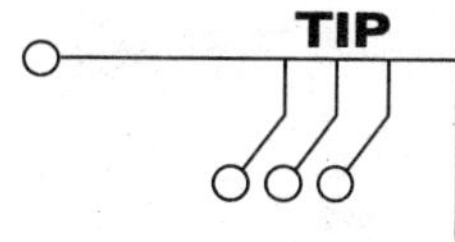

The number in the filename for the .REV file matches the first digits of the site's IP address (192.5.29). You can use a different name for the .REV file; however, I recommend that you name your .REV file ARPA-nnn.REV, where nnn is the first octet of your site's IP address.

The file, ARPA-192.REV, is the reverse domain lookup file. This file matches an IP address to a domain name. The ARPA-192.REV file is logically the reverse of the place.dom file (described above) in that place.dom looks up an IP address for a known domain name, while ARPA-192.REV looks up a domain name for a known IP address.

As with the place.dom file, create your own .REV file. If you rename the .REV file or add additional .REV files, make sure the BOOT file refers to them appropriately.

The Domain Name Service Manager

The Domain Name Service Manager (DNS Manager) is a program that you use to manage your DNS server. The DNS Manager handles multiple DNS servers, making management of multiple DNS server sites simpler. This program is relatively easy to use, provided you know and understand what a DNS is, how a DNS works, and the specific information regarding your specific implementation (such as node names and addresses).

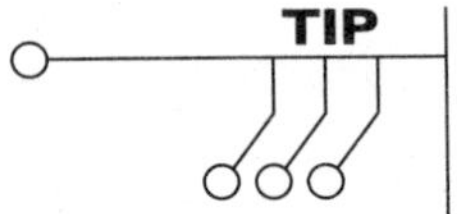

TIP

To use Domain Name Service Manager you must have already started the DNS server, either locally or on a remote DNS Server. If you have installed a DNS Server, and the DNS Server is not started, start DNS from the Control Panel's Services applet.

Shown in Figure 5-22 is the Domain Name Service Manager program's main window. This figure shows the DNS server as installed on DORA, our Windows NT 4 Server.

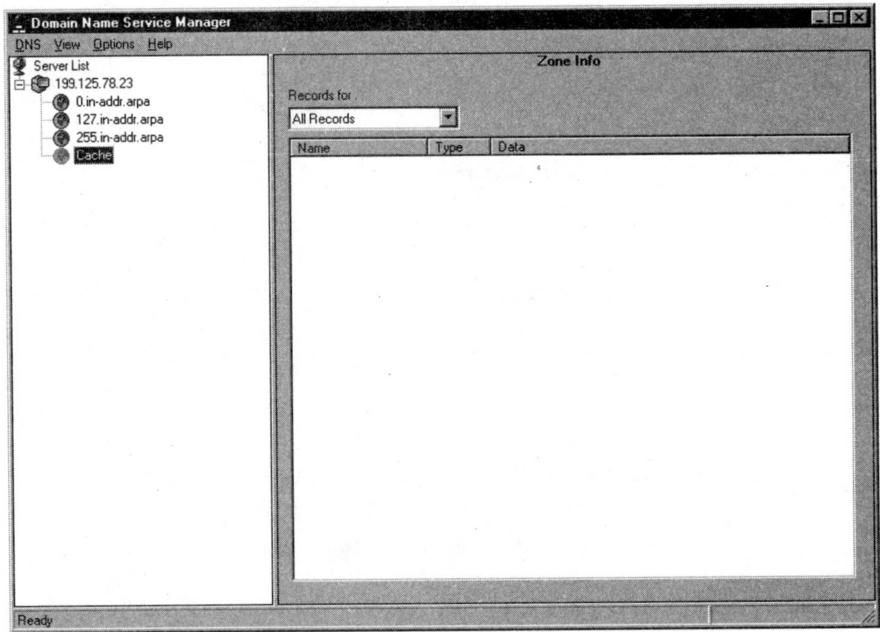

Figure 5-22: The Domain Name Service Manager on DORA.

Notice that in Figure 5-22, DORA's address is a numerical IP address rather than a domain name. This is normal.

Setting DNS Options

The Domain Name Service Manager is the best way to set various DNS options. The Domain Name Service Manager menu allows you to perform virtually all tasks and functions needed to manage your DNS.

The main menu for the DNS Manager allows you to make many of the routine changes to the configuration files described above. Prior to modifying a DNS configuration file manually with an editor, verify that you can't make the change using the DNS Manager.

To add an additional server to the group of DNS servers that the DNS Manager is currently managing, select DNS | New Server. The DNS Manager is able to manage multiple DNS Servers, making management of multiple DNS Server sites simpler.

DNS uses zones to manage computers on the network. A zone is a collection of computers (like a workgroup). When you create a zone, you can make the zone geographically based, functionally based, or a combination of the two. Windows NT 4 Server prefers compact, concise, hierarchically based zones. To create a new zone, use the DNS | New Zone menu selection. This menu selection modifies the configuration files to add the zone. Pausing a zone allows you to take a DNS zone offline, allowing the zone to be managed (the effect is immediate). Use the DNS | Pause Zone menu selection to take a zone offline.

As with creating a new zone, to create a new domain, use the DNS | New Domain menu selection. Use the DNS | New Host to create a new host DNS site.

To delete any selected item, use the DNS | Delete menu selection.

The Domain Name Service Manager updates the various DNS configuration files when it exits. The actual DNS configuration files (BOOT, CACHE, and so on) can be manually updated using DNS | Update Server Data Files. This command immediately updates the configuration files.

To display the properties of the current selection, use the DNS | Properties menu selection. To display the properties, you must have a current selection.

If it is necessary at any time to update the DNS Manager's main screen, use View | Refresh (the shortcut is F5). Otherwise, the information displayed on the screen is updated at regular intervals.

The View | Preferences menu selection allows you to set the DNS Manager's preferences. The Preferences dialog box is shown in Figure 5-23. You can set two items: "Auto Refresh," which allows you to specify the interval between refreshes (you can manually refresh at any time by pressing F5), and "Allow Duplicate Resource Records," which allows the DNS Manager to handle duplicate resource records.

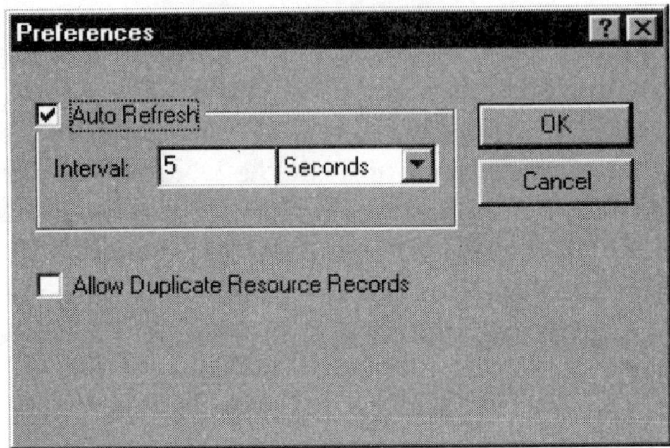

Figure 5-23: The DNS Manager's Preferences dialog box.

The Domain Name Service Manager program makes management of the various aspects of the DNS server more visual and easier to understand.

Domain Server Records

All Domain Name Servers use a standardized set of records to describe the names and IP addresses managed by the DNS. As new computers and IP addresses are added to the network, the DNS database must be updated to reflect these additions.

With the DNS | New Record menu selection, you are able to insert a new record into the DNS configuration. Typically, you add NS, A, PTR (In-addr.arpa domains only), CNAME, and MX records. The records you add using DNS | New Record include:

- CNAME—A CNAME record adds a canonical name. This record creates a synonymous name for the specified computer or device.
- MX—An MX record for an e-mail exchanger. This record specifies a mail exchange server for a DNS domain name.

- RT—An RT record specifies a routing record that defines hosts that route TCP/IP packets to the final destination.
- A—An A record specifies an IP address to a computer or other device (such as a router).
- PTR—A PTR record (which is the opposite of the A record) maps a computer or other device to an IP address.

Configuring Windows Internet Name Service (WINS)

A WINS server is a Windows NT 4 Server that uses the TCP/IP protocol and has WINS installed and running. The WINS server creates and populates a database that links computer names to specific TCP/IP addresses. By using WINS, you can connect more easily to specific computers using TCP/IP. WINS servers must have fixed IP addresses, and a WINS server should not be a DHCP client.

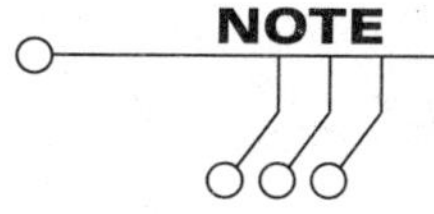

When your WINS server has more than one NIC, do not alter the binding order for TCP/IP. The WINS server is known to fail if this happens.

The WINS Manager configures and manages WINS. To access WINS Manager, click the Start Menu | Programs | Administrative Tools (Common) | WINS Manager.

Configure the WINS service prior to use. To configure it, you need to start the WINS Manager program, as shown in Figure 5-24.

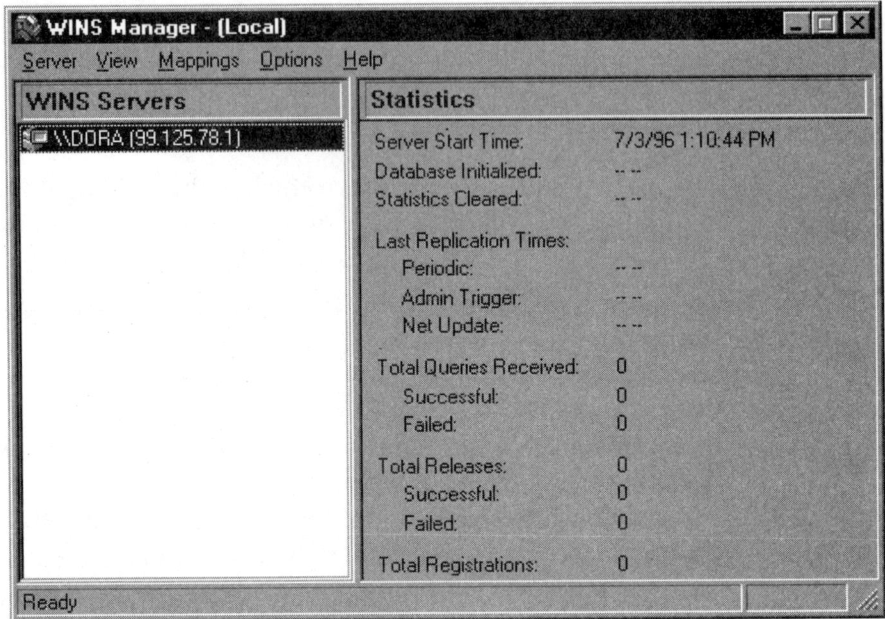

Figure 5-24: The WINS Manager program.

Setting WINS Options

A WINS server is a Windows NT Server computer running Microsoft TCP/IP and the Windows Internet Name Service (WINS) server software. WINS servers maintain a database that maps computer names to TCP/IP addresses, allowing users to easily communicate with other computers while gaining all the benefits of TCP/IP.

You can manage the WINS server with the WINS Manager. This program is easy to use, and displays information about each WINS server. The WINS Manager also lists WINS server statistics such as the Server Start Time, Last Replication Times, Total Queries Received, Total Releases, and Total Registrations.

When starting WINS Manager, select the menu item Server | Add WINS Server to add servers. The WINS Manager program allows you to remotely administer WINS servers. To remove a WINS Server from the WINS Manager program, select the Server | Delete WINS Server. This option deletes the selected WINS server.

WINS Manager can display the Detailed Information dialog box for each WINS Server. The Detailed Information dialog box, as shown in Figure 5-25, displays information about the currently selected WINS server.

Detailed Information

WINS Server Address
Computer Name: \\DORA
IP Address: 99.125.78.1
Connected Via: NetBIOS
Connected Since: 7/2/96 7:51:30 PM
Last Address Change: -- --

Last Scavenging Times:
Periodic: -- --
Admin Trigger: -- --
Extinction: -- --
Verification: -- --

Unique Registrations: 0
Conflicts: 0
Renewals: 288

Group Registrations: 0
Conflicts: 0
Renewals: 288

Close
Help

Figure 5-25: The WINS Manager Detailed Information dialog box.

The Detailed Information dialog box presents information about the WINS Server, including IP addressing information, and information about registrations.

To configure a specific WINS Server, follow the steps below:

1. Select the Server | Configuration menu selection. The WINS Manager Configuration dialog box appears.
2. Set parameters such as timeout values using the dialog box provided (see Figure 5-26).
3. Click the Advanced button to set additional, advanced items.

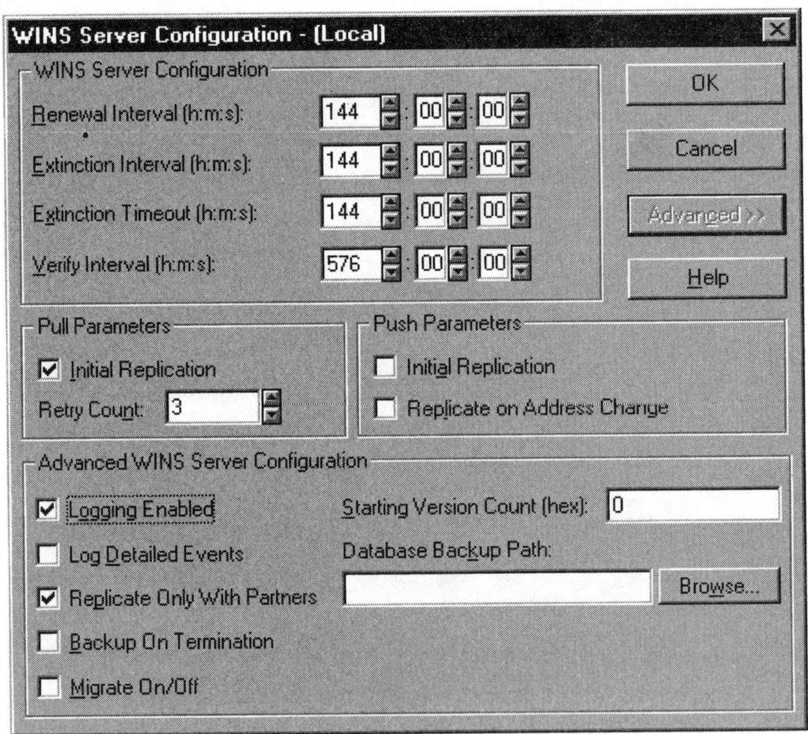

Figure 5-26: The WINS Manager Configuration dialog box.

Parameters in the WINS Server Configuration dialog box include:

- WINS Server Configuration—This option allows setting the time interval for Renewal, Extinction, Extinction Timeout, and Verify. Default values are six days for all values except for the Verify Interval, which defaults to 24 days.

- Pull Parameters—Both Initial Replication (a check box) and a Retry Count are set in this section.
- Push Parameters—Both Initial Replication and Replication on Address Change (both check boxes) can be set in this section.
- Advanced WINS Server Configuration—All the advanced items for the WINS Server are set in this section. Items such as logging (and the detail of events logged), replication restrictions (allow replication only with partners), backup, and migration are among the items that can be set.

The Server | Replication Partners menu selection displays the Replication Partners dialog box. A replication partner is another WINS server that replicates (copies) the WINS database. This process is similar to the way that the PDC (Primary Domain Controller) and BDC (Backup Domain Controllers) work. You can add and configure Replication Partners from this dialog box (see Figure 5-27).

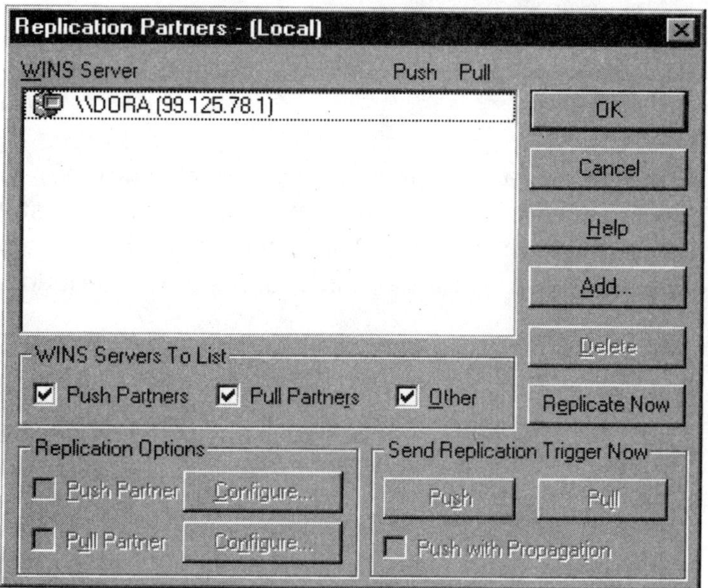

Figure 5-27: The WINS Manager Replication Partners dialog box.

In the WINS Manager Replication Partners dialog box, you can add and delete replication partners. After establishing a replication partner, configure the partner. Configure both push partners and pull partners (a partner can be both) separately.

A WINS server that is a pull partner pulls in database replicas from its push partner. It accomplishes this by requesting and then accepting replicas of any new database entries. This process synchronizes the pull partner's database with the push partner's database. The push partner sends notifications to the pull partner whenever there are changes to the WINS database.

Shown in Figure 5-28 is the configuration for a push partner. The only option you can set for a push partner is the update count.

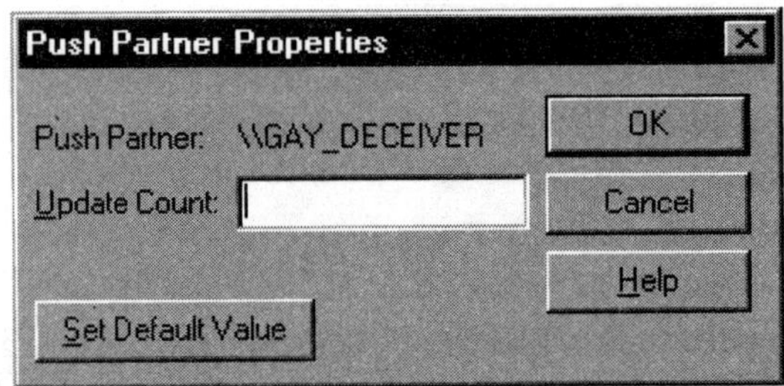

Figure 5-28: The WINS Manager Push Partner Properties dialog box.

The configuration for a pull partner is shown in Figure 5-29. The options you can set for a pull partner are the start time and the replication interval. Do not set the replication interval to an excessively short time period, as this may overload the system.

Figure 5-29: The WINS Manager Pull Partner Properties dialog box.

In the WINS Manager, you can clear the current statistics by selecting the View | Clear Statistics menu item. To refresh the display, select View | Refresh Statistics (the shortcut key is F5).

The Mappings | Show Database menu selection displays the WINS database, including mappings, as shown in Figure 5-30.

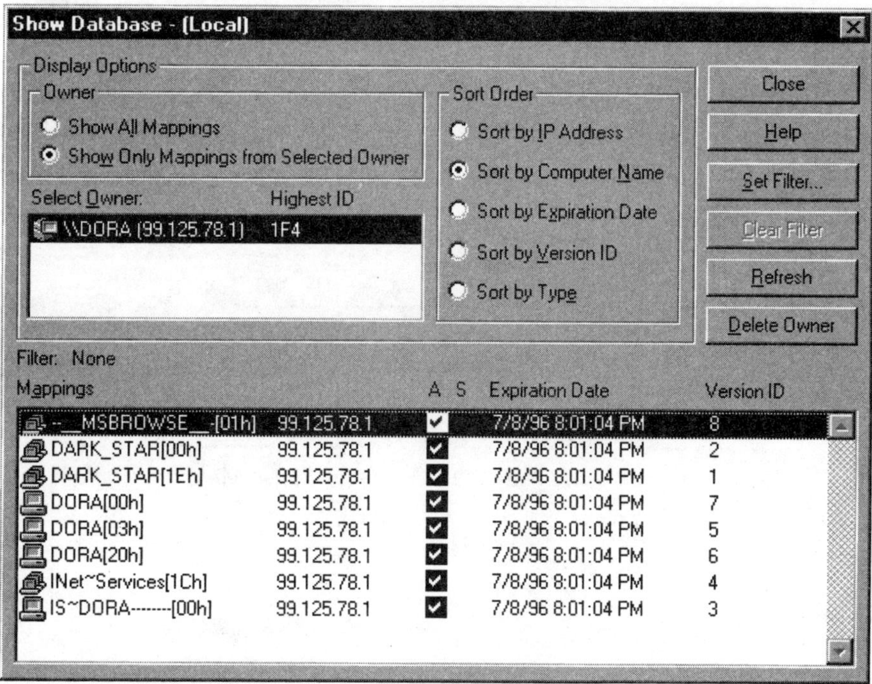

Figure 5-30: The WINS Manager database display dialog box.

The Show Database dialog box is primarily a data viewer. The only action possible from this dialog box is to delete the owner, using the Delete Owner button.

To queue a scavenging command, select the Mappings | Initiate Scavenging menu selection. The scavenging command is then placed in the queue.

Use the Mappings | Static Mappings menu selection to configure Static Mappings. The Static Mappings dialog box appears, as shown in Figure 5-31. You use the Static Mappings dialog box to add, import, delete, or edit static mappings. You can set a filter to limit the display of static mapping data using the Set Filter button.

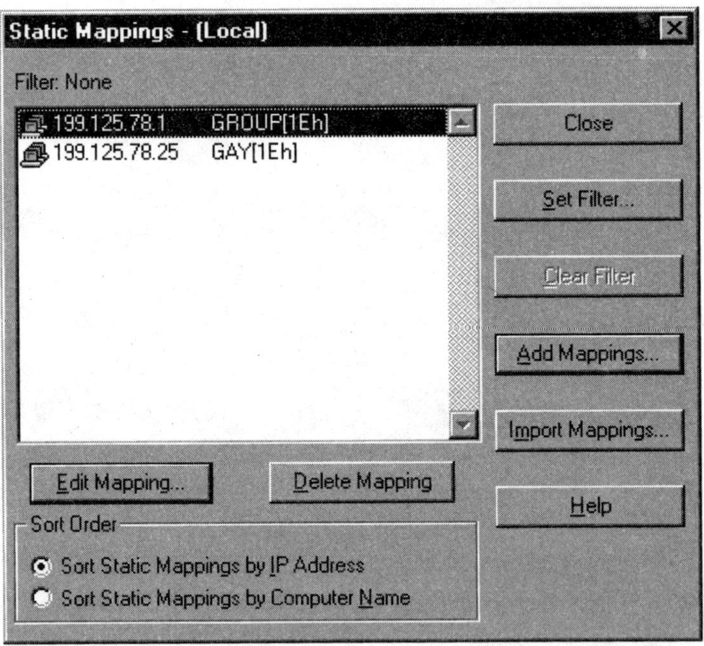

Figure 5-31: The WINS Manager Static Mappings dialog box.

To back up the mappings database, select the Mappings | Backup Database menu selection. The WINS Manager prompts you to select the folder in which you want to back up the database. After backing up the database, you can restore the database using the Mappings | Restore Local Database menu selection. As with backing up, the WINS Manager presents you with a folder selection dialog box.

To configure the WINS Manager's user interface, and how information is presented, select the Options | Preferences menu selection. The Preferences dialog box appears, as shown in Figure 5-32.

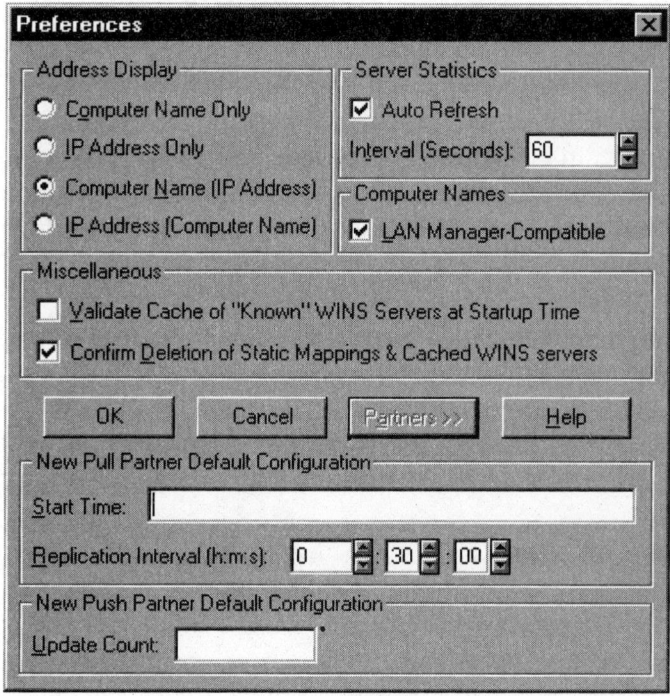

Figure 5-32: The WINS Manager Preferences dialog box.

Items that you may configure in the Preferences dialog box include the address display mode—I favor "Computer Name (IP Address)"—(though you may find the other display modes more readable) and statistics refresh interval (again, don't set this to an excessively low value). You can also set items such as cache validation, confirmations, and default values for the WINS Manager Pull Partner Properties dialog box, and the WINS Manager Push Partner Properties dialog box (see Figures 5-28 and 5-29).

Moving On

Covered in this chapter were TCP/IP, RIP for Internet Protocol, Simple TCP/IP services, DHCP, DNS, and WINS. We discussed the installation steps that will hopefully have you up and running in the shortest time possible!

Next, in Chapter 6, "Interacting With Other LANs," we will cover connectivity with Novell's NetWare, Banyan, and the Macintosh Services that Windows NT 4 Server provides.

6

Interacting With Other LANs

This chapter covers some of the components supplied with Windows NT 4 Server that allow you to work with other LANs. When I say "other LANs," I mean Novell NetWare, Apple Macintosh Networks, and Banyan VINES Networks.

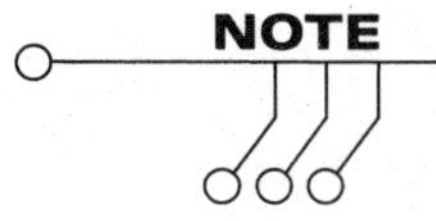

Both Windows NT 4 Server's native networking and the networking that comes with OS/2 are similar to each other, and are covered in other parts of this book.

The services you can configure include:

- Novell's NetWare—These services include the gateway (and client) services that make it easier for Windows NT clients to access NetWare shares on the network, the RIP (Routing Information Protocol) services that exchange information between routers, and the SAP agent that resolves names on NetWare networks.
- Apple Macintosh Networks—These services include the File Server service that allows Apple Macintosh clients to access the Windows NT 4 Server shared drives and the Print Server service that allows Apple Macintosh clients to access the Windows NT 4 Server shared printer queues.

- Banyan VINES Networks—These services enable and support the RPC (Remote Procedure Call) protocol on Banyan VINES Networks.

Unless otherwise specified, you can install each of the components using the Control Panel's Network applet. To select services to install, follow the steps below:

1. Start the Control Panel's Network applet.
2. Select the Services tab.
3. Click the Add button. The Select Network Service dialog box appears.
4. Select the services component you wish to install from the Network Service list.

If you are not using NetWare, Macintosh, or Banyan LANs, there is no need to consider installing, configuring, or tuning any of these services. Installing unneeded network components can create problems, as each protocol consumes system resources, including network bandwidth.

Configuration is often a part of installation; here it is a critical step in getting Windows NT 4 Server up and running effectively. Windows NT 4 Server usually performs much better if you, the system administrator, optimally configure the system. First you install, then you configure the installation, and finally you tune the configuration for optimal performance.

Configuration and tuning are interrelated to a certain extent. For example, it is common for changes in the configuration to affect system performance. If, and when, you make changes in the configuration, especially when adding new services (and servers, such as IIS) you need to consider the impact on system performance.

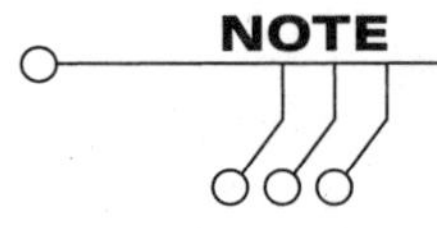

There is nothing to prevent you from having multiple installations of Windows NT Server on a single computer. You can have one installation that you keep relatively simple, and another installation that you are tuning and customizing. That way you have a system to fall back on, in case a change made while tuning adversely affects the server's reliability or performance.

Configuring NetWare Services

Novell's NetWare is currently the most used microcomputer network on the market. Though Windows NT 4 Server is making significant inroads into the NetWare market, NetWare will be around for some time to come.

It is often necessary to run both a NetWare server and a Windows NT 4 Server on a single network. There are applications that look for NetWare networks as well; when converting from NetWare to Windows NT 4 Server, both networks should be run together until you can determine that the Windows NT 4 Server is working correctly.

Configuring Gateway Services

The Gateway Service for NetWare allows Windows NT 4 Server to perform as a gateway for a Novell NetWare network. This allows the Windows client users to access the NetWare resources even if the clients are not running a NetWare redirector.

You can install the Gateway Services for NetWare at the time Windows NT 4 Server is installed, or later, using the Control Panel's Network Applet.

To install the Gateway Service for NetWare after installing Windows NT 4 Server, follow the steps below:

1. Start the Control Panel's Network applet.
2. Select the Services tab.
3. Click the Add button. The Select Network Service dialog box appears.
4. Select the Gateway Service for NetWare from the Network Service list. Windows NT 4 Server then prompts you to reboot.
5. Reboot your computer.
6. Log back onto Windows NT 4 Server. The Gateway Service for NetWare automatically displays the Select Preferred Server for NetWare dialog box, as shown in Figure 6-1. The options in this dialog box are similar to those in the Gateway Service for NetWare dialog box shown in Figure 6-2.

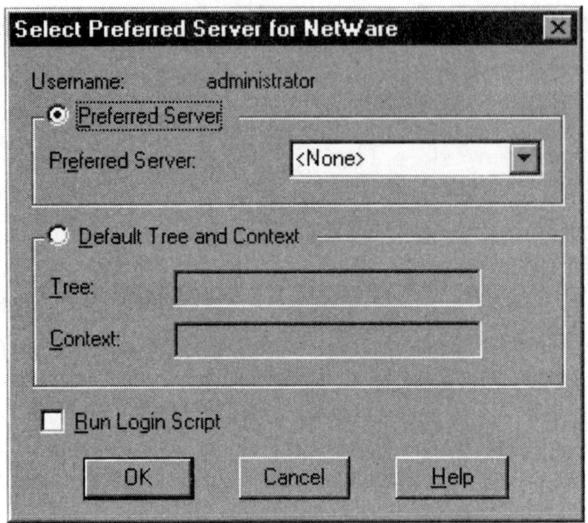

Figure 6-1: The Select Preferred Server for NetWare.

The NetWare gateway is intended to allow sites that must utilize both Windows NT and NetWare networks to perform efficiently.

To start the NetWare gateway, from a command prompt, follow the steps below:

1. Issue the command:

```
net start "gateway service for netware"
```

2. Press Enter. The NetWare gateway starts. Issuing the net start command starts the NetWare gateway only for the current session.

To start the NetWare gateway using the Windows NT 4 Server Control Panel, follow the steps below:

1. Start the Control Panel's Services applet. The Services dialog box appears.
2. Click the Startup button.
3. Click the Automatic radio button in the Service dialog's Startup Type group box. When a service's startup is set to Automatic, the service starts each time that Windows NT 4 Server is booted.

4. Set up user accounts and groups to configure the gateway service for NetWare.
5. Configure the gateway service for NetWare, following the addition of user accounts, using the Control Panel's Gateway Service for NetWare dialog box as shown in Figure 6-2.

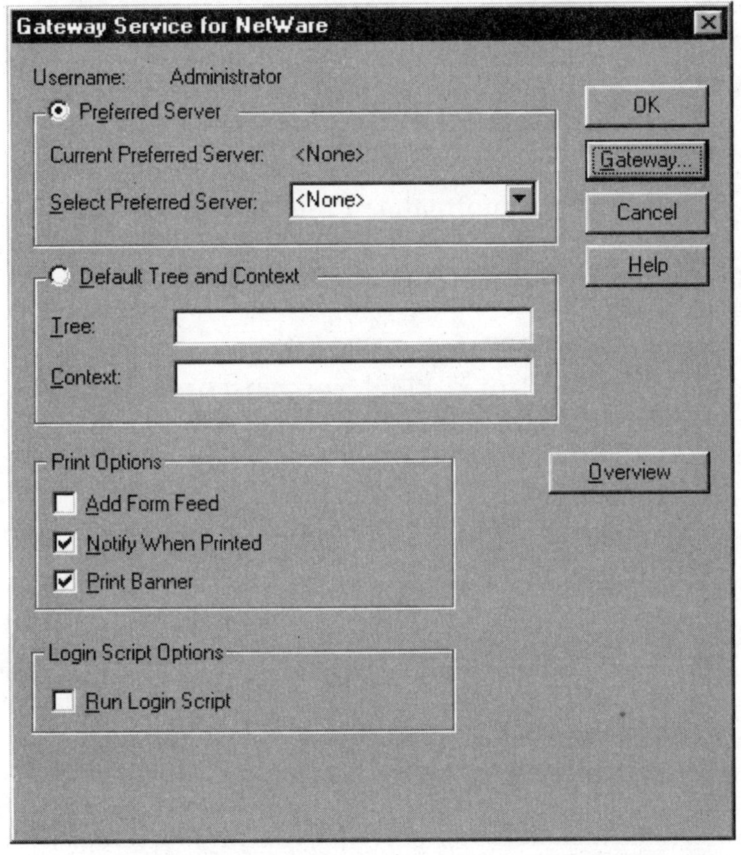

Figure 6-2: The Control Panel Gateway Service for NetWare dialog box.

6. Set the preferred server (the current NetWare server, if there is one, is shown for reference). The preferred server is the server to which the Gateway Service for NetWare connects.

7. Optionally, set the Default Tree and Context, which allows you to set both the Tree and the Name Context. The Default Tree and Context options are new to Windows NT 4.
8. Specify the desired print options. The Print Options, "Add Form Feed," "Notify When Printed," and "Print Banner" all apply to printer output.
9. Choose, if desired, to require a client user to use a NetWare login script by clicking the Run Login Script check box.

Configuring RIP Services

RIP (Routing Information Protocol) for NWLink IPX/SPX Compatible Transport, which I call "RIP for NWLink," allows NetWare routers to share routing information.

Installing RIP for NWLink

To install RIP for NWLink you must have the NWLink IPX/SPX Compatible Transport (IPX/SPX) protocol installed. When the IPX/SPX protocol is installed, NWLink NetBIOS is installed automatically.

To install RIP for NWLink, follow the steps below:

1. Select the Control Panel's Network applet.
2. Select the Services tab.
3. Click the Add button. The Select Network Service dialog box appears.
4. Select RIP for NWLink IPX/SPX compatible transport from the Network Service list.

The installation process for RIP for NWLink is simple. A single prompt is made: "NetBIOS Broadcast Propagation (broadcast of type 20 packets) is currently disabled. Do you want to enable it?" (see Figure 6-3). When using NetBIOS over IPX, or if you are not certain whether you need this feature, you should enable the NetBIOS Broadcast Propagation.

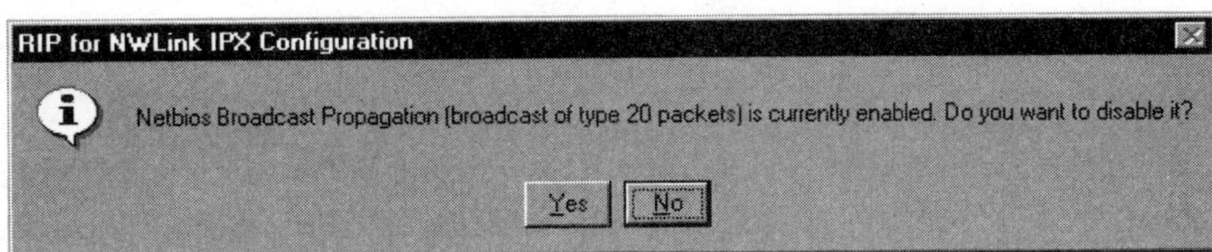

Figure 6-3: The RIP for NWLink IPX Configuration message box.

Later, if you decide you don't want NetBIOS Broadcast Propagation, follow the steps below:

1. Select the Control Panel's Network applet.
2. Select the Services tab.
3. Select the RIP for NWLink IPX.
4. Select Properties.
5. Respond to the message box that prompts you to enable (or disable) NetBIOS Broadcast Propagation.

Using the IPXROUTE Utility

To manage RIP for NWLink, you use the command line IPXROUTE utility. This utility allows you to configure, and otherwise manage, RIP for NWLink. An example of IPXROUTE is shown in Figure 6-4.

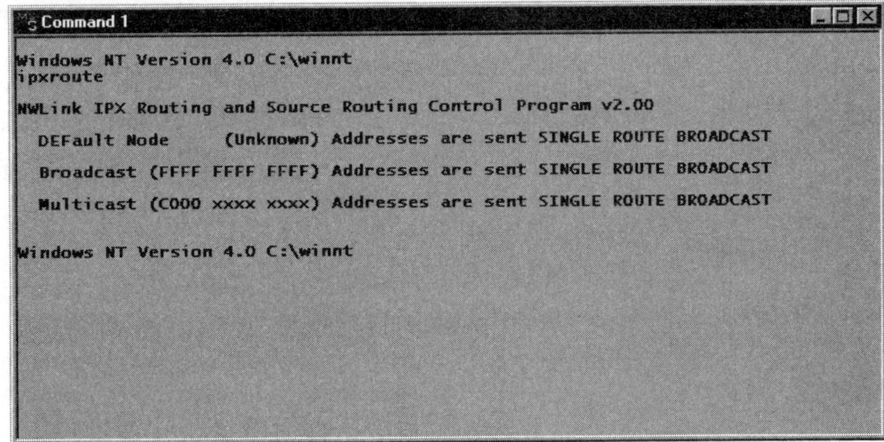

Figure 6-4: The IPXROUTE utility showing defaults.

The IPXROUTE program allows you to configure RIP for NWLink. You display and modify information contained in the routing tables using the IPXROUTE program.

Entering the command "IPXROUTE servers" displays a line of information about each server. For example, the output that I received was:

```
IPX Address                    Server Type   Server Name
-----------------------------
00000000.00a0246b331f          1600          DORA
```

Limit the types of servers listed with the /type= qualifier (for example, IPXROUTE servers /type=1600 limits the servers to type 1600).

Issuing the IPXROUTE table command lists the current routing table. The list is empty if there are no entries in the routing table.

Configuring your IPX routing with the IPXROUTE config command, with board=n (where n is a zero-based index to the NIC (Network Interface Card) to configure) provides optional support for the following options:

- clear—Clears the existing routing table.
- def—Sends packets destined to all unknown addresses (using an ALL ROUTE broadcast).
- gbr—Sends packets destined for the address FFFF-FFFF-FFFF (using an ALL ROUTE broadcast).
- mbr—Sends packets for the multi-cast address C000-xxxx-xxxx (using an ALL ROUTE broadcast).
- remove=xxxxxxxxxxxx—Removes the mac specified by the address xxxxxxxxxxxx from the routing table.

When entering parameters, they should be separated by spaces.

Configuring SAP Agent

NetWare clients use SAP (Service Advertising Protocol) when it is necessary to resolve names on a NetWare-compatible network. A NetWare-compatible server broadcasts SAP messages. IPX routers and servers then store both the broadcasting server's name and address for later use.

To install the SAP Agent, follow the steps below:

1. Start the Control Panel's Network applet.
2. Select the Services tab.
3. Click the Add button. The Select Network Service dialog box appears.
4. Select SAP Agent.
5. Click OK.

To remove SAP Agent, follow the steps below:

1. Select the Control Panel's Network applet.
2. Select the Services tab.
3. Select SAP Agent. Then click the Remove button to remove the service.

The SAP Agent is not configurable. Your only options are to install or remove the service. Removing SAP Agent can cause problems if any services that use SAP Agent are not removed at the same time.

Configuring SNMP Service

Microsoft Simple Network Management Protocol (SNMP) is a network management protocol. SNMP manages both TCP/IP networks and networks using the IPX protocol.

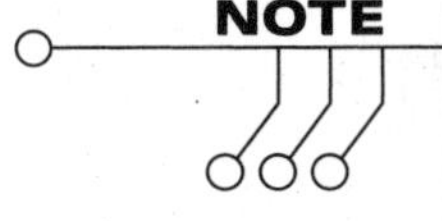

SNMP is a large and complex component of Windows NT 4 Server. You can obtain more information on SNMP from the Microsoft Windows NT 4 Resource Kit.

We use SNMP to communicate between the SNMP management program and an SNMP agent program (which runs on the host system). SNMP is a standard defined by a number of RFCs (Request for Comments).

The first step in configuring SNMP is to install the service. You can install SNMP at the same time that Windows NT 4 Server is installed, or at a later time, using the Control Panel's Network applet. The two methods are identical and produce the same results.

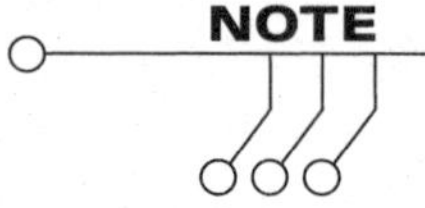

To install SNMP for the IPX protocol, you also need to install the TCP/IP protocol.

You must install SNMP on all Windows NT 4 Servers that use SNMP, and on any Windows NT 4 Workstations that act as SNMP agents.

To install SNMP, follow the steps below:

1. Start the Control Panel's Network applet.
2. Select the Services tab.
3. Select SNMP Service. The SNMP configuration dialog box appears. The Agent tab is shown in Figure 6-5.

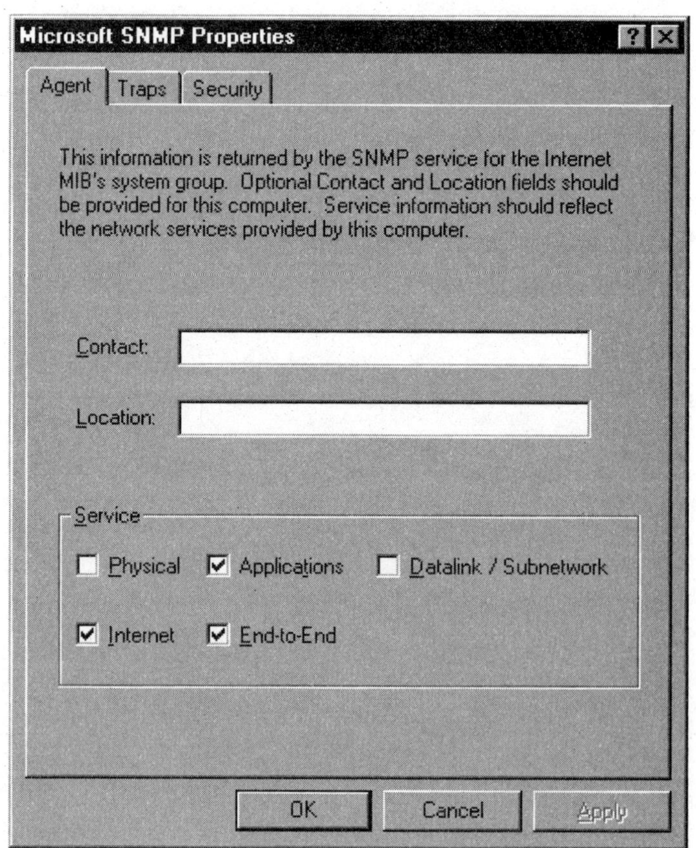

Figure 6-5: The Microsoft SNMP Properties dialog, Agent tab.

4. Use the Agent tab to establish the contact and location for the monitor agent. Both the Contact and Location are optional; however, you must select the applicable Service items as needed.
5. Use the Traps tab, as shown in Figure 6-6, to configure the trap destinations. A trap destination can be a name, IP address, or an IPX address. A community name is a group of hosts to which a server, running the SNMP service, belongs. This name is then placed in SNMP packets when traps are sent. The default community name is "Public," which is defined in the RFC as the community that is common to all hosts.

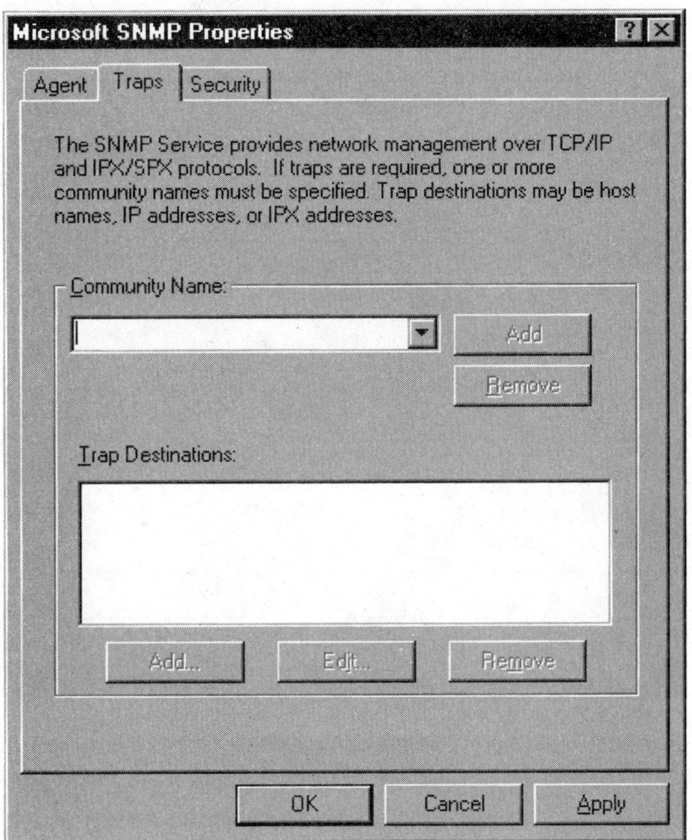

Figure 6-6: The Microsoft SNMP Properties dialog, Traps tab.

6. Use the Security tab, shown in Figure 6-7, to configure SNMP security. In the Security tab, you can select community names (which you may have created in the Traps tab, or here in the Security tab). You also select to have Authentication Traps sent (when an authentication request is rejected). The Security tab also allows you to select to receive SNMP packets from either all hosts or only from a specified group of hosts.

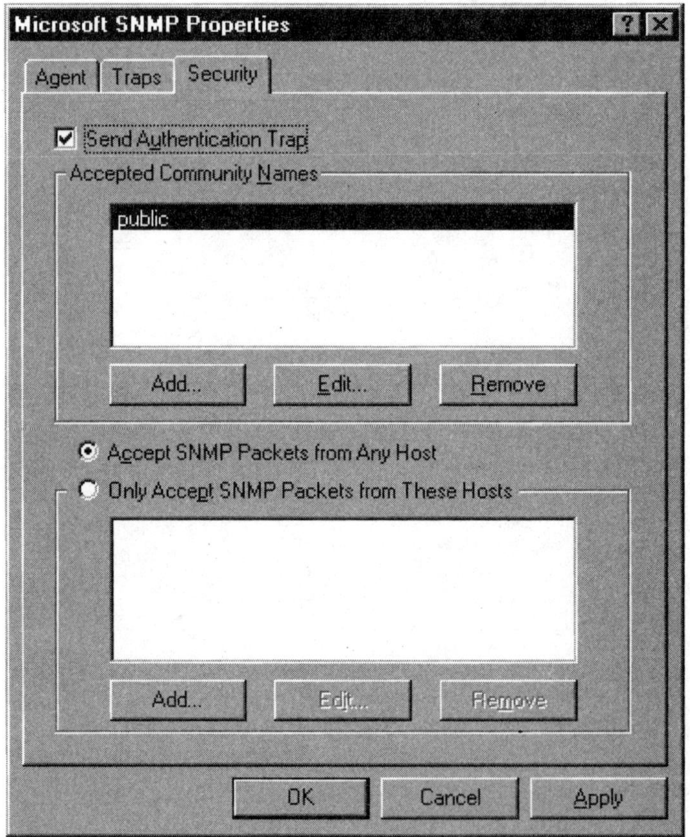

Figure 6-7: The Microsoft SNMP Properties dialog, Security tab.

You can reconfigure SNMP as needed at any time, using the Control Panel's Network Applet.

Configuring Macintosh File Servers & Print Servers

When the Services for Macintosh are installed, two services are added to the Control Panel's Services applet:

- File Server for Macintosh—The applet that allows the system to manage Apple Macintosh clients' access to Windows NT 4 Server shared Macintosh volumes.
- Print Server for Macintosh—The applet that allows the system to manage Apple Macintosh clients' access to Windows NT 4 Server shared printer queues.

You can configure each of these services to start automatically, manually, or be disabled. The default is that the Services for Macintosh start automatically at system startup time.

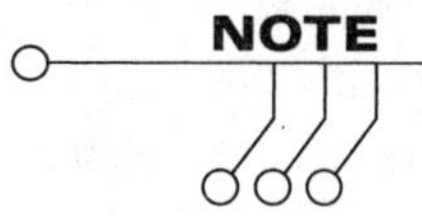

Apple Macintosh users may access only Macintosh-compatible volumes. The Services for Macintosh configure a Macintosh-compatible volume for you, as part of the installation process.

Configuring Connections to Macintosh Clients

Additionally, a new Control Panel applet, called MacFile, is created. The MacFile applet allows you to configure the connection to Apple Macintosh clients. Starting the MacFile applet displays the main window shown in Figure 6-8.

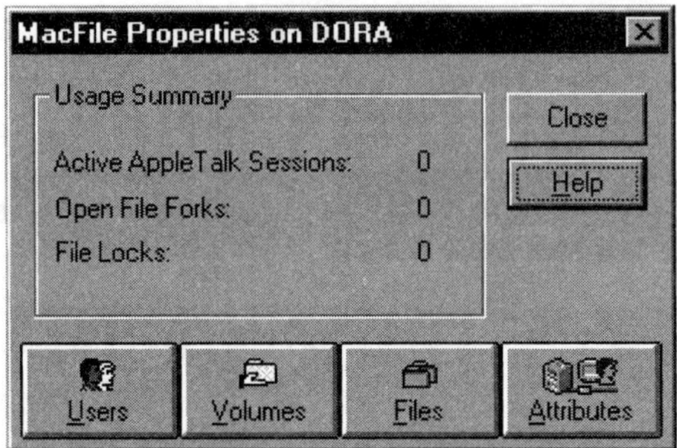

Figure 6-8: The MacFile properties dialog box.

The MacFile window has three items in the Usage Summary area. All three show numeric counts:

- Active AppleTalk Sessions—The Active AppleTalk Sessions counter allows you to determine how many actual connections to Apple Macintosh clients have been established.
- Open File Forks—The Open File Forks counter indicates how many files, resource and data forks combined, are currently open.
- File Locks—The File Locks counter indicates how many file forks are currently locked by Apple Macintosh clients.

Using the MacFile window, you can configure users, volumes, files, and attributes of a Macintosh LAN from Windows NT 4 Server:

- Users—Click the Users button to display the Macintosh Users dialog box. Use this dialog box to determine which users are currently connected to the system and how many volumes are open. You can view, disconnect, and send messages to a single user or multiple users.
- Volumes—Click the Volumes button to display the Macintosh-Accessible Volumes dialog box. This dialog box shows the Macintosh volumes that Macintosh clients can access. A Macintosh volume is typically created at the same time that the Services for Macintosh is installed.

- Files—Click the Files button to display the Files Opened by Macintosh Users dialog box. This dialog box shows the Macintosh files currently open by Macintosh clients. A Macintosh file is located on a Macintosh-accessible volume, as described above.
- Attributes—Click the Attributes button to display the MacFile Attributes dialog box. This dialog box shows the server configuration for Macintosh clients. Generally, the MacFile attributes are similar to those for the Windows NT 4 Server.

Configuring Services for Banyan

The Banyan Visual Networking System (VINES) supports multitasking for multiple users. Although VINES was designed using the UNIX operating system, a VINES LAN can also support DOS, OS/2-based, and Macintosh workstations. VINES' ability to move across operating system platforms makes network building with VINES an easy task. You can add RPC (Remote Procedure Call) support for Banyan using the Windows NT 4 Server Control Panel.

To install the RPC support for Banyan, follow the steps below:

1. Start the Control Panel's Network applet.
2. Select the Services tab.
3. Click the Add button. The Select Network Service dialog box appears.
4. Select RPC support for Banyan from the Network Service list.
5. Click OK.

To remove RPC support for Banyan, follow the steps below:

1. Start the Control Panel's Network applet.
2. Select the Services tab.

3. Select RPC support for Banyan.
4. Click the Remove button.

The RPC support for Banyan is not configurable. Your only options are to install or remove the service.

Moving On

We just showed you how to make it easier for Windows NT clients to access some of the most popular network services. The services we chose are Novell NetWare, Apple Macintosh Networks, and Banyan VINES. In this chapter we explained how to access Novell NetWare shares on the network, how to give Apple Macintosh Networks clients access to the Windows NT 4 Server shared drives and shared printer queues, and how to enable RPC protocol on Banyan VINES networks.

Now it's time to move on to Chapter 7, "Configuring Dial-Up Networking." Windows NT 4 Server allows you to take advantage of two additional optional services, collectively called RAS/DUN. RAS (Remote Access Server) is for incoming connections (the server side), while DUN (Dial-Up Networking) is for outgoing connections (the client side). Chapter 7 shows you how to configure RAS/DUN to use TCP/IP, NetBEUI, or IPX/SPX-compatible protocols.

7 Configuring Dial-Up Networking

Dial-up networking adds a valuable service to Windows NT 4 Server. With dial-up networking, users can dial into the server and have full access to all network facilities. Dial-up networking is divided into two parts: RAS (Remote Access Service), which allows users to dial into the server, and DUN (Dial-Up Networking), which allows a local user to dial into a remote network such as another Windows NT 4 Server or an ISP (Internet Service Provider). In Chapter 5, "Configuring TCP/IP Services," we discussed how the TCP/IP protocol was configured and used. In this chapter we cover Windows NT 4 Server's use of the TCP/IP protocol for RAS and DUN. You can have a RAS connection that uses either the IPX/SPX-compatible or NetBEUI protocols, but TCP/IP is more common.

Unless otherwise specified, you can install each of these services of Windows NT 4 Server using the Control Panel's Network applet. To select services to install, follow the steps below:

1. Start the Control Panel's Network applet.
2. Select the Services tab.

3. Click the Add button. The Select Network Service dialog box appears.
4. Select the services component that you wish to install from the Network Service list.

If you are not using RAS or DUN, then there is no need to consider installing, configuring, or tuning these services.

Configuration is often a part of installation; here it is a critical step in getting Windows NT 4 Server up and running effectively. Windows NT 4 Server usually performs much better if you, the system administrator, optimally configure the system. First you install, then you configure the installation, and finally you tune the configuration for optimal performance.

Configuration and tuning are interrelated to a certain extent. For example, it is common for changes in the configuration to affect system performance. If, and when, you make changes in the configuration, especially when adding new services (and servers, such as IIS), you need to consider the impact on system performance.

Configuring Dial-Up Networking (DUN)

You can configure both RAS and DUN to use TCP/IP, NetBEUI, or IPX/SPX-compatible protocols. Neither NetBEUI nor IPX/SPX are difficult to configure. However, TCP/IP seems to be more complex and daunting to users who are less experienced.

Unlike TCP/IP for a NIC, TCP/IP for DUN is not configured under the Control Panel's Network applet. Rather, to configure TCP/IP for DUN, follow the steps below:

1. Access the Dial-Up Network program. (Start Menu | Programs | Applications | Dial-Up Networking. See Figure 7-1.)

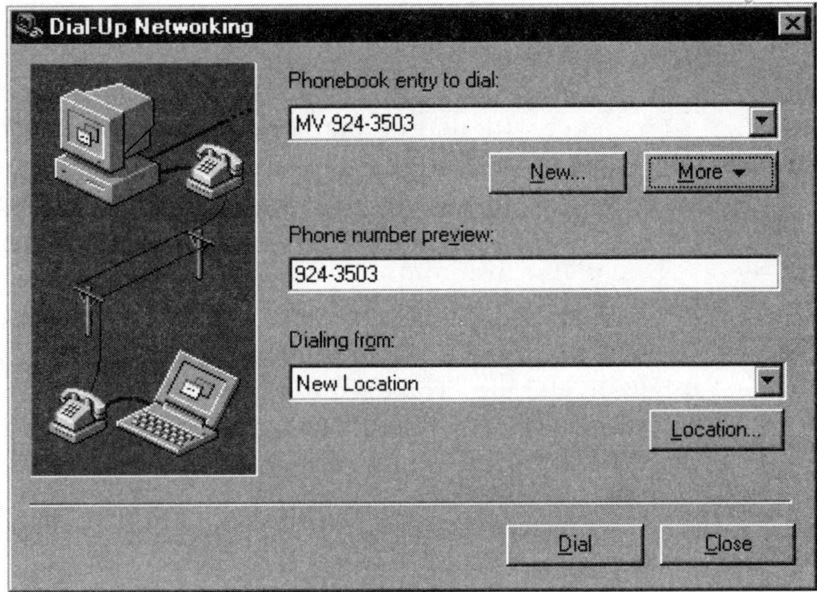

Figure 7-1: The Dial-Up Networking program.

What Is RAS & Where Did DUN Come From?

With Windows NT 4 Server, RAS (Remote Access Server) is for incoming connections (the server side), while DUN (Dial-Up Networking) is for outgoing connections (the client side). Collectively, the two are usually called RAS/DUN. DUN is configured with the Dial-Up Networking Administrator while RAS is configured from the Control Panel's Network applet's Services tab.

2. With the Dial-Up Networking program, you can add, configure, or remove dial-up connections, and set phone numbers and dialing locations. Readers who have experience with dial-up networking for Windows 95 will find many of the concepts in the DUN program for Windows NT 4 Server familiar. As well, future releases of Windows 95 will strive toward making the DUN program in both platforms uniform.

As Figure 7-1 shows, the Dial-Up Networking program allows you to select an existing configuration or to create a new configuration. In all cases, you need to know the telephone number to call (for outgoing DUN connections), the protocol of the receiving end (such as PPP), and other configuration information such as the TCP/IP parameters.

3. In the Dial-Up Networking program, you can also configure the modem properties. You can have as many modems connected to your system as you have serial ports. Most users have only one (or perhaps two modems); however, some systems have multiple modems, perhaps of differing types. You can attach any modem to a phone book entry as desired, and you can have more than one phonebook entry for each modem.

Creating a DUN Configuration

A DUN configuration describes a logical connection to a remote host. The configuration includes information about the modem to be used, telephone numbers, and host configuration.

In this section, you will learn to create a new DUN configuration (called a phonebook entry), using the name "Internet-1." This phonebook entry is the one that I actually use when I connect to the Internet using my ISP's dial-up PPP service.

Specifying an Entry Name

To create a new phonebook entry, select the New button. The New Phonebook Entry Wizard displays, as shown in Figure 7-2.

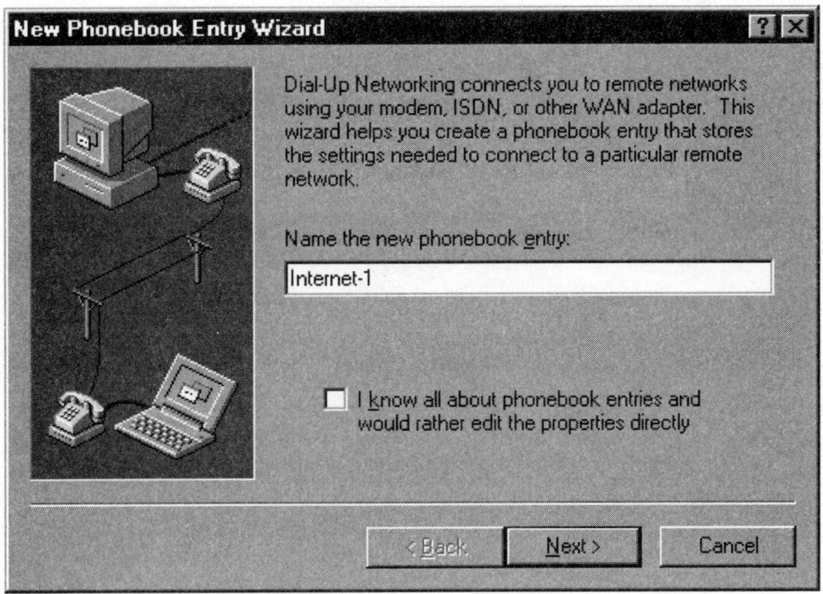

Figure 7-2: The New Phonebook Entry Wizard's first dialog box.

To specify a phonebook entry name, follow the steps below:

1. In the first dialog box of the New Phonebook Entry Wizard, you must enter the name for this entry (Internet-1).
2. Do not click the "I know all about phonebook entries and would rather edit the properties directly" check box. If you do, you will have to manually specify the properties for the phonebook (DUN) entry.
3. Click Next to set the Server options.

Specifying Server Options

On the next dialog box of the New Phonebook Entry Wizard (titled "Server" and shown in Figure 7-3) you can specify options for calling an Internet provider.

1. Use the check boxes provided to specify the following server options:
   - Whether you are calling an Internet provider (in many cases this will be true).

- Whether you want to send logon information like the password as plain text (many Internet providers don't support encrypted logons).
- Whether the server you are connecting to can provide TCP/IP configuration (such as the assigned node address) or not.

2. When you are finished, click Next.

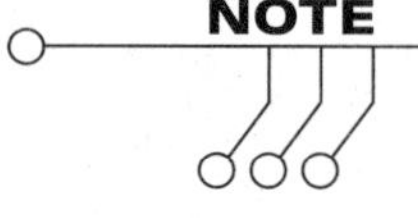

If in doubt as to whether to select these items or not, you can experiment: don't select "Send my plain text password..." but do select the "The non-Windows NT server I am calling..." button. If you are unable to successfully connect to your server, then try different combinations of these two options.

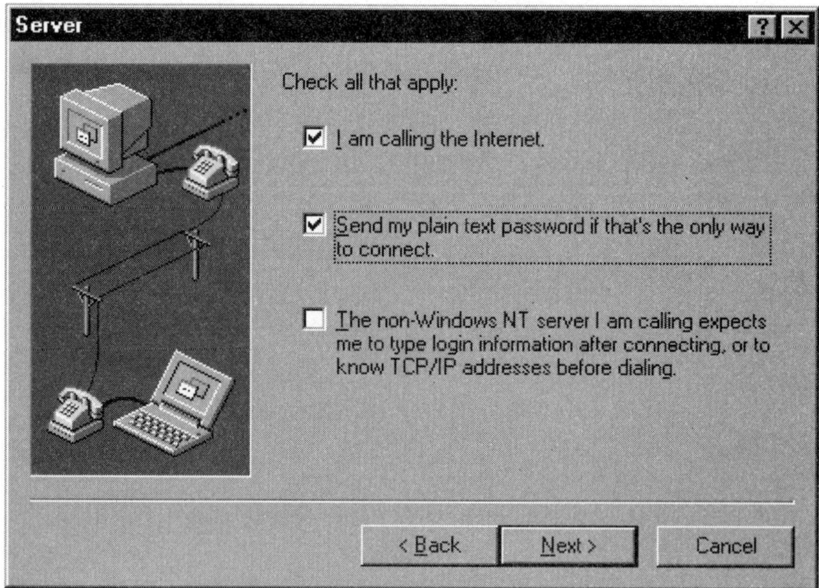

Figure 7-3: The New Phonebook Entry Wizard's second dialog box, titled Server.

Specifying Phone Numbers

To specify phone numbers to use to connect to the server, follow the steps below:

1. On the next dialog box of the New Entry Wizard (Figure 7-4), enter the telephone numbers to connect to the server. You can enter one or more numbers.
2. To enter alternate numbers, click the Alternates button. DUN dials the first number, and if DUN cannot connect (if the line is busy, for example) then DUN attempts to connect to the second number.

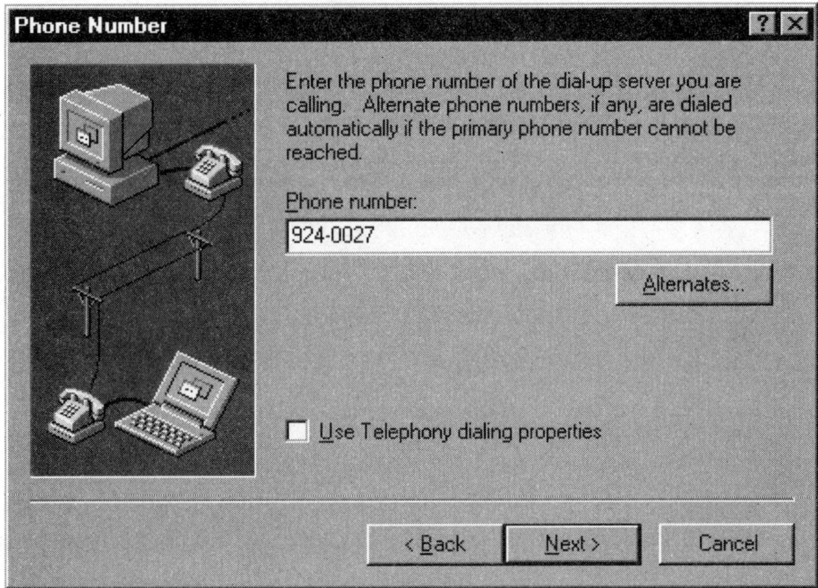

Figure 7-4: The New Phonebook Entry Wizard's third dialog box, titled Phone Number.

Using two numbers can be useful when your server has two types of modems (such as 28.8 and 14.4), each type with its own telephone number. DUN first calls the number that matches your modem, and if that number fails, it then calls the second number. Connecting to the second number might mean that you have to accept the possibility of degraded performance if the second number connects to less capable modems.

3. Additionally, you can select the "Use Telephony dialing properties" check box. The established dialing properties are used if you choose this option. This feature is useful for long distance numbers or for numbers that have special dialing requirements.

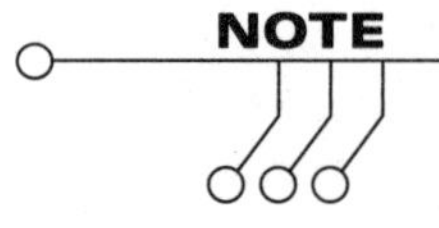

You can also configure Telephony Dialing Properties using the Control Panel's Modems applet. To configure Telephony Dialing Properties, follow the steps below:

1. *Select the Control Panel's Modems applet. The main window for the Modems Properties dialog box appears.*
2. *Click the Dialing Properties button to display the Dialing Properties dialog box.*

Finishing & Configuring DUN Entries

The next screen of the New Phonebook Entry Wizard (see Figure 7-5) simply shows you that the setup of the new phonebook entry "Internet-1" is complete. Click the Finish button to save "Internet-1."

If you need to go back and make a change, click the Back button to go back and change any parameter. If you wish you never set up the new phonebook entry, click Cancel to delete the new entry.

Figure 7-5: The New Phonebook Entry Wizard's fourth and final dialog box.

After creating a phonebook entry, you can edit the entry's properties. Generally, all entries require some manual configuration. To select an entry to edit, follow the steps below:

1. Access the Dial-Up Network program (Start Menu | Programs | Applications | Dial-Up Networking). See Figure 7-1.
2. Select an entry's name in the Phonebook entry to dial: drop-down list box.

The More button on the main Dial-Up Networking program dialog box, as shown in Figure 7-1, displays a pop-up menu with the following choices:

- Edit Entry and Modem Properties—Allows you to change DUN entry properties. See the section, "Setting DUN Properties," for more information.
- Clone Entry and Modem Properties—Copies a DUN entry and allows you to modify the entry immediately.
- Delete Entry—Deletes an entry.

- Create Shortcut to Entry—Creates a shortcut for the DUN entry on your desktop or in the Start program.
- Monitor Status—Monitors the DUN connection.
- Operator Assisted or Manual Dialing—Allows you to manually dial the number, such as when you are on a laptop computer in a hotel, or when making an international call.
- User Preferences—Specify general options for the DUN entry.
- Logon Preferences—Specify system administrator options.
- Help—Find more information about the DUN program options.

Editing DUN Properties

DUN properties are set using a standard Windows tabbed dialog box. This dialog box is displayed by selecting More | Edit Entry and Modem Properties.

The Edit Entry and Modem Properties dialog has five tabs:

- The Basic tab includes general information about the DUN entry, such as the name and phone number.
- The Server tab includes specific server settings, such as the type of connection and network protocol used.
- The Script tab allows you to create a logon script that makes non-automatic logon much easier.
- The Security tab includes authentication properties.
- The X.25 tab includes options for the X.25 protocol, which is only supported by a few ISPs, including CompuServe and SprintNet.

Configuring Remote Access Service (RAS)

The previous section describes the procedures for configuring DUN (Dial-Up Networking). This section describes configuration of RAS (Remote Access Service). There is substantial overlap between RAS and DUN: it is common to refer to both together as RAS/DUN, though the configuration of each is slightly different.

As we mentioned above, RAS is the server side, just as DUN is the client side of networking by modem. Both RAS and DUN interact, are able to use the same modems, and share similar properties and configurations. However there are differences, and in this section we cover some of these differences.

To configure RAS, follow the steps below:

1. Select the Control Panel's Network applet.
2. Select the Services tab.
3. Select Remote Access Service from the Network Services list, as shown in Figure 7-6.

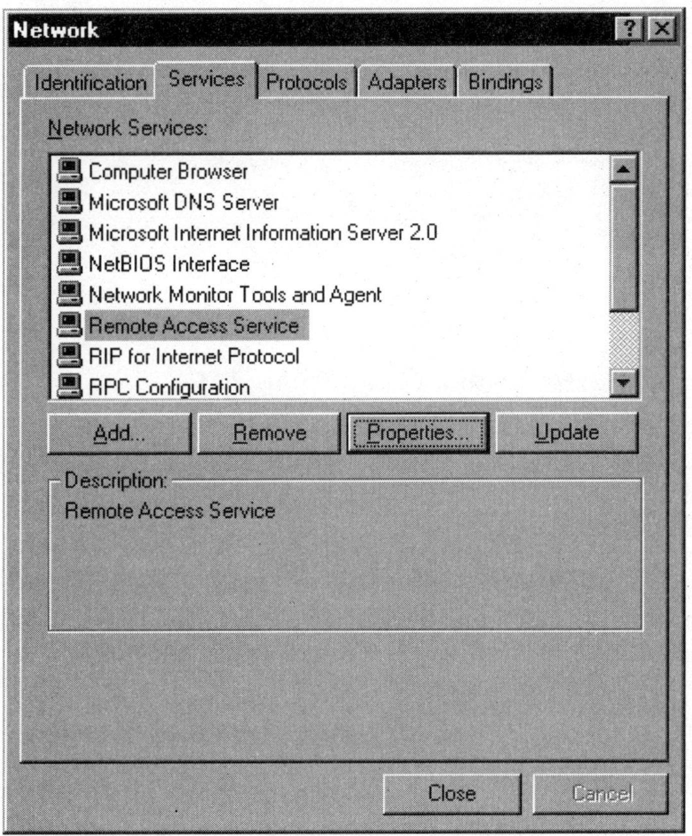

Figure 7-6: The Network Services list box with Remote Access Service highlighted.

4. Select the Properties button. The Remote Access Setup dialog displays, as shown in Figure 7-7. This dialog box lists each port that is configured for RAS, the device connected to the port (typically, the modem), and the type of device (such as Modem, though other devices such as ISDN are also supported).

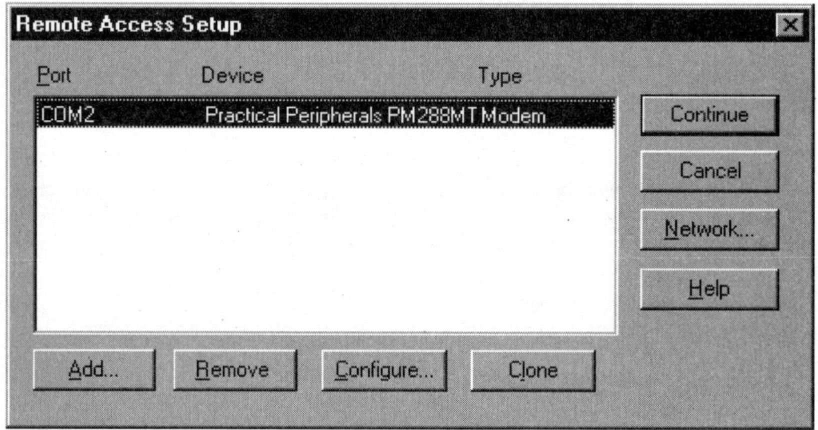

Figure 7-7: A single modem is listed on this Remote Access Setup dialog box.

From the Remote Access Setup dialog, you can add, remove, clone, and configure ports.

Configuring a RAS Port

To configure a Remote Access Setup port, follow the steps below:

1. Select the port using the Remote Access Setup dialog box.
2. Click the Configure button. The Configure Port Usage dialog displays, as shown in Figure 7-8.

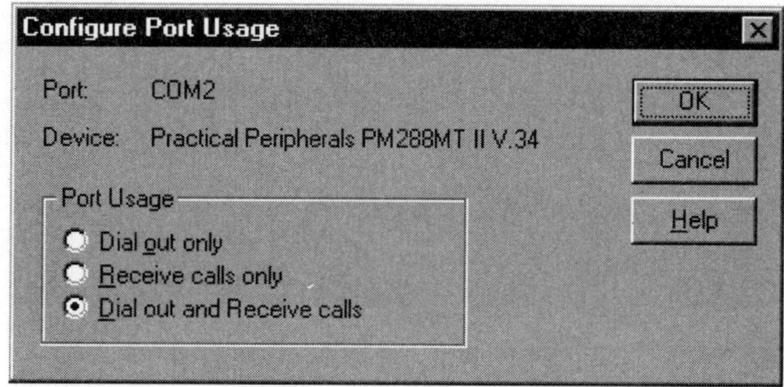

Figure 7-8: The Configure Port Usage dialog.

The Configure Port Usage dialog allows you to dedicate the port to RAS (Receive calls only), DUN (Dial out only), or both. When a port is configured as both, the modem both receives calls and places calls, as was done in our example.

The modem doesn't answer calls if the RAS service has not been started. You can set RAS to start automatically (use the Control Panel's Services applet), or manually (using the RAS Monitor program).

Configuring Network Protocols for the Port

Once the ports have been configured, you can then set the network configuration. To do this, follow the steps below:

1. Click the Network button on the Remote Access Setup dialog box. The Network Configuration dialog box displays, as shown in Figure 7-9.

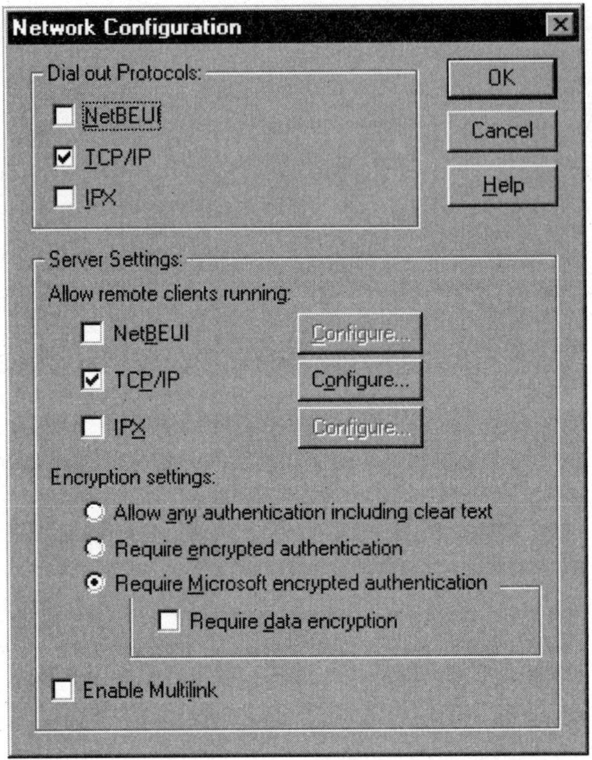

Figure 7-9: The Network Configuration dialog box.

2. Set the DUN and RAS network protocols on the Network Configuration dialog box. Typically, you specify TCP/IP, but NetBEUI and IPX protocols are also supported. Select those protocols that you are relatively certain the server supports, because DUN attempts to negotiate each protocol, which may seriously impact the performance at logon time.

Configuring NetBEUI

To configure the NetBEUI protocol, follow the steps below:

1. Click the Configure button next to the NetBEUI check box in Server Settings on the Network Configuration dialog box. (See Figure 7-9.) The RAS Server NetBEUI Configuration dialog box appears, as shown in Figure 7-10.

2. Use the RAS Server NetBEUI Configuration dialog box to restrict a NetBEUI client to accessing resources on this server only, or to allow the client to access resources across your entire network.

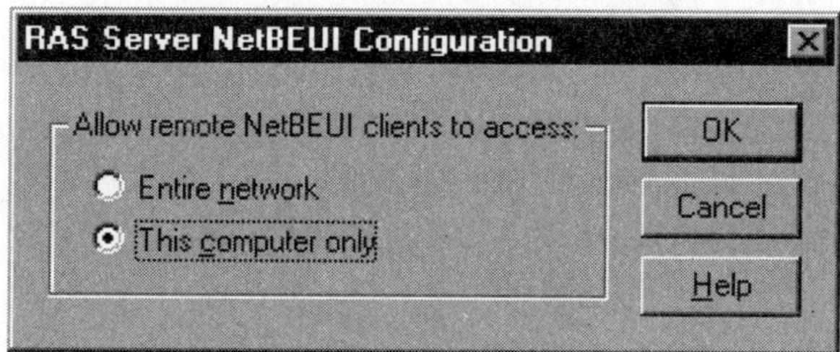

Figure 7-10: The RAS Server NetBEUI Configuration dialog.

Configuring TCP/IP

To configure the TCP/IP protocol, follow the steps below:

1. Click the Configure button next to the TCP/IP check box in Server Settings on the Network Configuration dialog box. (See Figure 7-9.) The RAS Server TCP/IP Configuration dialog box appears, as shown in Figure 7-11.
2. Use the RAS Server TCP/IP Configuration dialog box to restrict a TCP/IP client to accessing resources on this server only or to allow the client to access resources across your entire network.

For the TCP/IP protocol, you can specify that the client receives an IP address from a DHCP server or from a static pool. As well, you can specify that a client user can request a specific IP address. (The latter option is useful for users who expect the same IP address assignment each time they connect.)

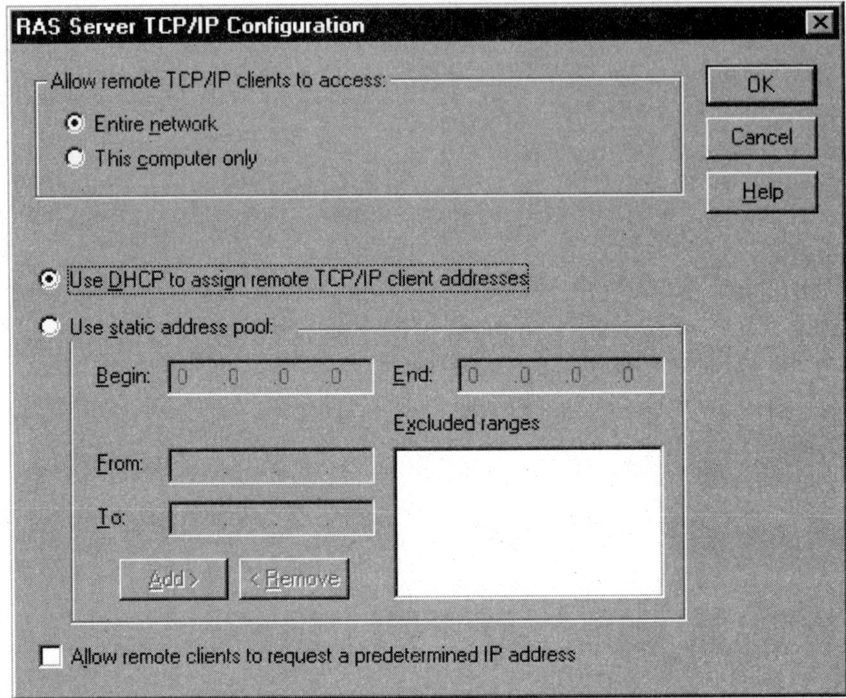

Figure 7-11: The RAS Server TCP/IP Configuration dialog.

Configuring IPX

To configure the IPX protocol, follow the steps below:

1. Click the Configure button next to the IPX check box in Server Settings on the Network Configuration dialog box. (See Figure 7-9.) The RAS Server IPX Configuration dialog box appears as shown in Figure 7-12.
2. Use the RAS Server IPX Configuration dialog box to restrict an IPX client to accessing resources on this server only or to allow the client to access resources across your entire network.

For the IPX protocol, you can specify that the client receives a network number automatically, or that network numbers are allocated from within the range you specify. Additional options allow assigning the same network number to all clients or to allow a client to request a specific IPX node number.

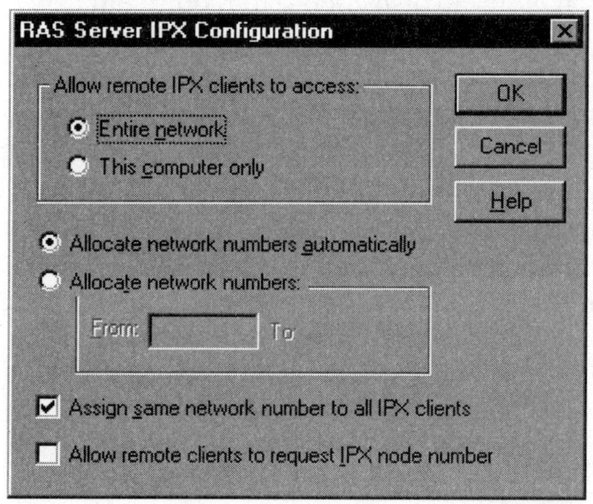

Figure 7-12: The RAS Server IPX Configuration dialog.

Be careful: allowing remote sites full access to your network can be dangerous! Remember, Windows NT 4 Server is a router and does not restrict access to other servers (including Windows NT 4 Workstation and Windows 95 clients who are sharing resources on the network)!

Setting Other Network Configuration Options

Other items in the Network Configuration dialog include Encryption settings, which enables the encryption used for authentication, and Enable Multilink, which allows a client to connect to the server using multiple ports.

To use the Encryption settings, follow the steps below:

1. You can choose between "Allow any authentication including clear text," "Require encrypted authentication," and "Require Microsoft Encrypted authentication."
2. If you choose to require Microsoft Encrypted authentication, you can also choose to require data encryption.

The final check box in the Network Configuration dialog box is Enable Multilink. Enable Multilink allows a client to connect to the server using multiple ports. Typically this is done using ISDN's multiple channel features; however, this facility is not restricted to ISDN—regular modem lines can also be multilinked. For example, a user can connect using two 28.8K modems and get a throughput of about 56K. The actual throughput may vary from the theoretical value for a number of reasons such as quality, server loading, and other factors that are not necessarily easily predicted.

Managing RAS/DUN

There are two programs, RASDIAL and RASADMIN, which allow console (typically a CMD window) interaction with RAS/DUN. Each of these programs may be called from other applications, or from a batch command file.

The RASDIAL Program

You can use the RASDIAL program to interact with RAS/DUN. It starts the RAS system and provides a connection to an entry that is specified.

With the RASDIAL program, you can dial a phonebook entry and make substitutions. You can issue the RASDIAL command from a command line, a batch command file, or as a call process from another application.

RASDIAL requires that you provide a Dial-Up Networking phonebook entry name. You usually have to provide a login username and password if either is different from your current Windows NT logon username and password. The user ID and the password would follow the phonebook entry name in the command:

```
RASDIAL PHONEBOOK USERID PASSWORD
```

When you use RASDIAL without any parameters, RASDIAL displays the status of any currently open RAS/DUN connections, as shown below:

```
Windows NT Version 4.0 C:\WinNT
Rasdial
Connected to
MV 924-3503
Command completed successfully.

Windows NT Version 4.0 C:\WinNT
```

Table 7-1 shows the various parameters you can specify on the RASDIAL program.

Option	Description
/domain	You can specify the /domain:domain option to allow the specification of a domain name. This parameter is optional, and is only used with servers that support domain names (such as Windows NT Server).
/phone	Specifying the /phone:phonenumber option allows you to override the telephone number in the phonebook entry. This parameter is optional.
/callback	The optional /callback:callbacknumber option allows the specification of a callback telephone number. The number specified overrides the number found in the phonebook entry.
/phonebook	You can override the current phonebook using the optional /phonebook:phonebookpath option.

Option	Description
/disconnect	You can disconnect from connections using the /disconnect option. You can specify the phonebook (connection) entry name to disconnect from a specific connection. The only other parameter you can specify with the /disconnect option is entryname.
/?	To receive online help for RASDIAL's command syntax, use the /? Help option.

Table 7-1: RASDIAL program parameters.

The RASADMIN Program

You can use the RASADMIN program to manage RAS/DUN connections (see Figure 7-13).

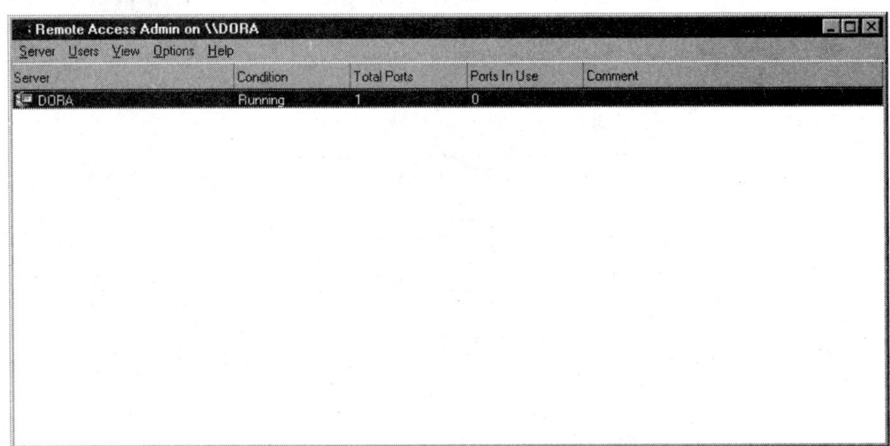

Figure 7-13: The RASADMIN program executing.

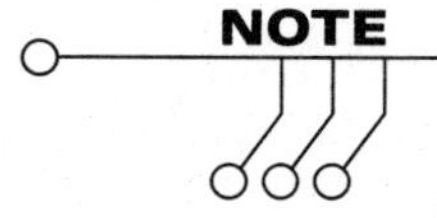

You can start RASADMIN from a command prompt with the command "RASADMIN" or from Start Menu | Programs | Administrative Tools (Common) | Remote Access Admin.

Figure 7-13 shows a single port active for dial-up users. Were a user to connect to my server (DORA) using this port, they would see my network as if they were locally connected, with the exception that they must set the Network Browsers for both Windows NT 4 Workstation and Windows 95 to browse a *slow* network.

RASADMIN allows the administrator to start, pause, or stop the Remote Access Services. Remember, RAS is incoming connections, while DUN is for outgoing connections. You can also use RASADMIN to configure ports and to view potential and current users.

The shortcut for RASADMIN is found in Start Menu | Programs | Administrative Tools (Common).

Moving On

This chapter covered both RAS (Remote Access Server) and DUN (Dial Up Networking). RAS allows a remote client user to connect to the Windows NT 4 Server using a telephone modem connection. With DUN, a locally logged-on user can connect to a remote server, again using a telephone modem connection.

The next chapter will cover how to configure the hardware for Windows NT 4 Server.

8

Configuring Hardware

This chapter covers the tuning of Windows NT 4 Server. Windows NT 4 Server runs reasonably well as installed; however, you can enhance performance using a number of basic tuning techniques.

You can make changes to Windows NT 4 Server's configuration to tune the system's performance. These changes can be as simple as setting the paging file size to an optimal value, to more complex decisions such as drive load sharing, selection of optimal partition formatting, or adjusting internal operating parameters by working directly with the Windows NT 4 Server registry.

Hardware Tuning

It is well beyond the scope of this book to delve deeply into hardware tuning. Hardware tuning is a complex topic and can be very time consuming. Some hardware tuning issues involve tweaking the CMOS BIOS settings (removing an unneeded wait state in the RAM access cycle can significantly enhance system performance but can also make that same system more prone to failure). However, we can cover some of the more common issues in tuning the hardware for maximum performance.

RAM & CPU Upgrades

Two of the most common quick fixes for sluggish performance are adding more memory (RAM) or replacing your motherboard (CPU).

- For systems with insufficient RAM, adding (likely doubling) RAM is easy and usually inexpensive (at mid-1996 RAM prices, RAM was selling at about $6/MB). RAM enhancements typically lead to more improvements in system performance than any other single change.
- For systems with an under-powered CPU, upgrading the CPU to a faster model is a viable alternative. Don't even consider upgrading using a "plug-in enhanced CPU." Replace the entire motherboard, and get the very best motherboard available. This computer is going to be a server—there is no justification for cutting corners here.

As a rule of thumb: Doubling the RAM in a system may well give the same performance increase as doubling the CPU speed. This is not a hard and fast rule, but it does work well in many situations where either RAM or CPU is lacking. Of course, increasing a lightly loaded (less than 25 active users) Windows NT 4 Server from 128MB of RAM to 256MB will probably go unnoticed. This perhaps is also true when upgrading CPUs—if the system's performance bottleneck is not the CPU, then upgrading the CPU will have little (or no) effect on system performance.

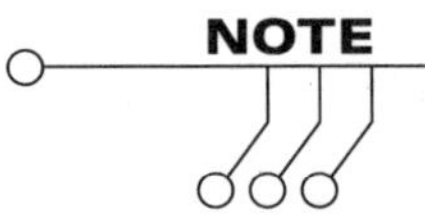

Some computers only cache 64 MB of RAM. Make sure that the system you are using caches all installed RAM. RAM that is not cached significantly slows the system. In many cases adding uncached RAM actually results in a decrease in system performance.

System Buses

System bus configuration is critical for servers. For example, one does not expect a great deal of performance from an ISA bus adapter—the speed of the standard AT ISA bus is limited to 8 MHz, with a maximum transfer width of 16 bits. That is fine for simple serial and parallel ports but is not adequate for either disk or network I/O.

As well, ISA adapters can only perform DMA (Direct Memory Access, which allows the adapter to directly read and write to memory) into the first 16MB of RAM on an ISA bus machine. If your Windows NT 4 Server is only an ISA bus machine, it may be a good investment to upgrade the motherboard to one that supports the PCI bus.

VESA/VLB bus machines were popular a few years back. Today, the PCI bus has all but taken over the bus market. Few if any adapter producers are creating new VESA/VLB bus adapters. New PCI bus cards are available daily, and any card designed for performance is released in a PCI version first. It is difficult to get a higher performance motherboard that is not PCI bus today.

Disk I/O

Servers that primarily function as file servers will benefit from enhanced disk I/O. Typically, these systems are SCSI-based (there are some IDE-based servers, but IDE is not designed for server-type applications, and IDE drives cannot equal the performance of a well-configured SCSI system). SCSI adapters such as Adaptec's 2940w (a single-channel, wide, SCSI 3 adapter) and Adaptec's 3940 (a dual-channel, wide, SCSI 3 adapter) are but two examples of higher performance SCSI systems.

High-Performance NICs

Virtually all servers benefit from high-performance Network Interface Cards (NICs). Examples are the high-performance PCI bus cards such as the 3Com 3C590 (which works with standard Ethernet installations) and similar NICs from SMC. Avoid low-cost, after-market clone NICs when configuring a Windows NT 4 Server. The price savings are nominal, while such lower-cost NICs do not perform nearly as well as their mainstream cousins.

Video Cards

For virtually all servers, video performance is not an issue. Installing a high-performance video card in a dedicated server is generally an unwise investment. Standard 1MB or 2MB VGA adapters (listed on the HCL) are adequate for most servers. If the server is being used in a non-dedicated mode running graphics applications, then the choice of video adapter is dictated by what other tasks the server must perform.

CD-ROM Drives

CD-ROMs, if shared, must be on drives that are as high in performance as possible. This is especially critical if more than one user at a time will access the CD-ROM. Regardless of whether the CD-ROM drive is shared or not, for most business applications quad-speed CD-ROM drives provide acceptable performance for single users, and 6X to 8X drives can handle two to four users without too much difficulty.

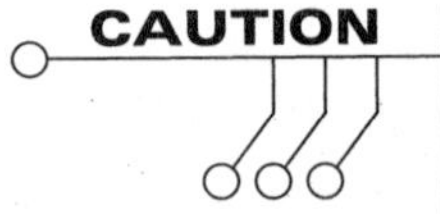

Never place an IDE CD-ROM drive on the same IDE port as an IDE hard drive. This configuration forces the port to run at the CD-ROM's speeds, significantly degrading the performance of the hard drive!

Most CD-ROM drives do not take well to being accessed by two different processes, or users. Seek times and CD-ROM organization make multiuser (or multiprocess) access slow, with the users or processes contending for a device with very limited performance. Solutions, where multiple users must share a single CD-ROM, include simply mirroring the CD-ROM to a networked hard drive, or the use of expensive, high-performance CD-ROM drives.

Modems & ISDN Lines

Modem sharing is virtually unheard of on today's PC-based networks. Typically, each user has a *dedicated* modem (modem costs are typically less than $100 for internal 28.8 modems). Dedicated modems allow each user to configure and use the modem however they desire. Shared modems may eventually lead to reliability problems: there is a vast array of communications programs, each of which may expect the modem to be in a predictable state, or if not, will configure the modem to their expectations or needs. These communications programs may also leave the modem in the same configuration and state that they used.

ISDN and other higher speed communications channels must be designed, and configured, on a case-by-case basis. Typically, if the connection is temporary—that is, the connection is made for a specific task or group of tasks, then the user treats the ISDN channel as though it were a dedicated, local modem. However, if the server is connected to an Internet Service Provider (ISP) on a full-time basis, then the IDSN channel is commonly connected to the server, and the client user accesses the Internet through Windows NT 4 Server's routing capabilities.

Hard Disks

Hard disks on servers need to be fast and large. Small- and medium-sized servers work well with standard SCSI II and SCSI III configurations. Medium to large servers work best with SCSI III RAID (or other high-performance) systems.

Having enough hard disk space is always an issue. How much is too much? With proper management, there will always be enough space on the server's drives.

IDE is not a viable alternative for hard disk resources, though there can be good arguments for using IDE for CD-ROM drives. If your server is IDE-based, one good move would be to switch to SCSI for the hard disk resources.

There are a number of high-performance SCSI adapters. Adaptec produces the 3940, a dual-channel, wide adapter that is an excellent choice for servers. The Adaptec 3985 is a high-performance PCI bus RAID adapter, and Mylex offers a similar product, the DAC960PL. Both these adapters offer enhanced data reliability and improved performance.

Using the Disk Administrator

Windows NT 4 Server includes a program called Disk Administrator. Disk Administrator performs both FDISK and Formatting functions. When you start Disk Administrator after installing a drive that has not been initialized, the Disk Administrator offers to configure the drive automatically.

Disk Administrator can also manage fault tolerance, format and manage drives, and check and repair errors on drives.

Any time you work with Disk Administrator you must be careful—it is possible, with just a few clicks of the mouse, to delete, format, or otherwise destroy the contents of a drive. Always, always, read all prompts, and be sure that your backup is current!

Working With Partitions

Working with partitions can be a daunting task for a system administrator. With MS-DOS, you can use a program called FDISK, which with a few keystrokes, wipes out a drive's data with little hope of recovery. As well, FDISK requires complicated keystroke sequences, munching of numbers, and is generally user-unfriendly.

Disk Administrator makes working with partitions much more user-friendly. Installing a new drive can be as simple as connecting the drive, running Disk Administrator, and creating a partition.

Creating & Deleting Partitions

To create a new partition, follow the steps below:

1. Select a drive that has not been completely allocated.
2. Select Partition | Create.
3. Create a new partition.

If the entire drive has been allocated to partitions, then you must delete a partition to be able to create a new one. Remember, deleting a partition deletes any data that has been written to that partition.

You can configure a drive into one or more partitions. When creating more than one partition, the second partition is called an extended partition. You must then divide the extended partition into multiple logical partitions that will appear as logical drives. Each logical drive will have a drive letter and will look to the user and operating system as a separate drive, even though the logical drive will not be on a separate physical drive. To create an extended partition, select Partition | Create Extended.

Sometimes it is necessary to either combine or split partitions that have already been created. An example of this is where you have created multiple, small, FAT-based partitions, and you wish to create a single large NTFS-based partition. To do this, follow the steps below:

1. Back up the data. (Do not skip this step! *Always* back up your data before working with partitions.)
2. Delete the existing partitions by selecting Partition | Delete.
3. Create the new partition.

Creating & Extending Volume Sets

There are times when you have a number of smaller drives such as three 2GB drives and you would really like to have a single 3GB drive. Sure, you could go and purchase a new drive, but for most of us, we would prefer to use the hardware that we already have.

With Windows NT 4 Server, we can combine multiple hard drives into a single logical drive. This logical drive is called a volume set. To combine multiple hard drives, follow the steps below:

1. Select the Disk Administrator's Partition | Create Volume Set.
2. Join two (or more) drives into a single, large, volume. The dialog box allows you to form a single logical drive from many small drives. The resulting logical volume has a storage size equal to the combined size of all the physical volumes that were joined.
3. A volume set must be formatted with the NTFS file system (Tools | Format) to use volume sets. Format prompts for the file system to use.

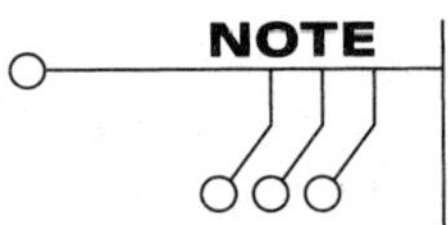

When creating a volume set, the component drives do not need to be the same size, nor do you need to allocate all the space on the component drives to the volume set—you can have a 4GB drive and a 2GB drive. On the first drive, you can allocate 1GB of the 4GB drive to be the C partition and allocate the remaining 3GB on the drive, along with the 2GB on the second drive, to create a 5GB volume set. You do have to format the resulting partition with NTFS.

Once you have a volume set, you can extend the size of your logical drive by adding more drives. This is done by selecting the Disk Administrator's Partition | Extend Volume Set. You can extend a volume set at any time, without the loss of data on the volume set.

Extending a volume set allows you to make an existing volume set larger by adding additional drives. However, once a drive has been included into a volume set, it cannot be removed without breaking the volume set and losing the volume set's data.

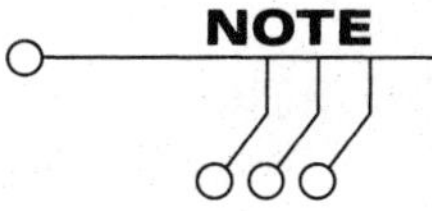

Volume sets are not compatible with MS-DOS or Windows 95. If you are dual booting your system to either of these operating systems, and anticipate needing to access the data on your volume set, do not create a volume set.

Creating Boot Partitions

One partition is used to boot or start a computer. This partition need not be the first partition (though it often is). Some systems have multiple, noncompatible (such as a Windows NT system and a UNIX system) operating systems, each installed on their own partition.

You can make a choice between two different, incompatible, operating systems by marking the partition that contains the desired operating system as active.

To mark a partition as active, use Partition | Mark Active. This defines which partition contains the operating system and startup files (and which partition boots).

If you mark more than one partition as active, then the first active partition is the partition that boots.

Saving Configurations

Save and restore the current drive configuration (partitions, drive letters, striping, volume sets, and so on) with Partition | Configuration. You should save the configuration before you upgrade to a different operating system version, and as a periodic measure to ease recovery in the event of an operating system failure.

To save your configuration information, follow the steps below:

1. Select Partition | Configuration | Save.
2. Insert a (blank) formatted floppy disk in drive A to save the current configuration. The configuration is automatically saved on the diskette in a file called SYSTEM.

After saving configuration information, you can recover the configuration. To do this, follow the steps below:

1. Select Partition | Configuration | Restore. The configuration is restored from the file called SYSTEM, contained on the floppy disk in drive A.
2. For users who have multiple installations of Windows NT, you can search for another installation of Windows NT and load that installation's configuration. To do this, select Partition | Configuration | Search. Drive letters, and so on, are restored but new partitions are not created or deleted.

When loading configurations, any changes made with Disk Administrator prior to searching (and loading a configuration) for another installation of Windows NT will be lost, with the possibility of data becoming inaccessible.

Committing Changes

Many of the changes to partitions and drives are not immediately written to the drive. To force Disk Administrator to write these changes, choose Partition | Commit Changes Now. This causes Disk Administrator to write all partition changes to the necessary locations. There is no going back once the changes have been committed!

If you do not commit changes, Disk Manager will prompt you to save (or discard) changes when you exit.

Working With Fault Tolerance

When your server reliability is a primary consideration, you may choose to either use a stripe set with parity (a RAID 5 implementation) or to create mirror sets.

RAID

RAID (Redundant Arrays of Inexpensive Disks) technology provides fault tolerance for Windows NT 4 Server (and other servers). The RAID technology works by using an array of inexpensive disks to store data. The following levels of fault tolerance are available with RAID systems, though Windows NT 4 Server only supports RAID levels 0, 1, and 5:

- RAID level 0—Disk striping only. Provides improved fixed-disk read performance by sequentially placing blocks of data on multiple disks. RAID level 0 disk striping by itself doesn't provide fault tolerance, only improved performance.
- RAID level 1—Disk mirroring. Uses a set of drives to store identical copies of data on two fixed disk drives. Each write to one member of the mirror set and is duplicated on the other member of the mirror set. If the drive in the mirror set fails, Windows NT 4 Server automatically uses the remaining operable disk.

  The advantage of disk mirroring is that only two drives are required, whereas RAID 5 requires three or more disks. If the drive that fails is the boot disk, you must boot from your ERD (Emergency Repair Disk) and refresh the operating system on the second drive.
- RAID level 2—Disk striping. Writes blocks of data across two or more drives. A third (and perhaps fourth) drive stores error-correction code. In the event of a failure, an error-correcting code regenerates data that was contained on the failed drive. Level 2 is faster when reading than level 1. Level 2 is not used in current RAID systems because of its inefficient method of storing data.
- RAID level 3—Disk striping. Works much like level 2. The costs of implementing level 2 are lower, as the error-correcting code is smaller. With level 3, one disk drive is required to store parity information that allows you to recover the data from the other drives. Level 3 is used for applications such as client-server (Microsoft SQL Server, for example) that use very large files.
- RAID level 4—Disk striping. Uses a technique similar to level 3, but the stripe blocks are larger for more efficiency.

- RAID level 5—Disk striping *with parity*. Level 5 uses level 4's larger blocks, and stripes the parity data across all disks, rather than storing parity information on a dedicated drive. The RAID system (Windows NT 4 Server) ensures that the parity and data are always stored on different drives. Though level 5 is slower writing data than level 1, the read performance is better.

Windows NT Server lets you choose either RAID level 0 (striping), 1 (mirroring), or RAID level 5 (striping with parity). Both RAID levels 1 and 5 offer redundancy to keep Windows NT 4 Server operating even when a drive fails. RAID level 5 is currently the favored method of providing disk drive fault tolerance; it is more efficient, though level 5 does require three (or more) drives.

If there are multiple drive failures, then the system will fail; Windows NT 4 Server is unable to reconstruct the missing data when more than one drive in a RAID system fails. Low-cost (well under $200 per gigabyte and still falling) fixed-disk drives that offer excellent reliability, with advertised MTBF (mean time between failures) rates of 800,000 to 1,000,000 hours are easily available.

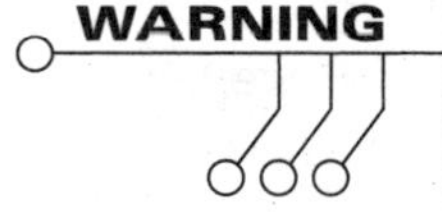

Regardless of what level of RAID is implemented, RAID isn't effective if multiple drives are damaged. Natural disasters, especially lightning and flooding, can easily destroy all the drives in a RAID system at once.

Infant mortality is the term used for failures early in the life of a drive. The failure rate is much higher for the first few months of a drive's life than at any other time (other than the first few seconds after being dropped on the floor). Be very aggressive with backups when new drives have been installed.

Adaptec and several other companies offer total RAID products, which consist of hardware (controllers, drives, cables, and so on), and software. These products are valuable for large Windows NT 4 Server installations, though there is no reason why you cannot create your own RAID system with standard components and Windows NT 4 Server's built-in RAID support.

Using Mirror Sets

A mirror set is a configuration where all data is duplicated on two different physical drives. A mirror set is RAID level 1. If either of the physical drives fails, you can quickly and easily extract the copy of the data on the second drive in the mirror set. For systems with online requirements (such as order processing and other real-time systems), a mirror set offers the highest degree of confidence in the system's data, with quick recovery times.

To create a mirror drive set, select Fault Tolerance | Establish Mirror. To establish a mirror, you must have a free space on another physical drive that is the same size (or larger) than the partition that you want to mirror. Both the primary partition and the mirror are referred to by the same drive letter. All data written to files on that drive letter are written to both physical drives.

If you have problems with the mirror set (or simply don't need to use mirroring for some reason) you can break apart the mirror volume set with Disk Administrator's Fault Tolerance | Break Mirror. This selection breaks the linkage between an existing mirrored drive set. The mirror (second drive) then is given its own drive letter. No files on either drive are lost; however, any writes to the original mirrored drive are no longer written to the mirror drive.

Stripe Sets

Similar to a volume set, stripe sets combine multiple hard drives into a single, large, logical volume. The differences between a stripe set and a volume set are:

- A stripe set requires that each component drive's space be identical in size. With volume set, each component can be different in size.
- A stripe set offers enhanced performance as data is spread effectively between multiple drives. With a volume set, the data can be spread between multiple drives, but this is not guaranteed, or even likely to happen.

- A stripe set is RAID level 0. RAID level 0 offers no enhanced data reliability. (RAID level 0 actually reduces data reliability, since if any part of a stripe set fails, the contents of the entire stripe set is lost.) A volume set is not part of the RAID specification.
- A stripe set can be created with parity, creating a RAID level 5 implementation, which offers enhanced reliability. More on this later!
- A failure of a stripe set drive, when the stripe set was generated without parity, usually results in the loss of all data in the stripe set. A failure of a stripe set drive, when the stripe set was generated with parity, often results in the loss of little or no data on the stripe set. A failure of a volume set drive typically results in the loss of at least some, and perhaps all data on the stripe set.

To create stripe sets, select Partition | Create Stripe Set. A stripe set is created in the same manner as a volume set. As mentioned above, there are additional restrictions to a stripe set: each member of the stripe set must be the same size, and on a different physical volume (Disk Administrator helps manage the size allocation for stripe sets).

For more information on stripe sets with parity, see the "Working With Fault Tolerance" section earlier in this chapter. Additional information on stripe sets with parity is found below, where we cover fault tolerance configurations.

Stripe Sets With Parity

As shown above, a stripe set (without parity) is created using two (or more) areas of free space, which are then built into a single larger volume. A basic stripe set has virtually no fault tolerance.

For a stripe set to have fault-tolerance protection, it is necessary to add parity-information stripes. In Windows NT 4 Server, disk striping with parity includes one parity stripe per row. A minimum of three physical drives is required when creating a stripe set with parity.

You can create a stripe set with parity, which implements RAID 5, using Fault Tolerance | Create Stripe Set with Parity.

Unlike mirrored sets which are quickly recovered, when a failure occurs in a stripe set with parity, the drive's contents must be recovered using Fault Tolerance | Regenerate. When a volume created as a stripe set fails (typically catastrophically), the stripe set becomes an orphan.

To recover the stripe set, you must regenerate the data from the parity stripe. To regenerate the stripe set, you must select a new area of free space that is either equal to or larger than the other stripe set members, and use Fault Tolerance | Regenerate.

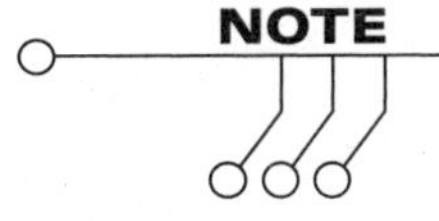

If you are using identical drives, then it is wise to have a spare drive (tested, formatted, and ready to use) in the event that you have a failure with your mirror or stripe set. Having a spare drive allows you to recover as quickly as possible, without having to purchase a new replacement drive.

Using the Disk Administrator's Tools

The Disk Administrator's Tools menu items allow you to manipulate drives. Functions for formatting, error checking, and setting the drive label and letter are available in the Tools menu. The Tools menu displays as the context menu when you right-click on a drive, making it easy to access these functions.

Formatting Drives

You must format both new drives that have never been formatted as well as drives that need to be *cleaned.* Cleaning is removing all files from the drive without using a delete command sequence.

To format a drive, select Tools | Change Format. You can format new drives as well as drives that were previously formatted. The Disk Administrator's format functionality is generally identical to the MS-DOS FORMAT command. The types of formatting supported include both FAT and NTFS for hard drives, and FAT for floppy drives. A floppy drive cannot be formatted using the NTFS file system.

Checking for Errors

Periodically, all drives should be checked for errors, especially drives that use the FAT file system. Generally, an NTFS file system drive is not as likely to fail, but you cannot go wrong checking NTFS drives. To check a drive, use Tools | Check for Errors. A drive can be checked for errors (using CHKDSK's functionality), and you can optionally repair any errors detected.

For those drives that are currently being used (typically there are open files on the drive), a check for errors can be scheduled for a later time. After the check, a report displays that can be printed or logged if you desire.

Labeling

The volume label for any drive (excluding diskettes) can be set using Tools | Set Volume Label.

For a FAT volume, the label can be no more than 11 characters, and NTFS volumes can have labels of 31 or fewer characters.

Assigning Drive Letters

You can modify the drive letter assigned to any hard drive or CD drive using Tools | Assign Drive Letter. For example, on our network, all CD-ROM drives use drive letters that range from S to Z. All clients establish links to the CD drives using the same letters, so that S is the same CD drive on all machines, both the server and the client users. However, be careful when changing a drive letter assignment, as many MS-DOS and Windows 95 applications assume that a drive is at a specific location.

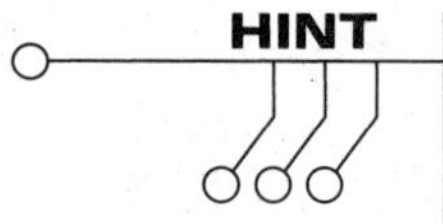

Assign your CD-ROM drives to higher letters (such as S, T, ...) so that added hard drives may be contiguous using lower letters (such as C, D, ...).

Viewing Properties

To display the properties of the current selection, use Tools | Properties. The Properties menu item displays the Volume Properties dialog box, as shown in Figure 8-1.

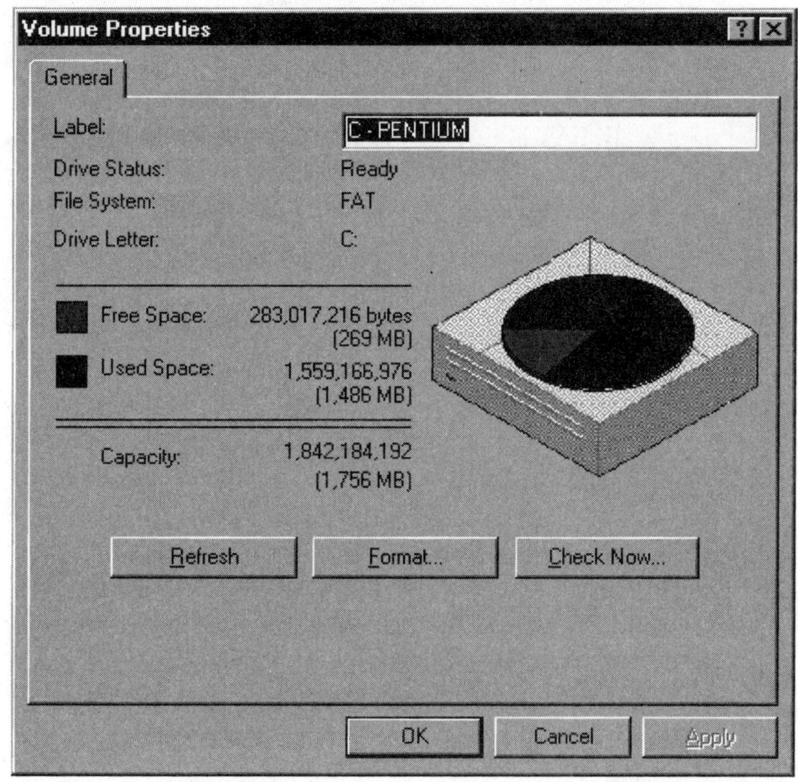

Figure 8-1: The Disk Administrator's Volume Properties dialog box.

File Formats

Windows NT 4 supports two file formats: NTFS (NT File System) and FAT (File Allocation Table). FAT has been used on PC-compatible computers since they were first developed. NTFS is newer, introduced by Microsoft with Windows NT.

FAT is suitable for smaller drives (FAT-16 will work only with smaller drives, and FAT-32 is not yet supported by Windows NT). As well, FAT is not secure and has a number of inefficiencies built-in, including excessive wasted space and an inefficient directory structure. The only benefits of FAT are that FAT is compatible with MS-DOS and Windows 95, and FAT may be faster on drives that are smaller than 500MB in size.

NTFS (NT File System) corrects the shortcomings of FAT, creating a file system that is secure (a necessity for any file server) and efficient.

Benefits of NTFS

The user interface with NTFS is very similar to that of FAT. Typically, a user will neither know nor care that files are stored on an NTFS volume rather than on a FAT volume. Although FAT volumes have a number of special items stored on the disk (such as the FAT and Root directory), NTFS does not allocate special areas to system overhead. With NTFS, there is no inherent requirement that the drive support 512 byte sectors, for example. This is critical for Windows NT 4 Server, which is defined as a portable operating system.

NTFS is intended to:

- Provide a reliable file system, designed for Windows NT Server (though usable with Windows NT Workstation).
- Be an extensible file system with optional features that can be added or removed as needed.
- Provide support for POSIX (Portable Operating System Interface).
- Not be limited by the restrictions of FAT-based file systems.

NTFS provides valuable reliability features. The ability to recover from a problem, the ability to "remove fatal single-sector errors," and support for "hot fixing" are all parts of the NTFS enhancements. NTFS keeps a record of transactions made on the volume. If there are problems with the NTFS volume, NTFS uses this record to recover from the errors.

Microsoft recommends that an NTFS volume be at least 400MB in size, or larger. This is because of the additional overhead that NTFS imposes for items such as the transaction log. As well, with NTFS, the file system does not degrade when the size of the volume increases.

Comparing NTFS to Other Formats

Selecting a partition or drive's file format is usually a simple task. There are several constraining factors. For example, FAT-16 limits partitions to 2 or 4GB. FAT-32 limits partitions to a much larger value—2TB. And NTFS allows partitions to be even larger in size—1.844674407371e+19 bytes.

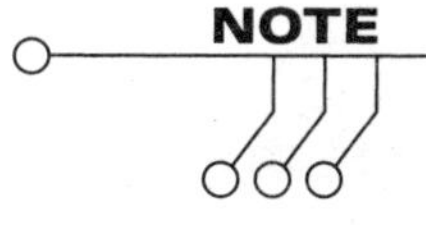

Just how big is a terabyte *(TB)? Try 1,000,000,000,000 (yep, that's one trillion, or one thousand gigabytes). Which leaves us with the issue of how large is the largest NTFS partition? Only about a million times larger, that's all. But no need to lose sleep today: no drive manufacturer has announced terabyte-sized drives, at least not yet!*

However, one must remember that if the computer is dual booted to Windows 95, MS-DOS, or any other operating system that does not support the NTFS file system, then NTFS partitions will not be visible to the Windows 95 operating system. If the system has Windows 95 already installed and is using DriveSpace 3 disk compression, then any drives compressed with DriveSpace 3 will not be accessible to Windows NT 4 Server.

Table 8-1, below, shows a comparison between FAT-16, FAT-32, NTFS, and HPFS. HPFS is shown only as it was supported with earlier versions of Windows NT Server—HPFS is no longer supported by Windows NT, as of Windows NT Version 4. Some of the specifications for FAT-32 were not available when this book was written. For a fuller review of FAT-32, check Microsoft's Internet WWW site. Search for the keyword FAT-32.

Attribute	Operating system			
	FAT-16 (Windows 95)	FAT-32 (Windows 95)	NTFS	HPFS*
Filename/ Directory length	255 UNICODE	255 UNICODE	255 UNICODE	254 DBCs
File size	2,147,483,648 bytes	(Not specified)	1.844674407371 ↵ e+19 bytes	About 4BG
Partition size	2,147,483,648 bytes	2 terabytes in size	1.844674407371 ↵ e+19 bytes	2^{41} bytes
Attributes	Fixed	Fixed	Extendible	Extendible
Directories	Unsorted	Unsorted	Btree	Btree
Allocation	Clusters	Clusters	Clusters	Sectors
Efficient for partition sizes of:	< 500MB	500MB - 10GB	> 400MB	200 to 400MB
Accessible through:	Windows 95, MS-DOS, and Windows NT	Windows 95, Windows NT 4 Server planned	Windows NT only (no Windows 95 support planned)	OS/2 only (no Windows NT 4 Server support)

Table 8-1: FAT-16, FAT-32, NTFS, and HPFS comparison.

Differences exist in the way these systems recover from errors. When you run CHKDSK on a FAT volume, the various pointers and structures are checked for consistency. If there are problems with a FAT volume, CHKDSK can only do a few nominal things to repair the damage. There is little or no record of transactions on a FAT volume. With an NTFS volume, the log of transactions is maintained. With this transaction log, CHKDSK is able to "roll back" the transactions and then recover the file system.

With FAT, if there are any hard read errors on any of the system areas (such as the FAT table or the root directory), then the entire contents of the drive may be lost. With NTFS, special system objects are generally avoided. Those necessary special objects (such as the NTFS Master File Table (MFT)) are protected in a number of ways, such as keeping multiple copies of the MFT. The actual number of copies of the MFT is dependent on the size of the NTFS volume.

Converting From FAT to NTFS

Users who have FAT- or HPFS-based file systems may find it advantageous to convert to NTFS. There are two methods of converting: destructively (by formatting) with Disk Administrator, and non-destructively using the CONVERT utility.

Typically, converting from a FAT-based file system to the NTFS file system is a straightforward process. When you install Windows NT 4 Server, the setup program prompts you to determine if you wish to convert the FAT volume to NTFS. If you have chosen to not convert to NTFS at installation time, you can convert at any later time that you desire, using Disk Administrator or the CONVERT utility.

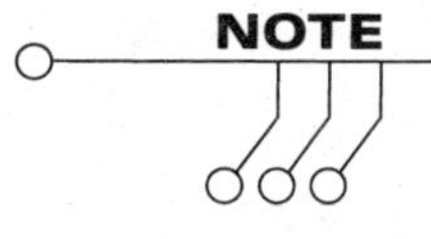

Don't convert to NTFS if you are planning to dual boot your system with either MS-DOS or Windows 95. Neither operating system can access NTFS volumes.

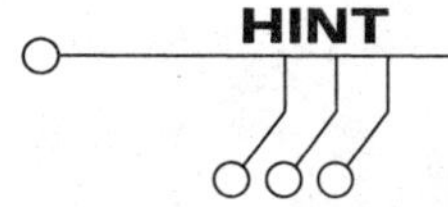

If you must read an NTFS partition using a system that is dual booted into either MS-DOS or Windows 95, you could try using the utility NTFSDOS Version 1.1, which you can obtain from the Internet site: ftp://ftp.ora.com/pub/examples/windows/win95.update/ntfsdos.html. *However, this utility allows the NTFS partition to be read only—you will not be able to write files to the NTFS drive.*

Using the Disk Administrator to Destructively Convert

Please remember that conversion from FAT to NTFS is destructive when the conversion is done with the Windows NT 4 Server's Disk Administrator. If you want to do a non-destructive conversion to NTFS, then you must use the CONVERT utility, which is described below.

When you format a drive or partition, you destroy all data on that drive or partition. If you do not want the data destroyed, use the CONVERT utility described in the next section.

To convert from FAT to NTFS, (or to simply reformat the volume) using Disk Administrator, follow the steps below:

1. Select the FAT volume you want to convert to NTFS.
2. Select the Tools menu selection Change Format.
3. The Change Format dialog box (see Figure 8-2) allows you to select either FAT or NTFS. Select the desired format, and respond to the confirmation prompt dialog.
4. The drive will be formatted. Note: you can select a quick format if the file format type is not being changed.

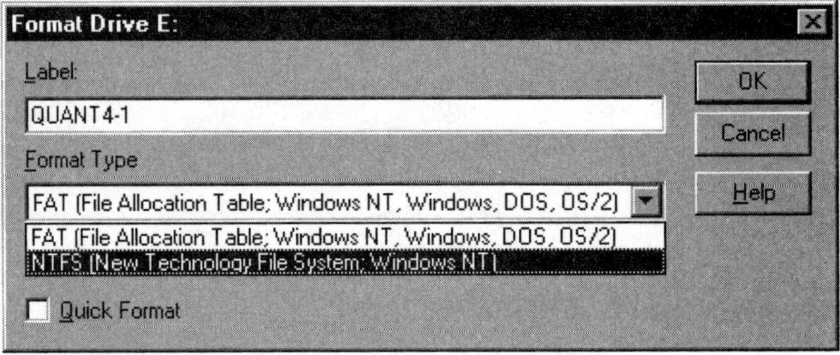

Figure 8-2: The Disk Administrator Format dialog.

Using the CONVERT Utility to Non-Destructively Convert

You can use the Windows NT 4 Server utility CONVERT to change a FAT volume to an NTFS volume. This utility is non-destructive (unlike Disk Manager's reformat, which destroys the drive's contents), making a conversion from FAT to NTFS easier.

To run CONVERT, use the following command line and arguments:

```
CONVERT drive: /FS:NTFS [/V]
```

Here is a breakdown of the command line:

- *drive:*—The drive to convert to NTFS. It is not possible to convert the current drive.
- */FS:NTFS*—Specifies that the volume will be converted to NTFS.
- */V*—The verbose mode, which provides progress information to the user.

If, for some reason, CONVERT is unable to exclusively lock the drive, then you will receive an error message, and CONVERT will prompt to schedule the conversion at the next boot time.

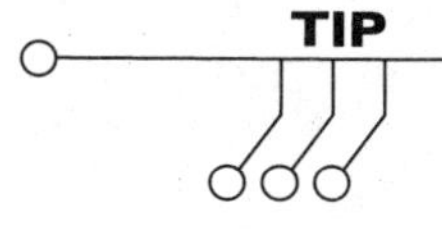

The most common reason that the drive cannot be locked is that the Windows NT 4 Server swap file is located on the drive. Check this first, and if the swap file can be moved, then move it, and retry the conversion.

Compressing Files Using Windows Explorer

One thing that Windows NT 4 Server Explorer manages under Windows NT 4 Server is compression. Unlike Windows 95 and FAT volumes, you can compress an NTFS volume on a file-by-file, directory-by-directory, or volume-by-volume basis.

The concept of compression is a bit different from that of DriveSpace in that the compression engine is built into the NTFS driver, and you will not receive much information about the effects of compression once the files on an NTFS volume have been compressed. For example, when you perform a DIR command on a compressed directory, you will see the same number of bytes in the files listed as you would have seen had the directory not been compressed.

As an example, I compressed an NTFS drive. This drive had almost 23,000 files. Under FAT, without compression, these files occupied 685MB of space on the drive. Under NTFS, again without compression, these same files occupied about the same amount of space. Once compressed, the numbers were quite different, with the files using only a bit over 350MB in disk space.

The count of files differs between a FAT volume and an NTFS volume. With NTFS volumes, folders are not counted towards the final file count, while with FAT, folders (directories and subdirectories) do count towards the final file count. Overall, NTFS compression gained about a 46% savings in free space on the drive. This is very competitive, though not as good, as compression with DriveSpace under Windows 95.

With the NTFS compression scheme, it can be difficult to determine what the free space on a drive is if you try to compute this value. You must, therefore, use the Windows NT 4 Server utilities (such as CHKDSK, DIR, or Explorer) to determine how much free space is available on a particular volume.

Compressing a File or Folder

To compress a file or folder, follow the steps below:

1. Select the object you want to compress in Explorer.
2. Display the object's properties, either by selecting Properties from the object's context menu, or by selecting File | Properties.
3. Select the General tab. (An example is shown in Figure 8-3).
4. Set Compressed in the Attributes section.
5. Click OK or Apply to compress the object. Click Cancel to discard your request.

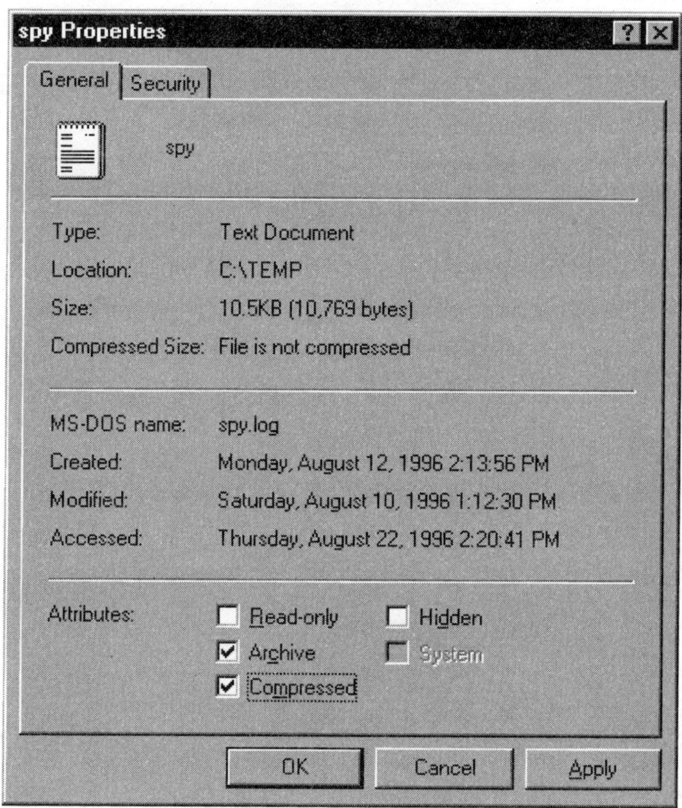

Figure 8-3: Properties, General tab, setting the Compressed Attribute for a file or folder.

Compressing a Drive

To compress a drive, follow the steps below:

1. Select the drive you want to compress in Explorer.
2. Display the drive's properties, either by selecting Properties from the drive's context menu or by selecting File | Properties.
3. Select the General tab. (An example is shown in Figure 8-4.)
4. Set Compressed in the Attributes section.

5. Click OK or Apply to compress the object. Click Cancel to discard your request. For a large volume, compression may take a long time.

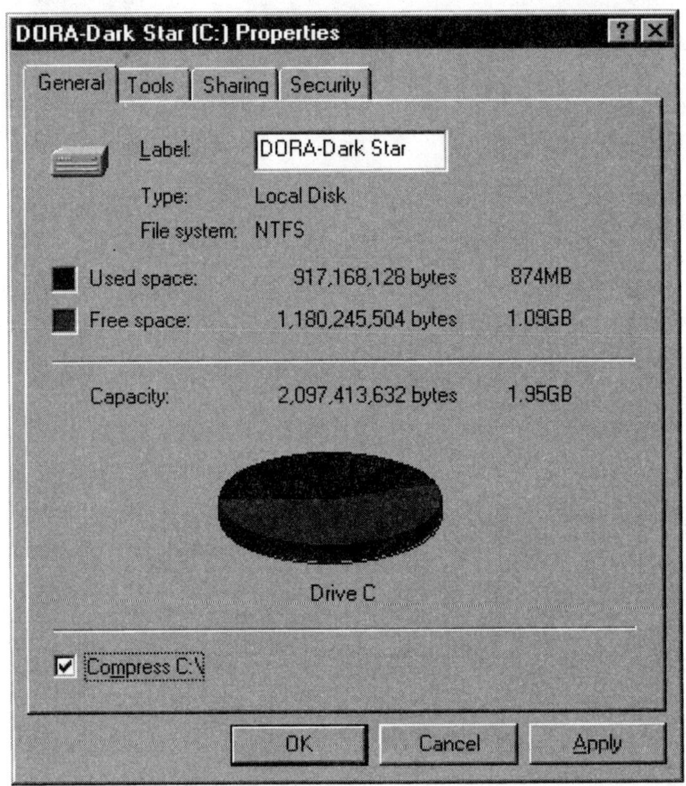

Figure 8-4: Properties, General tab, setting the Compressed Attribute for a drive.

When you compress either a folder or a drive, it can take some time for Windows NT 4 Server to do the compression.

Moving On

In this chapter, I showed you how to improve the performance and reliability of your Windows NT 4 Server system by using NTFS and RAID. Improvements to systems such as using NTFS and striping, monitoring, and configuration all help improve the system's performance.

The next chapter, "Monitoring Windows NT 4 Server Performance," delves into the Performance Monitor, the Network Monitor, and the Windows NT Task Manager (which has simple performance-monitoring capabilities).

9

Monitoring Windows NT 4 Server Perfomance

In this chapter, I'll cover several of the tools that allow us to monitor the performance of Windows NT 4 Server:

- The Network Monitor, which monitors the status and efficiency of the network.
- The Performance Monitor, a powerful, extensible, monitoring tool that monitors every facet of the Windows NT 4 Server operating system.
- The Task Manager, a program that provides a quick look at the system's performance and determines whether there are any applications that are utilizing excessive system resources.

Monitoring a system is only part of the battle. Once you have information about system performance, you must then decide how best to use this data! Pretty graphics, charts, and large files containing data won't make your system work any better. What will help is thoughtful evaluation of the data, which this chapter helps you accomplish.

There is an old saying that "you can never be too rich or too beautiful." Well, with system performance monitoring for Windows NT 4 Server, you certainly can have too much data. The Performance Monitor allows you to monitor aspects of the system's performance that are not, for the great majority of us, too useful. I'll cover the most useful data you'll encounter, then if you still need more, we'll delve deeper into the Performance Monitor objects and functions.

The Network Monitor

The Network Monitor Tools and Agent component includes the Network Monitor Agent and the Network Monitor program. You can install both programs or install just the Network Monitor Agent.

Network Monitor Agent is used to monitor performance remotely. If your network has multiple servers, you can monitor the performance of each server from a single location. If the network has only one server, then Network Monitor Agent is not needed.

As with other Windows NT 4 Server tools and components, you may install Network Monitor Agent and the Network Monitor program either when initially installing Windows NT 4 Server, or at a later time, as described below.

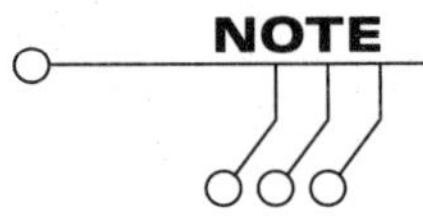

Systems Management Server (SMS) comes with a version of Network Monitor Agent. SMS is described in Chapter 10, "Microsoft Back Office."

Generally, you should install both the Monitor program and the Monitor Agent, so that you are able to run the Network Monitor program at the Windows NT 4 Server, or perhaps at a remote location.

Installing the Network Monitor Agent and Tools

To install Network Monitor Agent and Network Monitor Tools after you have installed Windows NT 4 Server, start the Control Panel's Network applet and follow the steps below:

1. Select the Services tab, and click the Add button.
2. In the Select Network Service dialog box, select "Network Monitor Tools and Agent."
3. Click OK.

To remove Network Monitor Agent, in the Control Panel's Network applet's Protocols tab, select "Network Monitor Agent." Then click the Remove button to remove the "Network Monitor Agent."

To remove Network Monitor Tools and Agent (if you have both installed), in the Control Panel's Network applet's Protocols tab, select "Network Monitor Tools and Agent." Then click the Remove button to remove the "Network Monitor Tools and Agent."

There is no automated uninstall for the Network Monitor Tools—these must be removed manually using either Explorer or a command prompt window.

Using the Network Monitor Program

The Network Monitor program allows you to monitor many of the aspects of the network. Figure 9-1 shows the Network Monitor running on a relatively lightly loaded network.

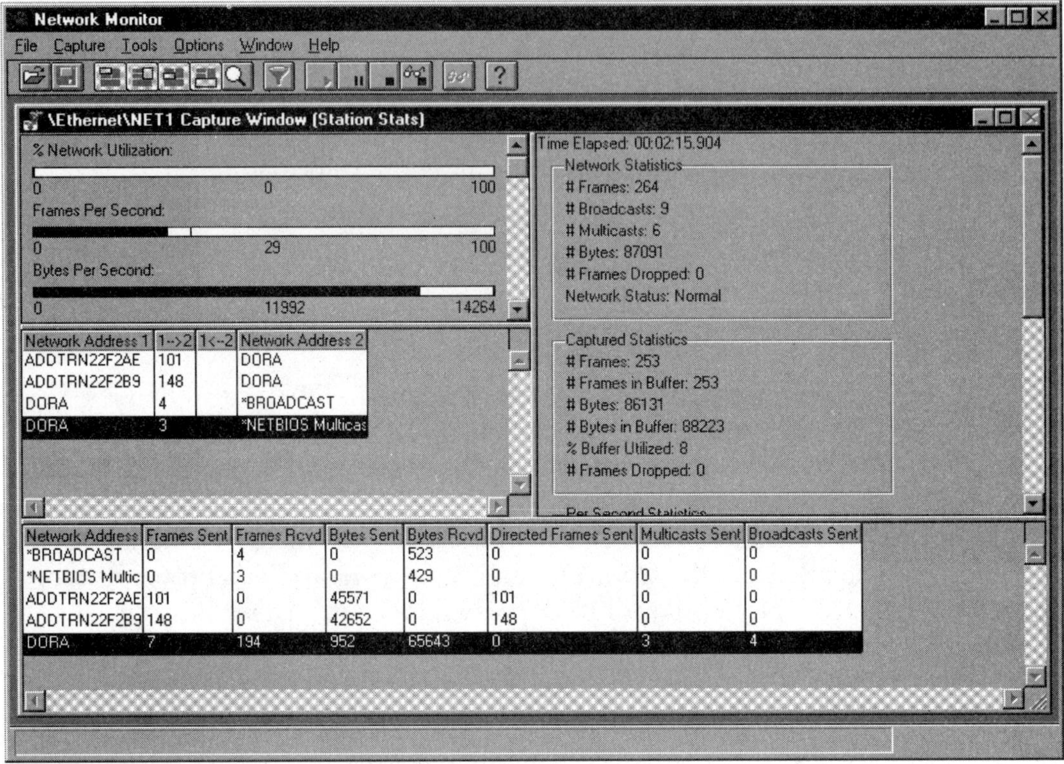

Figure 9-1: The Network Monitor program.

The Network Monitor program has a number of built-in tools. You start each tool by using the Network Monitor's Tools menu selection. Below are listed the Network Monitor tools and their functionality.

- Identify Network Monitor Users—Finds Network Monitor Users, including yourself, using the Other Network Monitor Installations dialog box (see Figure 9-2).
- Find Routers—Finds routers on your network, if there are any. If you do not have any routers on your network, this menu selection is disabled.
- Tools | Performance Monitor—Launches the Windows NT 4 Server Performance Monitor. You may select various parameters to monitor (both network and general system oriented).

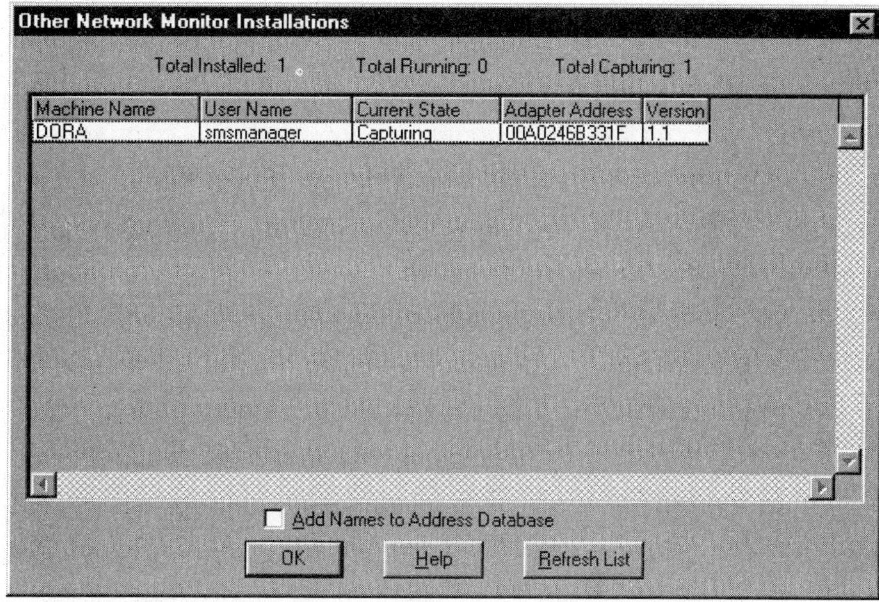

Figure 9-2: The Other Network Monitor Installations dialog box.

The Network Monitor program serves as a valuable tool in monitoring the performance of your network.

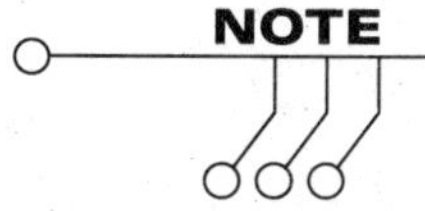

There is a version of Network Monitor for Windows 95, which allows remote monitoring of the network's status.

With the Network Monitor Agent running on a remote Windows NT 4 Server, an SMS (System Management Services) administrator can use the Network Monitor utility to capture network activity seen by the other system's network adapter card.

When using Network Monitor, the NIC in the system that runs the Network Monitoring Agent must support promiscuous mode. Network Monitor is typically used to determine whether systems are broadcasting excessively on the network.

Configuring the Network Monitor Agent

Configuring the Network Monitor Agent is not difficult. You must only supply optional passwords and descriptive names for your network adapters. To configure the Network Monitor Agent, open the Control Panel and start the Monitoring Agent applet. Figure 9-3 shows the main screen for this applet, which is titled "Configure Network Monitoring Agent." On this screen are three buttons (Change Password, Describe Net Cards, and Reset Defaults).

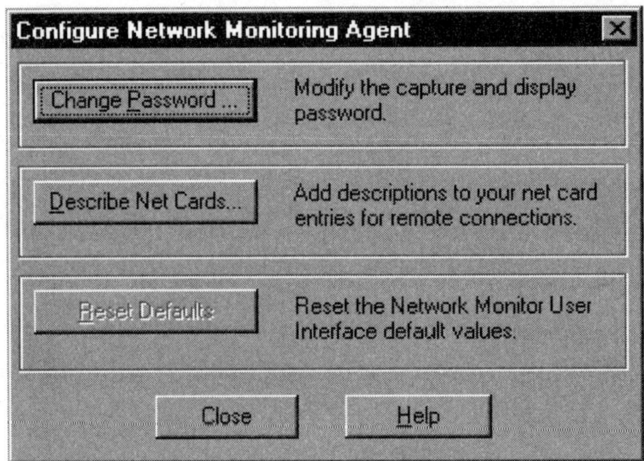

Figure 9-3: Configure Network Monitoring Agent.

When you select the Change Password button on this window, the Network Monitoring Password Change dialog box displays (see Figure 9-4). You can enter new or changed passwords for each functionality, or choose to not use passwords at all.

When you select Describe Network, the Describe Net Cards dialog box displays (see Figure 9-5). You may enter new or changed descriptions for each network card by using the Edit Description button. A simple change name dialog box allows you to provide the description.

Network Monitoring Password Change

You can control access to Network Monitor with two types of passwords. The Display password will restrict a user to viewing only previously saved capture files. The Capture password allows the user to capture data, as well as to view capture files.

Old Capture Password

Password: ***** — Enter the old capture password for validation.

Display Password

Password: *****

Confirm: ***** — This password will only grant permission to view previously saved capture files.

Capture Password

Password: *****

Confirm: ***** — This password will grant permission to capture frames and to view capture files.

OK | Cancel | No Password | Help

Figure 9-4: Network Monitoring Password Change.

Describe Net Cards

The following is a list and description of the network cards installed on your system.

When another computer connects to this computer to use it as a Network Monitoring Agent, the card description entered below will be displayed on the connecting computer.

To edit the card descriptions below, highlight the card and push the Edit Description button.

Network Adapters

El59x1 3Com 3C590 Combo

NdisWan2 WAN

OK | Cancel | Edit Description

Figure 9-5: Describe Net Cards dialog.

The adapter "3Com 3C590 Combo" is an Ethernet card that connects to twisted pair, coax, or thicknet cable. Coax is the term used to refer to coaxial cable, where there is a center conductor surrounded by an outer shielding conductor.

Twisted Pair?

What the heck is twisted pair? Well, take it from me, it is not a new rock band. Rather, twisted pair (usually called UTP (Unshielded Twisted Pair)) is becoming very popular as a replacement for Ethernet's thin coax. UTP works differently from coax: while coax connects the workstations and servers to a single "backbone" cable, UTP connects network servers and workstations to hubs, in a star arrangement.

With coax, any break in the network cable can bring the entire network down. Inexperienced users who sometimes disconnect the two cables from the T connector on the NIC usually disrupt perhaps hundreds of network users! Construction work and other accidents that damage the coax are often costly experiences.

With UTP, a broken cable affects only the computer that is connected to the cable, and no other users (of course, if the cable that is damaged is to the server, then disaster results, as the server will be out of service). Users don't have to contend with multiple network cables to their computers, either—a single wire, with a telephone-like connector, is easy to connect and disconnect, allowing users to add and remove workstations to the network quickly, without inconveniencing other users.

Monitoring Performance With the Network Monitor

Now that you have seen the Network Monitor, let's take a look at some of the important things you can see while actually *running* Network Monitor. You must consider your network topology.

- Ethernet comes in two main flavors, each offering two speeds: 10Base2 and 10BaseT (which offer network performance of 10 Mbps), and 100Base2 and 100BaseT (which offer speeds of about 100 Mbps). If you are creating a network that serves a large number of client users, then moving directly into 100Base2 or 100BaseT is a wise move.
- Token Ring, which is used to connect IBM computers. Speeds for Token Ring are slower, 4 or 16 Mbps.
- ArcNet, a declining standard (most ArcNet users are moving to Ethernet), offers only a fraction of the performance of Ethernet.

These figures point out that standard Ethernet can move at a maximum of about 1.2 MB per second. It doesn't take long to figure out that for a network with a large number of users, this rate of performance will not be appreciated by users. High-speed Ethernet, however, can move as much as 12 MB per second, a much better rate of data transfer. Token Ring can move perhaps a bit more than Ethernet; however, in practice, Token Ring's performance is not any better even when comparing the faster Token Ring performance with the slower version of Ethernet's performance.

What does this mean to us as system administrators? Performance wise, that is? First, we need to look at the Network Monitor's performance data.

Performance

The first piece of information presented by Network Monitor is called "% Network Utilization," and even with a moderately loaded network, it rarely exceeds a few percent. Were your network to have a relatively high value here, this could point to some very unusual network traffic. Even with DORA's network delivering over 550KB per second, the network utilization is only 4%. This indicates that the network is, basically, underutilized.

The second piece of information presented by Network Monitor is "Frames Per Second," which tells how many "packets" are being sent between the server and the client workstations. Values here, for a network supporting several workstations doing large data transfers across the network, may range from 350 to 500 frames per second, while Figure 9-6 shows just under 575 frames per second.

The third piece of information presented by Network Monitor is "Bytes Per Second." This information is probably the most important item to monitor in a network. On DORA, when two workstations simultaneously copy a large block of files from the server's drive to a drive local to the workstation, I see transfer rates of 250 to 500KB per second (Figure 9-6 shows a transfer rate of almost 570KB). This figure tells me that my 10Base2 Ethernet installation is running at about 25% to 50% of rated capacity. In a real-world situation, the network would have some difficulty reaching the theoretical maximum: a practical maximum would be somewhat less than the rated maximum. Figure 9-6 shows Network Monitor after a few busy minutes.

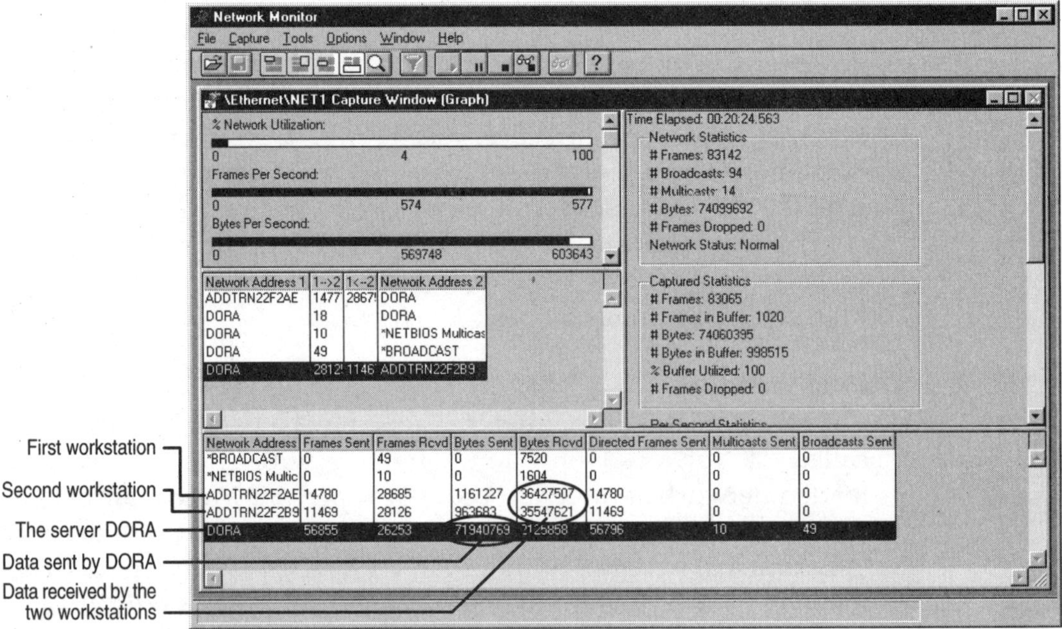

Network Address 1	1-->2	1<--2	Network Address 2
ADDTRN22F2AE	1477	2867	DORA
DORA	18		DORA
DORA	10		*NETBIOS Multicas
DORA	49		*BROADCAST
DORA	2812	1146	ADDTRN22F2B9

Network Address	Frames Sent	Frames Rcvd	Bytes Sent	Bytes Rcvd	Directed Frames Sent	Multicasts Sent	Broadcasts Sent
*BROADCAST	0	49	0	7520	0	0	0
*NETBIOS Multic	0	10	0	1604	0	0	0
ADDTRN22F2AE	14780	28685	1161227	36427507	14780	0	0
ADDTRN22F2B9	11469	28126	963683	35547621	11469	0	0
DORA	56855	26253	71940769	2125858	56796	10	49

Figure 9-6: Network Monitor after two workstations hog the network.

OK, so you constantly see transfer rates 50% to 80% of the maximum, what next? Several issues are important here:

- Can you change where files are located? Does one workstation constantly access a file that is not used by anyone else? Maybe this file could be placed locally to the workstation.
- Can the network be split? Windows NT 4 Server supports multiple NICs. By splitting your network load across two network segments, you can gain substantial performance increases. Since Windows NT 4 Server is able to route between the two (or more) network segments, users probably will not even know that there are multiple segments.
- Faster Ethernet... Moving from 10Base2 (or 10BaseT) to 100Base2 (or 100BaseT) can increase throughput by a factor of ten. This can be costly, however. You would need to replace the network interface cards in both the server(s) and in the workstations. As well, you may need to upgrade the network cabling, especially if the network is twisted pair Ethernet!
- Seek out workstations that utilize most of the network's bandwidth. Network Monitor offers the Station Stats window, which shows each node on the network. Figure 9-6 shows the Station Stats window: two workstations (network addresses ADDTRN22F2AE and ADDTRN22F2B9) are connected to the server DORA, and between them they have received a total of over 71 MB of data. That's a lot of bytes moved across the network.
- In Figure 9-6, we see that the first workstation at ADDTRN22F2AE has received about 36 MB of data. This may be more than your network should be sending: can the work that the workstation is doing over the network be moved to a local drive? Is the workstation reading temporary work files from the network drives that could be read from the workstation's local drive? Is there an imbalance between bytes received and bytes sent by a workstation? This could indicate that the workstation's file access could be better arranged.

When determining performance faults with a network, be careful that you interpret the data correctly. Don't look at peak periods and evaluate the network's performance based on the peak times; rather, take a moving average and use that figure. A big spike in network utilization at 4:55 PM is probably not a reason to upgrade the network!

Faster Networks or It's All in the Wire!

Today we speed up networks by using faster transmission rates. Twisted pair networks cable is rated Level 1 through Level 5, which specifies the speed at which data may be transferred through a cable.

Level 1 and Level 2 are not often used today. Level 1 is suitable only for analog telephone service and should never be used for networks. Level 2 is suitable only for very slow networks, and is typically used only for service with digital telephones.

Most businesses (and many homes) are now wired with Level 3 as a minimum. This means that a small twisted pair 10BaseT network should work with few problems. Any problems noted should be traced to a single workstation without too much problem.

The speed differences between Level 3 and Level 4 do not normally justify the installation of Level 4 cables for 10BaseT installations. When installing 100BaseT, Level 5 wiring is mandatory. Level 4 cable, if it works at all, will probably introduce an unacceptable number of damaged packets in the network.

Data rates for UTP cables are as follows:

- Level 1 is not rated except for analog phone service.
- Level 2 is rated well under 10 Mbps, and should not be used for networks.
- Level 3 is rated at 16 Mbps, and is acceptable for 10BaseT. Do not use Level 3 or Level 4 for new installations—instead, use Level 5.

- Level 4 is rated at 20 Mbps.
- Level 5 is rated at 100 Mbps.

Oh, and those big 25 pair cables that are commonly found in commercial buildings... They are usually rated as Level 1, sometimes Level 2, and they won't work for networks (or for most digital phones, either!).

Errors

Errors. Yes, errors. Look for errors. Check the Network Monitor's Network Card (MAC) Error Statistics (Figure 9-7). *CRC Errors* almost always indicate a cable problem. *Frames Dropped (No Buffers)* are usually a configuration issue—you need to have more buffer space allocated. *Frames Dropped (Hardware)* could indicate any of a number of problems including a hardware problem, misconfigured hardware, or even a cable problem.

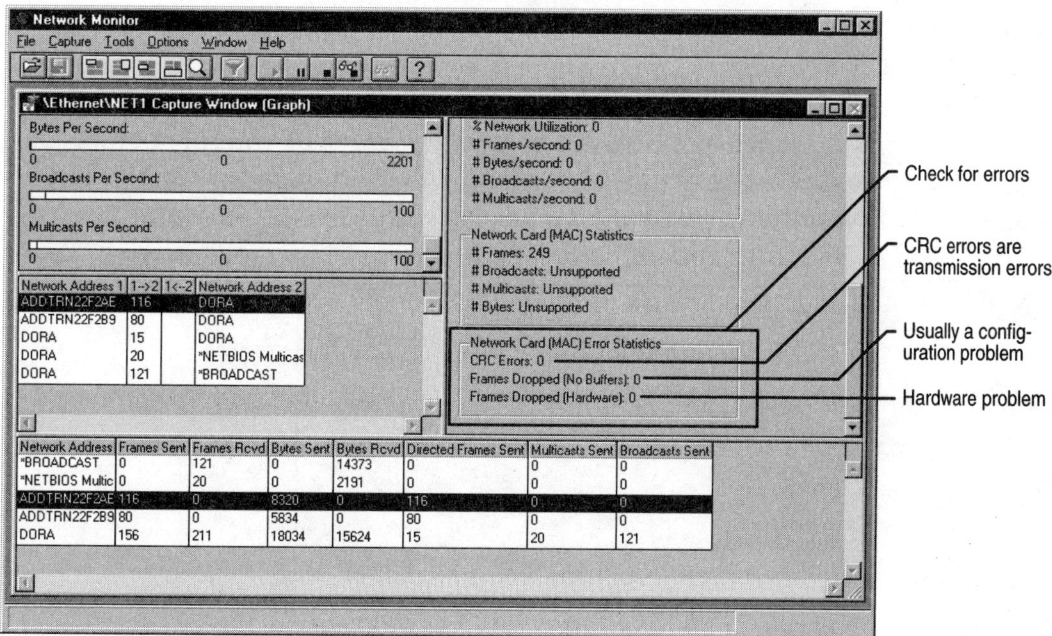

Figure 9-7: Error statistics show where to look for problems.

You must perform an analysis of the network's error rate. You should, if the network is currently running well, obtain some benchmark rates for errors—this will give you a standard to work from in the future when there are problems.

When a network is not working well and the error rate increases, find out why.

- If the network is UTP, is one workstation affected or many?
- If only one workstation is being affected, check the workstation and the cabling between the hub and the workstation.
- If many workstations are affected, are they all on the same hub? Then check the hub, and the cable between the hub and the next point—the next hub or the server.
- If many workstations are being affected, and they are on different hubs, check software configurations, NIC card problems (do all affected workstations have the same NIC?), and other common factors such as locations.

As a test, a two-computer UTP network can be set up without using a hub. This is done using a "cross-over" cable that is wired as shown in Table 9-1. Of course, you must be careful not to use this cable for any use other than a two-computer, no-hub, UTP-connected "network"!

RJ45 pin	RJ45 pin
1 - [TX+]	[RX+] - 3
2 - [TX-]	[RX-] - 6
3 - [RX+]	[TX+] - 1
6 - [RX-]	[TX-] - 2

Table 9-1: Null UTP cable (eliminates the hub for two computers connected with 10BaseT).

This configuration is useful when you need to test the workstation's hardware and software in order to isolate the problem without interfering with the network itself.

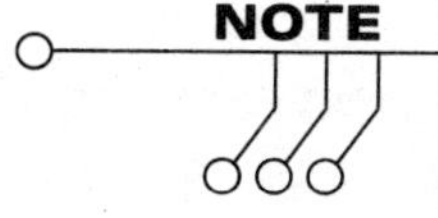

An excellent source of information is "Ethernet Network Questions and Answers" at http://pc-78-120.udac.se:8001/. There is a ton of information in this document!

The Performance Monitor

Starting Performance Monitor

The Windows NT 4 Server Performance Monitor supplements the Network Monitor described above. Much of what the Network Monitor does can be done with the Windows NT 4 Server Performance Monitor. However, the Network Monitor is better adapted to monitoring network-related performance.

To start the Performance Monitor, look in the Start Menu | Programs | Administrative Tools (Common). Once Performance Monitor has started, you will see a blank monitor screen. As with most Windows programs, the Windows NT 4 Server Performance Monitor accepts a command line parameter that allows you to specify a chart settings file. You can then create desktop icons (or place links in the Start Menu) for commonly used charts.

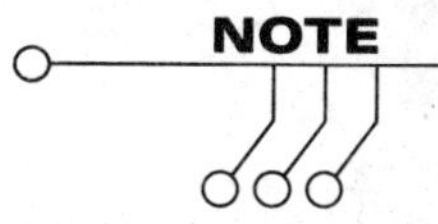

Some examples of using Performance Monitor with saved settings are given in Chapter 11, "Microsoft Exchange Server & Client."

Viewing the Data

The Windows NT 4 Server Performance Monitor can present output in two modes: Histogram view, where the data is presented as a histogram (bar chart), and Graph view, where data is presented as a line chart.

To select the desired view, select Options | Chart from the menu. In the Chart Options dialog box's Gallery group box, click either Histogram (Figure 9-8) or Graph (Figure 9-10).

Histogram View

The histogram view presents data as a set of vertical bars, one for each counter. The bars are sorted in counter order, and all are of the same width.

The histogram view always renders an *instantaneous* view of the counters—there is no history displayed in this mode! Now, why would you want to view data using the histogram?

Graph View

The graph view presents data in a line chart mode. This mode allows you to view data over a period of time. The graph view mode is the default, and most often used mode, mostly because many users don't understand how to get the maximum information from the histogram view.

The graph view is very useful for counters that quickly and constantly change and when a view of how the counters change over a period of time is needed.

Saving Chart Settings

Windows NT 4 Server Performance Monitor saves settings in a file called a chart settings file. You may save any number of chart settings files, and load these files as described below.

Performance Monitor also saves a file called a *workspace*. A workspace defines not only the objects and counters being monitored, but also the visual configuration of Performance Monitor (such as chart type and size).

Chart settings or workspace files are loaded using File | Open.

Counters and Objects

What the Windows NT 4 Server Performance Monitor is monitoring is based on a hierarchy of objects and counters found in objects. As mentioned above, when components are added to the system, they may add new objects and counters.

All objects are made up of one or more counters.

Counters

Counters are what the Performance Monitor uses to determine system performance. Each part of Windows NT 4 Server, and many applications, save performance information in performance counters.

Some counters show factors of an entity. For example, in the System object, there are the following counters that all indicate processor usage (for different types of tasks):

- % Total DPC Time
- % Total Interrupt Time
- % Privileged Time
- % Total User Time

Each of these counters are summed into the counter % Total Processor Time (notice that % Total Processor Time doesn't include idle time, however). Presenting the four components in a histogram allows you to see the relationships between each counter quickly and visually, as Figure 9-8 shows.

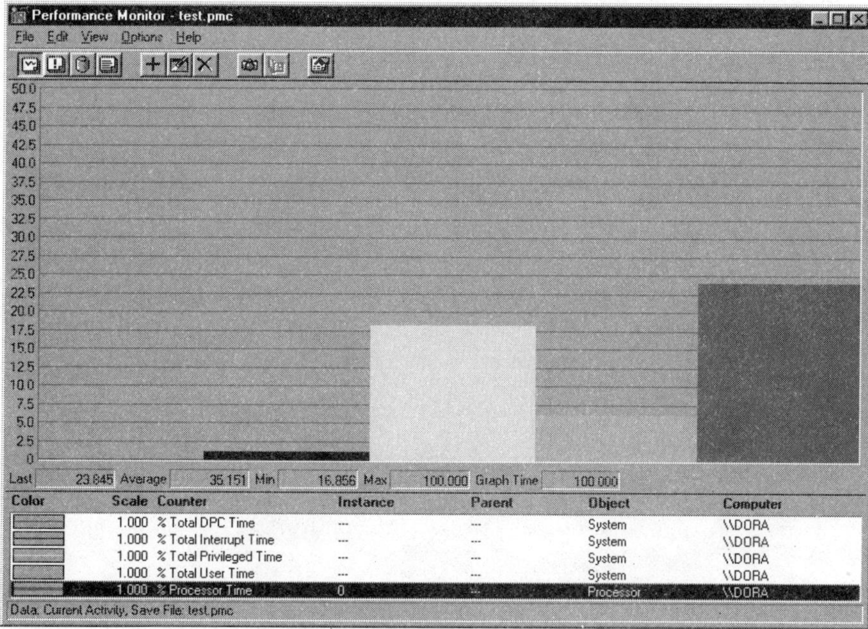

Figure 9-8: A histogram of processor usage.

Another example is to monitor all running applications. Some counters allow you to select an *instance* for the counter. An instance may be a task or process, or a specific CPU (in multi-processor environments).

An example of counters with instances is shown in Figure 9-9. In this figure, I am monitoring 36 processes. The important process in this window is WINWORD, which is shown as having 46% of the processor's time allocated (the initial bar shows the total of all processes). Now, were I having performance problems with my server, I would have to suspect that WINWORD was a problem application. Now, what about that rather tall bar in the middle of the histogram? Well, actually, Windows NT 4 Server Performance Monitor was monitoring itself there! At the time the figure was created, the performance monitor was using a substantial amount of the processor's resources as well.

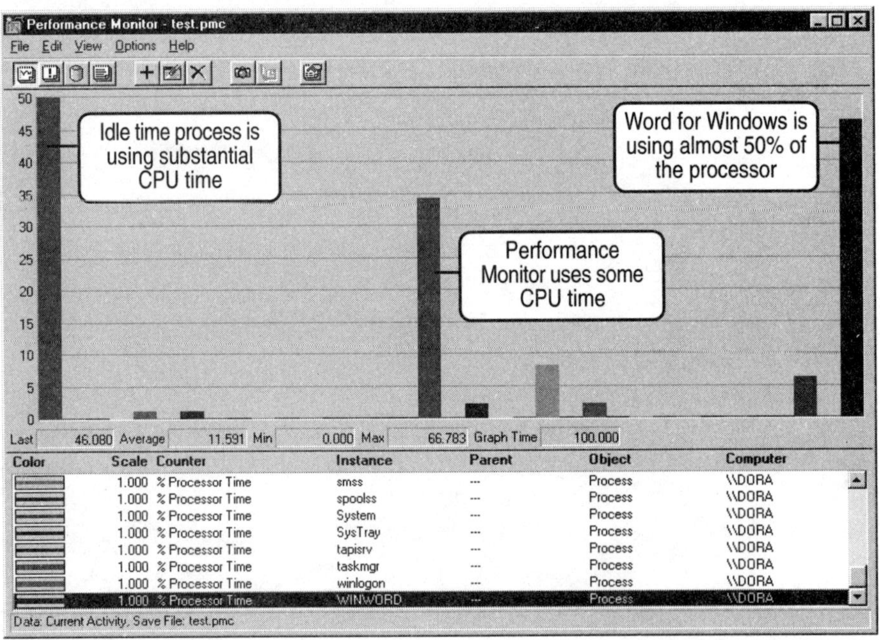

Figure 9-9: Processes usage—WINWORD is using a lot of processor time here!

The above examples show two uses for the histogram view—there are others. Monitoring the different network I/O rates (or disk I/O rates) using a histogram view can be instructive in showing possible bottlenecks in the system. Be creative: try the histogram view. If you find you need more historical data (usually because the bars are constantly changing), then switch back to the graph view.

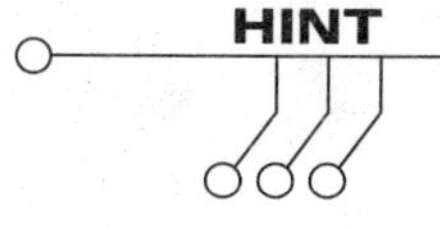

Try monitoring network users using a histogram. You may quickly find which users are "hogging" the system! Specific users who are using a lot of network resources should be checked—can their usage be moved to local resources? Applications that use excessive memory or CPU resources could be moved to other servers or workstations.

Processes and services that are not specific to a given user (or group of users), and are not user processes on the server are candidates for removal to a different server. For example, if SMS server or Microsoft SQL server were utilizing too many resources, this could indicate that now is the time for a new server!

Objects

Objects are collections of counters. Arranged by functionality, each counter in an object is selected for monitoring separately. Use objects to quickly locate a counter to be monitored.

Configuring Performance Monitor

Figure 9-10 shows the Performance Monitor displaying a listing of the CPU and memory usage. These two counters, "% Processor Time," and "% Committed Bytes in Use," provide information about overall system utilization.

- % Processor Time—Indicates the time that the processor is processing non-idle time tasks. Notice how this line shows definite peaks and valleys.
- % Committed Bytes in Use—Indicates the number of bytes of virtual (not physical) memory that have been committed. Virtual memory changes only when an application's memory needs change, such as when applications start, end, or open a document.

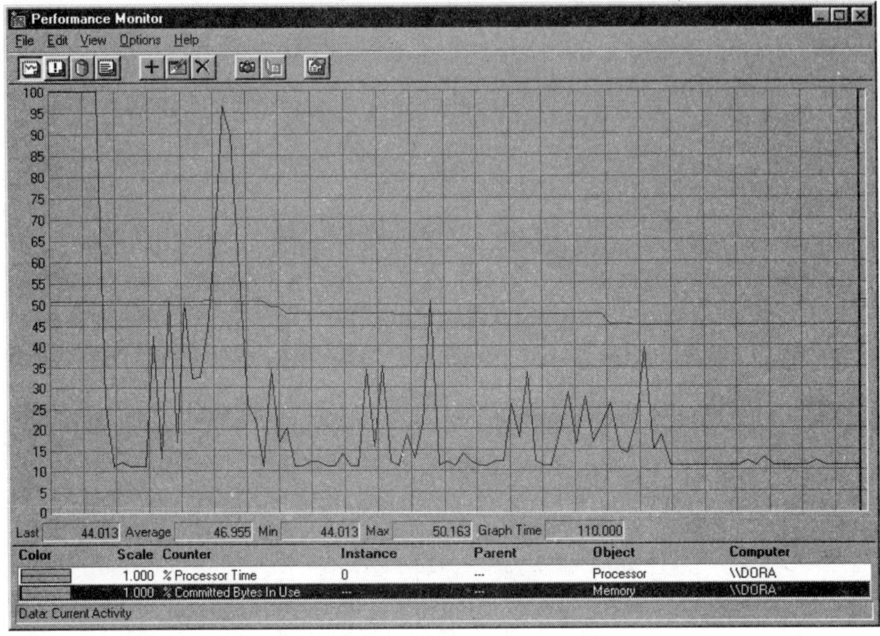

Figure 9-10: Performance Monitor monitoring processor and memory usage.

To add items to the current list of object counters being displayed, you would use the Add to Chart dialog box, which is accessed using the Edit | Add to Chart (the shortcut key is CTRL-I) menu selection. Figure 9-11 shows the Add to Chart dialog box.

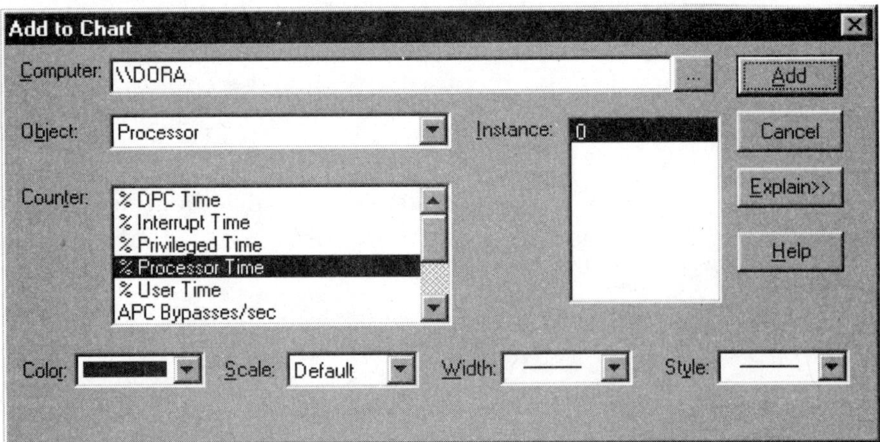

Figure 9-11: Adding the Processor object's "% Processor Time" to the chart.

The Performance Monitor can monitor a vast number of system parameters. As well, components of Windows NT 4 Server, Microsoft BackOffice, Microsoft Exchange Server, and other systems are able to add new objects and counters to Performance Monitor when they are installed.

Objects and Counters in Performance Monitor

It is well beyond the scope of this book to cover all possible monitor objects—in fact, there is no way to even know which applications and systems add new objects until the application or system is installed.

Instead, I've covered some of the more significant objects that Windows NT 4 Server uses. If you have installed items such as Microsoft Exchange Server, monitor these items as well. On dedicated servers, launching multiple Performance Monitors is one way to monitor several objects at one time without the display of monitored objects and counters becoming too complex. A graph with more than a few items can become very confusing quickly; however, selecting the Histogram display (use the Chart Options dialog, by selecting Options | Chart) allows the display of perhaps 15 to 20 items if necessary.

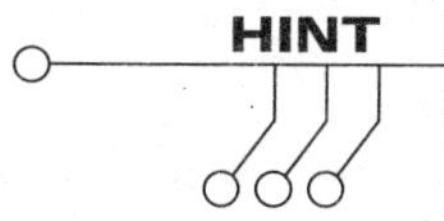

Performance Monitor is extensible. However, extending Performance Monitor requires a competent programmer who can create the necessary DLL files. To learn more about Windows NT 4 Server Performance Monitor DLLs and creating monitors, refer to the Windows NT Server Device Driver Kit (DDK).

Microsoft has made the source code for the Windows NT 4 Server Performance Monitor available as sample code included with the Windows NT SDK. You can therefore have your programming staff rewrite or redesign the Windows NT 4 Server Performance Monitor to suit your specific needs.

Below are listed some of the more important objects and the counters that are found in these objects. You could include all objects and counters and later eliminate those that do not provide significant data.

Some counters won't seem to move or change. This is generally because the event the counter is monitoring is not happening—you are probably looking in the wrong place. Other counters change in spurts and jumps. Counters for network activity follow the client user's network usage. Counters for processor and memory usage may reflect both network client usage and local server usage.

The Browser Object's Counters

The Browser object allows you to monitor the network browser. The network browser is usually not a major problem for most Windows NT 4 Server networks; however, it can cause problems if improperly tuned.

Below I've listed counters found in the Performance Monitor Browser object. You should look under the description column to see which counters may be likely candidates for monitoring:

- Announcements Domain/sec—Counts the number of times that the domain has announced itself on the network. If the number is high, then check to see why there are excessive browser announcements.
- Announcements Server/sec—Counts the number of times that the domain has announced itself to this server. Like domain announcements, check to see why the server is announcing so frequently.
- Announcements Total/sec—The sum of Announcements Domain/sec and Announcements Server/sec.
- Duplicate Master Announcements—Counts the number of times that the master browser detects the presence of another master browser on the same domain. Sometimes there are two master browsers, and one will (typically) demote itself from being the master browser.
- Election Packets/sec—The number of browser election packets that are received.
- Enumerations Domain/sec—Counts the number of domain browse request messages received.
- Enumerations Other/sec—Counts the number of non-domain and non-server browse request messages received.

- Enumerations Server/sec—Counts the number of server browse request messages received.
- Enumerations Total/sec—Enumerations Total/sec is the sum of Enumerations Server/sec, Enumerations Domain/sec, and Enumerations Other/sec.
- Illegal Datagrams/sec—A count of the number of invalid datagrams received. If high, indicates possible hardware problems, or perhaps some (really) strange software problem. Invalid datagrams are unusual!
- Mailslot Allocations Failed—Counts the number of times that user mail-slot writes failed due to insufficient memory.
- Mailslot Opens Failed/sec—A count of the mail-slot messages received for mail-slots that do not exist.
- Mailslot Receives Failed—Count of the number of times that user mail-slot reads failed due to various transport errors.
- Mailslot Writes Failed—Count of mail-slot messages that were received, but could not be written.
- Mailslot Writes/sec—The number of writes per second to Mailslots.
- Missed Mailslot Datagrams—Counts the number of Mailslot Datagrams that are deleted due to configuration or allocation problems.
- Missed Server Announcements—Count of the number of server announcements missed due to configuration or allocation problems.
- Missed Server List Requests—Counts the number of times the system needed to request the list of browser servers that were not processed because of configuration or allocation problems.
- Server Announce Allocations Failed/sec—Indicates the rate at which the server or domain announcements fail due to insufficient memory.
- Server List Requests/sec—A count of browser server list retrieval requests.

The Cache Object's Counters

The cache is used by the system to cache (buffer) data being transferred to and from the hard drive. Cache is critical to system performance when there is substantial disk I/O being performed by either a local user or task, or by network client users.

I've shown counters found in the Performance Monitor's Cache object below:

- Async Copy Reads/sec—An indicator of cache page reads, for applications.
- Async Data Maps/sec—An indicator of the frequency at which the file system is using the NTFS file system to map pages.
- Async Fast Reads/sec—Indicator of reads that do not go through the file system. Fast reads are good (performance-wise), as compared to reads that do go through the file system.
- Async MDL Reads/sec—An indicator of the number of reads from cache done using the MDL (Memory Descriptor List).
- Async Pin Reads/sec—An indicator of the number of reads of data into cache, before the data is written to the disk.
- Copy Read Hits %—Indicates the percentage of Cache Copy Reads that are still within the cache.
- Copy Reads/sec—The reads from data that is still within the cache.
- Data Flush Pages/sec—Indicates the number of pages flushed, either by a flush request or a write-through request. Pages are flushed for a variety of reasons, such as age, or the need for the memory that the page occupied.
- Data Flushes/sec—A count of how many times the cache is flushed. The cache gets flushed periodically.
- Data Map Hits %—Indicates the percent of reads that could be retrieved from the cache.
- Data Map Pins/sec—Data Map Pins/sec indicates the number of times a page is locked into the cache.

- Data Maps/sec—The number of NTFS file system mapped pages that are read.
- Fast Read Not Possibles/sec—Indicates that the application attempted to get cached data, and could not without file system assistance. If this is a frequent occurrence, it could indicate a problem; however, you would have to investigate the reason why the file system was needed.
- Fast Read Resource Misses/sec—A count of the number of cache read failures that are due to lack of resources.
- Fast Reads/sec—Count of the number of reads that do not use the file system to read the data.
- Lazy Write Flushes/sec—The level of activity for the lazy write thread for writes. Lazy write (which allows a process to write to the cache) and the cached page are later written (flushed) to the device. Lots of flushes per second may indicate a need for more cache memory.
- Lazy Write Pages/sec—Level of activity for the lazy write thread for reads. Like the lazy write flushes, this counter indicates activity of the cache.
- MDL Read Hits %—Indicates the number of cache requests that could be fulfilled without a disk I/O.
- MDL Reads/sec—Counts the number of read requests handled using the MDL list.
- Pin Read Hits %—Indicates the percentage of pin read hits.
- Pin Reads/sec—Indicates the count of pin read hits.
- Read Aheads/sec—Indicates when the cache manager sees that the application is sequentially reading a file, and caches pages that have not yet been requested.
- Sync Copy Reads/sec—How often a read is made from the cache to the application.
- Sync Data Maps/sec—How often the NTFS file system maps a page.
- Sync Fast Reads/sec—Counts how frequently the file system is bypassed.

- Sync MDL Reads/sec—Indicates the usage of MDL list pages used to access the cache.
- Sync Pin Reads/sec—Indicates how often data is read into the cache prior to being written to the disk.

The Logical Disk Object's Counters

Logical Disks are usually hard disk drives, though other devices (removable optical drives, CD-ROM drives, and so on) are also covered under this object. Problems that the Logical Disk object points out may be related to the disk, or to the way the cache is configured.

Generally I would recommend monitoring counters for the cache and the physical drives in addition to the Logical Disk object.

Each of the counters may be either a total for all drives, or for an individual drive. Selecting the drives where specific applications, databases, or other information resides can tell what items may result in excessive I/O rates.

I have listed counters found in the Performance Monitor Logical Disk object below:

- % Disk Read Time—Indicates the percentage of time that the drive is busy servicing read requests. If high, then the system is perhaps overloaded. Redesigning the server's drive layout may help, splitting the load between two servers, or even two SCSI chains may be useful.
- % Disk Write Time—Indicates the percentage of time that the drive is busy servicing write requests. If high, then the system is perhaps overloaded. Redesigning the server's drive layout may help, splitting the load between two servers, or even two SCSI chains may be useful.
- % Disk Time—The sum of % Disk Read Time and % Disk Write Time.
- % Free Space—Indicates the percentage of free drive space. You select the drive, or all drives. Low free space values can indicate lots of problems, the least of which is that you need more disk space! As disks get full, the efficiency of the system decreases, too. FAT systems tend to fragment when drives are too full.

- Avg. Disk Bytes/Read—Indicates the disk read rate. If the read counter is low, then running diagnostics and checking the drive I/O rate may be in order. Drives fail in many, many ways—one failure is that the drive slows down. (This is caused by the drive having too many soft read errors.)
- Avg. Disk Bytes/Transfer—Indicates the disk read/write rate.
- Avg. Disk Bytes/Write—The disk write rate. If the write counter is low, then running diagnostics and checking the drive I/O rate may be in order. Drives fail in many, many ways—one failure is that the drive slows down. (This is caused by the drive having too many verify errors, with possible remapping of defective areas.)
- Avg. Disk Queue Length—The number of read/write requests currently queued. A large queue value indicates that your disk system may be overloaded. Splitting the load between two servers, or even an additional SCSI bus may help.
- Avg. Disk Read Queue Length—Indicates the number of read requests currently queued. A large queue value indicates that your disk system may be overloaded.
- Avg. Disk sec/Read—The average time (in seconds) for a read. This value should be low. If it is high, then you must monitor other counters to determine why!
- Avg. Disk sec/Transfer—The average time (in seconds) for a read or write. This value should be low. If it is high, then you must monitor other counters to determine why!
- Avg. Disk sec/Write—Average time (in seconds) for a write. This value should be low. If it is high, then you must monitor other counters to determine why!
- Avg. Disk Write Queue Length—Indicates the number of write requests currently queued. A large queue value indicates that your disk system may be overloaded.

- Current Disk Queue Length—The number of currently unfulfilled I/O requests. A large queue value indicates that your disk system may be overloaded. Splitting the load between two servers, or even an additional SCSI bus may help.
- Disk Bytes/sec—Rate that data is transferred to and from the disk. This value should, on a heavily loaded system, approach the theoretical maximum for your hardware. But it will only approach maximum when the system is loaded; if the system is not heavily loaded, then this number will be lower.
- Disk Read Bytes/sec—Rate that data is read from the disk. Reads, like writes, are indicators of the drive's transfer rate.
- Disk Reads/sec—Number of reads from the disk.
- Disk Transfers/sec—Number of reads and writes.
- Disk Write Bytes/sec—Rate that bytes are written to the disk.
- Disk Writes/sec—Number of writes to the disk.
- Free Megabytes—Free space on the drive specified. Not as meaningful as the % free space counter, this counter must be considered with the size of the drive in mind. 300MB free on a 1GB drive is much different from 300MB free on a 9GB drive!

The Memory Object's Counters

The memory object is used to monitor usage of system RAM. Indicators can show that there needs to be more system RAM (rarely will you see situations where there is too much system RAM, but it is possible).

Most of the time, when we are trying to enhance system performance, we start with two objects: memory and CPU. Memory, especially if you suspect that you have insufficient RAM, is a good logical starting point.

I've listed the counters found in the Performance Monitor Memory object below:

- % Committed Bytes In Use—Indicator of the amount of memory that is actually committed, compared to the commit limit. In my server, the maximum commit is about 130MB (system memory plus total paging file size). Of this value, I have 65MB (about) in use, resulting in 50% committed. This is a good ratio, as it was taken when the system was being used in a typical manner. If the in-use percentage is high, then allocate more paging space; if the percentage is low, then you may be using more disk space for paging than necessary.
- Available Bytes—Number of bytes of available memory. If low, consider the possibility that you need more RAM.
- Cache Bytes—Number of bytes of memory used by the cache.
- Cache Bytes Peak—Number of bytes used by the cache to buffer received data.
- Cache Faults/sec— Indicates the number of pages that are not available from the cache without a file I/O.
- Commit Limit—Maximum number of bytes of virtual memory that may be allocated without expanding the paging file. Remember that you specify the paging file(s) size and location in the Control Panel's System applet's Virtual Memory dialog. Hint: put your paging files on drives other than the system drive, or a drive that will have substantial I/O demands.
- Committed Bytes—Indicates the number of bytes of memory that have been allocated. This value should not approach the commit limit! If the committed bytes is close to the commit limit, system performance is impaired, and applications may not run due to insufficient memory. Fixes include increasing the commit limit, and, even better, adding more system memory.

- Demand Zero Faults/sec—Count of the number of zeroed pages requested. Pages are zeroed as a security measure. This prevents applications from gaining information from discarded pages from other applications or the system.
- Free System Page Table Entries—Count of how many system page table entries are not being used by the system.
- Page Faults/sec—Count of the number of processor page faults. High values usually indicate the need for more physical memory.
- Page Reads/sec—Count of the number of page reads. High values usually indicate the need for more physical memory.
- Page Writes/sec—Count of the number of page writes. High values usually indicate the need for more physical memory.
- Pages Input/sec—Count of the number of pages that had to be read from the disk to satisfy page faults.
- Pages Output/sec—Count of modified pages that had to be written to the disk.
- Pages/sec—Count of the number of pages written or read.
- Pool Nonpaged Allocs—Indicates how often the system receives requests to allocate from the non-paged pool.
- Pool Nonpaged Bytes—Indicates the number of bytes in the non-paged pool.
- Pool Paged Allocs—Indicates the number of requests for the paged pool.
- Pool Paged Bytes—Indicates the number of bytes in the paged pool.
- Pool Paged Resident Bytes—Indicates the number of bytes present in the system paged pool.
- System Cache Resident Bytes—Indicates the number of bytes that are located in the disk cache.
- System Code Resident Bytes—Indicates the number of bytes of system code currently being used.

- System Code Total Bytes—Indicates the number of bytes of memory in the kernel, boot drivers, and other areas that were loaded by NTLDR or OSLOADER.
- System Driver Resident Bytes—Counter of device driver code that is pageable, and resident.
- System Driver Total Bytes—Indicates the number of total (in memory and paged) bytes of system drivers.
- Transition Faults/sec—The number of times that a page fault was recovered from a page as it was being written to cache.
- Write Copies/sec—Indicates that a shared page was actually written to. Memory can be shared between processes. However, should a process write to a shared page, the shared page first is copied so that only the writing process actually writes to the page.

The Paging File Object's Counters

Below are the counters found in the Performance Monitor Paging File object. The Paging File object monitors the system's paging file(s). Insufficient space allocated to paging files, and having paging files located on drives that have a high I/O rate (such as the system drive), are problems that often confront Windows NT 4 Server administrators.

The Paging File object allows you to monitor specific paging files (you may, with Windows NT 4 Server, have more than one paging file), or you may monitor the usage percentage for all paging files.

- % Usage—An indicator of how much of the specified paging file (or all paging files) was actually being used. Look at the most used paging files—and then check the other usage for these drives: drives that have substantial other I/O activity should be avoided as paging file devices if possible.
- % Usage Peak—An indicator of the peak usage of the specified paging file (or all paging files) that was actually being used. The peak value should be cleared so that you can assess peak usage times.

The Physical Disk Object's Counters

Below are the counters found in the Performance Monitor Physical Disk object. The Physical Disk object reports on physical disks, just as the Logical Disk object reports on logical disks. High values indicate a possibly excessive I/O rate.

Counters are maintained for each physical disk (remember, a physical disk may have multiple logical drives) and there is a total counter as well.

- % Disk Read Time—An indicator of the amount of time that the drive was actually reading data.
- % Disk Time—The sum of both read and write times.
- % Disk Write Time—An indicator of the amount of time that the drive was actually writing data.
- Avg. Disk Bytes/Read—The average number of bytes read from the drive, per I/O request.
- Avg. Disk Bytes/Transfer—The average number of bytes read from or written to the drive, per I/O request.
- Avg. Disk Bytes/Write—The average number of bytes written to the drive, per I/O request.
- Avg. Disk Queue Length—The average number of I/O requests that are queued.
- Avg. Disk Read Queue Length—The average number of read requests that are queued.
- Avg. Disk sec/Read—The average read time.
- Avg. Disk sec/Transfer—The average I/O time.
- Avg. Disk sec/Write—The average write time.
- Avg. Disk Write Queue Length—The average number of write requests that are queued.
- Current Disk Queue Length—The average number of I/O requests that are queued.
- Disk Bytes/sec—The disk I/O transfer rate.
- Disk Read Bytes/sec—The disk read input rate.

- Disk Reads/sec—The number of reads per second for the drive.
- Disk Transfers/sec—The number of I/Os for the drive.
- Disk Write Bytes/sec—The number of writes for the drive.
- Disk Writes/sec—The disk write output rate.

The Process Object's Counters

Below are the counters found in the Performance Monitor Process object. The Process object shows information about the work that the CPU is currently doing. Also see the Thread object, below.

The Process object maintains counters for each and every process (see Figure 9-9, which shows the counters for 36 different processes). There are also counters for the total of all processes. This makes it easy to determine whether a specific process is causing problems.

- % Processor Time—An indicator of the amount of time that the processor is performing non-idle time tasks. Yes, even the most heavily used server will have some idle time. Generally, a server that seems to perform poorly but has a high idle time value is probably suffering from a disk, network, or video bottleneck.
- % Privileged Time—The amount of time that the processor performs privileged tasks. Typically 10% to 15%, you may see peaks of up to 50%.
- % User Time—The amount of time that the processor performs user tasks. User tasks take many forms. The Task Manager may help figure which user task is utilizing the system.
- Elapsed Time—The time that the processor has been running. Not a terribly useful performance counter.
- Handle Count—The number of currently allocated handles for the specified process.
- ID Process—Process IDs are unique, reusable identifiers for processes. This counter counts the number of Process IDs, which indicates how many processes are running.

- Page Faults/sec—Counter of page faults. High page fault rates may indicate the need for more memory.
- Page File Bytes—A counter of bytes paged by the specified process, or all processes.
- Page File Bytes Peak—Indicates the maximum number of page file bytes for the process.
- Pool Nonpaged Bytes—Indicates the number of bytes in the non-paged pool.
- Pool Paged Bytes—Indicates the number of bytes in the paged pool.
- Priority Base—Indicates the current priority base for the process.
- Private Bytes—A count of non-sharable bytes owned by the indicated process.
- Thread Count—A count of the number of threads in the indicated process. A process will have one or more threads. First isolate the process that is using excessive resources, then attempt to isolate the thread.
- Virtual Bytes—The number of bytes of virtual memory currently allocated to the process.
- Virtual Bytes Peak—The maximum number of bytes of virtual memory that have been allocated to the process.
- Working Set—Indicates the number of bytes in the process's working set.
- Working Set Peak—The maximum number of bytes in the process's working set.

The Processor Object's Counters

Below are the counters found in the Performance Monitor Processor object. The Processor object is used to monitor the actual processor usage.

There are counters for each processor. If you have a multiprocessor (MPU) server, then you can determine the actual loading of each CPU.

- % DPC Time—Indicates the amount of time that the processor spends on deferred procedure calls. Rarely over a few percent in most systems.
- % Interrupt Time—Indicates the amount of time that the processor spends on interrupt service handling. Like DPC time, interrupt time normally is not a big item. If too large, you must determine why—reasons might include hardware problems.
- % Privileged Time—Indicates the amount of time that the processor spends on privileged processes. Privileged tasks are operating system work. User applications don't get privileged time directly.
- % Processor Time—Indicates the total amount of time that the processor spends on non-idle time procedure calls. There is a process called System Idle Process, which "eats" processor time that is not used for any other task. The processor never "sleeps"—rather, processor time that is unused is simply "wasted" by the idle process.
- % User Time—Indicates the amount of time that the processor spends on user application processes. User tasks are typically applications and non-privileged system processes.
- APC Bypasses/sec—Indicates the current rate of asynchronous procedure calls bypassed.
- DPC Bypasses/sec—Indicates the current rate of deferred procedure calls bypasses.
- DPC Rate—Indicates the deferred procedure calls handled rate.
- DPCs Queued/sec—Indicates the number of queued deferred procedure calls.
- Interrupts/sec—The number of interrupts the processor is servicing. You should investigate excessive interrupts. They can be indicative of a hardware problem or a tuning issue.

The Server Object's Counters

The Server object is used to monitor the server portion of Windows NT 4 Server. Servers that perform different tasks, (such as file servers, or servers such as Exchange server) affect Windows NT 4 Server's performance differently.

The server component of Windows NT 4 Server is probably the most critical part of Windows NT 4 Server—after all, we are running a server here! However, server-related performance issues are probably secondary to hardware problems (disk, processor, and memory) when it comes to affecting system performance.

The Network Monitor may work (either directly or indirectly) on many of the items that Windows NT 4 Server Performance Monitor monitors for the server object. Consider using Windows NT 4 Server Performance Monitor and Network Monitor together to help diagnose Windows NT 4 Server performance problems. Below are the counters found in the Performance Monitor Server object.

- Blocking Requests Rejected—Indicates the number of blocking server message blocks.
- Bytes Received/sec—Indicates the number of bytes read from the network. I/O rates that are too low (despite a known demand) usually indicate a hardware fault: either the server's NIC cannot handle the throughput, or the network itself is too slow. If you're running a 10 Mbps Ethernet, consider an upgrade to 100 Mbps as one possibility. Load sharing between multiple NICs and network legs is another idea to consider.
- Bytes Total/sec—The number of bytes read from or written to the network. Basic I/O rate, this number may approach the theoretical limits of the hardware for a well-tuned and well-running system.
- Bytes Transmitted/sec—Indicates the number of bytes written to the network.
- Context Blocks Queued/sec—Indicates the loading of the servers queue.
- Errors Access Permissions—Counts the number of times that client accesses failed due to failure to grant permission. This is often an indicator that there may be attempts to

breach system security—it would be wise to check where the errors originate. This counter is incremented by users who are logged on so it is probable that the person who is attempting to breach security has been logged on successfully. Setting a trigger on this value may be necessary.

- Errors Granted Access—Indicates that files were opened but access was denied. May indicate that there have been attempts to breach system security—it would be wise to check where the errors originate. Typically, however, this is caused by users attempting to access files for which they do not have permissions. Setting a trigger on this value may be necessary.
- Errors Logon—Count of logon errors, indicates that attempts were made to logon with an invalid password. Indicates that there may have been attempts to breach system security—it would be wise to check where the errors originate. This counter is incremented by users who are NOT logged on so it is possible that the person attempting to breach security is not part of the organization. Setting a trigger on this value may be necessary. Also, consider tracking the times that these errors occur. If they appear at specific times, this may help identify the person who is attempting to logon without proper passwords.
- Errors System—Indicates system-level errors. The server is quite possibly suffering from hardware problems when this counter exceeds normal values. To determine normal values, some historical data is useful.
- File Directory Searches—A counter of the number of searches for files on the server. May be useful to determine that users are "searching" for information.
- Files Open—A counter of the number of currently opened files on the server. Large numbers of open files can indicate overloading of the server.
- Files Opened Total—A cumulative counter of file open requests. Very dependent on the type of work that users are doing—each instance may need to be investigated.

- Logon Total—The number of logon attempts since the system was started. Failed and successful, failed should be few and far between!
- Logon/sec—The number of logons per second. Logons per second? Many network logons per minute are normal. If you suddenly find that you are faced with large numbers of logons per second, you should investigate. Common causes include user error and incorrectly configured clients that time out on logons.
- Pool Nonpaged Bytes—The count of bytes in the non-paged area.
- Pool Nonpaged Failures—The count of allocation failures in the non-paged area.
- Pool Nonpaged Peak—The count of the maximum number of bytes in the non-paged area.
- Pool Paged Bytes—The count of bytes in the non-paged area.
- Pool Paged Failures—The count of allocation failures in the non-paged area.
- Pool Paged Peak—The count of the maximum number of bytes in the non-paged area.
- Server Sessions—A count of the current sessions on the server. Usually one, but can be higher if there have been multiple logons.
- Sessions Errored Out—A count of the number of sessions that errored out on the server. All error types listed here.
- Sessions Forced Off—A count of the sessions that have been forced off the server for any reason.
- Sessions Logged Off—A count of the sessions that logged off the server. These sessions were dropped by the client.
- Sessions Timed Out—A count of the number of sessions that timed out on the server. Time out values can be useful when users "walk away" and don't properly terminate their session.

- Work Item Shortages—A counter of the number of instances that the message STATUS_DATA_NOT_ACCEPTED was returned. Typically, this indicates that the server is either overloaded or needs tuning.

The Work Queues Object's Counters

The Server Work Queues object monitors the interaction between the server and threads that utilize the server. Some of the information found in the Work Queues counters can be found in other objects and in the Network Monitor.

Below are the counters found in the Performance Monitor Server Work Queues object.

- Active Threads—A count of the number of threads that are currently active in the queue.
- Available Threads—A count of the threads that are not currently active.
- Available Work Items—A count of client requests.
- Borrowed Work Items—A count of work items that have been "borrowed" from another CPU. "Excuse me dear, but could I borrow a cup of sugar, and a few work items." Scary thought, but in a multi-processor environment, this is basically what happens… OK, I made up the sugar part.
- Bytes Received/sec—The number of bytes that have been received from the clients. Again, basic I/O rates, but this is a sum since the last time the counters were cleared.
- Bytes Sent/sec—The number of bytes sent to the clients. Again, basic I/O rates, but this is a sum since the last time the counters were cleared.
- Bytes Transferred/sec—The total client I/O rate. Again, basic I/O rates for read and write, but this is a sum since the last time the counters were cleared.
- Context Blocks Queued/sec—Indicates the number of context blocks that have been queued.
- Current Clients—The current number of client users being managed by this CPU.

- Queue Length—The length of the server queue.
- Read Bytes/sec—The number of bytes from files being sent to clients. Bytes per second is a better indicator of performance than total bytes.
- Read Operations/sec—Indicates the number of file read requests from clients. Operations per second is a better indicator of performance than total operations.
- Total Bytes/sec—The total client file I/O rate. File I/O and print queue I/O are the two major items in most networks. Some networks don't have much print queue I/O, and may have more non-file based I/O (directory searches and such).
- Total Operations/sec—An indicator of the total number of operations (file I/O). Operations per second is a better indicator of performance than total operations.
- Work Item Shortages—This indicates that there was a shortage of work items.
- Write Bytes/sec—The number of bytes written for clients. Bytes per second is a better indicator of performance than total bytes.
- Write Operations/sec—The number of write operations performed for clients. Operations per second is a better indicator of performance than total operations.

The System Object's Counters

Below are the counters found in the Performance Monitor System object. The System object is used to monitor Windows NT 4 Server overall.

The System object's counters mimic many of the counters found in other objects. For example, the monitoring of processor times may also be found in the Processor object.

- % Registry Quota In Use—Indicates the amount of the registry quota that has been used. You may control how large the registry may grow. If this value is approaching 100%, you must either reduce your registry size (be very, very careful, make sure you have adequate backups first), or (safest) increase the maximum registry size. Set the registry size in the Control Panel's System applet. Click the Virtual Memory button in the Performance tab, and make the change in the Virtual Memory dialog.

- % Total DPC Time—The total Deferred Procedure Call total time.
- % Total Interrupt Time—Indicates the average time spent processing interrupts.
- % Total Privileged Time—Indicates the average time spent processing privileged processing.
- % Total Processor Time—Indicates the average time the processor is in use.
- % Total User Time—The average time spent processing user code.
- Alignment Fixups/sec—The number of alignment fixups performed. Check the application that is generating the fixup errors. May indicate that an application was written for a different CPU in the same family (written for a 386 and being run on a Pentium). Some processors do not allow alignment fixups.
- Context Switches/sec—The number of context (thread to thread) switches.
- Exception Dispatches/sec—Indicates the system exception rate.
- File Control Bytes/sec—Indicates the non-I/O bytes transferred made to the file system.
- File Control Operations/sec—Indicates the non-I/O requests made to the file system.
- File Data Operations/sec—Indicates the rate of file I/O operations.
- File Read Bytes/sec—The file read rate.
- File Read Operations/sec—Indicates the number of read operations.
- File Write Bytes/sec—Indicates the file write rate.

- File Write Operations/sec—Indicates the number of bytes written to files.
- Floating Emulations/sec—Indicates the number of floating point math operations that were emulated by the operating system. For systems that do not have functional FPU (Floating Point Unit) hardware, the operating system is able to emulate floating point hardware. However, this emulation is costly in terms of system performance. Typically happens when a defective FPU in a CPU is discovered.
- Processor Queue Length—Indicates the queue length.
- System Calls/sec—The number of system calls made.
- System Up Time—The amount of time that the system has been operating.
- Total APC Bypasses/sec—Indicates the number of asynchronous procedure calls that have been bypassed.
- Total DPC Bypasses/sec—Indicates the number of deferred procedure calls that have been bypassed.
- Total DPC Rate—The number of deferred procedure calls.
- Total DPCs Queued/sec—Indicates the number of deferred procedure calls that have been queued.
- Total Interrupts/sec—Indicates the interrupt rate for the system.

The Threads Object's Counters

Below are the counters found in the Performance Monitor Thread object. The Thread object provides information about the execution of threads in the system.

Threads are the smallest dispatchable item. A process has one or more threads. Again, items in the thread object are similar to their counterparts in the processor object.

Counters are maintained for each thread in every process. If you have a normally active system, it will not be possible to monitor each and every thread in every process! There might be hundreds. Rather, monitor the processes first. Find which processes are using excessive system resources, then consider monitoring the threads in the processes that you suspect are causing problems.

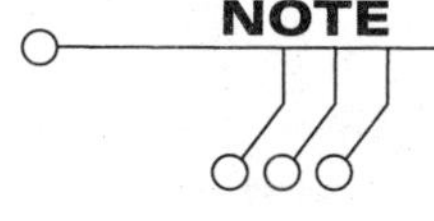

I'm not going to assume that you will be able to do anything about programs at the thread level! However, for applications that have been developed in-house, you can provide information for the programming staff about the application's performance.

- % Privileged Time—An indicator of the amount of time that the processor performs privileged tasks.
- % Processor Time—An indicator of the amount of time that the processor performs non-idle time tasks.
- % User Time—An indicator of the amount of time that the processor performs user tasks.
- Context Switches/sec—Indicates the number of context (thread to thread) switches.
- Elapsed Time—The time that the thread has been running.
- ID Process—Process IDs are unique, reusable identifiers for processes. This counter counts the number of Process IDs.
- ID Thread—Thread IDs are unique, reusable identifiers for threads. This counter counts the number of Thread IDs.
- Priority Base—Used to indicate the base priority for the specified thread.
- Priority Current—Used to indicate the current priority for the specified thread.
- Start Address—The starting address for the thread.
- Thread State—The thread's current state.
- Thread Wait Reason—Indicates the thread's wait state.

The Windows NT Task Manager

The Windows NT Task Manager (right-click on any blank area on the task bar, then select Task Manager from the pop-up context menu) is a quick way to see how the currently logged on user is affecting system performance.

The Windows NT Task Manager has three tabs:

- Applications—A display of all currently running applications (but not system tasks, services, or other non-user items). Each task is listed with its status. Right-clicking will bring up a pop-up menu that allows you to switch to, minimize, maximize, bring to front, end the task, or go to the process. You can end tasks, switch to tasks, or start new tasks from this tab (see Figure 9-12).

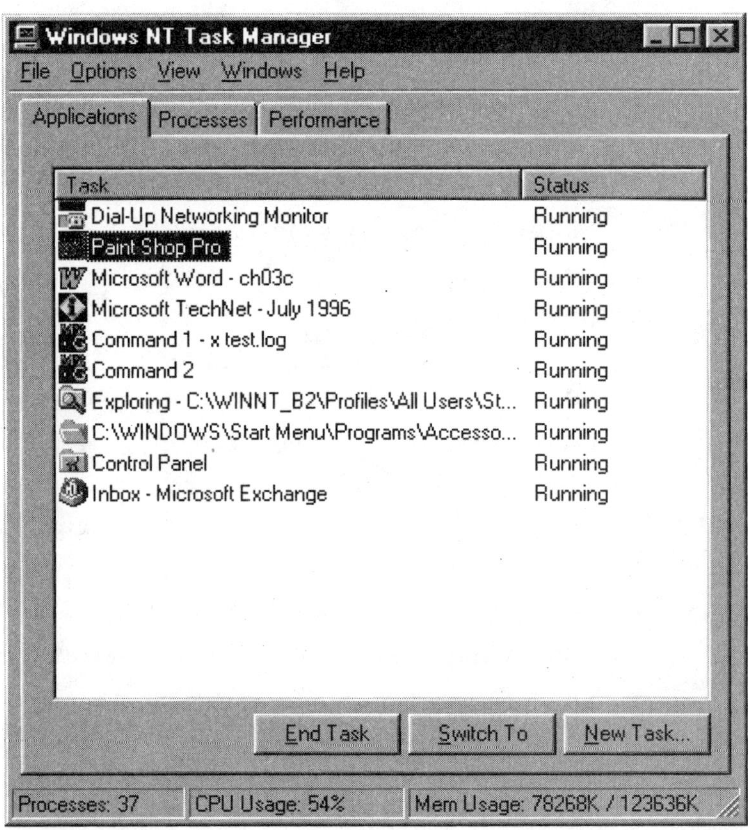

Figure 9-12: The Task Manager's Applications tab.

- Processes—Lists all processes, with columns to display Image Name, PID, CPU (current CPU utilization), CPU Time (cumulative CPU time), Mem Usage (how much memory is allocated to the processes). Each column may be sorted in either ascending or descending order. You can end the currently selected process from this tab (see Figure 9-13).

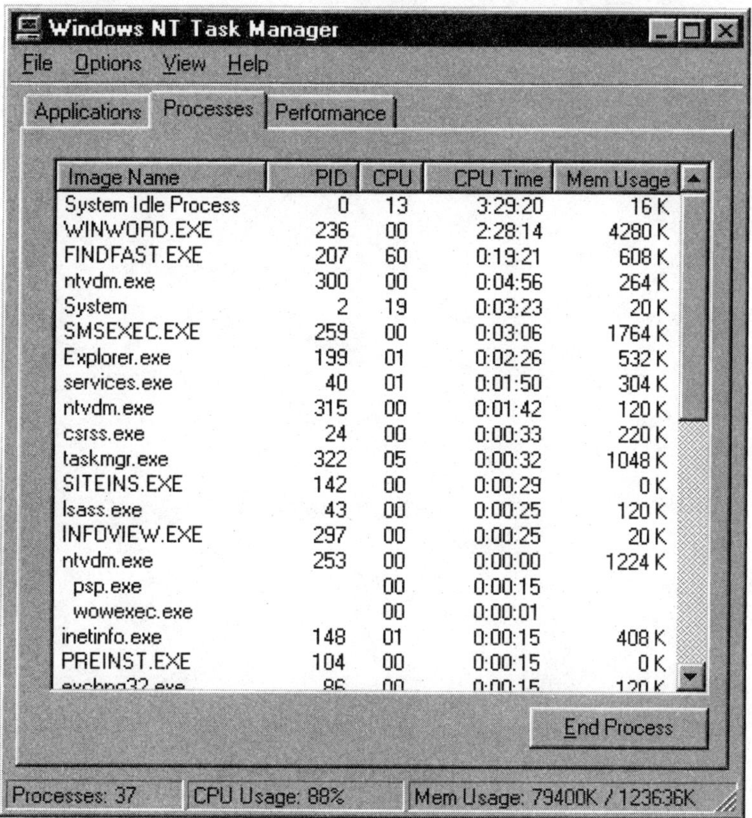

Figure 9-13: The Task Manager's Processes tab.

- Performance—Shows, graphically, both CPU usage (non-idle time usage) and memory usage. They are shown both as a bar chart and as a scrolling line chart. The Performance tab is shown in Figure 9-14.

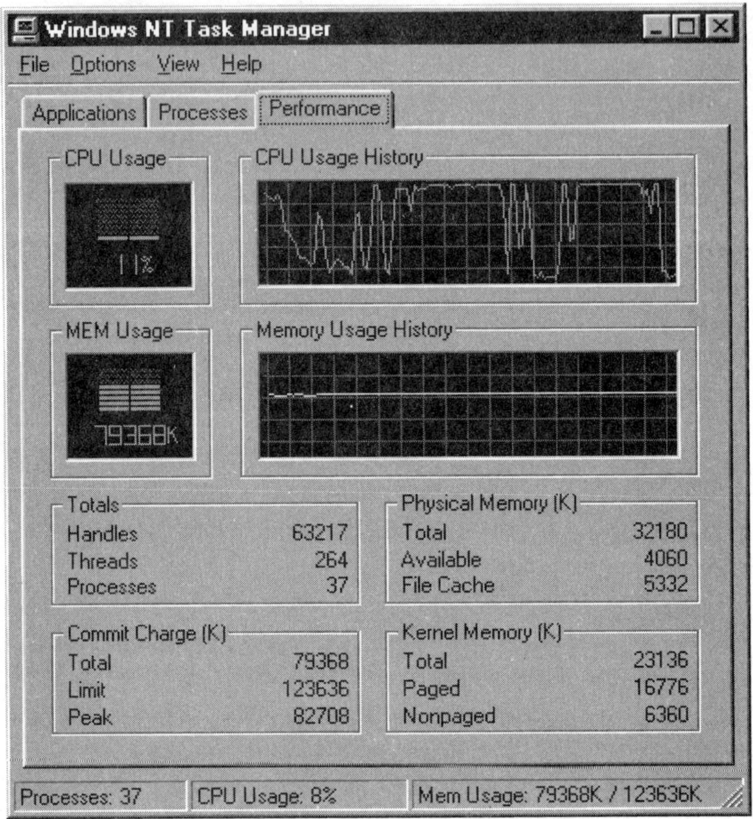

Figure 9-14: The Task Manager's Performance tab.

Task Manager is small and easy to use. In some cases smaller is better.

For example, Task Manager has proven very valuable in fixing some performance problems on the server DORA. If you look at Figure 9-14, you will see a group marked "Commit Charge (K)." The value in the Total field is the amount of virtual memory that has been allocated. The field "Limit" is the maximum virtual memory possible (limited by the paging file size).

In one case, I was able to quickly see that the Total field was almost as large as the Limit field—I was running out of memory! (Could this be why each time I tried to launch a new program I got the message "Insufficient memory to complete task, try closing one or more applications"?)

Valuable, also, is the "Physical Memory (K)" fields. In this section you can see how your physical memory is being allocated. In the machine that produced Figure 9-14, there is 32M of physical RAM. Of this figure, a bit over 5M was allocated to the file cache, 4M was free, and the remainder was allocated.

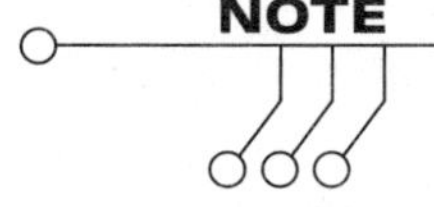

In Figure 9-14, the CPU Usage bar chart (upper left) shows 11% CPU utilization, while the status bar's CPU Usage figure shows 8%. As luck would have it, the screen shot was captured after the bar chart was updated, and before the status bar's figure had been changed.

Moving On

This chapter covered the Network Monitor, the Windows NT Performance Monitor, and the Windows NT Task Manager. The Network Monitor is capable of monitoring all aspects of network performance, both for the server and for each client workstation. For the Windows NT Performance Monitor, many of the major objects and counters were documented. The Windows NT Task Manager allows you to quickly see what is happening on your computer—and just as quickly terminate a process!

This chapter concludes the first part of our book. The next part, "Optional at Extra Cost," introduces components that make Windows NT 4 Server really work for you, including the Microsoft BackOffice suite of server applications, Microsoft SQL Server, Microsoft Exchange, and the Microsoft Internet Information Server, which just happens to be, in my opinion, one of the most exciting additions to Windows NT 4 Server!

SECTION II

Optional at Extra Cost

10

Microsoft BackOffice

In this chapter we describe Microsoft BackOffice. To use the products included with Microsoft BackOffice, you must first install the Microsoft BackOffice product. Then you can install and configure the individual products included with Microsoft BackOffice. Many different server products comprise BackOffice and are covered either directly in this chapter or elsewhere in this section. The components in Microsoft BackOffice include:

- Microsoft SNA Server, covered in this chapter.
- Microsoft Systems Management Server, covered in this chapter.
- Microsoft Exchange Server, which I cover in Chapter 11.
- Microsoft SQL Server, covered in Chapter 12.
- Microsoft Internet Information Server, which I cover in the next section, in Chapters 13 through 15.
- Windows NT Server, the subject of this entire book!

Microsoft BackOffice includes a copy of Windows NT Server. Version 2 of Microsoft BackOffice (which was the latest version of Microsoft BackOffice as of this writing) includes Microsoft Windows NT 3.51. There is nothing to prevent you from installing other components of Microsoft BackOffice under Windows NT 4 Server. Just don't install the copy of Windows NT 3.51 Server!

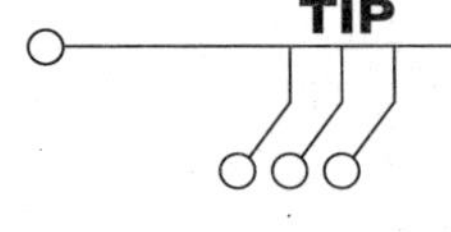

Windows NT 4 Server includes a more recent version of Microsoft Internet Information Server (IIS). So, when choosing components to install from BackOffice, IIS should not *be one of the components you install.*

You may not need to install all the components of Microsoft BackOffice. For example, some sites may wish to install only SQL Server and Exchange Server. Other sites may find that they need to implement the Microsoft Systems Management Server. Each installation will be somewhat unique in terms of which components are installed and how these components are configured and used.

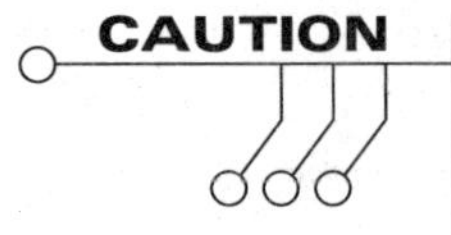

The license agreement for Microsoft BackOffice does not allow you to split the various parts of Microsoft BackOffice between multiple servers. All Microsoft BackOffice components must be installed on a single server, or additional Microsoft BackOffice licenses must be purchased.

The versions of the various components included with Microsoft BackOffice are the standard versions. If you need functionality that is available only with the Enterprise editions of a Microsoft BackOffice component, then you will need to obtain the Enterprise edition of the product.

Of Mice and Versions*

The microcomputer market changes practically on a daily basis. Microsoft will create a new version of Microsoft BackOffice that will better match Windows NT 4 Server.

However, the question of when a new version of Microsoft BackOffice will be released is anyone's guess. We can assume that as long as IIS is included with Windows NT 4 Server, that it will not be part of Microsoft BackOffice. We can also expect that Systems Management Server and Exchange Server will both be upgraded, and that possibly Microsoft SQL Server will also be modified somewhat.

However, even with changes you will find that the differences are not going to be too difficult. Do read this chapter even if you have a newer version of Microsoft BackOffice.

*With profound apologies to John Steinbeck...

Microsoft SNA Server

IBM uses SNA (Systems Network Architecture) to communicate between mini- and mainframe computers (and to communicate with peripherals).

Microsoft SNA Server is an important part of Microsoft BackOffice in environments where an IBM mainframe, AS/400, or other IBM PC computers are connected using SNA. In the remainder of this section we will refer to the IBM mainframe, AS/400, or other SNA-compatible computers simply as the "mainframe."

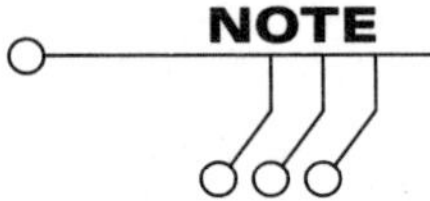

Microsoft SNA Server has not appreciably changed in the last few years, nor are any major improvements expected in Microsoft SNA Server in the foreseeable future.

Microsoft SNA Server connects client workstations running Windows NT 4 Server, Windows NT 4 Workstation, Windows 95, or other supported client operating systems to the mainframe. Additional applications (typically 3270 or 5250 terminal emulator programs) run on client workstations to allow users to interact with the mainframe as if the client user were using a directly connected, dedicated terminal.

With Microsoft SNA Server, you are able to emulate a 3270 terminal, a 5250 terminal, APPC, CPI-C, communications that use LUAs, or other IBM-specific communications techniques.

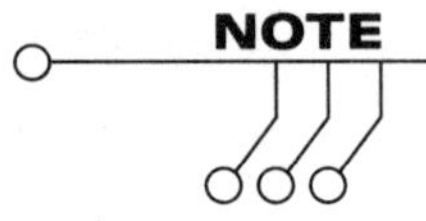

The 3270 interface requires that you install and configure the TN3270 service.

Readers who have no IBM SNA experience, and have no requirements to implement Microsoft SNA Server, may be happier if they skip this section—they may find it filled with confusing terminology and issues!

Installing SNA Server

You install the Microsoft SNA Server from either the Microsoft SNA Server distribution media or from the Microsoft BackOffice media. This chapter assumes that you're installing from the Microsoft BackOffice media; other than starting the installation program, there are no significant differences between the two versions.

You will be confronted with two typical Microsoft SNA Server configurations. The first configuration is called "centralized servers," where all the Microsoft SNA servers are located at one site, typically wherever the mainframe computer is located. The client users may be located locally to the Microsoft SNA Server or remotely (using some form of WAN, SDLC (Synchronous Data Link Control) bridge, router, or perhaps the Internet).

In the second type of configuration, the Microsoft SNA servers are remotely located near the client sites. Each Microsoft SNA Server connects to the mainframe computer through a communications link that supports SDLC. Each Microsoft SNA Server supports a single, isolated, LAN.

When only a single site exists to house both the mainframe and the client users, then configuration is the "centralized server" method, but without any remotely connected clients.

You must also configure the mainframe to support Microsoft SNA Server. The necessary LUs (Logical Units), terminal definitions, and such must be completed in order for the system to work. Configuring a mainframe computer is beyond the scope of this book; however, the techniques are very similar to adding local terminals.

Using the Microsoft SNA Server Admin Program

The Microsoft SNA Server Admin program is the main tool for managing the Microsoft SNA Server. The Microsoft SNA Server Admin program allows the administrator to configure:

- Servers and Connections
- LU Pools
- Users and Groups

To provide a smooth user interface, the Microsoft SNA Server Admin program dynamically modifies its menu structure. Generally, when changing tasks, the View menu item's contents change, and new menu items are added depending on the current task.

Common Administration Functions

Figure 10-1 shows the Microsoft SNA Server Admin program, with the Servers and Connections window active.

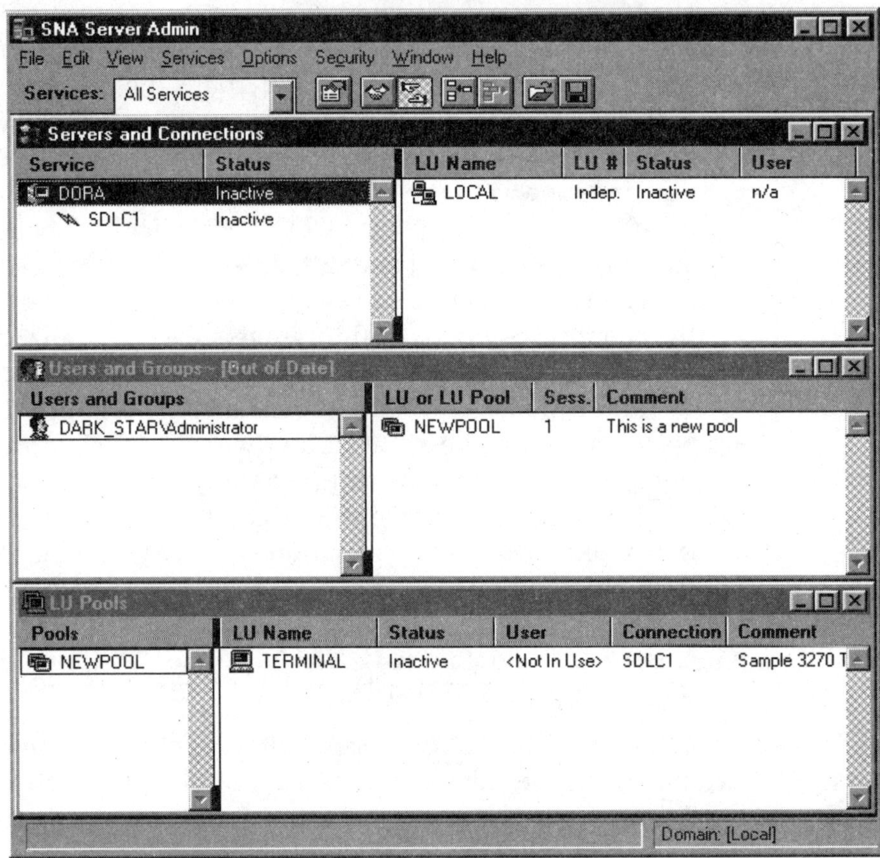

Figure 10-1: The Microsoft SNA Server Admin program with Servers and Connections window active.

The File, Edit, Options, Security, Window, and Help menu items for the Microsoft SNA Server Admin program are not modified dynamically when tasks are changed (other than when the Microsoft SNA Server Admin program is running without being connected to a Microsoft SNA Server).

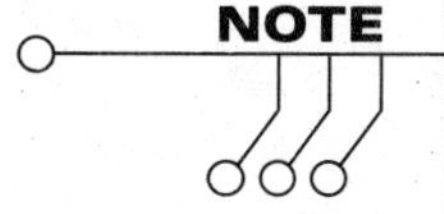

When the SNA Server Admin program starts, but is not yet connected to an SNA Server, the Files menu displays the Microsoft standard "Open" menu selection, which allows the user to connect to an SNA server.

You can use the File menu to open, reopen, save, back up, and restore configurations. You can also specify a different domain name to administer.

You can use the Edit menu to add a new connection, LU, or user; delete the current selection; or select all objects currently displayed. The Insert menu does not work like the typical Windows application in that it does not insert information from the clipboard but instead opens a dialog box for you to use to insert a specific object.

You can use the Options menu to set up the following:

- NetView, data from IBM's NetView product, a reporting system running on IBM mainframes. NetView forwards alerts that help the SNA administrator manage operations, diagnose problems, and improve system performance.
- RTM Triggers, available via 3270 emulators that receive RTM data. RTM monitors the time it takes for the host to interact with the user in a virtual 3270 session, using the 3270 terminal and NetView facility.
- Logs, which are the Windows NT 4 Server event logs.
- CPIC (Common Programming Interface for Communications) Names. This interface is used by APPC and is available for application programs.
- Display Verbs, used to specify a connection.
- Server Broadcasts, which control broadcasting to other network types (such as Novell NetWare, Vines, and Microsoft Networking).

You can also use the Options menu to set preferences for how the SNA Server Admin program looks and feels.

You use the Security menu to set server domain permissions, domain auditing, and domain owners.

Administering LU Pools

When the Microsoft SNA Server Admin program is in the LU Pools mode (Figure 10-2) (select this mode by making the LU Pools window active), the following functionalities (and menu items) are available. The View menu item has different items in it when tasks are changed, and a fourth menu item titled Pools is available.

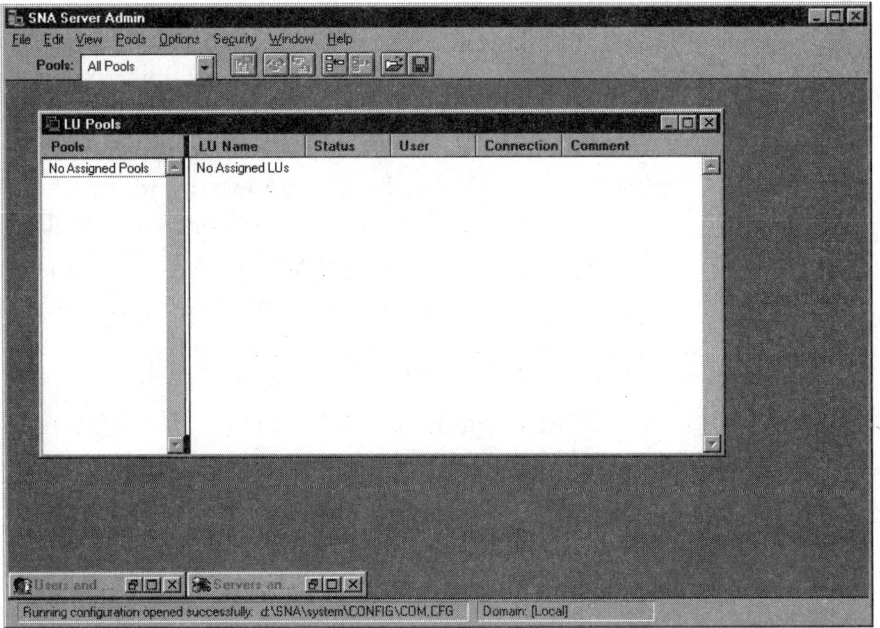

Figure 10-2: The SNA Server Admin program's LU Pools window.

You use the View menu to see only certain pools at one time, such as 3270 Pools, LU pools, or downstream pools.

You use the Pools menu to reset LUs, create new pools, assign LUs to a pool, move LUs to other pools, and display properties on a selected pool.

Administering Servers and Connections

Put Microsoft SNA Server Admin in the Servers and Connections mode (see Figure 10-3). You select this mode by making the Servers and Connections window active. The View menu has different items in it, and there is a new fourth menu item titled Services. The View menu exposes a number of functionalities.

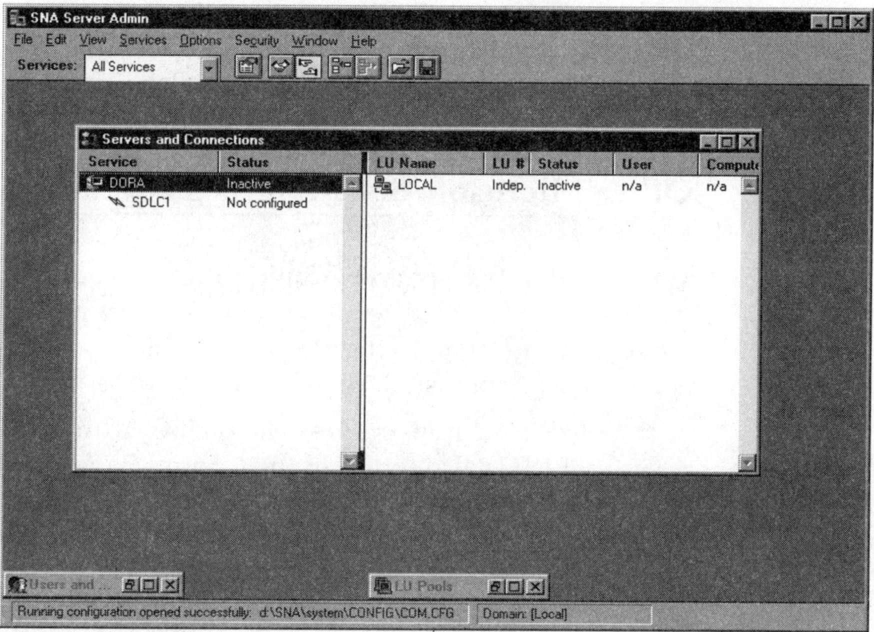

Figure 10-3: The SNA Server Admin program's Servers and Connections window.

You use the View menu to display active and inactive services and sort the list of LUs.

You use the Services menu to create, start, and stop SNA services. You can also assign, move, reorder, and copy LUs as appropriate. Finally, you can display properties of the currently selected object.

Administering Users and Groups

When the Microsoft SNA Server Admin program is in the Users and Groups mode (by making the Users and Groups window active), the View menu has different items, and there is a fourth menu item titled Users.

You use the View menu to display information about configured users or active users.

The Users menu allows you to create new users (or groups), assign LU (pool) sessions to a user, reorder LUs, or copy properties from one user to another. You can also display the properties of the currently selected user.

Other Microsoft SNA Server Program Items

The Microsoft SNA Server Admin program allows you to configure Microsoft SNA Server. Additionally, there are a number of other items installed in the Start Menu folder for Microsoft SNA Server when you install Microsoft SNA Server:

- ODBC Administrator—The ODBC Administrator program (which is also found in the Control Panel) is accessible from the Microsoft SNA Server (Common) group. The ODBC Administrator manages the StarSQL ODBC driver, which is supplied with Microsoft SNA Server.
- SNA Server 3270 Applet—This program emulates a 3270 display terminal, and is shown in Figure 10-4. A 3270 series terminal is typically connected to IBM mainframe computers.

Figure 10-4: The SNA Server 3270 Applet.

- SNA Server 5250 Applet—This program emulates a 5250 display terminal. A 5250 series terminal is typically connected to IBM mini-computers (such as the AS/400 series).
- SNA Server Documentation—An extensive help file for the Microsoft SNA Server product.
- SNA Server KnowledgeBase—An extensive help file, extracted from Microsoft's KnowledgeBase, for the Microsoft SNA Server product.
- SNA Server Modem Monitor—A program that monitors modems used by SNA dial-up clients.
- SNA Server Read Me—A read-me file for Microsoft SNA Server.

- SNA Server Service Pack #1—The documentation for the first (and currently only) service pack for Microsoft SNA Server.
- SNA Server Setup—The setup program for Microsoft SNA Server.
- SNA Server Trace—An application that allows you to set trace options. This functionality is also available in the Microsoft SNA Server Admin program.

Microsoft Systems Management Server

Microsoft Systems Management Server is an important part of Microsoft BackOffice in environments where there are systems that must be managed from a central location.

Microsoft Systems Management Server is able to monitor both hardware and software, distribute software (and upgrades), and audit the usage of software.

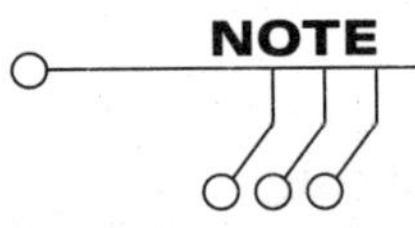

Microsoft Systems Management Server is a very large system. Microsoft Systems Management Server requires that Microsoft SQL Server be installed (and running). See Chapter 12, "Microsoft SQL Server 6.5," for information about installing Microsoft SQL Server. "Installing Microsoft Systems Management Server," later in this chapter, contains more information.

Microsoft Systems Management Server supports a number of different clients, including:

- Windows NT Server and Windows NT Workstation.
- Microsoft LAN Manager 2.1 (and later), with OS/2, DOS, and/or Windows 3.x clients.
- Microsoft Network Client for MS-DOS 3.0.

- NetWare 3.1x with MS-DOS and/or Windows 3.x clients.
- NetWare 4.x with MS-DOS clients.
- Apple Macintosh System 7.x clients.
- IBM LAN Server 3.0/3.1 running OS/2 clients.

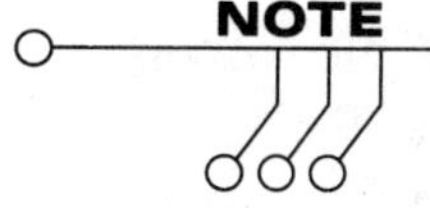

Microsoft Systems Management Server and its documentation was produced prior to the release of Windows 95. Although Windows 95 clients are not specifically listed, Windows 95 is supported. One of the few times that Windows 95 is mentioned is in the discussion about managing the distribution of the update to Windows 95 using SMS.

Installing Microsoft Systems Management Server

Microsoft Systems Management Server is a large product and requires substantial system resources. Microsoft suggests that an Intel 486 might run Microsoft Systems Management Server, though not well.

Even a mid-range Pentium (100 MHz) processor and 32MB of RAM may become bogged down running Microsoft Systems Management Server, especially if Microsoft SQL Server must also run on the same CPU. However, if you run Microsoft SQL Server on a computer other than Microsoft Systems Management Server, you may find that a lower-powered system is adequate.

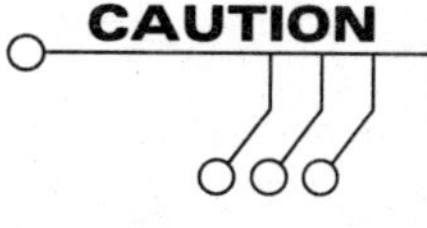

Only the very brave, or foolish, attempt to run Microsoft Exchange Server, Microsoft SNA Server, and Microsoft SQL Server at the same time on the same Pentium uni-processor server. To do this you need to have a very fast Pentium (at least 200 MHz) and a minimum of 128MB of RAM.

To install Microsoft Systems Management Server (SMS), you must first install Microsoft SQL Server. Additionally, you must do the following:

1. Create an account (using the Windows NT 4 Server's User Manager for Domains program) for the SMS Administrator program to use. This account is used by the SMS Administrator program, and typically not directly by the system administrator. Often this account would be named "smsadmin," and would need to have Administrative privileges, and the Log On As A Service rights privilege.
2. Create an account on your Microsoft SQL Server for the Microsoft Systems Management Server Administrator program to use. This account must have Create Database, Dump Database, and Dump Transaction permissions for the master database. The default administration login for Microsoft SQL Server, the "sa" (system administrator) account, also has these privileges.
3. Ensure that you have sufficient disk space for the Microsoft Systems Management Server product. A typical installation occupies about 60MB of disk space. You should also make sure that the Microsoft SQL Server database is large enough to hold the anticipated information that will be stored in it. (Microsoft Systems Management Server setup allocates about 53MB for the SMS SQL database.)

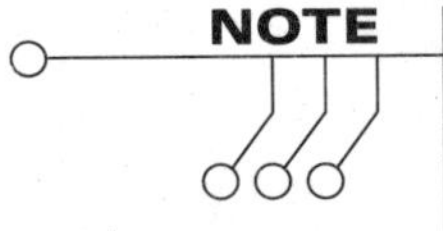

The version of Microsoft Systems Management Server shown in this example is from Microsoft BackOffice. The stand-alone version of Microsoft Systems Management Server may have slight differences.

Once you have prepared your system (installed Microsoft SQL Server and set up the necessary user ID), you may begin the installation of Microsoft Systems Management Server. To install, you should either start the Microsoft BackOffice setup program (if you are using the Microsoft BackOffice version) or the Microsoft Systems Management Server setup program (if you are using the stand-alone version).

You receive the typical prompts for user ID, organization, and product serial number. The first significant dialog that the Microsoft Systems Management Server setup program presents is the Primary Site Configuration Information dialog box, shown in Figure 10-5.

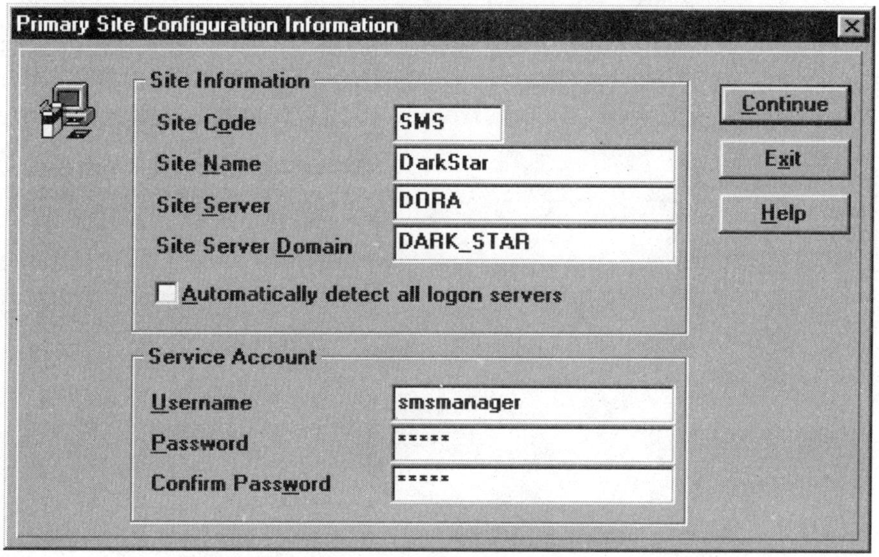

Figure 10-5: The Primary Site Configuration dialog.

You need to provide several pieces of information in this dialog box. First, create a three-character Site Code. This code uniquely identifies this Microsoft Systems Management Server site, and therefore you must take steps to ensure that the Site Code itself is unique. The Site Name is the "people readable" name that labels the site. The Site Name should be meaningful (for example, "Sales" for the sales office). Both Site Server and Site Server Domain are filled in with default values, which for the majority of the sites is acceptable. Change these names if desired.

You may also choose to check the "Automatically detect all logon servers." This configures Microsoft Systems Management Server to check for additional logon servers.

You will need to provide the Windows NT 4 Server user ID that was created to manage Microsoft Systems Management Server. Make sure you enter the correct password for this account.

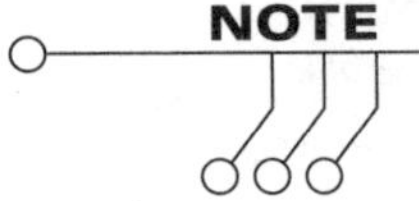

The Confirm Password edit box ensures that you typed the same password two times. It does not ensure the password is the correct one for Windows NT 4 Server.

The Microsoft Systems Management Server setup program displays a Setup Progress dialog. This dialog box displays the progress as Setup progresses. Shown in Figure 10-6 is the Setup Progress dialog, from an installation that is about 50% finished.

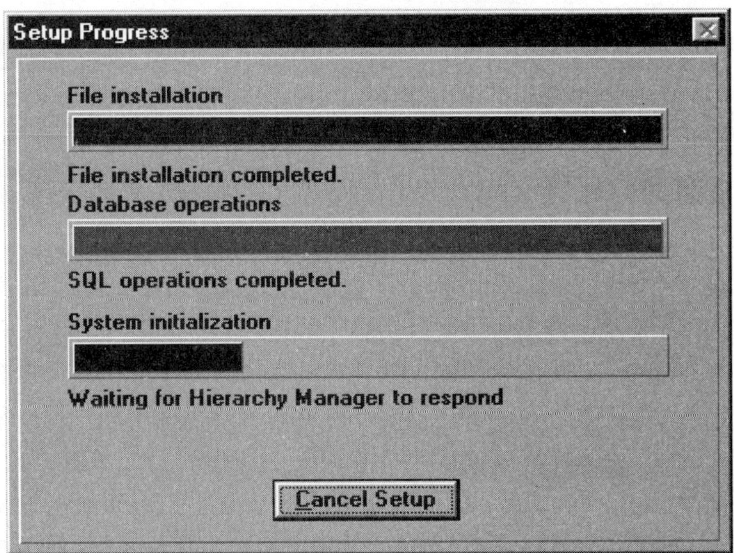

Figure 10-6: The Setup Progress dialog.

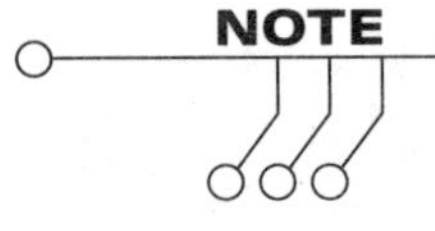

If you get a message that the Hierarchy Manager doesn't respond, check the user ID that you provided in the Primary Site Configuration Information dialog and make sure that it has the necessary privileges. Remember, a user ID may not be saved to the system until the User Manager for Domains program exits.

If you do not have the Network Monitor Driver installed, then you will need to add the Network Monitor Driver near the end of the setup process. The Microsoft Systems Management Server setup program prompts you (see Figure 10-7) to do this installation, and you may activate the Control Panel at this stage in the setup and add the Network Monitor Driver.

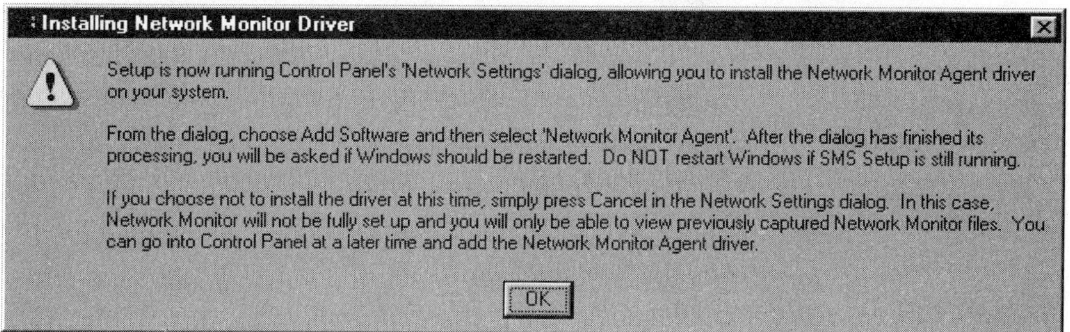

Figure 10-7: Prompt to add the Network Monitor Driver.

The prompt to add the Network Monitor Driver is not quite correct for Windows NT 4 Server (it was written for Windows NT 3.5x Server). Figure 10-8 shows the Control Panel's Network applet, with the Services tab displayed. You will need to click the Add button in the Services tab to install the Network Monitor Agent.

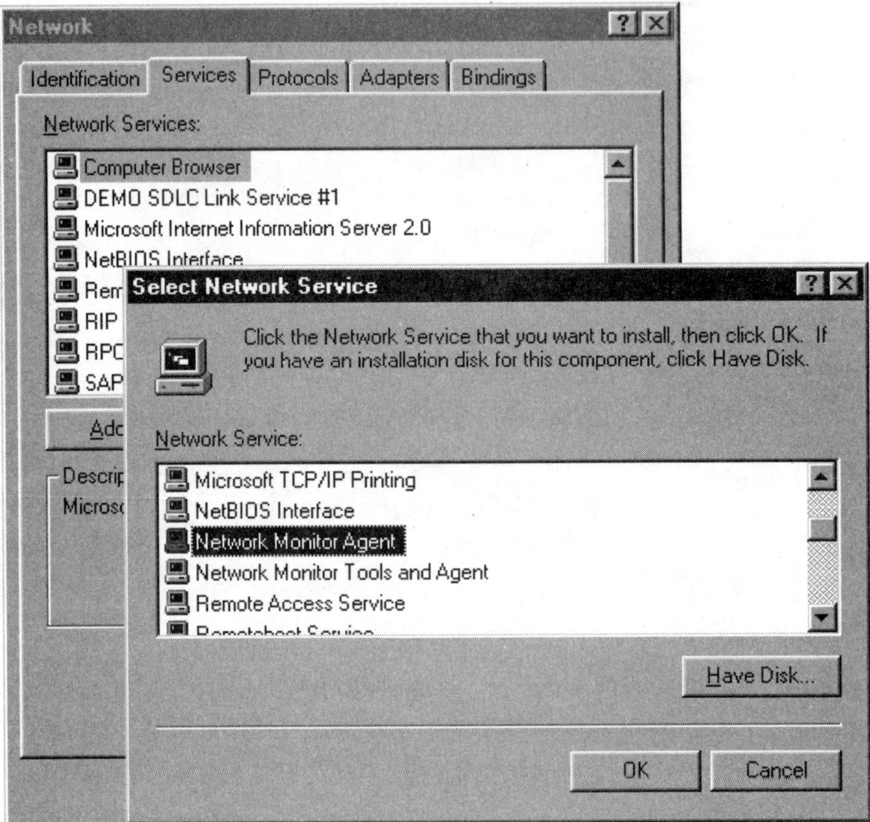

Figure 10-8: The Control Panel's Network applet.

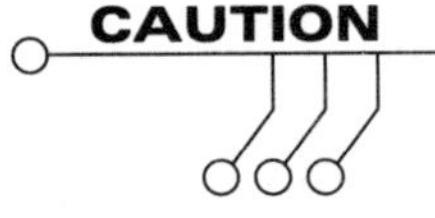

As the message shown in Figure 10-7 states, when the Control Panel's Network applet is closed, it will prompt to restart the system. Do NOT restart Windows NT 4 Server at this time—wait until the Microsoft Systems Management Server setup program has finished!

After you have installed all the component parts of Microsoft Systems Management Server, the setup program displays its completion dialog box. Once you dismiss the completion dialog box, restart Windows NT 4 Server to complete the installation of the Network Monitor Driver.

Installing Microsoft Systems Management Server Clients

Installing clients for Microsoft Systems Management Server requires an initial visit to each workstation. The client part of Microsoft Systems Management Server may be installed either by the system administrator or by the user (if the user is comfortable with such a task).

In the main Microsoft Systems Management Server folder (called SMS by default) is a folder called \sms\site.srv\maincfg.box\client.src. The necessary files needed to install the SMS clients for most operating environments and to run the Macintosh Installer command are located in this client.src folder. A Macintosh client requires special handling, using the Services for Macintosh (see Chapter 6, "Interacting with Other LANs," for details on the Services for Macintosh).

Throughout this section, we assume that you installed Microsoft Systems Management Server in the default \sms folder. The Microsoft Systems Management Server setup program creates several shares for you, sms_shr, sms_shrd, and sms_site. These shares allow clients (and other Microsoft Systems Management Servers) to access your Microsoft Systems Management Server.

In this section I provide an overview of the installation of a "DOS" client that is really being installed on a Windows 95 system. The installation is simple, requiring a batch command to be run from a DOS command window. Below, in Table 10-1, are the batch commands for all the different operating environments.

Command	Environment
RUNSMS.BAT	DOS, Windows 95, Windows 3.x, and Windows NT
RUNSMS.CMD	OS/2 (no versions are specified)

Table 10-1: Commands to install Microsoft Systems Management Server clients.

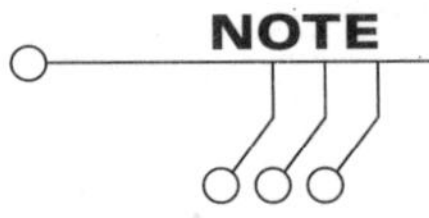

NOTE

When you install Microsoft Systems Management Server on an NTFS partition, check to make sure that client users have permission to access the Microsoft Systems Management Server folder(s).

If the user doesn't have the necessary permissions, then they will not be able to access the SMS system correctly.

To install the Microsoft Systems Management Server client for Windows 95, follow these steps:

1. On the client machine, establish a link to the sms_shr folder (which is created by the Microsoft Systems Management Server setup program), assigning this folder a drive letter (for this example, we will use L).
2. Open an Explorer window for the sms_shr folder and run the command to install the Microsoft Systems Management Server client setup program: runsms.bat.
3. The runsms client setup program then installs the necessary files and prompts the user for any required user actions. With most environments, you have to restart the client system to complete the installation.

If at any time you change your mind about the Microsoft Systems Management Server client software, you can use the "deinstal" command to remove the client software from the system.

After the installation of Microsoft Systems Management Server client software is complete, it performs an inventory of the client system.

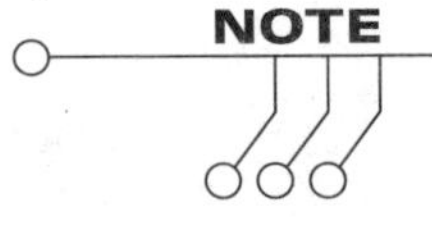

NOTE

The inventory of the client system may not be as accurate as, for example, the Windows 95 Control Panel's inventory. Minor differences may be noted; for example, one Windows 95 client with a Microsoft mouse installed was listed as having no mouse.

From the Systems Management Server client, there are many properties (see Figure 10-9) about their system including, but not limited to, the following: processor information, network information, disk and memory information, and other hardware-related information. There are also several diagnostic properties available, such as the Network Monitor (see Figure 10-10).

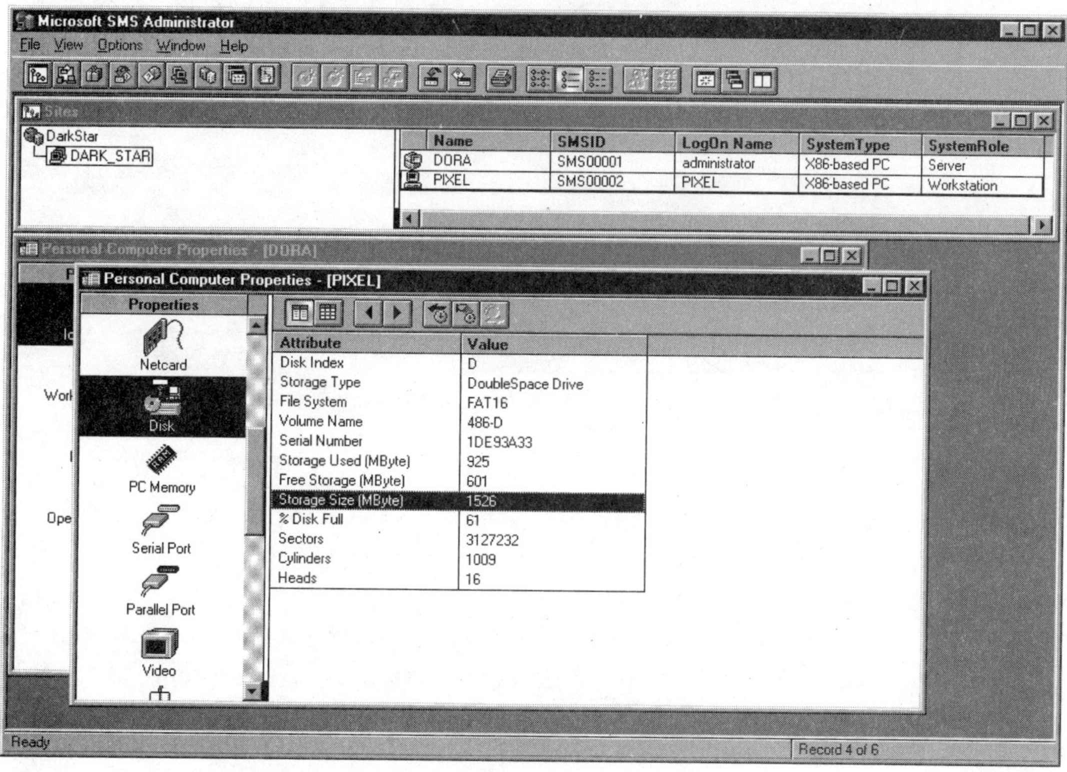

Figure 10-9: The Personal Computer Properties dialog.

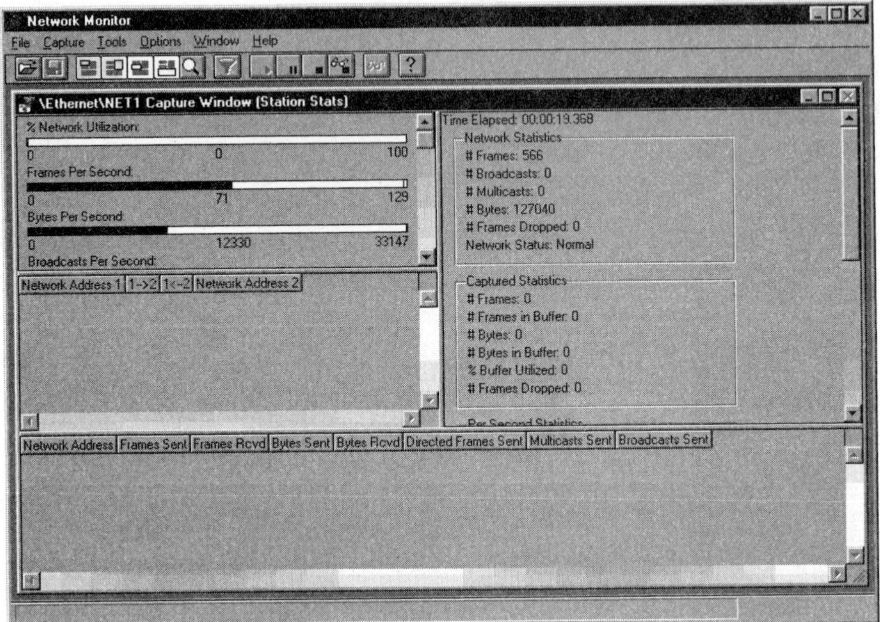

Figure 10-10: The Network Monitor following a client workstation's network activity.

Using the Microsoft Systems Management Server Administrator

The Microsoft Systems Management Server Administrator (which we will refer to as the SMS Administrator for the remainder of this chapter) program is the main interface with Microsoft Systems Management Server. This section provides an overview of the SMS Administrator and how it is used.

We can cover only a very limited subset of the Microsoft Systems Management Server and the SMS Administrator program in this book. Microsoft Systems Management Server is such a large product that readers needing more information should seek out publications dedicated to Microsoft Systems Management Server, and also check Microsoft's TechNet CD for the latest information on the SMS product.

Some of the topics in the SMS Administrator we cover are queries and informational displays.

Submitting Queries

Microsoft Systems Management Server allows you to easily interact with the Microsoft Systems Management Server SQL database, and provides a number of pre-defined queries for your use.

To perform a query, use the File | Execute Query menu, which displays the Execute Query dialog box (see Figure 10-11). In the Execute Query dialog box, you may choose which query to execute (choosing from a number of predefined queries, or by creating an ad-hoc query). You may also limit the queries search to specific sites. Some queries have different formats for the results.

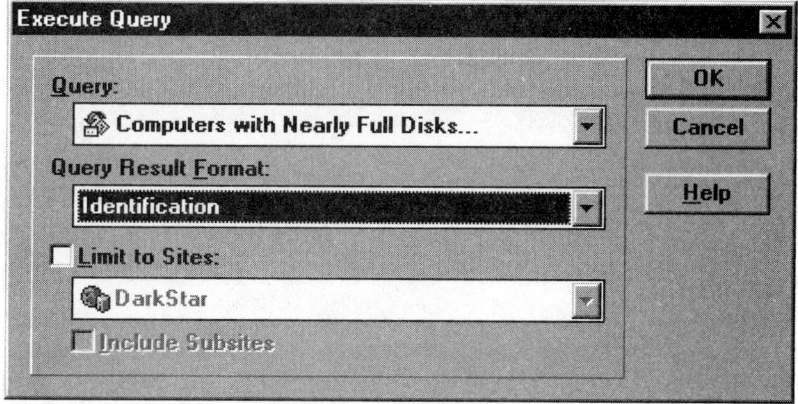

Figure 10-11: The Execute Query dialog box.

An example query: Search for all computers with disks that are more than 80% full (an easy search at the DarkStar domain, since all drives seem to be full most of the time); you would select "Computers with Nearly Full Disks." After you click the OK button, Microsoft Systems Management Server presents a dialog box that prompts for how full, in a percentage, the disks need to be. In this example, we specified 80%. The results of the query are shown in Figure 10-12.

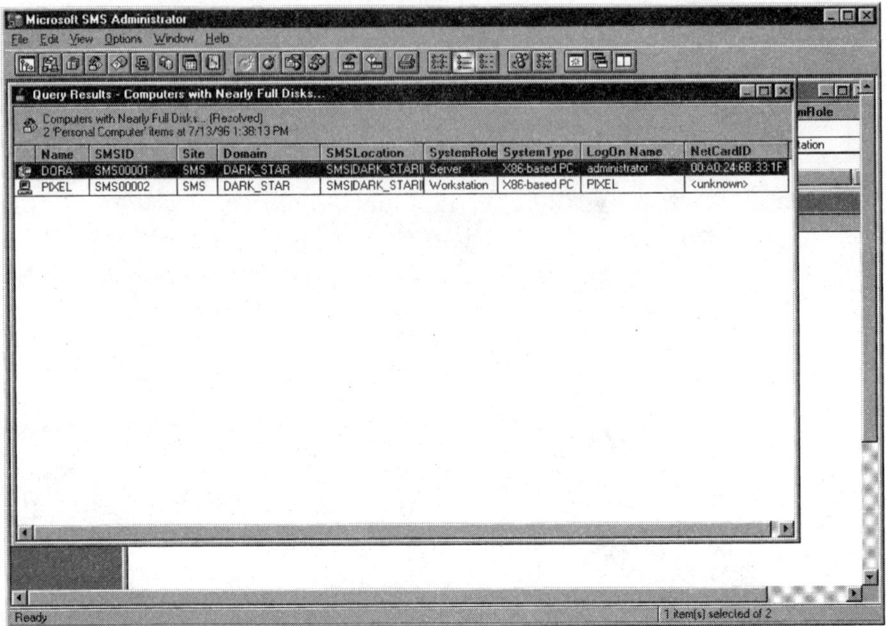

Figure 10-12: Results of a Computers with Nearly Full Disks query.

Displaying Queries

Microsoft Systems Management Server has the Queries window to display (select File | Open in the SMS Administrator's menu) the available queries on the Microsoft Systems Management Server database. Figure 10-13 shows the default queries that come with Microsoft Systems Management Server.

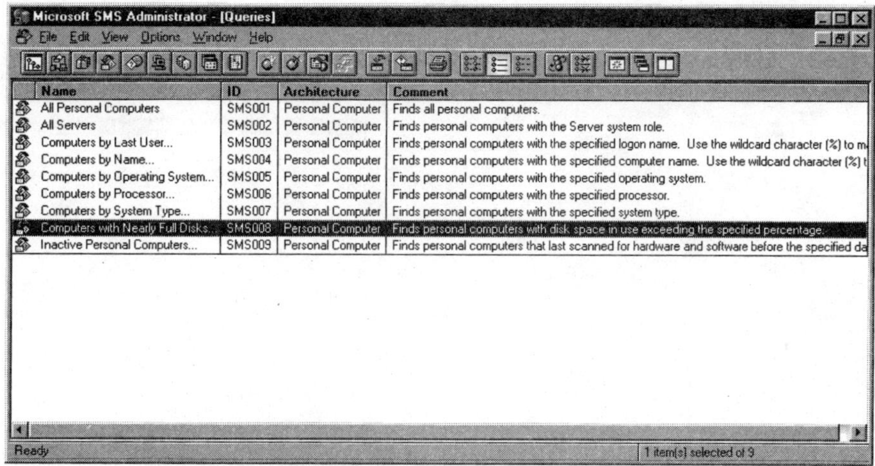

Figure 10-13: The Queries window.

In addition to the queries supplied with Microsoft Systems Management Server, you may create additional queries. The supplied queries may be customized as well. Customization might include limiting the scope of the query or limiting the output information.

Listing Sites in the SMS Hierarchy

Microsoft Systems Management Server's Sites window (select File | Open in the SMS Administrator's menu) displays a listing of the sites in the Microsoft Systems Management Server's hierarchy. Figure 10-14 shows an example of the Sites window.

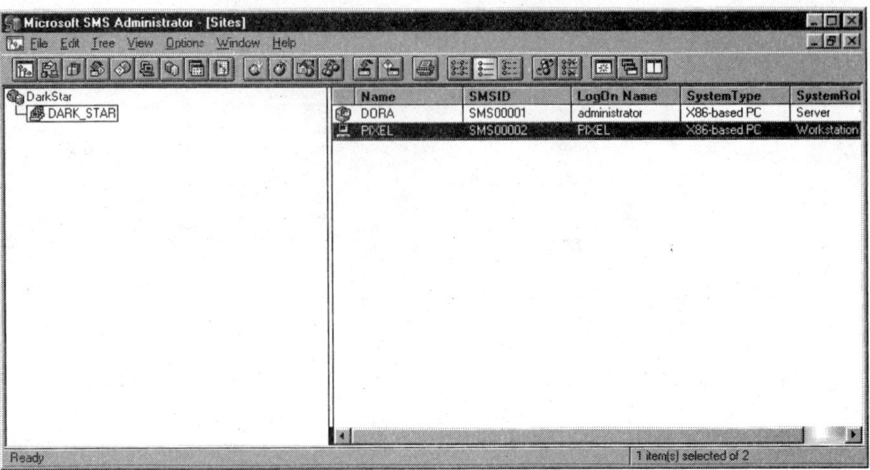

Figure 10-14: The Sites window.

Generally, all systems in the site are listed in the Sites window, and you use the Sites window when adding to Machine Groups and the Site Groups (both Machine Groups and Site Groups are described below). Most SMS Administrator users leave the Sites window open all the time, as it is frequently used.

Displaying and Creating Packages

Microsoft Systems Management Server's Packages window (select File | Open in the SMS Administrator's menu) displays the currently defined packages. A package is an action that you want to take place on the client systems. You define the command to be executed, where the command will be found (the command's path), and what platform the command is intended to run on when creating a package.

Figure 10-15 shows a list of packages defined in our example installation.

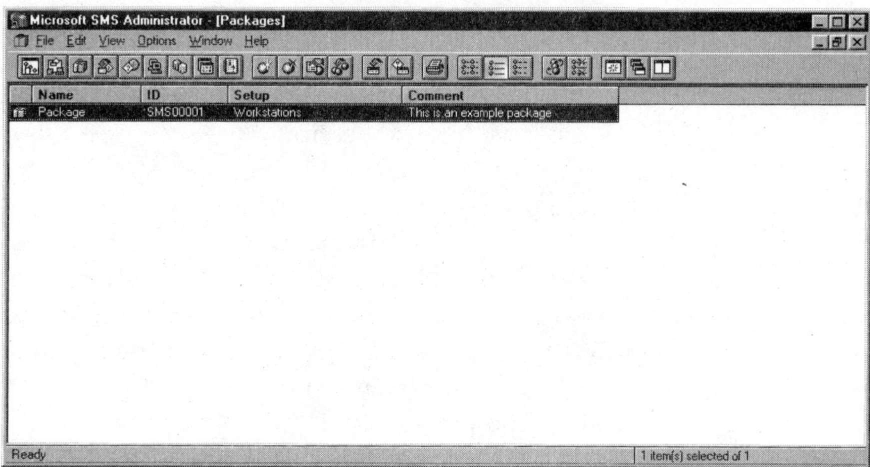

Figure 10-15: The Packages window.

When creating a package you are presented with several configuration dialog boxes. Figure 10-16 shows the Command Line Properties dialog box. This dialog box defines the actual command that executes. You also specify the platform for the command as well—in our example we can only execute the Pinball game under Windows 95 and Windows NT.

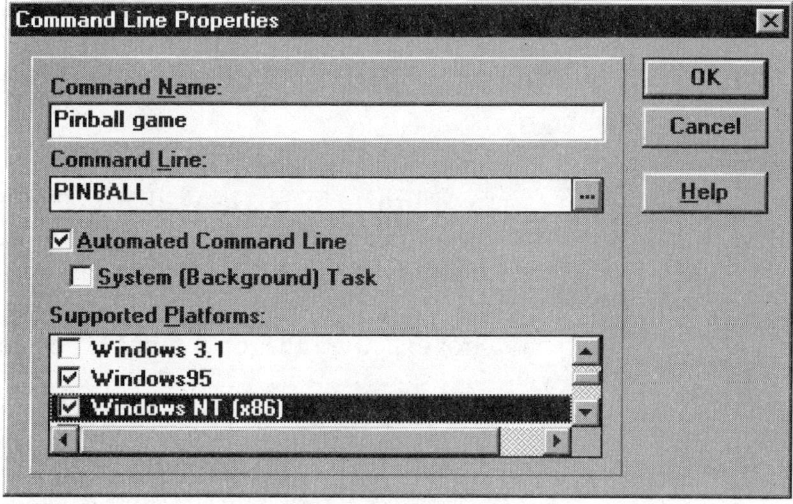

Figure 10-16: The Command Line Properties window.

Typical uses for packages include installing or upgrading software, testing, and running other administrative tasks. To enable a package to be executed on clients, you have to create a job, the topic of the next section.

Displaying and Creating Jobs

Microsoft Systems Management Server has the Jobs window (select File | Open in the SMS Administrator's menu) to display the status of any existing jobs. Jobs are created by opening the Jobs window, then selecting File | New from the menu.

Prior to creating jobs, you must create a package (which is the task that the job performs). Figure 10-17 shows the Jobs window.

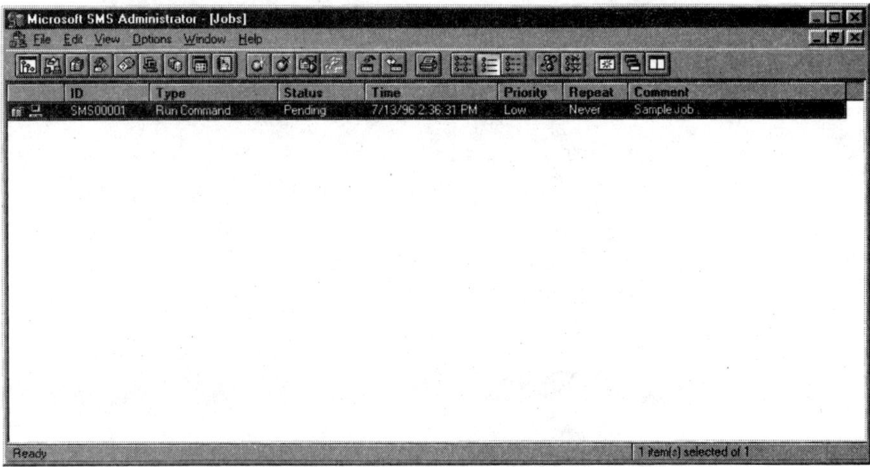

Figure 10-17: The Jobs window.

You can assign priorities to jobs as well as manipulate the schedule for the jobs. For example, you may make the execution of a job optional for a period of time, then mandatory after a certain date. At some later date, you may want the job to expire—any users who have not executed the job by that time probably won't.

Displaying and Creating Alerts

Microsoft Systems Management Server's Alerts window (select File | Open in the SMS Administrator's menu) displays information about alerts that have been created. To create an alert, open the Alerts window, and from the menu select Files | New. The Alerts window is shown in Figure 10-18.

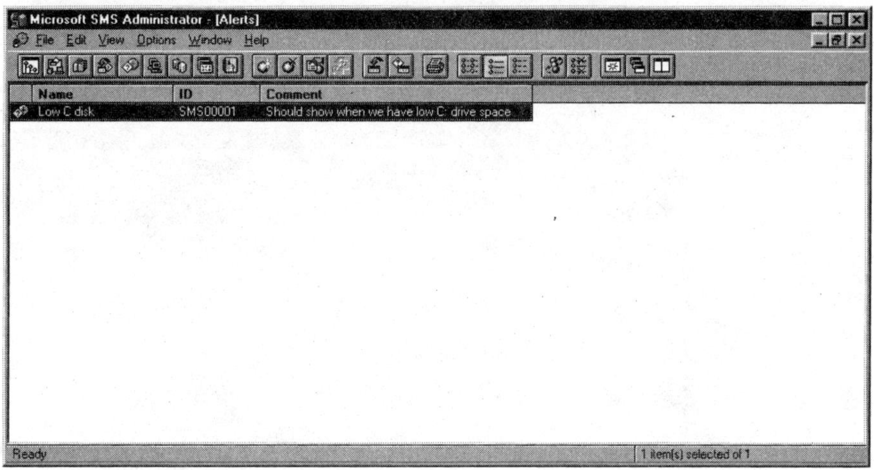

Figure 10-18: The Alerts window.

An alert could be as simple as checking the hard drives on the client systems to ensure that there is sufficient free space. For example, the alert shown in Figure 10-18 produced the message box shown in Figure 10-19.

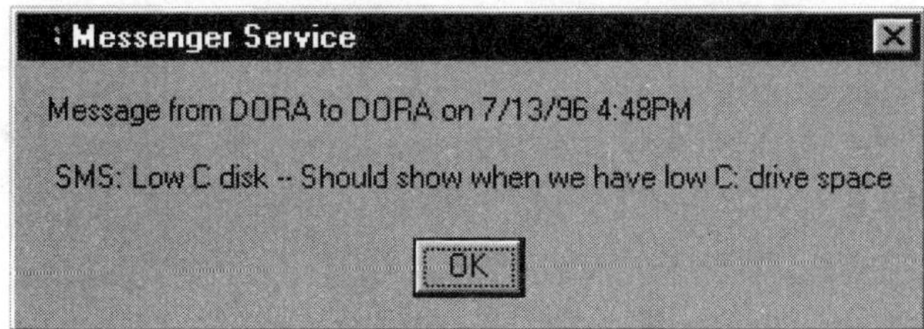

Figure 10-19: An alert message.

Notice how both the alert name and the comment are incorporated into the message: good reason to make sure both the name and comment make sense and are accurate.

Displaying and Creating Machine Groups

Microsoft Systems Management Server's Machine Groups window (select File | Open in the SMS Administrator's menu) displays information about Machine Groups. Machine Groups create a logical grouping of a number of machines. For example, there might be a Machine Group for the R&D group, a Machine Group for the Accounting group, and a Machine Group for the Administrative group. Figure 10-20 shows the Machine Groups window, with a single group (called "Group 1") comprised of two machines.

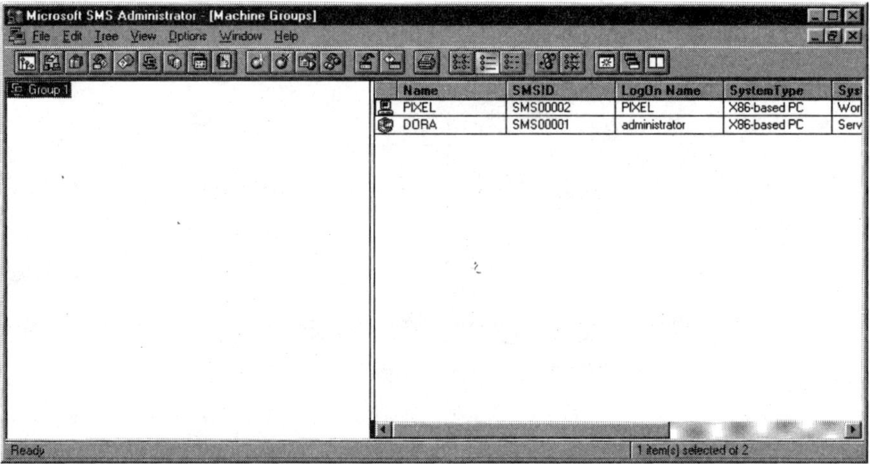

Figure 10-20: The Machine Groups window.

Displaying Site Groups

Microsoft Systems Management Server's Site Groups window (select File | Open in the SMS Administrator's menu) displays information about sites. Generally (but not always), sites are geographically separated parts of your organization.

Figure 10-21 shows the Site Groups window, with a single site defined. (Well, actually the DarkStar site is it—the only location on my system!)

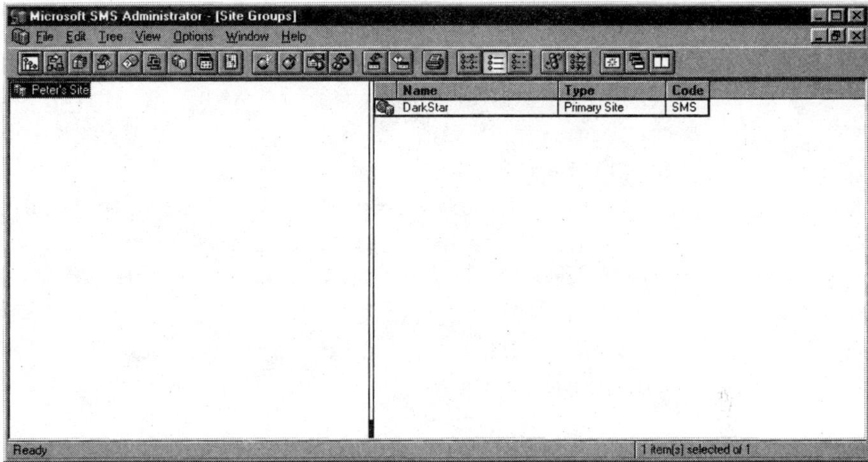

Figure 10-21: The Site Groups window.

Displaying Program Groups

Microsoft Systems Management Server's Program Groups (select File | Open in the SMS Administrator's menu) window displays information about Program Groups. Programs Groups manage programs.

Figure 10-22 shows the Program Groups window, with a single Program Group defined.

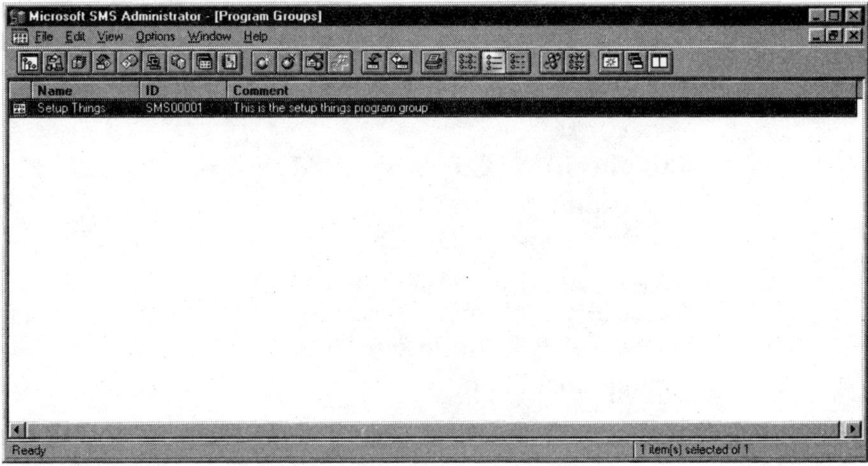

Figure 10-22: The Program Groups window.

Displaying Events

Microsoft Systems Management Server's Events window (select File | Open in the SMS Administrator's menu) displays information about events that have occurred in the Microsoft Systems Management Server. Event information is extracted from the Windows NT 4 Server event log (filtered, so that only event information relevant to Microsoft Systems Management Server is displayed). This is done by selecting events of the "SMSEvent" type.

Figure 10-23 shows the Events Window, with a number of events listed. You can then query each event to determine whether it is significant, or may be safely ignored.

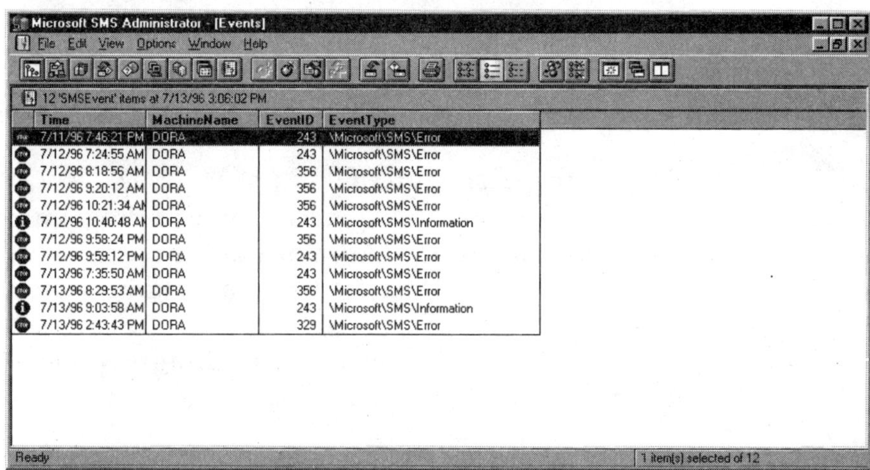

Figure 10-23: The Events window.

Displaying SQL Server Messages

Microsoft Systems Management Server's SQL Server Messages window (select File | Open in the SMS Administrator's menu) displays any message received from the Microsoft SQL Server. Generally such messages are important, so you should monitor the SQL Error window frequently when using Microsoft Systems Management Server.

Figure 10-24 shows the SQL Server Messages window, with one entry: "7/13/96 3:07:09 PM - 0 new entries." Bottom line with this entry: there is nothing wrong with the SQL Server!

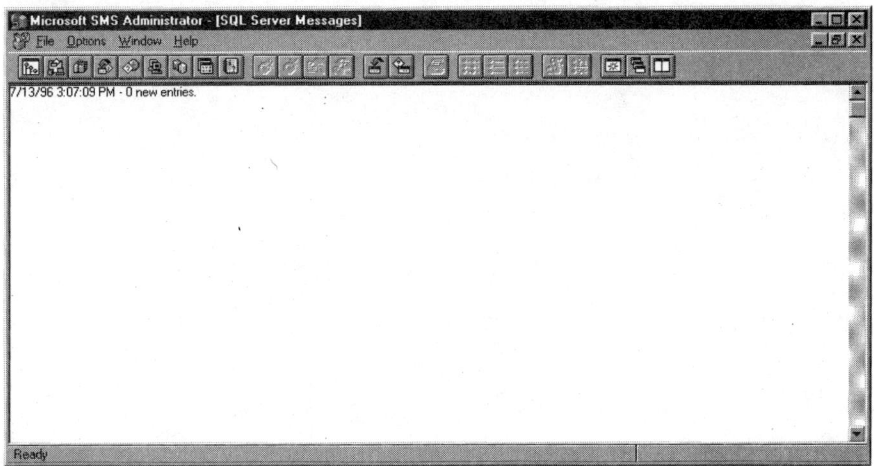

Figure 10-24: The SQL Server Messages window.

Moving On

This chapter introduced Microsoft BackOffice; we showed you how to install, configure, and use a number of components that are part of Microsoft BackOffice, such as Microsoft Systems Management Server and Microsoft SNA Server.

In the next few chapters, I will cover the Microsoft Exchange Server and Client and Microsoft SQL Server.

11

Microsoft Exchange Server & Client

Microsoft Exchange Server is Microsoft's replacement for MS Mail, which is part of Microsoft BackOffice 1.5. Microsoft Exchange Server 4.0 is an advanced, powerful, enterprise e-mail server.

Microsoft Exchange Client has been a valuable part of Windows 95, and will become a useful addition to both Windows NT 4 Server and Windows NT 4 Workstation. Windows NT 4 Server comes with basic Microsoft Exchange Client software.

Microsoft Exchange Server, which is available as either a separate product or as part of Microsoft BackOffice, includes a more advanced version of the Microsoft Exchange Client software.

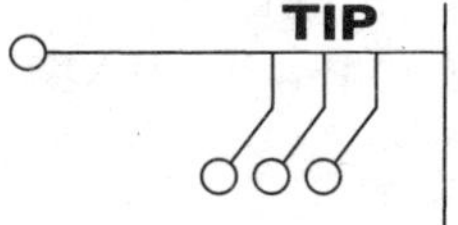

It is beyond the scope of this chapter to provide a complete reference to Microsoft Exchange Server. If you are working on an implementation of Microsoft Exchange Server, then I recommend that you purchase the printed documentation for Microsoft Exchange Server. Also, Appendix B lists some books that cover Microsoft Exchange Server.

Included with Microsoft Exchange Server are clients for Windows 95, Windows NT, DOS, and 16-bit versions of Windows.

Microsoft Exchange Server can be purchased either as a component of Microsoft BackOffice or separately as an individual product. There may be financial advantages to using Microsoft BackOffice—you may find that purchasing Microsoft BackOffice is less expensive than purchasing two or more products separately.

The license agreement for Microsoft BackOffice does not allow you to split the various parts of Microsoft BackOffice between servers. All Microsoft BackOffice components must be installed on a single server, or additional Microsoft BackOffice licenses must be purchased.

Installation Requirements

Microsoft Exchange Server is a large product. Minimum system requirements for Microsoft Exchange Server include:

- An Intel 486 (or better) or an RISC-based microprocessor (including the MIPS R4000, Digital Alpha AXP, or PowerPC).
- A minimum of 250MB free space on the server's drive(s).
- Additional space for the Windows NT 4 Server paging file. Generally, you need to add about 50MB of additional paging file space when running Microsoft Exchange Server.
- A minimum of 24 MB RAM, with 32MB recommended for Intel platforms. For RISC platforms, 32MB RAM, with 48MB recommended.

The above requirements are *minimum* values. To garner maximum performance from Microsoft Exchange Server, configure the Microsoft Exchange Server's computer to have the following:

- Use an Intel Pentium 90 or a Pentium Pro. Alternatively, you can use an RISC computer.

- Hard disk space for all folders and other information including user's e-mail. Consider the issues of holidays, large e-mail message attachments, and users who do not properly delete their e-mail from the server.
- The use of several physical drives (and multi-channel SCSI controllers) to enhance I/O interleaving and performance. (I/O interleaving rearranges I/O to optimize seeks done with hardware.)
- A striped drive set, which also enhances disk I/O performance. Striping (RAID Level 0) is described in Chapter 8, "Configuring Hardware."
- Additional paging file space. (Typically, Microsoft recommends 100MB in addition to the amount of RAM installed. I recommend 150MB in addition to the amount of RAM installed, if possible.)
- A minimum of 32MB RAM, preferably 48; 64MB RAM will perform even better. For RISC systems, 48MB minimum, preferably 64 or even 128MB for better performance.

Virtually all installations will be different. Variations will include number of users, amount and type of e-mail traffic, and other habits. Because of these variations, you should study and follow the recommendations found in the Microsoft Exchange Server Books Online volumes: "Installation Guide" and "Concepts and Planning Guide."

Installing Microsoft Exchange

Microsoft Exchange Server is installable on either a Primary Domain Server (PDC) or a Backup Domain Server (BDC). If Windows NT 4 Server is a stand-alone server, then you will need to reinstall Windows NT 4 Server as a PDC.

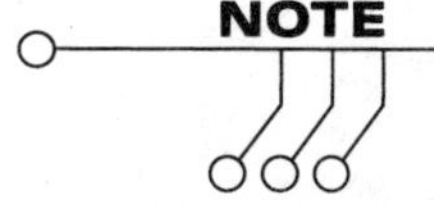

There is no way to upgrade from a stand-alone server to a PDC/BDC configuration other than to reinstall Windows NT 4 Server.

A typical installation of Microsoft Exchange Server starts with setup from the Microsoft Exchange Server distribution CD-ROM. Insert the CD into the drive and run setup from the correct folder. (There are versions of Microsoft Exchange Server for Intel, MIPS, and Alpha processors.)

When Microsoft Exchange Server is installed, a copy of Microsoft Exchange Client is also installed.

In this book, the version of Microsoft Exchange Server installed was the stand-alone product (as compared to the version that is part of Microsoft BackOffice). The version supplied with Microsoft BackOffice is virtually identical—the only difference is that you start the Microsoft BackOffice version of Microsoft Exchange Server's setup program from Microsoft BackOffice Setup.

Figure 11-1 shows the Microsoft Exchange Server setup program. You must click either Typical, Complete/Custom, or Minimum. Be careful: the Change Directory button in the Microsoft Exchange Server Setup window is the only way to modify the folder (directory) where Microsoft Exchange Server will be installed.

Figure 11-1: The Microsoft Exchange Server Setup, first screen—selecting the type of setup.

As shown in Figure 11-2, Microsoft Exchange Server consists of three installable components:

- Microsoft Exchange Server—This option installs the actual server portion of Microsoft Exchange Server. The server may be locally or remotely administered, using the Microsoft Exchange Administrator program.
- Microsoft Exchange Administrator—This option installs the administrator for Microsoft Exchange Server. The administration of Microsoft Exchange Server may be either at the server, or on a remote administration machine.
- Microsoft Exchange Server Books Online—This option installs the extended online help system. When installing either Microsoft Exchange Server or Microsoft Exchange Administrator, it is best to install this component.

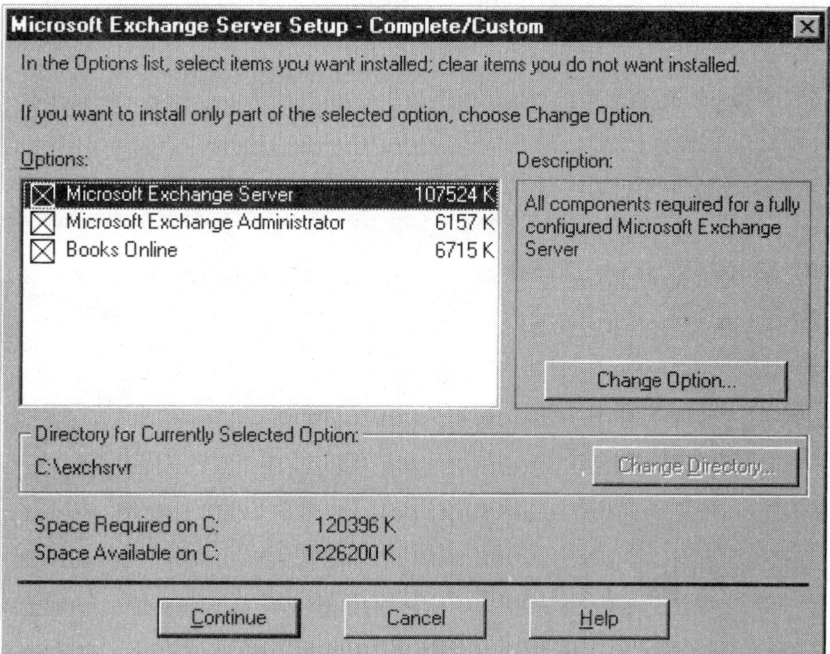

Figure 11-2: Selecting Microsoft Exchange Server options.

On the server, install Microsoft Exchange Server and Microsoft Exchange Administrator. Where Microsoft Exchange Server is being installed on one server, and will be administered from another server or workstation, install Microsoft Exchange Administrator on a second system being used for administration.

If you have access to the printed Microsoft Exchange Server documentation, then installing the Books Online may be redundant. However, if the Microsoft Exchange Server printed documentation is unavailable, then installing the Books Online represents a wise choice—Microsoft Exchange Server is a complex and difficult to manage system.

Installing Microsoft Exchange Server requires substantial planning. Microsoft provides a number of worksheets to assist in planning the Microsoft Exchange Server installation. These worksheets (for an example, see Figure 11-3) may be printed from the Books Online (search for the topics "Organization Planning Worksheet," "Site Planning Worksheet," and "Server Planning Worksheet").

Microsoft server products require that you select a licensing mode at installation time. The two choices, Per Server and Per Seat, should be familiar. If in doubt when installing Microsoft Exchange, select the Per Server licensing mode—your license agreement allows a one-time change from Per Server to Per Seat.

Installation Guide

File Edit Contents Bookmark Options Help

Contents | Index | Back | Print | << | >> | Glossary

2 Planning Your Organization 7 of 9

Planning Worksheets

Organization Planning Worksheet

Use this worksheet to record your organization setup.

Organization Name: ______________________

Site Names: ______________________

Windows NT Domain Names: ______________________

Server Names: ______________________

Naming Convention:

Display Name: ______________________

Alias: ______________________

Directory Name: ______________________

Connectors to Install:

☐ Site ☐ Dynamic RAS ☐ Internet Mail

☐ X.400 ☐ MS Mail (PC) ☐ MS Mail (AppleTalk)

☐ Other

Clients to Support

☐ Roving

☐ Remote

Connect via:

☐ Shiva ☐ RAS ☐ Modem

Figure 11-3: Microsoft Exchange Server installation worksheets help with installation.

If there is an existing site on another server, Microsoft Exchange Server can be installed as a member of the same site. The alternative is to create a new site (the most popular choice). Creating a new site requires you to provide two pieces of information:

- Organization Name—The name of your organization, which is used to form e-mail addresses.
- Site Name—The name of the site being installed, which is combined with Organization Name to form part of Microsoft Exchange Server's e-mail addresses.

The Organization Name and the Site Name form a default e-mail address, such as *Organization_Name.Site_name*.com, where *Organization_name*, and *Site_name* are the names you entered in the Organization and Site dialog box (see Figure 11-4).

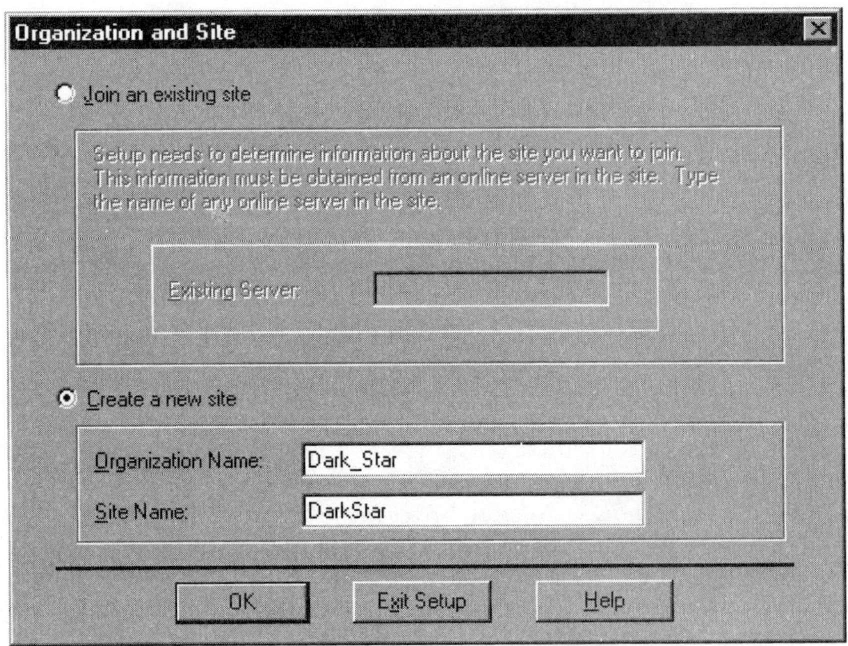

Figure 11-4: Entering the Organization Name and Site Name.

Microsoft Exchange Server's setup program prompts for any other needed information. After installing Microsoft Exchange Server, setup prompts to run the Microsoft Exchange Performance Optimizer (Figure 11-5).

Figure 11-5: Running Microsoft Exchange Server Optimizer for the first time.

If you do not optimize Microsoft Exchange Server during installation, then you should definitely do so before putting the Exchange Server to use.

Optimizing Performance

The Microsoft Exchange Performance Optimizer is a wizard that analyzes the disk resources on the server and determines the optimal placement for Microsoft Exchange Server files. Shown in Figure 11-6 is Microsoft Exchange Performance Optimizer's first screen.

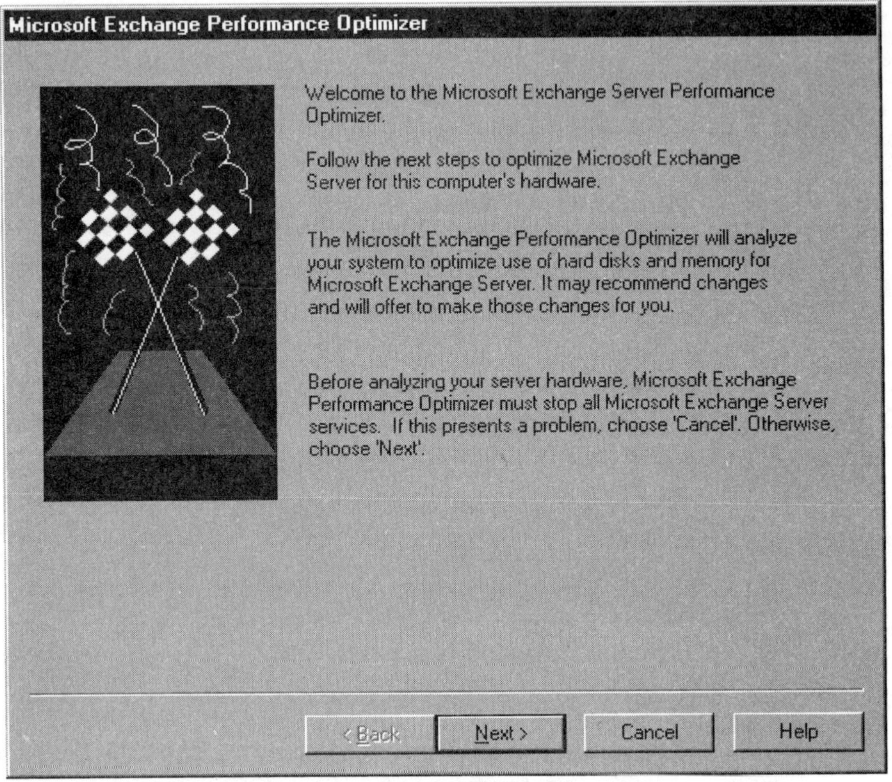

Figure 11-6: Microsoft Exchange Performance Optimizer's first screen.

For example, DORA has five hard drives (C:, D:, E:, F:, and G:), each of which has different performance factors and space availability.

Microsoft Exchange Performance Optimizer needs information about the size of your Microsoft Exchange Server site. You need to *estimate* the number of users, type of usage, and size of the organization, as Figure 11-7 shows.

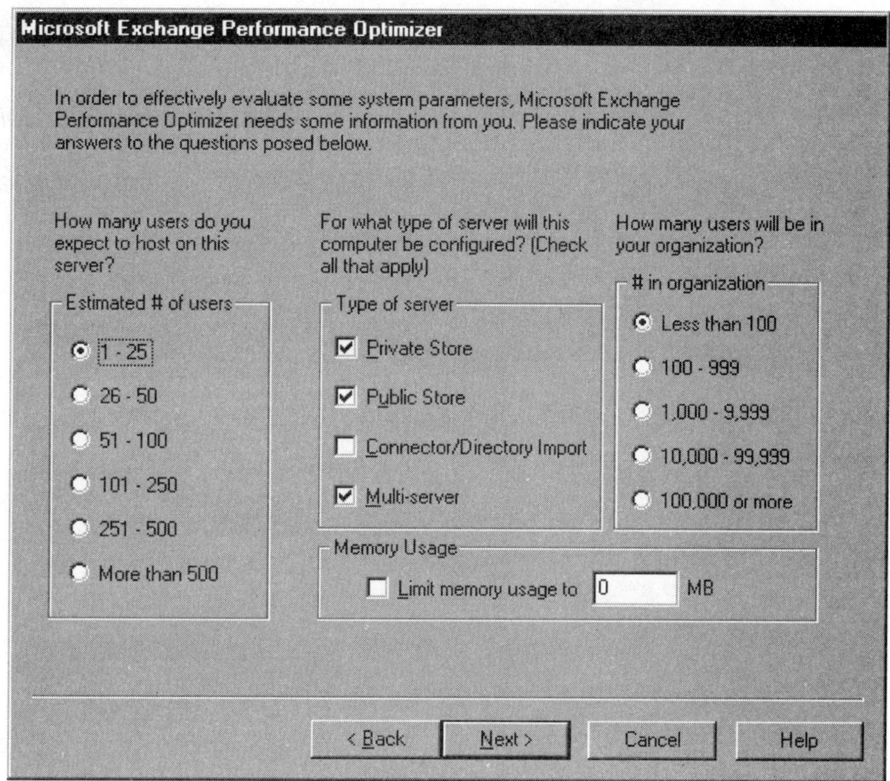

Figure 11-7: Telling Microsoft Exchange Performance Optimizer how big you are.

Once Microsoft Exchange Performance Optimizer has analyzed the hardware, it suggests new locations for a number of items. Figure 11-8 shows the results of running Microsoft Exchange Performance Optimizer on DORA: the optimizer used four of the five drives on DORA. Hopefully, Microsoft Exchange Performance Optimizer spread the load effectively between the different drives.

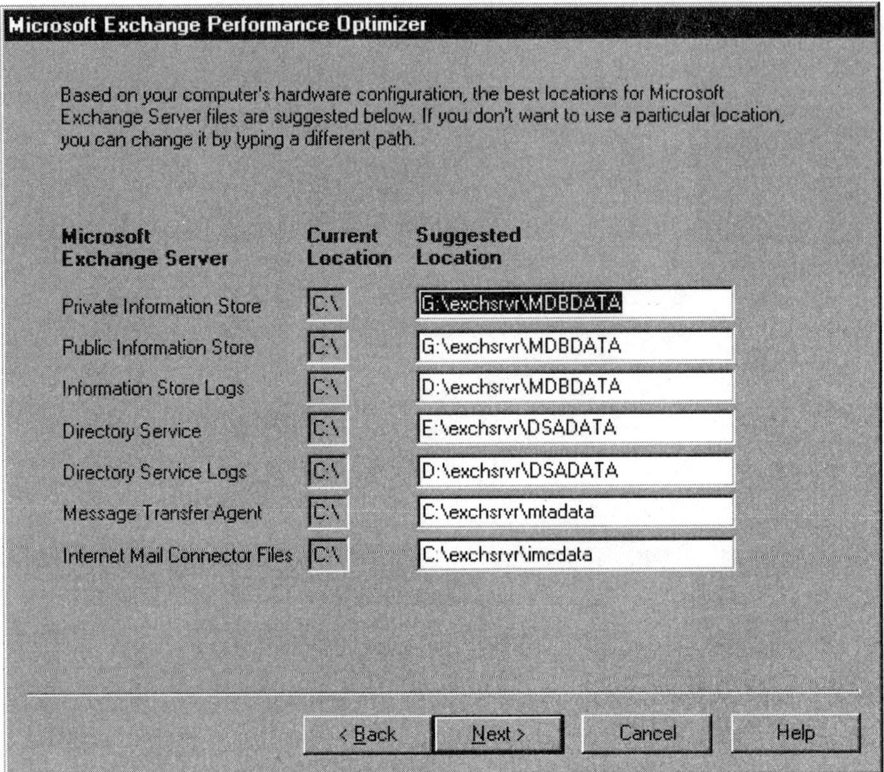

Figure 11-8: Microsoft Exchange Performance Optimizer suggests moving a few files.

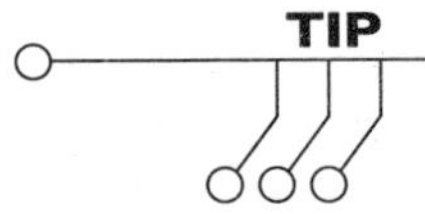

If you are running Microsoft Exchange Performance Optimizer as part of a new installation, you do not need to back up these files before moving them. However, if you are running Microsoft Exchange Performance Optimizer on a running Microsoft Exchange Server system, make sure you have adequate backups of all files being moved! Microsoft Exchange Performance Optimizer is able to move these files automatically (this is recommended).

Components of the Microsoft Exchange Server & Client

Once you have installed Exchange, you have a new Start Menu folder, called Microsoft Exchange. Shown in Figure 11-9 is a typical Microsoft Exchange management folder.

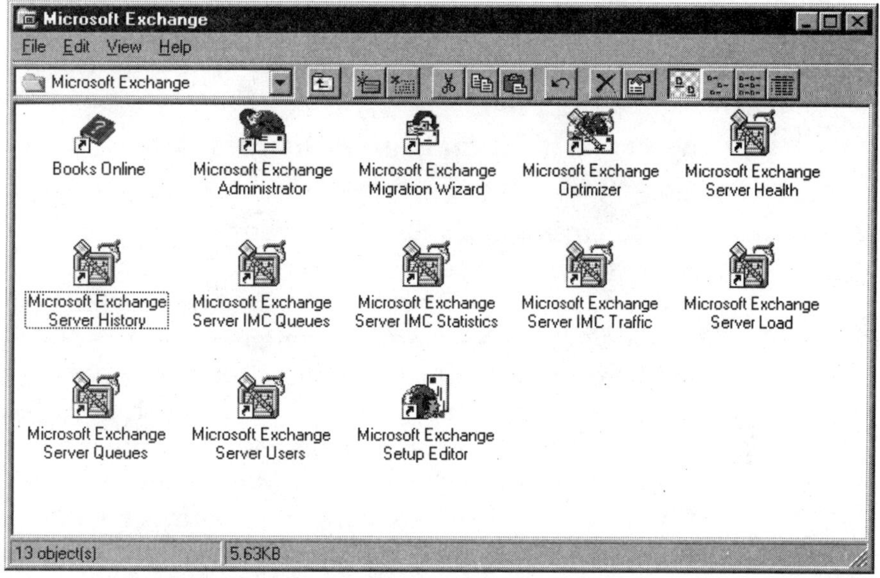

Figure 11-9: The Microsoft Exchange folder.

Microsoft Exchange Server Books Online

The Microsoft Exchange Server Books Online is the main online documentation for Microsoft Exchange Server. Books Online is composed of four books:

- Installation Guide—Documents the first step in installing Microsoft Exchange Server. Reading through the Installation Guide is an excellent idea, as it is a short volume.

- Concepts and Planning Guide—Explains how Microsoft Exchange Server works, and includes an overview of the Microsoft Exchange Server product.
- Administrator's Guide—Provides instructions on how to use the Microsoft Exchange Server Administrator program, and how to administer a Microsoft Exchange Server installation. This book is the most valuable resource in the Microsoft Exchange Server documentation.
- Application Designer's Guide—Covers the design of custom Microsoft Exchange applications.

Microsoft Exchange Administrator

The Microsoft Exchange Administrator program manages Microsoft Exchange Server. Start the Microsoft Exchange Administrator program (in Start Menu | Programs | Microsoft Exchange), and log on to a Microsoft Exchange Server to administer.

Microsoft Exchange Administrator has a user interface similar to that of Microsoft SQL Server's Administrator (described in Chapter 12, "Microsoft SQL Server 6.5"). The main window shows a pair of panes, the left showing a tree view of Microsoft Exchange Server, and the right showing detail/property information. Microsoft Exchange Administrator is shown in Figure 11-10.

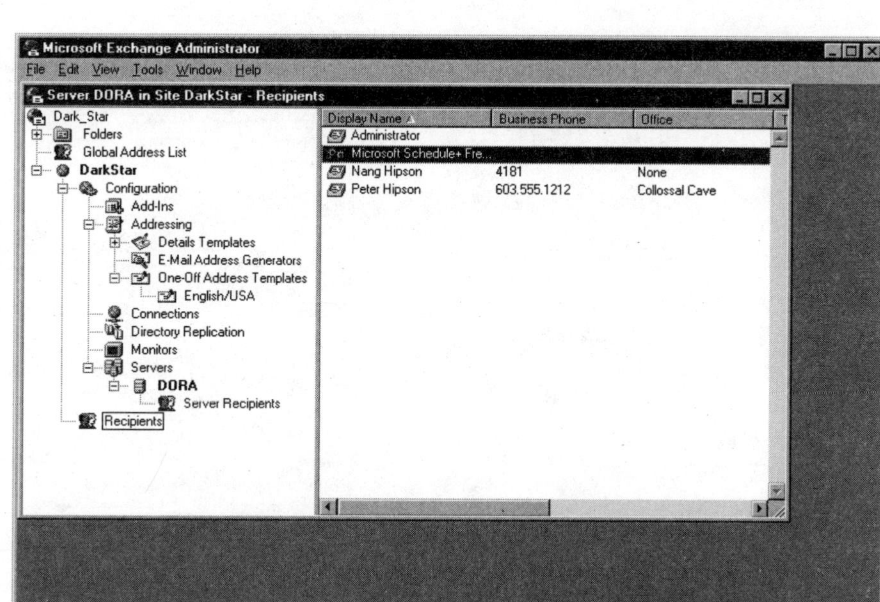

Figure 11-10: Microsoft Exchange Administrator for Dark_Star.

Figure 11-10 shows the relationship between the Organization Name, Site Name, and server. You use the Administrator program to create new mailboxes, new distribution lists, and other supporting services.

New Mailboxes

Each Microsoft Exchange client user must have a mailbox. Selecting File | New Mailboxes from Microsoft Exchange Administrator's menu displays the mailbox Properties dialog (Figure 11-11).

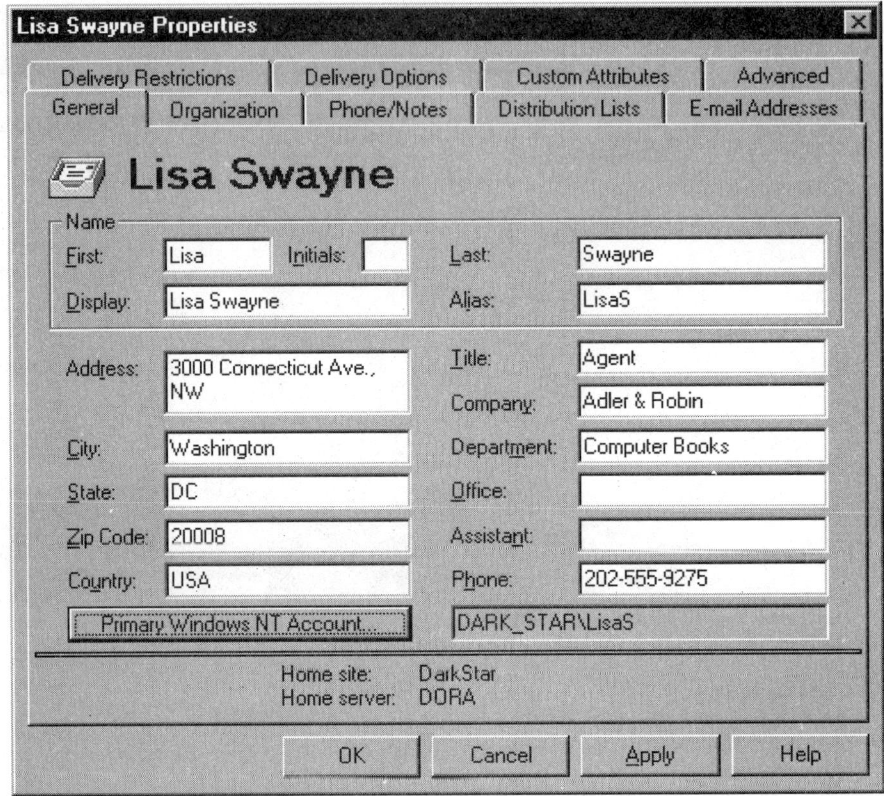

Figure 11-11: The mailbox Properties dialog box for user "Lisa Swayne."

The mailbox Properties dialog has nine tabs:

- General contains information about the user, including physical address, Windows NT 4 Server account name, and other miscellaneous information.
- Organization contains information about who the mailbox owner's manager is, and who reports to the mailbox owner. Each person named in the Organization tab is listed by their Microsoft Exchange Server user name.
- Phone/Notes lists all phone numbers for the mailbox owner. You can also save a note about this user.
- Use Distribution Lists to add this mailbox to distribution lists.

- E-mail Addresses lists the various e-mail addresses assigned to this user. Edit or delete each e-mail address as necessary.
- Delivery Restrictions allows e-mail to be restricted. You may have both Accept messages from, and Reject messages from lists. (It makes no sense to have both!) In our example, the user is only able to receive messages from three users!
- Delivery Options allows the mailbox user to send messages on behalf of other users. The ability to automatically "CC" another mailbox account to receive messages for this mailbox is included.
- Custom Attributes allows you to set custom attributes (such as employee number or office number) for each mailbox.
- Advanced allows you to set a variety of more advanced options. With the Advanced tab, you can set the mailbox user's simple display name (which defaults to the Directory name), trust level (defaults to 20), Home server, message sizes, and storage limits.

After entering the mailbox user's information, click OK to save the information.

New Distribution Lists

A distribution list is a method to send a piece of e-mail to more than one user. For example, I have a distribution list called "Everyone" that can send e-mail to everyone with a mailbox defined on my Microsoft Exchange Server.

If my company were larger, I would create distribution lists for the various departments (such as R&D, Accounting, Marketing, Sales, Administration, and Customer Support). A distribution list can be as flexible as you need!

Figure 11-12 shows the properties dialog for the distribution list "Everyone."

Figure 11-12: The distribution list for "Everyone."

There are six tabs in the distribution list properties dialog:

- The General tab (shown in Figure 11-12) has both the distribution list's name, alias, owner, notes, and a list of members.
- The Distribution Lists tab allows you to add additional distribution lists. This feature allows a hierarchical arrangement of distribution lists (such as having an R&D distribution list composed of the "Hardware Development" and "Software Development" distribution lists).
- The E-mail Addresses tab allows modification of the distribution list's e-mail addresses.

- Delivery Restrictions allows e-mail to be restricted. You may have either Accept messages from, or Reject messages from lists. (It makes no sense to have both!) The Delivery Restrictions for distribution lists works exactly the same as delivery restrictions for mailboxes.
- Custom Attributes allow you to set custom attributes (such as employee number or office number) for each mailbox.
- The Advanced tab allows you to set a simple display name, limit message sizes, and pick various distribution list options.

Do you see the potential for distribution lists? A simple mail list configuration can be made with little effort: each user on the system can send messages to an entire group using a single name.

New Custom Recipient

The File | New Custom Recipient menu selection allows you to create an e-mail address for a client user, of any supported type. When you create a custom recipient, a recipient who is not one of the standard types (Internet, Microsoft Mail, and so on), there is a prompt to provide the e-mail address type (see Figure 11-13), and then Microsoft Exchange Administrator displays the mailbox properties dialog box.

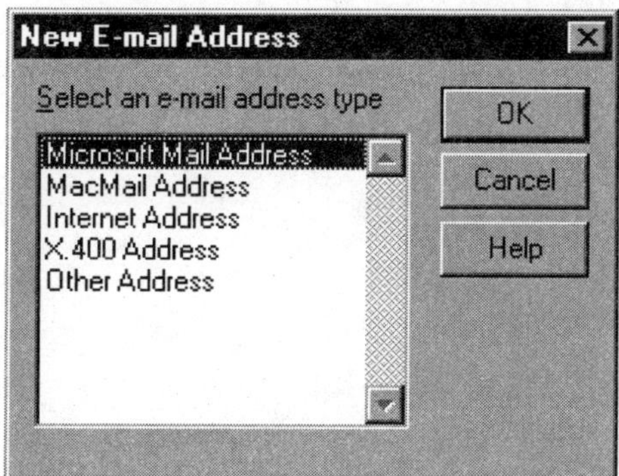

Figure 11-13: Select the custom recipient's e-mail type.

New Other

Found in Microsoft Exchange Administrator's File menu is a submenu called "New Other." Create each of the following items with the New Other selection:

- Server Monitor—Creates a new server alert or warning monitor. When a monitor event happens, the action taken is to either send a message, create a Windows NT Alert, or launch a process.
- Link Monitor—Creates a new bounced message alert or warning monitor. When a monitor event happens, the action taken is to either send a message, create a Windows NT Alert, or launch a process.
- Recipients Container—Creates a new container that can be used to hold recipients.
- MTA Transport Stack—Used to create a new MTA (Mail Transfer Agent) stack. Choices include "Eicon X.25 MTA Transport Stack," "RAS MTA Transport Stack," "TCP/IP MTA Transport Stack," and "TP4 MTA Transport Stack."
- X.400 Connector—Creates a new X.400 connector. Prior to creating an X.400 connector, you must create an MTA transport stack.
- Dynamic RAS Connector—Creates a RAS connector. A suitable MTA transport stack must be created first. Use the RAS connector to connect, on a schedule, to a remote mail site.
- Site Connector—Creates a connector to another Microsoft Exchange Server site.

- Directory Replication Connector—Creates a directory replication connector. A Site Connector must be created prior to creating a replication connector.
- Dirsync Requestor—Creates a dirsync requestor, which periodically queries the Microsoft Exchange Server directory to determine whether there are any changes to recipient information.
- Dirsync Server—Creates a dirsync server that processes updates from directory requestors. The results of the updates are placed in the directory as custom recipient objects.
- Remote Dirsync Requestor—Creates a remote dirsync requestor, which periodically queries the Microsoft Exchange Server directory to determine whether there are any changes to recipient information.
- Information Store—Creates a new information store, the location where objects are stored on the server.

Microsoft Exchange Migration Wizard

The Microsoft Exchange Migration Wizard automates your migration from either MS Mail for PC Networks or Lotus cc:Mail. If you have either of these e-mail systems installed and you wish to convert them to Microsoft Exchange Server, then the Microsoft Exchange Migration Wizard is the tool to use.

Figure 11-14 shows Microsoft Exchange Migration Wizard's first screen, which prompts for the type of system to migrate from.

Figure 11-14: Migrating MS Mail and Lotus cc:Mail systems.

Be sure to back up your files before running Microsoft Exchange Migration Wizard, just in case.

Microsoft Exchange Optimizer

The Microsoft Exchange Optimizer is identical to the Microsoft Exchange Performance Optimizer, described above under installation.

Use the Microsoft Exchange Optimizer whenever there are changes in the hard drive configuration; otherwise the usage of Microsoft Exchange Server changes significantly.

Monitoring Microsoft Exchange Server

Five pre-configured Windows NT 4 Server Monitor workspace files assist in measuring Microsoft Exchange Server's usage: Server Health, Server History, Server Queues, Server Users, and Server Load.

Microsoft Exchange Server Health

Microsoft Exchange Server Health starts Windows NT 4 Server Monitor, with the EXHEALTH.PMW performance monitor workspace file. Figure 11-15 shows Microsoft Exchange Server Health running.

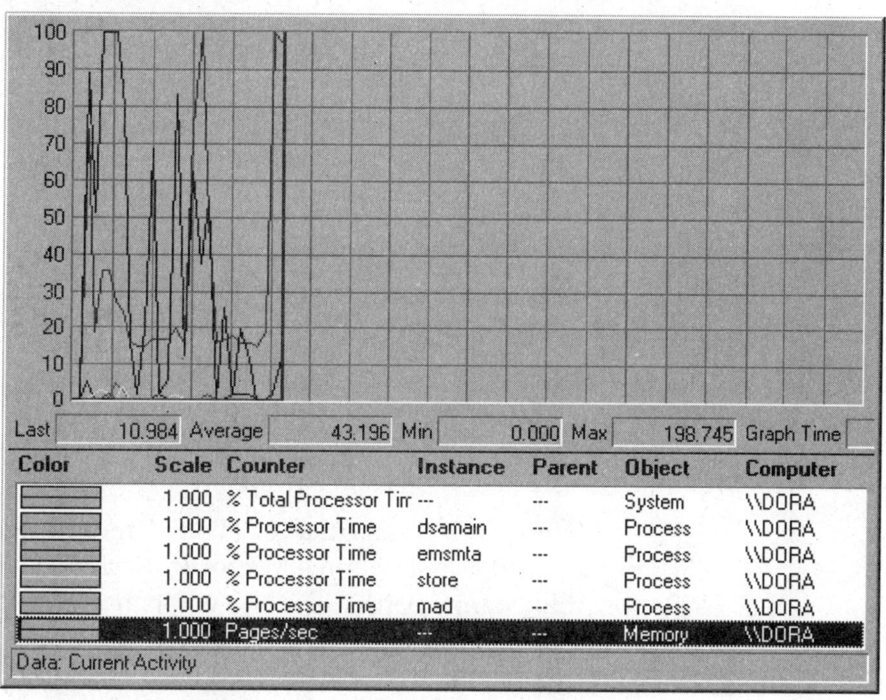

Figure 11-15: Monitoring the health of Microsoft Exchange.

Microsoft Exchange Server History

Microsoft Exchange Server History starts Windows NT 4 Server Monitor, with the EXHIST.PMW performance monitor workspace file. Figure 11-16 shows Microsoft Exchange Server History running.

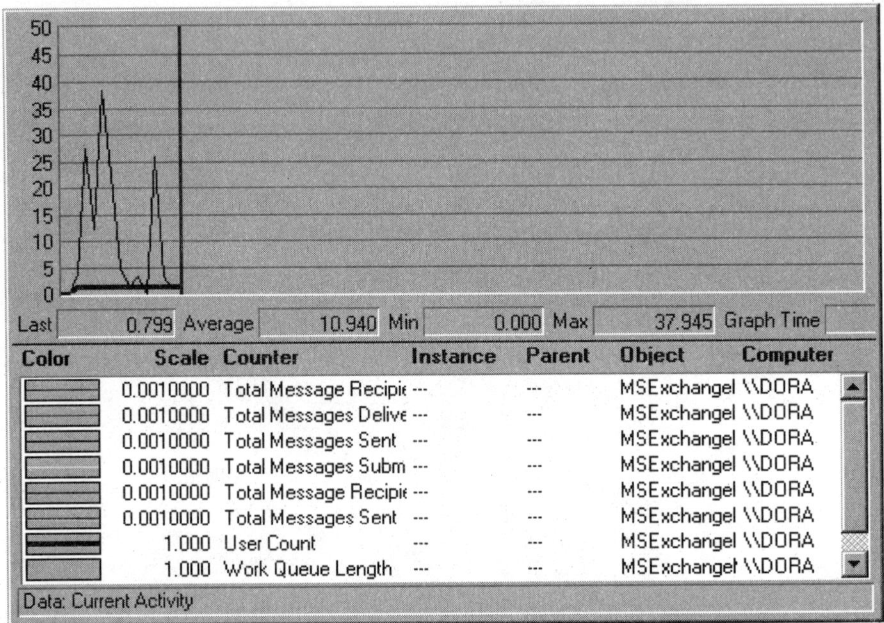

Figure 11-16: Monitoring the history of Microsoft Exchange.

The Microsoft Exchange Server History monitor is very useful when you need to re-optimize Microsoft Exchange Server. With Microsoft Exchange Server History, you can determine Microsoft Exchange Server's usage.

Microsoft Exchange Server Queues

Microsoft Exchange Server Queues starts Windows NT 4 Server Monitor, with the EXQUEUE.PMW performance monitor workspace file. Figure 11-17 shows Microsoft Exchange Server backlog.

The five bars in the Server Queues performance monitor (all are set to zero in this example) show:

- Work Queue Length
- Send Queue Length
- Send Queue Size
- Receive Queue Size
- Receive Queue Size

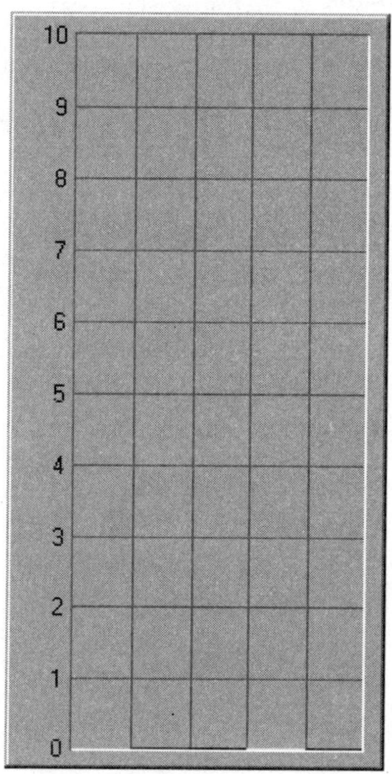

Figure 11-17: Server Queues shows Microsoft Exchange Server backlog.

With Microsoft Exchange Server 4.0, the Receive Queue Size is monitored twice, while Send Queue Size is not monitored at all. This error can be corrected by adding the "Send Queue Size" counter (found in the "MSExchangeIS Public" object) to the chart, and deleting the extra "Receive Queue Size" counter. Chapter 9, "Monitoring Windows NT 4 Server Performance," explains how to add and remove Windows NT Performance Monitor counters.

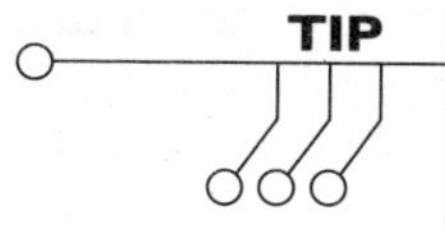

Performance Monitor does not prompt to save the workspace—make sure you save any changes you make!

Microsoft Exchange Server Users

Microsoft Exchange Server Users starts Windows NT 4 Server Monitor, with the EXUSER.PMW performance monitor workspace file. Figure 11-18 shows Microsoft Exchange Server with the number of connected users displayed.

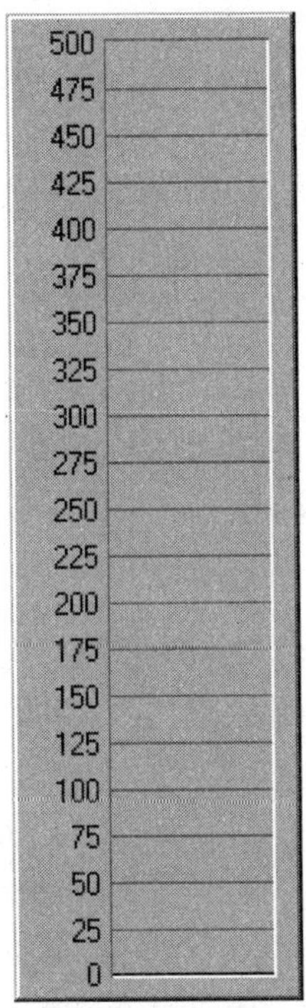

Figure 11-18: Server Users shows the number of users connected to Microsoft Exchange Server.

The one bar in the Server Users performance monitor shows the count of users. This example shows a very lightly loaded Exchange Server—none!

Microsoft Exchange Server Load

Microsoft Exchange Server Load starts Windows NT 4 Server Monitor, with the EXLOAD.PMW performance monitor workspace file. Figure 11-19 shows Microsoft Exchange Server IMC Traffic running.

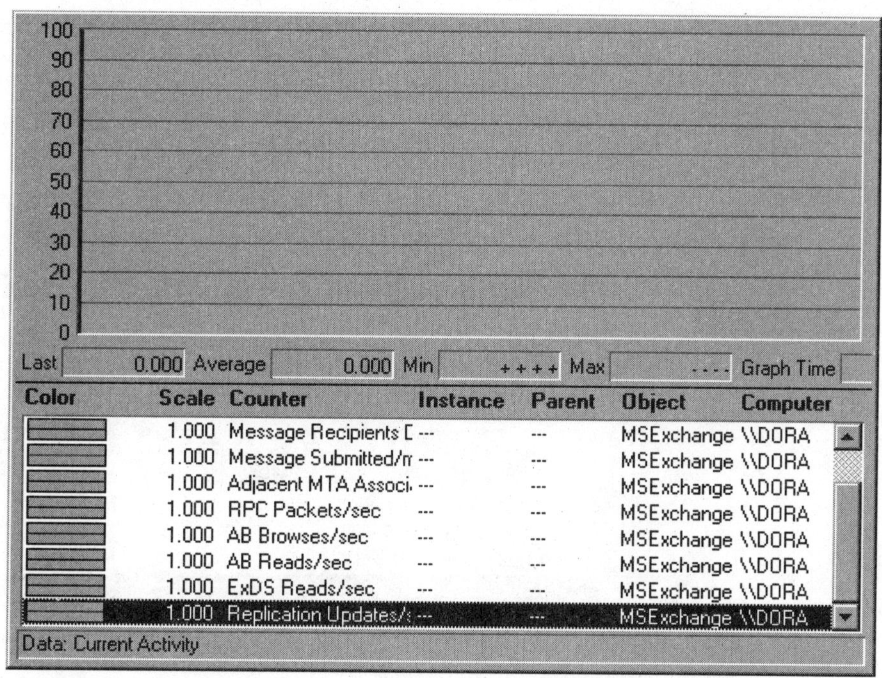

Figure 11-19: Server Load shows Microsoft Exchange Server activity.

Internet Mail Connector Monitoring

Three pre-configured Windows NT 4 Server Monitor workspace files are used to assist in measuring Microsoft Exchange Server's Internet Mail Connector (IMC): IMC Queues, IMC Statistics, and IMC Traffic.

Microsoft Exchange Server IMC Queues

Microsoft Exchange Server IMC Queues starts Windows NT 4 Server Monitor, with the IMCQUEUE.PMW performance monitor workspace file. Figure 11-20 shows Microsoft Exchange Server IMC Queues running.

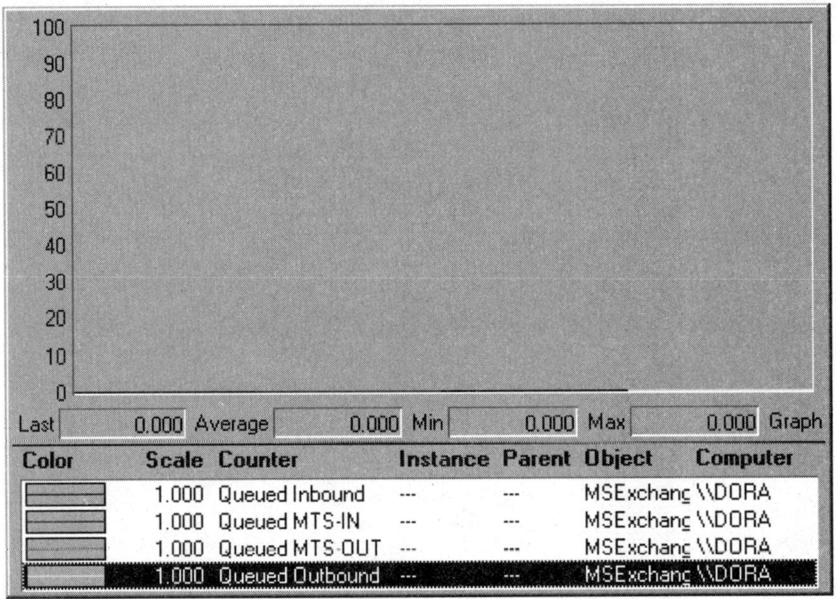

Figure 11-20: Monitoring IMC Queues shows how much Internet mail is being processed.

The Microsoft Exchange Server IMC Queues monitor helps manage Internet e-mail traffic.

Microsoft Exchange Server IMC Statistics

Microsoft Exchange Server IMC Statistics starts Windows NT 4 Server Monitor, with the IMCSTATS.PMW performance monitor workspace file. Figure 11-21 shows Microsoft Exchange Server IMC Statistics running.

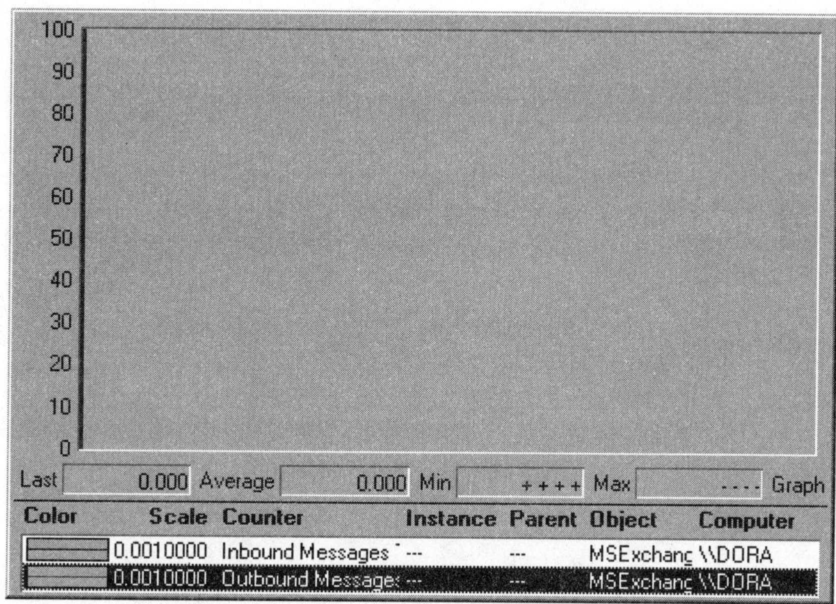

Figure 11-21: Monitoring IMC Statistics shows performance of the Internet Mail Connector.

Both incoming and outgoing e-mail counts are monitored.

Microsoft Exchange Server IMC Traffic

Microsoft Exchange Server IMC Traffic starts Windows NT 4 Server Monitor, with the IMCFLOW.PMW performance monitor workspace file. Figure 11-22 shows Microsoft Exchange Server IMC Traffic running.

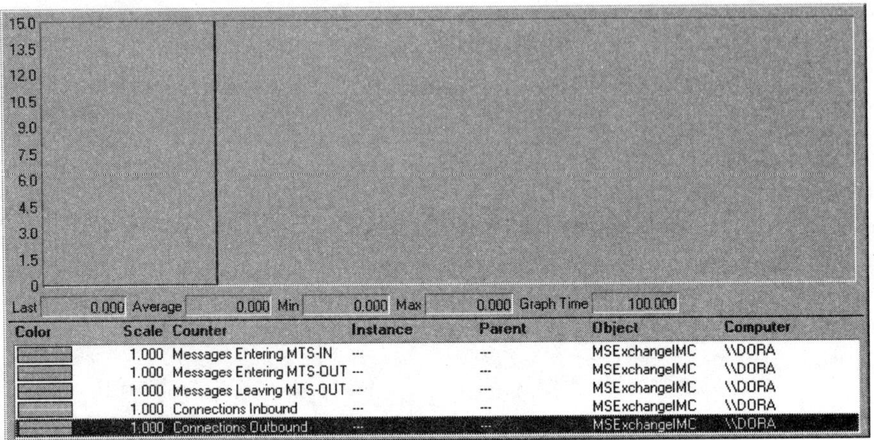

Figure 11-22: Monitoring IMC's traffic.

Microsoft Exchange Setup Editor

At the beginning of this chapter, I noted that there are two components of Microsoft Exchange: Microsoft Exchange Server and Microsoft Exchange Client. Some operating systems (Windows NT 4 Server, Windows NT 4 Workstation, and Windows 95) come with default Microsoft Exchange Client software.

Microsoft Exchange comes with a new version of Microsoft Exchange Client. This version may be installed on workstations using the Microsoft Exchange Setup Editor.

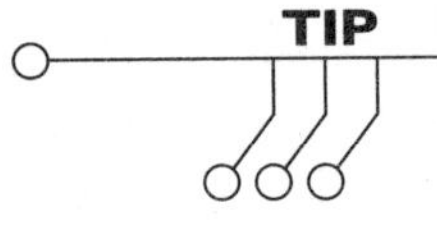

Be careful to avoid installing an older version of Microsoft Exchange Client on a system that already has a newer version of Microsoft Exchange Client installed. For example, Microsoft will probably release a new version of Windows 95 in late 1996, and the new version of Windows 95 will probably have an updated Microsoft Exchange Client.

Check the currently installed version of Microsoft Exchange Client, and if it is later than the version with Microsoft Exchange, don't upgrade it!

The Microsoft Exchange Setup Editor is used to modify a client installation setup. To create a client setup point (the shared folder that Microsoft Exchange Client will be installed from), first refer to the Microsoft Exchange Installation Guide, Chapter 4, "Setting Up Clients," and follow the steps outlined there to create a client setup point.

Once the client setup point has been set up, then you can run the Microsoft Exchange Setup Editor to modify the configuration. You can set up many things, including but not limited to: allowing complete and custom setups, options, folders, and icons.

Moving On

In this chapter we introduced Microsoft Exchange. Microsoft Exchange Server is one of the most complex server components that runs under Windows NT 4 Server. Microsoft Exchange Server, for organizations that are able to embrace the Microsoft Exchange Clients (which are available for virtually all platforms), is an excellent choice for e-mail management.

The next chapter introduces Microsoft SQL Server 6.5, the backbone of Microsoft's client/server platform.

12 Microsoft SQL Server 6.5

To fully understand what Microsoft SQL Server is, you must understand the differences between a client/server database and a shared (or distributed) database. The differences lie in where the "work" is being done.

In a client/server database system, the database is located on a server. The server also hosts a software system that interfaces the clients with the database. All the clients do (typically) is take the information that the server provides and format/display the data for the user. Typically, little or no processing of data is done by the client.

Microsoft SQL Server 6.5 and Oracle Server are just two examples of client/server database servers. Generally, despite the fact that the server does much of the work in a client/server system, client/server systems are generally more robust, and offer better performance when faced with greater loads. In a client/server environment, it is most unusual for a server to be developed in-house, whereas the client side software is typically developed in-house.

In a shared or distributed database, the data is usually found on one (or more, if distributed) servers, but all the processing is done at the client site. The client retrieves, sorts, and processes records, and the server(s) merely function as file servers, sharing the database with the client users. Microsoft Access is an example of a shared database system. Designed as a desktop database system, Access is actually able to serve well in a lightly loaded environment. However, when the number of concurrent users increases, the performance of a multi-user Access database system falters.

In this chapter we look into the Microsoft SQL Server 6.5 product. Available both as a stand-alone product and as part of the integrated Microsoft BackOffice server package, Microsoft SQL Server 6.5 is a leading contender in the client/server database world.

Installing SQL Server 6.5

Installation of Microsoft SQL Server 6.5 is straightforward. First, virtually all users install from a CD, though a few use network connections (usually from a networked CD-ROM drive, but possibly from a temporary directory). Regardless of where Microsoft SQL Server 6.5 is installed from, the process is basically the same: you will need to place the CD-ROM in your CD-ROM drive and run the Setup program (SETUP.EXE) from the CD. Make sure you run the correct version—there is a folder for each CPU architecture (I386 for Intel, MIPS, ALPHA, and PPC).

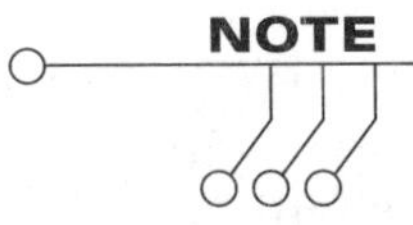

NOTE *Like other Windows NT server products, Microsoft SQL Server 6.5 is available in versions to support all of the current Windows NT 4 Server platforms, including Digital Alpha, MIPS, and Intel.*

Starting the Setup

The Setup program is straightforward. Figure 12-1 shows the initial screen, which the user sees when running Setup for the first time. Users who are upgrading from Microsoft SQL Server 6.0 will notice that there are few differences in the Setup program between the two versions of Microsoft SQL Server.

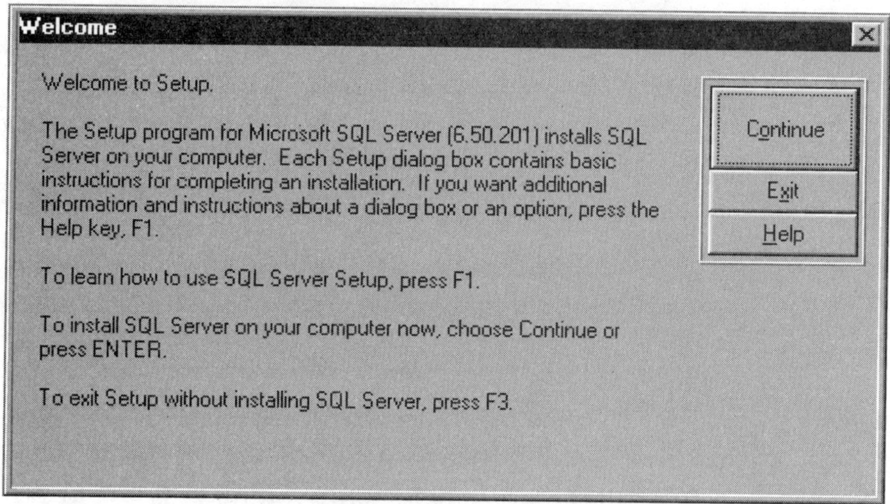

Figure 12-1: Welcome to the Microsoft SQL Server Setup.

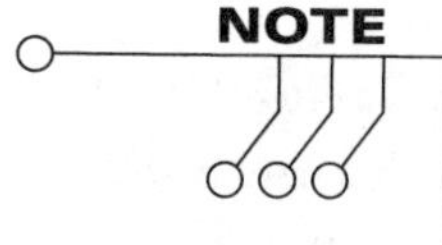

Prompts for installation vary slightly depending on which options are selected. In this chapter I cover new installations only, outlining the steps that the Microsoft SQL Server Setup program takes to install Microsoft SQL Server.

Once Setup starts, you are prompted for your Name, Company, and Product ID (found on the back of the CD holder).

Setup Options

Once Name, Company, and Product ID information have been entered and confirmed, the Microsoft SQL Server 6.5 - Options dialog box appears, as shown in Figure 12-2.

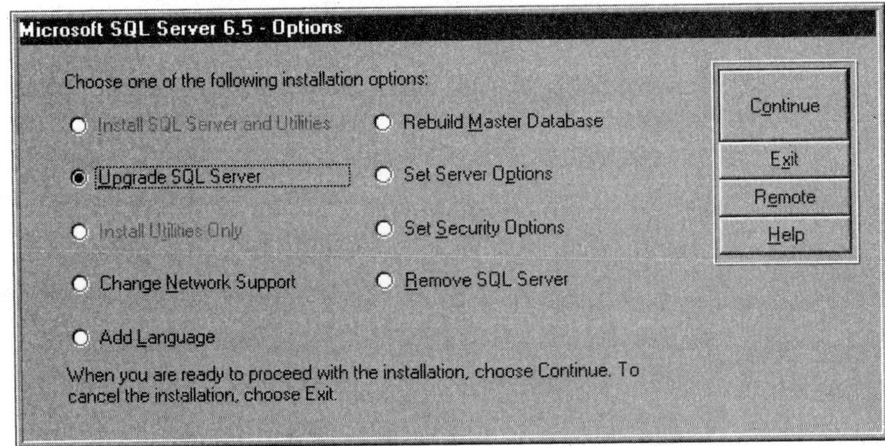

Figure 12-2: The Microsoft SQL Server 6.5 - Options dialog.

In the Options dialog box, you may choose to perform any of the following tasks. You may perform only one task at a time; however, the Setup program redisplays the Options dialog box after performing each task. In the Options dialog, you are presented with nine options:

- Install SQL Server and Utilities—This option is available only if you do not already have a copy of Microsoft SQL Server installed. With this option, you create a new installation of Microsoft SQL Server.
- Upgrade SQL Server—The upgrade option is available only if there is an existing installation of Microsoft SQL Server (any upgradeable version). The currently installed version of Microsoft SQL Server i upgrades to Microsoft SQL Server 6.5.

- Install Utilities Only—This option allows you to install the support utilities. If you have an existing installation of Microsoft SQL Server then this option is disabled. In most situations, the utilities are installed at the same time as the SQL server.
- Change Network Support—With this option, you can change the net library options. Select help for more information about this or any other option.
- Add Language—To add support for a different language, use this option.
- Rebuild Master Database—The master database, if damaged, may be rebuilt using the Setup program. You can also change character sets and sort orders with this option.
- Set Server Options—This option allows you to set different server options.
- Set Security Options—The security options: login mode, mappings, and auditing may be changed with this selection.
- Remove SQL Server—When you decide to "get rid" of SQL Server, use the Remove SQL Server option. This option deletes most of the Microsoft SQL Server files and cleans the registry as needed.

Most installations consist of either a clean installation of Microsoft SQL Server or an upgrade of an existing Microsoft SQL Server installation.

Setting the Licensing Mode

Microsoft server products require that you select a licensing mode at installation time. The two choices, Per Server and Per Seat, should be familiar. If in doubt when installing Microsoft SQL Server, select the Per Server licensing mode—your license agreement allows a one-time change from Per Server to Per Seat.

When you choose the licensing mode, you must also indicate how many client licenses you have purchased. Since Microsoft SQL Server is sold in a number of different packages (most of which vary only in the number of bundled client licenses included), you should review the product you have purchased and coordinate with your management to ensure that the correct number of client licenses have been obtained.

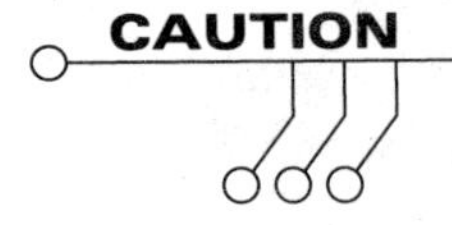

Licensing Microsoft SQL Server clients is a complex affair. In some cases you do not need to have a client license. Consult the current Microsoft EULA (End-User License Agreement) and your management to determine what your license requirements are—there is no reason to purchase more client licenses than you are required to obtain.

The next prompt in the installation is the installation path. The Setup program prompts with C:\MSSQL, although you may choose any drive and folder to install Microsoft SQL Server into. However, I recommend that you use the folder \MSSQL for your installation—this will make future maintenance easier.

The SQL Master Database

Microsoft SQL Server stores all of your data and other information in a master database file. This file is created by the Setup program, and you are prompted for the initial size for this file. Later, should your needs grow, you may expand this file's size. However, try to anticipate your initial requirements, and set the file's size to this requirement. The Setup program recommends a minimum size of 25MB. However, I recommend that you set the size between 35 and 50MB for the initial database, more if you are planning to import a large dataset from another source.

Microsoft SQL Documentation—Books Online

Most of the documentation for Microsoft SQL Server is contained in a Books Online database. You can choose to install the entire set of documentation on your hard drive, or execute the Books Online from the CD. If you plan on having the Microsoft SQL Server CD available when running Microsoft SQL Server, then running from the CD is acceptable; however, if your CD-ROM drive resources are limited, then I recommend that you install the Books Online on the hard drive. You can choose not to install the Books Online; however, there are very few Microsoft SQL Server users who are experienced enough that they don't need assistance.

Installation options, which you choose after determining the location for the Books Online, allow you to set the character set (for American users, select English) and sort orders (generally, if you are not using English, review the sort order to make sure it matches the language you are using, otherwise select the default). You may also choose to install additional network support at this stage. Two final options: "Auto Start SQL Server at boot time" and "Auto Start SQL Executive at boot time" allow you to choose to have Microsoft SQL Server started automatically each time the system is booted (not when you logon, but when Windows NT 4 Server is started) and to have the Microsoft SQL Server Executive program run at boot time as well.

The Administrator's User ID

The final required information is the user ID for the installation user. Setup must logon as this user to complete the setup. The default is your user ID (which should have Administrative privileges) for which you must supply the password. Once the user ID and password have been verified, the Setup program installs Microsoft SQL Server, generally with no further prompts.

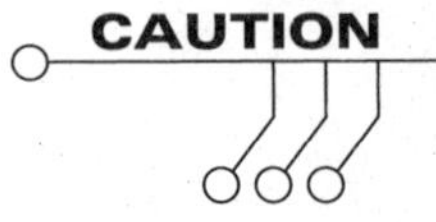

If, at a point near the end of the installation, you receive a critical error message that a file with the extension .CPL could not be copied to the SYSTEM32 folder, then you probably have the Control Panel program running. Close Control Panel, and click the "Retry" button. If you click "Cancel," then Setup will not correctly complete.

When Setup is finished, you should have a fully functional installation of Microsoft SQL Server. You will have, in the "All Users" group, a program group called "Microsoft SQL Server 6.5."

The Microsoft SQL Server 6.5 system consists of the actual SQL server and a set of utilities and programs that assist the user and administrator in using Microsoft SQL Server 6.5. The rest of the chapter looks at each of these utilities, what they do, and how they are used.

Again, this chapter cannot be an all-inclusive reference to Microsoft SQL Server 6.5. Rather, it provides an overview of the major components that make up Microsoft SQL Server 6.5. A good book dedicated completely to Microsoft SQL Server 6.5 might be a wise investment for anyone who is serious about working with Microsoft SQL Server 6.5.

All the component parts of Microsoft SQL Server may be found in the Start Menu, under Programs | Microsoft SQL Server 6.5.

ISQL/w

The ISQL/w utility queries an SQL Server. To start the ISQL/w utility, select ISQL_w in the Start Menu | Programs | Microsoft SQL Server 6.5 group. You can do an analysis and view statistical information about the query. ISQL/w is able to perform more than one query at a given time. ISQL/w is shown in Figure 12-3, with an example query being executed.

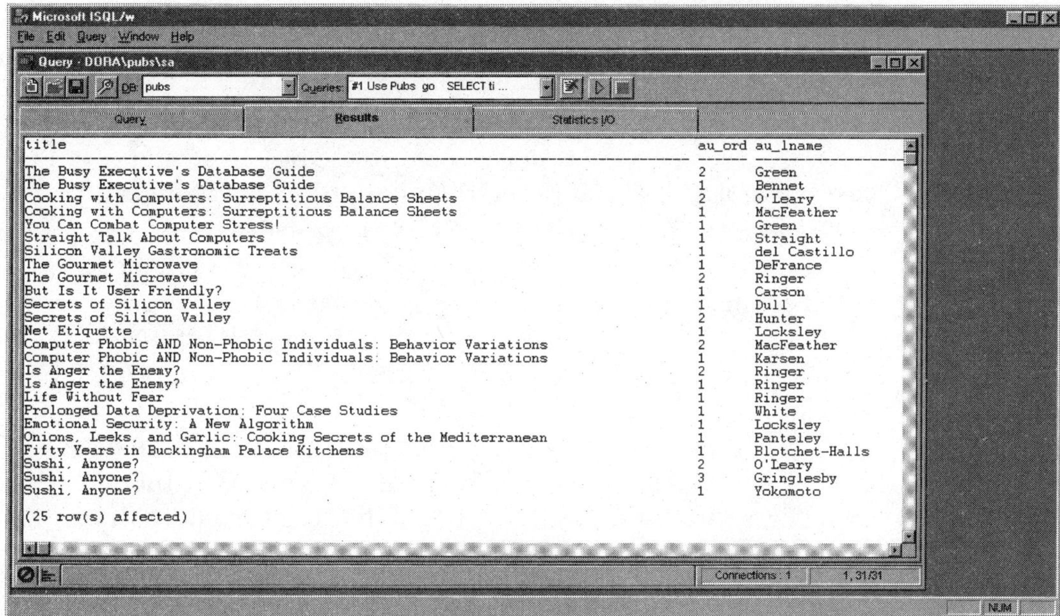

Figure 12-3: ISQL/w with a query's result set.

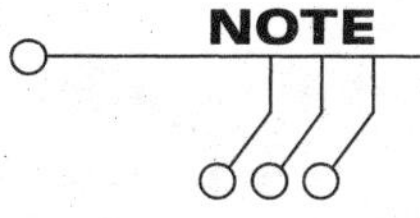

Unlike MS Query, ISQL/w works only with Microsoft SQL Server databases. If you need to perform queries on any other ODBC data source, you will need to use MS Query rather than ISQL/w.

ISQL/w has a toolbar and status bar available in each query window.

You can use the File menu to connect to and disconnect from servers, create new queries, open and close existing queries, and configure the look and feel of ISQL/w. You can use the Query menu to execute and cancel a query (which you would want to do if the query is not responding correctly or is returning excessive amounts of data). Many of the menus are represented in a toolbar, which unfortunately cannot be customized.

Microsoft ODBC SQL Server Driver Help File

The Microsoft ODBC SQL Server Driver help file is used when you need assistance on topics related to ODBC. To start the Microsoft ODBC SQL Server Driver help file, select Microsoft ODBC SQL Server Driver in the Start Menu | Programs | Microsoft SQL Server 6.5 group. ODBC is the engine that clients use to connect to a data source such as Microsoft SQL Server 6.5.

While ODBC is used only by clients, it is important that a Microsoft SQL Server 6.5 administrator understand how ODBC works.

Microsoft SQL Server 6.5 is a multi-user, relational database management system (DBMS). There are 16-bit and 32-bit ODBC drivers for Microsoft SQL Server 6.5. The 16-bit ODBC drivers are used with 16-bit applications (typically those applications written for Windows 3.x and which have not yet been ported to the 32-bit world of Windows 95 and Windows NT).

Microsoft SQL Server 6.5 uses SQL to access data in a SQL Server database. Typically a client would communicate with Microsoft SQL Server 6.5 using a network, including LANs, WANs, and even the Internet.

Any, and hopefully all, questions about ODBC as it pertains to Microsoft SQL Server 6.5 are answered with the Microsoft ODBC SQL Server Driver help file.

MS Query

Microsoft Query (often referred to as MS Query) is a general-purpose query tool. To start Microsoft Query, select MS Query in the Start Menu | Programs | Microsoft SQL Server 6.5 group. Not only is it usable with Microsoft SQL Server 6.5, MS Query is also able to query any data source in which there exists an ODBC driver.

MS Query is a reasonably flexible tool. It is available in both 16- and 32-bit versions (though you would be less likely to utilize the 16-bit versions of MS Query).

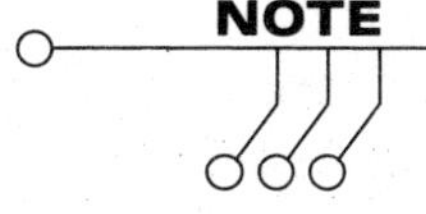

MS Query is typically installed in the C:\WINNT\MSAPPS\MSQUERY folder (where C:\WINNT is the drive and folder where Windows NT 4 Server has been installed), and not in your Microsoft SQL Server 6.5 base directory.

Like ISQL/w, MS Query is basically a menu-driven application. Figure 12-4 shows MS Query after a basic query has been executed. This simple query (which lists all the data in the Authors table), in native SQL format, is:

```
SELECT authors.au_id, authors.au_fname,
   authors.au_lname, authors.address,
   authors.city, authors.state, authors.zip,
   authors.phone, authors.contract
   FROM "pubs.dbo".authors authors
```

File Edit View Format Table Criteria Records Window Help

Query1

authors
address
au_fname
au_id
au_lname
city

au_id	au_fname	au_lname	address	city	state	zip	phone	contract
172-32-1176	Johnson	White	10932 Bigge Rd.	Menlo Park	CA	94025	408 496-7223	1
213-46-8915	Marjorie	Green	309 63rd St. #411	Oakland	CA	94618	415 986-7020	1
238-95-7766	Cheryl	Carson	589 Darwin Ln.	Berkeley	CA	94705	415 548-7723	1
267-41-2394	Michael	O'Leary	22 Cleveland Av. #14	San Jose	CA	95128	408 286-2428	1
274-80-9391	Dean	Straight	5420 College Av.	Oakland	CA	94609	415 834-2919	1
341-22-1782	Meander	Smith	10 Mississippi Dr.	Lawrence	KS	66044	913 843-0462	0
409-56-7008	Abraham	Bennet	6223 Bateman St.	Berkeley	CA	94705	415 658-9932	1
427-17-2319	Ann	Dull	3410 Blonde St.	Palo Alto	CA	94301	415 836-7128	1
472-27-2349	Burt	Gringlesby	PO Box 792	Covelo	CA	95428	707 938-6445	1
486-29-1786	Charlene	Locksley	18 Broadway Av.	San Francisco	CA	94130	415 585-4620	1
527-72-3246	Morningstar	Greene	22 Graybar House Rd.	Nashville	TN	37215	615 297-2723	0
648-92-1872	Reginald	Blotchet-Halls	55 Hillsdale Bl.	Corvallis	OR	97330	503 745-6402	1
672-71-3249	Akiko	Yokomoto	3 Silver Ct.	Walnut Creek	CA	94595	415 935-4228	1
712-45-1867	Innes	del Castillo	2286 Cram Pl. #86	Ann Arbor	MI	48105	615 996-8275	1
722-51-5454	Michel	DeFrance	3 Balding Pl.	Gary	IN	46403	219 547-9982	1
724-08-9931	Dirk	Stringer	5420 Telegraph Av.	Oakland	CA	94609	415 843-2991	0
724-80-9391	Stearns	MacFeather	44 Upland Hts.	Oakland	CA	94612	415 354-7128	1
756-30-7391	Livia	Karsen	5720 McAuley St.	Oakland	CA	94609	415 534-9219	1

Record:

Select View Criteria to show/edit criteria limiting records shown   NUM

Figure 12-4: MS Query with results of a simple query.

Generally, MS Query displays the query graphically. To view the actual SQL statement, click the SQL button in the toolbar. This displays the SQL dialog, as shown in Figure 12-5. It is possible to modify this SQL statement, and when the OK button is selected, the modified SQL statement executes.

Figure 12-5: MS Query SQL dialog.

MS Query has a toolbar and status bar to make interacting with it very easy.

You can use the File menu to create and save a new query, open or close an existing query, execute a query, and view a table definition. You can use the View menu to add new tables to your query and view SQL statements that fetch data. You can use the Table menu to add or remove tables or create, remove, or reorder joins between tables. The Records menu allows you to add, remove, or edit columns, sort data, go to a specific location in the data, enable editing of records in the database, perform a query immediately, and perform a query immediately after it has changed.

MS Query is a rather powerful tool, which makes it very useful for developing client applications. MS Query is also part of many of the other Microsoft applications such as Microsoft Office, Access, Visual C++, and Visual Basic, environments where front-end applications are typically developed.

The Readme File

The readme.txt file is an important part of any software package. Contained within this file are a number of important topics:

- Installing or upgrading SQL Server 6.5.
- Xp_sqlregister extended stored procedure.
- Running SQLOLE65.SQL.
- Using Microsoft distributed transaction coordinator.

SQL Client Configuration Utility

Started from the Start Menu | Programs | Microsoft SQL Server 6.5 group, the SQL Client Configuration Utility displays, as its main window, a tabbed dialog box. The three tabs in this dialog box are:

- DBLibrary—Configures the DB Library.
- Net Library—Configures the network library.
- Advanced—Configures the advanced client options.

In the SQL Client Configuration Utility there is also a button labeled Locate. This button searches the system for the libraries used by SQL Client Configuration Utility and Microsoft SQL Server 6.5. Selecting Locate displays the dialog box shown in Figure 12-6.

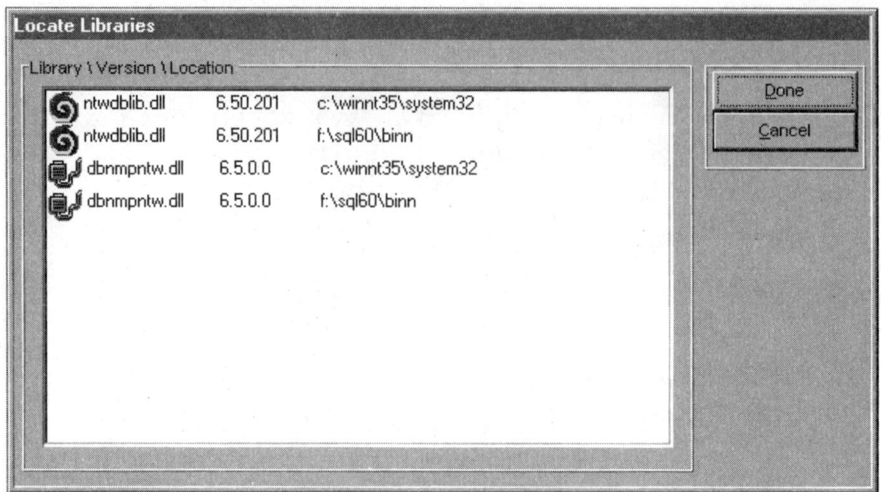

Figure 12-6: The SQL Client Configuration Utility Locate Libraries dialog.

The Locate Libraries dialog has no controls other than Done and Cancel. With the Locate Libraries dialog you can specify a library (click on the library name or icon in the list) other than the default library that SQL Client Configuration Utility names. Once you have selected a library, click the Done button.

The DBLibrary Tab

The DBLibrary tab (see Figure 12-7) configures the DB (database) library options. There are two options in this tab:

- Automatic ANSI to OEM, which enables the automatic conversion of objects from ANSI character sets to OEM character sets. It is useful when the OEM line drawing characters have been used in an object.
- Use International Settings, which enables international settings for the DB library.

In addition to the above two options, you are also presented with statistical information about the DB library.

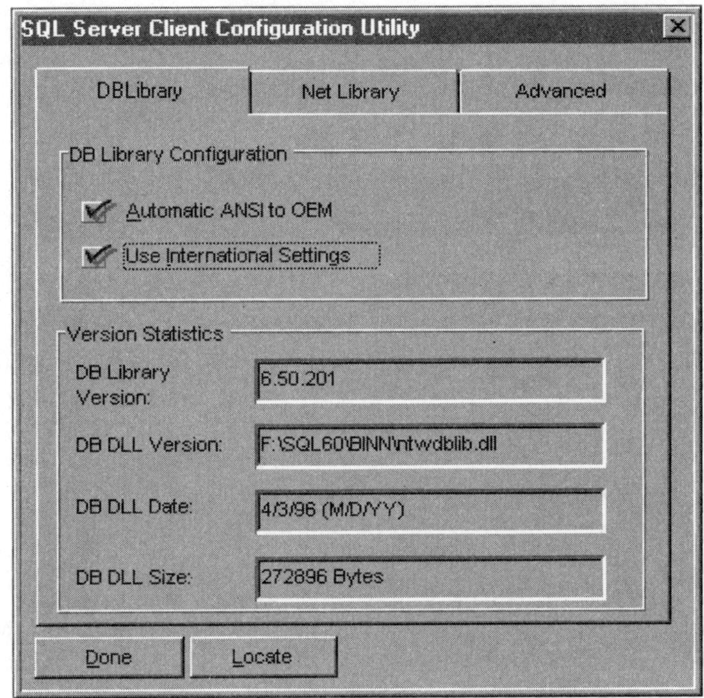

Figure 12-7: The SQL Server Client Configuration Utility DBLibrary tab.

The Net Library Tab

The Net Library tab (see Figure 12-8) allows you to configure the network protocol for Microsoft SQL Server 6.5. The Net Library tab has only one option that can be set: Default Network. In the Default Network, you can choose one of the following network protocols:

- Named Pipes
- Multi-protocol
- NWLink IPX/SPX
- TCP/IP Sockets
- Banyan VINES

The default is Named Pipes, which will serve for most installations. There is no "Defaults" button in the SQL Client Configuration Utility, so be sure to note what the current default is.

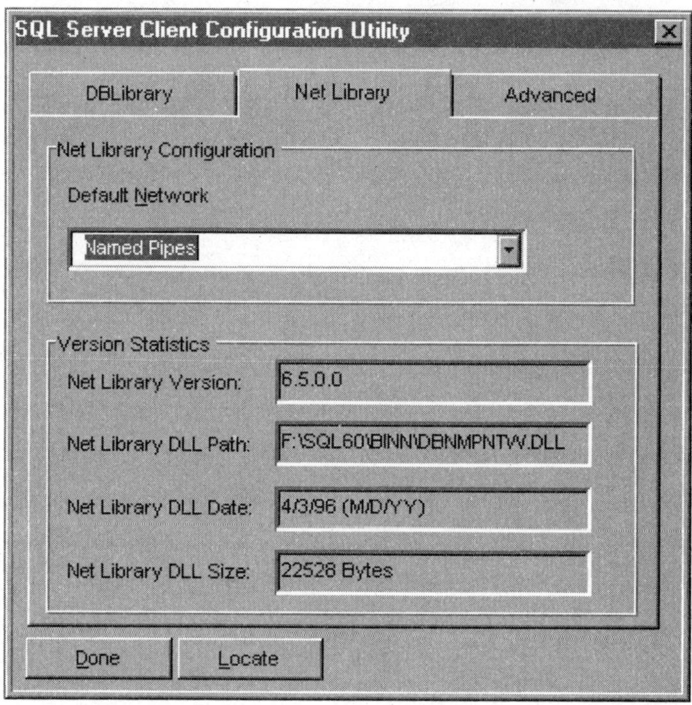

Figure 12-8: The SQL Server Client Configuration Utility Net Library tab.

The Advanced Tab

The SQL Client Configuration Utility Advanced tab (see Figure 12-9) configures advanced options. You are able to set the configuration for multiple servers in this tab by specifying both a server name and a DLL name (which is actually the protocol as described previously in Net Library tab).

Using the Advanced tab, you are able to specify different Net Protocols for different servers, if this is necessary. You may also specify a connect string for each entry.

The process for using the Advanced tab is to fill in both the Server and DLL Name boxes in the Client Configuration group box. You may optionally fill in a Connection String, too. After filling in the Server and DLL Name, select Add/Modify to add the entry to the list of current entries.

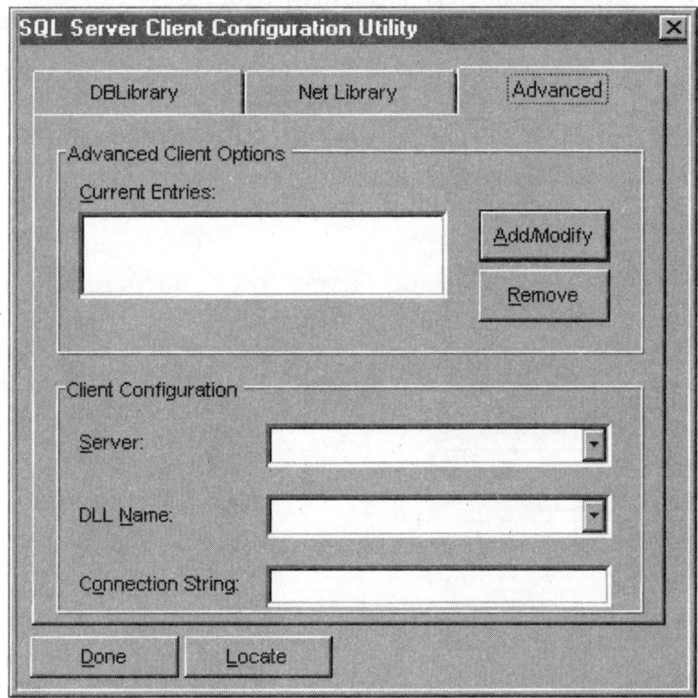

Figure 12-9: The SQL Server Client Configuration Utility Advanced tab.

SQL Distributed Management Objects Help

The SQL Distributed Management Objects help file contains descriptive text for each of the object classes in Microsoft SQL Server 6.5. To start the SQL Distributed Management Objects help file, select SQL Distributed Management Objects in the Start Menu | Programs | Microsoft SQL Server 6.5 group. Descriptions of the objects are given for both Visual Basic and Visual C++ (MFC) contexts whenever appropriate.

Figure 12-10 illustrates the application-related objects. When in SQL Distributed Management Objects, you are able to click on any object and a hypertext jump will take you to the description of the object.

Each of the following three figures shows relationships between various objects in the SQL hierarchy.

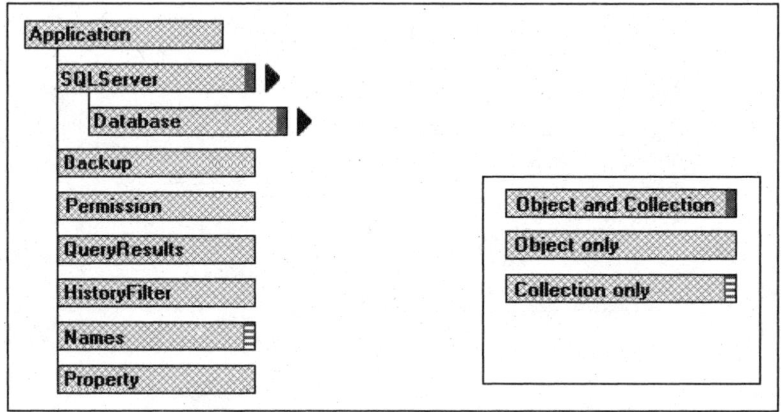

Figure 12-10: SQL Distributed Management Objects application objects.

Figure 12-11 illustrates server-related objects.

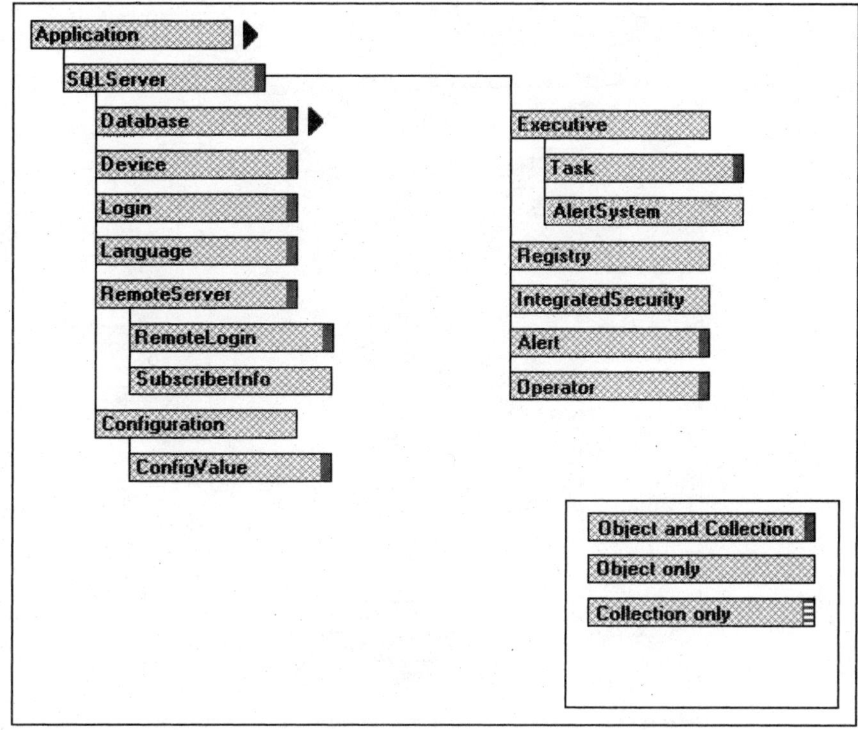

Figure 12-11: SQL Distributed Management Objects server objects.

Figure 12-12 illustrates database-related objects.

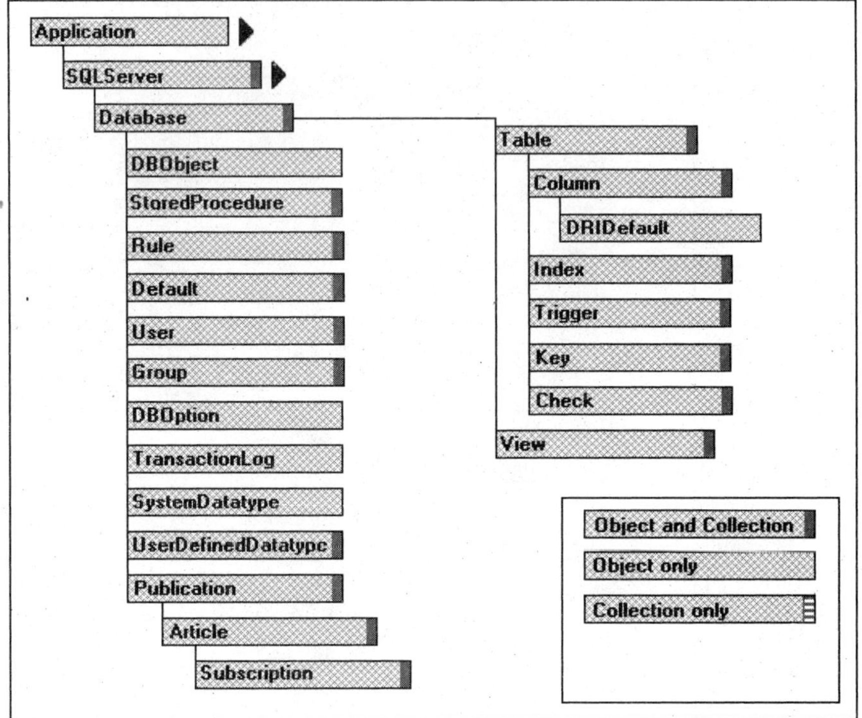

Figure 12-12: SQL Distributed Management Objects database objects.

The SQL Distributed Management Objects help file is useful when designing and programming Microsoft SQL Server 6.5. There are examples for most items for Visual Basic programmers, as well as for those of us who are addicted to Visual C++.

As an example, an important database design tool would be the ability to insert a new column of information into an existing table. The InsertColumn Method allows you to do this, as shown in Figure 12-13. To use InsertColumn, complete the following steps:

1. Select Database in the Contents page (see Figure 12-12).
2. Click on the Table box.
3. After the Table Object page is shown, click on the Methods hyperlink. This displays a list of all the table methods.

4. Click the InsertColumn item in the list. Voila! You now have a new column.

In this figure you see the description for the InsertColumn method, examples of both Visual Basic and Visual C++ usage, and descriptions of the elements of the InsertColumn method.

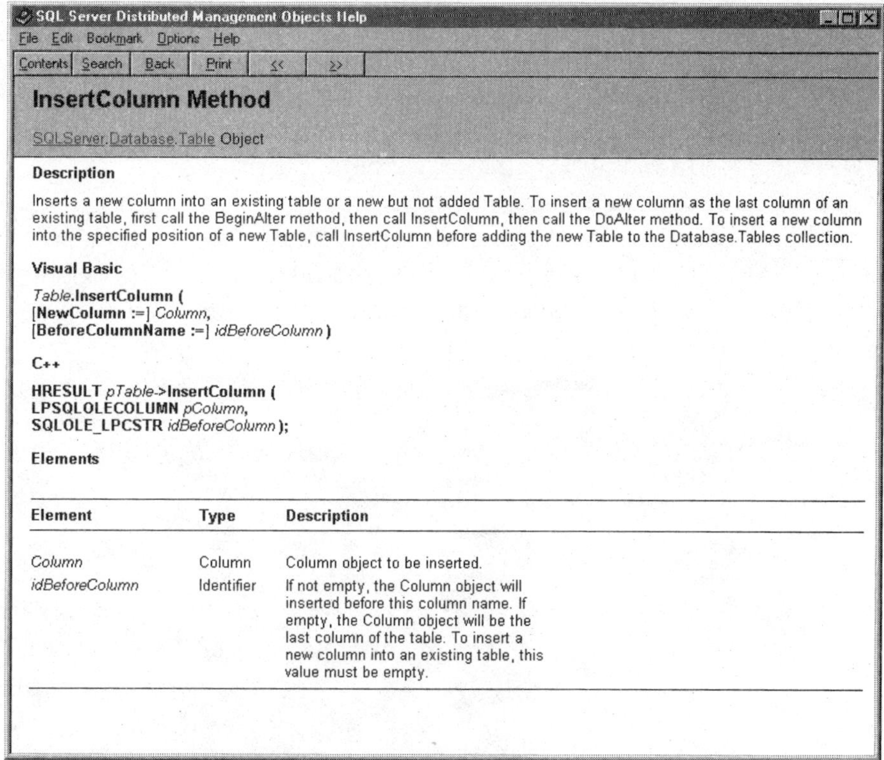

Figure 12-13: SQL Distributed Management Objects documenting the InsertColumn method.

If you are not programming Microsoft SQL Server 6.5 using Visual Basic or Visual C++, then you will probably not find much use for the SQL Distributed Management Objects help file.

SQL Enterprise Manager

The SQL Enterprise Manager is the core management tool for Microsoft SQL Server 6.5. The SQL Enterprise Manager is the tool that modifies, backs up, and generally interacts with Microsoft SQL Server 6.5. You launch SQL Enterprise Manager from the Start Menu, using the Programs | Microsoft SQL Server 6.5 group.

SQL Enterprise Manager is a complex program with many options and features. Due to SQL Enterprise Manager's complexity, this chapter only presents an overview of what SQL Enterprise Manager is capable of doing.

When launched, SQL Enterprise Manager presents a display similar to the one shown in Figure 12-14 (the displayed data will reflect your server's configuration). This figure shows SQL Enterprise Manager managing the Microsoft SQL Server 6.5 on DORA.

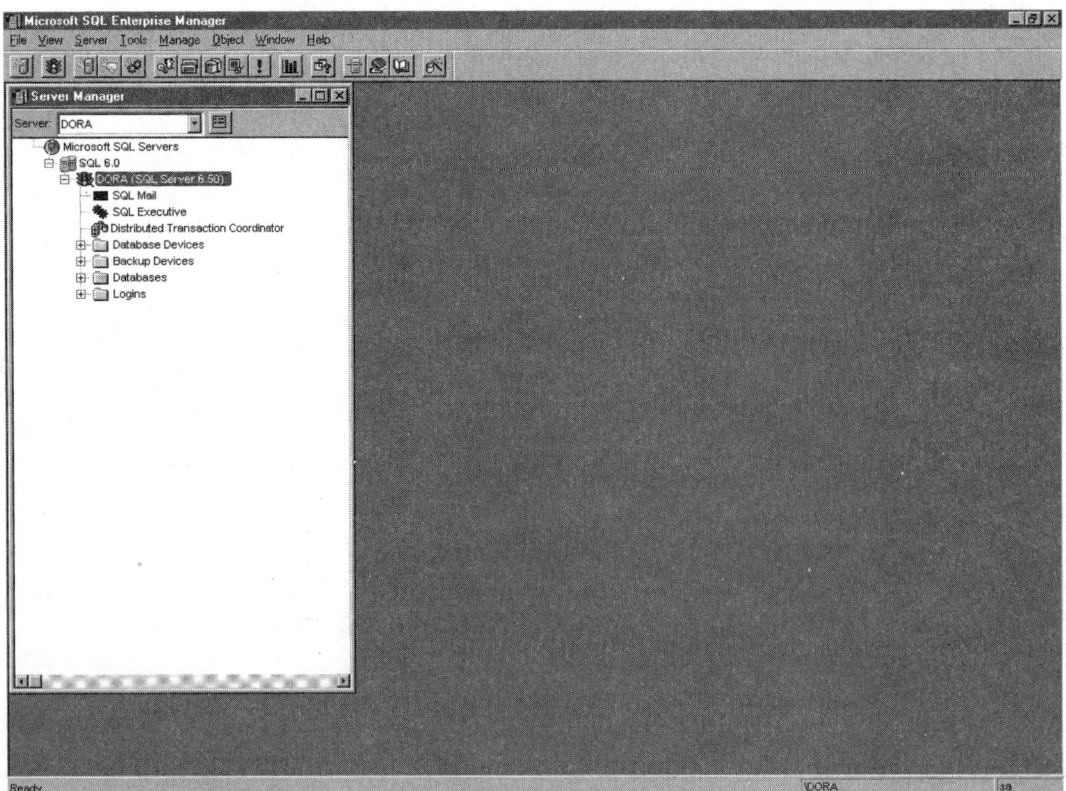

Figure 12-14: SQL Enterprise Manager managing Microsoft SQL Server 6.5 on DORA.

Notice in Figure 12-14 that only the SQL Server has been started. The SQL Mail, SQL Executive, and the Distributed Transaction Coordinator (DTC) have not been started. If you wanted to start these services, you would start them in SQL Enterprise Manager or in the SQL Service Manager. To start an SQL service (the SQL Server), right-click on the service and choose "Start" from the context menu that is displayed.

Also shown in Figure 12-14 are four other services, which I will cover shortly.

When connected to an SQL server, the SQL Enterprise Manager program has a complex menu structure, described below.

One thing that this chapter doesn't cover is the proliferation of context menus. There are approximately 35 different context menus—some of which are actually dynamically constructed based on need at the time of display.

SQL Enterprise Manager uses a relatively standard menu structure. However, because SQL Enterprise Manager is such a complex program, it is easy to "lose" functionality.

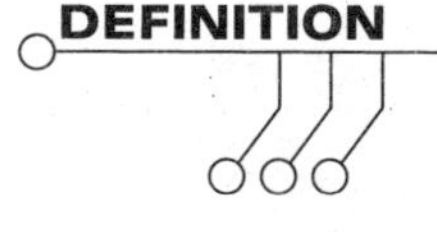

LFD—Lost Functionality Disorder, a condition that strikes accomplished computer users, is usually diagnosed when they are discovered mumbling at their desks: "I know how to do it, I just don't know where to find it." The current treatment is rest, and soothing words.

From the Server menu, you can manage SQL servers, SQL mail, SQL executive, and distributed transaction coordination. From the Manage menu, you can work with logins, devices, disks, replications, users, groups, and indexes, among other things. From the Objects menu, you can work with permissions, dependencies, and the like.

Database Devices

If you click the plus sign next to the Database Devices item in the tree shown at the left side of Figure 12-14, it expands into a set of sub items: master, MSDBData, and MSDBLog. The master device is the master database, the MSDBData device is the scheduling database, and the MDSBLog device is the transaction log.

Each of the Database Devices items, when double-clicked (or when you choose "Edit" from the context menu), displays a dialog box similar to the one shown in Figure 12-15.

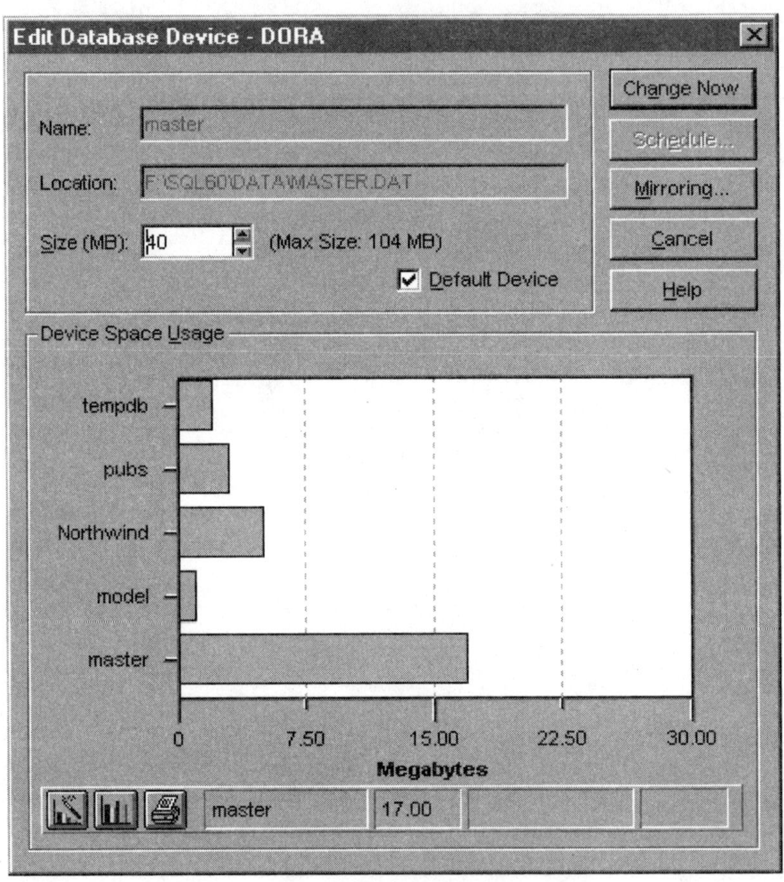

Figure 12-15: The Edit Database Device dialog.

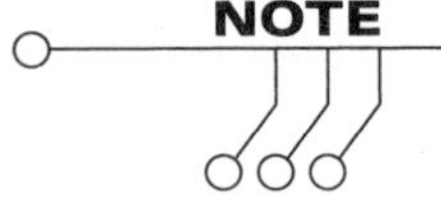

NOTE

You are not able to change the location of the Database Services items from the Edit Database Device dialog box. Use the New Device selection to create a new Database Services item on a different drive.

You can use the context menus to add new devices, edit and delete existing devices, and mirror existing devices.

Backup Devices

Backup devices allow you to back up your SQL database. Your choices include both tape and disk storage. When using disk storage to back up, it is possible to choose any local hard drive. You cannot select networked devices, nor are diskette drives selectable in this context. When selecting tape devices you can choose to skip headers.

Using the context menu you can create new backup devices, delete existing backup devices, restore devices, and refresh the list of backup devices.

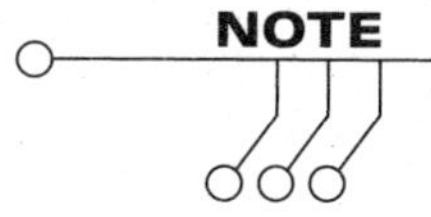

It does not make a great deal of sense to back up a file to the same drive. If the drive were to fail, then both copies of the file would be lost. No security there!

Databases

In the SQL Enterprise Manager's Server Manager window (shown in Figure 12-14), click the plus sign next to the Databases folder.

Data in Microsoft SQL Server 6.5 is stored in a hierarchical manner. The highest level is a database object. Stored in the database in Microsoft SQL Server 6.5 are Groups/Users and Objects. Under Objects comes Tables. Within Tables are columns and rows of data. Figure 12-16 shows the hierarchy for the "Pubs" database, a sample database of publisher data.

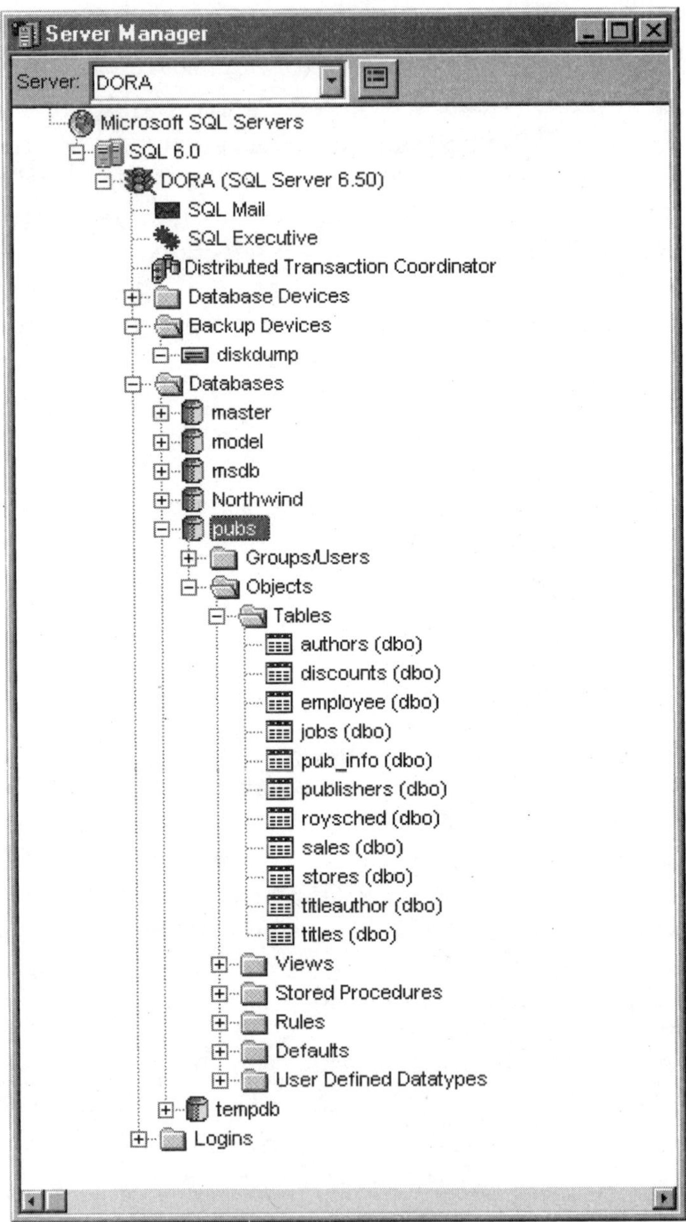

Figure 12-16: The Pubs database in Microsoft SQL Server 6.5.

Also note that there are a number of other items stored under the Objects tree item in addition to Tables. Table 12-1 describes the items in the Objects tree.

Item	Description
Tables	A table contains rows of data. Each row consists of one or more columns, each column having a particular set of attributes, such as name and datatype. A row of data is usually referred to as a record in the database.
Views	A view is a virtual table that represents an alternative way of looking at the data in one (or more) tables. A typical use is to allow a user to see some but not all of the data contained in a table. For example, you may allow users to see employee names and titles, but not to see salary information. To do this, create a view that contains only the information that you wish the user to see.
Stored Procedures	A stored procedure is a set of commands saved with the database in the Microsoft SQL Server 6.5. Stored procedures offer improved performance as they execute at the server rather than the client.
Rules	Rules, which are bound to columns or user-defined datatypes, specify acceptable values that can be inserted into a column or user-defined datatype.
Defaults	Defaults allow you to specify a default value when the user fails to provide data for a column or a user-defined datatype.
User-Defined Datatypes	A user-defined datatype is created by the user and is defined in terms of existing system datatypes.

Table 12-1: Items in the Objects tree.

Figure 12-17 shows the user-defined datatypes from the pubs database. In pubs there are three user-defined datatypes, "empid," "id," and "tid."

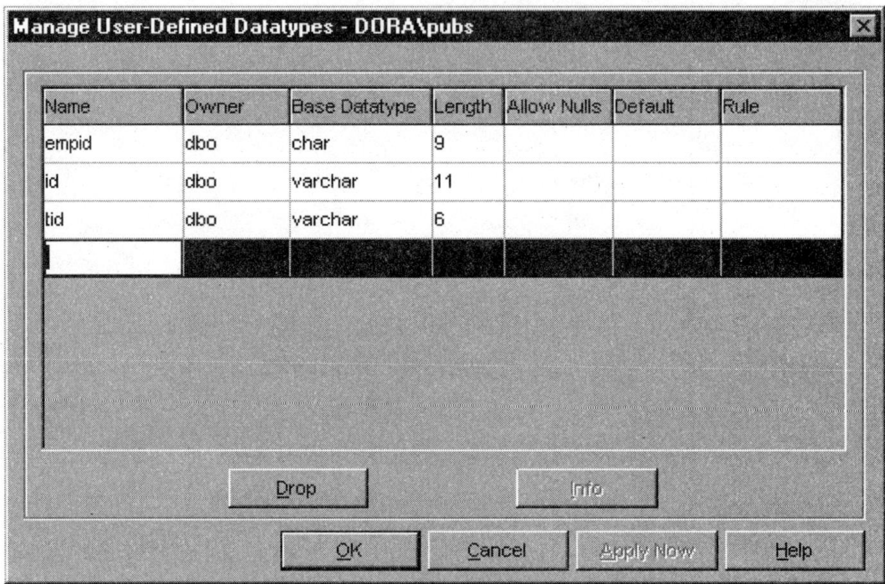

Figure 12-17: The three user-defined datatypes in pubs.

Generally, user-defined datatypes are simply a way to qualify an existing datatype. For example, in Figure 12-17, the tid datatype is simply a varchar type with its length defined as six characters. Each database could have zero, one, or more user-defined datatypes.

Logins

The last item in the Service Manager window tree is Logins. Logins contains the status of all authorized users. Each user may be queried using the context menu's Edit selection (or simply double-click a user's name to display the Manage Logins dialog box). Figure 12-18 shows the "sa" login. Note that this dialog shows what privileges each login ID has.

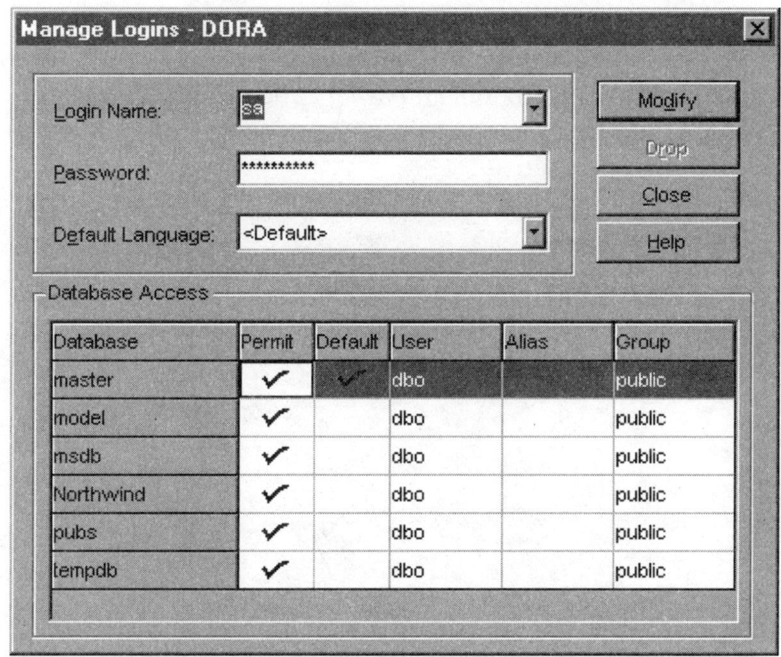

Figure 12-18: The Manage Logins dialog box.

SQL Performance Monitor

The SQL Performance Monitor is a powerful system-monitoring tool that monitors the performance of Microsoft SQL Server 6.5 as well as Windows NT 4 Server's performance.

To start the SQL Performance Monitor, click the SQL Performance Monitor in the Start Menu | Programs | Microsoft SQL Server 6.5 group. SQL Performance Monitor is actually a call to Windows NT 4 Server's Performance Monitor using a modified parameter file to include monitoring of Microsoft SQL Server 6.5 parameters. You can display performance data in a number of formats.

The SQL Performance Monitor is a powerful application with many options. As it is simply a monitoring tool (and therefore rather benign), it is an easy application to "play" with. Starting SQL Performance Monitor launches it in the graph mode, as shown in Figure 12-19.

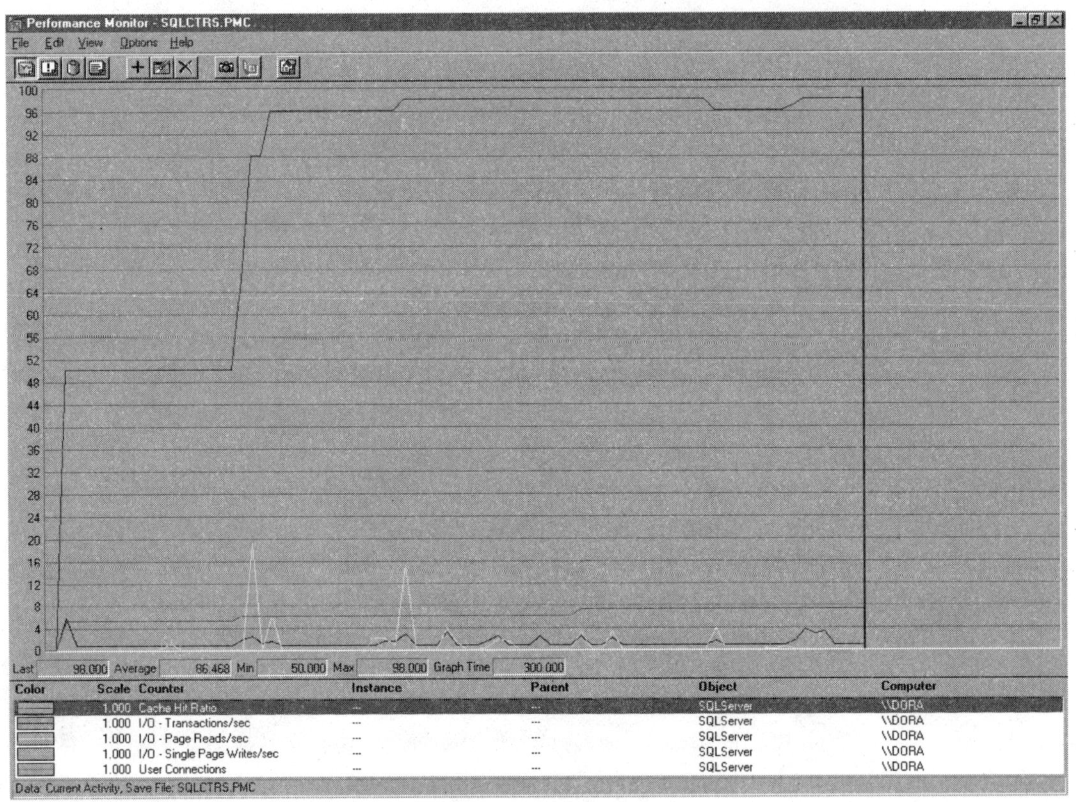

Figure 12-19: The SQL Performance Monitor main window.

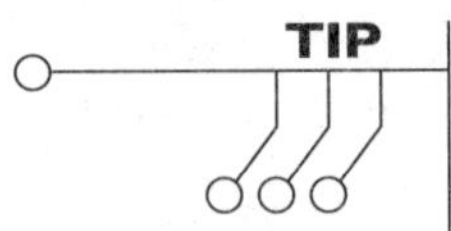

Because SQL Performance Monitor is Windows NT 4 Server's performance monitor, it may make sense to include this application in your startup group, especially at times when you are optimizing server performance.

With the SQL Performance Monitor, you can monitor parameters in the following categories: processor, cache, Internet services, network services, and many SQL Server services, among others.

To add a parameter to the SQL Performance Monitor, select Edit | Add to Chart (the shortcut key is CTRL-I). This displays the Add to Chart dialog box, as shown in Figure 12-20.

Each of these categories has between 10 and 30 sub-items that can be selected. There is descriptive text for each item as well, as shown in Figure 12-20.

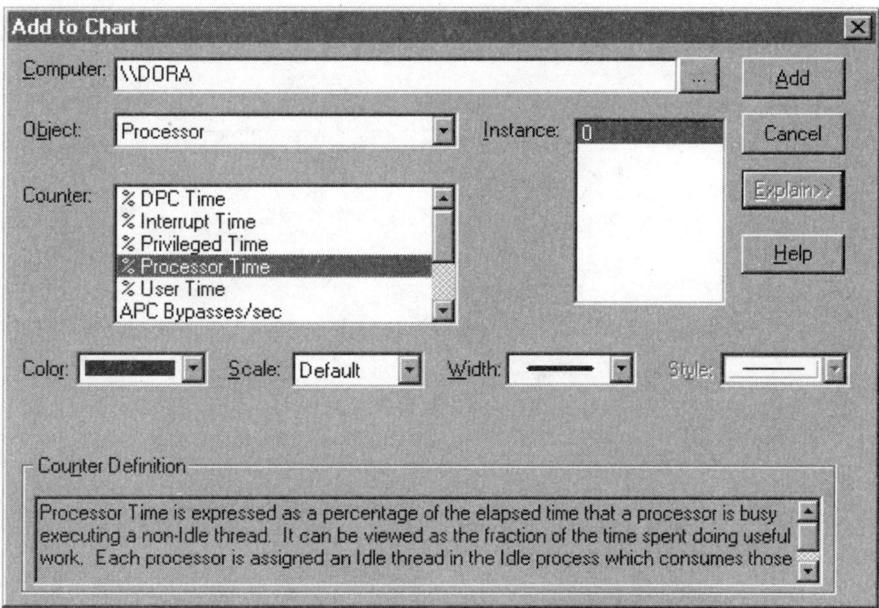

Figure 12-20: The SQL Performance Monitor Add to Chart dialog.

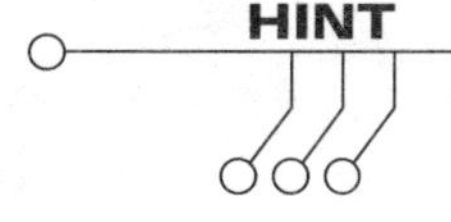

For more information about the Windows NT 4 Server Performance Monitor, see Chapter 8, "Configuring Hardware," and Chapter 9, "Monitoring Windows NT 4 Server Performance."

SQL Security Manager

The SQL Security Manager manages Microsoft SQL Server's security features. Start SQL Security Manager from the Microsoft SQL Server program group (Start Menu | Programs | Microsoft SQL Server 6.5). Microsoft SQL Server 6.5 Security Manager allows you to manage Microsoft SQL Server users and defaults. Shown in Figure 12-21 is SQL Security Manager's main window, with users displayed.

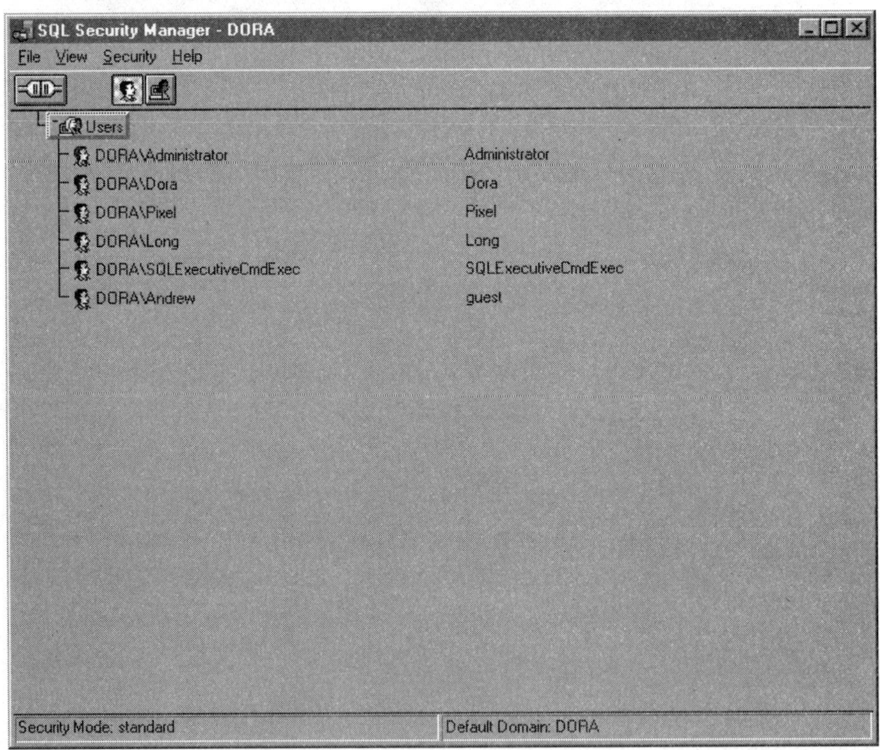

Figure 12-21: The SQL Security Manager main window.

SQL Security Manager shows both users and administrators for the Microsoft SQL Server. Administrators are defined as users who have "sa" privilege (sa: system administrator), while users have no special privileges.

To add Windows NT 4 Server users to the list of allowed Microsoft SQL Server users, select the Security | Grant New menu selection. In the Grant User Privilege dialog that displays, select "Users" in the Grant Privilege list, then click the Grant button. The SQL Security Manager then enumerates the Windows NT 4 Server user list, and adds new users to the list of SQL user IDs.

In the menu for SQL Security Manager you can select File | Configure, and SQL Security Manager displays the Configure dialog box, as shown in Figure 12-22.

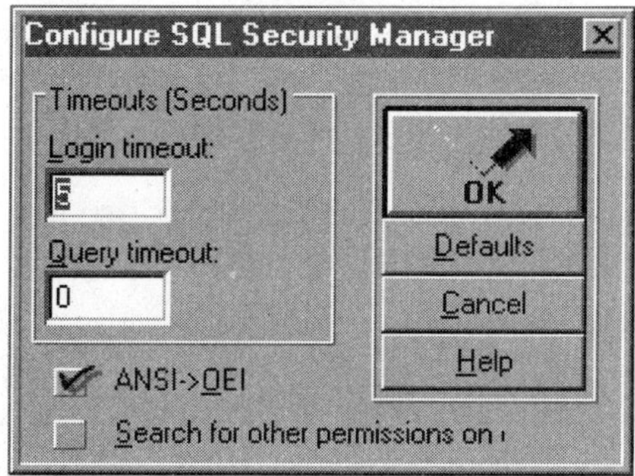

Figure 12-22: The SQL Security Manager Configure dialog box.

This dialog box has the following options:

- The Login timeout text box specifies the time, in seconds, that Microsoft SQL Server 6.5 waits prior to terminating an incomplete login attempt.
- The Query timeout text box specifies the time, in seconds, that Microsoft SQL Server 6.5 waits to retrieve a query result.
- The ANSI->OEM check box enables or disables the automatic ANSI to OEM character set conversion. The conversion assists in correcting any problems that may arise when displaying extended characters as graphics. Normally these characters display as letters with diacritical marks on Windows NT-based computers. You need to disconnect and then reconnect to Microsoft SQL Server 6.5 for this selection to take effect.

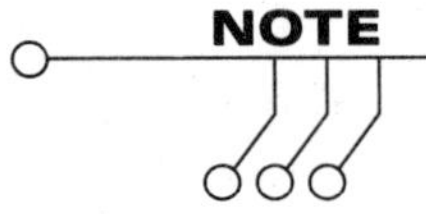

This option affects not only Microsoft SQL Server 6.5 but also all Windows- and Windows NT-based applications using the DB Library API.

- The "Search for other permissions on drop" check box indicates to Microsoft SQL Server 6.5 that when a login ID is dropped, all permission paths are searched. If any other permission paths exist, they are dropped as well.

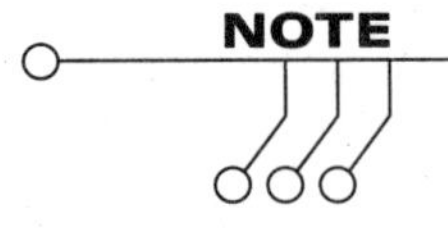

Selecting the Search for other permissions on drop option may result in a performance degradation of Microsoft SQL Server 6.5.

- You can use the Defaults button to restore the SQL Security Manager to the default values for these options.

For user-level accounts you can display account details: simply double-click on a user's name in the Users tree. The Account Details dialog box is shown in Figure 12-23. This dialog displays a number of pieces of information about the user, as the figure shows.

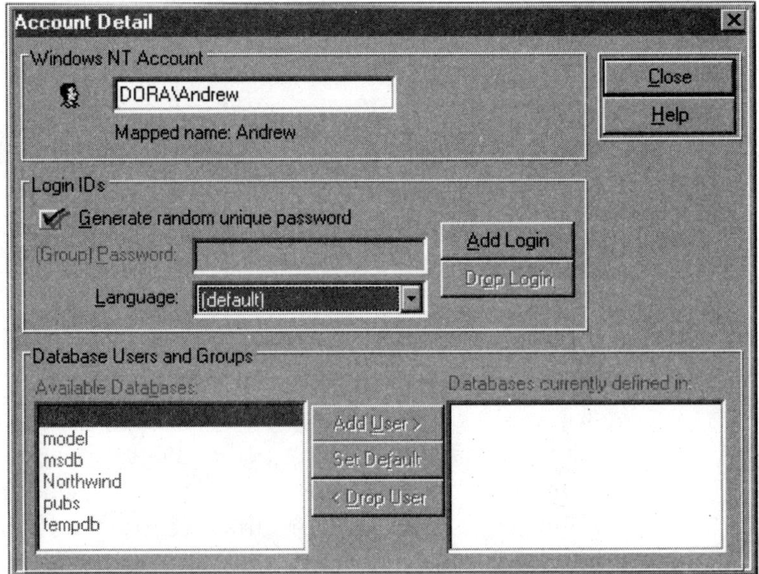

Figure 12-23: The SQL Security Manager Account Detail dialog box.

SQL Server Books Online

SQL Server Books Online offers a full set of documentation for Microsoft SQL Server 6.5. To start the SQL Server Books Online, select SQL Server Books Online in the Start Menu | Programs | Microsoft SQL Server 6.5 group. When using SQL Server Books Online you are presented with the standard "Books Online" program, used with many of Microsoft's products.

Each of the books offers a vast number of topics and valuable information. Whenever you need to find an answer about Microsoft SQL Server 6.5 and are not certain where to look, check SQL Server Books Online. Odds are, this is where you will find your answers!

SQL Server Web Assistant

The SQL Server Web Assistant is a very useful tool if you are interfacing your Web site with Microsoft SQL Server 6.5. With SQL Server Web Assistant you are able to automatically publish tables as Web pages.

The entire SQL Server Web Assistant program is a wizard. That is, you will be prompted for various information and when the SQL Server Web Assistant program completes, it generates the necessary Web page and the program ends.

Running SQL Server Web Assistant is easy:

1. Select the SQL Server Web Assistant icon in the Start Menu | Programs | Microsoft SQL Server 6.5 group.
2. The application launches with the window shown in Figure 12-24.

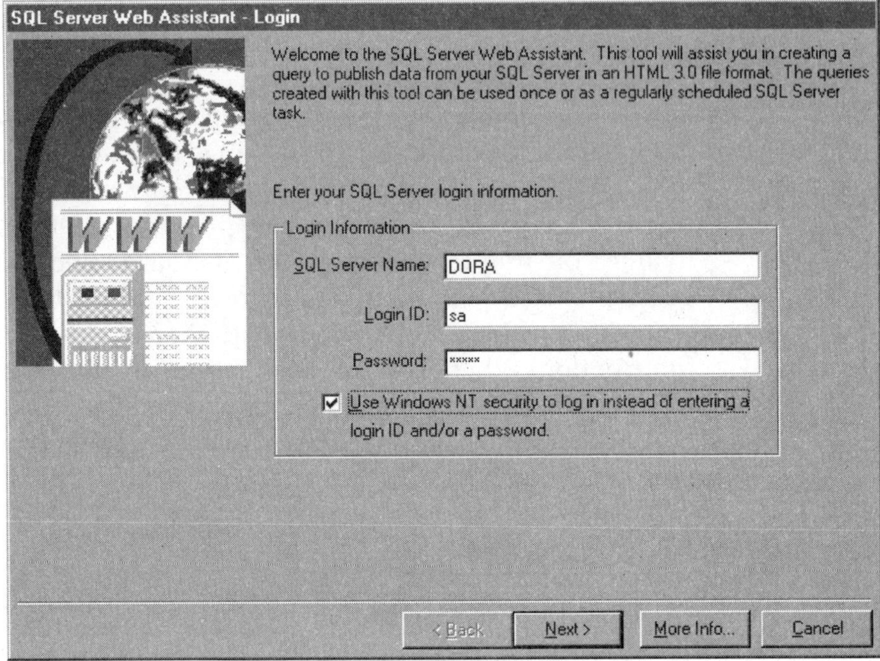

Figure 12-24: SQL Server Web Assistant - Login window.

3. In this window, enter Microsoft SQL Server 6.5 login information, including a server name, login name, and password. You may choose to use Windows NT's security rather than using Microsoft SQL Server 6.5 security.

Using Windows NT's security means that you will be logged on to the SQL server using your current logon user ID and password. After entering the necessary login information, click the Next button.

The second window, after SQL Server Web Assistant logs into Microsoft SQL Server 6.5, displays a tree view of the different databases available. Figure 12-25 shows this window, with the pubs database tree opened. Not shown in Figure 12-25 are the titles table and the title, ytd_sales, and pubdate columns in the titles table that I selected to be included in my query. I've not selected any other criteria, but you probably would want a WHERE clause, and perhaps a SORTED BY clause, too.

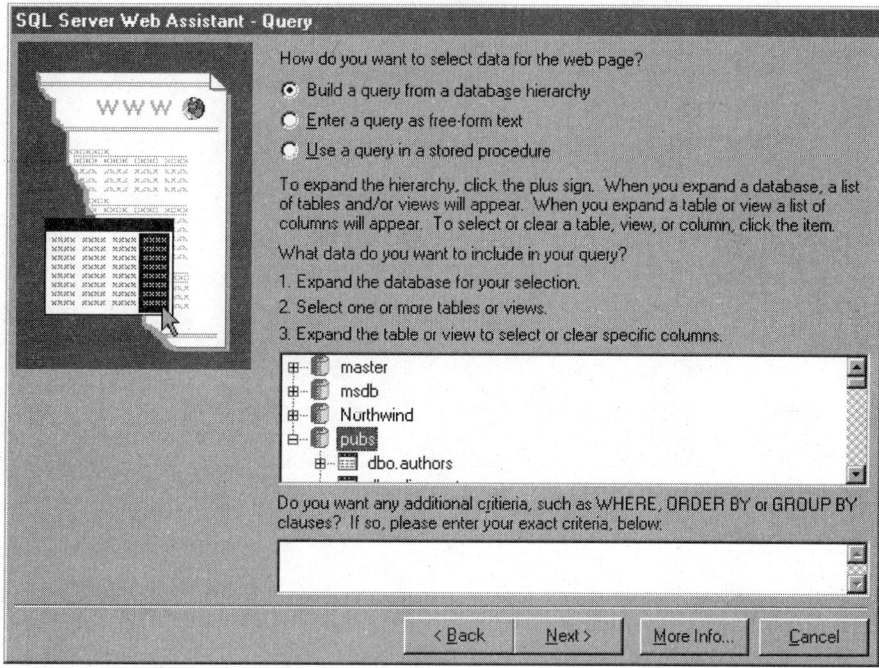

Figure 12-25: The SQL Server Web Assistant - Query window.

Once you have selected the tables (and columns if you do not want all columns in the selected tables) and entered any optional criteria, then click the Next button. The third wizard window, shown in Figure 12-26, allows you to set scheduling options.

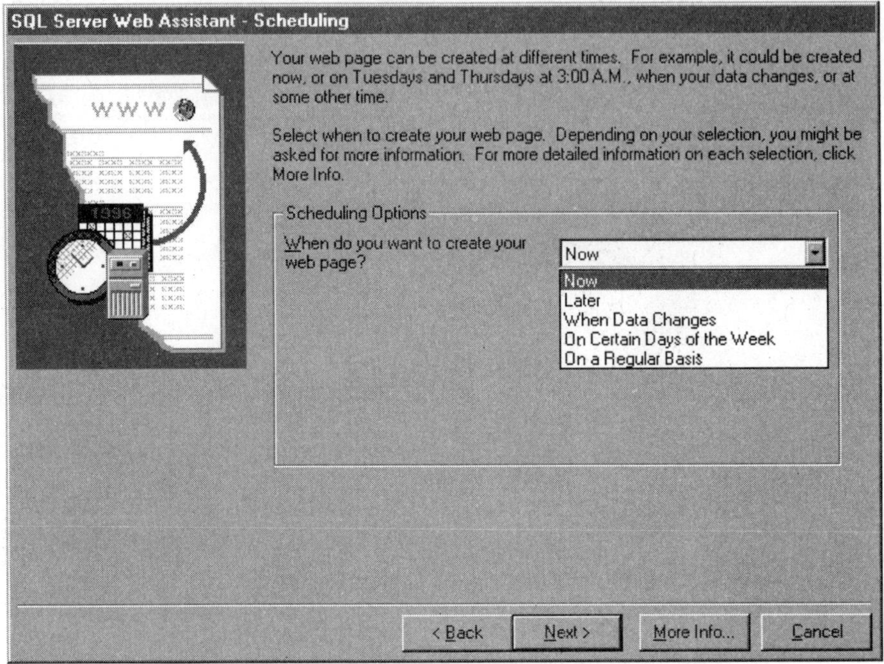

Figure 12-26: The SQL Server Web Assistant - Scheduling window.

You have five choices in the SQL Server Web Assistant - Scheduling window:

- Now—The query executes immediately, and the Web page is generated from this query.
- Later—The query executes at a later time. You specify the date (and time) for the query to execute.
- When Data Changes—The query executes when data in the column(s) you specify changes.
- On Certain Days of the Week—The query executes on the day (or days) and time specified.
- On a Regular Basis—The query executes at the specified interval. For example, every two hours, or every day at a given time.

Select a schedule option that reflects the volatility of your data—if your data changes frequently, schedule the page to be updated more frequently. If the data is relatively static, then a less frequent updating is required. Once you have selected the schedule (and provided any schedule-specific information required, such as day, time, or interval), click the Next button.

The fourth window, shown in Figure 12-27, defines the final format for your Web page. You specify a name for this page, a source template or title and table information, and whether you wish to have any URL (Uniform Resource Locator) information included in your Web page.

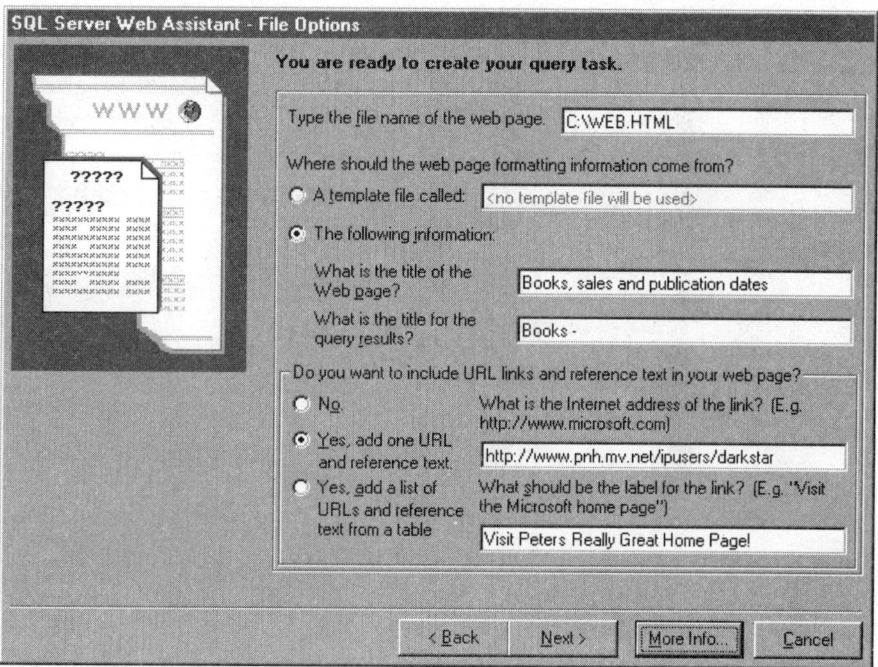

Figure 12-27: The SQL Server Web Assistant - File Options window.

In the File Options window is a radio button labeled "A template file called," which is followed by a text box. You can specify a template file to have the results table inserted into it. The template file is for a standard HTML document, with a marker <%insert_data_here%>. Where the <%insert_data_here%> marker is found, the table created by the query is inserted. This lets you customize a complex HTML document by (dynamically) adding data from a Microsoft SQL Server 6.5 database table.

When you specify a template file, then all other options in the File Options dialog box (except for the Web page name) are disabled.

The fifth, and final, window in SQL Server Web Assistant is the Formatting window, shown in Figure 12-28. This window allows you to specify the appearance of your Web page, including the title format and level (Header 1 through Header 6), and the font and attributes of the data table. You can also specify whether you want a time and date stamp, column or view column names, and whether you wish to limit the number of rows returned by the query.

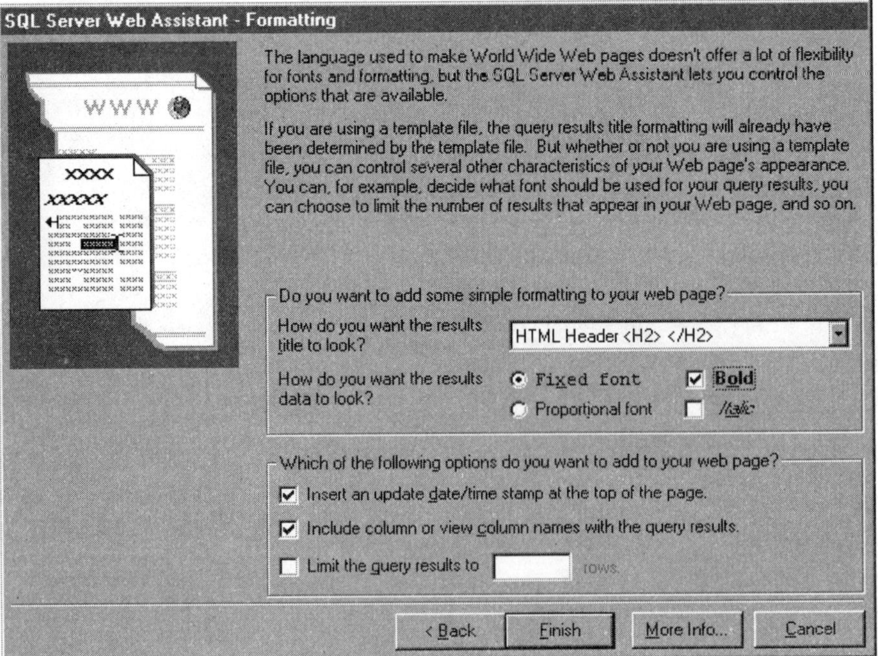

Figure 12-28: The SQL Server Web Assistant - Formatting window.

The final results (as seen using Microsoft Internet Explorer) are shown in Figure 12-29. The Web page shows information about books, and includes the link to my home page.

This page would be much more complex if a template were designed and used. The technique for using a template is simple and effective, allowing you to use your background, text, footers, headers, and so on. For professional results, a template is recommended.

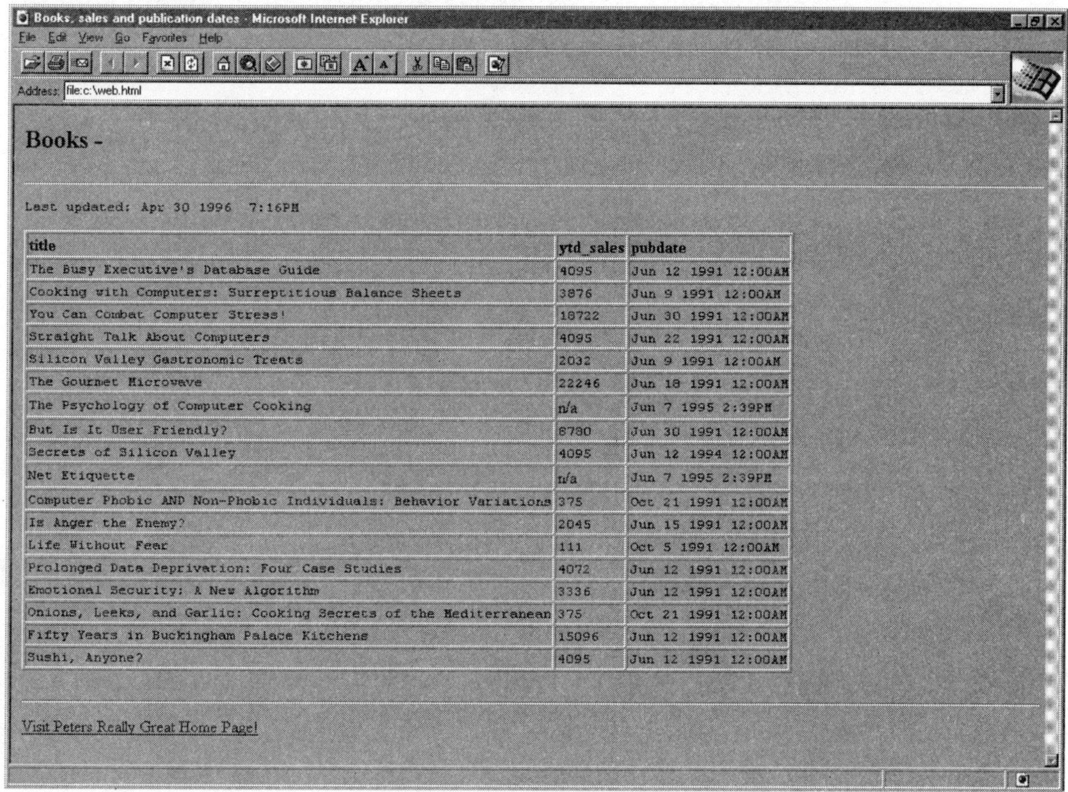

title	ytd_sales	pubdate
The Busy Executive's Database Guide	4095	Jun 12 1991 12:00AM
Cooking with Computers: Surreptitious Balance Sheets	3876	Jun 9 1991 12:00AM
You Can Combat Computer Stress!	18722	Jun 30 1991 12:00AM
Straight Talk About Computers	4095	Jun 22 1991 12:00AM
Silicon Valley Gastronomic Treats	2032	Jun 9 1991 12:00AM
The Gourmet Microwave	22246	Jun 18 1991 12:00AM
The Psychology of Computer Cooking	n/a	Jun 7 1995 2:39PM
But Is It User Friendly?	8780	Jun 30 1991 12:00AM
Secrets of Silicon Valley	4095	Jun 12 1994 12:00AM
Net Etiquette	n/a	Jun 7 1995 2:39PM
Computer Phobic AND Non-Phobic Individuals: Behavior Variations	375	Oct 21 1991 12:00AM
Is Anger the Enemy?	2045	Jun 15 1991 12:00AM
Life Without Fear	111	Oct 5 1991 12:00AM
Prolonged Data Deprivation: Four Case Studies	4072	Jun 12 1991 12:00AM
Emotional Security: A New Algorithm	3336	Jun 12 1991 12:00AM
Onions, Leeks, and Garlic: Cooking Secrets of the Mediterranean	375	Oct 21 1991 12:00AM
Fifty Years in Buckingham Palace Kitchens	15096	Jun 12 1991 12:00AM
Sushi, Anyone?	4095	Jun 12 1991 12:00AM

Figure 12-29: The SQL Server Web Assistant-created web.html document.

SQL Service Manager

The SQL Service Manager is the initial interface with Microsoft SQL Server 6.5. The SQL Service Manager is the way the administrator starts, stops, or pauses Microsoft SQL Server 6.5. You launch SQL Service Manager from the Start Menu, using the "Programs | Microsoft SQL Server 6.5" group.

Using SQL Service Manager is easy. The user interface consists of a "traffic signal" type control (a frequently used control with Microsoft SQL Server 6.5) with three buttons: red, yellow, and green. The functionality of each button is documented right in the control:

- Red—stop Microsoft SQL Server 6.5.
- Yellow—pause Microsoft SQL Server 6.5.
- Green—start Microsoft SQL Server 6.5.

The current state of Microsoft SQL Server 6.5 is indicated by whichever button is brighter, and is also shown in the status bar at the bottom of the SQL Service Manager main window, as shown in Figure 12-30.

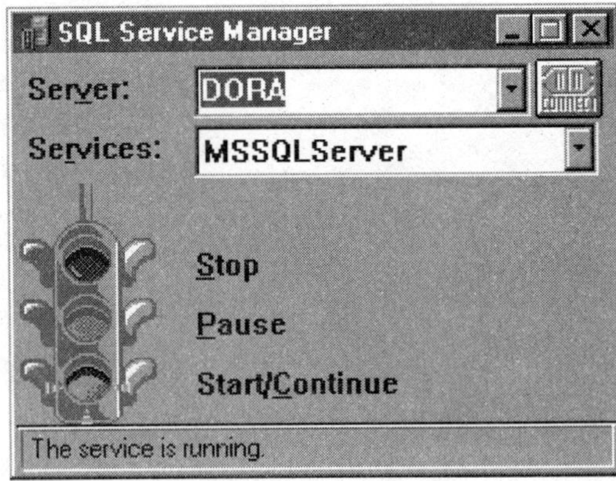

Figure 12-30: SQL Service Manager's main window.

The Microsoft SQL Service Manager allows you to connect to and manage SQL Servers remotely. Shown in Figure 12-30 are two drop-down lists: Server and Services. A button allows you to connect to a server (which is disabled in Figure 12-30) when you select a remote server that is not currently connected in the Server combo box control.

Use the Server drop-down list to work with either a local Microsoft SQL Server or a remote Microsoft SQL Server. When you select a server, you must then connect to that server, supplying the necessary password and other logon information as necessary.

The Services drop-down list allows you to Stop, Pause, or Start/ Continue the following services:

- MSDTC—The Microsoft Distributed Transaction Coordinator (MSDTC) coordinates transactions across a network of Windows NT and Windows 95 clients and servers. Using MSDTC, Microsoft SQL Server 6.5 is able to do several things. Using MSDTC, it is possible to update data that resides on two or more Microsoft SQL Server 6.5 systems. It is also possible to participate in transactions controlled by X/Open DTP XA-compliant transaction-processing monitors. MSDTC provides a graphical user interface for distributed transactions.
- MSSQLServer—The Microsoft SQL Server is the core component of Microsoft SQL Server 6.5.
- SQLExecutive—The SQLExecutive is the service for the SQL executive. SQLExecutive resides on the Windows NT 4 Server on which Microsoft SQL Server 6.5 runs. SQLExecutive provides the Microsoft SQL Server 6.5 scheduling engine, and offers robust and varied task scheduling and alerting abilities. SQLExecutive is able to work in large client/server environments. SQLExecutive is also sometimes referred to as SQL Executive both in this book and in the Microsoft SQL Server 6.5 documentation and programs.

Once you've selected the server and services, to manage them you double-click on the start, pause, and stop buttons.

SQL Setup

The SQL Setup utility is the same program that you used to install Microsoft SQL Server 6.5. The Setup program can be re-run at any time to refresh, modify, or totally reinstall Microsoft SQL Server 6.5 if desired.

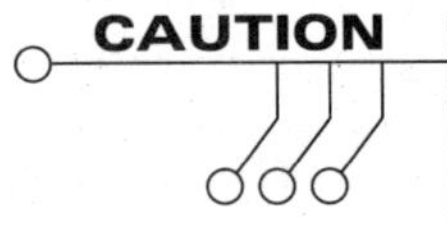

Use caution when you have an actively used database. Make sure you have adequate backups of all the information in the database: schema, miscellaneous items, data—all must be backed up, and frequently.

Most options may be specified whenever SQL Setup is re-run. This gives the user the opportunity to change basic Microsoft SQL Server 6.5 options, if desired.

Though it is not a good idea to reinstall a product arbitrarily, if you find that your installation is not reliable, has unexplained crashes, or hangs for no apparent reason, a reinstall may be in order. If you find that more than one application fails, however, check hardware or other system components for the problem area.

SQL Trace

The SQL Trace utility monitors Microsoft SQL Server 6.5. To start the SQL Trace utility, select SQL Trace in the Start Menu | Programs | Microsoft SQL Server 6.5 group. You may choose which events you wish to monitor (the defaults are to monitor virtually everything) and how you wish the monitoring to be performed.

Figure 12-31 shows the SQL Trace utility tracing the execution of a simple SQL query. This query successfully returned a number of rows of information to the user.

```
SQL Trace - DORA  [Example]
File  Edit  View  Tools  Window  Help
go
-- 5/1/96 12:14:02.986 SQL (ID=3, SPID=12, User=sa(DORA\administrator), App='MS SQLEW', Host='DORA'(fc) )
select o.name, user_name(o.uid), o.crdate, o.id, o.category from sysobjects o where sysstat & 0xf = 2 and o.name not like '#%
go
-- 5/1/96 12:14:03.026 SQL (ID=3, SPID=12, User=sa(DORA\administrator), App='MS SQLEW', Host='DORA'(fc) )
select name, owner = user_name(uid), crdate, objtype = sysstat & 0xf, id, deltrig from sysobjects o where power(2, sysstat &
go
-- 5/1/96 12:14:03.046 SQL (ID=3, SPID=12, User=sa(DORA\administrator), App='MS SQLEW', Host='DORA'(fc) )
select name, owner = user_name(uid), crdate, objtype = sysstat & 0xf, id, deltrig from sysobjects o where power(2, sysstat &
go
-- 5/1/96 12:14:07.573 SQL (ID=3, SPID=12, User=sa(DORA\administrator), App='MS SQLEW', Host='DORA'(fc) )
select o.name, user_name(o.uid), o.crdate, o.id, o.category from sysobjects o where sysstat & 0xf = 2 and o.name not like '#%
go
-- 5/1/96 12:14:07.593 SQL (ID=3, SPID=12, User=sa(DORA\administrator), App='MS SQLEW', Host='DORA'(fc) )
select name, owner = user_name(uid), crdate, objtype = sysstat & 0xf, id, deltrig from sysobjects o where power(2, sysstat &
go
-- 5/1/96 12:14:07.603 SQL (ID=3, SPID=12, User=sa(DORA\administrator), App='MS SQLEW', Host='DORA'(fc) )
select name, owner = user_name(uid), crdate, objtype = sysstat & 0xf, id, deltrig from sysobjects o where power(2, sysstat &
go
-- 5/1/96 12:14:07.813 SQL (ID=3, SPID=12, User=sa(DORA\administrator), App='MS SQLEW', Host='DORA'(fc) )
if exists (select * from syscomments where id=object_id('dbo.titleview') and texttype & 4 <> 0) select text='<Encrypted>', nu
go
-- 5/1/96 12:14:07.903 SQL (ID=3, SPID=12, User=sa(DORA\administrator), App='MS SQLEW', Host='DORA'(fc) )
 exec sp_MSobjectprivs 'dbo.titleview'
go
-- 5/1/96 12:14:22.013 New connection (ID=4, SPID=13, User=sa(DORA\administrator), App='MS SQLEW', Host='DORA'(fc) )
-- 5/1/96 12:14:22.123 SQL (ID=4, SPID=13, User=sa(DORA\administrator), App='MS SQLEW', Host='DORA'(fc) )
exec sp_server_info 18
go
-- 5/1/96 12:14:22.173 SQL (ID=4, SPID=13, User=sa(DORA\administrator), App='MS SQLEW', Host='DORA'(fc) )
 set textsize 64512 use pubs
go
-- 5/1/96 12:14:22.173 SQL (ID=4, SPID=13, User=sa(DORA\administrator), App='MS SQLEW', Host='DORA'(fc) )
select suser_name()
go
-- 5/1/96 12:14:22.183 SQL (ID=4, SPID=13, User=sa(DORA\administrator), App='MS SQLEW', Host='DORA'(fc) )
select @@microsoftversion
go
-- 5/1/96 12:14:22.183 SQL (ID=4, SPID=13, User=sa(DORA\administrator), App='MS SQLEW', Host='DORA'(fc) )
select name from master..sysdatabases order by name
go
-- 5/1/96 12:14:24.530 SQL (ID=4, SPID=13, User=sa(DORA\administrator), App='MS SQLEW', Host='DORA'(fc) )
select suser_name()
go
-- 5/1/96 12:14:24.550 SQL (ID=4, SPID=13, User=sa(DORA\administrator), App='MS SQLEW', Host='DORA'(fc) )
SELECT title, au_ord, au_lname, price, ytd_sales, pub_id
FROM authors, titles, titleauthor
WHERE authors.au_id = titleauthor.au_id
       AND titles.title_id = titleauthor.title_id
go
Active filters 1
```

Figure 12-31: SQL Trace at work.

The SQL Trace program has a number of options, described below.

To connect to an SQL server, use the File | Connect menu selection. Once you make a connection, then you can begin tracing operations. Also, when finished tracing a specific SQL Server, select the File | Disconnect to disconnect from the currently connected SQL Server.

You can use the File menu to create new filters, modify or delete existing filters, or start, pause, or stop tracing with existing filters. You can use the View menu to monitor the filter that is currently being used in the tracing. The Tools menu lets you audit or monitor the SQL Server, put the results in a file, and configure what is traced. Many of these menu items are represented on a toolbar, which unfortunately cannot be customized.

Moving On

In this chapter I covered the Microsoft SQL Server 6.5 system. Microsoft SQL Server 6.5 is part of the Microsoft BackOffice product, and forms the cornerstone of Microsoft's Client/Server thrust.

Using Microsoft SQL Server allows organizations to completely manage data access. Microsoft SQL Server and Client applications can be made to do most any information management task that could be needed.

This chapter ends the second part of the book. Chapters in the next section, "Windows NT 4 and the Internet," introduce Microsoft Internet Information Server (IIS) and discuss the three IIS services: Web, Gopher, and FTP.

SECTION III

Windows NT 4 and the Internet

13

The Microsoft Internet Information Server

First, a little background information. In keeping with Microsoft's goal to move fully into the world of the Internet, the Microsoft Internet Information Server (IIS) was provided as an optional feature for Windows NT 3.51 Server. IIS is also supplied as part of the Microsoft BackOffice 2.0 product. IIS version 2.0 is now included as a part of Windows NT 4 Server. Microsoft is offering a limited-feature version of IIS for use with Windows NT 4 Workstation and plans a future version of IIS for Windows 95.

Now, what can you do with Microsoft IIS? You can use Microsoft IIS to establish a company on the Internet or to set up an intranet. In case you missed our introduction to the Internet and intranets in earlier chapters, an intranet is a network like the Internet, but totally private, usually limited to a single company, corporation, or organization. The Internet, on the other hand, is global (really, worldwide!), public, and for all intents and purposes, offers unlimited access to its users!

Microsoft IIS consists of three separate server services:

- Gopher
- FTP
- World Wide Web (WWW)

With IIS there are also a few other supporting software applications, files, and sample Web site file components you can install.

First Things First

Don't worry too much about setting up an individual IIS service. Simply load the example files and start with them. Later, you can customize (or just replace) the Microsoft-provided Web pages!

Neither the FTP nor the Gopher service has sample files. If you don't provide sample files, the services still work correctly, but users don't get anything! No problem. You can add files to the FTP and Gopher services at any time.

The Microsoft IIS administrator can set a number of options to configure each of the IIS services. Of these three servers, the Web server is probably the most customized by users—Web pages encourage a great deal of Web site individuality and creativity.

This chapter introduces both IIS and the Internet Service Manager. The chapters listed below cover the other servers:

- Chapter 14, "The Microsoft IIS Gopher & FTP Services"
- Chapter 15, "The Microsoft IIS WWW Service"

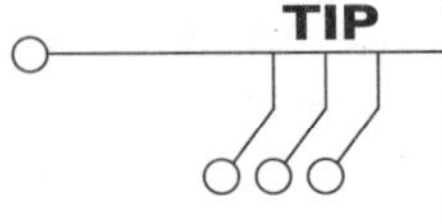

Microsoft distributed free beta versions of IIS that worked with Windows NT 3.51. If you have IIS installed under Windows NT 3.51 Server, be sure to allow setup to install the new version of IIS that comes with Windows NT 4 Server.

Installing Microsoft IIS

Installing IIS is relatively easy. There are a number of ways to install IIS. Each method, however, will run the same Setup program. The only difference between the different installation methods is how the IIS Setup program is run.

When Windows NT 4 Server is installed, Setup Wizard prompts you to install IIS. If you do not choose to install IIS at Windows NT 4 Server installation time, the Setup Wizard places, on your Windows NT desktop, an icon for installing IIS. When installing IIS, you must decide on a location for the IIS product (typically IIS is installed in a default location, the Windows NT folder: C:\winnt\system32\inetsrv).

One suggestion is to install IIS on an NTFS partition. If Windows NT 4 Server is installed on an NTFS partition, then installing IIS in the default folder is likely the best choice. Using an NTFS partition enhances security for the files IIS uses (NTFS partitions have better security)—an important consideration when connecting to the Internet.

If you do not install Microsoft IIS when installing Windows NT 4 Server, then you have three choices on how to install IIS:

- You can select the IIS installation icon that Windows NT 4 Server setup has placed on your desktop. This will run the IIS Setup program.
- You can run the IIS Setup program from the Control Panel, as described below.
- You can run the IIS Setup program from the Windows NT 4 Server distribution CD-ROM. The Setup program, INETSTP.EXE, is found in the INETSRV folder.

Installing IIS From the Desktop

To install Microsoft IIS using the icon placed on the desktop by the Windows NT 4 Server Setup program, simply double-click the IIS installation icon. If for any reason you do not have an IIS installation icon (maybe it was deleted), then use one of the two following methods.

Installing IIS From the Control Panel

To install IIS using the Control Panel, follow the steps below:

1. Start the Control Panel's Network applet.
2. Select the Services tab.
3. Click the Add button. The Select Network Service dialog box appears.
4. Select Microsoft Internet Information Server 2.0 from the Network Service list, and click OK.

Installing IIS From the Windows NT 4 Server CD-ROM

To install Microsoft IIS from the Windows NT 4 Server distribution CD-ROM, follow the steps below:

1. On the CD-ROM, change the current IIS folder to the correct folder for your processor (for Intel, the I386\inetsrv folder).
2. Run the Setup program INETSTP (which is the name of the IIS Setup program) to install, remove, or modify the current installation of IIS.
3. Follow the prompts to complete the installation of IIS. The setup is identical to setup started from the Control Panel's Network applet, as described below.

The IIS Setup Program

Whichever method you choose to begin installation, the Microsoft Internet Information Server 2.0 Setup program's welcome dialog box appears as shown in Figure 13-1.

The Setup program allows you to select which IIS components are to be installed (you may elect to install Web, FTP, and Gopher services). None of the Microsoft Internet Information Server components are large. In fact, the entire IIS system occupies less than 5MB, including all of the example HTML pages! The author recommends installing all, then simply stopping those services that are not desired.

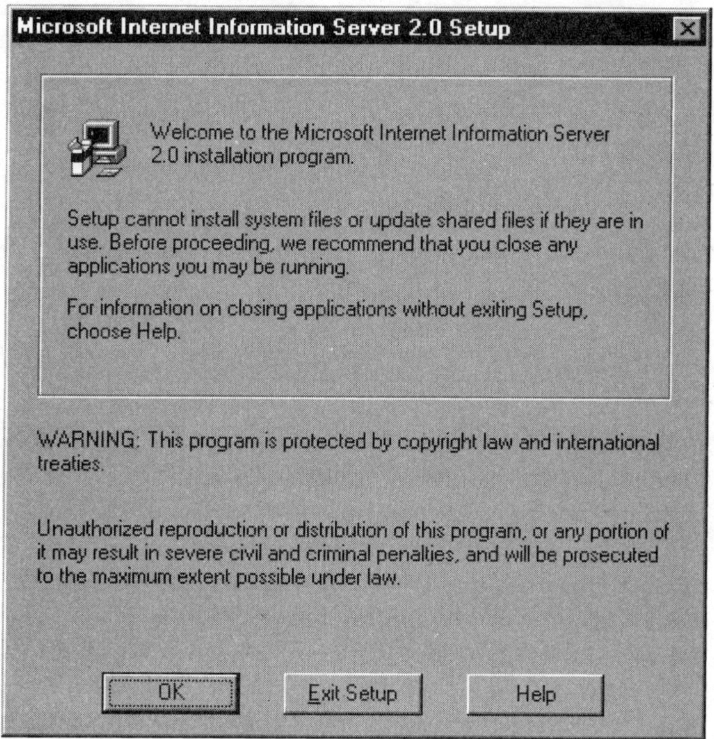

Figure 13-1: The Microsoft Internet Information Server 2.0 Setup dialog box.

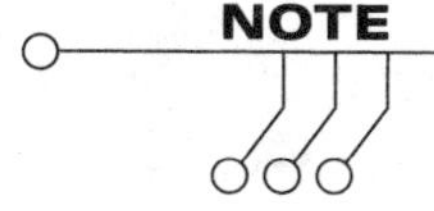

When IIS is installed after Windows NT 4 Server has been installed and you use the method described in the steps above, you may come across a problem. Installing IIS requires that you start the Control Panel's Network applet. The Microsoft IIS Setup program, however, needs to update the Control Panel, which cannot be updated while the Control Panel is open. If the somewhat cryptic message displays, stating that a .CPL file cannot be copied (yes, this happens often when installing Windows NT 4 Server components), as shown in Figure 13-2, simply close the Control Panel and click the Retry button.

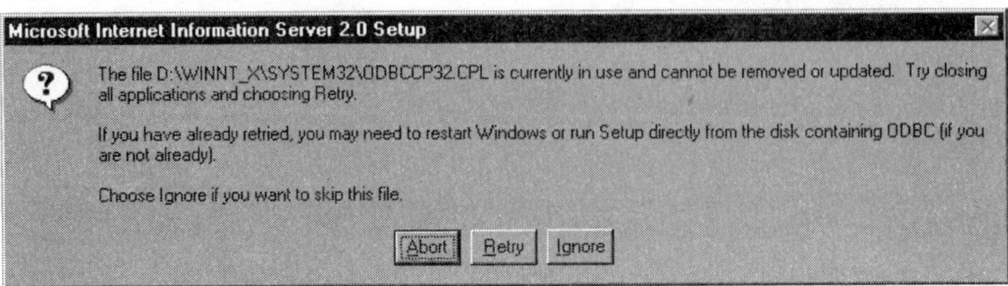

Figure 13-2: IIS Setup error—the Control Panel can't be updated!

The installation process is simple and quick. Once completed, you should restart Windows NT 4 Server, which will start the IIS services.

Setting Up & Configuring IIS

The initial folders used to publish on the Internet are created by the IIS Setup program. For the World Wide Web Publishing Directory, the IIS Setup program writes (if the help and sample files are installed) several HTML examples. The FTP and Gopher publishing folders do not contain any sample files. If you modify any of the example Web pages that are installed by IIS, and at a later time you reinstall IIS, your modifications will be lost.

Whenever using the Internet, you must define a Domain Name Server (DNS). If you have not specified a DNS, the IIS Setup program cautions you to configure the DNS entry in the Control Panel's Network applet. The IIS Setup program prompts if the DNS entries are not set correctly!

IIS can use ODBC, SQL Server, or text files (the default) to store the IIS logs. There is a prompt to install the SQL Server ODBC driver, if ODBC Drivers & Administrator was selected.

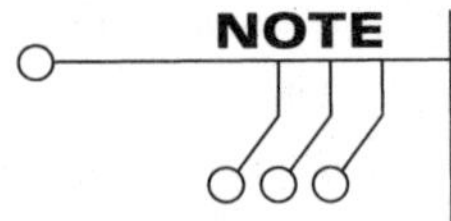

You are not limited to using SQL Server as your IIS logging device—the default logging device is a comma-delimited text file.

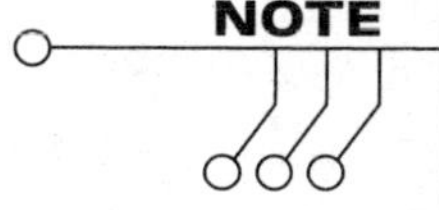

Microsoft has created a version of IIS that does run on Windows NT 4 Workstation and Windows 95, but with reduced functionality.

Microsoft had planned to limit Windows NT 4 Workstation to a maximum of ten unique incoming IP addresses; however, an announcement in mid-July 1996 indicated that Microsoft has decided not to limit Windows NT 4 Workstation in this way. Windows NT 4 Workstation installs IIS from the inetsrv folder using the same procedure as Windows NT 4 Server.

Microsoft IIS is configured using the Microsoft Internet Information Server Manager program—the topic of the next section.

The Microsoft Internet Information Server Manager

After you install Microsoft IIS, there will be a new item in Start Menu | Programs. This item is called Microsoft Internet Server and contains five items:

- Internet Information Server Setup
- Microsoft Internet Explorer
- Product Documentation
- Internet Service Manager
- Key Manager

The Internet Information Server setup was described in the previous section.

The Microsoft Internet Explorer included with Windows NT 4 Server is version 2, which has since been replaced with version 3. I recommend that you download and use the latest version of Internet Explorer, rather than using the older version. For the current version of Internet Explorer, check http://www.microsoft.com.

The IIS product documentation consists of a help file that contains the documentation you'll need to use and manage IIS.

The Key Manager program is used to manage security keys for IIS. With the Key Manager you can create new key requests and manage keys. You can find more information on keys in Chapter 15, "The Microsoft WWW Service."

Microsoft IIS is managed by the Internet Service Manager application. Launch this application using the Start Menu | Programs | Microsoft Internet Server | Internet Service Manager selection.

The Internet Service Manager application manages and customizes each of the servers that make up IIS. Management typically consists of starting or shutting down the various servers as needed. For example, if the Gopher server will not be used at your site, simply stop the Gopher server. Each of the IIS servers are independent—and you can start or stop them as needed without affecting the other servers.

Use the Internet Service Manager window (see Figure 13-3) to work with various servers or services. The list below describes the functionality available from the Properties and View menus.

- From the Properties menu, you can configure each service (locally or remotely), make connections to specific servers, locate servers, and display properties of a service. You can also start, stop, and pause services using the service's context menu.
- From the View menu, you can specify how you want the information presented, by individual service or sorted by field.
    - The Servers view is the default view.
    - Services view and Reports view offer other presentations of the same information.

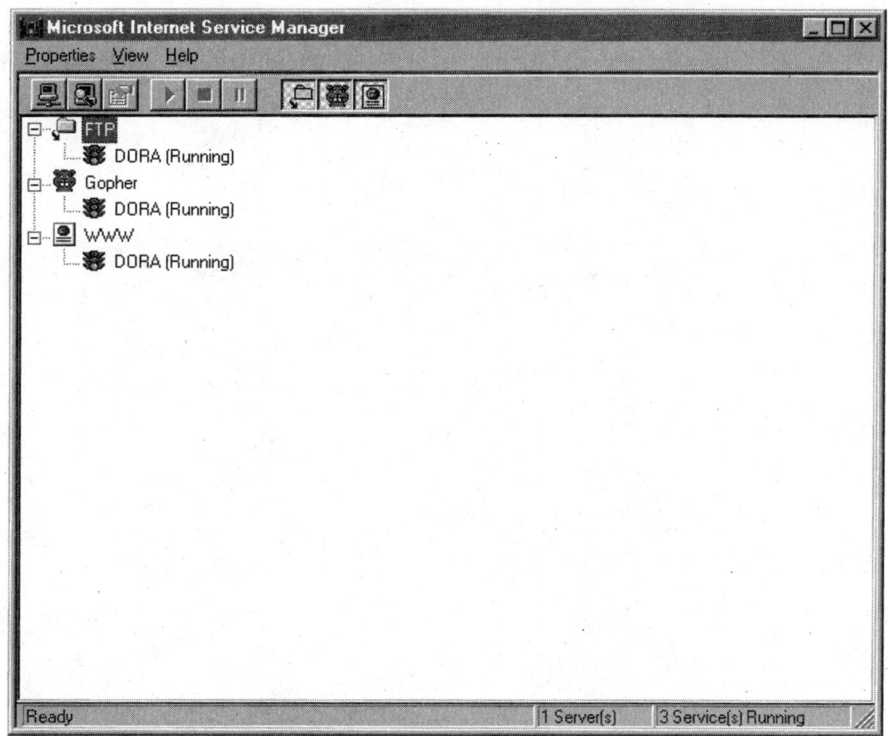

Figure 13-3: The Microsoft Internet Service Manager main window.

Configuring each service is usually simple. Designing the information that the service will publish may be more difficult. Fortunately, there are many excellent books out on this topic. Try *Looking Good Online*, by Steve Bain, or *Ten Secrets for Web Success*, by Bryan Pfaffenberger, both from Ventana.

Configuring the FTP, Gopher & Web Servers

You must configure each of the three IIS Services before placing them in service. Configuration is not too difficult. Each service uses a similar Setup program (minor differences, unique to specific service are noted).

The FTP Service Properties dialog box, in Figure 13-4, has five tabs: Service, Messages, Directories, Logging, and Advanced. The Gopher and Web Service Properties dialog boxes have four tabs: Service, Directories, Logging, and Advanced. The Messages tab is found only in the FTP Service Properties dialog box.

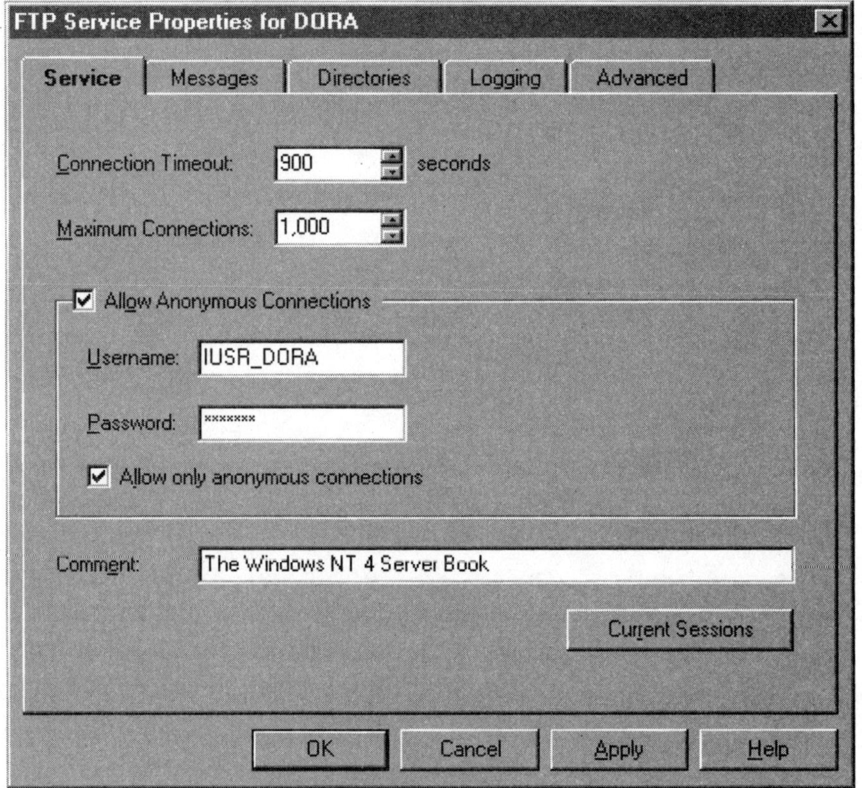

Figure 13-4: The Internet Service Manager FTP Service Properties dialog.

The FTP Service Properties tab functionality is described in detail below. You can accept many of the defaults for an initial installation of IIS and later, as you become more comfortable with administrating your site, you can customize more and more of your installation.

Setting Up the Services

The Service tab allows configuration of the Service. You can set values for Connection Timeout and Maximum Connections, you can choose whether to allow anonymous connections, and you can add the service's comment (which displays in the IIS Manager program).

Connection Timeout

Use the Connection Timeout control to set the number of seconds the service will maintain an inactive connection. Connections become inactive for several reasons, such as when users begin perusing a file or talking on the telephone, but the most common is when the client drops the connection without properly terminating the session.

Having a Connection Timeout value that is too high will result in resources being consumed by connections that are possibly no longer active. If the Connection Timeout value is too low, then clients who are still working with the service may find themselves disconnected. Therefore, you must use a sensible median value for the Connection Timeout. The default value of 900 seconds is reasonable—if a client has not responded in 15 minutes, then it can be safely assumed that the client is no longer actively using the service.

Maximum Connections

Use the Maximum Connections control to set the maximum total number of simultaneous connections that this server will allow. Typically, unless you are planning a large site, you will not exceed the default of 1,000 concurrent connections.

It may be worthwhile to consider reducing the Maximum Connections to a lower value if your Internet connection is slower than a T1 line. If your system uses a fractional T1 or ISDN connection, you may want to set the Maximum Connections parameter to 50 or 100. For dial-up connections, you may wish to be even more conservative: 5 to 25 connections are all that most dial-up connections can handle.

Anonymous Connections

Both Gopher and WWW (Web) services use anonymous connections. As well, you can configure the FTP service to allow anonymous connections. The IIS Setup program provides a default anonymous user ID and password, and you do not need to change this field.

The service uses the anonymous user ID and password to access files for the client user. Remember, the service is a system task and does not run using your logon user ID.

The FTP service allows three choices for anonymous users:

- **Do not allow anonymous connections**. Set by unchecking the Allow Anonymous Connections radio button. Any user who wants to connect to the FTP server must have a user ID assigned just as if the user were a local user. This mode allows the highest degree of security but does not allow anyone without a Windows NT 4 Server user ID to connect to the FTP server.
- **Allow only anonymous connections**. Set by checking the Allow only anonymous connections radio button. In this configuration, all users must logon as anonymous, and all users will have the same privileges.
- **Allow both anonymous and non-anonymous connections.** Set by checking the Allow Anonymous Connections radio button and unchecking the Allow only anonymous connections radio button. This setting allows anyone to connect as anonymous, and users who have a user ID on the server to connect using their user IDs. This mode allows the most flexibility: anonymous users can have limited (read-only, perhaps) access, while users with a Windows NT 4 Server user ID can be granted more privileges.

The Username field contains the default IIS anonymous user ID. You can change this user ID if you desire; however, neither Microsoft nor I recommend using a different Username unless you have determined that a different name is necessary.

The Username determines permissions of all anonymous connections. Since the great majority of your users will connect with an anonymous connection, the Username is important! By default, Internet Information Server Setup program creates and uses the account IUSR_computername.

In Figure 13-4, the Username is IUSR_DORA, as the computer name is DORA. Note that anonymous users do not know, or log on using the Username.

Figure 13-5 shows the Windows NT 4 Server's User Manager with the properties for the IUSR_DORA displayed. Since a user would never (typically) logon using this user ID, the password is not critical. However, to minimize the risks of a security attack on your IIS system, you must use a non-trivial password. IIS Setup assigns an initial password, which you do not need to change.

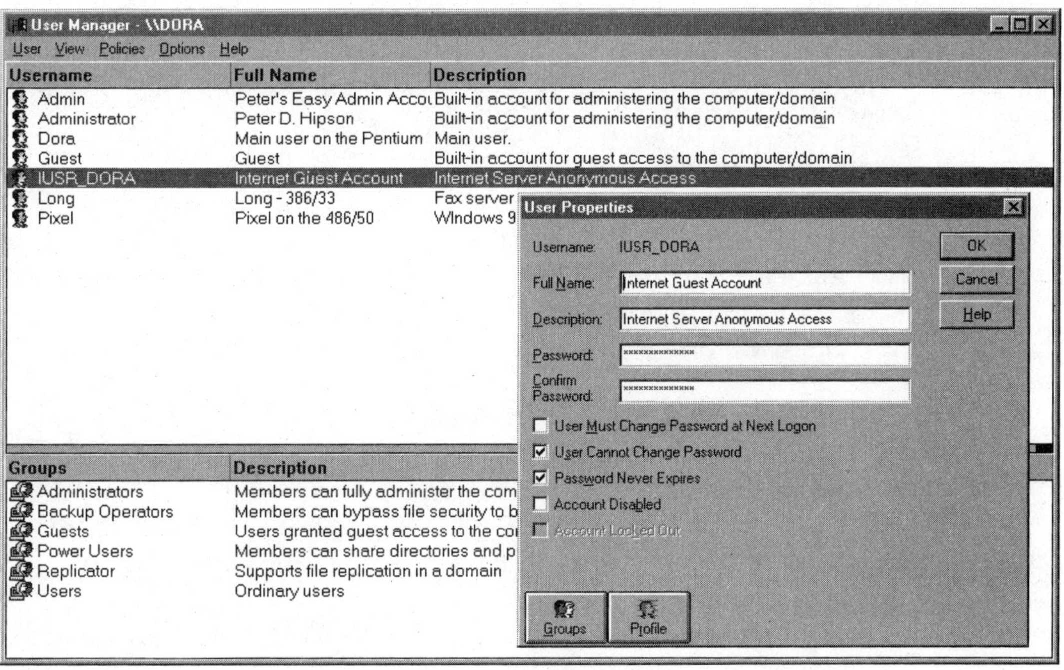

Figure 13-5: The Windows NT 4 Server User Manager.

The Microsoft IIS installation process creates the initial user ID (IUSR_computername) for you. If you change the Username field, you must manage this user ID yourself.

If you change the Username, follow the steps below:

1. Start User Manager for Domains application in the Start Menu | Programs | Administrative Tools (Common) group.
2. Create a new user.
3. Assign the user a password (make sure you select the User Cannot Change Password and Password Never Expires check boxes).
4. Place the new user in the Guests and Domain Users groups, but assign no other group memberships to this user ID.

Comment

The Comment text box enables you to specify the text string you want to display in the Internet Service Manager's Report View mode. If you anticipate managing more than one service, then you can use the Comment parameter to differentiate between the different servers.

As we said earlier, each service uses a similar Setup program. The FTP setup we just described is very much like the Gopher setup. However, I now want to introduce you to fields found only on the Gopher Service Properties' Service tab, the Service Administrator's Name and Email fields.

Gopher's Service Administrator

When configuring the Gopher service, the name and an e-mail address of the administrator must be provided in the Service Administrator box. Some Gopher clients can retrieve this information, allowing the client user to contact the Gopher site's administrator.

In the Name field, enter the administrator's name. (That often is your name). This is a "people"-readable field, so spell your name as you want people to use it. In Figure 13-6, the name field contains my name: "Peter D. Hipson."

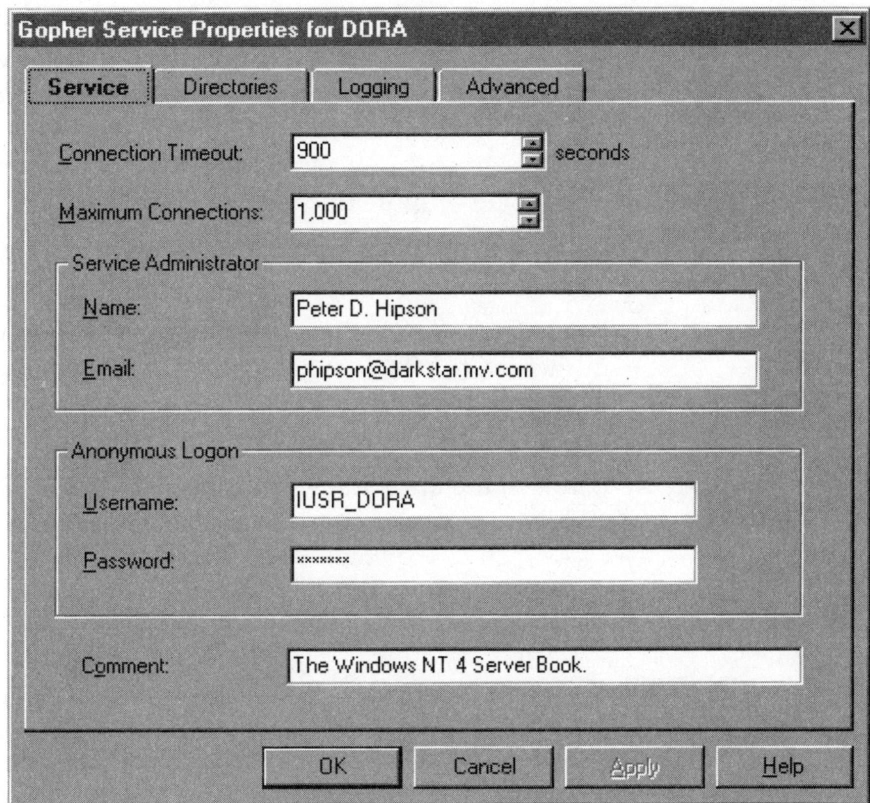

Figure 13-6: The Gopher Service tab.

The Email field holds the administrator's e-mail address. Some administrators create a special e-mail account for each server, such as: *gopher_admin*@site.organization.com. Be sure that whatever e-mail address you enter exists! No sense in your users sending e-mail to the Internet e-mail black hole! The e-mail address should be in standard Internet format. Try to avoid complex e-mail addresses if possible, as it is possible that users will have to retype this field when sending you e-mail. In Figure 13-6, the Name field contains my e-mail address: phipson@darkstar.mv.com.

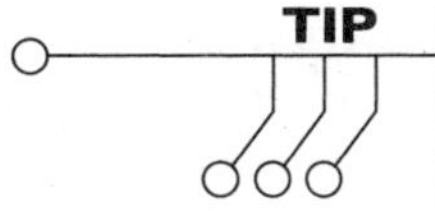

Don't use my name and e-mail address when you set up your Gopher service—I won't know what to do with your e-mail!

WWW's Password Authentication

The WWW setup, similar to FTP and Gopher, has several unique fields you must fill in. Below, I introduce you to fields found on the WWW Service Properties' Service tab.

The WWW service allows you to configure password authentication. Select one or more of the three choices:

- Allow Anonymous—permits anyone to connect to the Web server.
- Basic (Clear Text)—if a user ID is used to connect, the authentication is done using a clear text protocol. This mode is not secure.
- Windows NT Challenge/Response—if a user ID is used to connect, the authentication is done with the Windows NT Challenge/Response protocol. This mode is secure.

Setting Up FTP Messages

Of the three services we've been discussing, FTP, Gopher, and WWW, only FTP Service Properties contains a Messages tab. The Messages tab in the FTP Service Properties dialog box allows you to configure the FTP Service's messages. Messages are given to users when they first connect to the FTP service, when they disconnect, and when the maximum number of connections has been reached and a user is attempting to connect.

Figure 13-7 shows the FTP Service Properties' Messages tab.

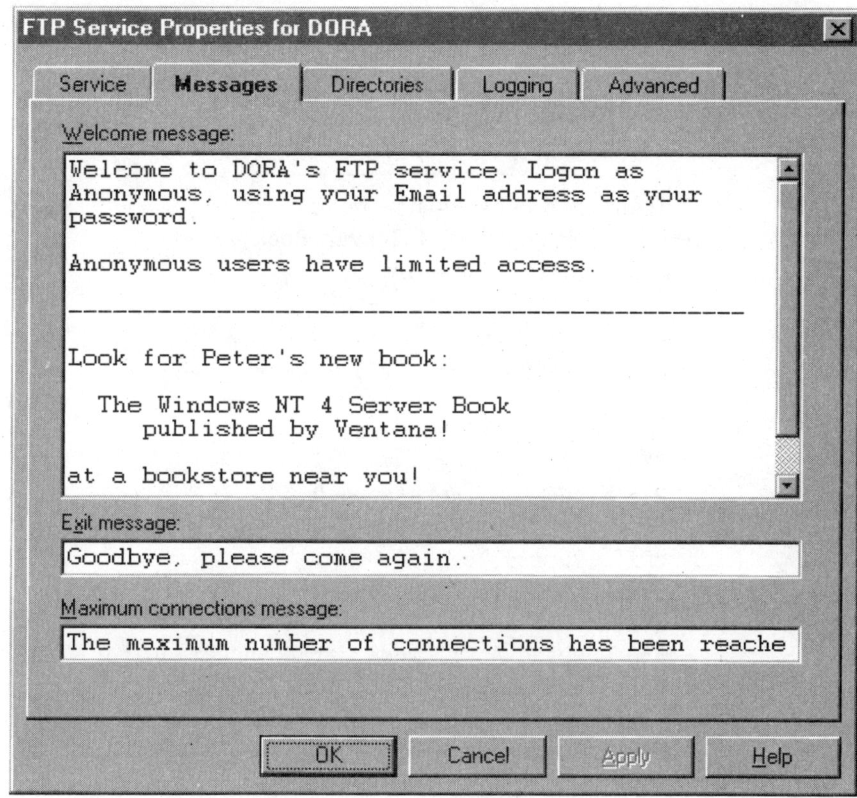

Figure 13-7: The FTP Service Properties' Messages tab.

Below is an example of an FTP session (using Junod's WS_FTP32 program). Notice that an anonymous user cannot create directories (or files, for that matter) in my FTP server:

```
WINSOCK.DLL: WinSock 2.0
WS_FTP32 94.11.28, Copyright © 1994 John A. Junod.
All rights reserved.
- -
connecting to 199.125.78.23 ...
<Computer CoConnected to 199.125.78.23 port 21
220 dora Microsoft FTP Service (Version 1.0).
USER anonymous
331 Anonymous access allowed,
send identity (e-mail name) as password.
```

```
PASS xxxxxx
230-Welcome to DORA's FTP service. Logon as
 Anonymous, using your Email address as your
 password.
 Anonymous users have limited access.
 ----------------------
 Look for Peter's new book:
   The Windows NT 4 Server Book
     published by Ventana!
 at a bookstore near you!
 ----------------------
230 Anonymous user logged in as IUSR_DORA.
PWD
257 "/" is current directory.
SYST
215 Windows_NT version 4.0
Host type (2): Windows NT
PORT 199,125,78,23,4,30
200 PORT command successful.
LIST
150 Opening ASCII mode data connection for /bin/ls.
Received 0 bytes in 0.1 secs, (0.00 bits/sec),   →
  transfer succeeded
226 Transfer complete.
MKD NoDo
550 NoDo: Access is denied.
QUIT
221 Goodbye, please come again.
```

As the example shows, your messages should provide useful information for your users. The Maximum connections message is more difficult to test—if you feel you really must test the Maximum connections message, set the Maximum Connections parameter to a number that you can easily exceed (such as one). Remember, however, that resetting a parameter even temporarily, such as for testing, can cause disruptions to legitimate users.

Welcome Message

The welcome message is presented to the user *after* they have successfully logged on to the FTP service. If you have configured your FTP service to accept anonymous logons, then the FTP service automatically sends the following prompt when a user attempts to logon using the "Anonymous" user ID:

```
331 Anonymous access allowed,
send identity (e-mail name) as password.
PASS
```

After logging on the user, the welcome message is then presented.

Many FTP servers have long welcome messages, but it is wise, if possible, to limit the welcome message to one screen (20 or 24 lines of 80 characters each) to avoid having the first part of the message scroll off the user's screen before it has been read.

Exit Message

The Exit message is sent to users when they use the FTP commands *quit* or *bye*. Limit the Exit message text you enter to one or two lines.

Any nice, pleasant message is appropriate here.

Maximum Connections Message

The Maximum Connections message is sent to users when they attempt to logon to the FTP server when the maximum number of users are already connected. The message text should state the problem ("Maximum number of users already connected") and suggest an action for the user to take, such as:

- "Wait and try later."
- "Other mirror FTP sites are..."
- Some other reasonable action.

Do be as polite as you can, as the user is going to be disappointed at their inability to connect.

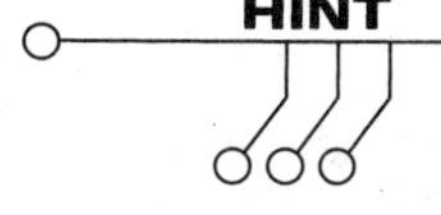

Consider including an e-mail address where users who receive the Maximum Connections message can e-mail you or the system administrator. This will give you an indication that your FTP service is overloaded. Try this for an example: "The maximum number of users are already connected. Try again, and if this error happens again, send me an e-mail at mail@darkstar.mv.com. Thank you!" (Don't use my e-mail address, however!)

Setting Up Directories

The Directories tab allows you to configure a service's directories. With this tab you configure directory names and properties for the directories. For each service there is typically one home directory and any number of virtual directories.

Remember security when setting up your directory structure. Be careful not to give access to directories you do not intend to share with clients.

Figure 13-8 shows the Directories tab, with a single home directory configured.

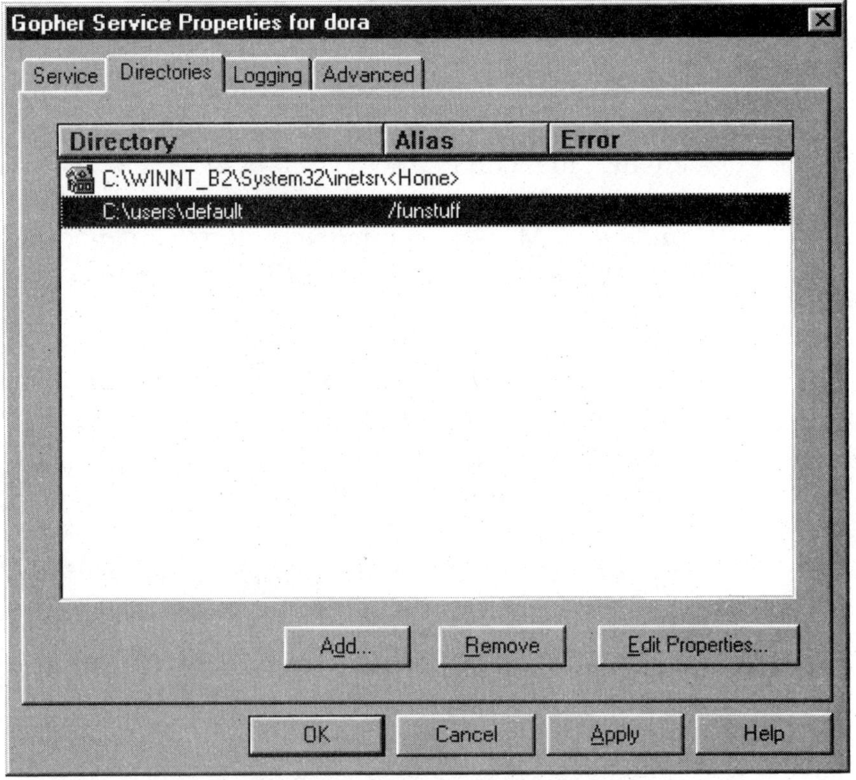

Figure 13-8: The Gopher Service Properties' Directories tab.

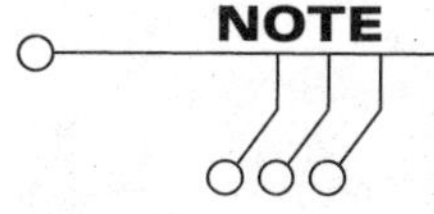

The IIS programs and documentation use the term directory when referring to a folder as defined in the Windows NT file structure.

The IIS installation program creates a set of folders used by the services. These default folders are:

- ftproot—used as the base directory for the FTP service.
- gophroot—used as the base directory for the Gopher service.
- iisadmin—contains administration files: this folder should not be accessible by FTP, Gopher, or Web users.
- scripts—contains script files used by the Web service.
- wwwroot—used as the base directory for the Web service.

The folders that end in *root* are the service's root directories. You can then create other folders for your servers, either nested within the service's home folder or in other locations as desired. You can define only one home folder. You must define all other folders as virtual folders.

There are three buttons, which control functionality, in the Directory tab: Add, Remove, and Edit Properties. Let's begin with the Add function.

Add

Each service, FTP, Gopher, and WWW, uses one or more directories. To add an additional directory to a service, follow the steps below:

1. Access the Directory Properties dialog box for the service to which you want to add a directory.
2. You can replace your current home directory or add additional virtual directories as desired. To add a new directory to your server's set of directories, click the Add button. The Internet Service Manager displays the Directory Properties dialog box (Figure 13-9).

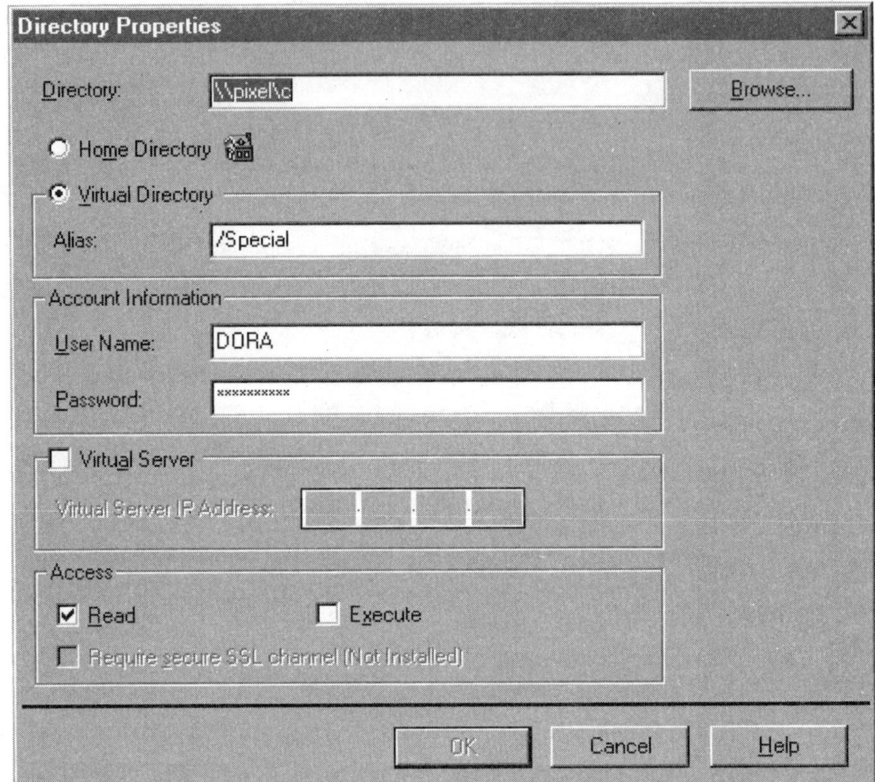

Figure 13-9: The Internet Service Manager Web Directory Properties dialog box.

Each service has a different Directory Properties dialog box. The fields you can configure for each directory are listed below:

- **Gopher Directory Properties**—You can configure the name of the directory, locate directories to work with, specify a directory as a home directory or a subdirectory under a home directory (as a virtual directory), and provide account information used to access a remote, shared, directory.

- **FTP Directory Properties**—Directory name, location, alias, and account information to access networked resources are specified for an FTP directory.

  Access to each FTP directory can be read, write, or read/ write.
- **Web Directory Properties**—Directory name, location, alias, and account information to access networked resources are specified for a Web directory. Additionally, for a Web directory, you can choose to associate the directory with a virtual server and to limit access to the directory.
- **Home Directory**—In the Directory Properties dialog, you can name the directory (giving the full path name) and assign the directories attributes. A service can have only *one* home directory; if you select the Home Directory radio button and you already have a home directory defined, this directory will *replace* your current home directory.
- **Virtual Directories & Their Aliases**—For all directories other than the home directory, you can specify an alias for the directory. The alias is a name that the client uses to access the directory, and it need not match the actual directory name.

  If you do not specify an alias, then Internet Service Manager creates an alias for you.

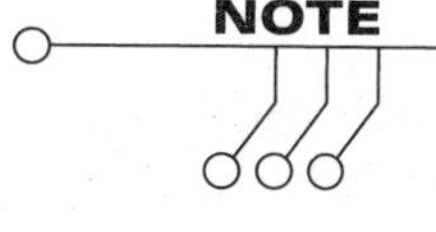

You enter a delimited path name in the Alias field, using UNIX conventions—a forward *slash between the names. For an example of an Alias name, see Figure 13-9. Note the leading forward slash indicating that "Special" is found under the Web root name.*

The use of an alias allows you to create a virtual directory structure for your service. For example, a Gopher user enters "gopher://darkstar.mv.com/funstuff" (in Internet Explorer for example), to access the virtual directory funstuff.

This implies that there is a subdirectory under my Gopher home directory called "funstuff." Actually, "funstuff" is an alias to a folder in a different directory tree, and the Gopher server creates the illusion that "funstuff" is actually a subdirectory under the Gopher root directory, even though it is not.

Virtual directories are always accessed using the alias in the URL as if the alias were a subdirectory of the home directory. That is, the virtual directory will seem to be a "subdirectory," even though it may actually be located on a different drive (and perhaps even on a different computer). This allows you to publish using other directories and have these directories be accessible from within the home directory.

When specifying a virtual directory (a subdirectory under a home directory), specify both the directory name and an "alias" that the client users must enter when referring to the directory.

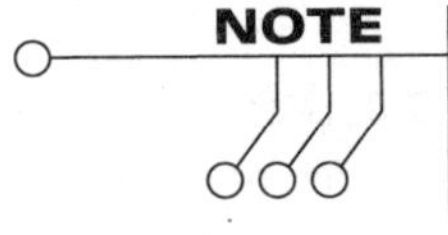

Gopher virtual directories do not appear in directory listings. To make a virtual directory appear in the directory listing, you need to create an explicit link in a tag file for Gopher clients to access virtual directories.

A Gopher user can type in the URL if they know the alias for the virtual directory. To do this, they must prefix the alias name with an 11/. For example, to access the virtual directory "funstuff" from your Gopher server that is named darkstar.mv.com, you use the following URL: gopher://darkstar.mv.com/11/funstuff.

You, the administrator, specify the actual location name of the virtual directory (such as c:\users\default) and the virtual name (alias). The alias is the directory name used by Gopher clients—in the above examples, the alias is "funstuff."

- **Directory Account Information**—When the directory is located on a machine other than the Gopher server, and is accessed using a Universal Naming Convention (UNC) server and share name, you must provide both a Username and Password to access the directory. Regardless, all virtual directories on networked drives must be on computers in the same Windows NT domain as the computer that is running Gopher server. An example of a networked virtual directory is shown in Figure 13-9.

The Account Information controls (User Name and Password) are active only if the connection is specified using a UNC server and share name, for example, \\Pixel\D\Letters. Enter the username and password that has permission to access this directory.

All accesses to a UNC-named virtual directory are made using the username and password that you specify. Be careful that you do not inadvertently create a security risk by allowing Gopher users to access directories that you do not want them to access!

- **Directory Virtual Server**—The Virtual Server check box allows you to create virtual servers, each of which can have its own unique URL (domain name and IP address). For example, your company is XYZ Corporation, and you have your Web home page at www.xyz.com. XYZ Corporation also has a subsidiary called the AlphaBeta Company, which has a Web home page, also. You set up a domain name for a unique IP address (for example www.alphabeta.com), and link the www.alphabeta.com's IP address to a virtual directory. This sets up two unique URLs (domain names) pointing to a single server. Each URL is separate (unless you point both to the same directory) and unique: users will never know that both URLs are being served by the same computer.

  When you have more than one domain name and IP address being serviced by your Web server, and if no IP address is specified for a specific directory, then the directory with no IP address specified is visible to all virtual servers. Default directories created during the IIS installation do not specify an IP address, and are therefore visible to all virtual servers.

If you are an Internet provider, or a Web provider, this feature can be an excellent way to minimize the hardware requirements while creating unique URLs for your customers.

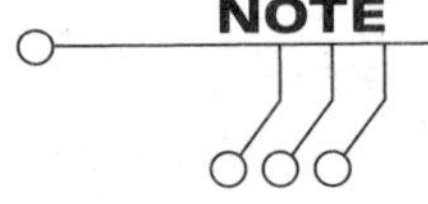

The IP address for the virtual server must be bound to the network card providing the service. Use the Network Applet in Control Panel to bind additional IP addresses to your network card. In addition, you need to specify a Class C Internet IP address, which consists of a total of 256 unique addresses in a range. You can route addresses not assigned to virtual Web servers to other machines (users) on the network for their use.

- **Directory Access**—The access level of permissions that users have to the directory is set using the three controls in the Access group box: Read, Execute, and Requires secure SSL channel. The following access levels are valid:
  - Read—Allows a user to view the files.
  - Execute—Allows clients to run programs in this directory. This access level should be selected for program directories. Typically, you would place your scripts and executable files into a directory with execute access.
  - Requires secure SSL channel—Selected when using SSL security to encrypt data transmissions.

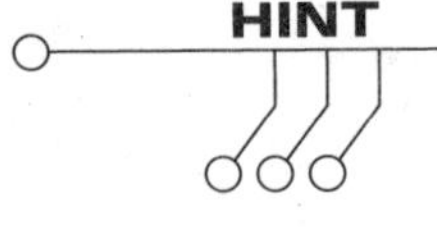

Do not select Execute access level for directories containing static content—use the Read access level for these directories.

Remove

Click the Remove button to remove the currently selected directory in the Gopher Service's directories list. This button is active only when a directory is selected. You can delete the home directory; however, the Gopher server does not function without a home directory.

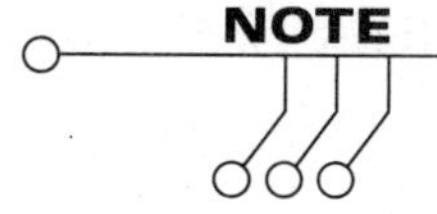

There is no confirmation with the Remove button. If you remove a directory in error, you need to use the Add button to re-add the directory to your Gopher Server's list of directories.

When you remove a directory from the list of directories, you don't actually remove the directory from the disk. If you no longer need the disk folder or directory, explicitly delete the folder or directory using Windows Explorer, or a command prompt window.

Edit Properties

Click the Edit properties button to change the properties of a Gopher directory.

You use the Internet Service Manager's Directory Properties dialog when you want to add a directory, or when you must change a directory's properties. This dialog box has several items in it. The Internet Service Manager's Directory Properties dialog box is shown in Figure 13-9.

FTP's Directory Listing Style

Each FTP directory can have a listing mode: UNIX or MS-DOS. The UNIX mode is more commonly used today; however, MS-DOS file modes are becoming more common as Windows NT 4 Server is used more and more for FTP servers.

Web Default Document

The Web service allows specification of a default document that displays if the user does not specify a document name. For example, if the default document on my Web service is Default.htm, and the user enters http://darkstar.mv.com/, then the user actually receives this document: http://darkstar.mv.com/default.htm.

A default document allows a user to connect to a site without knowing what the highest-level document is. Virtually all Web servers have a default document; the two most commonly used default document names are "default.htm" and "index.htm."

Web Directory Browsing Allowed

Though not often used, directory browsing is sometimes used to allow a user to explore the Web site. I recommend that Directory Browsing not be allowed unless you have a specific need that requires Directory Browsing.

Setting Up Logging

The Logging tab of the Properties dialog box allows you to configure each service's logging of information such as errors and accesses. With this tab you configure where you want to maintain logging, and where you want to place the logging information (either in a file or to an SQL/ODBC database).

Logging can be critical to maintaining statistics for your Internet servers. You should maintain a log, if only to determine who is using your server.

Many sites maintain the log to collect information about which components of their sites are most popular—a frequently active area with lots of return visits indicates an area to which users are drawn; an area that is infrequently visited, and which never generates return visits, is an area that you probably can remove.

Enable Logging

Click the Enable Logging check box to have the server log information.

Logging collects information about all clients who connect to your server. A logging entry contains the user's IP address, time of connection, and other information about the transaction (see Table 13-1 for a list of all information that is logged).

You can have separate logging files for each of the IIS services, or you can use a combined logging file. There is sufficient information in the log file entries that you can determine which service generated the entry.

Log to File

Click Log to File to have the server log information to a file. You must then specify how often to open a new file, where to place the file, and a filename if you want it named a specific name.

When logging to a text file, the file is written in comma-delimited format. The format of this file is slightly different from the columns written to an SQL/ODBC database. Table 13-1 shows each column and a description of the column's data:

Column Name	Datatype	Description
ClientHost	Character data	Name of the client machine, or the client's IP address.
Username	Character data	The client's username.
LogDate	Character data	The date the item was logged.
LogTime	Character data	The time the item was logged.
Service	Character data	The service requested, such as "GopherSvc" for a Gopher request.
Machine	Character data	The machine used to process the request.
Serverip	Character data	The server's IP address.
Processingtime	Numeric data	Time spent processing this request.
Bytesrecvd	Numeric data	The number of bytes that were received.
Bytessent	Numeric data	The number of bytes that were sent to the client.
Servicestatus	Numeric data	The service status flag.
Win32status	Numeric data	The Windows Win32 status.

➡

Column Name	Datatype	Description
Operation	Character data	The requested operation, such as "GET," "Dir," "File," or "Error."
Target	Character data	The target name or directory.
Parameters	Character data	Any parameters supplied, or a "-" if none.
Blank	Character data	Blank, empty column.

Table 13-1: Columns in the Log to file log.

Log to SQL/ODBC Database

Click Log to SQL/ODBC Database to have the server log information to either an SQL Server database or any other ODBC database. For those users who are not using SQL Server, then logging to an ODBC Access database can be an excellent choice, as Access is capable of producing reports and summary information.

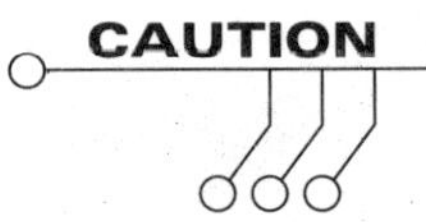

If IIS is being logged to a local SQL Server, and IIS starts prior to SQL Server, then an error condition occurs and no logging is done. This condition can be corrected by telling Windows NT 4 Server that SQL Server must be fully started before starting IIS. This is done by setting the registry key

```
HKEY_LOCAL_MACHINE\System\CurrentControlSet\Services\<service>
```

where <service> is W3SVC for the Web server, MSFTPSVC for the FTP server, and GOPHERSVC for the Gopher server. In this key is a value called "DependOnService" that typically contains two null terminated strings: "RPCSS" and "NTLMSSP." Add the string "MSSQLServer" to this list, and restart the system.

As always, changes in the registry are dangerous—use extreme caution, and back up critical information!

Within the Log to SQL/ODBC Database group box are four text boxes that become enabled after you select the Log to SQL/ODBC Database. Enter the information that applies into each text box. These text boxes are:

- ODBC Data Source Name (DSN), which is the DSN that you have created as a system DSN. For an Access file, the DSN is the name of your database.
- Table, which is the table in the DSN in which logging information is saved.
- User Name, which is the username for the DSN.
- Password, which is User Name's password for the DSN.

The table in the DSN must contain the columns shown in Table 13-2.

Column Name	Datatype	Description
ClientHost	varchar(255)	Name of the client machine, or the client's IP address.
username	varchar(255)	The client's username.
LogTime	datetime	The date and time the item was logged.
service	varchar(255)	The service requested, such as "GopherSvc" for a Gopher request.
machine	varchar(255)	The machine used to process the request.
serverip	varchar(50)	The server's IP address.
processingtime	int	Time spent processing this request.
bytesrecvd	int	The number of bytes that were received.
bytessent	int	The number of bytes that were sent to the client.

➡

Column Name	Datatype	Description
servicestatus	int	The service status flag.
win32status	int	The Windows Win32 status.
operation	varchar(255)	The requested operation, such as "GET," "Dir," "File," or "Error."
target	varchar(255)	The target name or directory.
parameters	varchar(255)	Any parameters supplied, or a "-" if none.

Table 13-2: Column names and specifications for ODBC logging.

Logging to an SQL database uses a different set of columns. In the IIS\SERVER subdirectory is an .SQL file called LOGTEMP.SQL. This file generates the necessary SQL table for IIS logging. Below is a listing of a somewhat better version of this SQL script:

```
if exists (select * from sysobjects where id =
     object_id('inetlog') and sysstat & 0xf = 3)
     drop table inetlog
GO
CREATE TABLE inetlog (
  ClientHost varchar(255),
  username varchar(255),
  LogTime datetime,
  service varchar(255),
  machine varchar(255),
  serverip varchar(50),
  processingtime int,
  bytesrecvd int,
  bytessent int,
  servicestatus int,
  win32status int,
  operation varchar(255),
  target varchar(255),
  parameters varchar(255)
)
GO
```

The script shown above is somewhat better than Microsoft's example—the Microsoft script fails when the table already exists.

Setting Up Access

The Advanced tab of the Properties dialog box allows you to configure access to each service. You can choose to exclude (deny access to) all users except for those you specifically authorize, or to include (grant access to) all users except for those you specifically exclude. As well, you can limit the total network throughput for *all* the IIS servers (Gopher, WWW, and FTP) in the Advanced tab (see Figure 13-10).

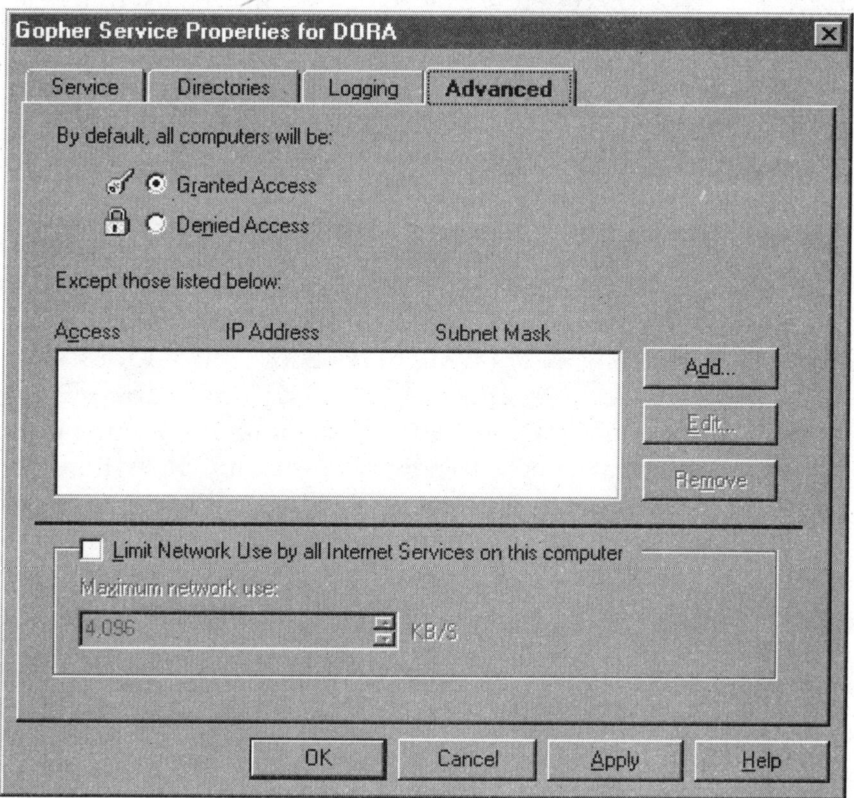

Figure 13-10: The Advanced tab.

Granted Access/Denied Access

Click Granted Access to tell Microsoft IIS to grant access to all users, except for those listed in the "Except those listed below" list. This is the normal mode of operation for IIS.

Click Denied Access to tell IIS to grant access to no users, except for those listed in the "Except those listed below" list. This mode of operation is used when the IIS site is *closed* to users other than those specifically authorized.

Except Those Listed Below

The "Except those listed below" list is a list of users who are either to be denied, or granted, access. The user's name, IP address, and subnet mask are all shown in this list.

You may choose to grant or deny based on groups of IP addresses, too! This way, you could exclude groups of people, without knowing their specific IP address.

To deny a group, you must know the Class A, B, or C IP address for the group to which you are denying access. For example, if the XYZ Corporation (your hated competitor) has a Class B IP address, and a domain name of xyz.com, you could use PING xyz.com, and you might get back an IP address of 204.146.46.133. This address indicates that XYZ Corporation's Class B IP address (which translates to 65536 IP addresses) is 204.146.xxx.xxx. You then can choose to deny access to anyone within that group with a single entry—such power! Figure 13-11 shows the entry for our fictional XYZ Corporation.

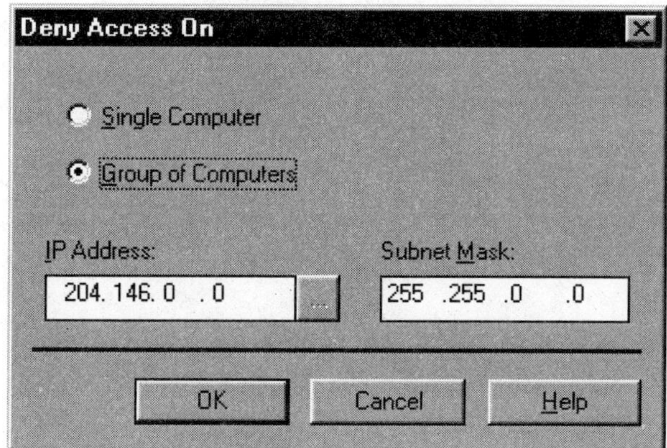

Figure 13-11: The Deny Access On dialog box.

You can add, edit, or remove users from the list using the appropriate buttons.

Limit Network Use by All Internet Services

The Limit Network Use by all Internet Services on this computer check box allows you to limit the amount of network I/O performed by the IIS to a value you specify. For example, if your site has a T3 connection to the Internet, and you need to limit the actual I/O to only use a small part of the T3 connection (to leave some bandwidth for other network tasks), set this to a value that reflects the amount of T3 connection usage that you wish to assign to the IIS services.

The default value is 4,096K. Is this default realistic? You must decide—how important is your Internet presence, how important is your non-IIS bandwidth, and what is the return on the investment for your communications? Table 13-3 shows the communications rate for various methods of communicating with remote networks (such as the Internet).

Type of Connection	Speed	Typical Number of Active Users
Dial-up	28,000	1-2
Frame Relay	56,000	5-10
ISDN	128,000	5-15
T1	1,500,000	25-100
Fractional T1	Varies as needed	Varies
T3	45,000,000	1,000+

Table 13-3: Remote communications speeds.

Reliability

We all strive for reliability. Let's face it—when our system is not reliable, we usually meet with some difficult work. All in all, the IIS server is simple. It is not a complex program (such as SQL Server), and it should not be prone to failures.

Right—not prone to failures—true, but what most often fails with Internet servers is neither the software nor the hardware. In all the time that I have been using IIS, I have yet to see it fail. Yes, when it was in beta it had its *glitches*, but IIS has been a very reliable product. The failure is typically the IIS administrator—us. (It was Pogo who said, "We have met the enemy and he is us.") We fail to make our site complete, we have links to *nowhere*, we have objects (such as FTP and Gopher files) that can't be found, we do all sorts of unexplainable things, most of which tend to convince the user that we are nothing more than a bunch of babbling idiots—when nothing could (we hope!) be further from the truth!

Most failures are caught and fixed quickly when administrators simply check their own work. Nothing is more frustrating to a client user than to click a link and get a message that the link is not valid, the page cannot be found, or the server doesn't exist.

Performance

If our Internet server is to be useful to client users, it must perform well. Long delays, error transmissions, and cryptic results all detract from the value of the site. Some of the things that can be done to make an Internet site perform better are:

- Don't run a serious Web site on a dial-up connection. Even a fast 28.8K modem can only keep up with one user. A minimum connection for a Web server is a 56K ISDN connection, and preferably a connection with twice that performance. Popular sites have thousands of "visitors" daily. Let's face it—there are not many "home" Internet sites using Windows NT 4 Server!
- Use the NTFS file system if possible for your data directories. NTFS offers enhanced security and reliability.
- Ensure that your server has sufficient RAM to do its job. Generally, IIS does not need large amounts of RAM; however, if you are running a complex server, perhaps with an SQL back end, RAM can be critical.
- Keep drives on SCSI interfaces and avoid, if possible, IDE drives for Windows NT 4 Server installations. IDE is fine for desktop applications, but not for servers.
- Don't serve files from a CD-ROM. CD-ROMs do not work well when more than one task or user is attempting to access files on the device.

Moving On

In this chapter we covered Microsoft Internet Information Server (IIS). This server consists of three main components: Web, FTP, and Gopher services, and an administration program to manage each of them.

The next chapter covers the Microsoft IIS Gopher and FTP services. And the Microsoft IIS Web service is covered in the chapter that follows.

14 The Microsoft IIS Gopher & FTP Services

In this chapter, both the Gopher and FTP services are described.

Gopher is a service that allows users to easily interact with the server and retrieve information. It is similar to the WWW, but is a text-based service and is no longer as popular on the Internet.

FTP (File Transfer Protocol) is *the* file transfer protocol for the Internet. Virtually all sites support FTP, and recent releases of all browsers support FTP.

Both FTP and Gopher are configured using the Internet Information Service Manager program, as described in Chapter 13, "The Microsoft Internet Information Server."

The IIS Gopher Service

Gopher is a client/server application that once found some popularity on the Internet. Combining some features of both Web pages and FTP, Gopher allows users to find and retrieve both information and files. Gopher services require more maintenance than FTP servers, but the management of a Gopher service is usually easier than maintaining a Web site—Gopher is text oriented!

When we talk about the IIS Gopher service, we usually call it a Gopher service or a Gopher site. You can use either term interchangeably. Oh, and some people call Gopher services "Gopher holes." I guess Gopher kind of grows on you after a while!

Why a Gopher server? In reality, Gopher servers are infrequently used and are not often implemented as part of new Internet sites. Part of this lack of popularity is the fact that Gopher servers are not well understood by users (not to mention administrators!), and there is a lack of good, quality, Gopher client software for the all-important Windows environment. However, many Internet sites support Gopher, if only to have a complete set of servers.

Although Microsoft Internet Explorer does access Gopher sites, it is not an optimal client for serious Gopher users.

Many Gopher sites are poorly maintained. We cannot fault many of these sites—they are run by students and volunteers at various universities and other noncommercial organizations, a transient population who often have conflicting priorities and excessive responsibilities.

A Gopher server is very similar to an FTP server. Both Gopher and FTP allow you to publish files. The differences between Gopher and FTP include:

- The Gopher service allows you to create links to other computers and services—FTP servers typically link to files and directories only.
- The Gopher service allows you to annotate the files and directories that are published—FTP limits file and directory information to their names.
- The Gopher service allows you to create custom menus—FTP menus are simply another word for directories.

The down side of all that Gopher functionality is that you must create the links, configure the folders and directories, and build your menus—manually. Unlike the Web service, there are no automated tools for creating Gopher sites.

The IIS Gopher Service supports all the standard Gopher services and features. Additionally, there is support for Gopher+

selector strings, which permit the Gopher server to provide additional information to the client, including items such as the Gopher server administrator's name, modification date, and MIME-type information.

Whether or not you decided to implement the IIS Gopher server is a decision you and your system administrator must make. You will find, however, that implementing a Gopher server takes little in the way of resources and is not too complicated, if you configure a simple Gopher site. Gopher can provide a better interface to the user, but it does require more effort to configure.

Some examples of the better-known Gopher sites on the Internet include:

- gopher://gopher.nstn.ca/1
- gopher://ukoln.bath.ac.uk/
- gopher://gopher.eff.org/

If you are not a Gopher expert (many of us are not) then use your Web browser to take a look at each of these sites. They give you some examples of what is done with a Gopher site. Remember, Gopher does not have the popularity that the WWW has: Web sites can have thousands of visitors each day; Gopher sites may have tens of visitors per day. A really popular Gopher site may have hundreds of visitors, but there are no published figures to tell us how much traffic there is to the popular Gopher sites.

Setting Up the Gopher Service

Setting up your Gopher service can be as simple as copying your files (and directories) to the Gopher service's root directory. This creates a simple Gopher server. Client users can then browse the Gopher directories using a Gopher client (such as Internet Explorer).

Additionally, you can enhance your site by creating tag files that enable links to other computers or services. Use these tag files to annotate your files and directories and to create custom menus, if desired. All the information that a Gopher client gets from your Gopher service comes from tag files.

A tag file usually contains the following items:

- Display name—The name displayed to the Gopher client. The display name is commonly called the "friendly" name.
- Host name—The name of the Gopher host.
- Port number—The port number (the default is 70) for the item.

Tag files are typically not edited or manipulated by hand. When written to an NTFS-formatted drive, the tag file is not available to the user. When a tag file is written to a FAT file system drive, the tag file has the hidden attribute set. Actually, under the FAT file system, a tag file is a simple text file:

```
C:\winnt\system32\inetsrv\gophroot>type att01t~1.gtg
0
GdsPriv=Gs1.0;07/25/96;19:20:43
Type=0
Name=Attachment file for Gopher.
AdmN=Peter D. Hipson
AdmE=phipson@darkstar.mv.com

C:\winnt\system32\inetsrv\gophroot>
```

If you are running Gopher+, you can add more information to each tag file, such as:

- The name and e-mail address of the server administrator, or the person responsible for the server.
- The creation and last modification dates of the file.

A tag file, under the FAT file system has the same name as the source file with a .GTG extension added. For example, the file "hipson.dat" has a tag file with the name of "hipson.dat.gtg."

When you are moving Gopher files with tag files on a FAT file system drive, you must also move the tag file. To move the tag files, follow the steps below:

1. It is necessary to first make the tag file visible (as it is hidden). Using Explorer, set the view to include all files.
2. Select the Gopher file you want to move, and the tag file, and move both of the files together (use a drag and drop or cut and paste).
3. Don't forget to rehide the tag file after moving it.

It is not possible to copy or move tag files between drives that are formatted with different file systems.

Some documentation with Microsoft IIS indicates that tag files stored on an NTFS volume can be either directly copied or unhidden. This is not true—the tag information is not directly accessible under NTFS. The tag information is not stored in a file; rather, it is stored in an alternate data stream.

When copying files that have tag information attached under the NTFS file system, the tag information is automatically copied also.

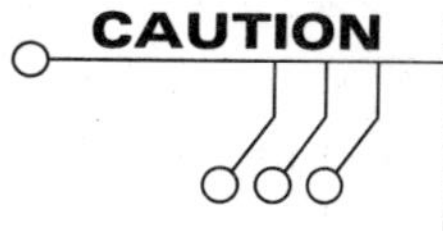

CAUTION

When you are short of disk space, be sure to consider the size of the tag files—though not large, tag files do require disk space.

Creating Tag Files

The program GDSSET creates a tag file. This program is run (typically) from a command prompt, and all parameters are entered on the command line. Though it is possible to run GDSSET using the Windows Run command (in the Start menu), it is not convenient to do so. The command syntax for the GDSSET command is:

```
gdsset -c -gn -f "description of file"
-a "administrator's name" -e e-mail filename
```

Table 14-1 lists the options for GDSSET. In all cases, when a parameter is required (such as the AdminName), and the parameter has embedded spaces, then the parameter must be quoted.

Option	Description
-c	Change the existing tag information. (Default is to create a new tag information.)
-r	Read and dump the tag information on console.
-G	Specifies the debug flags to be used.
-D	Specifies the directory for the given file.

Option	Description
-d	Specifies that the given file is actually a directory.
-g	The option specifies the file's type, as from Table 14-2. This value is a single digit or character. The default, if this option is omitted, is "9," a binary file. (Not valid when the -r option is used.)
-f<FriendlyName>	Specifies Friendly Name for object (valid when -r is not used).
-l	Specifies that link information is to be set for write (valid when -r is not used).
-s<Selector>	Specifies the selector for link (valid when -l is used).
-h<HostName>	Specifies the Host for link (valid when -l is used).
-p<PortNumber>	Specifies the Port number for link (valid when -l is used).
-a<AdminName>	The administrator's name (in quotes, if there are embedded spaces). When this option is omitted, then the name in the Service tab of the Internet Service Manager is used.
-e<Adminemail>	The administrator's e-mail address. When this option is omitted, then the e-mail address in the Service tab of the Internet Service Manager is used.

Table 14-1: GDSSET options.

When you run GDSSET, the tag file is automatically hidden. When the tag file is on a FAT volume, then you can unhide and view this file using the ATTRIB command or Explorer. For tag files on NTFS volumes, the tag file is contained in a second data stream. You cannot view or edit tag files on NTFS volumes directly—instead, use GDSSET -r to view the tag file's contents.

If you must create a number of tag files, it is possible to use a batch file to do this. For example, the following command creates a series of tag files of the same type:

```
for %1 in (*.txt) do <echo %i&& gdsset -c -gn -f %i %i
```

Table 14-2 lists the allowed Gopher file types. Not all Gopher clients (especially older clients) recognize *all* the types listed, but most current Gopher clients recognize the types listed in this table.

Type	Description
0	A nonspecific file, typically a flat text file
1	A Gopher directory file
2	A CSO (qi) phonebook server file
3	Error
4	A BinHexed Macintosh file
5	An MS-DOS binary archive
6	A UNIX Uuencoded file
7	An Index-Search server
8	A text-based Telnet session
9	A binary file
c	A calendar or calendar of events
g	A Graphic Interchange File (GIF) graphics file
h	An WWW HTML hypertext page
I	An image file (generally other than GIF)
m	A BSD format mbox file
P	A PDF document
T	A TN3270 (IBM) mainframe connection session
:	A bitmap image (it is necessary to use Gopher+ information to determine the actual image type)

Table 14-2: Gopher file type codes.

In short, to set up your Gopher Service files, follow the steps below:

1. Copy the actual files to the Gopher root directory (and subdirectories, as desired).
2. Use GDSSET to create tag files for each Gopher file.

Using Tag Files

Once you have created the tag files, a Gopher client can see the friendly name and file type. To see an example, take a look at my Gopher site, shown in Figure 14-1.

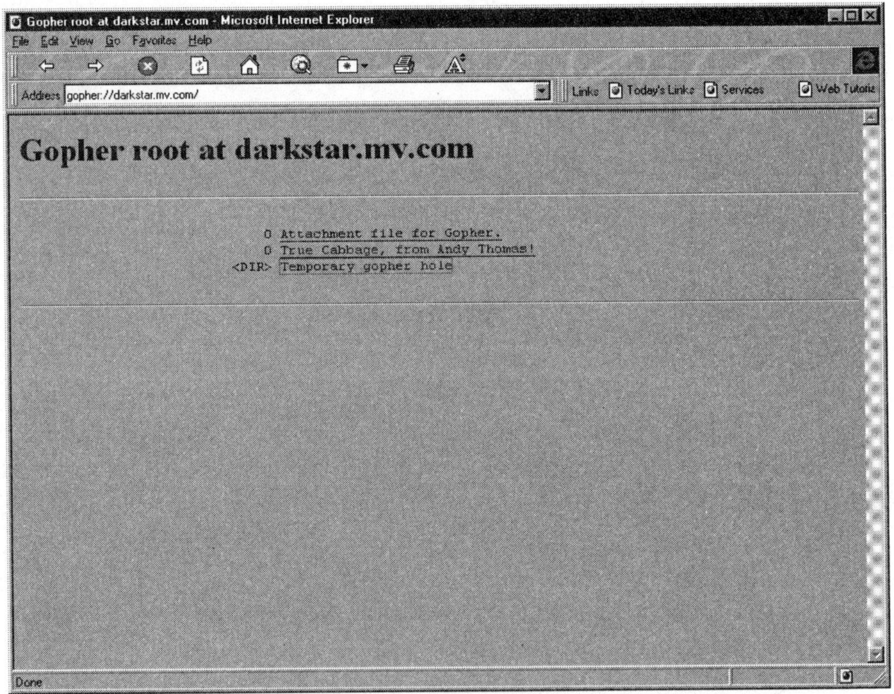

Figure 14-1: Internet Explorer looking at my Gopher site.

Notice how the friendly name displays, and also notice the number beside the two files: the "0" specifies that the file is "A nonspecific file, typically a flat text file" type of file. The <DIR> before "Temporary gopher hole" tells you that this file is actually a directory the user can open.

Curiosity having gotten the better of me, I wondered just what is "Pure Cabbage." I clicked "Pure Cabbage, from Andy Thomas," and saw the contents of the file cabbage.txt, as shown in Figure 14-2.

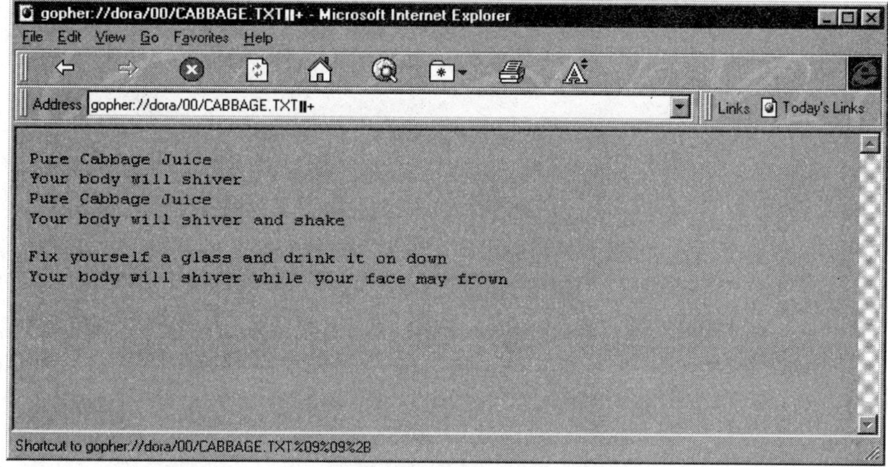

Figure 14-2: Gopher file: "Pure Cabbage, from Andy Thomas."

Andy is a musician and is rightfully proud of his music. He has a style of his own! For an excerpt of the song, take a look at http:// www.emmemm.com.

And if you click on the "Temporary gopher hole," you can see the contents of this directory, as shown in Figure 14-3. Notice that the files listed in this figure are formatted differently from those in Figure 14-1 because the files in the "Temporary gopher hole" didn't have tag files!

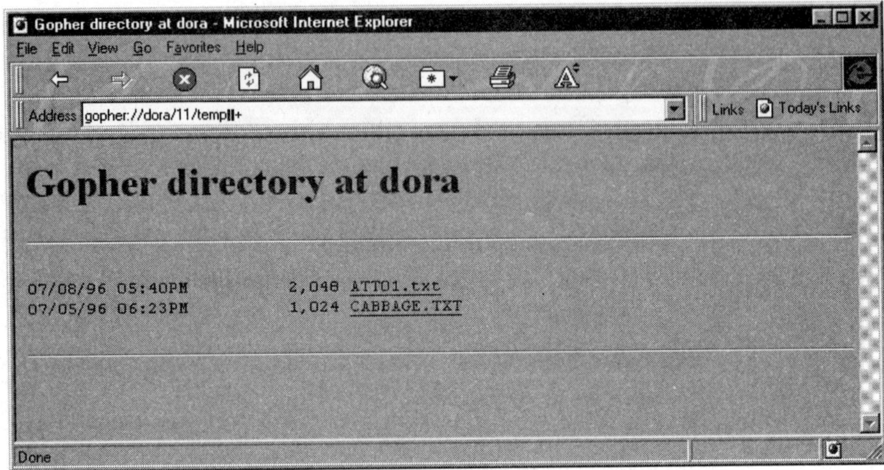

Figure 14-3: The "Temporary gopher hole" directory.

The actual steps I took in creating the tag file information for Figures 14-1, 14-2, and 14-3 are:

1. I created tag file information at the command prompt (items I entered are shown in bold) for each of the files, and the subdirectory in the gophroot folder:

```
C:\winnt\system32\inetsrv\gophroot>gdsset -e
"phipson@darkstar.mv.com" -a "Peter D. Hipson"
-g0  att01.txt
Enter the Gopher Friendly Name for File( att01.txt)
Attachment file for Gopher.

C:\winnt\system32\inetsrv\gophroot>gdsset -e
"phipson@darkstar.mv.com" -a "Peter D. Hipson"
-g0  cabbage.txt
Enter the Gopher Friendly Name for File( cabbage.txt)
Pure Cabbage, from Andy Thomas!

C:\winnt\system32\inetsrv\gophroot>gdsset -g1  -d temp
Enter the Gopher Friendly Name for File( temp)
Temporary gopher hole
```

2. I started Microsoft Internet Explorer, connected to my Gopher site, and created Figures 14-1, 14-2, and 14-3.
3. After making the figures, I returned to the command prompt and listed the tag file information (items I entered are shown in bold):

```
C:\winnt\system32\inetsrv\gophroot>gdsset -r temp
Tag information for C:\winnt\system32\inetsrv\gophroot\temp
Object Type  = 1; Friendly Name = Temporary gopher hole
Administrator Name =
Administrator Email =

C:\winnt\system32\inetsrv\gophroot>gdsset -r att01.txt
Tag information for
C:\winnt\system32\inetsrv\gophroot\att01.txt
Object Type  = 0; Friendly Name = Attachment file for Gopher.
Administrator Name = Peter D. Hipson
Administrator Email = phipson@darkstar.mv.com

C:\winnt\system32\inetsrv\gophroot>gdsset -r cabbage.txt
Tag information for
C:\winnt\system32\inetsrv\gophroot\cabbage.txt
Object Type  = 0; Friendly Name = Pure Cabbage, from Andy
Thomas!
Administrator Name = Peter D. Hipson
Administrator Email = phipson@darkstar.mv.com
```

A directory listing for my gophroot folder shows us that there are only a few files there. The gophroot folder is on an NTFS drive, so I told the DIR command to show all files, including the hidden tag files.

```
C:\winnt\system32\inetsrv\gophroot>dir /AD /AH /AA  /s
 Volume in drive C is C - PENTIUM
 Volume Serial Number is 0F44-19DC


 Directory of C:\winnt\system32\inetsrv\gophroot

07/05/96  03:34p        <DIR>           .
07/05/96  03:34p        <DIR>           ..
```

```
07/25/96  08:08p       <DIR>              temp
07/08/96  01:40p                  2,225   ATT01.txt
07/25/96  08:24p                    130   att01.txt.gtg
07/05/96  02:23p                    194   CABBAGE.TXT
07/25/96  08:41p                    132   cabbage.txt.gtg
07/25/96  08:11p                     72   temp.gtg
               5 File(s)          2,753 bytes

 Directory of C:\winnt\system32\inetsrv\gophroot\temp

07/25/96  08:08p       <DIR>              .
07/25/96  08:08p       <DIR>              ..
07/08/96  01:40p                  2,225   ATT01.txt
07/05/96  02:23p                    194   CABBAGE.TXT
               2 File(s)          2,419 bytes

     Total Files Listed:
               7 File(s)          5,172 bytes
                            235,634,688 bytes free

C:\winnt\system32\inetsrv\gophroot>
```

The IIS FTP Server

FTP (File Transfer Protocol) is the Internet's way of moving files between servers and clients. Of the three servers in Microsoft IIS, the FTP server is the easiest to configure; but then, as it involves strictly text and a limited user interface that consists of directory listings of file names and little more, FTP is the most inflexible of the protocols and services on the Internet. Basic configuration of the FTP server is covered in Chapter 13, "The Microsoft Internet Information Server." FTP, however, remains popular, mostly by supporting file downloads for Web sites.

Unlike Gopher servers, FTP servers are much more common and more easily understood both by administrators and users. Virtually everyone who is on the Internet has experienced FTP file transfers.

(That can't be said about Gopher!) There are many competent FTP client programs available to users, including Junod's WS_FTP32 program, the Windows NT 4 FTP command, and, though limited, Internet Explorer does serve as an FTP client also.

Many WWW sites also host an FTP server to allow clients to download files from the server. FTP sites can be open (allowing anonymous logons) or closed (requiring a preassigned user ID and a password to log on). FTP has been around for a very long time and has its roots in UNIX. When using the Windows NT FTP command you will see, full well, FTP's UNIX parentage.

An FTP Server is quite similar to a Gopher server in that both allow the user to access files. However, a Gopher server only transfers files to the client site, whereas FTP can both send and receive files from clients.

The IIS FTP Service supports all the standard FTP services and features. As the IIS FTP server is Windows NT-based, the configuration is slightly different from that of an FTP server running under UNIX. As well, the IIS FTP server supports long file names, something that many non-Windows NT servers have difficulty doing.

Whether or not you decide to implement the IIS FTP server is a decision you and your system administrator must make. You will find, however, that implementing an FTP server takes virtually no time to set up, and requires little in the way of resources.

Setting Up an FTP Site

Setting up your FTP server can be as simple as copying your files (and directories) to the FTP root directory. This creates a simple FTP server, which client users can then browse. The client user could use any FTP client (such as Internet Explorer).

As well, you can set up other virtual directories as needed. You can use virtual directories to create private areas where users may save files.

Security for an FTP server is based on how a user accesses your FTP server—if anonymous access is used then allow only read-only access. Users who have a Windows NT 4 Server user ID can be granted read/write access as necessary.

CAUTION

Be very careful about allowing anonymous FTP users write access. There are numerous instances where anonymous users have uploaded "pirated" software to FTP sites for other users to download. This practice could result in civil liability, if it happens to your site!

Another problem with allowing anonymous users to upload files is the possibility that an executable file with a virus may be uploaded. If for any reason you allow anonymous users to upload files, use a virus scanner frequently to protect both yourself and your users from viruses.

Moving On

In this chapter, we covered the Microsoft Internet Server (IIS) Gopher and FTP services.

Gopher allows users to easily interact with the server and retrieve information. While Gopher is similar to the WWW, it is a text-based service and is now less popular on the Internet.

FTP (File Transfer Protocol) is *the* file transfer protocol for the Internet. Virtually all sites support FTP, and recent releases of all browsers support FTP.

The next chapter covers using the Microsoft IIS WWW server. The Web has become the most popular feature of the Internet, with a substantial amount of the usage of the Internet being dedicated to WWW transactions.

15

The Microsoft IIS WWW Server

The World Wide Web (WWW), often called the "Web," is the Internet's hypermedia information network. Virtually every user on the Internet today has a Web page somewhere. Conservative estimates are that over half of the Internet's traffic consists of transfers between Web servers and Web clients (also called Web browsers).

Web usage dwarfs the next most often used Internet service, FTP. The Web browser wars of mid-1996 pitted Microsoft against Netscape, with each company churning out new releases of their respective products on a two- to four-month basis. The fighting over the browser market has been fierce, with Microsoft essentially giving away Internet Explorer to Windows 95 and Windows NT users. At one point, Microsoft was beta testing several consecutive releases of their product at the same time!

This chapter guides you in setting up your IIS WWW Server. I won't try to tell you how to design a specific Web page—heck, I'm not an artist. I will give you some information about tools that can assist you in creating Web pages, but you and your system administrator will have to take it to the next level.

The IIS WWW Server

A Web server is the most popular Internet server. Management screams for it, users demand it, and corporate images live on the Web today. For organizations configuring intranet web sites, IIS is an excellent choice for the server.

Though many Internet users do not initially set up FTP and Gopher servers, virtually all set up Web servers first. Many Web servers also host an FTP server to allow clients to download files from the server, and some even have Gopher servers. Many Web browsers are capable of working with FTP, News Groups, and Gopher servers. Web transactions can be secure, though frequently they are not.

A popular Web site can generate thousands (the most popular Web sites receive millions) of *hits*, or accesses, each day. It is now routine for a popular Web site to find that its popularity is its undoing: the server, or the communications link, is unable to keep up with the demand and system performance fails.

Exotic server systems, including multiple IP addresses (and servers) assigned to a single URL, are being developed to cope with the issues of the high demands placed on popular Web servers. For most of us, communications bandwidth is a problem we must overcome, a topic covered later in this chapter.

A Web server is a bit different from FTP and Gopher servers—WWW clients do not think in terms of files and directories, though in reality these elements are as basic to the Web as they are to FTP and Gopher. Rather, a Web client "thinks" in terms of resources, links, objects, and other abstract items. These items are what make the Web work, and you therefore need to understand what HTML (HyperText Markup Language) is.

The IIS WWW Server supports all the standard Web services and features. As the IIS WWW Server is Windows NT-based, the configuration is slightly different than a Web server running under UNIX—these differences are not significant enough to

warrant discussion (some issues are simply items such as differences in file-naming conventions between UNIX and Windows NT). As well, the IIS WWW Server supports long file names, something that many non-Windows NT servers have difficulty doing. Keep any names the user must type as short as possible. After all, nothing is more disheartening than to type a long URL and have it fail because of a trivial typing error.

Whether or not you decide to implement the IIS WWW Server is a decision you and your system administrator must make. The basic implementation of an IIS WWW Server takes virtually no time to set up, and little in the way of resources. However, a professional set of Web pages take planning and work, the amount of effort being governed by how much you wish to invest in your Web pages.

Setting Up a Web Site

Setting up your Web site can be as simple as modifying the example Web pages that come with the IIS WWW Server. This is perhaps only a temporary solution, however, as Web pages are typically very individualized and customized for each site.

Many Web sites employ a person who is skilled in the creation of Web pages. Such a person has artistic as well as computer skills. For a company that is making its presence on the Web known, hiring a professional Web page designer may be a very good idea!

As well as having a single Web page, you can set up other, virtual directories as Web pages. When working with large systems, you can use virtual directories to create areas for products, news, and other information as desired. We discussed virtual directories in Chapter 13, "The Microsoft Internet Information Server."

IIS WWW Server Samples

Microsoft provides with IIS WWW Server a set of Web pages and applications you can customize and work with to assist in learning how the IIS Web Server works. These examples are found in the inetsrv\wwwroot\samples folder.

Sample applications include an example Web site for a fictitious company, several database examples, some programming examples, and HTML example source code.

In addition to these examples, the Microsoft Web site (http://www.microsoft.com) contains many examples. The FrontPage program (included with Windows NT 4 Server) also makes much of the development of your Web page simpler.

Sample IIS WWW Server Pages

Microsoft supplies sample Web pages with the IIS WWW Server. These sample pages are divided into four broad categories: sample HTML site, database, programming, and sample HTML styles.

SampSite—An HTML Sample Site

The heart of the SampSite HTML example is a fictitious company called the Volcano Coffee Company (see Figure 15-1). This company's business is coffee over the Internet, and the example pages have a number of interesting features. The user can:

- Order a sample of coffee. The user enters data into an HTML form. The data is returned to the Web server for processing. The coffee company ships the sample to the user's address.
- Request specific information. The user enters their name and e-mail address. The Web server adds this name and address to a mailing list. The coffee company sends out the requested information.

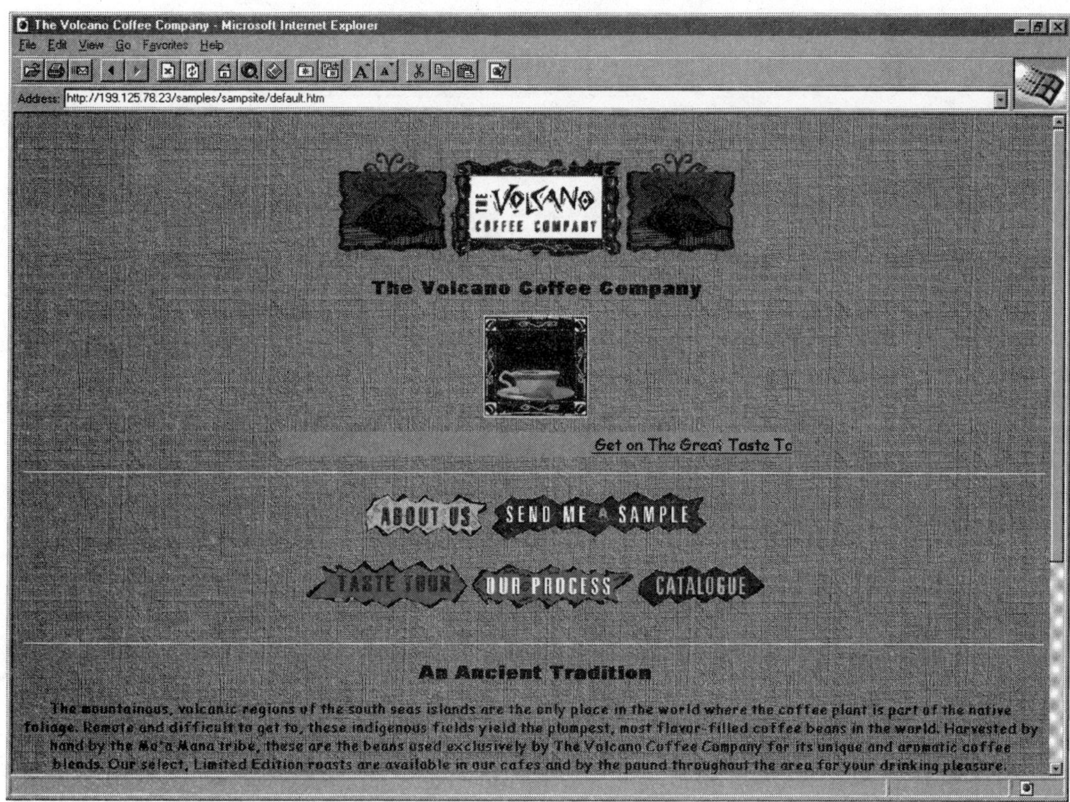

Figure 15-1: The Volcano Coffee Company on the Web.

Database

The database examples are all linked to Microsoft SQL Server. Figure 15-2 shows part of the introduction HTML that the Web server administrator uses to set up the database examples.

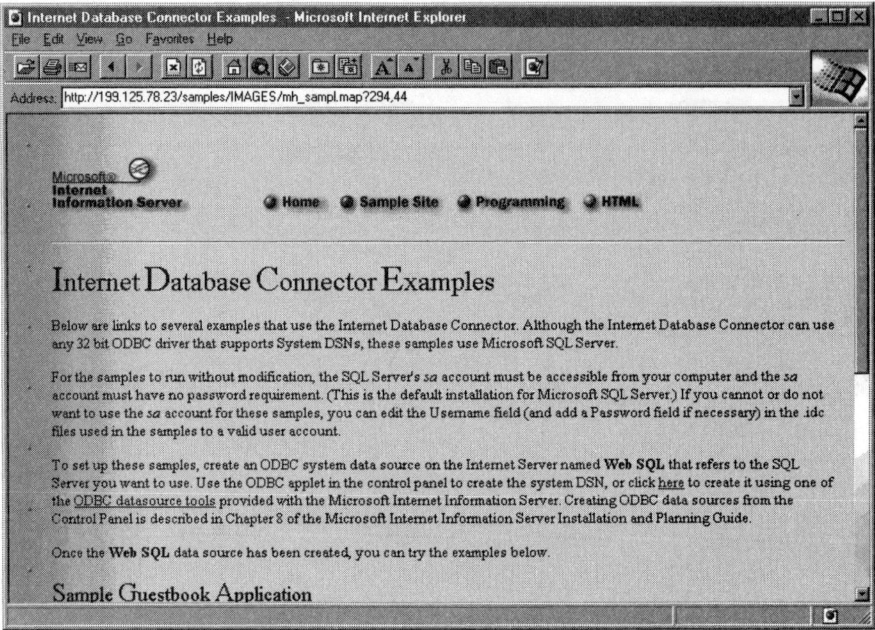

Figure 15-2: The database example—interfacing with SQL Server.

The database examples include:

- Guestbook—An application where client users "sign in" using an HTML form. This information is then sent to the SQL Server where it is saved in a table.
- Query—An application that allows the client user to make a simple free format query on the database.
- FormQuery—An application that allows the client user to make a simple query on the database. This query is form-based.
- Query, return as a hyperlink—An application that allows users to make a query and have the results returned as a hyperlink.

All of the database-based HTML examples use Microsoft SQL Server as their database engine. If you are not using SQL Server, use the programming examples as a starting point for accessing other data sources using ODBC (Open Database Connectivity).

Programming

The programming examples offer two different capabilities:

- A search function—Allows the client user to search for text in this site.
- A "Favorite Sites Bulletin Board" (see Figure 15-3)—Allows users to leave information about their *favorite site*. One should expect a bit of horn blowing here, touting one's own site, but that's life. All users can access the list of favorite sites. These favorite sites are saved in the file wwwroot\samples\isapi\drop.htm.

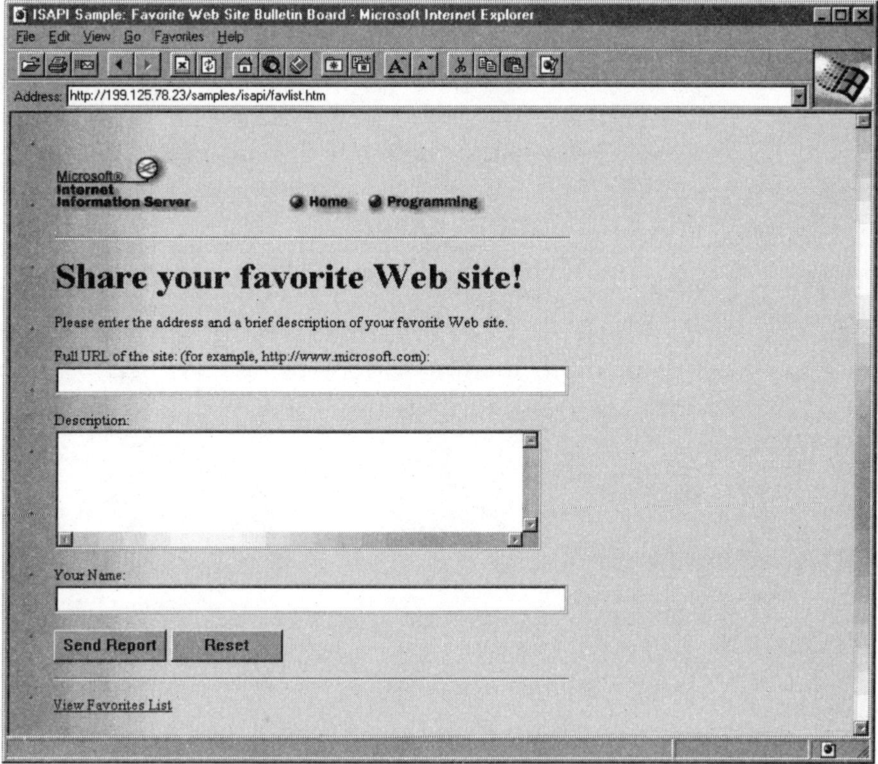

Figure 15-3: The Favorite Sites Bulletin Board form.

As well as these two programming examples, users of Visual C++ 4.1 (and later) will also find other programming examples supplied with Visual C++. Two noteworthy examples supplied with Visual C++ 4.1 include:

- HTTPSRV—A simple Web server (no, this program doesn't compete with Microsoft's IIS WWW Server) that runs under both Windows NT 4 and Windows 95. This server is basic, and the code shows how simple it is to create a basic server for the Internet.
- WWWQUOTE—A simple stock quote program that queries a database of stock prices and returns information from the query to the client user. The data is *canned*, and in a real application is replaced with an actively updated database.

In Visual C++ 4.1, there is also an example of a filter, which converts text to uppercase. Filters are an advanced programming topic, well beyond the scope of this book.

HTML Sample Sheets

The HTML sample sheets (see Figure 15-4) demonstrate styles for tables, headings, lists, and such. Generally, using Internet Assistant is an easy way to format your HTML documents, where most (if not all) formatting is done using a WYSIWYG (What You See Is What You Get) format.

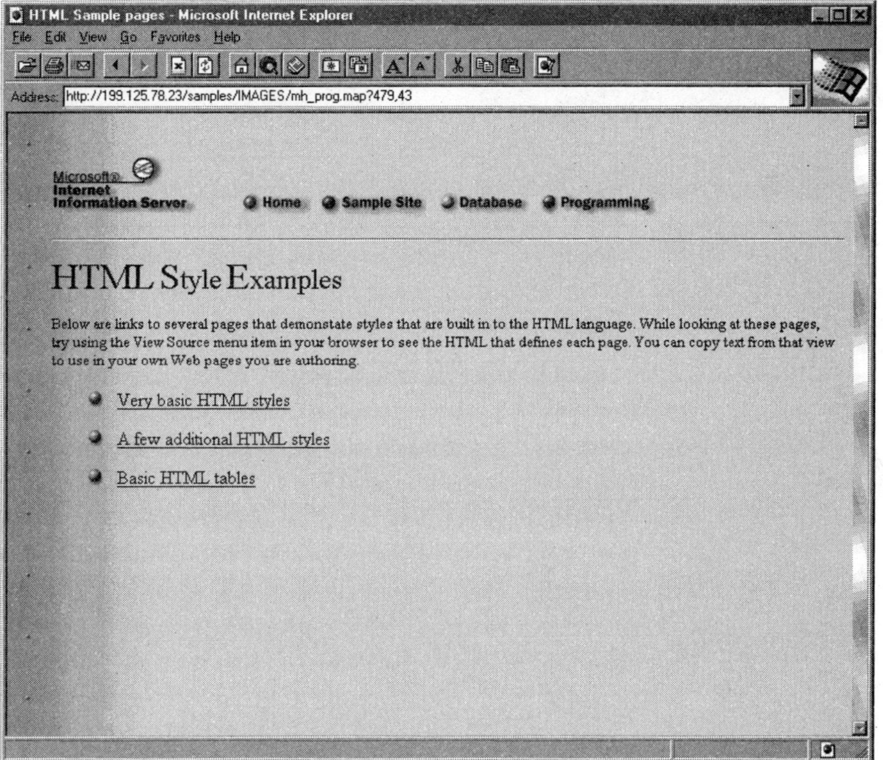

Figure 15-4: The HTML sample style sheets introduction page.

Creating Initial WWW HTML Pages

Web pages are created in a format called HyperText Markup Language (HTML). Though HTML is a text-based format that you can edit using simple editors such as Notepad, it is much easier to create and edit your HTML documents using an editor that understands HTML and edits HTML directly, and allows you to work using a WYSIWYG format.

The process of creating a Web page is complex. A good Web page must have a number of attributes, including being attractive and easy to work with, and having the best mixture of graphics and text.

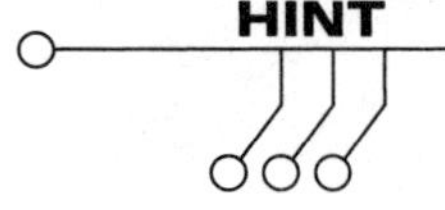

Many Web pages have too many large graphic images. Many users are still accessing the Web at speeds of 28K or slower. When a Web page has too many, or large graphic images, the time to transfer the page to the user's computer can be excessive. Each image must be separately requested, and large images compound the problem. A Web page should transfer, at 28K modem speeds, in less than five seconds if possible. Large images, if necessary, can be presented in lower resolution, with a link to a higher-resolution version.

In the next part of this chapter, I provide some methods for creating HTML documents and describe some tools that you can use to create and maintain your HTML documents.

First, we look at Microsoft's Internet Assistant, a product you can download from Microsoft's Internet site. Another product you can use is Microsoft FrontPage, which is included with Windows NT 4 Server.

There are a number of excellent references on creating Web documents. Several from Ventana that come to mind are:

- *HTML Publishing With Internet Assistant* by Kidder and Harris.
- *Looking Good Online* by Steve Bain.
- *Ten Secrets to Web Success* by Bryan Pfaffenberger.

Using Microsoft Internet Assistant

Microsoft has created a tool to allow Word for Windows to create and edit HTML documents. This tool, called Internet Assistant version 2 (IA for Word 95) is available from Microsoft at their Internet site at http://www.microsoft.com.

Internet Assistant for Microsoft Word for Windows 95 (Word 95 also runs under Windows NT 4) is an add-on available from Microsoft at no charge. Internet Assistant allows users to create and edit HTML documents for the Internet using Microsoft Word for Windows. Internet Assistant is a full-featured Internet authoring tool that can convert a Word file to HTML and provide users with a toolbar (and menu), and an interface for inserting hyperlinks, images, and forms into HTML documents.

Using Internet Assistant, a Web page designer can create a richly formatted HTML document without having to understand the complicated code associated with HTML.

Internet Assistant is available as specified, from the following locations:

- At URL http://198.105.232.4/kb/softlib/mslfiles/WRDInternet Assistant20Z.EXE.
- On the TechNet CD.
- Downloaded from the keyword "Free Stuff" on the Microsoft Network (MSN).
- On the CompuServe MSWORD forum.
- A disk version can also be ordered from Microsoft, at 1-800-426-9400, for the cost of shipping and handling.

Using Internet Assistant is simple. First, you install Internet Assistant. Next, execute the file that contains Internet Assistant, WRDInternet Assistant2Z.EXE (after you have installed Word for Windows). The installation program then installs the necessary files for Internet Assistant to work.

Internet Assistant has the advantage of supporting the HTML tags that are most often used. It is very easy to create hyperlinks and Internet forms with Internet Assistant, since hyperlinks may be inserted in compound Word documents. You can even use Internet Assistant to view and edit all your source code. Figure 15-5 shows a Web page from the Volcano Coffee Shop loaded in Word for Windows with Internet Assistant.

Your work in creating a set of Web pages isn't finished until you have tested the work using as many Web browsers as possible. Always test using both Internet Explorer and Netscape as a minimum. You should make sure that features supported by one browser and not supported by other Web browsers degrade gracefully. You should view the Web page in a text-only browser, too.

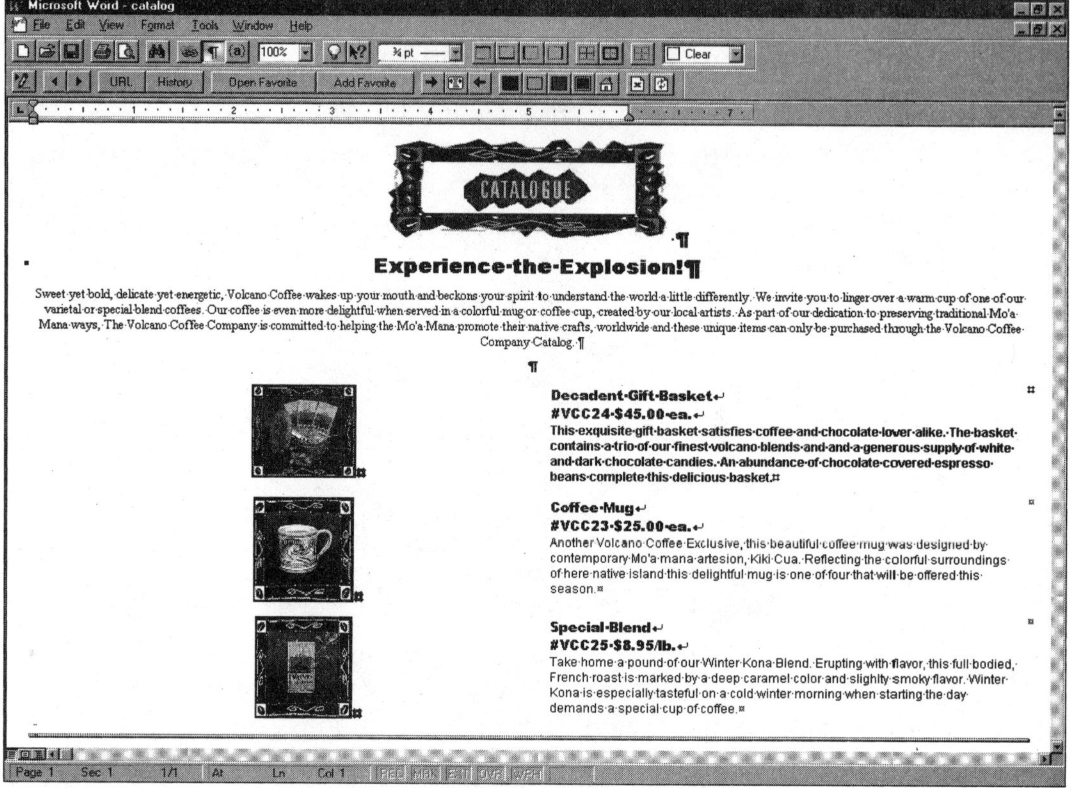

Figure 15-5: Internet Assistant at work editing catalog.html.

Using Microsoft FrontPage

Microsoft, at the 11th hour, decided to include the Microsoft FrontPage product with Windows NT 4 Server. FrontPage allows creation and management of Web sites and offers the following features:

- FrontPage Editor—Edits HTML (HyperText Markup Language) documents. The FrontPage Editor is patterned after Microsoft Word for Windows and has a very similar user interface.

- FrontPage Explorer—Browses Web pages both in the normal display mode and in link and outline views.
- Summary—Provides property information about each page.
- FrontPage TCP/IP tester—Tests the implementation of WinSock (Windows Sockets, the programming interface to TCP/IP).
- Server Administrator—Interfaces FrontPage with your Web server. Web servers supported include: FrontPage Personal Web Server, Netscape Commerce Server, Netscape Communication Server, and WebSite.

The Secure Sockets Layer (SSL)

Chapter 13, "The Microsoft Internet Information Server," introduces securing your Microsoft Information Internet Server against unauthorized access. This section discusses protocols that use cryptography to secure data transmissions to and from your server.

Microsoft IIS provides users with a secure communication channel through support for Secure Sockets Layer (SSL) and RSA Data Security, Inc.'s encryption.

SSL protocol provides secure data communication through data encryption and decryption. The security provided by SSL is rather good, providing an avenue for commercial transactions on the Web. With SSL, you are able to transact business, including credit card transactions, with little risk of a security breach on the network. The IIS WWW Server can send and receive private communications across the Internet to any SSL-enabled client such as Microsoft Internet Explorer version 2.0 for Windows 95 and Windows NT. As well, Netscape has an SSL-enabled browser available.

Defined as a protocol layer between the TCP/IP layer and the application layer (HTTP), SSL provides server authentication, encryption, and data integrity. Server authentication assures the client user that they are indeed connected to the correct server. Encryption ensures both the client and the server that their communications are as confidential as possible. Data integrity ensures that information passed between the server and the client has not been modified, either intentionally or unintentionally.

Enabling SSL Security

To enable SSL security on the IIS WWW Server, follow the steps below:

1. Use the KEYGEN utility to create a key pair file and request file.
2. Request a certificate from a certification authority such as VeriSign for your system. See the section below, "Obtaining an SSL Certificate," for more information on requesting a certificate. You must pay for the certificate.
3. Install the certificate on your server.
4. Activate SSL security on a Web service directory in the IIS WWW Server configuration dialog. See the "Setting Up Directories" section of Chapter 13, "The Microsoft Internet Information Server," for an example of where SSL is used with the IIS WWW Server.

You must do the following when you enable SSL security on your IIS Web server:

- In either your Web server's root directory, or in one (or more) of the Web server's virtual directories you must enable SSL security. You do not need to use SSL security for your entire Web site, however.
- After you configure and enable your SSL directories, then only those clients that have support for SSL security can use these directories.
- Make references to those directories that are SSL-enabled using https:// and not http://. Links made using http:// to documents in an SSL-enabled directory do not work!

- You can enable and disable the use of SSL on directories using the Internet Service Manager. The process for enabling and disabling SSL security for a specific directory is described in the "Setting Up Directories" section of Chapter 13.

Obtaining an SSL Certificate

You must obtain an SSL certificate. This certificate is issued from one of the certifying authorities, such as VeriSign. Below is listed the complete process to obtain an SSL certificate. However, before investing a substantial amount of time in completing these steps, contact the certificate issuer. The certificate issuer may have other requirements or information that must be supplied. To obtain a certificate, follow these steps below:

1. Go to the directory where you have installed IIS. This directory is usually C:\Inetsrv\Server. In this directory are two utilities that manage SSL security certificates. The KEYGEN.EXE program generates a key request. The SETKEY.EXE program installs the certificate key once it has been returned from the certificate issuer.
2. Use the KEYGEN.EXE program to generate the two files described below. The first file is the key file that contains the key pairs. The second file is the key request file. The key request file is a text file that you can either e-mail or otherwise transmit to the certificate issuer. Display the parameters for the KEYGEN.EXE program using the command KEYGEN (without any arguments) from a command prompt.

   The following example shows how to create a set of SSL key files, based on the DORA server. The example shows how to create two files, the KEYPAIR.KEY file (which contains the key pair) and the KEYREQUES.TXT file (which contains the request for the certificate). When KEYGEN runs, it generates these files in the current directory. (Also see the KEYGEN reference, below.)

   The execution of KEYGEN is shown in Figure 15-6.

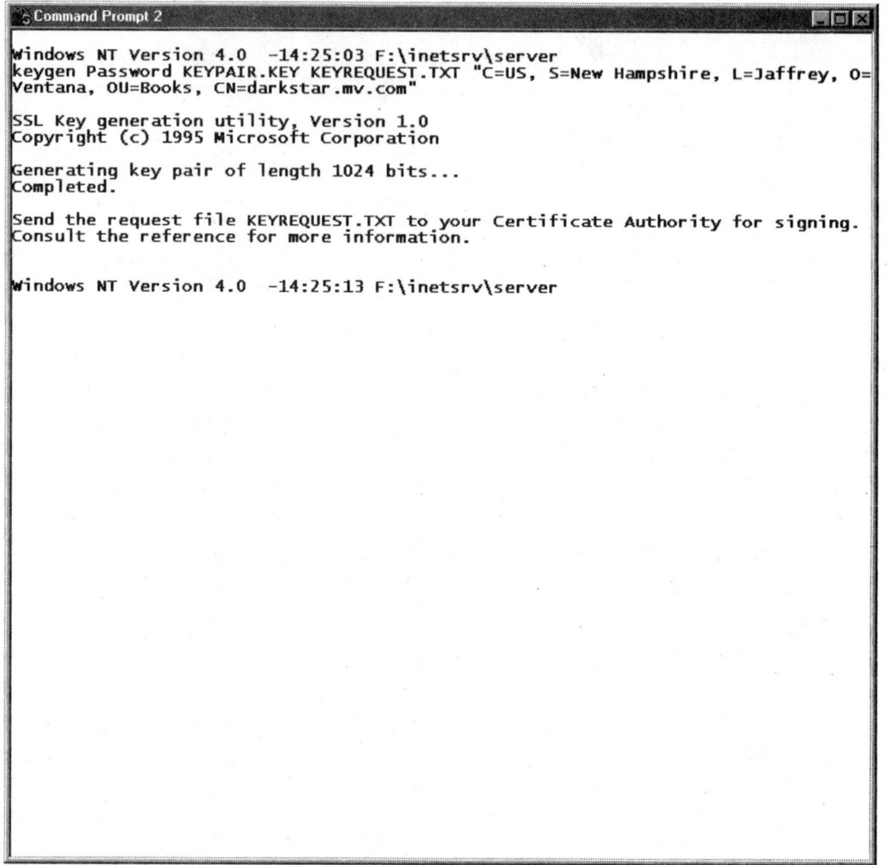

Figure 15-6: KEYGEN generating key files in a CMD window.

3. To use SSL, you need to obtain a certificate for your system from a certifying authority such as VeriSign. You can find instructions for acquiring a VeriSign certificate on VeriSign's Web site (start at http://www.verisign.com).
4. You must send your key request to the certificate issuing authority (such as VeriSign). Use e-mail to submit your request to the certificate issuing authority. Note, however, that you may need to address other issues, including payment for the certificate. You should also provide a copy

of the command line instructions that generate the key request file (see Figure 15-6, above). Don't send your password, however—the password is confidential! The resultant file from the KEYGEN execution is shown below in Figure 15-7.

Figure 15-7: The results of running KEYGEN.

5. It is easy to cut and paste the command line instructions (don't retype it, you may make a typing error!) to the beginning of this file as shown in Figure 15-8.

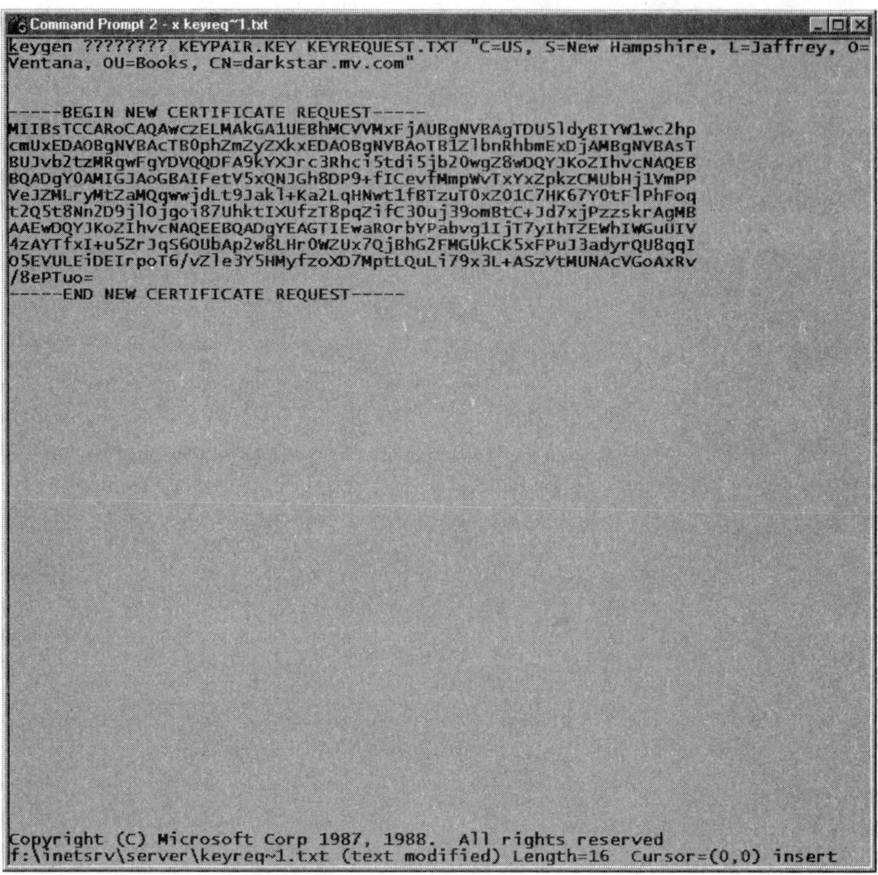

Figure 15-8: The key request file ready to send to the certificate issuer.

Installing the SSL Certificate

Once you have completed these steps, the certificate issuer processes your request and then sends you some form of communication containing information about your actual key. The certificate response you receive (perhaps an e-mail response) may look similar to the one shown in Figure 15-9.

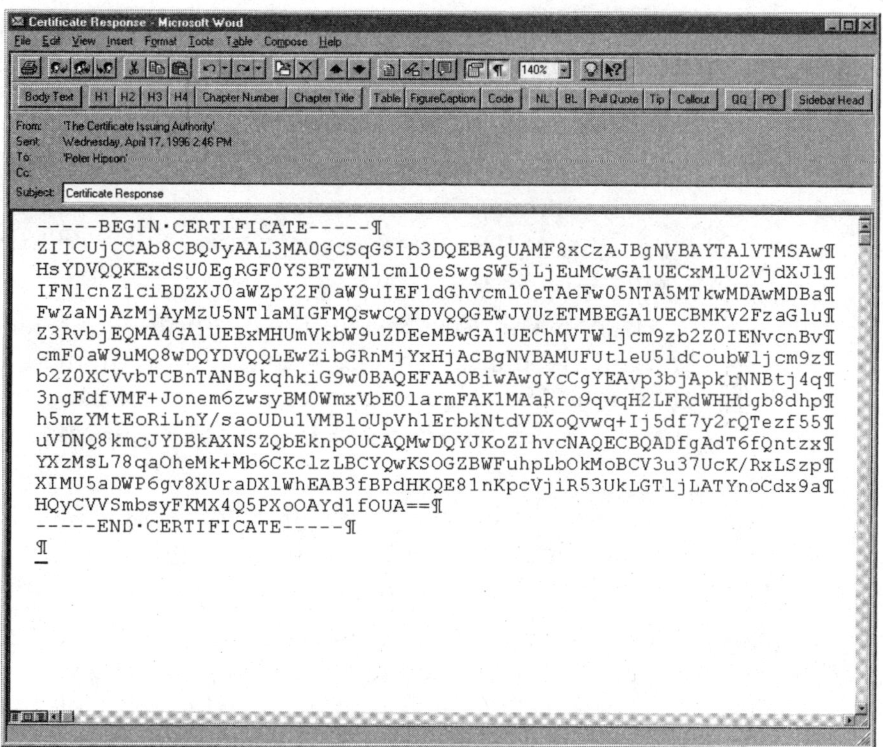

Figure 15-9: Response from the certificate issuing authority.

To copy the key text and install the certificate for your server, follow the steps below:

1. Use the Windows clipboard to copy the key text (but not the lines that contain the "-----BEGIN CERTIFICATE-----" or the "-----END CERTIFICATE-----" text) into a file. Use Notepad or some other simple text file editor. Word for Windows can be used, if you remember to save the file as a text-formatted file with line breaks.
2. Save the file with a meaningful name, such as CERTIFICATE.TXT.
3. Use SETKEY.EXE to install the certificate for your server. (Also see the SETKEY reference, below.) To install an SSL key using SETKEY, enter the command as SETKEY \\server

password key certificate IP_Address where \\server is the name of your server (for the examples in this book, the server is \\DORA). The password parameter is the password that you use to generate the key. The key parameter is the result of running KEYGEN, and IP_Address is the IP address on which the key is used. When all IP addresses are to use the same certificate, you don't need to specify the IP address parameter.

The above process installs the certificate. Once installed, you can use the Internet Service Manager to configure the Web service to support SSL. There are several important issues when telling Internet Service Manager to use an SSL certificate:

- To use the same certificate on more than one virtual Web server, do not specify an IP address or domain name when running SETKEY. When no IP address is specified, the certificate is applied to all servers.
- Use Internet Service Manager to set the Require Secure SSL Channel option for directories that you want to protect by using SSL. See Chapter 13, "The Microsoft Internet Information Server," in the section titled "Setting Up Directories," for information on the Require Secure SSL Channel check box.
- In their documentation, Microsoft suggests that you use different directories for the secure and nonsecure pages on your Web server.

Microsoft states: "It is important to avoid having a server directory not protected by SSL as a parent for a secure directory."

- Do not lose your key pair file (as generated by KEYGEN). Back up this file. Also do not forget the password that you used to generate this file! Backing up to a diskette is a very good idea, and keeping this diskette secure is a wise move.

SETKEY Reference

Usage:

```
setkey [\\server] password private_key
certificate [IP_Address]
```

or

```
setkey -d [\\server]
```

Where:

[\\server]	The Windows NT server that the IIS Web server is running on. Server must not be specified when administrating a Web server on the local machine. This parameter is used when remotely administering an IIS server.
Password	Password used to create keys with KEYGEN.
private_key	The file name for the file that contains the key file: KEYPAIR.KEY.
certificate	The file name of the file contains the returned key certificate from the certificate issuer.
[IP_Address]	The IP address for the virtual server using this SSL certificate. If no IP address is specified, then this key is applied to all virtual servers.
-d	Tells SETKEY to delete all currently installed keys.

Examples:

```
setkey OurUnsecurePassword c:\keys\serverkey
c:\keys\certificate
setkey \\RemoteServer OurUnsecurePassword C:\keys\serverkey
c:\keys\certificate 199.231.22.1
```

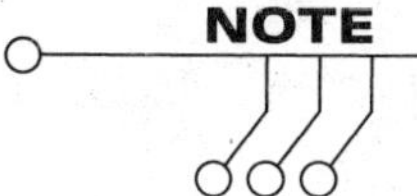

You must restart the IIS WWW Server when you change the SSL configuration.

KEYGEN Reference

Usage:

[-bits bits]	KEYGEN can generate keys of 512, 768, or 1,024 bits in length. This optional parameter specifies the size of the key, in bits. The default is 1,024 bit keys.
password	Your password to encrypt the private key.
private_key	The filename for the file (typically KEYPAIR.KEY) where the encrypted private key is stored.
request File	The filename where Certificate Request is stored.
dist_name	Distinguished name for the key, in the following format: C=<Country>, where <country> is the two-letter ISO country designation (for example, US, FR, AU, UK, DE) O=<Organization>, (Preferably ISO-registered top-level organization or company name) OU=<Organization Unit> S=<State/Province>, where <State/Province> is the state or province (for example, Washington, Alberta, or California. Do not abbreviate!) L=<Locality/Town>, (for example, Redmond, Jaffrey, Calgary, or Redwood City) CN=<net address>, (Domain Name of server, for example, www.darkstar.com)

Example:

```
keygen Password Key Request "C=US, O=Marie's Bike Shop, S=New
Hampshire, L=Pelham, CN=barber.com"
```

Notes:

By default, KEYGEN generates keys 1,024 bits long.

The argument in quotation marks in the Keygen.exe command line ("C=US, S=Washington, L=Redmond, O=Example, OU=Marketing, CN=www.mycompany.com") specifies several fields for the certificate request related to your organization and server. Do not embed commas in any field.

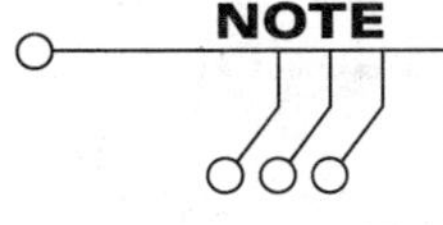

Do not use commas (such as "Smith, Jones, and Company") in any field. Commas are interpreted as the end of that field and generate a bad request without warning. Simply spell the name without commas: "Smith Jones and Company."

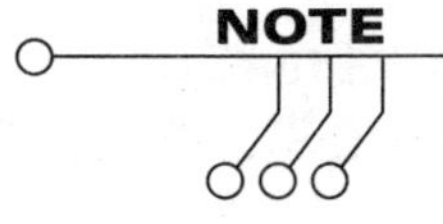

Running KEYGEN two times with the same files results in an error. You must delete the files created by KEYGEN prior to rerunning (if you are rerunning with output to the same files).

Reliability

All Web sites must be constantly maintained and upgraded. The "browser wars" result in new Web browser features every few months, and other parts of the Web change frequently.

To make your Internet site more reliable, consider the following:

- Test all changes fully. Don't assume that since a change to a Web page looks good with Internet Explorer, that it will look good with Mosaic or Netscape.
- Keep a list of all external HTTP links, and check them frequently. Links, names, and addresses change constantly. The Web is a living, evolving, growing thing, and links go out of date constantly. To check Web links for validity, a program such as FrontPage can be used.

- Make sure that links to your own Web pages are valid. Nothing is more likely to create a bad impression than to have a button that, when used, results in a "not found" message.
- Use whatever features of HTML that you need. Don't make things more complex, fancy, or whatever, just for the sake of being different. Like any other publishing task, use moderation—limit yourself to one or two fonts, keep the images sensible (in size and complexity), and don't use a riot of color.
- Don't use a busy background with your Web pages. Be careful that your background doesn't overpower your message.
- If you use sounds (such as those supported by Internet Explorer) use a MIDI file, not a .WAV file. MIDI files are much smaller and take much less time to transfer to the user's system.
- Be careful of copyright issues: Don't use clip art, sound clips, or other objects unless you either own them or have permission. A common misconception is that if the sound clip is short, you can use it—not true!
- Use the NTFS file system for as many of your directories as possible. NTFS offers enhanced security, performance, and reliability.

In addition to reliability, a Web site must perform well. See the "Performance" section at the end of Chapter 13, "The Microsoft Internet Information Server," for ideas on how to make your Internet site perform better.

Moving On

In this chapter, we covered the Microsoft Internet Information Server's WWW Server and discussed some of the issues in creating Web pages. The sample pages provided with IIS WWW Server and the sample Web applications were covered in this chapter. Also covered was SSL, the Secure Sockets Layer.

This chapter concludes our coverage of Windows NT 4 Server and the Internet.

The next chapter introduces sharing, both file and printer resources.

SECTION IV

Advanced Windows NT 4

16

Sharing

This chapter covers issues in sharing a server's resources. Sharing is usually a simple process, provided you are organized.

Of all the talents you possess, being organized is the one you need to exercise now. Whether or not you set up your server in an organized fashion will most certainly affect the security of your assets, including your expensive hardware and software!

Most servers share *some* disk resources. You can set up your server in such a way that *entire* drives and folders are shared with client users. When the shared drive or folder is on an NTFS-formatted volume, you can assign permissions based on users or groups.

Many servers also share one or more printers. Printers are relatively expensive devices, and are therefore ideal candidates for sharing among users.

Security (which we cover in the next chapter) is usually very important—client users should only be allowed to access resources they have a need to access.

Sharing Files

Most servers are file servers—they share disk or folder resources with client users. Large networks do have dedicated print servers (which we talk about later in this chapter), and other servers (such as Exchange servers or Microsoft SQL servers), but even these installations have one or more file servers.

Using Explorer

File sharing is managed using the Microsoft Explorer program (use Start Menu | Programs | Explorer). Explorer is a vital part of Windows NT 4 Server—it is the replacement for Windows NT 3.x's File Manager.

NTFS, Sharing & Security

NTFS offers a more powerful security sub-system for sharing. With NTFS you set permissions on a file-by-file basis, with FAT you can set permissions for folders only.

Generally, if you have a file server, you want to run NTFS as your primary file system; though FAT file systems are suitable for single user systems, any network gains substantial advantages in performance and security using NTFS.

Using Microsoft Explorer is not difficult. Designed to be user-friendly, Microsoft Explorer manages a number of different areas. With Explorer, you can easily review and set properties (such as sharing) for files and folders.

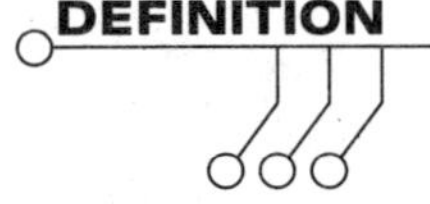

I'll refer to files, folders, and volumes together as objects. *Then, when there are differences between files, folders, or volumes, I will be specific.*

Let's start by opening Microsoft Explorer and selecting a folder on an NTFS volume that has some files we would like to share—Figure 16-1 shows Microsoft Explorer with my "Example" folder opened.

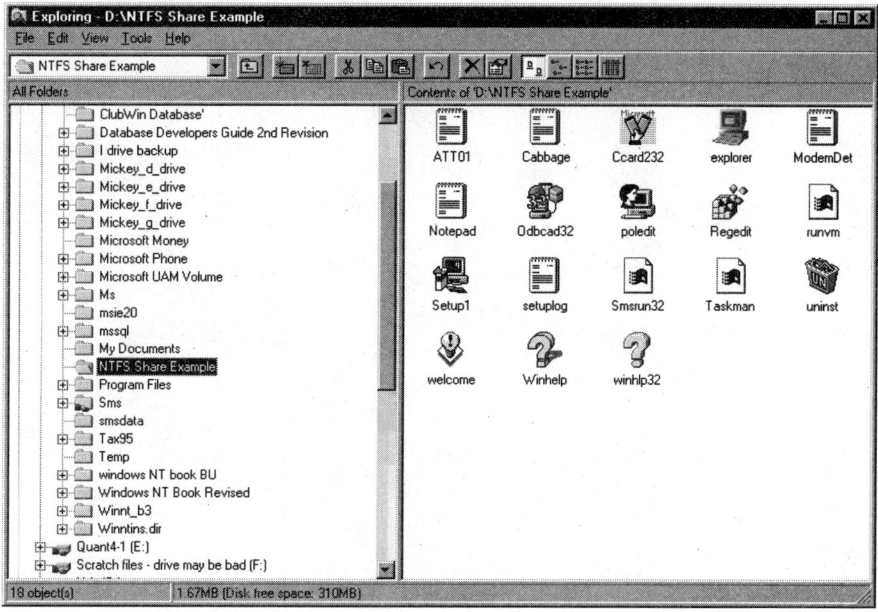

Figure 16-1: Microsoft Explorer NTFS Share Example.

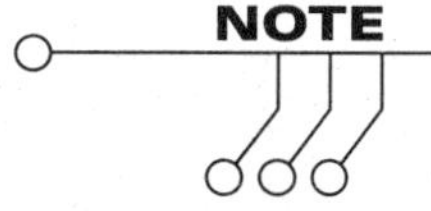

For files, folders, and volumes that are NTFS, a third tab in the Microsoft Explorer Properties dialog, Security, is present. Using the Security tab is a topic in Chapter 17, "Security & Users."

To share an object, open the Properties dialog for the object you want to share. For example, in Microsoft Explorer, I highlight, then right-click the object I want to share. This action causes a list of options to appear. I then can select either Sharing or Properties. Both selections display the Properties dialog; however, selecting "Sharing" displays the Properties dialog with the Sharing tab already selected for me, as shown in Figure 16-2.

The default sharing for any object is that the object is *not shared*. By not sharing by default, you don't inadvertently share confidential objects.

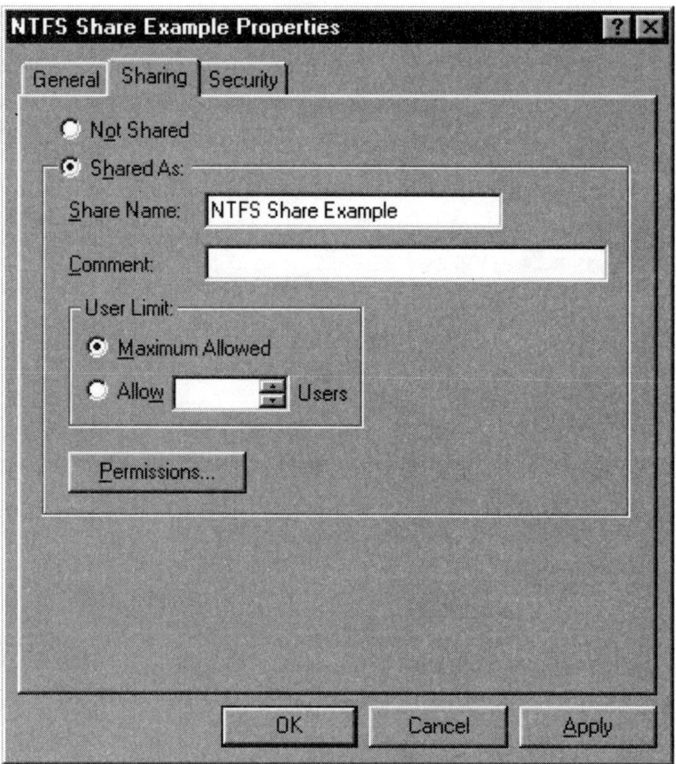

Figure 16-2: The Sharing tab in the Properties dialog.

To set up a new share of an object that has not been shared, select the object's properties dialog in Microsoft Explorer and follow the steps below:

1. Click the Shared As radio button in the Properties dialog box.
2. Specify a meaningful name in the Share Name field.
3. Specify a description of the object in the Comment field.

4. If you want to restrict the number of users who can concurrently access the shared object, specify that number in the User Limit field. Remember, this user limit is not tied to the Windows NT 4 Server client license limit. The user limit is an additional limitation you can place on the concurrent accesses to a share.

To set up a new, additional share of an object that already has an existing share, select the object's properties dialog in Microsoft Explorer and follow the steps below:

1. Click the New Shared button in the Properties dialog box.
2. Specify a meaningful name in the Share Name field in the New Share dialog box.
3. Specify a description of the object in the Comment field in the New Share dialog box.
4. If you want to restrict the number of users who can concurrently access the shared object, specify that number in the User Limit field. Remember, this user limit is not tied to the Windows NT 4 Server client license limit. The user limit is an additional limitation you can place on the concurrent accesses to a share.

You can also limit access to a shared object by specifying permissions by users or by groups. You can specify no access, read (can see, but not make changes), change (can see and make changes), and full control (like administrative control). Let's look at an example. As Figure 16-3 shows, you can set access permissions for groups, or specific users (by specifying the user's logon name). Permissions I've set include:

- Administrators have full control. Generally, Administrators (a group) are trustworthy and have the ability to set permissions.
- Andrew (andrew) is a member of the Users group and has no access. In this case, this is a user who is not an employee, hence, this user's access is very limited.
- SYSTEM is the operating system, and is generally not needed for most shares. Only when you have specific needs do you need to specify SYSTEM.

- Users constitutes the general user community. Client users are members of the Users group and have read access.
- Wadman (Barry Wadman) has read access, but cannot write to the share.

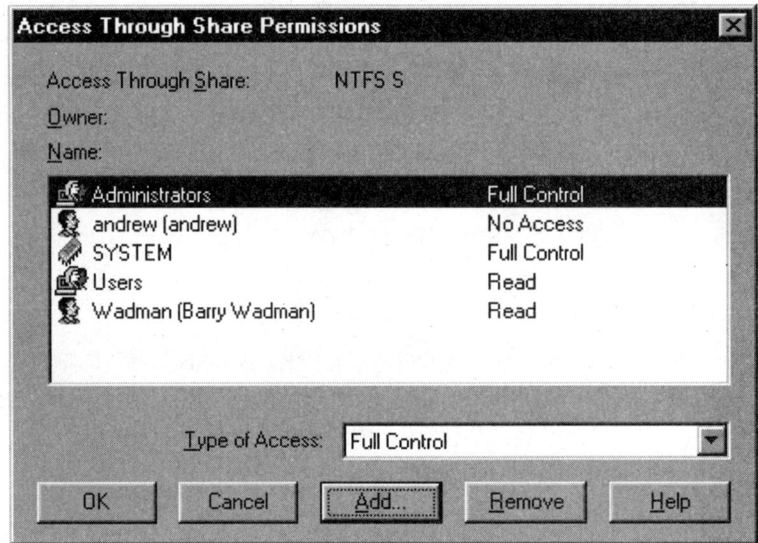

Figure 16-3: The Access Through Share Permissions dialog box.

The above list leaves a few gray areas: first, when you specify a specific user (such as the user andrew (andrew)) that conflicts with a group specification (andrew is a member of the Users group), the user specification takes precedence.

The same rule applies to user Wadman (Barry Wadman). He is allowed read privileges since he must access items in this folder. Any user who is in the Administrators group has full control over this share, and may read, write, or delete objects in this folder as desired.

The Good Old Days...
For the history buffs, do you remember the "good old days" when that server we were using prompted us for each directory on the volume whenever we changed permissions for a volume level share? If there were a thousand directories on the volume, you got a thousand prompts. With that operating system, changing permissions was something you did not do unless it was unavoidable—Windows NT 4 Server has been much better in that respect.

Using the Server Manager or, Who's Using the Share?

Finding out who is using a specific share can be useful. Finding the status of much of what the Windows NT 4 Server is making available on the network is vital! Unfortunately, Server Manager is an example of an application that does not follow the object/folder paradigm—directories are still the word in Server Manager.

Server Manager is capable of doing truly nasty things—you can disconnect a user from a share that has opened files. This may result in the user losing data, and possibly in the file being totally corrupted.

You start the Server Manager program by selecting the Start Menu | Programs | Administrative Tools (Common) | Server Manager. This runs the Server Manager program, as shown in Figure 16-4.

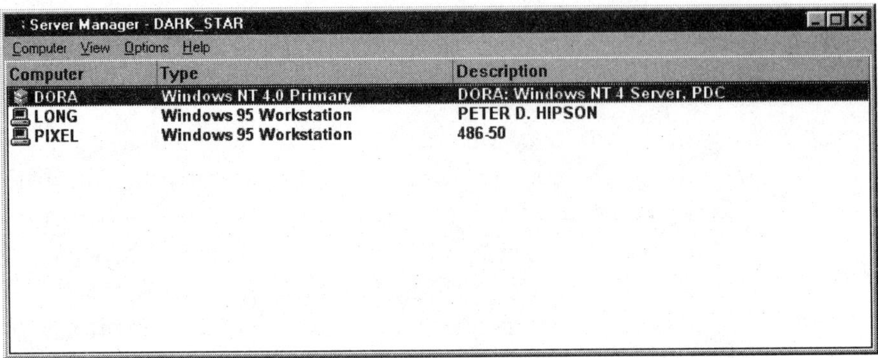

Figure 16-4: Server Manager with one server and two client workstations.

The Server Manager allows you to remotely administer a server too. However, you cannot remotely administer a Windows 95 workstation, since Windows 95 is not a true server and is not configured for remote administration.

The Server Manager program brings together all the server's administration. The Server Manager is a very useful tool that allows the system administrator to view shares, users, and domains.

To view a server's properties with Server Manager, select Computer | Properties from the Server Manager's menu. For example, the Properties for DORA dialog box (see Figure 16-5) allows you to quickly see the number of Sessions, Open Files, File Locks, and Opened Named Pipes.

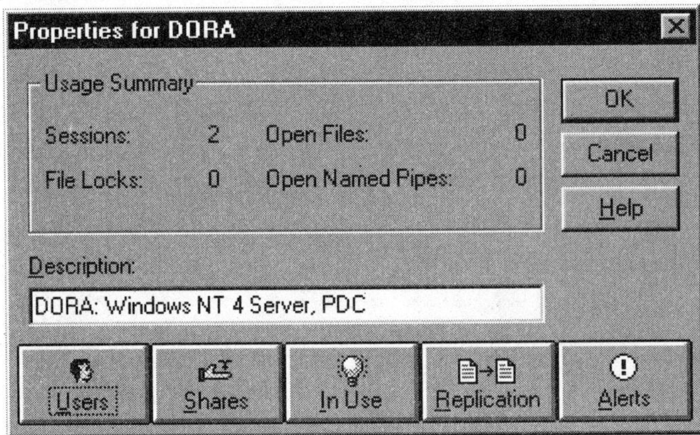

Figure 16-5: The Properties for DORA dialog box.

The server's description is available (and can be reset) in the Properties dialog box. This allows you to rename the server as needed. At the bottom of the Properties dialog box are five buttons. Each button activates a dialog box to help you manage the server. The buttons are as follows:

- Users
- Shares
- In Use
- Replication
- Alerts

Managing Users

To determine what users are currently connected to the server, from the Properties dialog, click the Users button. A User Session dialog appears; for an example, see the User Sessions on DORA dialog box shown in Figure 16-6.

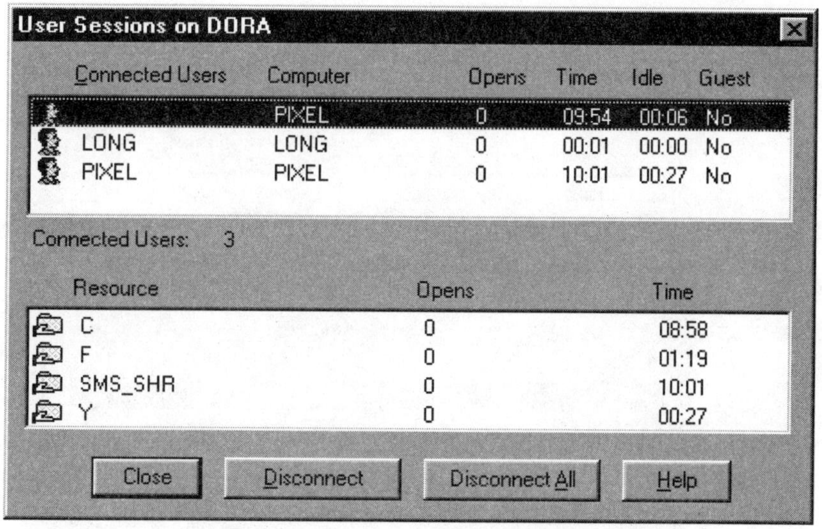

Figure 16-6: The User Sessions on DORA dialog box.

The User Sessions dialog box provides you with a list of connected users and a list of shared resources with the number of opens on each resource. Selecting a connected user in the upper list displays information about connections for the selected user. Many applications only open a file when I/O is being performed; when the file is not being directly used, the file is closed.

Each share indicates how many (if any) files are actually opened by the user. Also indicated is the connect time for the user and the share. The Idle time is useful in determining whether the user is actually using the share.

You can disconnect one or all connected users. However, make sure that users are aware that they may lose data when you disconnect them (i.e., give them the chance to save any data before you disconnect them).

Managing Shares

On the Properties dialog (as shown in 16-5), click the Shares button to display the Shared Resources dialog box. An example of this dialog box is shown in Figure 16-7. The Shared Resources dialog box allows you to manage specific shares.

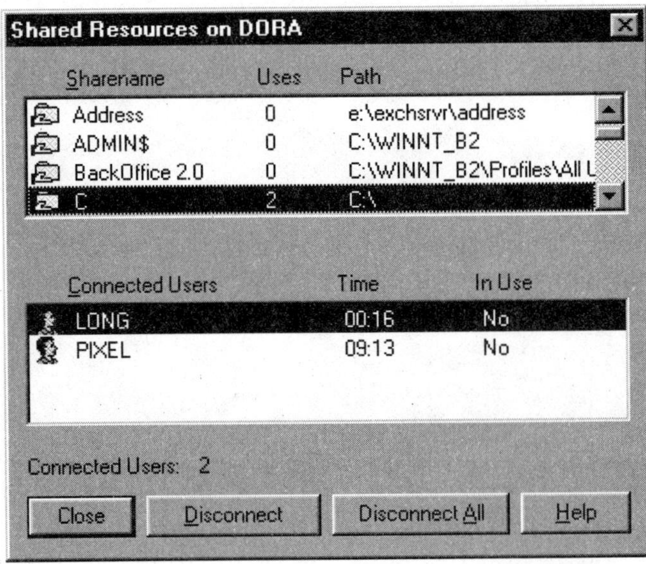

Figure 16-7: The Shared Resources on DORA dialog box.

Listed in the Shared Resources dialog box are shares, number of users of the share (Uses), and the path of the share. For each share you can see who is connected and the amount of time that the user has been connected to the share.

You can disconnect one or all connected users from their shared objects. Again, make sure that your users are aware that they may lose data when you do this.

Managing Objects That Are in Use

On the Properties dialog box (as shown in 16-5), click the In Use button to display the Open Resources dialog box (see Figure 16-8), which shows what objects are actually open (yes, a folder can be *open*, but that is an exceptional condition).

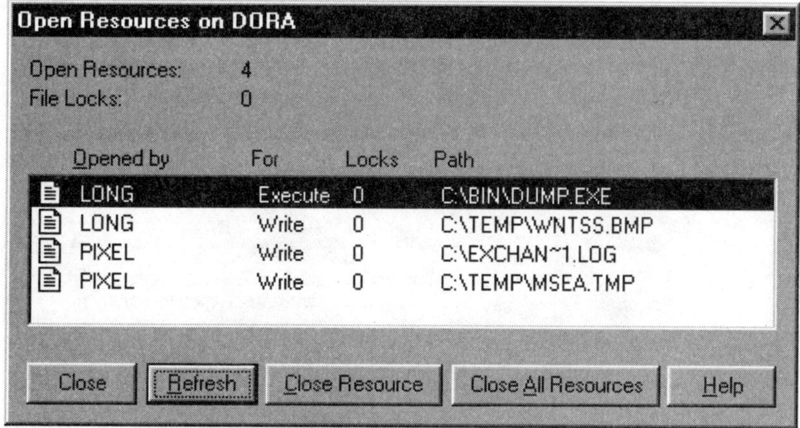

Figure 16-8: The Open Resources on DORA dialog box.

Notice in the example that four items are open. The first item in the list, with the path of C:\BIN\DUMP.EXE, is an application opened in Execute mode. The other three files are currently opened in Write mode.

From the Open Resources dialog, you can close one or all resources. Again, be sure to warn your users that they may lose data when you perform this option. You can refresh the list of resources, too.

Replicating Directories

On the Properties dialog box (as shown in 16-5), click the Replication button to create a duplicate of a directory on a second server (or workstation) and let Windows NT 4 Server update the data contained in the replicated directory. An example of the Directory Replication dialog box is shown in Figure 16-9.

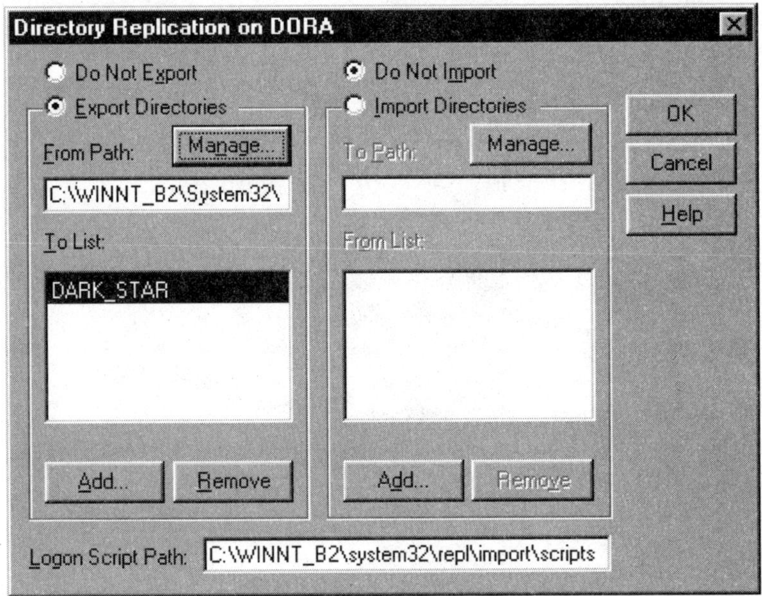

Figure 16-9: The Directory Replication on DORA dialog box.

Windows NT 4 Server supports both import and export directory replication. Click the Manage button to display the Manage Exported Directories or Manage Imported Directories dialog box. In the Manage directories dialog boxes, you choose which directories you wish to have replicated.

Managing Alerts

On the Properties dialog box (as shown in 16-5), click the Alerts button to display the Alerts dialog box. An example of the Alerts dialog box is shown in Figure 16-10. Use the Alerts dialog box to

manage messages that are sent (generally automatically) when an event occurs. For example, an alert might be sent in response to a specified event, such as a drive being nearly full.

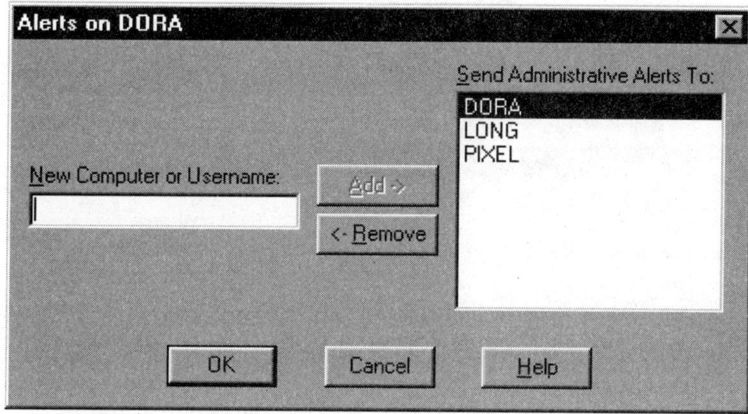

Figure 16-10: The Alerts on DORA dialog box.

For the recipient of an alert message to receive the message, the Messenger service must be running. Be sure to start the Alerter service on the computer that is to originate the alert.

Figure 16-11 shows an administrative alert that I received telling me that the C drive was almost full. Yes, the message does say that I only have 161MB of free space, but percentage-wise, that is less than 10% free!

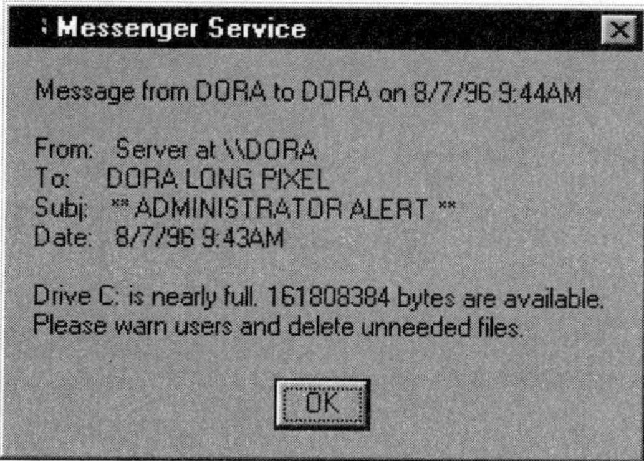

Figure 16-11: An alert message from Messenger Service.

Managing Shared Directories

Use the Server Manager's Computer | Shared Directories menu to display the Shared Directories dialog box. An example of the Shared Directories dialog box is shown in Figure 16-12.

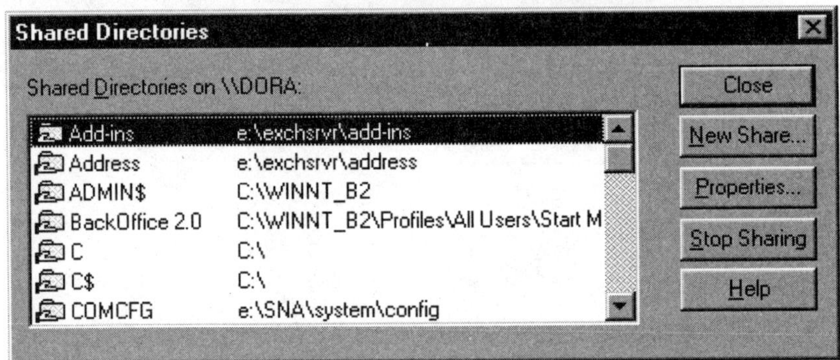

Figure 16-12: The Shared Directories on \\DORA dialog box.

The Shared Directories dialog box lists all shared directories and other shared objects, such as IPCs (InterProcess Calls) and printers. Shared printers are not manageable under the Server Manager—you must use the Printer Manager program (Start Menu | Settings | Printers) to manage shared printers.

You can create a new share, stop sharing a directory, and display the properties of shared directories. The properties, with the exception of the share name, are all modifiable using the Share Properties dialog (Figure 16-13). Once a share has been created, the only way to change the name is to create a new share with identical properties to the old share, then delete the old share.

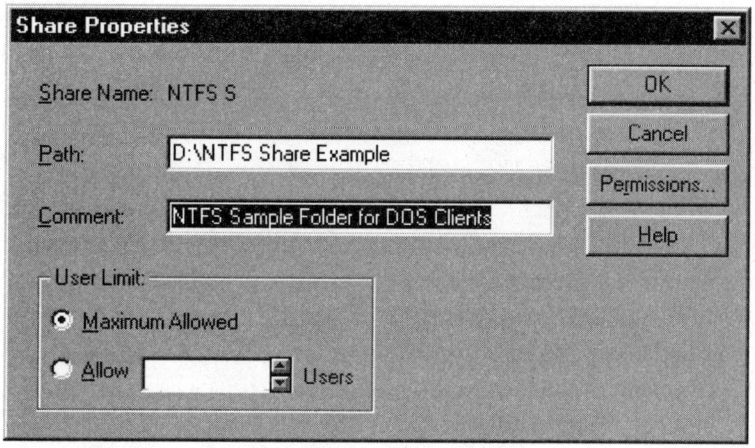

Share Properties

Share Name: NTFS S

Path: D:\NTFS Share Example

Comment: NTFS Sample Folder for DOS Clients

User Limit:

Maximum Allowed

Allow Users

OK

Cancel

Permissions...

Help

Figure 16-13: The Share Properties dialog box.

Managing Services

The Server Manager manages services on the server. Use the menu selection Computer | Services to display the Services dialog box. An example of the Services dialog box is shown in Figure 16-14.

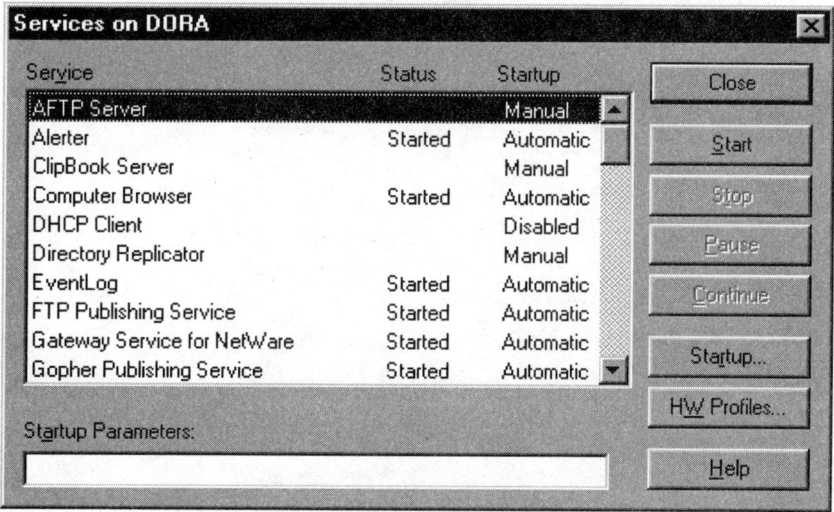

Figure 16-14: The Services on DORA dialog box.

You can manage each service in the same way that you manage services from the Control Panel's Services applet. In fact, the user interface is identical for both!

You can start, stop, pause, or continue any service. You can start a service that is not started. You can stop or pause a service that has been started. Lastly, you can continue a service that has been paused.

Click the Startup button on the Service dialog box, as shown in Figure 16-14, to display the Service dialog box. An example of the Service dialog box is shown in Figure 16-15. The Service dialog box allows you to set or provide the following:

- How the service is started (either automatically, manually, or disabled).
- Whether the service will use the system account (most services do).
- When using the system account—whether the service is allowed to interact with the desktop (most services do not).
- For services that do not use the system account, you must provide an account name and password for the service.

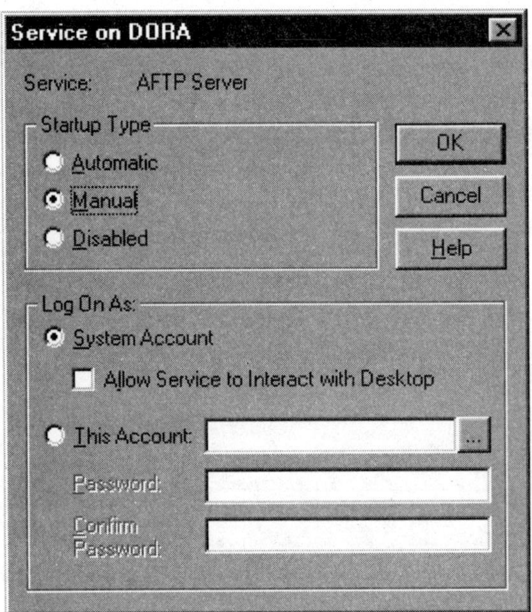

Figure 16-15: The Service on DORA (for AFTP Server) dialog box.

Sending Messages

The Send Message feature of Server Manager allows you to send a message to all users who are connected to the server that Server Manager is currently managing. You provide the message's text, as Figure 16-16 shows. To send messages, select Computer | Send Message from the menu.

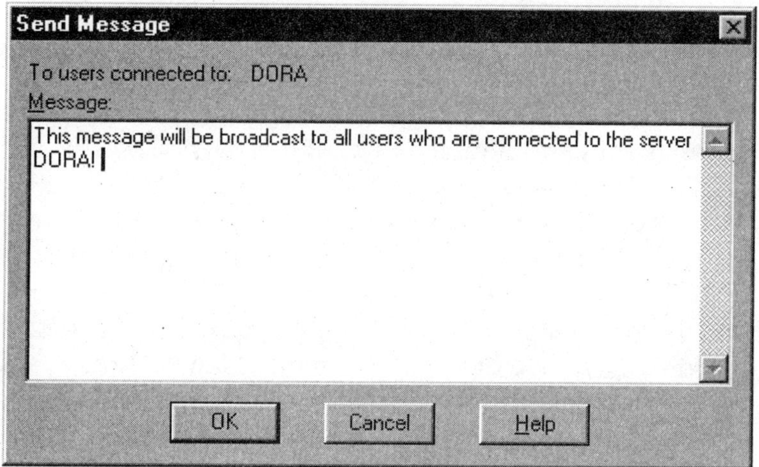

Figure 16-16: The Send Message dialog box.

The result of the message in Figure 16-16 is shown in Figure 16-17.

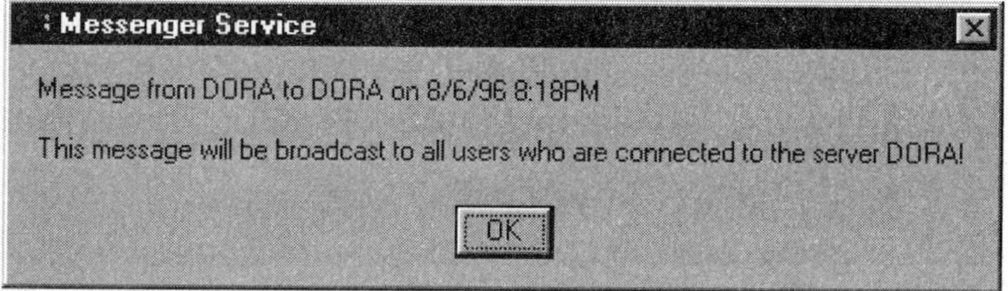

Figure 16-17: The Messenger Service displaying a message.

Fortunately, I was the only user connected to DORA that evening!

Working With Primary Domain Controllers

Use the Server Manager's Computer | Promote to Primary Domain Controller menu selection to promote the currently managed computer (which must be a backup domain controller, or BDC) to function as the primary domain controller, or PDC.

Setting up a server as a PDC or BDC is covered in Chapter 3, "Installing Windows NT 4 Server."

If the currently managed server is already the PDC, then this menu selection is disabled. If, for some reason, the network detects that the PDC has failed, then a BDC is automatically promoted if possible. You can make the domain controller switch easier by manually promoting a BDC. If there is no PDC, users may experience difficulties logging on and using shares.

Two scenarios are possible: The current PDC is automatically demoted to a BDC when you manually promote a BDC to the PDC. A PDC that fails is automatically demoted to a BDC, and if there is an available BDC, it is automatically promoted. You can only have one PDC on a network. Hence, if the system cannot automatically demote the current PDC, then *you* must do so manually. Select the PDC you want to demote, and select Computer | Demote to Backup Domain Controller.

Use the Server Manager's Computer | Synchronize Entire Domain and Computer | Synchronize with Primary Domain Controller menu selections to either synchronize the entire domain or synchronize a specific server with the PDC.

Generally, this task is done by the network automatically; however, due to errors (such as the inability to connect to the PDC) synchronization may not take place.

Not all networks have both a PDC and a BDC—a network with a single server has a PDC without a BDC. Domains enhance security for Windows 95, for example.

Working With Domains

You can add a computer (a Windows NT 4 Server or Windows NT 4 Workstation), or a BDC (Windows NT 4 Server) to the domain, using the Computer | Add to Domain menu selection.

The Add Computer To Domain dialog box, shown in Figure 16-18, allows you to specify the computer type (only add Windows NT computers, which are part of the Windows NT domain security), and the Computer Name.

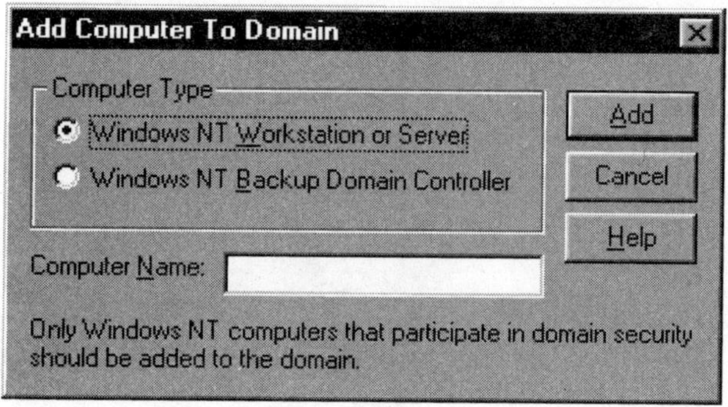

Figure 16-18: The Add Computer To Domain dialog box.

You do not need to add Windows 95 clients to the domain.

To remove a computer from the domain, select the computer in the list, and then select Computer | Remove from Domain from Server Manager's menu.

Once the computer has been removed from the domain, then the user must remove the computer from their workstation (using the Control Panel's Network applet) and specify a new domain (or work group).

The Server Manager's Computer | Select Domain menu selection displays the Select Domain dialog box (see Figure 16-19). Select the domain from the Select Domain dialog box.

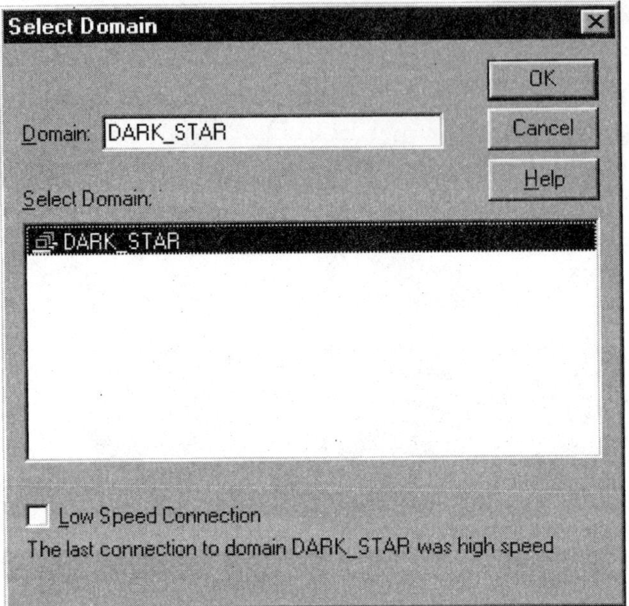

Figure 16-19: The Select Domain dialog box.

You can establish the connection to the domain as either low or high speed. For most, directly connected networks (which are not going through slow modems), do not select the Low Speed Connection check box. Server Manager also reminds you of the speed of the previous connection.

Sharing Printers

Sharing printers is the second most common server task that a general purpose server does. Though it is common for a file server to also function as a printer server, there is no reason why you cannot have a dedicated printer server when you have a large number of printers and a lot of printer output.

Windows NT 4 Server is capable of remote printer management and supports network-connected printers. It is common to have laser printers with standard network interface cards built in. A networked printer has a network address (which is given to Windows NT 4 Server) and then Windows NT 4 Server spools printer output to the networked printer.

Spooling

If you are new to the network environment (and didn't work with large computers years ago) the term *spool* may be new to you. The term comes from the "good old days" when large mainframe computers would temporarily write printer output to reel-to-reel tapes (which look like spools) for later printing. The process was called spooling, and usually there was a spooling operator who managed printer output. We don't store printer output to tape anymore, but we continue to use the term.

All printer sharing management is done from the Printers management program. Select Start Menu | Settings | Printers to start the Printer Manager.

The Printer Manager, like many parts of Windows NT 4 Server, is an Explorer-based application—a standardized user interface allows you to quickly learn how to display information (large icons, small icons, list, or details), and how to manipulate each object.

In the Printer Manager (see Figure 16-20), there is an object titled "Add Printer," which allows you to quickly configure a new printer. There is also an object for each printer you have defined. The icon indicates, with a hand, that the printer is shared—both printers in Figure 16-20 are shared.

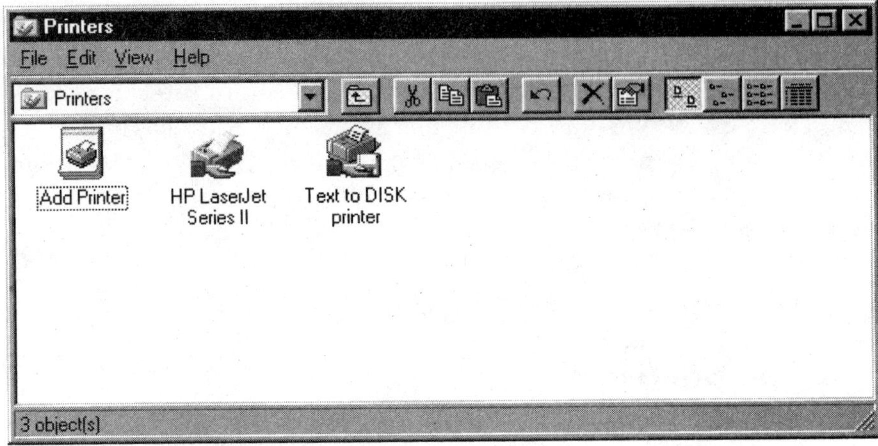

Figure 16-20: The Printers Manager dialog box.

Adding Printers

The Add Printer Wizard steps you through the process of creating a printer. You can add both locally connected printers and networked printer servers. Using a network-connected printer server allows you to print documents remotely, as any client workstation does.

The first page in the Add Printer Wizard is shown in Figure 16-21. In this example, I am going to install a locally connected printer (an IBM Lexmark 4039), and share this printer with workstations on the network. In Figure 16-21, I click the My Computer radio button, then click the Next button.

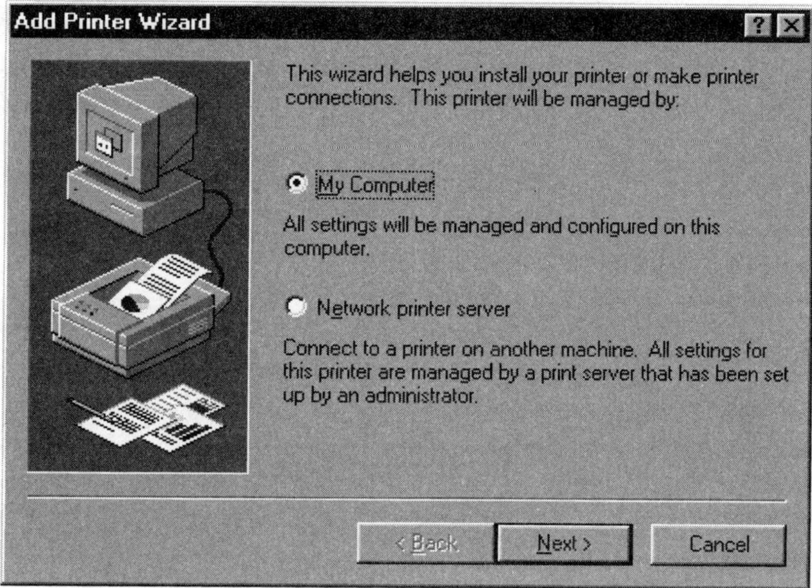

Figure 16-21: The Add Printer Wizard, page one.

Specifying the Printer Port

The second page in the Add Printer Wizard (Figure 16-22) requires that you select the port to which the printer is connected. Most printers are connected to LPT1; however, for installations that have multiple printers, Windows NT 4 Server supports both serial and parallel ports.

You can select the FILE: port, also. When a printer is connected to the FILE: port, all output is written to the disk (with a filename that the user specifies) in print image format. Later, you can copy this file to the actual device for printing. This technique is useful when you need to print the output at a different site.

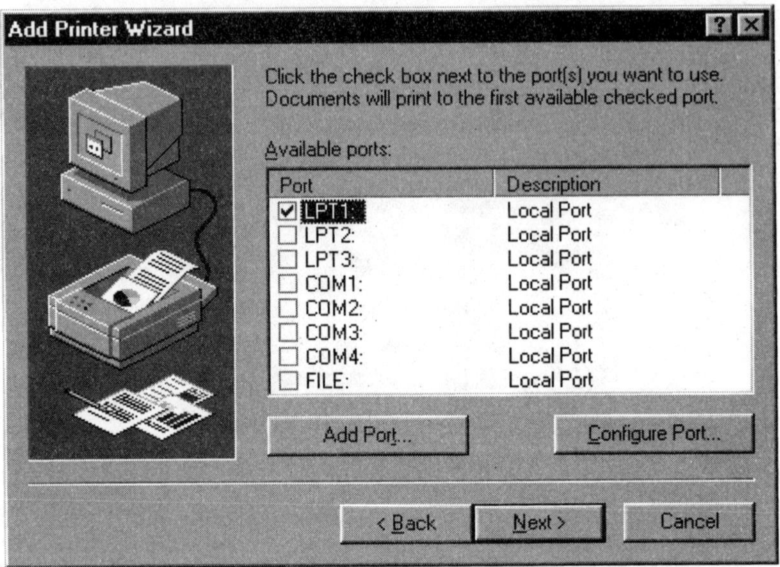

Figure 16-22: The Add Printer Wizard, page two.

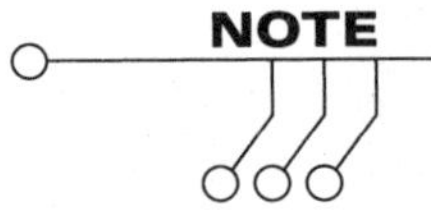

With output to FILE:, some printers generate large output files. Make sure that sufficient disk space exists for the output file.

You can add new ports (some systems have more serial or parallel ports than are indicated, or if there is a need for a special port, such as described below) and you can configure the ports as well.

Default port types supported by Windows NT 4 Server include local ports, Digital Network Port, and PJL Language Monitor ports. Figure 16-23 shows the Printer Ports dialog, where I am adding a Digital Network Port. The Digital Network Port is a printer connected to the server using the TCP/IP Ethernet network.

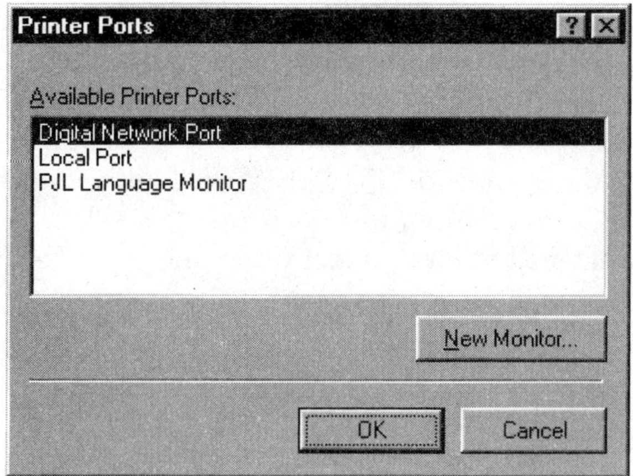

Figure 16-23: The Printer Ports dialog, adding a Digital Network Port.

When I select OK, the Add Port - Digital Network Port dialog box (Figure 16-24) displays. In this dialog box, select the Port Type (you can select from a number of different printer types, or a generic PrintServer compatible printer). Also fill in the Port Information's Name and Address fields. The Port Name defaults to the Port Information's Name field; however, you can override this setting if desired. Click the Options button to set the printer options (printer options vary with each port type selected).

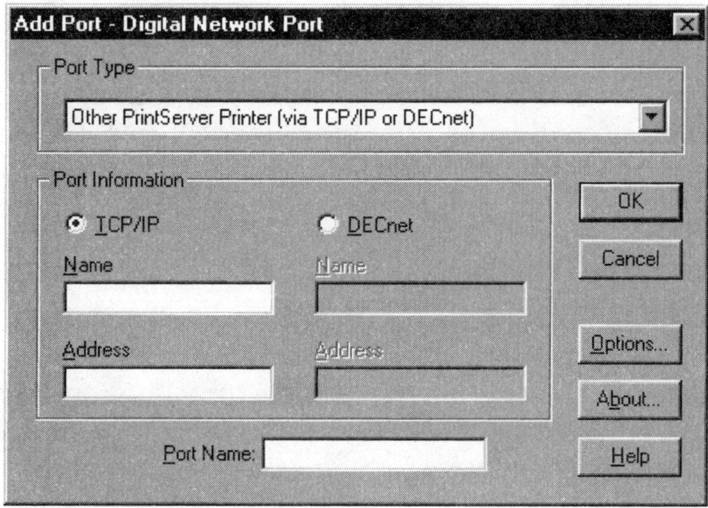

Figure 16-24: The Add Port - Digital Network Port dialog box.

Once you have added a port, select (and configure, if desired) the port in the Add Printer Wizard second page.

Specifying the Type of Printer

The third page in the Add Printer Wizard allows you to select the printer type. First, in the Manufacturers list, select the manufacturer of your printer. Next select the specific printer from the Printers list.

What happens when your printer manufacturer or printer type is not listed?

Not every printer manufacturer or printer type is listed. Though we all would like to have our printers listed, sometimes this just doesn't happen!

The first thing to do is to see if the printer manufacturer has written a Windows NT 4 driver for your printer. If so, then you can use the Have Disk button to add this printer driver to your system.

Second, if the printer manufacturer has not written a Windows NT 4 driver for your printer (usually because the printer is either too new or too old) then you should consult the printer documentation to see if the printer *emulates* any other printer types. If the printer does emulate a printer that is listed in the Add Printer Wizard list of printers, then you can select the emulated printer type and get the same features that are available on the printer that your printer emulates.

Third, if the printer does not emulate any supported printers, then you can try a bit of hit-or-miss. Select a similar printer from the same manufacturer. Try the printer (print a few test documents) and see if it works. If it does, then great, if not then select another printer type. If you are lucky you may find a driver that you can use even though it is for a different printer!

Finally, you could sell the printer and buy one that is supported by Windows NT 4 Server. Drastic measure!

In our example, we select the Lexmark 4039 LaserPrinter Plus printer, as Figure 16-25 shows.

Figure 16-25: The Lexmark 4039 selected in the Add Printer Wizard, page three.

Once you have found and selected your printer, click the Next button to display the Add Printer Wizard's fourth page (Figure 16-26).

Specifying a Printer Name & Sharing Options

In the fourth page (see Figure 16-26), you must specify a printer name (or accept the default). You must also decide if you want this printer to be the default printer for all of your Windows-based programs. This selection has no effect on users who connect to the printer using the network—it is only for your applications! You can have only one default printer defined. Setting a new printer as the default overrides the existing default printer, if there is one.

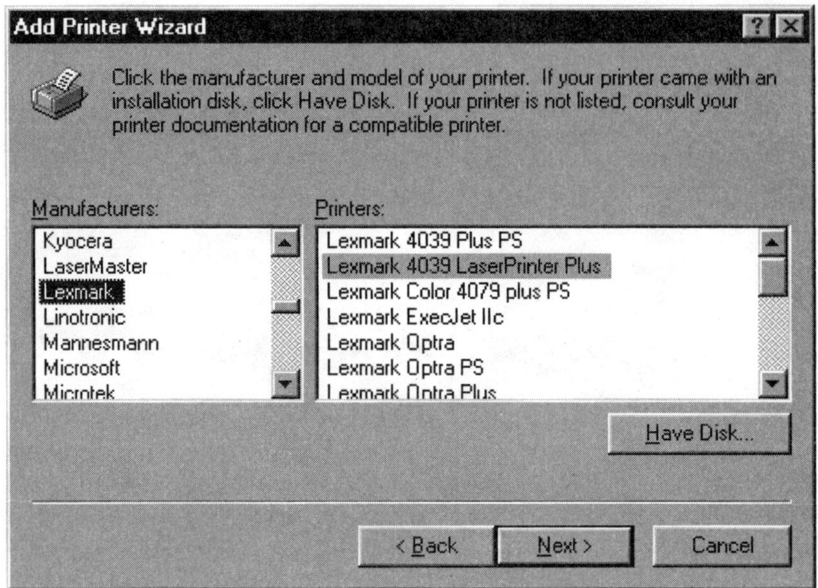

Figure 16-26: The Add Printer Wizard, fourth page.

The fifth page of the Add Printer Wizard allows you to set the sharing options. Generally (this is a server, after all!) you share your printers. You must click the Shared radio button and provide a share name (or accept the default). You must also indicate what type of network clients will use this printer. Choices for network clients include Windows 95, Windows NT 3.1, Windows NT 3.5x, or Windows NT 4.0 (both Intel and RISC processors). Select *all* applicable clients from the list, as shown in Figure 16-27.

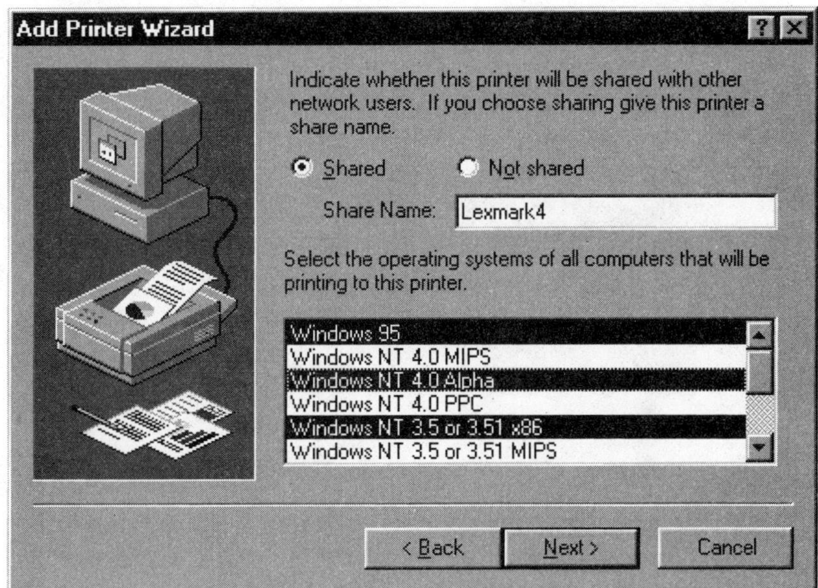

Figure 16-27: Add Printer Wizard sharing page, fifth page.

Printing a Test Page

The sixth page of the Add Printer Wizard (Figure 16-28) prompts you to print a test page. If the printer is connected and ready to print it is a good idea to print the test page. Testing the printer driver and port configuration ensures that all is working correctly! If you don't have the printer connected and ready, do not attempt to print a test page! Click the Finish button when you have finished.

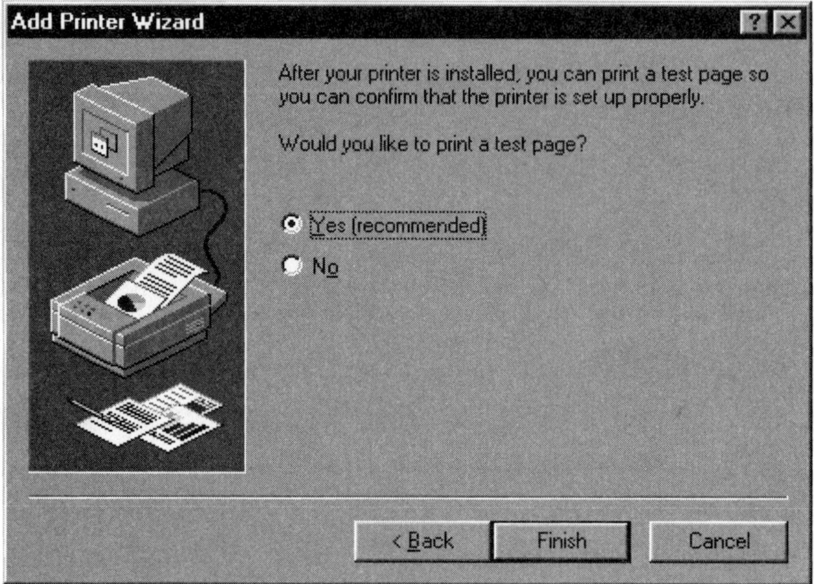

Figure 16-28: Add Printer Wizard: Print a test page?

Specifying Printer Properties

Once you have completed the installation, the necessary files are copied from the installation CD. The Printer's Properties dialog box displays, allowing you to configure the printer to your specific needs.

The Properties dialog box (though each printer may have a slightly different properties dialog, it is usually similar to the example we use here) for the HP LaserJet II printer (which is one of the most commonly used printer types today) is shown below in Figure 16-29.

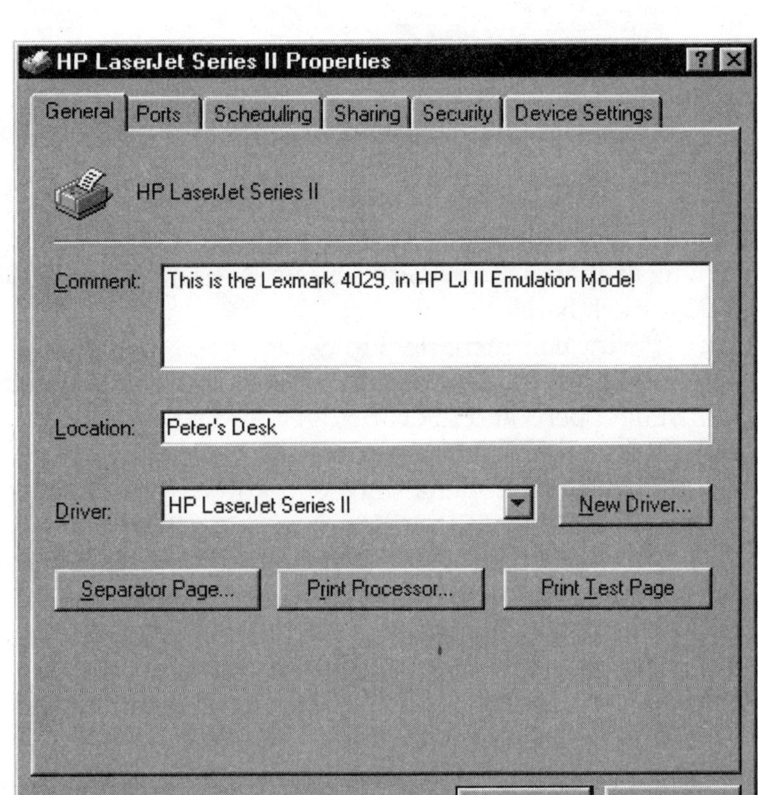

Figure 16-29: The HP LaserJet Series II Properties dialog box.

The printer properties dialog box has six tabs. Each of the following tabs is covered below:

- General
- Ports
- Scheduling
- Sharing
- Security
- Device Settings

General Tab

Use the printer properties General tab (Figure 16-29) to set the printer's comment, location, and driver. Generally, both the comment and location describe the printer and the printer's location. Printers do get lost, so a meaningful location is useful—tying the printer's location to a person (as I did) is only good as long as that person doesn't move. Around here, that is a given—I'm stuck here!

Use the comment field to describe any special feature that this printer supports, including installed font and memory cartridges, installed pens and ink cartridges, and so on.

Use the Driver drop-down list to select any currently installed printer driver. If there is no compatible printer driver installed, then you can install a new driver using the New Driver button.

Use the Separator Page button to specify a separator page. The separator page is placed at the beginning of each print job, allowing multiple users to easily identify their output. Separator pages are stored in text files with the extension of .SEP, usually in the WinNT\System32 folder. There are three default separator pages supplied with Windows NT 4 Server.

- SYSPRINT.SEP—A Postscript separator page. Prints a page before each printed document. This page contains user and job information that identifies print jobs.
- PCL.SEP—A Postscript separator page. Enables PCL on dual-language HP LaserJet printers.
- PSCRIPT.SEP—A PCL separator page. Enables PostScript on dual-language HP LaserJet printers.

You can create separator pages yourself, using any text-based editor. The PCL escape codes described below (in Table 16-1) are used to create the separator page. (For PostScript separator pages, see the SYSPRINT.SEP separator file.)

Escape string	Description
\	The escape character begins the separator file. The first nonblank character in the file is defined as the escape character. Microsoft conventions set the escape character as a backslash, which this book uses also. All other escape strings start with the escape character.
\B\M	The \B\M escape string causes text to print double-width characters. This mode is canceled with the \U escape code.
\B\S	The \B\S escape string causes text to print single-width characters. This mode is cancelled with the \U escape code.
\D	The print job's date prints when you use \D. The format of the date is the same format you define with the Control Panel's Regional Settings applet.
\E	The \E page eject escape string is used to eject the separator page from the printer. The separator page can actually be more than one page long. Be sure to force an eject at the end of the separator page.
\Fpathandfilename	Used to print the contents of the file specified (use a fully qualified filename). A new line is printed on the separator page, then the file's contents are printed, without any processing.
\Hxx	The \Hxx sends a nonprintable character code xx, specified in hexadecimal, to the printer. The use of this escape string is dependent on your understanding of the printer's actions upon receipt of special characters.
\I	To print the print job number, use \I.

Escape string	Description
\Labcd	Prints literal text (represented by abcd in the example). All text following the \L escape string, until the next escape character, is printed.
\N	To print the name of the user who printed the job, use \N (again, where \ is the escape character).
n	The *n* escape string (where n is between 0 and 9), causes the printer to eject one or more lines. Specifying zero causes printing to begin on the next line.
\T	The print job's time can be printed using \T. The format of the date is the same format you define with the Control Panel's Regional Settings applet.
\U	The \U escape string turns off the \B\M and \B\S escape modes.
\W*nn*	The width of the separator page is defined with the \W*nn* escape string. Width can be up to 256 characters, though the default of 80 is adequate for most jobs.

Table 16-1: PCL escape codes.

You can specify only one separator page for a printer. To have multiple separator pages, you must create a custom separator page that incorporates all the features you need.

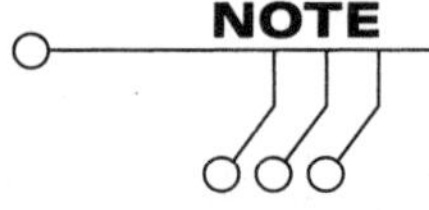

You can define multiple printers for a single device, each printer having a different separator page. One printer could be defined to have special paper requirements, another could have a different default font, and so forth.

The Print Processor button is used to specify the print processor (or datatypes) for this printer. Unless an application or system specifically needs to change the print processor, you should use the default.

The Print Test Page button allows you to print a test page to the printer.

Ports Tab

Use the Ports tab, as shown in Figure 16-30, to reset the physical port to which the printer is connected. This tab works exactly like the second page in the Add Printer Wizard (Figure 16-22), with one exception: you can enable bi-directional printing for those printers that support this mode.

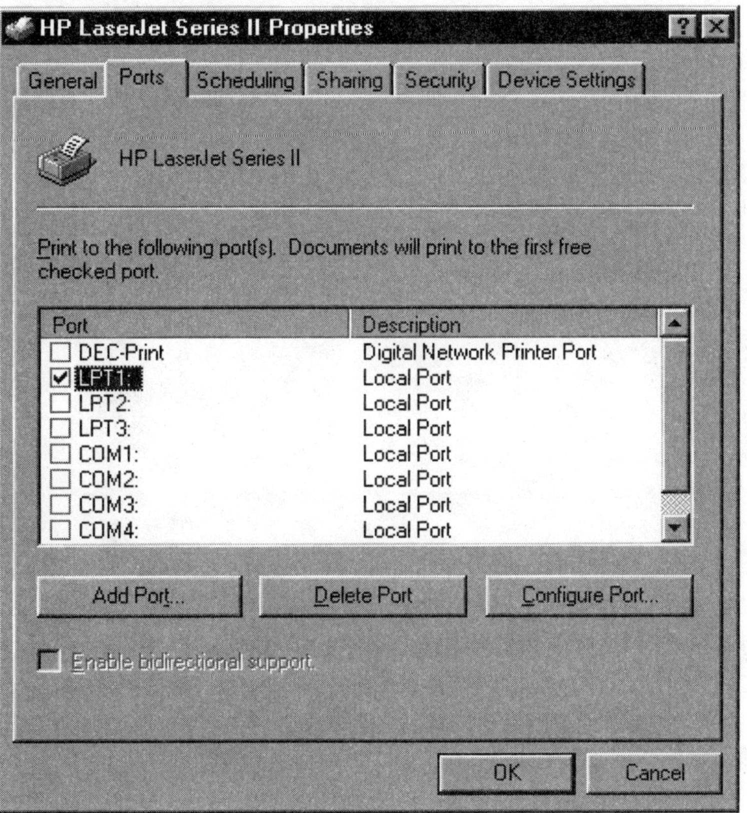

Figure 16-30: The Printer Properties, Ports tab.

Scheduling Tab

Use the Scheduling tab, as shown in Figure 16-31, to schedule when the printer is available, the printer's priority, how spooled documents are printed (either as soon as there are pages to print, or only after the entire job has been received), and other miscellaneous scheduling options.

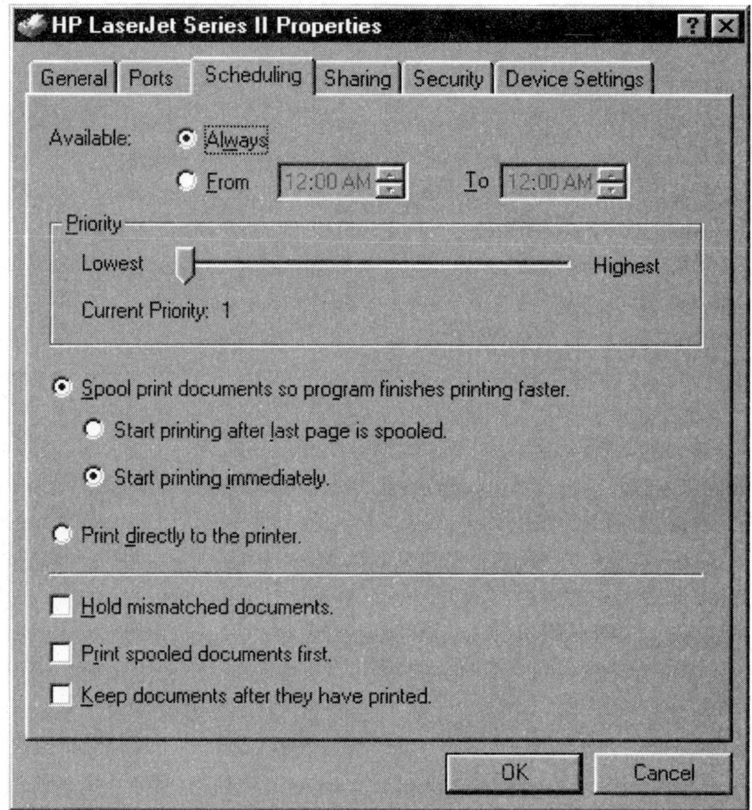

Figure 16-31: The Printer Properties, Scheduling tab.

A few hints for the Scheduling tab: First, for larger networks where the printers are generally busy, set the printer to "Start printing after the last page is spooled" so that other users won't have to wait for a slow application. Avoid "Print directly to the printer" unless you are experiencing some difficulties in getting the printer to print correctly. Don't select "Keep documents after they have printed" unless you have a very large hard drive available.

Sharing Tab

Use the Sharing tab, as shown in Figure 16-32, to reset the sharing properties for the printer. The Sharing tab works like the fifth page of the Add Printer Wizard, as shown in Figure 16-27.

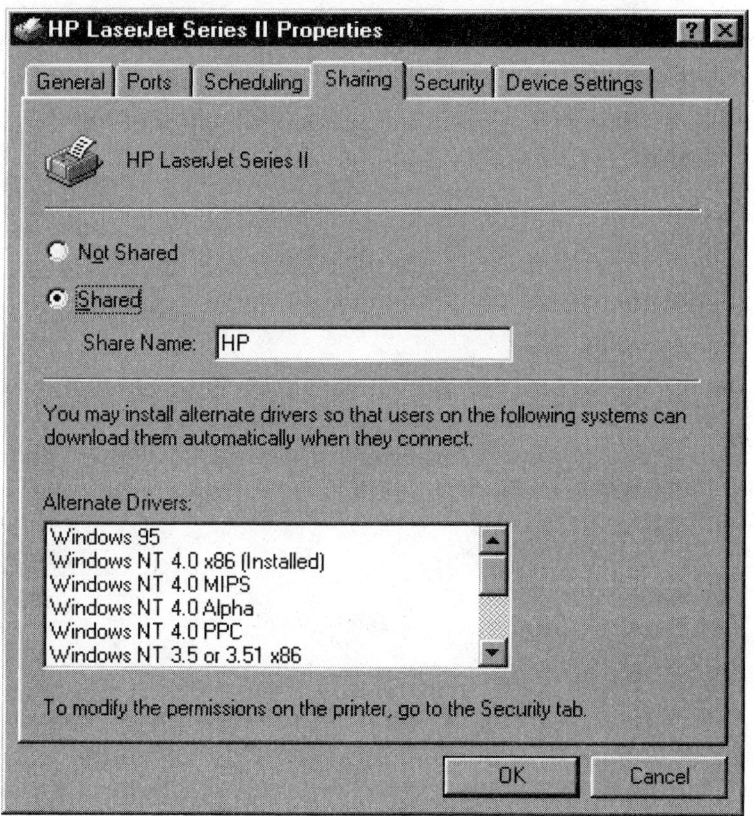

Figure 16-32: The Printer Properties, Sharing tab.

When you installed the printer, if you did not select the correct clients, the Sharing tab will allow you to add new client drivers.

Security Tab

Use the Security tab, as shown in Figure 16-33, to set the permissions, auditing, and ownership for the printer. Chapter 17, "Security & Users," describes security.

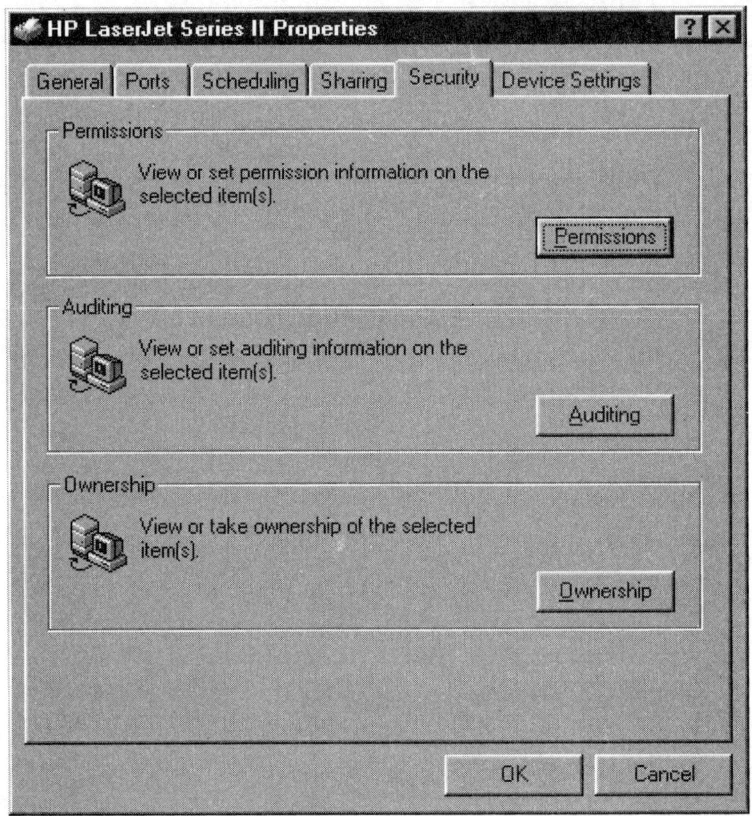

Figure 16-33: The Printer Properties, Security tab.

Device Settings Tab

Use the Device Settings tab, as shown in Figure 16-34, to set the printers' settings. Each printer can be different (some printers have only one paper source, some do not have font cartridges, some have fixed memory), but generally the concepts for this page remain the same—you are defining the printer's paper, fonts, memory, and graphics. Color printers may also allow you to define color-related items, while PostScript printers usually allow setting Job timeout and Wait timeout values.

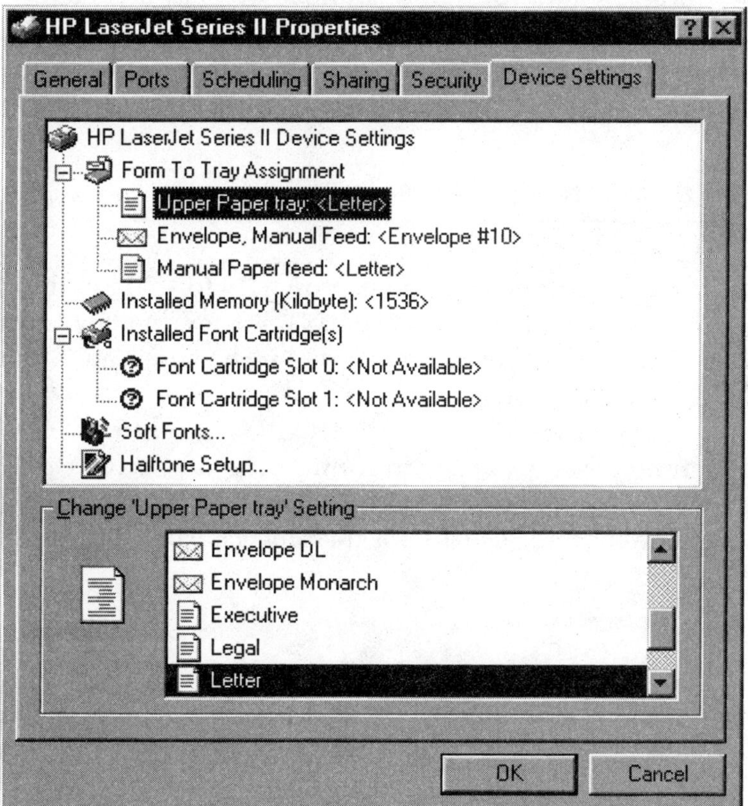

Figure 16-34: The Printer Properties, Device Settings tab.

Other Sharing

In addition to the items covered in this chapter, you may wish to review the topic "Configuring Services for Macintosh" in Chapter 6, "Interacting With Other LANs." File resources shared to Macintosh clients are slightly different than for a PC.

IPCs (InterProcess Calls) are shared as well. There is, with a domain controller (but not with a stand-alone server) a share created by the system called IPC$, which helps manage logon authentication. You do not need to make any changes to this share.

An excellent description of IPCs is found in the TechNet (see Appendix B for information about TechNet) document "Operating Characteristics and Restrictions of Named Pipes."

Moving On

In this chapter we showed you how to share both printers and files. Virtually all Windows NT 4 Server installations share files, and many share printers as well. Sharing is an important part of any network server.

The next chapter, "Security & Users," moves into setting up users, user groups, and configuring the security on your Windows NT 4 Server system. Security issues between NTFS and FAT file systems and security for the physical site are also addressed in the next chapter.

17

Security & Users

In this chapter, I cover both system and physical security, users, groups, permissions, ownership, and other issues related to security.

Security is paramount to networks. Whenever a server is used, there is a need to maintain confidentiality for both user and corporate data.

Threats to security come from both inside the organization (disgruntled or simply unethical employees) and outside (hackers, visitors, and others who may or may not have a relationship with the organization).

System Security

When I say system security, I am talking about non-physical security. System security means securing from hackers and other people who should not have access.

Many companies take the mistaken attitude that "break-ins happen to the other guy." Heck, *someone* has to be that other guy! And since I've protected my system, it may well be you who gets hit.

What happens, and why? System attacks can come from outside sources (usually through either your RAS dial-in connection, perhaps a permanent Internet connection), while internal attacks can result from a number of factors, most of which are easily prevented:

- Employees whose employment is being terminated, either by their choice, or the company's. Many companies tend to think that an employee who has resigned is not a threat. Wrong. More than one company has lost their customer list to a competitor when a departing sales manager carries the list to their new job. Whenever an employee leaves, immediately remove their computer access privileges!

  We won't even discuss what happens when an employee has been dismissed, and that employee's computer access privileges have not been terminated—files, entire drives formatted, subtle changes made in databases and accounting systems, and all sorts of vandalism and mischief are frequent.

- Dissatisfied and unethical employees are a constant threat. Oftentimes these people are not recognized—audit policies (discussed below) can be an effective tool in spotting misdeeds and trespasses by employees.

- Outside vendors and other non-employees who have access to the system should be monitored. Be cautious about items being removed from the computer room, especially when critical or sensitive data is being managed.

- When a drive fails, it is usually possible that the data on the drive can be recovered. You may choose not to bother recovering the data (possibly an expensive task, unnecessary if there are adequate backups of the data). The drive, if returned to a dealer, given away, or tossed in the trash, could have the data recovered, thereby compromising your security.

- When a drive is removed from service, radical steps, including physical destruction of the drive, may be called for. A few well-placed whacks with the office hammer will render the typical hard drive permanently, and irrevocably, unreadable!

If the drive must be returned to the manufacturer for warranty service, ship it directly to the manufacturer yourself if possible: don't delegate this task to the dealer, as you have no control over what happens to the drive once it leaves your premises.

Network Security

Is your network secure? Probably not. Cables and wires often go to unused offices (that may not even be located in your company). Imagine this: someone moves into an office, plugs into the network jack on the wall, and ends up connected to the network for the company next door! If you are that company next door, this can be a problem!

With 10BaseT and other UTP (Unshielded Twisted Pair) networks, which use cabling that resembles telephone wires, the cables are frequently all routed to a "cable closet" that is connected with similar "cable closets" on other floors in the building. It is easy to inadvertently connect to the wrong cable and find your network routed to virtually any location in the building. Frequent cable audits, determining that each hub jack is routed to a workstation you can account for, are necessary. Unannounced spot checks can be useful in detecting problems.

Networks made of fiber optic media are much more secure—it is very difficult to "tap" into a fiber optic connection.

Wireless networks are becoming more common. Once considered toys, a wireless network today can save literally 50% of the cost of wiring a complex network. Most wireless networks are reasonably secure; however, you must evaluate security on a case-by-case basis.

Wireless networks come in two varieties: infrared and radio-based. Both cover a limited area, but the radio-based units are better able to penetrate walls, floors, and ceilings. Infrared units don't go through walls (though some windows may allow some signal to escape); however, infrared units are typically useable only where there are cubicles with open areas through which the infrared signal can pass—infrared is really "line of sight."

Internet and Intranets

Today it seems that everyone's goal is to be "on the information superhighway," the Internet. This book has devoted lots of coverage to Internet topics, and I am sure your computer, if it's not already connected to the Internet, will be connected one day.

The Internet is so big that it is difficult to estimate its size. On the Internet are students, hackers, children, even politicians! The bottom line is that there are people out there who are just waiting for your computer to be placed on the Internet so they can try to break into it. With Windows NT you are at a slight advantage—many of the evildoers are oriented towards UNIX-based computers (once almost 100% UNIX-based, the Internet continues to have a very large community of UNIX machines).

The most common protection against an attack via the Internet is a device called a *firewall*. This device is placed between your network and the Internet. Programmed with the IP addresses of those networks and computers that are not considered to be a security risk, the firewall totally blocks attempts to access your network from the Internet by others.

A number of companies produce firewalls, including Cisco, 3Com, Cypress, and Network 1. You should contact each of these companies to determine their offerings.

Securing RAS

RAS (Remote Access Service) can be made very secure if you are able to work with the restrictions that security requires. First, when configuring RAS you may choose to allow only those clients that follow the Windows NT security model.

First, you manage RAS configuration from the Control Panel's Network applet, by setting the Remote Access Server network service's properties. Figure 17-1 shows the Remote Access Setup dialog that displays when you click Properties in the Network applet.

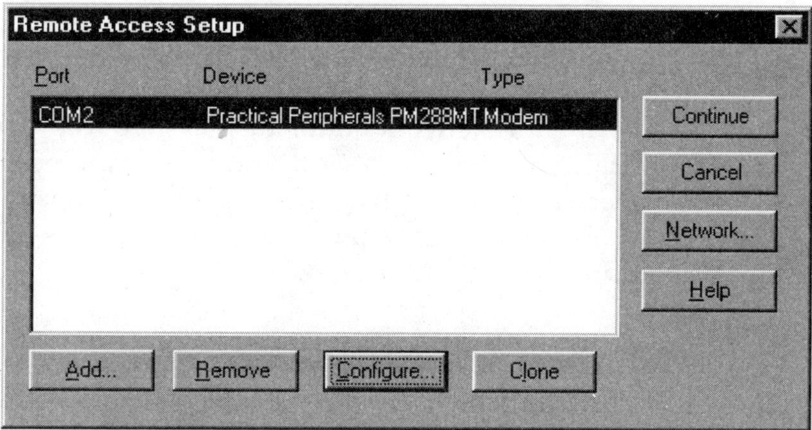

Figure 17-1: The Remote Access Setup dialog box.

As Figure 17-2 shows, each modem (there is one modem, connected to COM2 in my example) in the RAS pool may be configured to:

- Dial out only—the modem is used for DUN (Dial-up Networking) only, and no incoming calls are received on this modem. The phone can ring for hours, Windows NT 4 Server won't answer.
- Receive calls only—the modem is used for RAS only, all incoming calls are answered, but users are unable to use this modem for dialing out.
- Dial out and Receive calls—allows both incoming and outgoing calls on this modem.

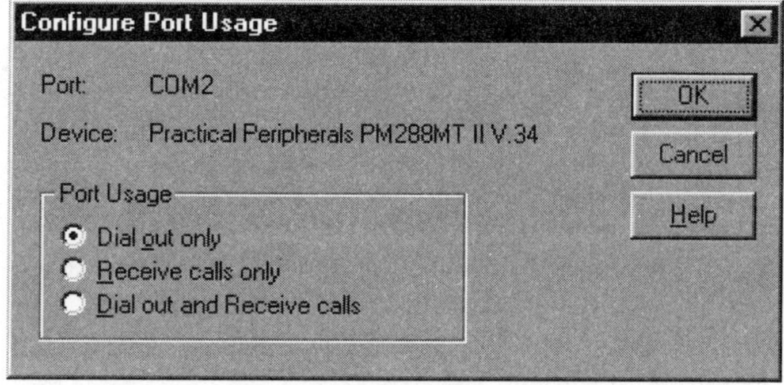

Figure 17-2: The Configure Port Usage dialog.

If you are not hosting clients (no one will be calling in to your computer) then set the modem to Dial out only. That way a hacker will not be able to enter your system from the modem.

Clicking the Network button displays the Network Configuration dialog box (Figure 17-3). Set only those protocols that are required. There is no advantage to offering an unsupported protocol—and this can lead to abuse if a hacker is able to use a protocol you don't need.

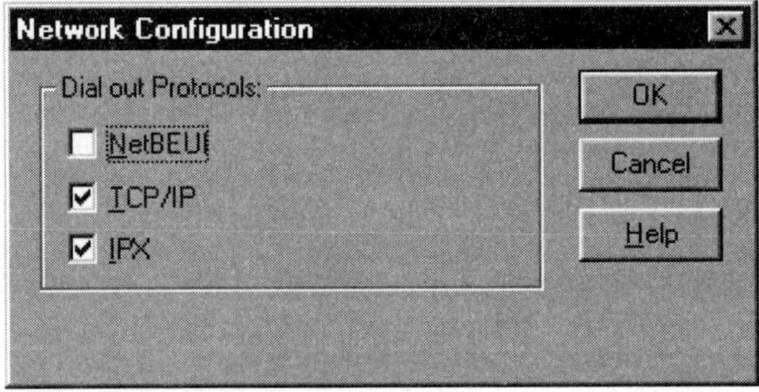

Figure 17-3: The Network Configuration dialog box when dial-in is not authorized.

When you check either "Receive calls only," or "Dial out and Receive calls" in the Configure Port Usage dialog box (Figure 17-2), then the Network Configuration Dialog box shown in Figure 17-4 displays.

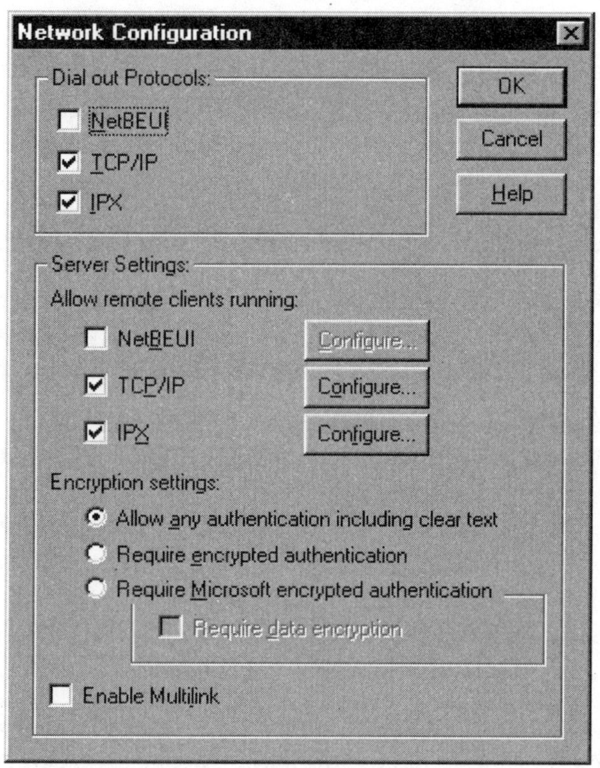

Figure 17-4: The Network Configuration dialog box when dial-in is authorized.

Most dial-up network connections to the Internet only need TCP/IP protocol. Some private connections use NetBEUI or IPX protocols also, so check all protocols that your installation needs to support. Configure each protocol by clicking the appropriate Configure button.

Encryption settings allow you to greatly enhance the security of your dial-in links. You may choose among the following:

- Allow any authentication (user ID and password) including clear text. This is the weakest level of security, and should be avoided if possible. Use this level of encryption only if you have clients that are not using Windows NT as their operating system.
- Require encrypted authentication allows you to restrict authentication to one of the encrypted protocols (except that PAP (Password Authentication Protocol) is not supported).
- Require Microsoft-encrypted authentication allows use of MS-CHAP (Challenge-Handshake Authentication Protocol) only. If you select this option, then you can choose to also encrypt the data being sent to the client—this enhances data security substantially! The encryption is the RSA Data Security, Inc.'s RC4 algorithm.

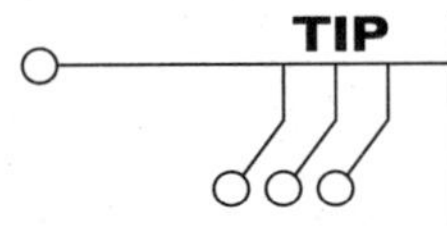

Need more information? Chapter 6, "Interacting With Other LANs," provides more information about configuration of RAS.

Configuring TCP/IP

When clients are allowed to dial into your Windows NT 4 Server, you must configure the incoming TCP/IP connections. This is done using the RAS Server TCP/IP Configuration dialog, shown in Figure 17-5. This dialog displays when you click the Configure button in the Network Configuration dialog (Figure 17-4).

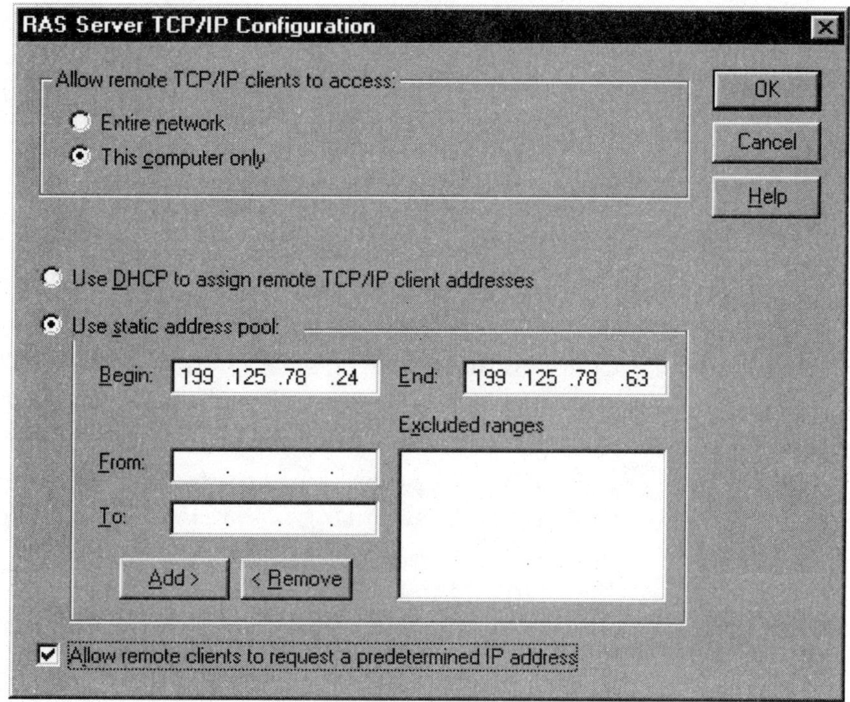

Figure 17-5: Configuring TCP/IP for RAS connections.

Problems... RAS won't start, you say?

If you get a message telling you that RAS will not start, and that RAS returned an error code, check the error log.

You can review the Windows NT 4 Server error log by selecting Start Menu | Programs | Administrative Tools (Common) | Event Viewer.

In the event log, you will see an entry with the same date and time as the attempt to start RAS. Open this event, and if the event ID is 7024, and the error returned is 1066, then the problem is simple to fix—RAS cannot start if you have not defined at least one modem with receive calls active!

For security, limit dial-in clients to resources found only on the Windows NT 4 Server. Do this by clicking the "This computer only" radio button. This protects other servers (and other workstations with shared resources over the network) from possible attack from dial-in clients.

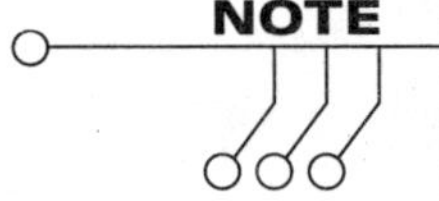

Disabling access to other resources on the network means that you're turning off Windows NT 4 Server's routing capabilities!

As well, you must specify how TCP/IP addresses are assigned to dial-in clients:

- TCP/IP addresses may be assigned using a DHCP server. If you have more than one Windows NT 4 Server with dial-in connections, then using a DHCP server is the most efficient method to assign TCP/IP addresses.
- TCP/IP addresses may be assigned from a fixed pool (generally a satisfactory solution if there is only one server used for dial-in clients). You must provide a beginning address, an ending address, and any addresses to be excluded from assignment.

You may choose to allow a dial-in client to specify their TCP/IP address. The address that the client specifies must be routed to the server.

Security considerations include making only this server's resources visible to the client, and perhaps using a fixed TCP/IP address.

Configuring IPX and NetBEUI

If you allow IPX or NetBEUI protocol clients, then you use their configuration dialogs. As with TCP/IP, you can limit dial-in clients to resources found only on the Windows NT 4 Server. Do this by clicking the "This computer only" radio button.

Like TCP/IP, IPX protocol assigns an address (called the "network number") to the client. You may choose to either allocate network numbers automatically, or restrict the network numbers to a specific range.

Remote Access Admin

You start the Windows NT 4 Server Remote Access Admin program by selecting Start Menu | Programs | Administrative Tools (Common) | Remote Access Admin. This program is also described in Chapter 7, "Configuring Dial-Up Networking."

There are several security-related functions in the Remote Access Admin program. Selecting Users | Permissions displays the Remote Access Permissions dialog box (see Figure 17-6). This dialog allows you to specify which of your Windows NT 4 Server users have permission to logon remotely using RAS. You may also set the user's call back status:

- No Call Back tells Remote Access Admin that this client user may connect directly. Often needed for client users who call from multiple locations (sales representatives, for example).
- Set by Caller tells Remote Access Admin that the client user will specify the call back number. This allows some after-the-fact auditing of phone numbers used to access the system. This option is useful in reducing costs, as the caller (Windows NT 4 Server) will be paying for the call, not the client user.
- Preset To forces the user to be at a specific number. RAS calls back to the preset number, and the client user's computer has to answer. This option is useful when access to the network must be strictly controlled.

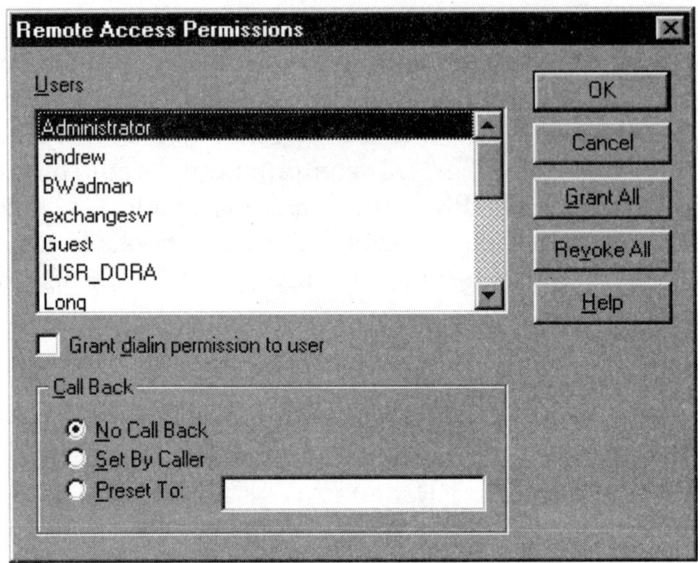

Figure 17-6: The Access Permissions dialog box.

RAS offers a great deal of flexibility, but it also exposes your server, and possibly your network, to compromise from outside. Don't configure or use RAS unless you understand the risks involved.

To enable logging for dial-in RAS client users, you must enable logging in the system registry. The key for logging is found in "HKEY_LOCAL_MACHINE\SYSTEM\CurrentControlSet\ServicesRasMan\PPP" as the variable "Logging." Set the Logging variable to 1 to enable logging of PPP connections. Figure 17-7 shows the Registry Editor with the logging variable selected.

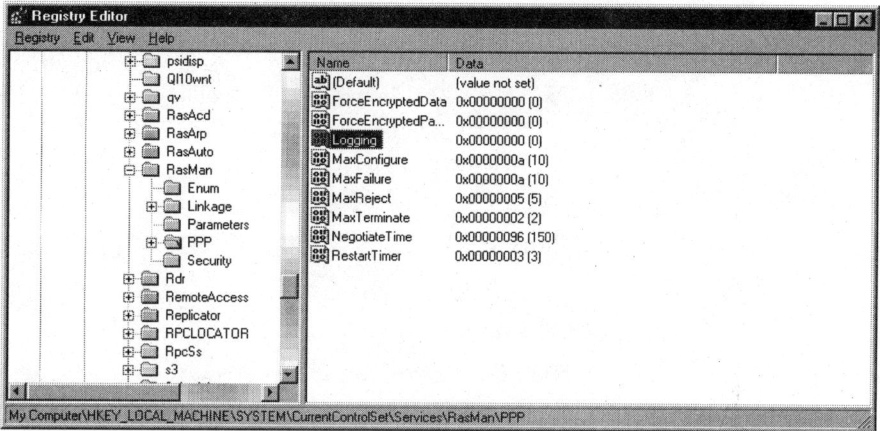

Figure 17-7: The Registry Editor, ready to change the RAS logging mode.

After setting the logging mode, you need to restart RAS for the change to take effect.

Groups

Once you have your system secured, you'll need to turn your attention to user security. Organizing users into logical groups helps manage users and security. A group doesn't have any special privileges initially; however, you may assign privileges to a group if desired.

To create a group, select User | New Global Group or User | New Local Group in User Manager for Domains. The main difference between a local group and a global group is that a local group can only be used in the database in which it was defined. A global group can be a member of a local group. There is no restriction on how many global or local groups you can create, but keep it to a manageable number. Members can be added to a group at any time.

Create groups for each part of your organization—for example, you may have groups for accounting, sales, administration, data processing, research and development, and so on. You may also create groups based on functionality, though Windows NT 4 Server has a number of pre-configured groups:

- *Account Operators,* users who can establish and modify user accounts.
- *Administrators,* who are able to administer the server and the domain.
- *Backup Operators,* who have the necessary privilege of accessing files for backup purposes.
- *Domain Admins,* a global group that consists of administrators who administer the domain.
- *Domain Guests,* a global group that consists of guests to the domain.
- *Domain Users,* a global group that consists of users in the domain.
- *Guests,* users with limited access to the computer and domain.
- *Print Operators,* who are allowed to administer print queues.
- *Replicator,* which supports file replication in a domain.
- *Server Operators,* who manage the domain servers.
- *Users,* users who have more privileges than a guest, but fewer privileges than administrators.

Groups may be assigned rights, as were described above in "Rights & Privileges."

Users

Simply put, users are why we are here. A user is anyone who either logs on directly to the server or makes a network connection to the server.

Users are given privileges and rights, and must be managed. Users who will be logging on locally may have a somewhat different configuration—for locally logged-on users, you may choose to create a profile. A profile defines how Windows NT 4 Server will appear to the user, and the user may choose to customize parts of the system (such as the desktop) to meet their own needs and desires.

To create a user account on Windows NT 4 Server you should have already created any groups to which you will be assigning the user. It is slightly easier to assign users to a group when creating user accounts than it is to assign users to a group when you create groups last.

Defining Users

To define a user account on Windows NT 4 Server, select the User Manager's User | New User menu selection. The New User dialog box (Figure 17-8) displays.

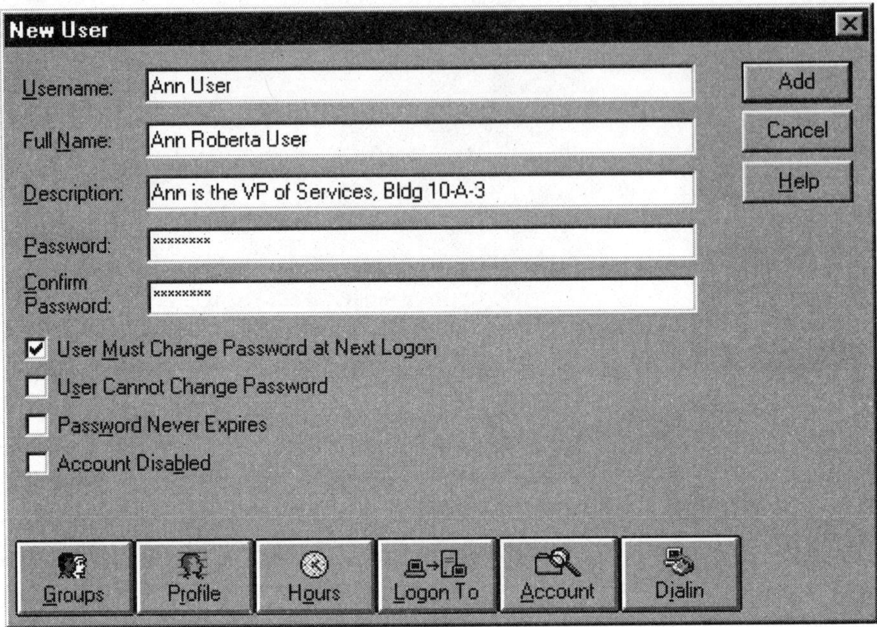

Figure 17-8: Adding a new user.

Fill in the Username, Full Name, Description, Password, and Confirm Password edit boxes. Even though a user account may be created without a password, I do not recommend that any accounts (even guest accounts that only have read-only privilege) be created without passwords. Also set, as appropriate, the "User Must Change Password at Next Logon," "User Cannot Change Password," "Password Never Expires," and "Account Disabled" check boxes.

At the bottom of the New User dialog box is a set of six buttons: Groups, Profile, Hours, Logon To, Account, and Dialin:

- The Groups button displays the Group Memberships dialog box. The default group is Domain Users. Add any other groups that you wish this user to be a member of. Remember, groups are not exclusive—a user account may be a member of multiple groups. If more than one group is selected, then one group may be selected as the primary group; if there are conflicting rights in groups assigned to the user, then the right specified in the primary group takes

precedence. More on groups in "Working With Users & Groups," later in this chapter.

- Click the Profile button to add profile information. The user must have been granted the right to "Logon locally" in order to use profiles. Profiles are discussed below, under "Profiles."
- The Hours button displays the Logon Hours dialog box. A user may be restricted to accessing the server only during certain hours—a user who is working on a shift basis may be restricted from working during shifts other than the one he or she is currently assigned to. All users may be restricted from accessing the server at certain hours for maintenance purposes. And some non-essential users may be restricted from accessing the server during peak load times.
- Click the Logon To button to restrict the user's access to the server from specific workstations. For example, you can restrict a person who is working in the R&D department to use workstations only in the R&D area (and not in Accounting, for example).
- Click the Account button to set account options. The Account Information dialog box allows you to set several options. A life span of an account can be set to either never expire or to expire on a specific date. You may also set the account type—either a domain (global) account, which will be used throughout the domain, or a local account.
- Click on the Dialin button to set the dial-in privileges for this user. Users may be prohibited from dialing into the server (using RAS). If a user is permitted to dial in to the server, then you may specify a call back protocol for this user—either No Call Back (the user dials in, and is connected directly to the server), Set By Caller (the user configures the call back number when they call in), or Preset To (the callback is fixed to a single number).

Once all necessary information for the user has been set, click the Add button to add the new user to the user database.

Defining Profiles

For users who have the right to logon locally you may establish a profile. Profiles contain information such as Application Data, Desktop, Favorites, Personal, SendTo, and the Start Menu. To enable profiles for a given user, go to the User Manager, select the user, and display the user's properties.

Not all users need to have a profile defined. If there is only a limited number of users with the right to logon locally (to actually logon at the server, in addition to logging on through a workstation), it may be best to establish a profile for each.

Using the User Environment Profile Dialog

When a user's properties are displayed (see Figure 17-9), you can click on the Profile button to display the User Environment Profile dialog box, shown in Figure 17-10.

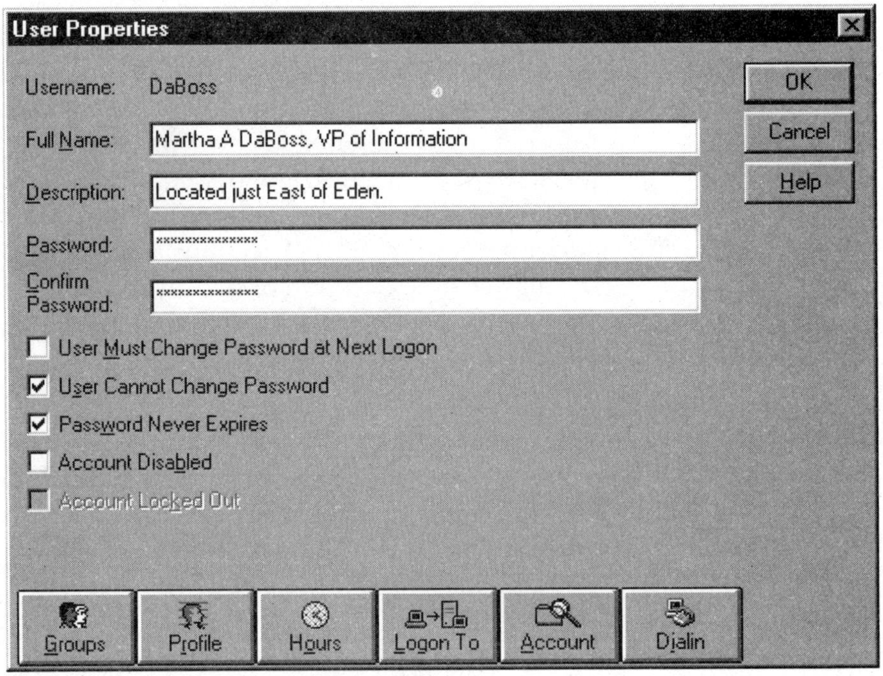

Figure 17-9: Properties for a typical user.

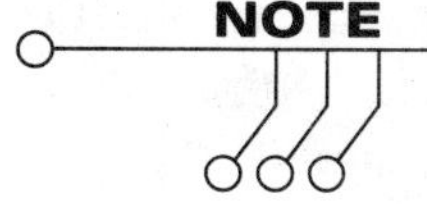

In Figure 17-9, the Account Locked Out button is enabled only when the account has been locked out. See the "Account Lockout" section for information about locking out users.

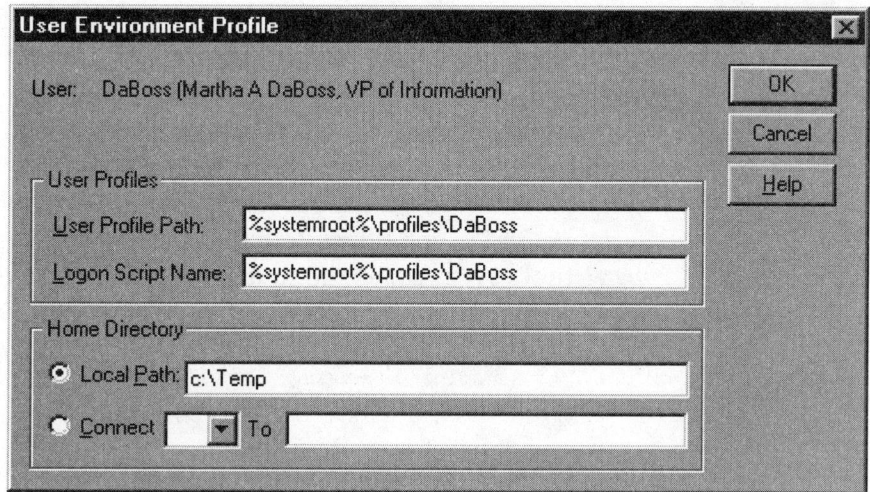

Figure 17-10: User Environment Profile—for DaBoss.

In the User Environment Profile dialog are three items:

- User Profile Path—a fully qualified path name where the user's profile will be stored. The default location is in the %systemroot%\system32 folder, which is not a good location for a profile. A better choice is the %systemroot%\profiles folder, which has been established for user profiles.

- Logon Script Name—a .BAT, .CMD, or other executable file name that executes whenever the user logs on. Maintenance, setup, and other commands can be placed in the Logon Script file. If the user logs on from a DOS-based workstation, then the logon script must be a .BAT file. The typical logon script path for users who logon remotely is \%systemroot%\system32\system32\repl\import\scripts, although you may establish a different path (such as the \users folder) for logon scripts.
- Home Directory—the initial folder whenever a File Open or File Save As dialog is displayed. As well, any CMD sessions also default to the Home Directory. Either a local folder (specified in the Local Path edit box) may be specified, or a virtual drive connected to a shared network folder. You may specify the environment variable %USERNAME% to insert the current user's name for the Home Directory: \users\%USERNAME%.

Using the System Applet

In the Control Panel's System Applet, select the tab marked "User Profiles." The System Properties dialog box (shown in Figure 17-11) shows four user profiles defined on the server DORA. One profile (Administrator) is the account that I use. DaBoss is the profile created for this chapter. The other two profiles, *exchangesvr* and *smsmanager*, are accounts created automatically by other installed products, Exchange Server and SMS Manager. Neither account is used by me very often though they are available if needed.

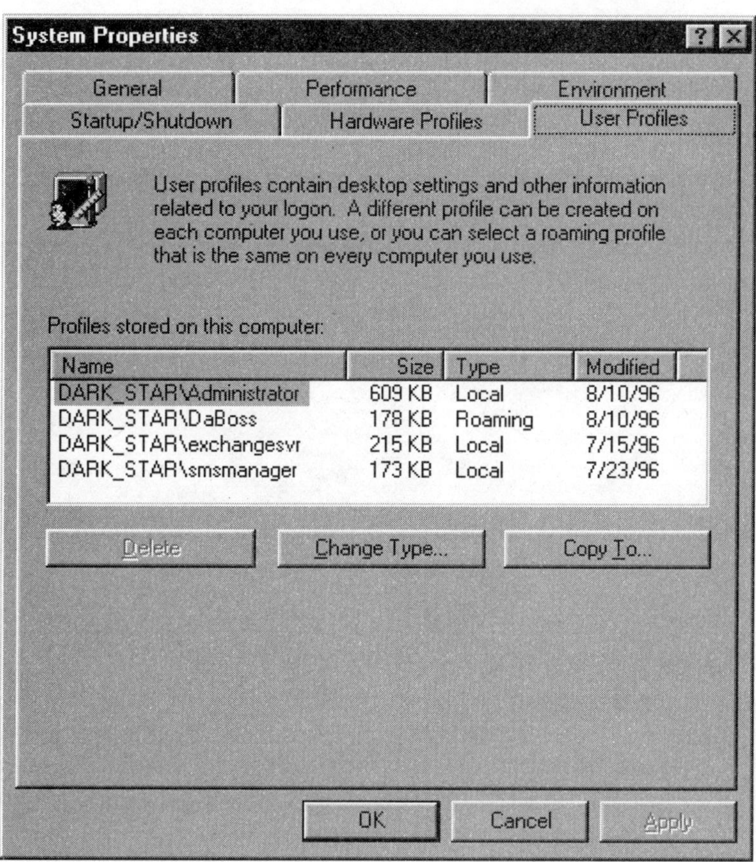

Figure 17-11: Four User Profiles in the Control Panel's System applet.

The type of profile may be changed as needed. For example, DaBoss's profile is currently roaming (a roaming profile is always retrieved from the server, if available), while Administrator's profile is local (a local profile is always loaded from the local machine). When using a roaming profile, you can specify the profile be cached to improve performance. If a roaming profile is not available then a local profile is used. If two users logon with the same roaming profile, the last user to logoff will be the one whose settings are saved.

Figure 17-12 shows the Change Type dialog box for user DaBoss. Specified for this user is a roaming profile, which will be cached if the connection is defined as slow.

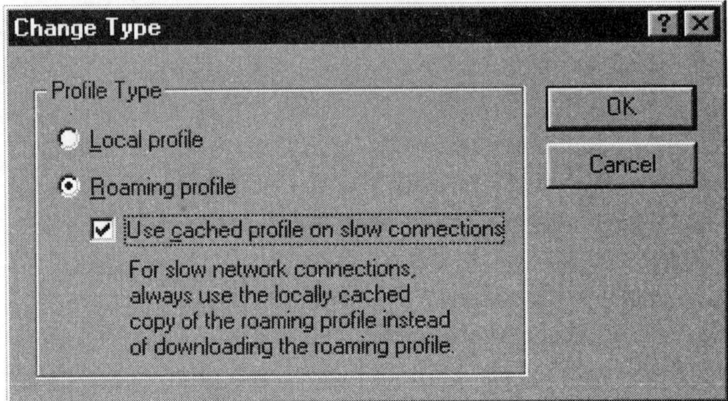

Figure 17-12: Changing a profile's type.

Working With Users & Groups

Maintaining control over users can be a difficult task. For large organizations, there can be thousands of users, creating a nightmare for the system administrator. In this book I assume that you have configured a domain, and that you are working on the primary domain server (PDS).

Fortunately, Windows NT 4 Server provides several features and tools to make user management less difficult. First, it is important to understand that *anyone* who interacts with Windows NT 4 Server is a user. You are a user, and everyone else is a user.

Groups are logical collections of users. A group may be managed as a whole, and members of a group may in turn be granted (or denied) privileges as needed.

Management of users is done using the User Manager for Domains program, found in Start Menu | Programs | Administrative Tools (Common) | User Manager for Domains. When the

User Manager for Domains program starts (Figure 17-13), a display of both users and groups will be provided. All users belong to one or more groups. For example, a user may be a member of both the Administrators group and the Domain Users group at the same time.

User Manager - DARK_STAR

User View Policies Options Exchange Help

Username	Full Name	Description
Administrator		Built-in account for administering the computer/domain
andrew	andrew	486/50-16
BWadman	Barry Wadman	
exchangesvr	Exchange Server Admin A	Exchange Server Admin Account
Guest		Built-in account for guest access to the computer/domain
IUSR_DORA	Internet Guest Account	Internet Server Anonymous Access
Long	Long	486/50-16
NangH	Nang Hipson	
NHipson	Nang Hipson	
Pixel	Pixel	386/33-16
smsmanager	Manager for SMS Server	manager
SQLExecutiveCmdExec	SQLExecutiveCmdExec	SQL Executive CmdExec Task Account
TWestheimer	Tom Westheimer	
Wadman	Barry Wadman	Barry's private Userid

Groups	Description
Account Operators	Members can administer domain user and group accounts
Administrators	Members can fully administer the computer/domain
Backup Operators	Members can bypass file security to back up files
Domain Admins	Designated administrators of the domain
Domain Guests	All domain guests
Domain Users	All domain users
Guests	Users granted guest access to the computer/domain
People	People who don't fit into groups
Print Operators	Members can administer domain printers
Replicator	Supports file replication in a domain
Server Operators	Members can administer domain servers
Users	Ordinary users

Figure 17-13: The User Manager.

Rights & Privileges

Both groups and users are assigned privileges called rights. Groups created by default have a set of default rights. New groups, which you create, do not have any special rights.

To grant your groups any special rights, select Policies | User Rights from the menu. Most groups do not need to have any special rights assigned. Most user base groups only need to have the "Access this computer from network" right.

Rights are categorized into two broad classifications: regular rights and advanced rights. Advanced rights include rights given to very special user accounts that must perform special tasks. Usually you will not have to assign advanced user rights—when an application or system requiring advanced user rights is installed, it will create a user account and assign whatever rights are needed. From time to time, however, you may need to know where advanced user rights are set: User Manager's Policies | User Rights menu selection displays the User Rights Policy dialog, as shown in Figure 17-14.

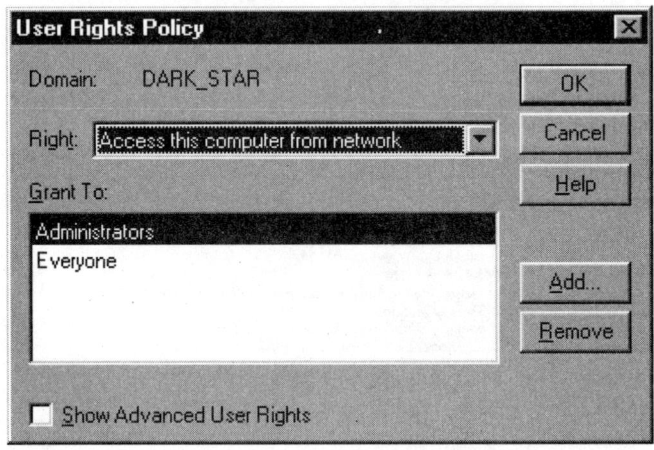

Figure 17-14: The User Rights Policy dialog lets you add and remove rights.

To grant a right to a group or a user, in the User Rights Policy dialog click the Add button, and in the Add Users and Groups dialog select the user account or group that you plan to grant the right to. To remove a right from a group or a user, select the user or group in the Grant To: list and then click the Remove button.

The various rights supported by Windows NT 4 Server are shown in Table 17-1. Rights should not be granted indiscriminately, as they can compromise system security if misused.

Right	Basic?	Notes
Access this computer from network	X	Everybody has this right. It is the default right for all users.
Act as part of the operating system		Used by services, and not by users.
Add workstations to domain	X	Usually domain account managers, if you have one.
Back up files and directories	X	Backup operators—you may define zero, one, or more backup operators.
Bypass traverse checking		Everybody has this right. It is the default right for all users.
Change the system time	X	Usually assigned to administrators and server operators, you may want to create other privileged users who are able to change system time. Be aware of the impact of an improper change of time—many transactions will be timestamped with the incorrect time.
Create a pagefile		Usually only administrators create pagefiles.
Create a token object		Creation of token objects is a special right that is normally assigned when the user who needs this right is created.
Create permanent shared objects		Creation of permanent shared objects is a special right that is normally assigned when the user who needs this right is created.
Debug programs		Normally only administrators are allowed to debug programs, but at times maintenance or development staff may need this right.

➡

Right	Basic?	Notes
Force shutdown from a remote system	X	Administrators and server operators are assigned this right. You would not normally want other user accounts to be able to shut down the server remotely.
Generate security audits		Not normally assigned, could be useful to administrators or server operators.
Increase quotas		This right is usually granted to administrators. It is possible that server operators may need this right; determine this on a case-by-case basis.
Increase scheduling priority		Administrators have this right, though server operators may benefit from being granted this right.
Load and unload device drivers	X	This right is assigned to administrators.
Lock pages in memory		This right is not assigned to any group or user by default.
Log on as a batch job		Assigned to individual user accounts as needed when these accounts are created. Not normally assigned manually; however, you may find a use for this right.
Log on as a service		The administrator group is given this right, and individual accounts created to work with services are also granted this right on a user-by-user basis.

Right	Basic?	Notes
Log on locally	X	Most administrative and operator user accounts may log on locally. As well, the IIS guest account has this right. This right can be assigned to many users who would have a need to logon at the server, but should not be granted indiscriminately.
Manage auditing and security log	X	Usually granted to administrators, the audit log is useful for monitoring security problems.
Modify firmware environment values		This right is usually granted only to administrators.
Profile single process		This right is usually granted only to administrators.
Profile system performance		This right is usually granted only to administrators.
Replace a process level token		This right is usually granted only to administrators.
Restore files and directories	X	Granted to administrators, backup operators, server operators, and individual user accounts who need this right.
Shut down the system	X	This right is usually granted only to administrators.
Take ownership of files or other objects	X	This right is usually granted only to administrators, though it may be granted to other trusted operators and users who need this privilege.

Table 17-1: User rights, both basic and advanced.

Printing a List of Users

Having a list of users is useful should the user database need to be re-created. By printing this list, it is possible to look up users and do other user management tasks even when access to the server is not available. The User Manager program is not able to print (or save to disk) the list of users. However, the command-based NET command does support listing user accounts and detailed information about user accounts. Though the process to produce a list of users is a bit convoluted (you must create a command file using an editor), it is possible, using the steps outlined below, to generate a list of all user accounts.

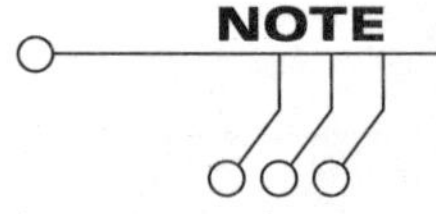

The same basic process can also be used to document groups.

To generate a detailed list of user accounts, follow these steps:

1. When logged on as an administrator, open a command prompt window.
2. Issue the command *"NET USERS >TEMP.BAT."* An example of the output from this command is shown in Figure 17-15.

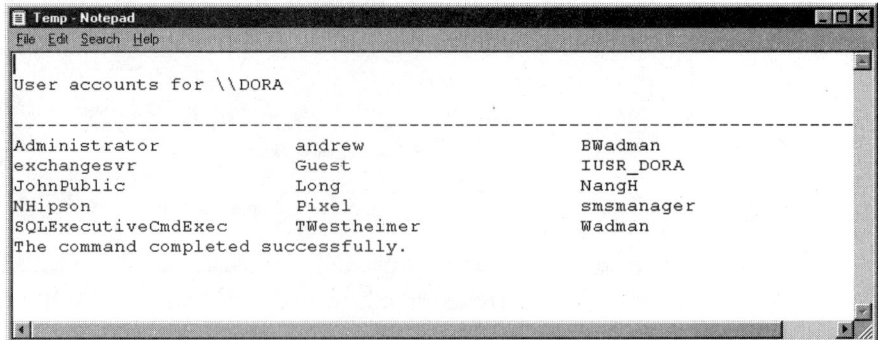

Figure 17-15: The output from NET USERS>TEMP.BAT.

3. Edit the output from the command (the file TEMP.BAT) using any text-based editor. Split the three columns of user account names into a single column, and delete all information from the file except for the user account names. Figure 17-16 shows the TEMP.BAT file after these changes.

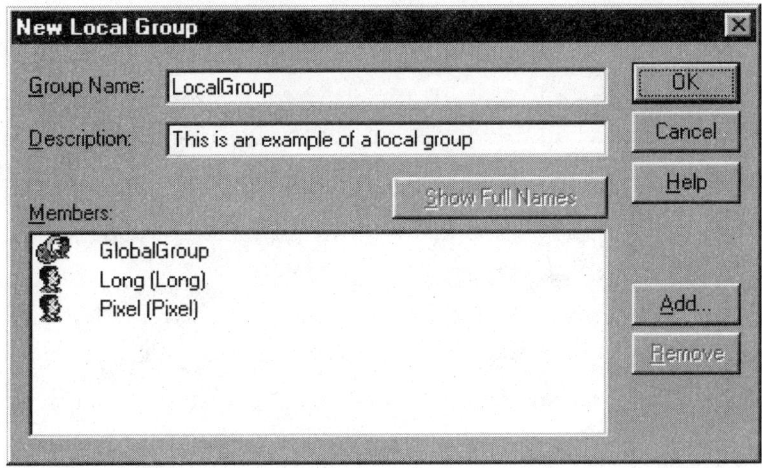

Figure 17-16: TEMP.BAT after editing.

4. Add, in front of each user account name, the command *"NET USERS ."* After each user account name, add " >> *USERLIST.DAT ."* Finally, add a header line at the beginning of the file: *"ECHO 'List of users as of (date)' > USERLIST.DAT."*
5. Save TEMP.BAT, and from your command prompt, execute it!
6. The file USERLIST.DAT will contain a detailed list of all user accounts.

Information contained in the user list could be used to compromise system security. Keep this list secure! When it is no longer needed, dispose of this list in a secure manner. Do NOT *leave the USERLIST.DAT file on the server without protecting it from access by unauthorized users!*

Backing Up the User List

OK, if we can print a list of users, can we back up the user database? The answer, short and sweet, is not really. However, Windows NT 4 Server does automatically back up the user account list when you have both a PDC (Primary Domain Controller) and a BDC (Backup Domain Controller) configured.

The whole purpose of a domain with PDCs and BDCs is to allow the account information to be maintained in one location, and be available from more than one location. If the PDC cannot function (for any reason, such as being shut down), then a BDC is promoted to become the PDC. The BDC has its own copy of user account information (this information is replicated between the PDC and any BDCs).

If for some reason you must create a new clean PDC installation, it is not necessary to re-enter the user information:

1. Create the new PDC server initially as a BDC.
2. Bring the new server up on the network.
3. The current PDC replicates the current user account information to the new server.
4. Manually promote the new server to be the PDC (this process automatically demotes the current PDC to be a BDC).

Voila! Your new server now has the complete list of user accounts (and all other security information such as groups and rights).

Account Policy

In Windows NT 4 Server, all accounts have a set of basic policies. These policies can be used to enhance system security, as shown below. Figure 17-17 shows the Account Policy dialog that displays when you select Policies | Account in User Manager.

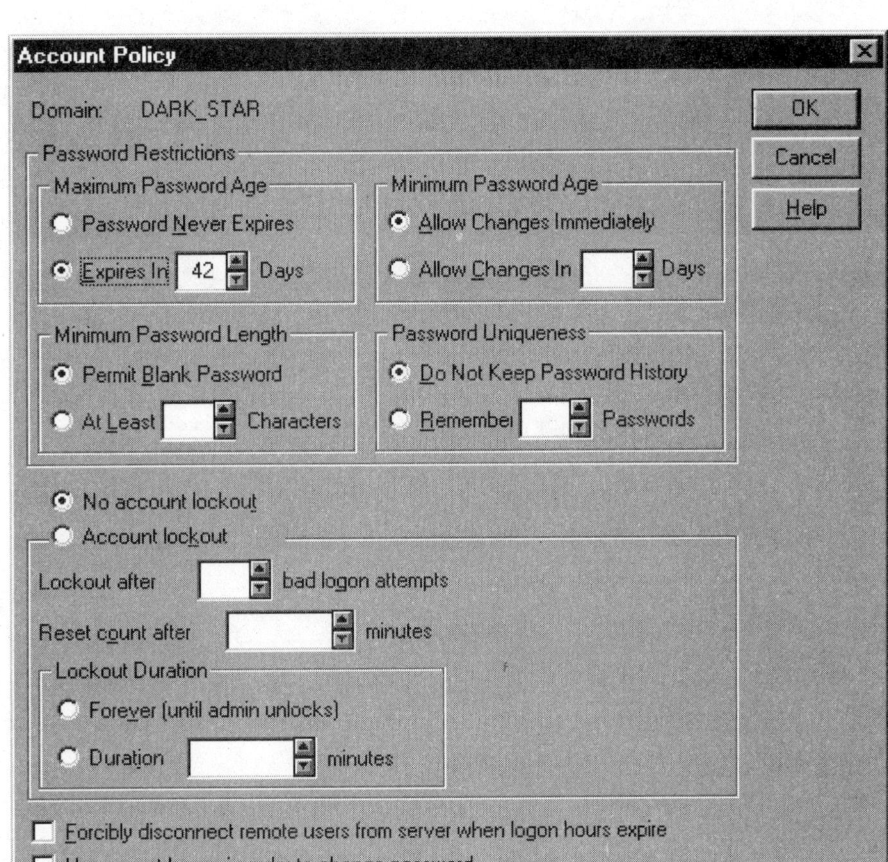

Figure 17-17: Default Account Policies.

Password Restrictions

For user accounts, you may set a number of password restrictions:

- Maximum Password Age allows you to force passwords to expire after a fixed period of time. Choosing Password Never Expires forces Windows NT 4 Server to never have a password expire. Most organizations find it advantageous to have passwords expire on a monthly basis.

- Minimum Password Age allows you to set the minimum amount of time the user must wait before changing their password. Most organizations don't restrict password changes.
- Minimum Password Length permits you to specify a minimum password size. You may specify either that the user may have a blank password (never a good idea, in my opinion), or that the password must have At Least <number> Characters. The minimum number of characters should be at least six, and preferably eight or more.
- Password Uniqueness helps prevent users from having fixed lists of passwords that they rotate on a regular basis. If you implement this feature, set the number of passwords remembered to at least eight! The typical number, four, is not sufficient.

Account Lockout

Locking out an account when there have been possible security violations is an effective tool in stopping such practices as password guessing.

If you set Account Lockout, you can specify that the account is locked out after a specified number of bad logon attempts (bad password attempts). The typical number of consecutive bad logon attempts permitted is four, though in organizations where security is critical this number may be set to two or even one.

The count of bad logon attempts is typically reset after a predefined period of time, typically 30 minutes. Some organizations set this time to as much as 24 hours.

Lockout duration can be either a fixed period of time (the default of 30 minutes is typical for many organizations), or "Forever." If forever is selected, then when an account has been locked out, the administrator must unlock the account using the Account Locked Out check box in the User Properties dialog box (see Figure 17-9).

For highest security, select "Forever (until admin unlocks)." This way, when a user's account is locked out, the administrator will always be aware of the situation.

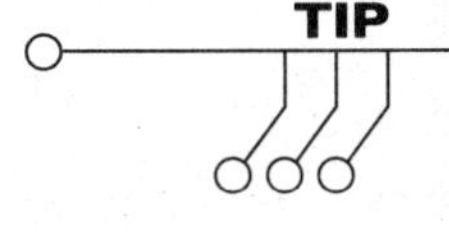

Just because a user's account has been locked doesn't mean that the user is doing anything wrong. There are a number of reasons for this to happen, including (in no particular order):

1. *The user has a poor memory for passwords.*
2. *The user has a problem typing passwords.*
3. *There is someone who is attempting to access the user's account improperly.*
4. *The user was given the wrong password.*
5. *There are network communication difficulties.*

A user may be restricted to a limited number of hours of connection to the server. When the connection hours have expired, the user is not to be allowed to logon again until either the next authorized time period or the authorized hours have been changed. You can tell Windows NT 4 Server to disconnect a user when the logon hours expire.

Users should always be required to logon to change passwords. This helps prevent someone from changing a password for a user account without authority.

Audit Policy

The Windows NT 4 Server audit facilities allow you to monitor a number of events. Events may be audited when successful or when there is a failure. Display the Audit Policy dialog box (Figure 17-18) by selecting Policies | Audit from the User Manager's menu.

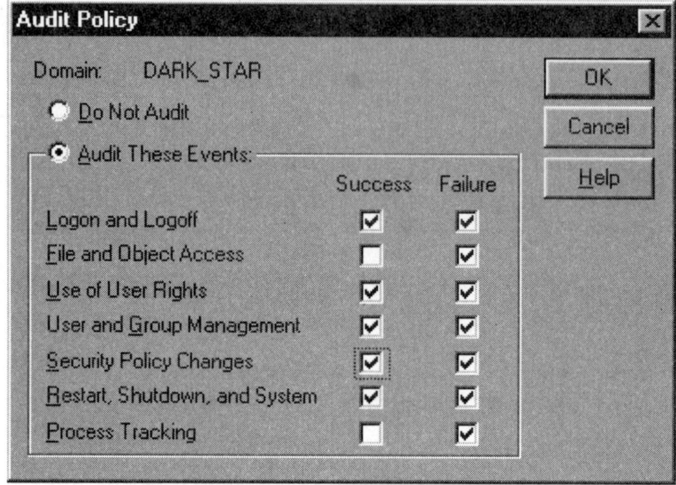

Figure 17-18: Establishing Audit policies.

Generally, if you are monitoring success, you should also monitor failure.

- *Logon and Logoff* audits user logon and logoff. When auditing success, you will be able to determine who is using the system. Auditing failure allows you to detect possible attempts to logon improperly.
- *File and Object Access* audits whenever files or objects are accessed from the server. The information from the success audit can be extensive. Failure information can help detect attempts to browse files and objects that are not permitted for the user.
- *Use of User Rights* audits any user rights other than logon or logoff.
- *User and Group Management* audits changes to users and groups.

- *Security Policy Changes* audits changes to user rights, audit, or trust relationship policies.
- *Restart, Shutdown, and System* audits starts, shutdowns, or any event that could compromise system security.
- *Process Tracking* audits actions related to program activation and termination and other related actions.

Auditing information is sent to the security log. Use the Event Viewer (Start Menu | Programs | Administrative Tools (Common) | Event Viewer) to view audit information.

Trust Relationships

A trust relationship is the method by which two separate domains establish that they "trust" each other. Creating a trust relationship is a two-stage process—each domain must configure the trust relationship.

The Trust Relationship dialog box (select Policies | Trust Relationships from the User Manager menu), shown in Figure 17-19, shows that no trust relationships have been established.

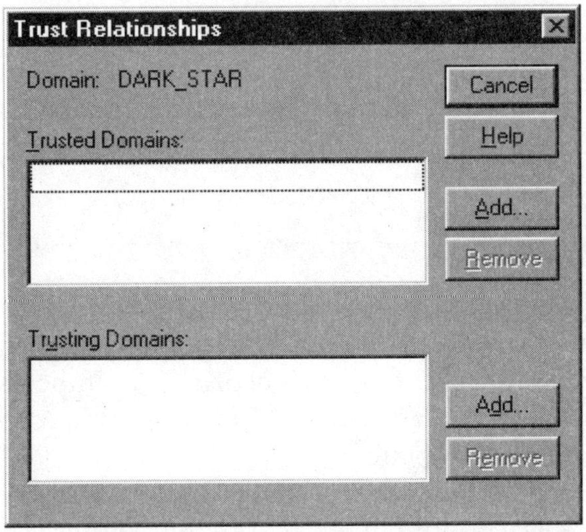

Figure 17-19: The Trust Relationship dialog box.

A trusted domain's users and groups are allowed user rights, resource permissions, and local group memberships on the trusting domain.

A trusting domain allows its users to have user rights, resource permissions, and local group memberships on the trusting domain.

To create a trust relationship you must:

1. On the domain that will be trusted, select the Add button next to the "Trusting Domains:" list and add a trusting domain.
2. On the domain that was added to the "Trusting Domain:" list in step one, you must start the User Manager, go to the Trust Relationships dialog, and add the trusted domain to the "Trusted Domains:" list by selecting the Add button next to the "Trusted Domains:" list.

Never, ever, remove one side of a trust relationship without removing the other side. Both sides (trusted and trusting) must agree on the relationship.

Physical Security

Most servers are shared resources. Generally, for most of us, we need to meet a set of conflicting goals—the server must be located convenient to administration, users, and other resources (including printers, power, and network connections).

Server Locations

Planning your server location and security may be difficult. Existing installations may dictate the server's location, smaller companies that are growing larger may feel security is unimportant (and will continue to feel this way until there is a security problem), and, let's face it, planning is difficult.

Even if operating systems claim to be secure, as Windows NT 4 Server does, the bottom line is that if your server is not physically secure then no amount of operating system security will make the system secure. Some physical security points of mine include:

- Place the servers, drives, backup devices, and backup media in a computer room that has restricted access.
- Use combination or electronic locks on the computer room. Like passwords, change the combinations frequently. Dual-lock the computer room for maximum security, so that it takes two people to open the door.
- Ensure that the computer room cannot be accessed through a raised computer room floor from outside the room.
- Check the ceilings! Dropped or suspended ceilings usually offer no barrier to people moving from room to room through the ceiling using only a simple stepladder.
- Windows in the computer room should be protected with alarms that cannot be disabled except by the security staff, whether the windows are internal or external.
- Secure your network cables. Be very cautious of network cables that run between discontinuous floors, or run through common raceways.
- A lot of damage can be done to a server by a remote user who is using an account with administrator privileges. Make sure passwords and user ID lists are kept confidential.
- Installed Microsoft SQL Server? Be sure the Microsoft SQL Server "sa" account has a password!

Power Security—the UPS

The first rumble of thunder, and you start getting nervous… Out goes the message, "There is a storm coming, save your data frequently." Well, for users that is half a solution.

Most network servers run with some form of Un-interruptible Power Supply (UPS). This device is typically a rechargeable battery and a converter that converts the battery's power to power that the server can use.

Windows NT 4 Server has UPS communications features, which are very useful. You can perform a number of tasks when power fails:

- Notify users that there has been a power failure at the server.
- If power is not restored in a reasonable period, begin a system shutdown.

Configuring a UPS requires that the UPS be able to send some form of message to the server that power has failed. This is done by connecting the UPS to the server using a serial cable. For example, many better UPS systems notify the server when power fails, when there is a low battery power condition, and when the UPS is shutting down (either because batteries have been exhausted or the UPS is overheating).

The Windows NT 4 Server Control Panel's UPS applet, shown in Figure 17-20, shows a typical configuration. Every UPS is unique, so you will need to consult with the documentation supplied with your UPS to determine which features are supported and how to configure these features.

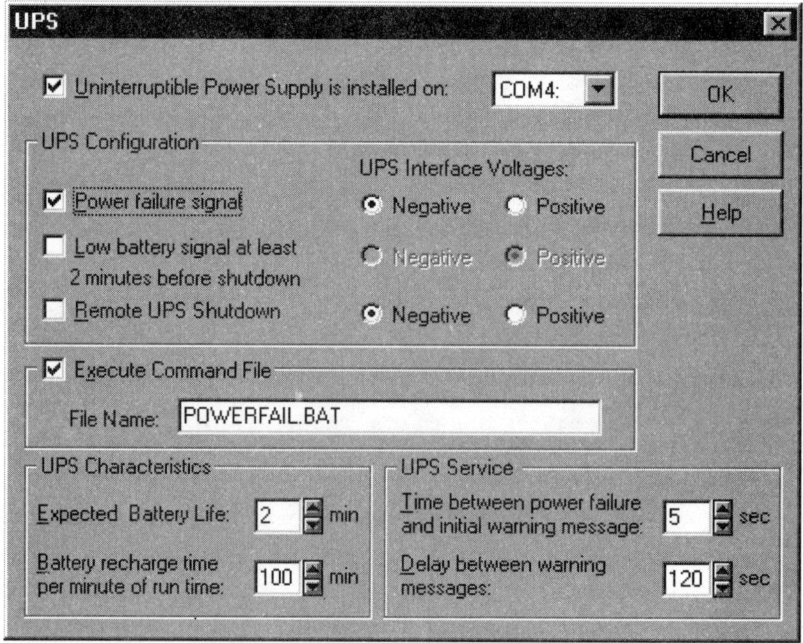

Figure 17-20: The Control Panel's UPS applet.

The UPS Configuration group box allows you to select which signals the UPS sends to the server. UPS communications are very simple, and as well, not all UPS systems support the different signals. You can select whichever signals your UPS provides, and configure for those signals. Make sure the UPS Interface Voltage polarity is set correctly!

UPS Communications

UPS systems communicate using the serial port's control lines. Each line is assigned a use by Windows NT 4 Server:

- **CTS** (Clear-to-send) signals that the power has failed. CTS will either go negative or positive when power fails. Enable the "Power failure signal" check box to use this feature.
- **DCD** (Data-carrier-detect) signals that the battery level is dropping to a critical level. Enable the "Low battery signal at least 2 minutes before shutdown" to use this feature.
- **DTR** (Data-terminal-ready) signals that the UPS is in the process of being shut down. Enable the "Remote UPS Shutdown" to use this feature.

If using any adapters or extension cables, make sure they correctly carry these signals! Test the installation: Pull the plug, and see what happens (but do this when there are no users on the server).

You can have the server automatically execute a command file (.EXE, .COM, .BAT, or .CMD) located in the WinNT\System32 folder. This command file executes just before the system is shut down when:

- The time limits specified expired.
- The UPS signaled that the system should shut down.

Microsoft states that the command file specified in Execute Command File must execute within 30 seconds or the server may not properly shut down. Making this command file as simple as possible is a wise idea!

A second part of the UPS system configuration is found in the Control Panel's Services applet, where you configure the UPS service "Startup Type" to "Automatic," as shown in Figure 17-21. The default, for most systems, is that the UPS service is manually started.

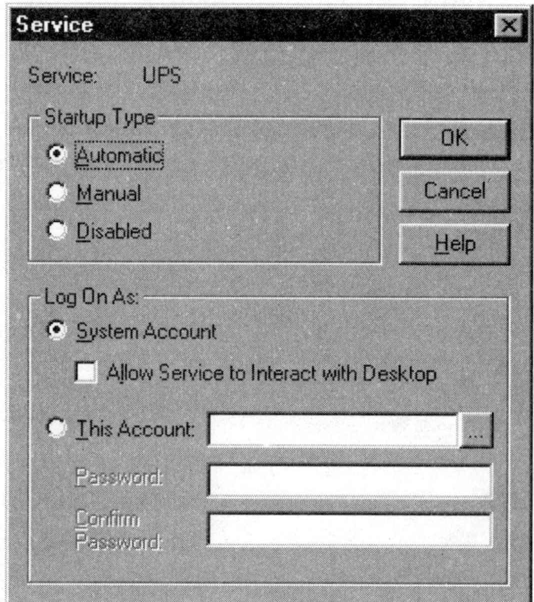

Figure 17-21: Changing UPS startup to Automatic.

Environmental Security

Ever wonder how hot it gets inside your server? Wonder how much dust those little fans deposit on the inside of the system? Wonder what would happen if your computer fell into a lake?

Temperature is a critical problem with computers. Back in the "good old days" we used huge air conditioners to cool the computers. Today, a small room air conditioner is all that is needed, but in many environments, some form of air conditioning is still needed. Generally, you should not have to worry about overheating if the ambient air temperature is about 70°F (or 22°C). When the air temperature exceeds this value by more than 15%, then overheating becomes a real threat.

Some hardware has overheating protection, but many servers do not have sufficient protection and should be monitored whenever possible. Even simple, electronic thermometers (such as what Radio Shack sells) monitor the temperature of a server adequately. In the two servers here at the Dark_Star domain, I continually monitor both the temperature near the CPU and the temperature of the power supply. Several fans have failed, and these monitors have helped prevent disaster! Give serious consideration to multiple fans. The external SCSI drive unit on the DORA server has five fans—a single fan failure will not cause immediate problems there!

Dust and dirt in the air is a major problem. Corrosive atmospheres can wreck havoc for computers—be certain that servers are not exposed to any substances (gases, salt air, and so on) that could cause corrosion. All computers, especially servers, should be taken apart at regular intervals and cleaned of dust. Dust traps air and can lead to overheating. A small air compressor, or canned air, is adequate to clean most computers. A carefully used vacuum cleaner can be used, but caution must be exercised so as not to damage components while cleaning.

Moving On

In this chapter we delved into users, groups, auditing, and security. For most organizations, security is a major part of the system administrator's job. Most Windows NT 4 Server security is managed using the Domain User Manager. Physical security is also an issue covered in this chapter—if you don't take physical security issues into consideration when planning your system, the most carefully managed Windows NT 4 Server will never be secure.

The next chapter, "Backing Up the System," covers how to make successful backups of the system and user information. Some backup issues include technology (tape drive technology changes every few years) and backup methodology.

18

Backing Up the System

In this chapter, I'll cover backing up both the system files for Windows NT 4 Server and client data. Not all applications and operating systems back up files the same way. For example, Microsoft SQL Server has its own built-in backup facilities. Many applications cannot be restored from backups when there is a clean Windows NT 4 Server installation.

Is Backing Up Worth It?

The day this chapter was supposed to be written, the Dark_Star server's C: drive failed. Multiple soft errors and hard errors in critical system areas made recovery or repair impossible.

Eventually, I low-level formatted the drive (with a SCSI drive this is not difficult), installed a new copy of Windows NT 4 Server, and reinstalled all applications. Finally, I restored user data and other files from *yesterday's* backup.

Result? A day's time, lost. But no data or files were lost! That wasn't luck—extensive backups make this type of potential disaster a mere inconvenience.

Backups consist of two different types:

- Archival backups store data that has been replaced or removed from the system. An archival backup is usually kept for long periods of time (years, perhaps even decades). The ability to later read archival data is a critical factor—retaining the backup program that created the archival backup is important, and, as well, compatible hardware must be available. The backup is useless if either compatible hardware or software is not available to read the backup!
- Security backups are backups of current data that is being used (perhaps on a daily basis). Security backups ensure that neither software nor hardware failures render data inaccessible. Since security backups are seldom kept for longer than a short period of time, the problem of having the appropriate software and hardware to read the backup media is less critical.

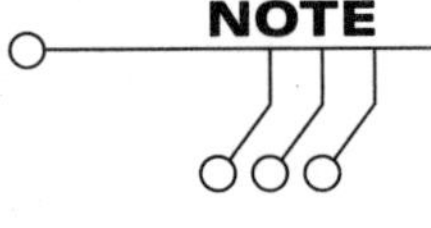

Whenever upgrading your backup technology (either hardware or software), make sure that you have a methodology to read existing backups, or all existing backups must be converted to the new technology. That one old tape that was not converted is the one you will need every time!

Backup Strategies

Backup strategies depend on how a backup is done. How often backups are done, whether the backup is complete or only backs up modified data, and how long a backup is retained are all backup strategies.

Frequency & Aging of Backups

How frequently should data be backed up? Until there is a failure of a drive, or another reason to seek to restore a file, backup frequency is usually not given much thought. A professional viewpoint is simply that backups should be performed frequently enough that the estimated value of data lost is less than the expense of backing up the data.

How long should you retain a backup of your data? At one time, I would have said "forever," but this is a frivolous answer.

The value of most data, and software, declines with age. Most applications and operating systems become worthless after a few years (as you upgrade to newer versions). User data, on the other hand, may continue to be valuable many years into the future.

One critical issue is how can the data be restored from (possibly old) backup media? Since you may have to restore the backup using the same backup application that wrote the tape, how do you back up the "backup program?" A few hints:

- First, mark your long-term backups, specifically indicating what is on them and what application created the backup.
- Save all backup programs with their original media for as long as you have backups written with the backup program.
- Determine how long you must keep backups. Do not hoard backups, generating tens, or even hundreds, of copies of data that don't need to be backed up more than one time.
- Consider legal ramifications of keeping the backup. Accounting and tax information may need to be retained for a certain period of time. Following this time period, such data may prove to be a liability—were the backup to be obtained by unscrupulous parties, the backup may actually cost your organization!
- Differentiate between security backups (which are used to restore the system in the event of a failure), and archival backups (which are, typically, the only copy of the data).

Physical Security of Backups

Make backups in sets of two (or more), with one set stored offsite. Smaller companies may choose to use a safety deposit box at a nearby bank, while larger companies can use either other corporate sites, or commercial data storage facilities.

Try, if possible, to physically isolate the second backup from the original. Don't choose a bank that is in the same building as your site! Any disaster that destroys the building may well affect both copies of your data.

Fireproof safes, vaults, and other containers can provide some protection; however, none of these devices should be considered replacements for offsite storage of backups.

For critical data, where the loss of a server may cause serious problems, an online backup (using replication) to an offsite server may be a wise investment. Even a backup server that is not directly connected to the main network may be adequate. A RAS dial-up connection used each night to transfer data may be practicable when the data that changes is not too large. With dial-up, a reliable 28.8 modem connection can transfer 10MB in an hour, and an ISDN connection two to four times that figure (20 to 40MB per hour).

What Do I Back Up?

Backups may consist of an entire server, drive, or only a selection of files. Virtually all backups are selections of files from one or more drives. There are two significant backup methodologies: complete backup and incremental backup. Many have debated the relative advantages and disadvantages of the two different backup methodologies.

A complete backup consists of all files that are to be backed up, whether the files have been modified since the last backup or not. Whenever files must be restored from a complete backup, only the most recent backup would be restored.

Incremental backups initially start by doing a complete backup. Further backups consist of only those files that have been modified since the last backup operation. With incremental backups, any unmodified files are simply recovered from earlier backups. When files are restored from an incremental backup, all backups from the first, complete backup to the last incremental backup are restored.

Each method has value, neither is exclusive; you may choose to perform both complete backups and incremental backups on a regular scheduled basis.

What About Application Software?

For any backup methodology, the question often asked is: "Do we back up our application software?" There is no hard and fast answer, but do take the following points into consideration when creating your backup policy:

- Realize that virtually all major applications must be reinstalled when you install a new operating system.
- There is a good possibility that the backed up application may be corrupted and fail to operate correctly, possibly damaging either the system or data.
- Many software license agreements limit backups of the application to a single backup copy.
- Virtually all major applications are distributed using CD-ROM media. Though CD-ROM media life is still unknown (estimates range from a low of 10 years to a high of over 50 years), you can reasonably expect the CD-ROM media (if properly cared for) to exceed the life span of the application.
- Backups of applications distributed on diskettes will generally be better if you back up the original distribution media, rather than the installed product.

Incremental Backups

Incremental backups are done by first making a complete backup, then, for a period of time, backing up only those files that have changed. Incremental backups work best when most files on the system don't change frequently. Many organizations do a complete backup one day each week and incremental backups the remaining days of the week. The process repeats itself, on a weekly basis.

If the original complete backup is lost, the incremental backup tapes will not contain enough information to restore the system. In fact, they may not contain sufficient information to even restore the parts of the system that have been backed up!

An incremental backup's weakness becomes apparent at file restoration time: you must first restore the original complete backup, then restore each (and every) incremental backup. This can be rather time consuming, especially when there are many incremental tapes.

Let's look at an example. You have five files (A through E), and you do your first complete backup, which creates an initial copy of all five files. The first week file A changes and is backed up on Week 1's tape. The second week file B and file D change and are backed up on Week 2's tape. The third week file A changes (again) and is backed up on Week 3's tape. The fourth week file D changes and is backed up on Week 4's tape.

Then disaster strikes, and in a really fumble-fingered move I drop the server out a 35th-story window, and it is totally destroyed (like the piano in the TV ad). To restore files C and E the initial tape is used (they never changed). To restore file B, Week 2's tape is used. To restore file A, Week 3's tape is used. To restore file D, Week 4's tape is used. The restoration process would be to simply restore each tape, in the order that they were made: this would result in the latest copy of each file being restored.

Advantages of incremental backups include reduced system overhead (the backup program and the system are working to back up only those files that have changes), and reduced cost (incremental backups don't require as many tapes as a complete backup).

Complete Backups

Complete backups are just that—all the files on the server are backed up each time a backup is performed. Each backup is a complete copy of all files, making management and restoration easier.

Complete backups can be time consuming (with tape changers and management systems, much of the effort can be automated); however, a restoration from a complete backup is typically much faster—only one tape set must be restored.

Hazards of a complete backup system include the possible loss of all files from a certain date if the backup procedure is not correctly managed.

The End of the World?

Sometimes data is corrupted, and this damage is not noticed immediately.

The biggest disaster that any backup scheme can perpetrate (with your help) is to back up "bad" data. As time progresses, old tapes are re-used to make new backups, and older uncorrupted data is overwritten with newer, corrupted data.

It has happened, more often than one would like to admit, that eventually all copies of a given data file have been corrupted! Restoration of the data becomes impossible, and the resulting costs of data re-creation may be very high.

Assuring that backups of files don't contain flaws that render the backup useless is difficult. Checksum routines may be able to determine that a file's contents have, or have not, been modified. For files that are frequently modified (such as accounting data), long-term backups (going back many years) may be the only solution. I back up my accounting data each month after the monthly accounting run. These backups are never overwritten.

Backup Hardware

Backup hardware for servers comprises a vast array of components. Simple systems consist of a single tape drive, manually operated, with few frills. More complex systems include changers automated to feed tapes on command into the drive from the backup software.

Windows NT 4 Server supports most simpler backup hardware systems virtually straight out of the box, though more complex hardware demands specialized software. Fortunately most systems supply the necessary backup software with the hardware.

There are questions about the life span of backup tapes. I certainly question the ability to read tapes when operating systems and backup software is updated. Frequently, we find that as the backup software is updated, our previous backups are no longer readable.

All server backup systems are SCSI interface. Floppy interface tape drives don't have sufficient I/O speed to perform in a server environment. Some low-cost tape backup systems are IDE (Integrated Drive Electronics) based; however, like floppy-based systems, neither tape drive capacity nor speed make these drives suitable for backing up servers.

Tape Technologies

Tape technologies have evolved from ½" 9-track reel-to-reel tapes (which held from 25 to almost 200MB of data) to ¼" cartridge tapes which held from 20 to 500MB of data. Today's tapes systems allow storage of gigabytes of data on a single cartridge.

Single-tape drives, in either a 3½ or 5¼ mounting size, are common and not expensive. Available from dealers, mail-order, and other sources, these drives require more manual intervention (tapes must be removed and inserted manually). All tape formats are available in single-tape drives.

Multi-tape changers allow you to back up with multiple tapes without having to "babysit" the backup process. With a multi-tape drive (usually called a changer), you can load up to 12 tapes, which are then selected into the drive under the backup program's control. Multi-tape changers can cost 50% more than a single-tape drive, but a tape changer's ease of use compensates for the increased cost.

There are four main technologies available today to microcomputer users: DLT, 4-MM, 8-MM, and DAT. Open-reel, QIC, and other older technologies are becoming much less popular, though for legacy backups, there may be support for old technologies.

DAT drives, capable of storing up to 8GB of data, usually cost between $500 and $1,000. DLT technology will back up about 6GB of data for about $1,000 to $1,500, and high-density DLT drives (storing as much as 20GB) cost about $3,000.

Drive changers can increase the speed of the backup and the amount of data you can back up.

DLT

Digital Linear Tape, or DLT, has been available on mini and mainframe computers for some time. Moving into the micro-server market, these drives offer superior reliability and convenience.

Currently the newest backup methodology, DLT drives are fast (many drives will back up at speeds of 50 to 150MB per minute), and DLT tapes hold 2.6GB of data.

8-MM

8-MM tape format uses the same tape-writing technology as a VCR: helical scanning that writes data on the tapes in tracks that are set at an angle to the edges of the tape.

Most 8-MM tapes hold 8GB (backup routines that compress may get as much as 16GB on a single tape).

4-MM

4-MM tape format, like 8-MM, also uses the same tape-writing technology as a VCR: helical scanning that writes data on the tapes in tracks that are set at an angle to the edges of the tape.

Most 4-MM tapes will hold either 3 or 4GB (backup routines that compress may get as much as 8GB on a single tape).

8-MM technology is better suited when backing up very large servers.

DAT

DAT (or Digital Audio Tape) is a technology that was originally developed to allow digital audio to be written to a small, easy-to-use tape. DAT never became popular in the audio industry (perhaps due to very restrictive legislation), but DAT technology did become popular as a backup media.

DAT tapes typically hold 2GB of data (with compression, a DAT tape may hold 4GB of data).

DAT's value is most apparent when it is necessary to exchange data between two systems. The DAT format and specifications have been standardized, allowing data to be transferred between drives made by companies such as Archive, Conner, HP, and WangDAT, and attached to a multitude of devices including graphic devices, CD duplicators, and data-conversion companies.

Optical Media

Though optical backups are not as popular as tapes, there are a number of choices in optical backup media. Some choices include:

- CDW (Writeable CD-ROM), which records on media that is compatible with standard CD-ROM drives. This backup technique is not often used, due to the difficulty of creating CD-ROMs (most CD-ROM writers require extensive supporting hardware). Writeable CD-ROMs are useful when the backup must be distributed to multiple sites, mainly because they are easy to ship. CD-ROMs are quick, easy to use, and have a very long life span. CD-ROMs hold between 600 and 700MB of data.
- WORM (Write Once, Read Many) and erasable optical drives offer a number of different storage capacities, ranging from a low of about 120MB up to a high of about 1.3GB. Typically, media costs are much higher than tape drives, but optical drives offer fast, random access to backed up data.

Diskettes

Don't laugh... Diskettes are a valuable backup media for many purposes. Small, high-value files may be easily backed up to diskettes, allowing multiple low-cost backup copies to be produced.

Though slow, the latest diskette technology may hold as much as 120MB of information (and more if compression is used), which can permit you a number of backup options. Even 1.44MB diskettes may prove valuable: a backup of this book takes eight 1.44 diskettes, including a copy of the software used to do the backup. The program (PKZIP) runs under virtually every version of DOS, Windows, and Windows NT. Speed, ease, and long-term system compatibility are a few of the advantages of diskette backup.

The easiest program to use to back up to diskettes is either PKZIP or WinZip. Both programs are available as shareware, and are easy to configure and use.

Hard Drive Backups

Hard drive backup? Automated with custom software, this amounts to simply copying critical files and folders to a second (or third) hard drive, either on the same server, or on another network resource.

Hard drive backups are usually done using two servers (or a server and a workstation) though there is no reason why a backup cannot be written to two different drives on the same computer. With hard drive backups, the backup is written to the second drive, either as a simple image (perhaps using a copy command), or by using a backup program that writes to a hard drive.

Though the Windows NT 4 Server backup program does not back up to a hard drive, the backup program included with Windows 95 does—allowing Windows 95 clients to back up both local and networked data to either local or networked drives.

Hard drive backups (which can be automatically produced by mirroring technology or replication) are the fastest way to back up data. Hard drive backups can also be the most expensive methodology for backing up!

Windows NT Backup

There are two alternatives for backup software: you can either use the backup program that comes with Windows NT 4 Server, or you can purchase a third-party application. This chapter focuses mainly on the program that comes with Windows NT 4 Server.

Windows NT 4 Server includes a basic tape backup program created by Arcada Software. This program is a good basic backup utility that supports hardware compression (but not software compression), multiple volume backups, and other features.

The Windows NT 4 Server backup program is a simple, easy-to-use program that will prove valuable to many users. Windows NT 4 Server backup does, however, have a few shortcomings:

- There is no software compression.
- There is support only for backing up to tape drives.
- There is no way to create exclusion lists.

The Windows NT 4 Server backup program is started by selecting Backup from the Start Menu | Programs | Administrative Tools (Common).

The Windows NT 4 backup program does not support backups to diskettes; however, for a server, diskette backups are not significant. Both PKZIP and WinZip are alternatives when diskette backup is necessary.

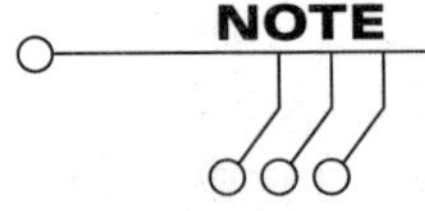

You must have a tape device connected to your system to use Backup. The best tape drive interface choices are SCSI connections, which support higher I/O rates than most other interfaces.

Installing Hardware

This section is not intended to be an all-inclusive installation guide for every tape device made. But for most tape devices, the following will help make things work better.

1. Physically install the drive, making sure that the drive itself is easily reached. Tapes must be inserted and removed on a regular basis when doing backups, so keep the tape device in a convenient location. I prefer external SCSI devices, as this allows the device to be easily moved as necessary.
2. Install the driver for your tape device. From the Control Panel, start the Tape Devices applet. The Tape Devices applet (Figure 18-1) is simple, with two tabs (Devices and Drivers).

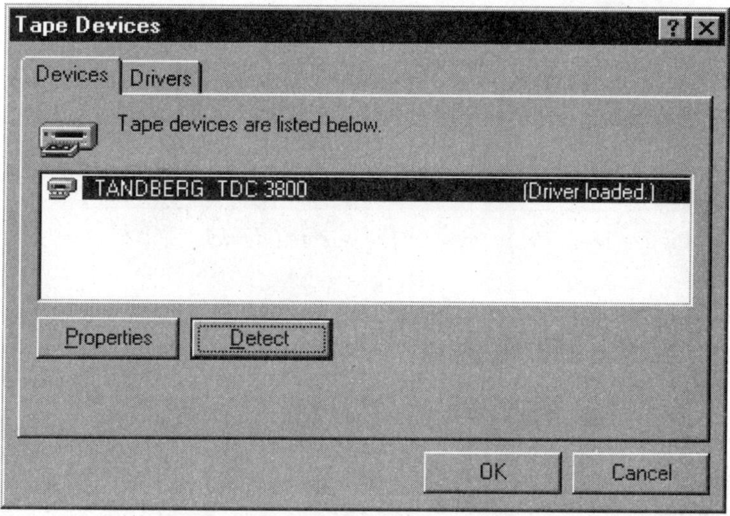

Figure 18-1: The Control Panel's Tape Devices applet.

3. The first tab, Devices, configures each tape device installed. Clicking on Properties displays a Properties dialog for the currently selected device (Figure 18-2). A tape device's properties include interface, manufacturer, and status information.

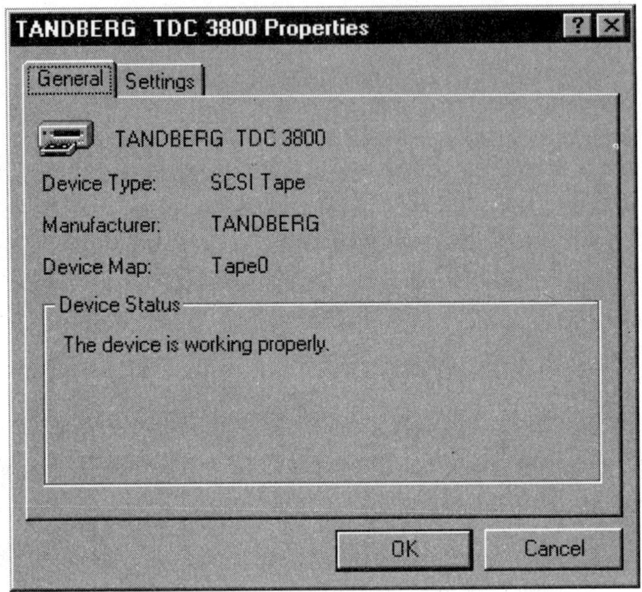

Figure 18-2: Properties for the selected device.

Clicking the Detect button causes Windows NT 4 Server to search for (new) tape devices. If any new devices are found, then Windows NT 4 Server prompts to install any needed drivers. A system may have more than one tape device installed.

4. The second tab, Drivers, displays each currently loaded drive. New drivers are added with the Add button, while existing drivers that are no longer needed are deleted using the Remove button.
5. After installing the device and using the Tape Devices applet to install the drivers, the hardware installation is complete!

Backing Up

Backing up consists of a few simple steps. Because the Backup application is easy to use, you won't have many problems once you have used it a few times.

There are decisions to make—first of all, you must decide what is being backed up. (Consider taking a look at the section "What Do I Back Up?") Selection can be any combination of drives, folders, and files. Figure 18-3 shows the drives window, with a drive (D:) opened.

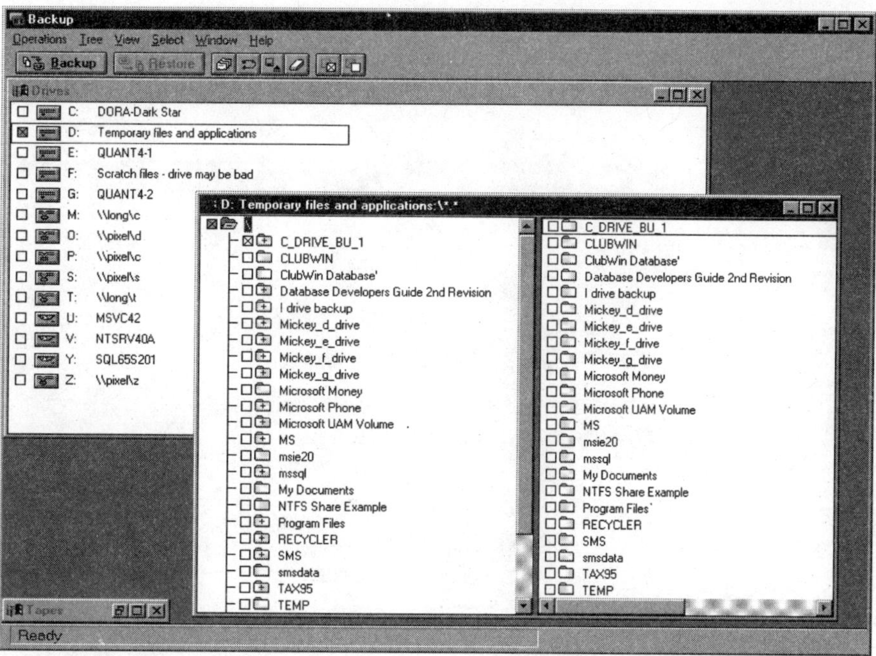

Figure 18-3: Drives window in the Backup program.

Backup has three main windows: the Drives window displays all drives available (including network resources). You can back up drives on other systems, and read-only (CD-ROM) drives, too!

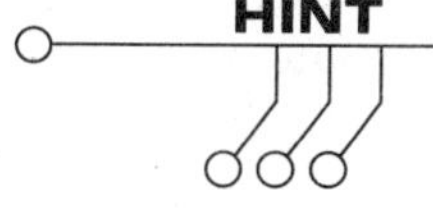

If you are planning to back up workstations on your network, then create a backup share on each workstation that will be backed up. This share allows access to the entire drive on the workstation for backup purposes.

The backup share is then accessed by the backup system to allow backing up of the workstation's data.

Double-clicking on any drive icon will open a window displaying the drive's contents. The Drive contents window has two panes: the left pane displays the folders on the drive, while the right pane displays folders and files. Both folders and files may be selected as desired. Select all drives, folders, and files you wish to back up!

Click the Backup button on the toolbar to start the backup. The Backup Information dialog box (Figure 18-4) displays. Items in Backup Information control how the backup is performed.

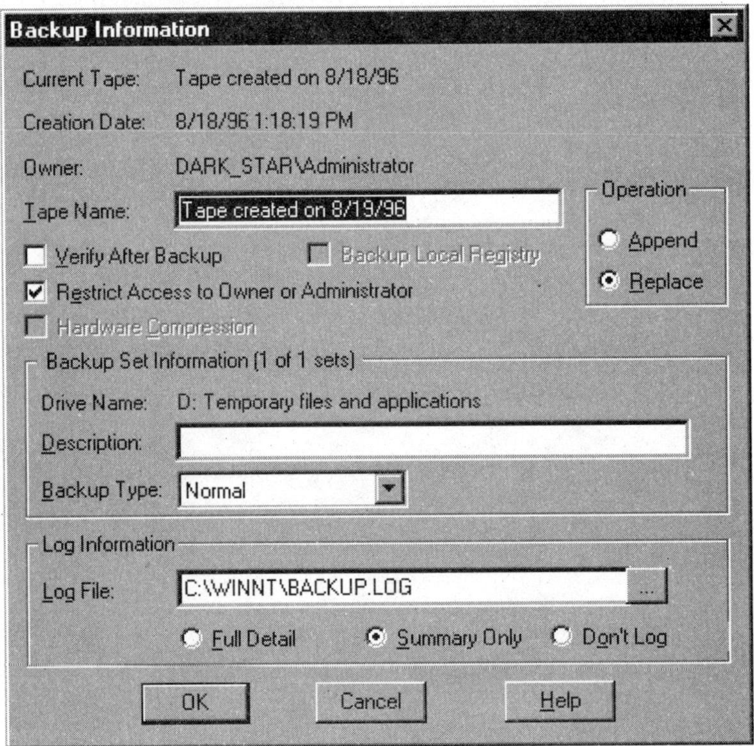

Figure 18-4: The Backup Information dialog box.

Specifying Tape Name and Options

Name each backup in the Tape Name edit box. Names should reflect the nature of the backup, though information such as the type, date, and time of the backup are also stored on the tape.

Tape Name information displays in the left pane of the Tapes window (see Figure 18-5).

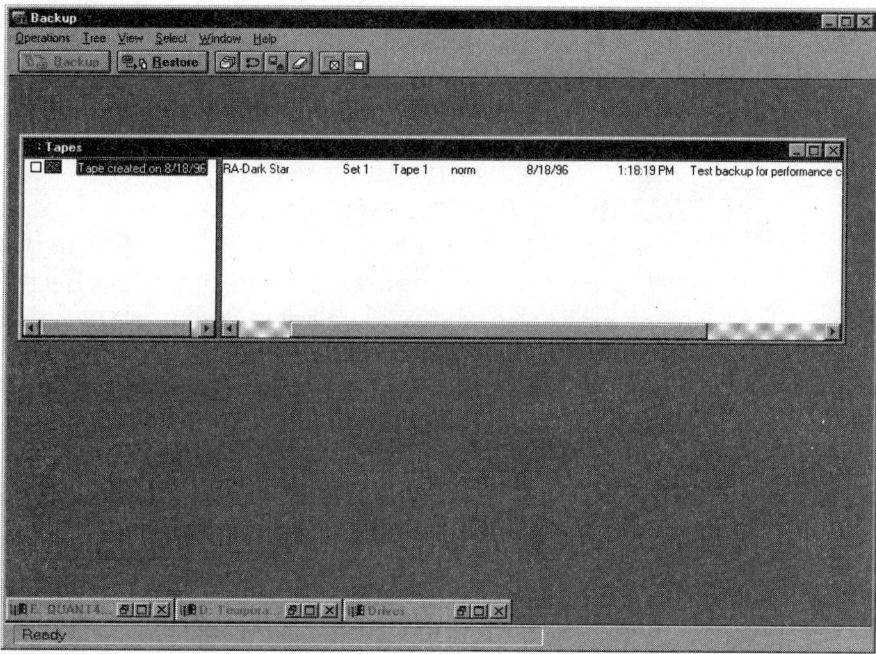

Figure 18-5: The Tapes window in Backup.

There are four check boxes that must be set or cleared:

- Verify After Backup—If this backup is critical, then verifying the backup against the original files ensures that the backup succeeded.
- Backup Local Registry—When the local boot drive has been selected, you can choose to back up the registry, too. Anytime you are doing backups, making a backup of the registry is a good idea.

- Restrict Access to Owner or Administrator—For any sensitive drives, folders, or files, restriction to either the administrator (any user with administrator privilege) or the owner is a wise idea.
- Hardware Compression—Drives that support compression can double the amount of information stored on the tape. Be cautious, as the tape usually has to be restored using the same type of drive if hardware compression is used.

To create a new backup, click the Replace button in the Operation groupbox. To append the new backup to an existing backup, select the Append button.

Specifying Backup Set Information

A backup set consists of a definition of what is to be backed up, including descriptions and other information. Each backup set has a description (each tape in a backup set may have a different description).

There are a number of philosophies for backing up data. No methodology can be said to be better than the other. For example, some methods take longer but are fast when a file must be restored. Other methods are quick on a daily basis, but restoring a file may take considerable effort.

How often do *you* have to restore? Yes, *you*… Not me, nor anyone else, but how often do you, in your organization, find that files must be restored from backup?

If your response is "frequently," then a philosophy that emphasizes quick restoration of files may be the best alternative for you. If your response is "seldom," then philosophies that reduce the time spent backing up may be the best.

When using Windows NT 4 Server's backup program, select the Backup Type to specify the philosophy you are using for a backup.

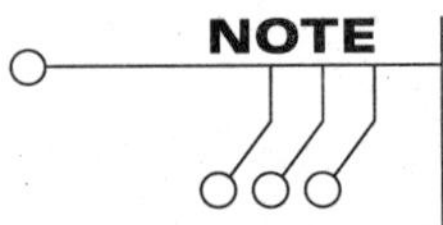

You cannot go wrong using the Normal philosophy (Normal backup type) when making a backup. This philosophy will back up all selected files, regardless of status, date, or any other factors.

- **Normal**—Backs up all files and folders selected in the Drives and Folder(s) windows. The backup is unconditional—the archive attribute, file's modification date, and other information is ignored. Once a file or folder is backed up, it is marked as having been backed up (the archive attribute is cleared).
- **Copy**—Copies all files and folders selected in the Drives and Folder(s) windows. The backup is unconditional—the archive attribute, file's modification date, and other information is ignored. The status of the archive attribute is not modified by Copy.
- **Incremental**—Backs up all files and folders selected in the Drives and Folder(s) windows. The backup is conditional: the archive attribute is used to determine whether a file should be backed up or not. If a file's archive attribute is set, the file is backed up. Once a file or folder is backed up, it is marked as having been backed up (the archive attribute is cleared).
- **Daily Copy**—Backs up all files and folders selected in the Drives and Folder(s) windows. The backup is conditional—the file's modification date must be equal to the current date, other information is ignored. The status of the archive attribute is not modified by Daily Copy.
- **Differential**—Backs up all files and folders selected in the Drives and Folder(s) windows. The backup is conditional—the archive attribute is used to determine whether a file should be backed up or not. If a file's archive attribute is set, the file is backed up. The status of the archive attribute is not modified by Differential.

Log Information

The Windows NT 4 Server backup program logs information for you, in a file you may specify. You can use either the default log file or specify a new log file name.

There are three logging options:

- Full Detail—Backup logs everything, including names, sizes, dates, and attributes of files and folders that have been backed up. Full Detail includes all information that is logged in the Summary Only logging mode, too.
- Summary Only—Backup logs significant events, such as tape status, and failures to open or backup files.
- Don't Log—Backup logs nothing.

All logging options are set in Backup Information dialog box.

Starting the Backup

Once the information in the Backup Information dialog box has been entered, clicking OK begins the backup. If the current tape is not blank, then a warning dialog (Figure 18-6) prompts, seeking confirmation that the current backup on the tape will be lost!

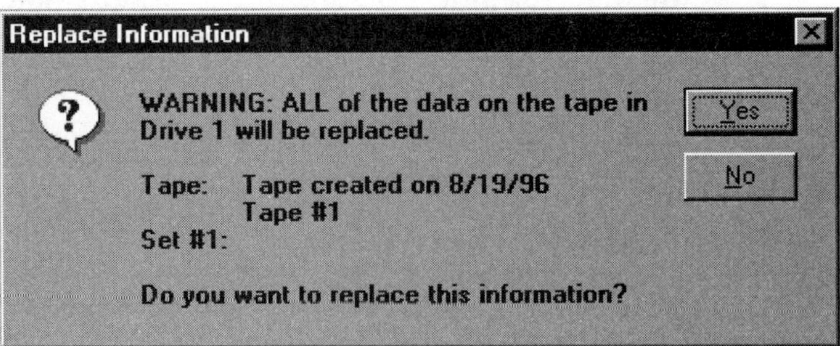

Figure 18-6: Data on the tape is about to be lost.

A backup's status is displayed in the Backup Status window (Figure 18-7).

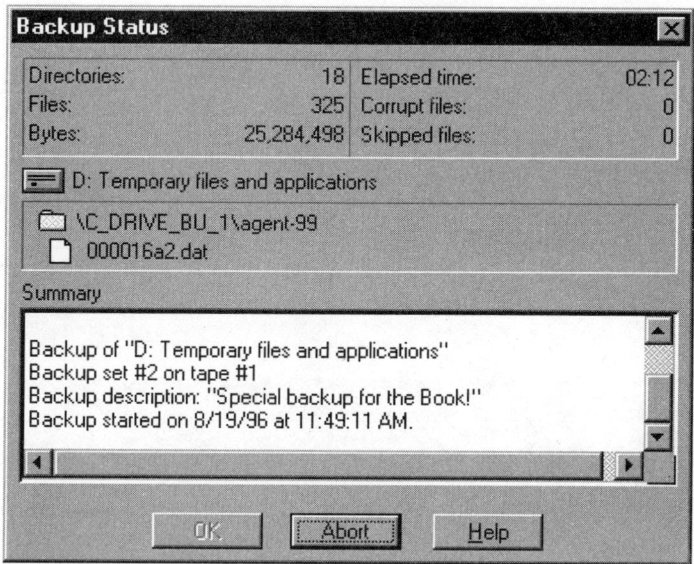

Figure 18-7: Backing up some files.

Once you have completed the backup (remember tape devices are slow, so a backup can take considerable time), the Backup Status window's OK button is enabled. If there are problems, the backup may be cancelled at any time. Anything that was already written to the tape is retained. When cancelling a backup, the file currently being written completes, if you choose it to.

If the backup requires more than one tape, Backup prompts for the next tape.

Restoring Backups

Backups are useful only if you can restore the files from the backup tape. After all, why back up if you can't restore?

The Tapes window (shown in Figure 18-5) lists the currently installed tape drives, the drive's status, and the installed tape (if any).

If there is a backup tape in the drive, Backup's mode is determined by which window has focus—if a drive window has focus, then Backup is in backup mode. If the Tape window has focus,

then Backup is in restore mode. If there is no tape, or the tape in the drive is not a backup tape, then Backup's mode is neither backup nor restore.

To restore, you perform the same process as a backup—you choose drives, folders, and files to restore. This is done by opening a backup set in the tapes window: double-click on the folder icon in the right pane of the Tapes window. A Tape backup set window (an example is shown in Figure 18-8) opens, displaying a directory of the contents of the tape.

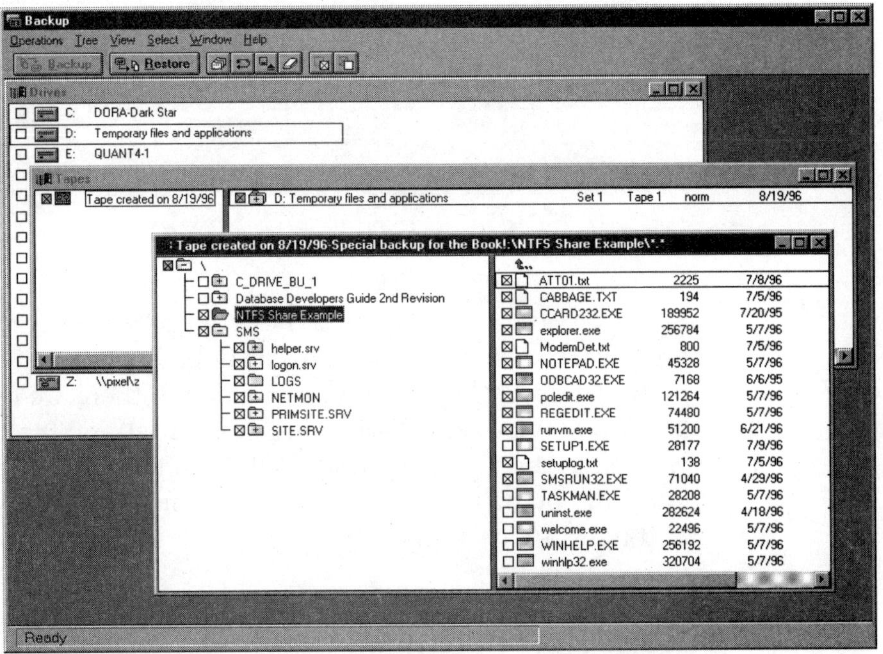

Figure 18-8: Window showing which files were written to the tape.

Select the drives, folders, and files to be restored. Any combination may be restored, and only the files selected will be restored. You do not have to restore an entire drive just to recover a single file!

Once the drives, folders, and files to be restored have been selected, click on the Restore button in the toolbar. The Restore Information dialog box (shown in Figure 18-9) displays, showing the name of the tape, the backup set name (remember, more than one backup set may be written to a single tape), the creation data, and owner's name.

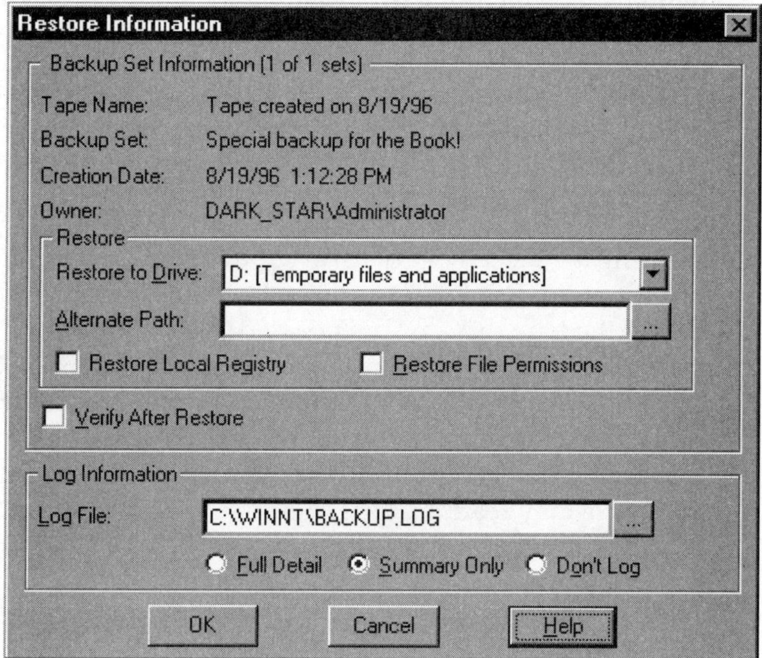

Figure 18-9: Restore Information, getting files back from the tape.

Also specified on the Restore Information dialog box is the destination for the restored files. You can choose to restore to the original path (drive or folder), or you may choose an alternate path. Using an alternate path is very useful when the current file's contents should not be overwritten. Restore to Drive specifies the drive to restore to, while Alternate Path allows the files being restored to be placed in a folder on the restore drive.

You may also choose to restore the Local Registry (don't, unless you are having problems with the registry—any changes made since the registry was backed up will be lost!) and restore the file permissions.

Choosing Verify After Restore tells Backup to check to make sure that the file(s) written are identical to the files on the tape.

Logging information may be customized, with optional file name and level of detail selections, as when doing a backup.

Once you click the OK button, Backup then restores the files to the location you specified.

A Final Note About Erasing Tapes

Erasing a tape can be necessary if the tape contains any sensitive information. Prior to discarding tapes they should either be erased using the tape drive or bulk erased.

Prior to giving a backup tape to a user, make sure the tape does not contain any information that could be compromised if the user obtains access to the information on the tape. Though the backup program you used to write the tape may have security, other software may read the tape, without regard to security!

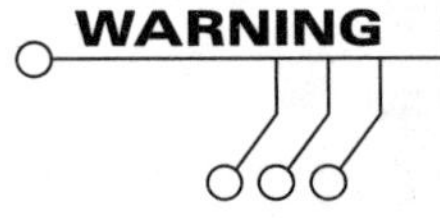

Bulk tape erasers may not perform as well as you think. Always check each *tape bulk erased to ensure that the tape cannot be read!*

Moving On

This chapter concentrated on backup techniques and described the Windows NT 4 Server backup program of the same name, Backup. Backups are usually made to tape devices (almost always cartridge tapes), though sometimes backups are made to other media including optical, diskette, and hard drives.

Windows NT 4 Server comes with a basic and easy-to-use backup program. For more advanced functionality, you will need an aftermarket product.

The next chapter, "The Registry," introduces the Windows NT registry, RegEdit, RegEdt32, and the BOOT.INI file. The Registry serves as the main repository for configuration for both Windows NT 4 Server and for many applications. The BOOT.INI file controls the Windows NT boot manager, allowing multiple boot configurations.

19 The Registry

In this chapter, I cover the Windows NT 4 Server registry, the BOOT.INI file, and a few simple modifications you can make to Windows NT 4 Server. Both the registry and BOOT.INI file are critical to the proper functioning of Windows NT 4 Server.

The registry serves as the central depository of information for Windows NT. Most applications store application-specific information in the registry, whereas Windows NT stores all of its configuration information in the registry.

The BOOT.INI file controls the Windows NT 4 Server boot manager. BOOT.INI is the key to being able to boot multiple versions of Windows NT and other operating systems.

The Windows NT 4 Server Registry

The Windows NT registry is a hierarchical (that is, tree-based) database containing virtually everything that Windows NT 4 Server needs to know in order to start and run. Information about applications, systems, servers, and services all resides in the registry.

If the Windows NT 4 Server registry is damaged, the result may well be a server that doesn't work. Sometimes the only fix is to install a clean copy of Windows NT 4 Server. Be very careful. Be very, very, careful when manually adding, changing, or deleting anything in the registry.

Why have a registry? Wouldn't Windows 3.x's .INI files work just as well, and not be as sensitive to damage? Can't the registry get so large that it becomes unmanageable? Are we not just putting "all our eggs in one basket?" These questions, and more, are answered in this chapter.

First, why have a registry? The registry serves as a centralized depository of information for Windows NT. This information is used by the operating system, and by applications, as needed. Neither Windows NT, nor applications, need to search for information—everything is in a known location—the registry.

The Registry and .INI Files

Windows 3.x (and earlier) used .INI files to store both system and application information. The files SYSTEM.INI and WIN.INI stored Windows 3.x operating system-specific information, and a myriad of application .INI files (sometimes hundreds of them) clogged the WINDOWS directory.

And, no, .INI files are not dead: there are still a few of them left in Windows NT 4 Server. As some applications are installed (such as Office 95, TechNet, MSDN, and others) they oftentimes write an .INI file, and many (if not all) 16-bit applications write .INI files, regardless of what operating system they were created for.

.INI files are generally text-based and can be edited with a text editor. The Windows NT registry, however, is a binary file that is not modifiable except by using the registry editors (RegEdit and RegEdt32). The registry, because it is a hierarchical database, won't become so large as to be unmanageable. In the old days, an .INI file, for example (the WIN.INI and SYSTEM.INI files in Windows 3.x), often became so large that searching for a specific piece of information was quite time consuming! A Windows 3.x system with a lot of fonts often suffered from this problem.

Files in the Registry

In Windows NT 4 Server, information contained in the registry is stored in a set of files. These files are not changed or edited directly by you; rather, you use a program such as RegEdit to make changes in the registry files.

The Windows NT registry's files are found in the %SystemRoot%\System32\Config folder. (%SystemRoot% is an environment variable, defined by Windows NT 4 Server, that contains the path to the Windows NT 4 Server folder.) An example of a typical set of files contained in the Config folder is shown in Figure 19-1.

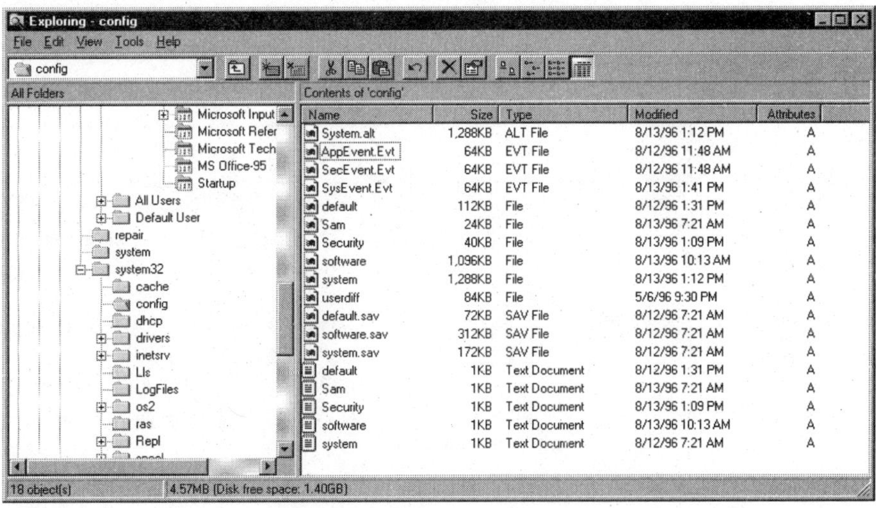

Figure 19-1: A typical Config folder—home of the registry!

In Chapter 18, "Backing Up the System," I mentioned that my computer's C: drive had failed just as I started to write the chapter. What happened? I started Windows NT 4 Server, and then got a message that the file %SystemRoot%\System32\Config\System could not be read. It turns out that this file is a major part of the registry! No wonder I could not even start the computer!

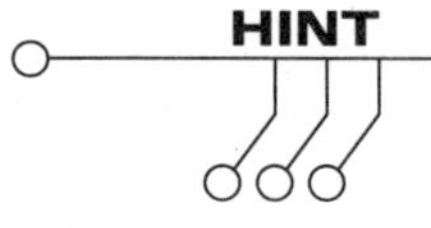

When part of the registry cannot be read, Windows NT 4 Server usually suggests that you repair your installation. This may work, or it may not—if there are problems with the drive (as in my case) then a more drastic solution may be needed. To repair your Windows NT 4 Server installation, run the Windows NT 4 Server installation program (boot the installation diskettes or CD-ROM) and select repair when prompted.

More drastic solution: for SCSI drives, a low-level format may be needed, followed by a complete reinstallation of Windows NT 4 Server.

In the %SystemRoot%\System32\Config folder, there are about twenty files. Table 19-1 lists many of these files, and describes the part that they play in the Windows NT 4 Server registry.

File	Description or Usage
SAM	SAM (Security Accounts Manager) contains information about user accounts. SAM authorizes logons and validates security.
system	Information about the system. This part of the registry is critical, so Windows NT 4 Server saves a copy as SYSTEM.ALT. If SYSTEM cannot be read, then Windows NT 4 Server automatically uses SYSTEM.ALT.
default	Default user settings.
SECURITY	The system security database.
software	Information about installed software.

File	Description or Usage
userdiff	Miscellaneous user information.
SYSTEM.ALT	A backup of the SYSTEM file.
AppEvent.Evt	The application event log file.
SecEvent.Evt	The security event log file.
SysEvent.Evt	The system event log file.
SAM.LOG	Record of modifications to the SAM file.
System.LOG	Record of modifications to the SYSTEM file.
Default.LOG	Record of modifications to the DEFAULT file.
SECURITY.LOG	Record of modifications to the SECURITY file.
software.LOG	Record of modifications to the SOFTWARE file.
system.sav	A forced backup of the SYSTEM file.
default.sav	A forced backup of the DEFAULT file.
software.sav	A forced backup of the SOFTWARE file.

Table 19-1: Files found in the %SystemRoot%\System32\Config folder.

Windows 95 users will remember that the Windows 95 registry is composed of two files, SYSTEM.DAT and USER.DAT, and has a structure that is very similar to Windows NT 4 Server's registry, though perhaps not as large.

There are two tools for working with the registry: RegEdit and RegEdt32. Either program produces the same results; however, the user interface and options are different for these two programs. We will talk about these two programs a bit later in this chapter.

Both RegEdit and RegEdt32 may be started from the Windows NT Start Menu's Run command—simply click Run, and type either RegEdit or RegEdt32 in the Open box, and click OK.

The registry files are made up of hives, keys, key values, values, and data.

Hives = Folders

So, then what in blue blazes is a hive? And where did that strange, non-computer name come from? (Trust me, it is a non-computer name!)

Just as files on your disk are arranged into a hierarchical fashion (using folders), items in the registry are arranged in the same way. For example, Windows NT 4 Server is installed in a folder, which has sub-folders, which in turn may have sub-folders of their own.

The registry's term for what you would call a folder is a *hive*. Well, don't blame me, I didn't name it! It seems that some unnamed programmer at Microsoft looked at the registry, and was reminded of a bee hive, and the name stuck. A hive consists of keys, subkeys, and values. Each hive is located in a file, as described below.

Because the term "hives" is not descriptive, it is most common to refer to registry entries as keys and key values (referred to collectively as keys) and values. RegEdt32 uses this terminology extensively.

Keys

A registry key is an entry that may contain either values or other keys. Similar to a folder on a disk (which may contain folders or files), registry keys consist of an identifier and an optional value.

For example, there is a key in the Windows NT 4 Server registry called *Identifier* which, for my computer, contains the value "x86 Family 5 Model 2 Stepping 4." When Windows NT boots, this value is placed in an environment variable called PROCESSOR_IDENTIFIER.

Key Values

A registry key is an identifier for an item in the registry. This item may be another key, or a value. A key value is a registry key that has some data assigned to it. It is common to refer to an entire key and its data value as just a key. For example,

```
HKEY_LOCAL_MACHINE\OWNERMAP\PCI_0_6 = \Device\ScsiPort1
```

HKEY_LOCAL_MACHINE\OWNERMAP is the key, and *PCI_0_6* is the key value that contains the data "*\Device\ScsiPort1*." However, the entire key (for example: *HKEY_LOCAL_MACHINE\OWNERMAP\PCI_0_6*), is usually referred to simply as the "registry key" for simplicity's sake.

Specific data is usually assigned to a key value. Some registry keys don't have a value set, which is also acceptable. Values have different types such as binary, numeric, and character.

So now we know that the registry is made up of keys, each of which may contain zero, one, or more data values. Each value may contain data whose type is predefined when the key is created.

Changing the Registry

Most, though not all, registry changes are done using parts of Windows NT 4 Server such as the Control Panel. For example, if you wanted to change the color of an inactive window's title text, you'd use the Control Panel's Display applet. However, since some registry changes can only be done manually, there just is no other way to make changes to many of the registry keys and their values other than to use RegEdit or RegEdt32.

The Display applet will then modify, in the registry, the key HKEY_USERS\S-1-5-21-891767030-446455771-1795632751-500\Control Panel\Colors, setting Colors from the original value of 192 192 192, to the new value "255 255 0," which is yellow. This key is shown in Figure 19-2.

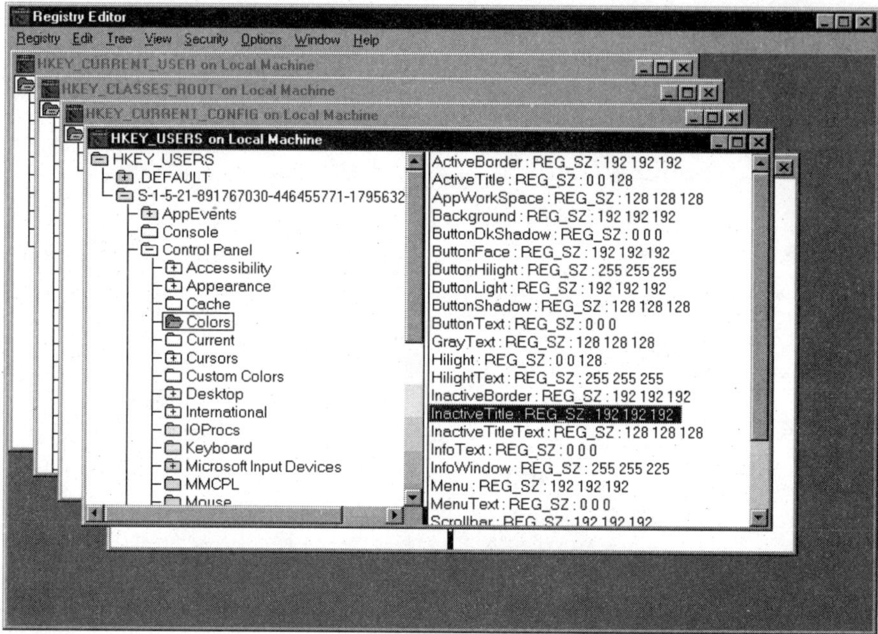

Figure 19-2: The inactive title's text color in the registry.

Wait a minute, how does that value relate to me? My user ID is *Administrator*! Well, Windows NT 4 Server maintains, for security, users as an identifier, not as the user name. For example, the number S-1-5-21-891767030-446455771-1795632751-500 was generated by Windows NT 4 Server as the user identifier for Administrator user ID when the Administrator account was created.

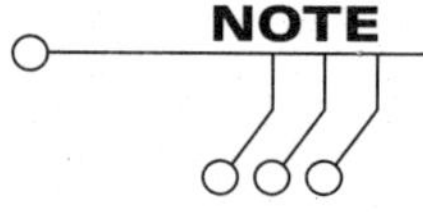

The mappings between user identifiers and user IDs are not accessible to anyone except the system.

If the registry can be modified by applications such as the Control Panel, then why use the registry editor? Well, there are two reasons to use the registry editor:

- Some system keys are not directly editable, except by using a registry editor. In fact, many keys are not accessible from the Control Panel, or from any other location.

- All application keys (yes, applications can, and do, store items in the registry) are accessible only by the application (using the application's configuration functionality), or by one of the registry editors.

Examples of Registry Changes

Microsoft maintains an extensive database of information documenting bugs, changes, enhancements, and other features or problems with each of their products. This database is called the Knowledge Base (often referred to as the KB), and each article is written concisely (most KB articles are only a page or two long). You'd use the registry editor to make the changes suggested in the KB article.

An example of a KB article is shown in Figure 19-3, where I've highlighted where a registry key must be changed to alter the way the system works. This article talks about adding a new value to a registry key to change the way that TCP/IP works.

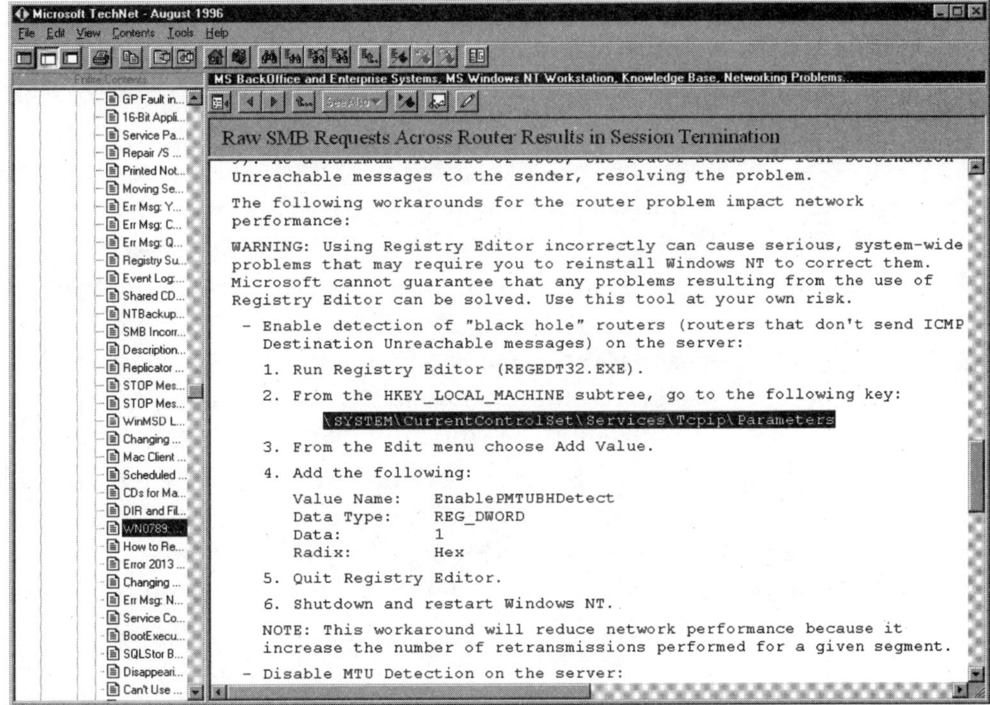

Figure 19-3: A Microsoft Knowledge Base article on setting a registry key.

Another example of changing a registry variable is with Windows NT 4 Server. The shutdown button on the logon screen is disabled. This is by design—after all, who wants their server shut down by anyone who can access the computer? For some environments, however, shutting down the server from the logon screen may be acceptable—and a quick change in a registry key allows this to be done.

Change the HKEY_LOCAL_MACHINE\SOFTWARE\Microsoft\Windows NT\CurrentVersion\Winlogon\ShutdownWithoutLogon key value to 1 (the default is 0), and the Shutdown button is enabled on Windows NT 4 Server. Handy if you don't have a security risk!

A couple of other interesting keys in *HKEY_LOCAL_MACHINE\SOFTWARE\Microsoft\Windows NT\CurrentVersion\Winlogon* include:

- *LegalNoticeText* is a text string displayed in a dialog box after the user presses Ctrl-Alt-Del, and before the Windows NT 4 Server logon dialog is displayed. Of course, the notice needn't be anything as ominous as a "legal" notice: it could be something as simple as a message stating that the server is being removed from service for maintenance at a specified time.
- *LegalNoticeCaption* is a title to the legal notice dialog box, displayed after the user presses Ctrl-Alt-Del, and before the Windows NT 4 Server logon dialog is displayed.
- *PowerdownAfterShutdown* tells Windows NT 4 Server that the computer supports software-controlled power down, and that the power down feature should be used. (Power down technology is usually found on notebook computers, though some desktop systems do support this feature.)

The above are but a few examples of some of the more interesting items that can be modified in the Windows NT 4 Server registry. For example, adding a "LegalNoticeCaption" allows you to provide text information to anyone who logs onto the server.

Using RegEdit

RegEdit and RegEdt32 perform similar functions, but have different interfaces to perform those functions. RegEdit displays a single, split-pane window showing the entire registry. You can manually search the various keys, add new keys, and change a key's data value using RegEdit.

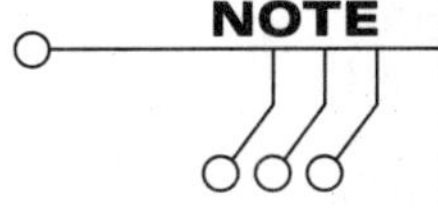

Both RegEdit and RegEdt32 identify themselves in the title bar as "Registry Editor." To avoid confusion, I'll refer to each by the executable file name (RegEdit or RegEdt32).

Figure 19-4 shows RegEdit's user interface. On the left side of RegEdit is a listing of keys, and on the right is a listing of values and their data, stored in keys.

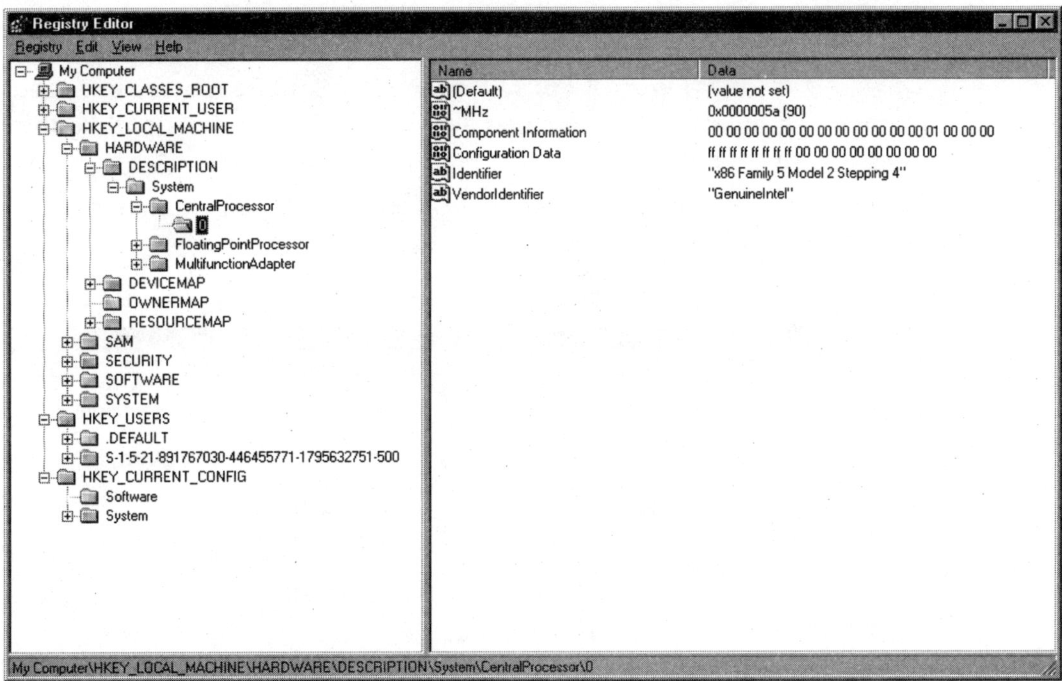

Figure 19-4: RegEdit's user interface.

To modify a value, simply double-click on it, and the edit dialog box (Figure 19-5) displays.

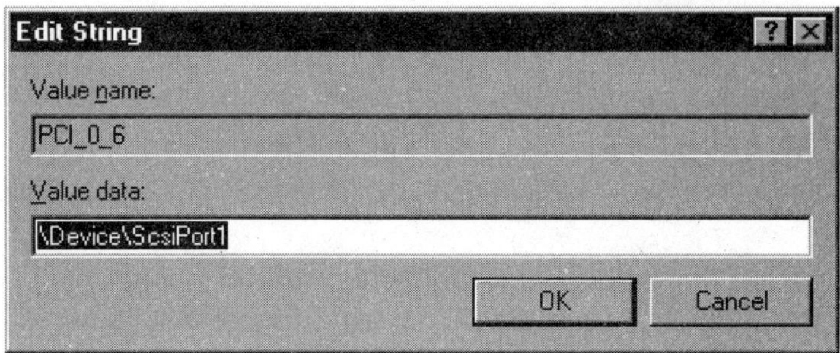

Figure 19-5: Editing a string value in RegEdit.

Adding a key (which you may have to do) is just as easy.

1. Select, from RegEdit's menu, Edit | New | Key. The new key is created, and you are then placed in the Rename mode (Figure 19-6) so that the key's name may be changed. Once you have created a new key, then you may add either new sub-keys or values to the key.
2. To add a sub-key, simply open the key you created, then select Edit | New | Key again.

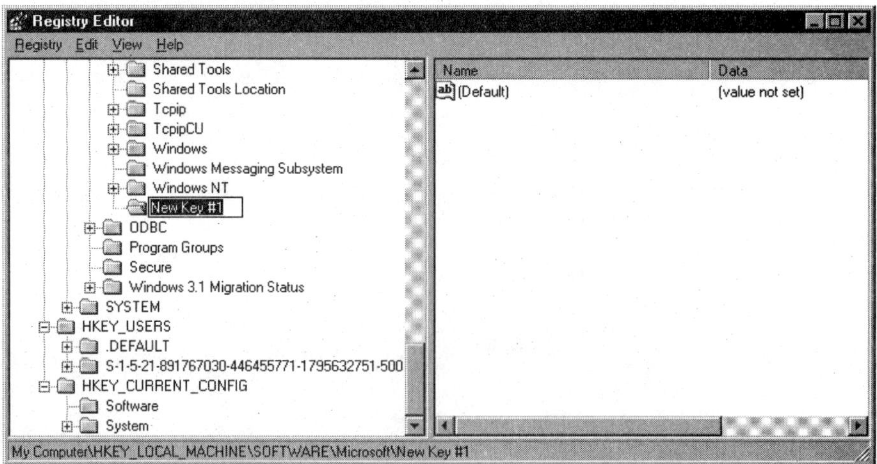

Figure 19-6: Naming a newly created key.

Adding a new value to a key is as easy as creating a key. Select, from RegEdit's menu, Edit | New | String Value, Edit | New | Binary Value, or Edit | New | DWORD Value, as appropriate for the type of data that will be stored in the value.

RegEdit allows you to delete, rename, and copy items, and you may search the registration database if desired.

Using RegEdt32

The other registration database editor is RegEdt32. This program offers a different user interface than RegEdit (described above). RegEdt32 has a somewhat more powerful user interface, and provides more flexibility by showing each of the HKEY_ hives as a separate window.

It is possible to search the various keys manually, add new keys, and change a key's data value using RegEdt32. Figure 19-7 shows RegEdt32's user interface. On the left side of each of RegEdt32's child windows is a listing of keys; on the right is a listing of values and data stored in keys.

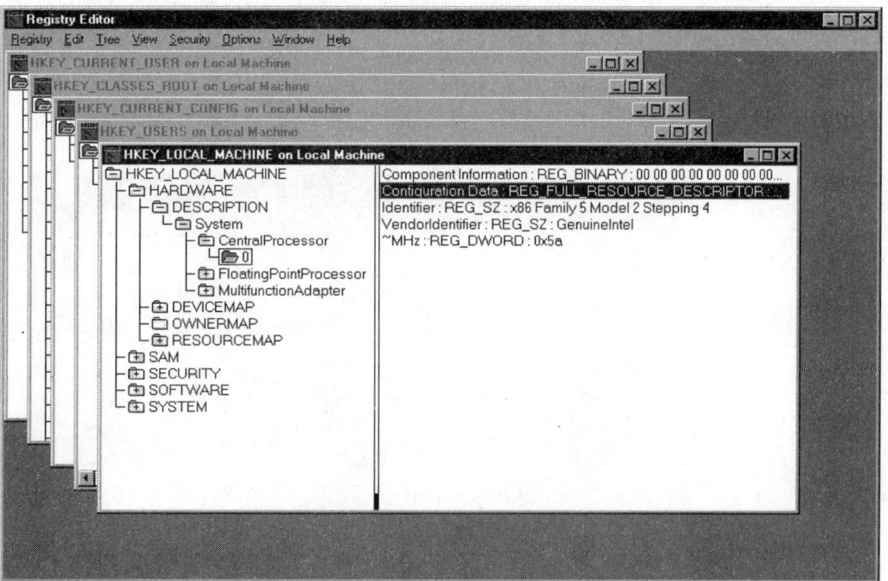

Figure 19-7: RegEdt32's MDI user interface.

To modify a value, simply double-click on it and the edit dialog box (Figure 19-8) displays. Notice that unlike RegEdit, this edit box doesn't show anything except for the data value.

Figure 19-8: Editing a string value in RegEdt32.

Adding a key is as easy here as it was with RegEdit.

1. Select, from RegEdt32's menu, Edit | Add Key. The Add Key dialog box (Figure 19-9) displays.
2. Enter the new key, and the optional Class, and click OK. The new key is created. Once you have created a new key, then you may add either new sub-keys or values to the key.
3. To add a sub-key, simply open the key you created, then select Edit | Add Key again.

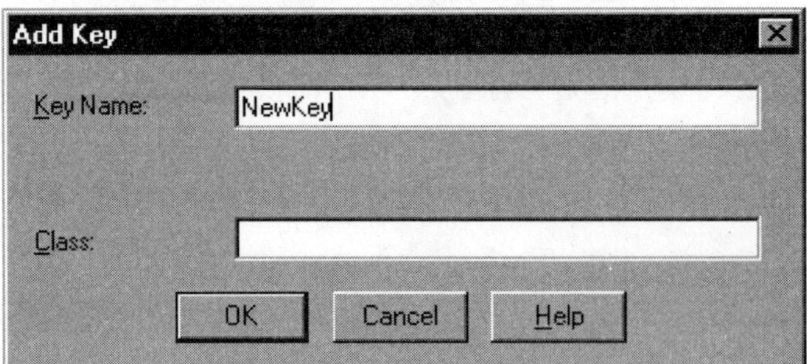

Figure 19-9: Adding a key using RegEdt32.

Adding a new value to a key is as easy as creating a key.

1. Select, from RegEdt32's menu, Edit | Add Value and the Add Value dialog box (Figure 19-10) displays.
2. In the Add Value dialog box, enter the value name and the data type for the value, and click the OK button. The appropriate edit dialog box (in my example, a REG_SZ string was created, so RegEdt32 displayed the String Editor) displays as shown in Figure 19-11.
3. Enter an appropriate data value, and click OK.

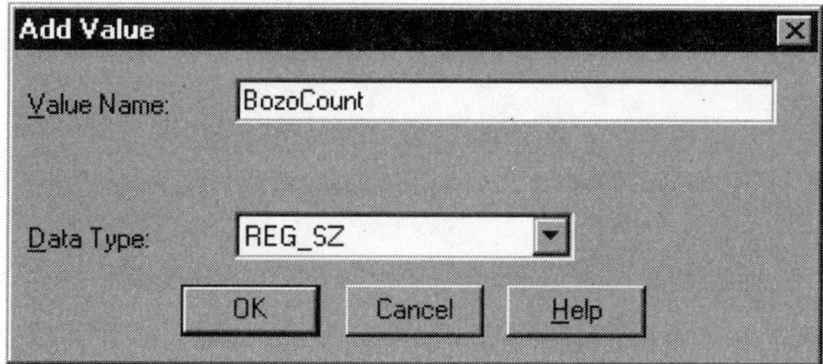

Figure 19-10: Creating a new value with RegEdt32.

Figure 19-11: Assigning data to the value created.

RegEdt32 allows you to delete, rename, and copy items, and you may search the registration database if desired.

RegEdt32 has security functions built in. For example, you can restrict a key's access to be read-only, full control, or special access (see Figure 19-12).

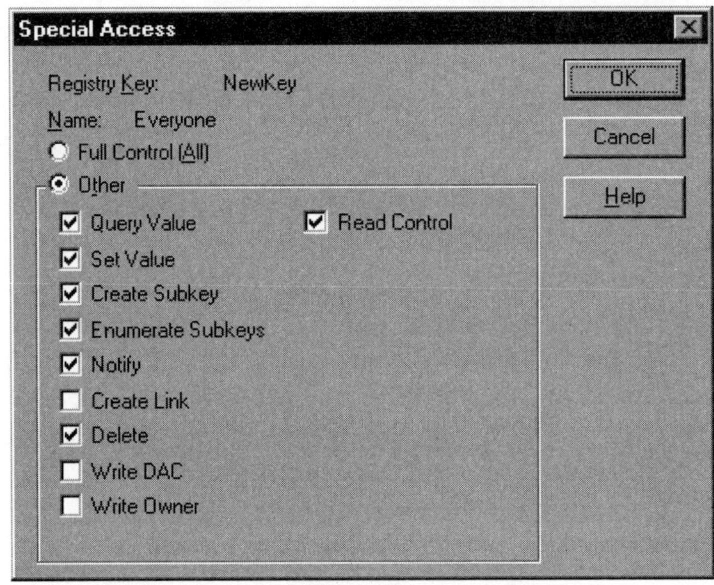

Figure 19-12: The RegEdt32 Special Access dialog box.

Registry Data Types

A registry key may have the following data types assigned to it. Both RegEdit and RegEdt32 manage most of these types of data.

- REG_BINARY is a binary value (entered either as hexadecimal or binary). Figure 19-13 shows the Binary Editor used to enter REG_BINARY data.

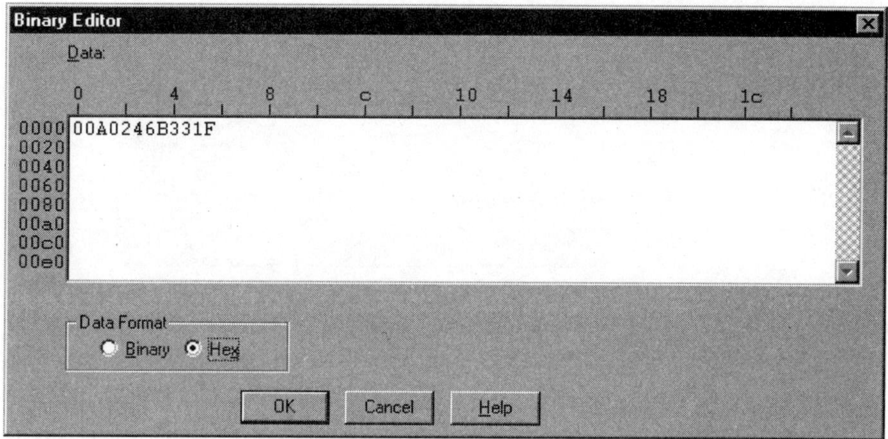

Figure 19-13: The REG_BINARY, binary data type edit box.

- REG_SZ is used for registry keys that contain strings. Figure 19-14 shows the String Editor used to enter REG_SZ data.

Figure 19-14 The REG_SZ, string data type edit box.

- REG_EXPAND_SZ is used if the key contains an expandable string. Since applications may frequently modify a given key, using expandable strings is more efficient; additional space is allocated for expansion. The same dialog as REG_SZ is used to enter a REG_EXPAND_SZ key.
- REG_DWORD is used to store a 32-bit value in the key, entered as decimal, hexadecimal, or binary. Figure 19-15 shows the DWORD Editor used to enter REG_DWORD data.

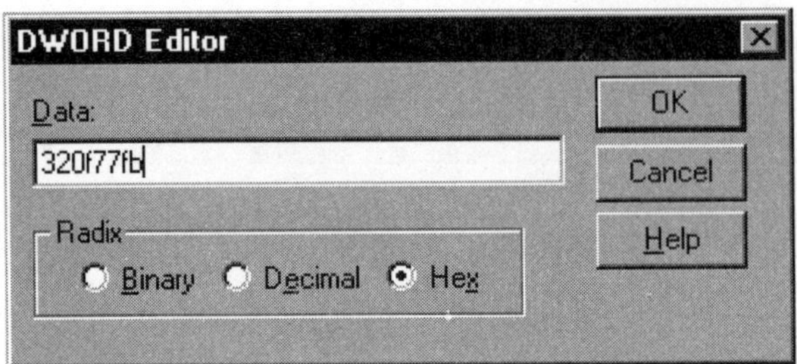

Figure 19-15: The REG_DWORD data type edit box.

- REG_MULTI_SZ stores multiple strings in a single registry key. Figure 19-16 shows the String Editor used to enter REG_MULTI_SZ data. Notice how multiple lines may be entered into the key.

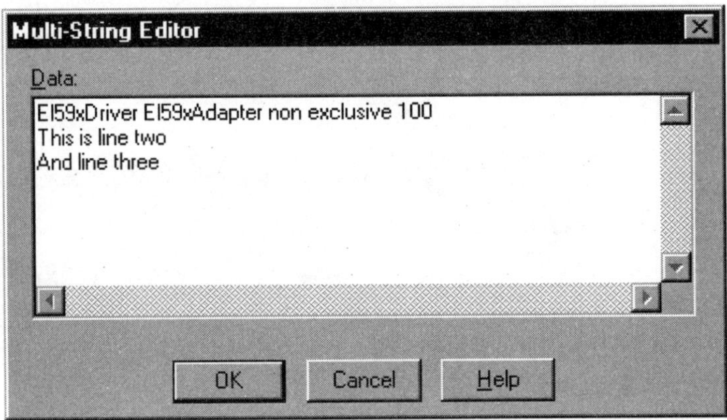

Figure 19-16: The REG_MULTI_SZ, multiple string data type edit box.

- REG_FULL_RESOURCE_DESCRIPTOR is used to manage information about hardware resources, as shown in Figure 19-17.

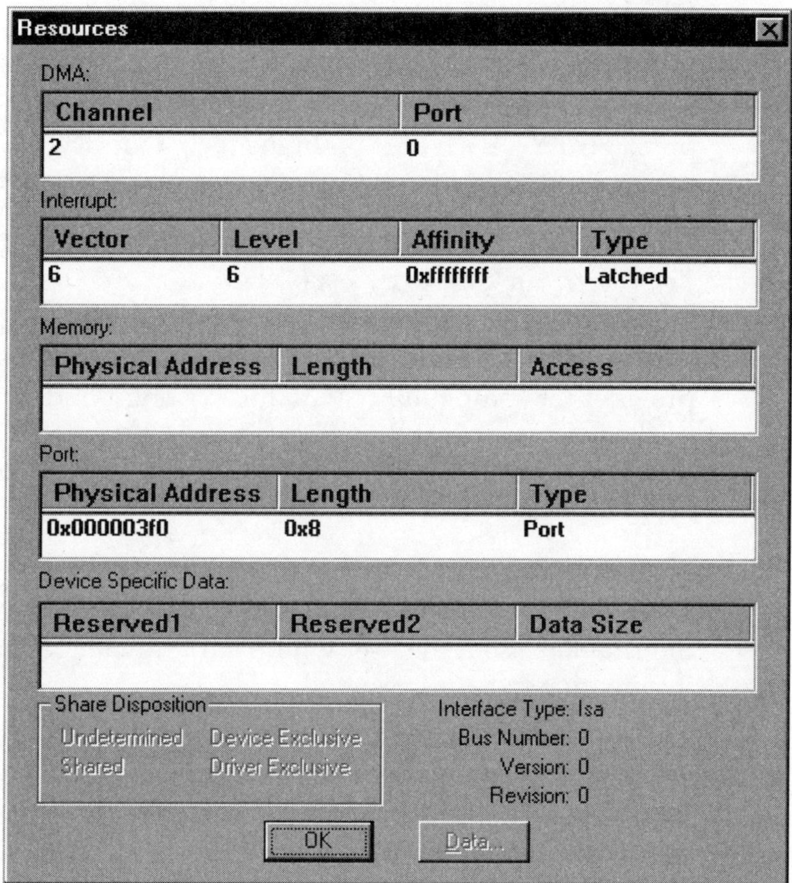

Figure 19-17: The REG_FULL_RESOURCE_DESCRIPTOR, hardware resource data type edit box.

- REG_NONE is an identifier used when there is no data stored in the key.
- REG_UNKNOWN is used when the key's datatype cannot be determined.

Major Keys in the Registry

The registry is divided into five major parts, each named with the prefix HKEY_. Each part (or branch) embodies a major section of the registry, with different functionality. Do we dare to guess that HKEY is short for *Hive KEY*?

HKEY_CLASSES_ROOT

The HKEY_CLASSES_ROOT branch contains information about both OLE and various file associations. HKEY_CLASSES_ROOT provides for compatibility with the existing Windows 3.x registry.

The information contained in HKEY_CLASSES_ROOT is identical to information found in HKEY_LOCAL_MACHINE\SOFTWARE.

HKEY_CURRENT_USER

The HKEY_CURRENT_USER branch is used to manage specific information about the user who is currently logged on. This information includes:

- The user's desktop, and the appearance and behavior of Windows NT 4 Server to the user.
- All connections to network devices, such as printers and shared disk resources.
- Desktop program items, application preferences, screen colors, and other personal preferences and security rights are stored for later retrieval by the system when the user logs on.
- All other environment settings are retained for future use.

By using the user profile (see Chapter 17, "Security & Users"), Windows NT is able to make any workstation the user logs onto appear the same to the user—domain users need not worry about having to "setup" or customize each possible workstation they will be using.

Information contained in HKEY_CURRENT_USER is updated as users make changes to their environment.

HKEY_LOCAL_MACHINE

The HKEY_LOCAL_MACHINE branch contains information about the actual computer. Information contained includes applications, drivers, and hardware. There are five separate keys contained within the HKEY_LOCAL_MACHINE:

- HARDWARE is used to store information about the system's actual hardware. This key is created when the system is booted (this allows new hardware to be easily added), so changes to this key are not retained. Contained within the HARDWARE key are four sub-keys:
    - DESCRIPTION contains information about the system, including the CPU, FPU (floating point unit), and the system bus. Under the system bus is information about various I/O, storage, and other devices.
    - DEVICEMAP contains information about devices (keyboard, printer ports, pointer, and so on).
    - OWNERMAP contains miscellaneous information about devices such as SCSI adapters.
    - RESOURCEMAP contains information about the HAL (Hardware Abstraction Layer), I/O devices, drivers, SCSI adapters, system resources, and video.
- SAM, the Security Account Manager, stores information about users and domains in the SAM key.
- SECURITY contains information about local security and user rights. A copy of the SAM key is found in the SECURITY key.
- SOFTWARE contains information about installed software, including descriptions. There should be sub-keys for each installed product where the product will store information, including preferences, configurations, and other modifiable items.
- SYSTEM contains information about the system startup, device drivers, services, and the Windows NT 4 Server configuration.

HKEY_USERS

The HKEY_USERS key contains information about each active user who has a user profile. There are a minimum of two keys in the HKEY_USERS key: .DEFAULT, and the ID for the currently logged on user (see "Changing the Registry," above, for information about a user's ID).

The .DEFAULT key provides information for users who logon without a profile.

Personal profiles are contained in the %SystemRoot%\Profiles folder.

HKEY_CURRENT_CONFIG

The HKEY_CURRENT_CONFIG key (which is new to Windows NT 4) contains information about the system's current configuration. This information is typically derived from HKEY_LOCAL_MACHINE\SYSTEM\ and HKEY_LOCAL_MACHINE\SOFTWARE, though HKEY_CURRENT_CONFIG does not contain all the information that the source keys do.

BOOT.INI

The BOOT.INI is a file found in the root folder of the primary boot drive. This file (which has the system and read-only attributes set), is loaded by NTLDR (the program that Windows NT uses to load, or boot, the operating system) to control which operating system (and options) will be loaded.

BOOT.INI is usually managed by the Control Panel's System applet (see Figure 19-18), which allows you to select the default operating system and the time delay before the default operating system is booted.

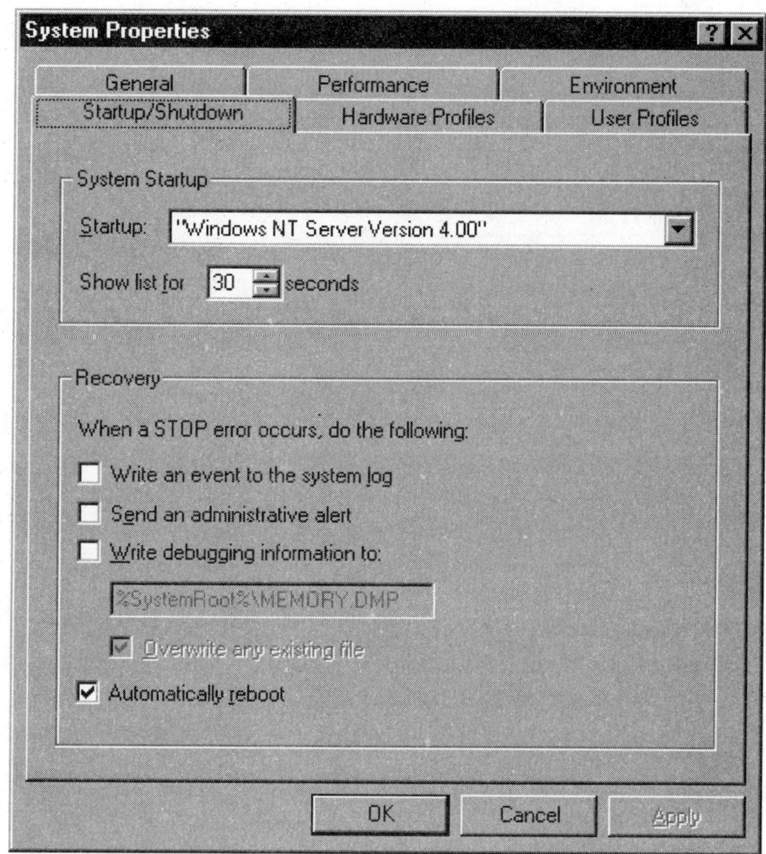

Figure 19-18: Setting the default operating system and time delay.

The BOOT.INI file can be modified manually if desired. First you must make the file accessible to your editor, by changing BOOT.INI's attributes. Open a command window and enter the command:

```
attrib -s -r %homedrive%\boot.ini
```

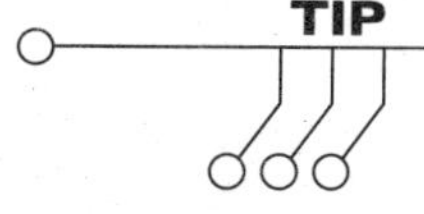

Explorer cannot be used to change the system *attribute on a file—only the ATTRIB command can set or reset the* system *attribute.*

Once the BOOT.INI file's attributes have been reset, you then may edit the file using any handy text editor, such as Notepad. Make whatever changes you need to make, then save the BOOT.INI file. After saving the BOOT.INI file, reset the attributes back to their original values:

```
attrib +s +r %homedrive%\boot.ini
```

Knowing how to modify the BOOT.INI file doesn't tell you what you can do with it. A simple BOOT.INI file contains:

```
[boot loader]
timeout=30
default=multi(0)disk(0)rdisk(0)partition(1)\WINNT
[operating systems]
multi(0)disk(0)rdisk(0)partition(1)\WINNT=<CC>
  "Windows NT Server Version 4.00"
multi(0)disk(0)rdisk(0)partition(1)\WINNT=<CC>
  "Windows NT Server Version 4.00 [VGA mode]"<CC>
  /basevideo /sos
```

In the above listing, the <CC> character indicates a line which, due to its length, had to be broken into two parts. In the actual file, this line is one single, long line.

If you had another operating system (say Windows 95, or another DOS-based operating system) already installed on the system when you installed Windows NT 4 Server, and you do not convert the file system to NTFS, then the Windows NT 4 Server installation creates a dual-boot system. A dual-boot system allows you to boot the previous operating system. For example, if you installed Windows NT 4 Server on a computer that already had a Windows 95 installation, a line would be placed into the BOOT.INI file, similar to:

```
C:\="Microsoft Windows 95"
```

The quoted text ("Microsoft Windows 95") in this line appears in the boot menu, allowing you to select Windows 95 to boot rather than Windows NT 4 Server. Magic? No—when "Microsoft Windows 95" is selected, NTLDR searches for the file BOOTSEC.DOS (which is the default boot sector when none is specified), and uses the contents of this file to boot from. Now, the question is: what the heck is BOOTSEC.DOS?

When a computer is booted, the following process takes place:

1. The first sector on the hard disk is read into memory by the BIOS, and a jump is made to a short program contained in the sector. This first sector is called the *boot sector*.
2. For Windows NT, the program in the first sector loads the NTLDR program.
3. NTLDR reads the BOOT.INI file and displays the choices of operating systems for the user to select from.
4. After the user selects the operating system, NTLDR calls NTDETECT.COM (which checks the hardware configuration).
5. If the user selected a Windows NT operating system, then NTOSKRNL.EXE loads to start Windows NT.
6. If the user selected a DOS-based operating system, then the proper boot sector file loads. If no boot sector file is specified, then the default file—BOOTSEC.DOS—loads.

Adding More Operating Systems

This section is an advanced topic. Don't try the below instructions unless you understand them, and have experience with this type of work!

You can modify the BOOT.INI file to allow for multiple booting. For instance, it may be possible to make a multiple boot which boots into a version of Unix, or even OS/2 if you need to.

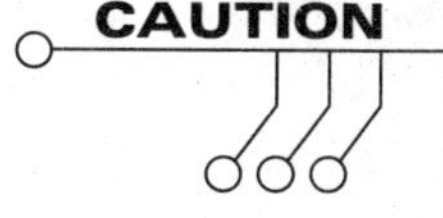

Make sure you have an emergency repair disk (ERD) before you start this procedure! If you did not create an ERD when installing Windows NT 4 Server, you should create one now *using the* rdisk *command. The ERD disk allows you to recover if you make an error when working with the BOOT.INI.*

Say you wanted to be able to choose between two versions of DOS (say DOS 6.2 and Windows 95). First, you would need the boot sectors from both of these operating systems. To get a boot sector, use a raw disk editor, or use the DOS debug command's *load* command. If you don't know how to do this, seek assistance—it is very easy to "blow," or otherwise damage your drive doing this.

Save the boot sector in a file. The file's name is not critical, though convention says name the file BOOTSEC.xxx where xxx is W95 for Windows 95, DOS for DOS (any version), or Dnn (DOS, where nn is the version number).

In your BOOT.INI file, add a line for each boot sector you have saved. For example, if you saved a Windows 95 boot sector into the file BOOTSEC.W95, and a DOS boot sector into the file BOOTSEC.DOS, then you would add the following to your BOOT.INI file:

```
c:\bootsec.w95="Windows 95" /win95dos
c:\bootsec.dos="Plain DOS" /dos
```

The folder name following the description (/win95dos and /dos) indicate the locations for the boot and operating system files.

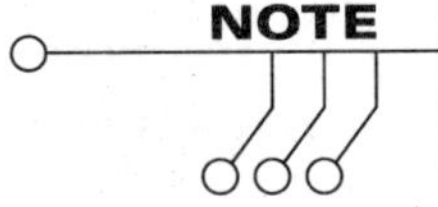

If you do damage your boot sector, you can boot from a Windows NT Emergency Repair Disk, and restore the system.

Windows NT Boot Options

When Windows NT boots, you can choose to set a number of options. These options are listed below in Table 19-2.

Option	Description
/debug	Implements the debugging mode. You may begin debugging by activating the debugger from the system connected to the computer being debugged. Debugging output will be written to the COM1 port, at the default speed (9600 for Intel-based systems, 19200 for most RISC-based systems).
/crashdebug	As with the /debug mode, with the /crashdebug mode the debugger is loaded when the system starts. The debugger is not activated until there is a kernel level error. Using /crashdebug is useful when the faults are random, and when there may be a significant time lapse between faults.
/debugport=comx	Specifying /debugport directs the debugging information to be sent to any suitable, unused, serial port.
/baudrate=<baudrate>	Specifying /baudrate=<baudrate> sets the speed at which the debugging information is sent to the debugging port. The default is either 9600 or 19200 baud, depending on whether the system is Intel- or RISC-based.
/SOS	The /SOS option tells the NTLDR to display a list of drivers as they are loaded. This option doesn't affect the operation of Windows NT, it only provides information about what drivers are being loaded.
/basevideo	Specifying /basevideo tells Windows NT 4 to load in the standard 640 x 480, 16-color video mode. This mode allows you to start Windows NT after changing the video adapter to a different type. This mode is similar to Windows 95's "Safe Mode" boot.

Table 19-2: Boot options for Windows NT 4.

Troubleshooting Hints & Tricks

Customizing BOOT.INI is not difficult, and if you are careful, you should have no problems. These hints and tricks may help you maintain your BOOT.INI file.

When the System Always Boots to the Non-Windows NT Operating System

The timeout value in the BOOT.INI controls how long the operating system selection boot menu displays. If the timeout value is set to zero, no operating selection boot menu displays. (This is definitely not recommended—it could cause the system to be inaccessible if the video system is changed.)

Normally this would not be a problem, but if you have a dual boot system, and the default operating system is not a version of Windows NT, you will not be able to boot to Windows NT! To fix this problem, do the following:

1. Set the BOOT.INI file's attributes to normal (not system, and not read-only).
2. Edit BOOT.INI, and manually change the *timeout* value from "0" to "30."
3. Save the BOOT.INI file, and reset the BOOT.INI file's attributes to system, read-only.
4. Reboot the system, and the operating system selection menu should appear for 30 seconds.

Changing the Name of the Bootable Operating Systems

To change the name displayed when you select which operating system to boot, edit the name in the BOOT.INI file:

1. Set the BOOT.INI file's attributes to normal (not system, and not read-only).

2. Edit BOOT.INI, and manually change the name (which is in quotes) to whatever name you wish. Make the name descriptive, if possible. For example:

```
multi(0)disk(0)rdisk(0)partition(1)\WINNT=<CC>
"Windows NT Server Version 4.00"
```

In the above listing, the <CC> character indicates a line which, due to its length, had to be broken into two parts. In the actual file, this line is one single, long line.

"*Windows NT Server Version 4.00*" may not be descriptive enough. Changing this to "*Working Version: Windows NT 4 Server*" may help an inexperienced user restart the system!

3. Save the BOOT.INI file, and reset the BOOT.INI file's attributes to system, read-only.
4. When the system is re-booted, the new name appears in the operating system selection menu.

Other Windows NT Customization

The (splash) screen shown when there is not a currently logged on user may be customized. The bitmap shown (centered) on the screen, which advertises Windows NT 4 Server, can be changed to your company's logo.

To customize the splash screen just follow these easy steps:

1. Create two copies of your logo, one in 16 colors, and another in 256 colors. Save both these files in the %SystemRoot% folder, as bitmaps, with ".BMP" as the extension.
2. Rename the LANMANNT.BMP file to LANMANNT.BAK.
3. Rename your 16-color bitmap logo to LANMANNT.BMP.
4. Rename the LANMA256.BMP file to LANMA256.BAK.
5. Rename your 256-color bitmap logo to LANMA256.BMP.

The next time you logoff (or restart the system), your logo bitmap will display while the user logs on!

Moving On

In this chapter we delved into the registry and the BOOT.INI file. The registry is the repository for virtually all system configuration information and most application configuration information. The BOOT.INI file controls the boot process for Windows NT 4 Server—and allows you to boot into other operating systems such as Windows 95 or even DOS.

The next and final chapter in our book, "Accessories, Toys, Fun & Games," digs deeply into the new accessories that come with Windows NT 4 Server.

Ching, ping, ding, ding, ding…

Pinball? Fun and games? Me play games?

Well, maybe not everyone has time to play games, but for those of us who can scrape together a few minutes of free time, Windows NT 4 Server comes with four games: Minesweeper, FreeCell, Solitaire, and Pinball. For action games, Pinball has my vote!

Let's get together in the next chapter for a bit of fun and some less serious Windows NT 4 Server accessories.

20 Accessories, Toys, Fun & Games

In this, the final chapter, I cover almost everything that is *not* necessary when using Windows NT 4 Server. Windows NT 4 Server comes with a host of utilities, accessories, and games, all of which are very useful (even the games are useful!) to a Windows NT user.

Games abound, accessories shine through, and I bet we'll find a few fun things in this chapter.

Accessories

Windows NT 4 Server comes with a suite of accessories. These accessories are installed when you install Windows NT 4 Server. Some of them are virtually identical to those accessories found in Windows NT 3.5x Server, while others have been almost totally rewritten. Not every system will be able to use all accessories. For example, if the system is not multimedia-equipped, then the multimedia accessories will not be of any value.

Calculator

The Calculator program has not changed much over the years. Figure 20-1 shows the Calculator program—its two views are standard (which basically has only four functions), and scientific mode, which offers a variety of math functions.

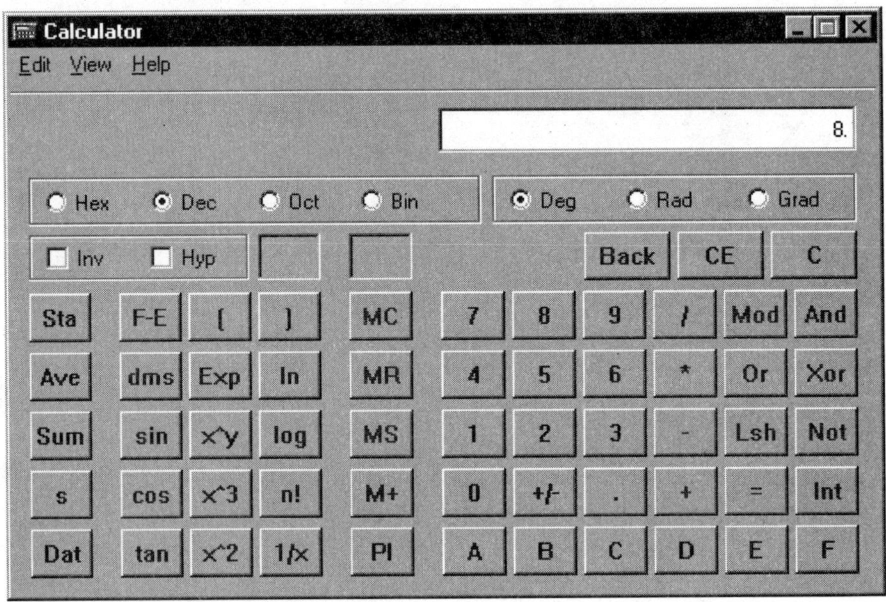

Figure 20-1: Windows NT's Calculator, in scientific mode.

Calculator reads numbers from, or places results into, the clipboard. This is handy since it allows you to cut, compute, and paste the results of a computation.

Character Map

The version of Character Map included with Windows NT 4 Server is Unicode-compatible. Character Map is very useful when there is a need for a special character and the character's value is unknown.

Figure 20-2 shows Character Map, with the Wingdings font displayed. To take a character from the Wingdings font and place it into a document (say with Wordpad), follow these steps:

1. Click the character desired.
2. Click the Select button (to place the character in the Characters to Copy edit control).
3. Click the Copy button (to copy the characters to the Windows NT clipboard).
4. Paste the characters in the other program.

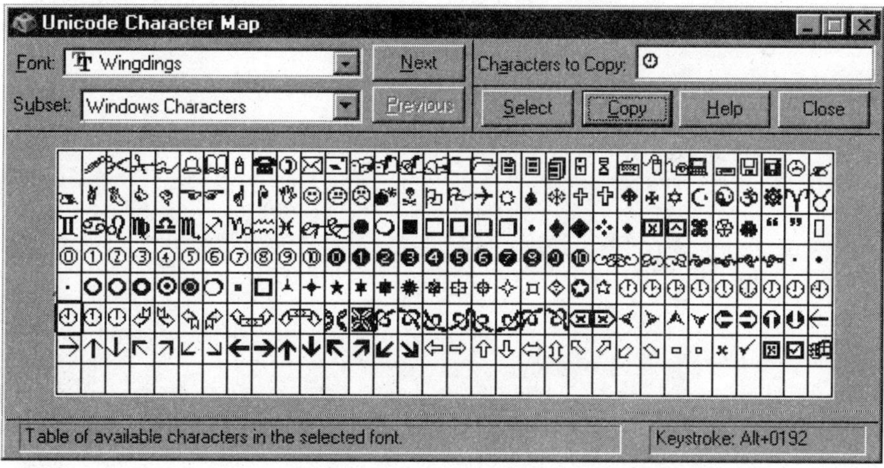

Figure 20-2: The Character Map program at work, copying a clock to the clipboard.

Chat

Gossip in the office? Or valuable tool? You decide.

The Chat program allows two workstations to carry on a typed conversation, as Figure 20-3 shows.

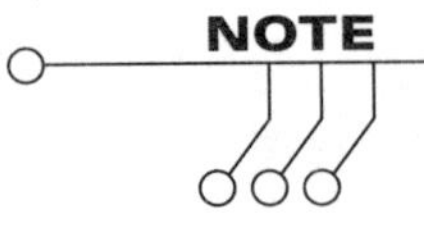

Windows 95, as used by client workstations, does not install the Chat application by default. See the Knowledge Base article PSS ID Number: Q141827 for more information about installing Chat for Windows 95.

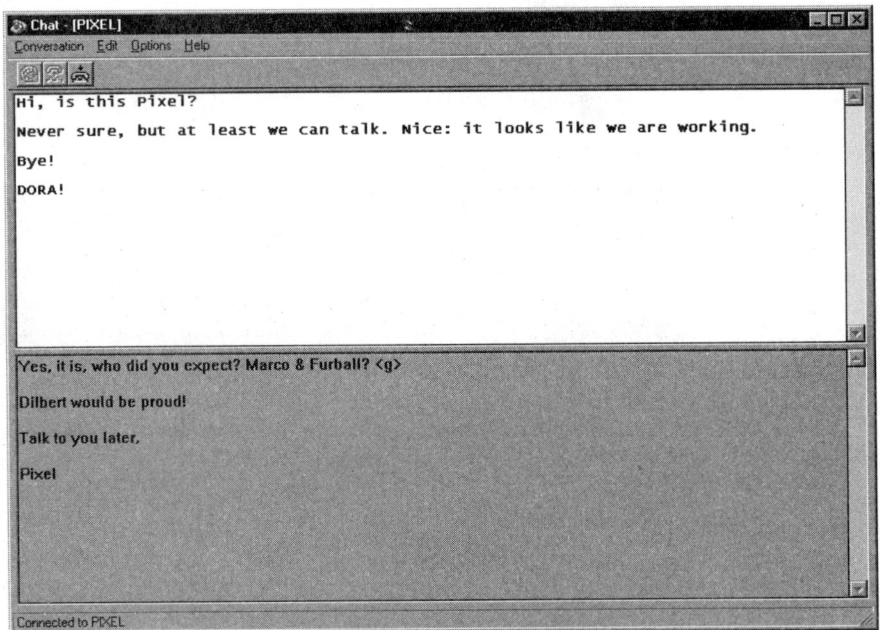

Figure 20-3: The Chat program—chatting up a storm.

To place a call with Chat, the recipient of the call must have Chat running. Chat will not automatically start, nor will Chat answer any calls unless the recipient specifically selects Conversation | Answer from Chat's menu.

Chat can be fun, but it can also prove highly useful within business environments. For example, Chat can be invaluable in setting up meetings, sending text to someone (where spelling might be a problem if given orally), or really any time written conversation would be useful. And by using the clipboard, you can save the conversation to any text editor such as Notepad.

Clipboard Viewer

The Clipboard Viewer, also known as ClipBook Viewer, is a nifty utility for working with the clipboard on the system, and for sharing clipboard contents with other computers on the network.

For example, you can capture an object to the clipboard on one computer and copy that object to another computer using Clipboard Viewer.

The text in Figure 20-4 is from the clipboard on another workstation. Clipboard Viewer then transferred the clipboard's contents to DORA.

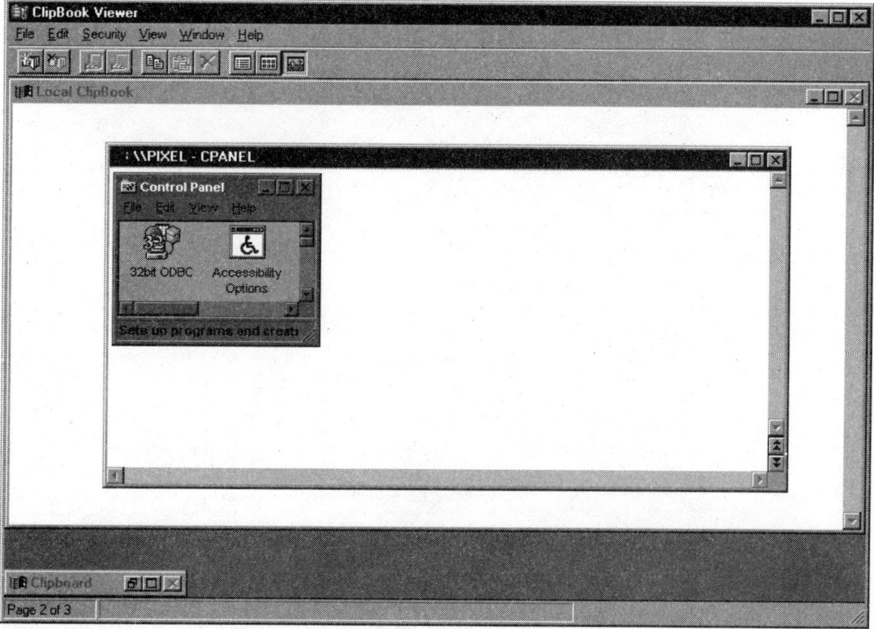

Figure 20-4: Clipboard Viewer.

Clock

The Clock program tells us the time. Windows NT 4 Server's clock has not changed much over the years. Heck, it is the same as the one that came with early versions of Windows. Here in Figure 20-5, without further ado, is Clock:

Figure 20-5: The Clock program, now if the big hand...

HyperTerminal

HyperTerminal is new to Windows NT 4 Server. Originally developed for Windows 95, HyperTerminal allows us to connect to remote computers and transfer files.

HyperTerminal replaces the old, featureless, Terminal program with a communications package that really does something. Figure 20-6 shows a connection to a bulletin board for a software company that sells geographic mapping software.

```
Main menu:

[M].............Message Menu          [F]..............Files Menu
[C]....Comments to the SYSOP          [B]...........Bulletin Menu
[P]...........Page the SYSOP          [I]...Initial Welcome Screen
[Q]...........Questionnaire           [V]...........Verify a User
[Y]...........Your Settings           [S]........System Statistics
[U]............Userlog List           [N]...............Newsletter
[G]........Goodbye & Log-Off          [H]..............Help Level
[?].............Command Help          [R]....Reports for the SYSOP

Conf: "[0] - General Mail Folder", time on 0, with 999 remaining.

Main menu: [M F C B P I Q V Y S U N G H ? R] ? _
```

Figure 20-6: HyperTerminal connected to a remote computer.

HyperTerminal transmits and receives files using 1K-Xmodem, Xmodem, Ymodem, Ymodem-G, Zmodem, Zmodem with Crash Recovery, and Kermit protocols.

HyperTerminal emulates a number of popular terminal types including:

- ANSI (the default)
- AutoDetect (which will select the correct emulation, if possible)
- Minitel (a French terminal type)
- TTY
- Viewdata
- VT-100
- VT-52 (both VT-100 and VT-52 are Digital terminal types)

The scroll back buffer (which saves the current session in a buffer, thus enabling the user to view a history of the session) has a default size of 500 lines. If necessary, the size of the scroll back buffer can be increased.

Set other configurations, typical to terminal emulator, and communications programs as needed. Most users of HyperTerminal find the default configuration adequate for most connections.

Fast, powerful, and most importantly, free, HyperTerminal is a very useful tool if you need to connect to remote computers.

Imaging

Well, you find something new in every operating system. The Imaging program is a scanner and image management program originally produced by Wang. The Imaging program is not capable of making image modifications other than to "annotate" the image—Imaging is not a "paint" type program. Imaging is able to load, save, send, annotate, and print existing images, and to scan (using any supported scanner) new images.

Figure 20-7 shows the Imaging program, with one of the figures for this chapter, the Clock application, loaded.

Figure 20-7: The Imaging program showing another figure from this book.

If I had a scanner, I could scan in a page with Imaging and save the image as a file.

Imaging is also able to annotate documents: you can overlay lines, freehand figures, and, my personal favorite, "rubber stamps."

Notepad

The Notepad program has not changed much over the years. Unlike the 16-bit Windows versions of Notepad, there are no practical limits (other than overall memory restrictions) to the size of the file that Notepad can edit.

Figure 20-8 shows Notepad with a letter to Mother.

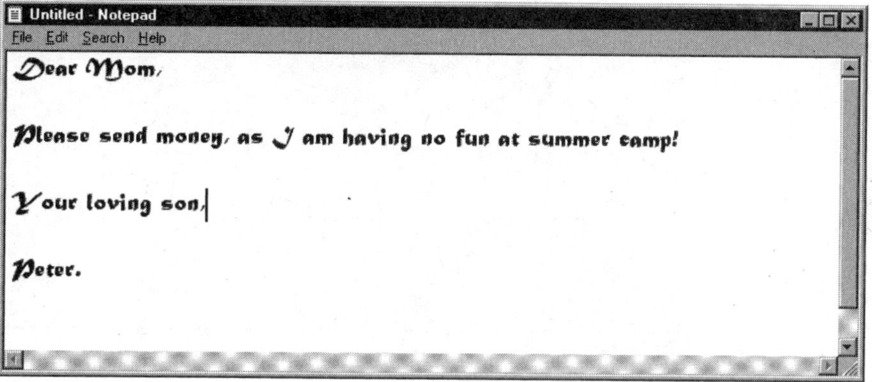

Figure 20-8: Notepad with a letter home—Dear Mom, please send money!

With Notepad, you can set the font for the entire document (though only text information, and not the font, will be saved). Notepad does simple string search and replace, using standard dialog boxes.

Notepad is really useful only for unformatted text files. Open all complex word-processing files (such as Word for Windows, and Write) using WordPad.

Object Packager

The Object Packager program creates an OLE object that you can insert into a document. Any application that supports OLE drag-and-drop can contain an object created using Object Packager.

Figure 20-9 shows Object Packager creating an object. This object could then be inserted into a Word for Windows (or WordPad) document. However, once the document has been printed, you would have difficulty clicking on the object.

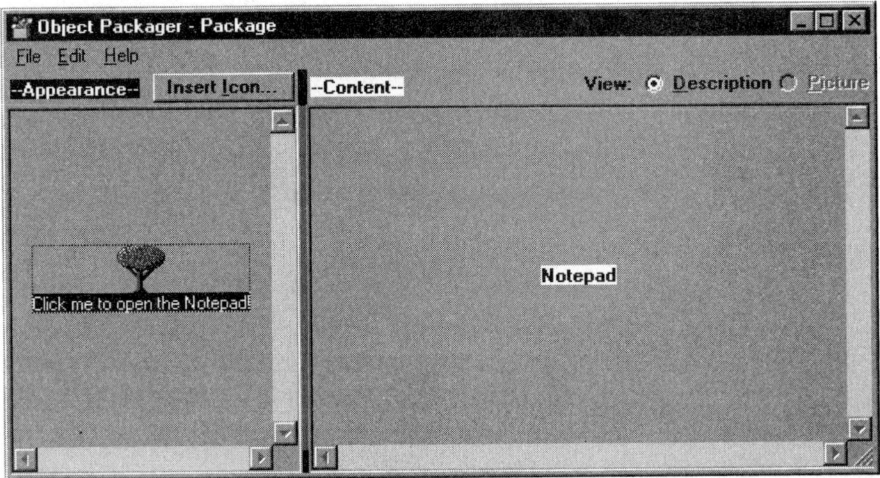

Figure 20-9: The Object Packager program creating a simple object.

Paint

Since Windows NT 3.5x days, the Paint program has been changed slightly. Paint loads both PCX and BMP images, and saves images in BMP format only. Paint also edits and prints images. Figure 20-10 shows Paint with another image loaded.

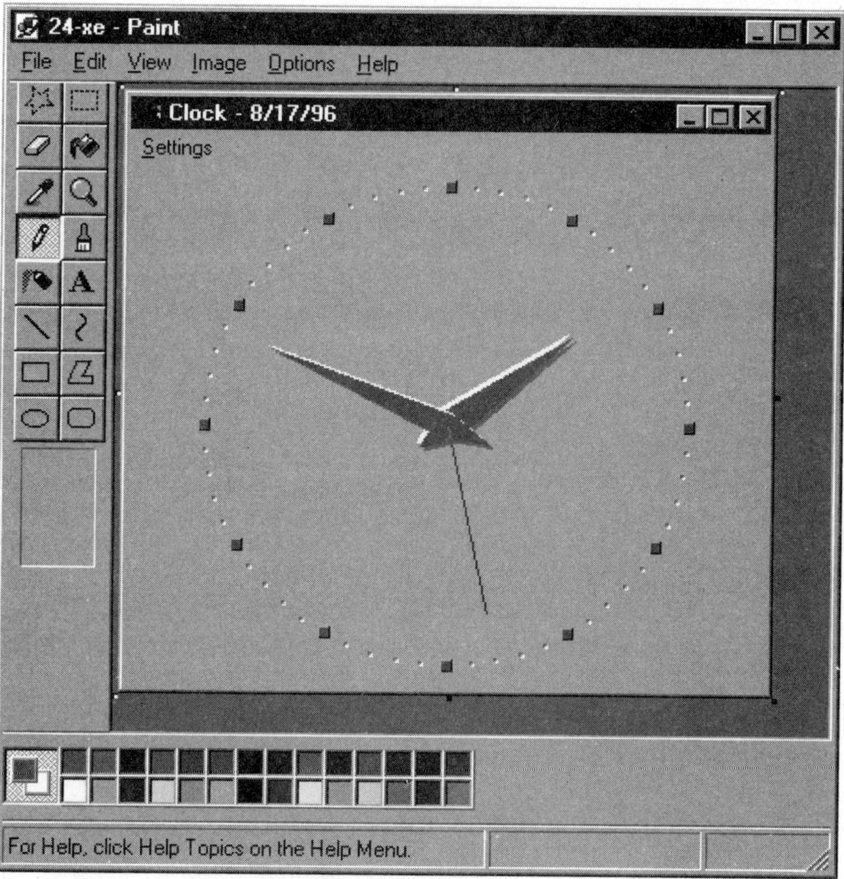

Figure 20-10: Paint editing the Clock image.

Not as full-featured as commercial programs, Paint is acceptable for occasional creation or modification of graphics images.

Phone Dialer

Windows NT 4 Server offers a telephone dialer program. The Phone Dialer requires that a modem be installed, and dials numbers using standard TAPI (check out Modems in the Control Panel) settings.

Figure 20-11 shows the Phone Dialer program.

Figure 20-11: Phone Dialer ready to dial a number.

Telnet

Telnet is the remote terminal protocol usually used by UNIX computers; it is also the name for a Telnet-compatible terminal program. Included with Windows NT 4 Server is a simple Telnet program that allows Windows NT to connect, in terminal mode, to any Telnet-compatible computer over the Internet.

Figure 20-12 shows Telnet connected to a computer, as part of an online session.

```
Telnet - metro.jussieu.fr
Connect  Edit  Terminal  Help
Do you want to continue [Yes] : y


Departure station [no default answer] : alewife
Arrival station [no default answer] : park

Several station names match what you typed (park)
They are:
(1) Forge Park/495      (3) Melrose/Cedar Park (5) Science Park
(2) Hyde Park           (4) Park Street

Choose (with its number) your station : 4

Estimated time = 15 minutes

Line 'Red', Direction 'Braintree' or 'Ashmont'
        Alewife
        Davis
        Porter
        Harvard Square
        Central
        Kendall/MIT
        Charles/Massachusetts General Hospital
        Park Street
Do you want to continue [Yes] :
```

Figure 20-12: A Telnet session to a computer telling me how to get somewhere via the Boston subway.

About that session shown in Figure 20-12… I connected to a computer located in France, and then was able to retrieve information about the Boston subway! How's that for international cooperation?

WordPad

I saved the best for last. WordPad, the replacement for Write, is a really effective basic word processor. Capable of reading and writing in a number of formats, WordPad is usable for many document creation tasks.

Figure 20-13 shows WordPad with a short section of a chapter in this book opened.

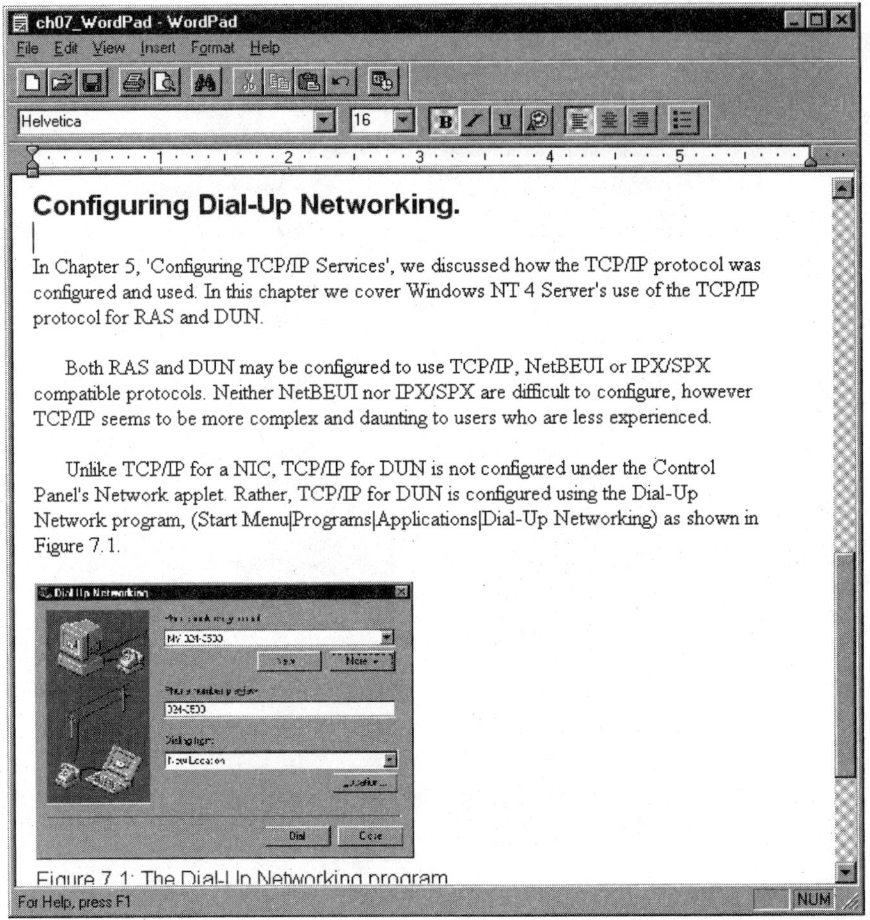

Figure 20-13: WordPad at its best—formatting and embedding graphics.

WordPad works internally as an RTF (Rich Text Format) editor—anything that cannot be done with RTF will not work with WordPad. Realize that WordPad is not a complete editor. In fact, WordPad does not support all RTF specifications (there is no support for footnotes, for example). But as a general, simple, all-around word processor, WordPad is hard to beat!

System Tool: Inbox Repair Tool

Maybe someday there will be more system tools. Windows 95 offers several more tools, but until we get a Windows NT 4 Server Resource Kit the only tool available is the Inbox Repair Tool.

The Inbox Repair Tool, the only tool found in the System Tools section, fixes inconsistencies in the Microsoft Exchange Client inbox files (.PST), and repairs any damage found.

All your e-mail is stored in the inbox file, and any problems with the file may make your e-mail inaccessible. If Exchange reports problems with the inbox file, then you should:

1. Back up the existing .PST file.
2. Run the Inbox Repair Tool on the .PST file that is failing.

If, after running the Inbox Repair Tool, Exchange still reports that the inbox file is not readable, then you must use Exchange to create a new inbox file.

Figure 20-14 shows a session of Inbox Repair Tool.

Running the Inbox Repair Tool on a large file can take a long time.

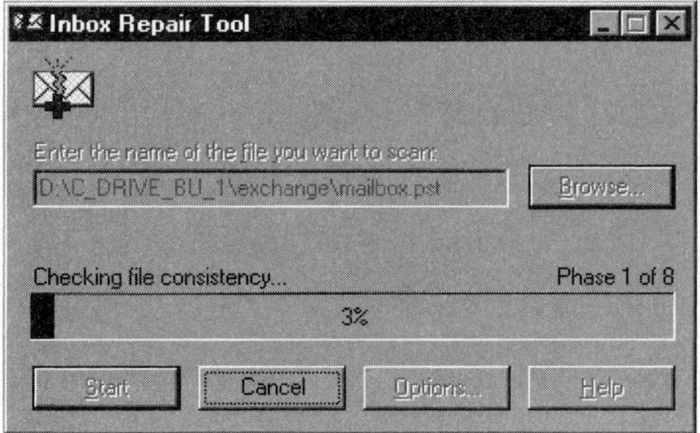

Figure 20-14: Inbox Repair Tool at work, repairing a damaged Microsoft Exchange inbox.

Multimedia

Multimedia tools interface with Windows NT 4 Server's multimedia support. To use most of these tools, you must have multimedia-compatible video and sound hardware installed. The CD Player requires that an audio-compatible CD-ROM drive be installed, something that virtually all Windows NT 4 Servers have.

CD Player

The CD Player program plays audio CDs using the computer's multimedia components. The user enters Artist, Title, and Tracks information, though CD Player provides defaults.

Figure 20-15 shows CD Player playing Kevin Clark's wonderful "New Orleans Trumpet" CD.

Figure 20-15: CD Player playing some jazz.

If you have multiple CD-ROM drives (DORA has three), then CD Player allows you to select the correct CD-ROM drive.

Media Player

Media Player allows you to work with sound (.WAV), video (.AVI), audio MIDI (.MDI), or CD-AUDIO. Figure 20-16 shows Media Player playing an AVI file from the Windows 95 CD.

Figure 20-16: Goodtimes playing in Media Player.

Sound Recorder

It is possible to create sound files (.WAV) using most sound cards, with either a microphone or auxiliary input. The Sound Recorder application is a simple program that allows you to record short bits of audio.

Figure 20-17 shows Sound Recorder recording a radio program. With most sound cards, anything recorded will be played back through the speakers: if you experience feedback when recording from a microphone, turn down the speaker volume or use head-sets to listen while recording.

Figure 20-17: Sound Recorder recording a radio show.

Volume Control

The Volume Control application controls audio levels. Volume Control controls the master speaker level and levels for Synthesizer, Microphone, CD Audio, and Wave Output. For the master speaker, you may also set tone controls by clicking on the Advanced button. For the microphone, you may set tone, and enable an automatic gain control.

Figure 20-18 shows the Volume Control application.

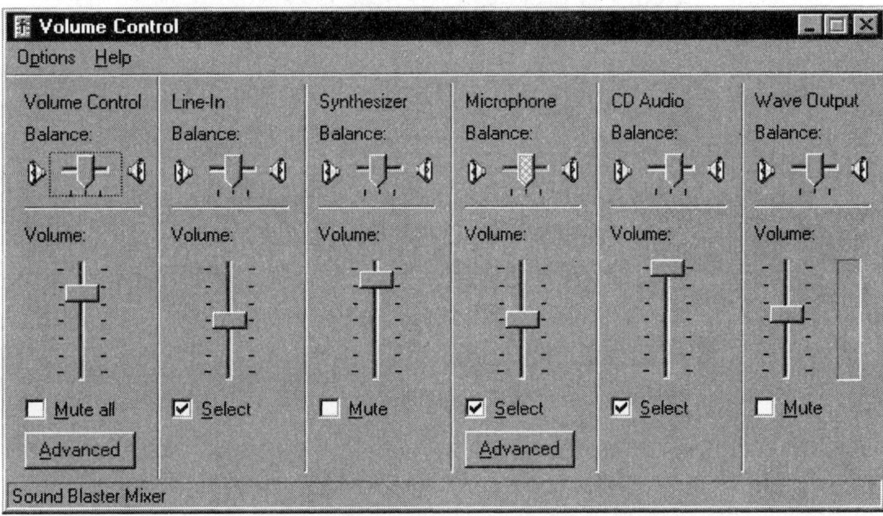

Figure 20-18: Setting sound volume levels with the Volume Control program.

Each volume control has a balance control and a Mute or Select control, as applicable.

Games

Sometimes we just have to play games. Here I am, writing away, and there is a FreeCell game active on one of the workstations. Well, I'm the only one here, so I must be the one playing games!

FreeCell

FreeCell is a solitaire game in which you play against luck. The theory is that "every game is winnable"—however, no one has proved this to be true or false.

Figure 20-19 shows a game of FreeCell being played. The object of the game is to move all the cards to the home cells (the four spots in the upper right) from either the free cells (the four spots in the upper left) or the playing area (lower piles). Each free cell may have one (and only one) card at a time. Cards are moved to other playing area piles based on a highest to lowest order, in alternating colors. For example, red ten goes on the black jack.

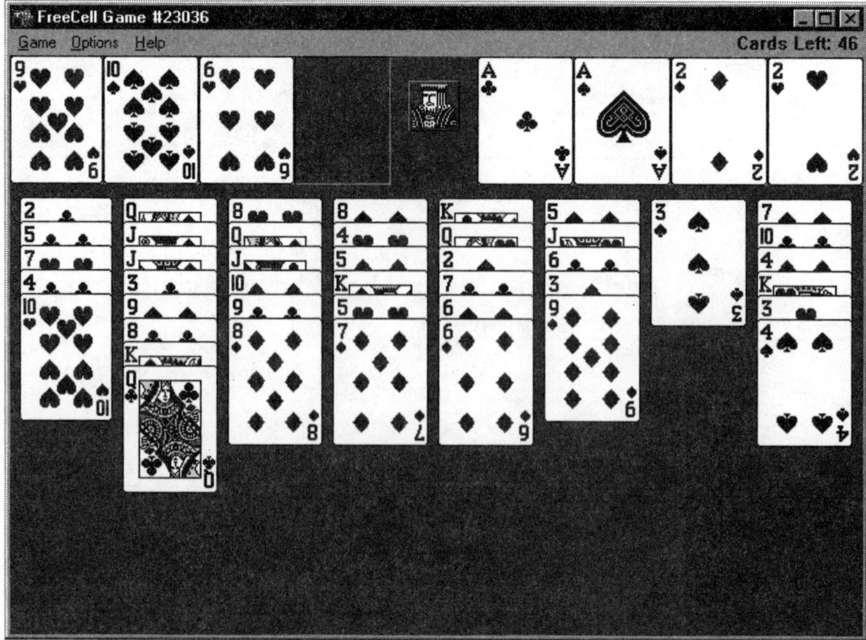

Figure 20-19: A FreeCell game (I lost!).

Minesweeper

Minesweeper is a game of logic. Virtually all games of Minesweeper may be won, if the player considers all clues provided by the game.

Figure 20-20 shows a Minesweeper game. I lost, again!

Figure 20-20: Minesweeper at the expert level.

Pinball

Pinball is *the* game. Fast, exciting, and addictive, Pinball is one game that may well beat Solitaire's record for most wasted corporate time.

In Figure 20-21 is a Pinball game in progress. Well, it has been a while since I've played Pinball, you will have to take me at my word that I've gotten higher scores!

Figure 20-21: Pinball, a game you can't lose.

Solitaire

Solitaire's claim to fame is that it is the game that has wasted more corporate time than any other computer game. Banned from computers in many companies, Solitaire is an addictive game. Figure 20-22 shows Solitaire, the traditional card game.

Figure 20-22: Solitaire, the traditional card game. I finally won!

Conclusion

And so concludes our book. If you have skipped around, and not read everything, that's OK—after all, not all chapters are important to everyone. You did read (I hope) this last chapter, so you know how to both work and enjoy yourself.

Now for the real truth: Windows NT 4 Server is not the end, it is only the beginning—already Microsoft is hinting (rather loudly, at that) about what is to come for Windows in the future. Oops, did I say Windows, without an NT? Yes, we can be sure that someday there will be only one version of Windows, probably available in three (or four) flavors: server, workstation, personal, and perhaps dedicated. But those products are yet to come—today we are using Windows NT 4 Server, and we have the best version of Windows NT yet!

Please, do feel free to contact me. Internet e-mail is the best way (phipson@darkstar.mv.com), though regular old snail mail (the USPS really *hates* it when we use that term!) to P.O. Box 88, West Peterborough NH, 03468-0088 will get to me. Enclosing a SASE will virtually guarantee a reply, too!

Thanks for reading *The Windows NT 4 Server Book*, and enjoy using Windows NT 4 Server!

SECTION V

Appendices

Windows NT 4 Server Resources

Below are companies, organizations, and places where you can find information, products, and help for Windows NT 4 Server.

Arcada Software

Arcada Software, Inc., develops data protection and storage management software for multiple desktop and client/server environments, including those from Microsoft, Novell, and IBM. Product: Storage Exec and Enterprise Backup with HSM capabilities.

Arcada Software
37 Skyline Drive, Suite 1101
Lake Mary, FL 32746
Phone—main: (407) 333-7500
Phone—sales: (800) 327-2232
Technical Support: (800) 468-2587
Fax: (407) 333-7770
BBS: (407) 444-9979
e-mail: CompuServe - GO ARCADA
http://www.arcada.com/

Ataman Software, Inc.

Ataman Software is a company with a few interesting products for the Windows NT 4 Server user.

Ataman Software, Inc.
749 S. Lemay Ave, Suite A3-411
Fort Collins, CO 80524
Telephone: (970) 225-9131
FAX: (970) 225-0335
http://www.ataman.com

Beverly Hills Software

In February 1995, Dave Baker resigned his position as Development Director for Symantec Corporation to pursue opportunities in the fast-growing Internet. One month later, Dave started Beverly Hills Software. His first Internet venture was the Windows NT Resource Center, initially a simple, one-page Web site. Within a few months it had evolved into an advanced, full-featured site that had become the number one site for Windows NT users.

Beverly Hills Software
8845 W. Olympic Blvd. Suite 200
Beverly Hills, CA 90211
Tel: (310) 358-8311
Fax: (310) 358-0326
http://www.bhs.com

Cheyenne Software, Inc.

A leader in the development of sophisticated local area network (LAN) management software. Products include ArcServe for Windows NT and other Backup software products.

Cheyenne Software, Inc.
3 Expressway Plaza
Roslyn Heights, NY 11577
http://www.cheyenne.com/

Digi International

Digi International is a leading ISO 9001-compliant provider of data communications hardware and software that delivers seamless connectivity solutions for multiuser environments, remote access, and LAN connect markets. The company markets its products through an international network of distributors and resellers, system integrators, and original equipment manufacturers (OEMs).

Digi International
11001 Bren Road E.
Minnetonka, MN 55343
Tel: (800) 344-4273 or (612) 912-3444
Fax: (612) 943-4952
http://www.dgii.com

EMWAC

The European Microsoft Windows NT Academic Centre (EMWAC) has been set up to support and act as a focus for Windows NT within academia. It is sponsored by Datalink Computers, Digital, Microsoft, Research Machines, Sequent, and the University of Edinburgh.

EMWAC provides an extensive library of free tools for Windows NT 4 Server. These tools are oriented towards ISPs, and several are very interesting to ISPs who are running Windows NT 4 Server.

EMWAC provides the following Internet tools for Windows NT 4 Server:

- Freeware HTTP Server—A Web server that provides basic Web publishing capabilities. Generally, most ISPs use IIS for this functionality.
- Freeware Gopher Server—A Gopher server that provides basic Gopher publishing capabilities. Generally, most ISPs use IIS for this functionality.
- Freeware WAIS Server—A WAIS (Wide Area Information Server) used to allow users to query indexes of distributed databases and retrieve data. Windows NT's Resource Kit included a WAIS server, and when Microsoft releases the Resource Kit for Windows NT 4 Server, a WAIS server should be included.
- WAIS Toolkit based on freeWAIS 0.3—A WAIS toolkit to assist in configuring and setting up freeWAIS 0.3 (the Freeware WAIS Server).
- Freeware Finger Server—A finger server that provides basic finger capabilities. Though finger is not supported by all Internet sites, it can be a useful service. Since the Freeware Finger Server is easy to obtain, install, and configure, running a finger server is not difficult.
- Freeware EMWAC Internet Mail Services—Internet mail (SMTP/POP-3) is necessary for all ISPs. Using Exchange is possible only if the client users are all using Microsoft Exchange, something public ISPs cannot be assured of.

- EMAIL—The EMWAC Internet Mail Services for Windows NT (known as "IMS") are a suite of server programs that allow you to use Windows NT as a mail server for Internet mail. The EMWAC IMS requires an NTFS partition and Windows NT 3.51 or higher. With IMS, your Windows NT machine can receive messages from Internet, put them in individual users' incoming mail boxes, accept outgoing mail from users, and relay that mail to its destination anywhere on the Internet. It supports mail aliases, and can also run (optionally moderated) mailing lists.

EMWAC Computing Services
30-38 George Square
Edinburgh EH8 9LJ
UK
Tel: +44 (0)131 650 6565
Fax: +44 (0)131 650 6464
FTP: emwac.ed.ac.uk
e-mail: emwac@ed.ac.uk
http://www.emwac.ed.ac.uk

Forté, Inc.

Forté is a privately held company with headquarters in Carlsbad, California, just north of San Diego. The company has grown from a staff of four people in 1987 to a 52-person staff with a variety of skills, talents, and backgrounds. Forté has offices in Carlsbad, California, and Ottawa, Canada. Forté's products include Agent and Free Agent.

Forté, Inc.
2141 Palomar Airport Road
Suite 100
Carlsbad, CA 92009
Tel: (619) 431-6400
Fax: (619) 431.6465
http://www.forteinc.com

Internet Shopper Ltd.

Internet Shopper Ltd. has been providing e-mail services since August 1995 (Internet Shopper Ltd. was the first with a SMTP/POP3 mail server for Windows NT). NTMail takes five minutes to set up, has an integral list server and supports multiple domains—and it is available for a free trial.

Internet Shopper Ltd.
PO Box 6064, London, SW12 9XG, UK
FAX: +44 181 673 2149
http://www.net-shopper.co.uk

Legato Systems, Inc.

Legato, located in Palo Alto, California, provides an integrated set of storage management services that simplify the administration of client/server computing.

They are a leading provider of network-wide data storage management software, whose goal is to simplify administration by providing a family of scalable storage management software products that deliver the right solution at the right price.

Legato Systems, Inc.
3210 Porter Drive
Palo Alto, CA 94304
Phone: (415) 812-6000
Fax: (415) 812-6032
Fax-on-demand: (415) 812-6156
Contact www@legato.com
http://www.legato.com

Microsoft Corporation

The world's leading software provider, Microsoft strives to continually produce innovative products that meet the evolving needs of customers. Their extensive commitment to research and development is coupled with dedicated responsiveness to customer feedback. This allows Microsoft to explore future technological advancements, while assuring that customers today receive the highest-quality software products.

Microsoft Corporation
One Microsoft Way
Redmond, WA 98052
http://www.microsoft.com

NetManage

NetManage, Inc. is the leading provider of standards-based intranet solutions, offering intranet software for information access, collaboration, communication, and management. By delivering standards-based technology for the corporate intranet—desktop applications, servers, development tools, and protocol extensions—NetManage is well positioned to meet the needs of the intranet explosion.

NetManage
10725 N. De Anza Blvd.
Cupertino, CA 95014
Phone: (408) 973-7171
Fax: (408) 257-6405
http://www.netmanage.com/

Nico Mak Computing, Inc.

WinZip brings the convenience of Windows to the use of ZIP files without requiring PKZIP and PKUNZIP. The new WinZip Wizard makes unzipping easier than ever. WinZip features built-in support for popular Internet file formats, including TAR, gzip, and Unix compress. ARJ, LZH, and ARC files are supported via external programs. WinZip interfaces to most virus scanners.

Nico Mak Computing, Inc.
PO Box 919
Bristol, CT 06011
http://www.winzip.com

Palindrome Corporation

Palindrome is a leading provider of LAN Storage Management Software. A Seagate Software Company, one product from Palindrome is Backup Director.

Palindrome Corporation
600 East Diehl Road
Naperville, IL 60563
Tel: (800) 288-4912 or (708) 505-3300
Fax: (708) 505-7917
e-mail: sales@palindrome.com
http://www.palindrome.com/

Queue Systems, Inc.

Queue can help you establish a presence on the Internet. Queue has over a decade of experience in implementing process control and supervisory systems and services for ALCOA, Bechtel, NASA, Omaha Public Power, Shell Oil, Weyerhauser, and others.

Queue Systems, Inc.
1800 Saint Julian Place, Ste. 304
Columbia, SC 29204
Tel: (803) 771-4100
Fax: (803) 771-0810
http://www.queuesys.com

Windows NT 4 Server as an ISP

Windows NT 4 Server is a logical choice as the platform to use when setting up an ISP (Internet Service Provider). Both Windows NT 4 Server and the PC and RISC platforms provide good support for supporting ISPs, and Windows NT 4 Server is becoming more popular with ISPs.

ISPs usually have client users who dial in. These client users can be the general public, or employees of the ISP—as in the case of an ISP seeking to simply expand utilization of their expensive Internet communications facilities. Client users are an ISP's customers. If an ISP company is well run, it will most likely have and enjoy a long-term source of income from loyal client users.

ISPs require a permanent connection to the Internet. Most connections are made through SprintLink, MCI, AT&T, Pacific Bell, TLC, other ISPs, or communications companies who offer connectivity services.

A Threat or a Promise?

The ISP business is a growing and changing business! The most common problem that new ISPs have is financial: rates are low, competition is fierce, and falling behind in customer billing is a sure way to run out of *cash*—the lifeblood of any business.

As with any business—make sure you have sufficient *working capital* to carry the business through whatever growth problems you may experience.

Install, and use, a competent accounting system. Billing systems based on flat rates or actual usage are most common. Some ISPs ask for (and usually get) *advance payments*, especially for their lower-rate or flat-rate fares. Consider ET (Electronic funds Transfers) or direct credit card billing as methods to ensure prompt payments from client users. Both your bank and the credit card companies can provide information on doing this.

Also, consider obtaining legal advice: *contracts* with client users should be written to limit the ISP's liability, regardless of fault.

Consider *insurance*—all kinds of insurance, including liability insurance, in case a customer files a lawsuit against the ISP. Property insurance is a wise investment.

Many ISPs start as small organizations and often are run from people's homes. Windows NT 4 Server makes an ideal platform for these new ISPs. Commonly available hardware and Windows NT 4 Server's ease of configuration are advantages that other systems may not offer. Small beginnings shouldn't limit your potential for growth. Many smaller communities may never be reached by the large ISPs (such as MSS, Sprint, or AT&T's WorldNet). A community of five to ten thousand homes can be a viable market for a small ISP.

One justification for setting up your company as an ISP is to help pay for a high-cost, high-speed connection to the Internet. For example, if your company has a T1 line, and this line is only used during business hours, then offering ISP services substantially increases the usage during evening hours. In this type of situation, an incentive to client users is to offer greatly reduced rates for those times when your company is not utilizing the full bandwidth of the connection to the Internet. Running your system as a private ISP, accessible only by your own employees during off hours (perhaps on a free or cost plus basis), provides an attractive fringe benefit.

Services & Host Protocols

Protocols an ISP should try to offer (and Windows NT 4 Server offers you) include:

- WWW (World Wide Web)—Provides a hypertext, multimedia database to Internet users. Many client users expect a WWW server to be active at the ISP's server site. Make provisions for client users' home pages.
- FTP (File Transfer Protocol)—Allows Internet users to transfer files between the server and an Internet client.
- Gopher—Allows users to view information from text documents easily. A somewhat better user interface than FTP, though not as useful as WWW.
- IRC (Internet Relay Chat)—The "CB radio" of the Internet. Allows interactive textual chat between two or more users. Similar to Windows NT 4 Server's Chat utility (see Chapter 20, "Accessories, Toys, Fun & Games"), IRC allows conversations to be many-sided. Other very popular things that users do on IRC besides textual chat is exchange and play waves (sound files) in the channels and exchange pictures and other files.

Other items you'll want to provide your users include:

- RA (Real Audio)—Allows client users to receive audio in real-time from an RA server.
- VDOLive (Streaming Video)—Allows client users to receive video from a VDOLive server.

Connecting to the Internet

An ISP must be reliably connected to the Internet. Such a connection must be fast enough to satisfy client user needs.

Connecting to the Internet is a two-part process: you must have an Internet site to connect to (called a PoP, or Point of Presence, which is different from POP—Post Office Protocol), and the physical connection (telephone line, optical cable, or satellite) must be established.

Most organizations (PoPs) connected to the Internet will assist you in negotiating with whatever entity (usually the telephone company) to provide you with the physical connection.

Connections to the Internet are measured by speed:

- Dial-up connections allow speeds of up to 28,000 bits per second. Not useful for connecting your site to the Internet, dial-up connections allow client users to connect to your site.
- ISDN allows speeds of 56,000 bps to 128,000 bps. Usable for very small ISP sites (isolated, small communities) and for client user dial-up.
- Frame Relay provides rates that are compatible with ISDN, with multiple circuits providing higher rates.
- T1 speeds are adequate for most small and mid-sized ISPs. T1 supports rates up to 1,500 Kbps, though you can configure "fractional" T1 circuits, which operate at slower speeds.
- T3 speeds are adequate for even large ISPs. Smaller sites will not find the performance of T3 worth the costs. When configuring T3, an ISP should consider the advantage of having multiple T1 lines to diverse sites—redundancy of connections can be very valuable. T3 speeds are 45,000 Kbps.
- FDDI is used only for the very largest ISPs and corporations. Speeds of 100,000 Kbps make these circuits fast, but expensive. Multiple T3 lines can be advantageous where reliability is a factor.

Many smaller ISPs start with a leased 56 Kbps line that can support a minimal number of users. An upgrade to T1 is made as soon as the client user load permits.

Incoming lines, connected to modems, connect client users with the Internet. When possible, make sure the lines are available and are in good condition. Be sure you have a firm commitment from the local telephone company before selecting your site: it may be possible that sufficient lines will not be available to your proposed site!

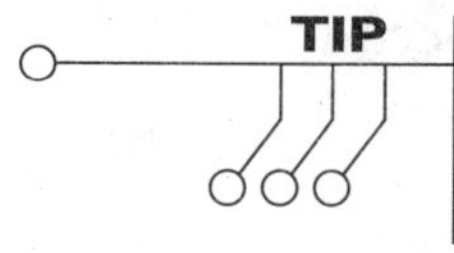

Don't short plan. *Many ISPs quickly grow to hundreds of incoming lines within a few weeks or months. If the telephone company cannot provide the necessary service, your organization will be in trouble!*

Connecting to a Point of Presence

Where you connect your system is called your Point of Presence (PoP). Larger ISPs usually try to connect to two different, geographically separate PoPs. If something happens to one connection to a PoP (such as a communications cable being cut), the other connection can continue to handle the workload.

PoPs range from other ISPs, large communications companies, and telephone companies, to interstate telephone carriers.

Connecting to Another ISP

The easiest way to get started is to forge an agreement with an ISP in a neighboring area. Carefully search out other ISPs:

- Look for a company that is not too remotely located (remember, costs for high-speed communications lines are based on distance).
- The ISP will become a silent, invisible "partner" in your operations. All your services will eventually feed through this ISP—if the ISP is unable to provide good service, this shortcoming will reflect badly on your operation.

- Consider expansion. Make sure that you and your PoP will not be competing for the same markets later. This type of situation can make a working relationship difficult.

Smaller (and often larger) ISPs are usually eager to find a way to increase their business.

Some hints that have led to successful ISP startups include:

- An ISP forged a relationship with a local college by providing services to the college in exchange for assistance in setting up, and providing a site and facilities. Then the college became the ISP's first (and largest) account.
- A partnership with an existing ISP in a neighboring town or area can be very helpful. Technology, infrastructure, support, and possibly even hardware can be among the benefits of such a relationship.

SprintLink

Sprint offers SprintLink, which provides a number of flexible connections to the Internet. Sprint is probably one of the largest players in the Internet game, and one of the best organized.

For many ISPs, Sprint can offer excellent connectivity: SprintLink has main hubs located in Anaheim, Atlanta, Cheyenne, Chicago, Fort Worth, Kansas City, Pennsylvania, Seattle, and Washington, DC.

In addition to SprintLink's main hubs, there are over 300 other SprintLink PoPs. ISPs can use each of these PoPs to connect to the Internet.

MCI

MCI Communications states that they are willing to provide support to ISPs up to and including providing equipment that has been configured and tested.

MCI also provides other support, such as assisting in providing Web page creation, and router and DNS setup.

Like SprintLink, MCI offers a large number of PoPs that ISPs can use to connect to the Internet.

Other PoPs

Some other companies offering Internet connectivity include:

- AT&T WorldNet—A competitor to both SprintLink and MCI, AT&T is becoming a noted player in the Internet connectivity market.
- TLC—HLC.internet is a company that specializes in network connectivity only. HLC.internet is not a long-distance carrier, and as such may be more focused on connecting to the Internet.
- Pacific Bell—PacBell is a "local" telephone company (local phone companies provide local telephone service) that has become a player in the PoP market. Unlike many other local telephone companies, PacBell has boldly moved into advanced communications, with an aggressive ISDN program.

There are other companies offering connectivity to the Internet than those listed above. One way to find which companies are establishing PoPs in your local area is to interview other ISPs in your region.

Multi-Homed Systems

Most ISPs try to connect to the Internet through two sites. Referred to as *multi-homing*, this allows some redundancy in the event of communications problems. However, connecting to two sites can increase the costs—especially if the communications costs are high.

An extreme in multi-homing is when the ISP maintains communications that are 100% separate. Communications to the two (or more) sites to which the ISP is connected leave the ISP's facilities from different locations (such as front and rear), so that there is no common point or location that could cause a disruption in communications. Splitting the dial-up client user access lines this way is also important—if your incoming dial-up lines fail, the effect is the same as if the link with the Internet is lost.

If your site is large enough, consider direct backup satellite communications. Generally considered too slow for main communications links, satellite communications can be an effective backup to land-based lines.

Factors that influence whether you wish to multi-home your system include the distance from the PoP (if the distance is very short, the risks of a catastrophic communications failure and the potential costs of an outage are somewhat reduced).

At the present time, many occasional (home) client users are accustomed to periodic failures and slowness in the Internet. Business users, however, expect a reliable connection. Well, actually we all are used to a certain amount of slowness and failure in connecting to the Internet. The Internet has grown noticeably slower in the past year, and continues to slow as heavy growth outstrips the ability of the Internet backbone to carry this increased traffic.

Domain Names

Domain names establish our identity on the Internet and are assigned by InterNIC. InterNIC maintains a Web site at http://www.internic.net/.

Registering a domain name is not difficult:

1. Set up your DNS servers to recognize the name. InterNIC checks to make sure this has been done, so configure the DNS first! Remember, a DNS is hierarchical in nature—coordinate your efforts with your PoP to ensure that their DNS has correct information, also!
2. At the Web site http://rs.internic.net/cgi-bin/itts/domain, fill in the registration form. InterNIC charges $100 for the initial registration (which includes a two-year registration), and $50 per year after the second year. InterNIC sends invoices, which can be paid by check or credit card.

What's a valid domain name? InterNIC provides the rules (length, valid characters, etc.), and you may search the database for your intended name to ensure that no other organization has registered the same name. If there is a registration of the same name, but with a different suffix ("yourname.net" already exists, where you want to register "yourname.com") you should try to find a different name to register. Consider adding a hyphen ("your-name.com") or spelling the name differently.

If your intended name is so important to you that no other name can be used, consider contacting the current holder of the name—you may be able to purchase rights to the name. Generally, Internet domain names are first come, first served. You may be able to force an existing user to cease using a name (if the name is your trademark, or your company name) but such an action is expensive and difficult.

ISPs register only their domain names, and maybe domain names of permanently connected commercial client users. Virtually all occasional client users use names that are under your domain name, and as such are not registered with InterNIC.

Each of your ISP client users has a name in your domain. For example, if your domain name is "ourtown.com," and you had a user named "Westheimer," then this user might be given the name "westheimer.ourtown.com." Of course an ISP should always work with the client user to make sure that the name is acceptable, and that there are no duplicates. Many ISPs have automated their database of client user records to allow quick searches for duplicate names.

Microsoft Windows NT 4 Server DNS

An ISP must have a Domain Name Server (DNS). There are several candidates for the job of DNS. However, Microsoft Windows NT 4 Server DNS is an excellent (and free) product that does the job. Like Windows NT 4 Server, DNS is easy to manage and configure (just use the DNS Manager).

As you add client users, you must add their names to your DNS system. Chapter 5, "Configuring TCP/IP Services," talks about the Microsoft DNS Server.

IP Address Allocations

As an ISP, you will have a group of IP addresses (probably a Class C, or a partial Class C address) which you can then assign to your client users.

ISPs assign IP addresses either statically or dynamically. All client software that connects with ISPs (such as Windows 95 and Windows NT's DUN) can handle dynamic IP address allocations.

Using a system such as Catapult allows you to isolate your client user's IP addresses from the Internet. This allows your ISP site to exist with a minimum number of assigned IP addresses—which makes management of the system much easier.

Making Connections

Gateways connect two networks together, using either hardware, software, or a combination of the two. Typically, a gateway provides protection from attack from outside, similar to a firewall.

Microsoft is producing a product to allow Windows NT 4 Server to perform the tasks of a gateway and a proxy server, and to do IP Spoofing—this product, currently in beta, is code-named Catapult.

Catapult server provides these benefits:

- Access control is managed by user, service, port, and Internet domain, for both inbound and outbound connections.
- Compatibility with most Internet protocols and Windows Sockets-based applications. On your Windows NT 4 Server, you can use both IPX/SPX and TCP/IP.
- Designed to be used with Windows NT 4 Server, Catapult is easily installed, with excellent linkages with Windows NT 4 Server's security, networking, and user interface.
- Catapult server offers speed, thereby making only small demands on the system, and users will not notice that they are isolated from the Internet.

- Security, preventing any access from external sources to your own private network. Catapult also isolates the client user from the Internet.
- Support for data encryption using Secure Sockets Layer (SSL) tunneling.

Catapult is currently in beta, available to MSDN subscribers. (MSDN, the Microsoft Developer Network, is a quarterly CD base information source for developers.) Catapult will probably be released both as a component of Microsoft BackOffice and as a separate product.

Gateways

A gateway is a hardware and/or software product that connects two networks. For example, gateways connect parts of the Internet together.

As an ISP, you would use a product such as Catapult to connect your client users with the Internet. Using Catapult, your network is isolated from users, yet users can transparently interact with the Internet.

IP Spoofing

IP Spoofing—My comment, when I first encountered the term *IP Spoofing*, was what the heck is this? Actually, IP Spoofing is one of the more interesting products around!

Earlier in this book were comments on the problems of "not enough IP addresses." As a result of this shortage, it can be difficult to obtain IP addresses to support an ISP's operations. Using IP Spoofing, you can circumvent this problem. With only one IP address, you can offer Internet connectivity to an almost unlimited number of client users!

With IP Spoofing, your server has one IP address on the Internet. All your users, however, have local, private IP addresses, that do not appear directly on the Internet; rather, all communications between your users and the Internet are routed through Catapult. Catapult receives requests from users and forwards these requests to the recipient on the Internet. Prior to forwarding these requests, however, Catapult changes the IP address from the client's local private IP address to the server's IP address. When information is received from the Internet, Catapult determines which user this information is intended for and forwards the information to the correct user.

IP Spoofing allows the ISP's server to have a single IP address on the Internet, while each and every user on the ISP's system seems to have their own IP address. A basic win/win situation—the Internet wins, only one IP address is allocated to your site. The user wins, as they are actually isolated behind your router and are impervious to any security risks from the Internet! You win, because you don't have to obtain separate IP addresses for each active client.

Proxy Servers

A proxy server provides a security barrier (firewall) between your Windows NT 4 Server and the Internet. This prevents other Internet sites from accessing information on your Windows NT 4 Server.

Working like a firewall, a proxy server allows no other user on the Internet to access any computers (client users) on your side of the proxy server, while at the same time passing legitimate information freely between the Internet and client users.

Windows NT 4 Server users can use WINS (Windows Internet Name Service) to implement a Proxy Server.

ISP Servers & Services

Each ISP must offer a number of services to the client users. Some of these services can be offered directly, others can be obtained from other ISPs, or PoPs.

News Servers

A news server is a product that allows a user to connect to the ISP's server and retrieve postings from newsgroups. A newsgroup is a collection of messages posted by users, arranged into categories. Client connection software includes: Microsoft's News Reader, Forté's Agent (available both in commercial and freeware versions), and WinVN, a public domain news reader.

There is no news server included with Windows NT 4 Server. Aftermarket products, such as NetManage's product, or a news server from Net-Shopper, is generally a satisfactory solution.

NetManage has released the commercial version of NNS USENET Network News Server. It is called the NetManage IntraNet Forum Server, which is included in the NetManage IntraNet Server.

This freeware version of the NetManage IntraNet Forum Server is a multi-threaded, standards-based, NNTP-compliant, fully integrated NT service. This server provides an organization fast access to create and/or participate in USENET News Groups, for public or private use. Using a standards-based NNTP news reader (such as NETNews, provided with NetManage Chameleon), your company can communicate in privately created newsgroup discussions or any of the 15,000+ established newsgroup discussions in the Internet community.

Telnet Servers for Windows NT 4 Server

Telnet provides a console interface with the server computer. With Windows NT 4 Server, the console interface is a CMD command prompt.

There is one company, Ataman, with a telnet server for Windows NT 4 Server. Telnet is very useful for remote administration over the Internet.

When users log on to the system using the telnet service, they are presented with a CMD prompt type interface. Users are given privileges based on the Windows NT 4 Server user ID's specified privileges.

The Ataman TCP Remote Logon Services (ATRLS) provide rlogind, telnetd, and rexecd services for Windows NT. Each remote user executes in their own security context. The ATRLS runs as Windows NT service—no one needs to be logged onto the console. Rlogind and telnetd services support full-screen console-mode apps.

Mail List Servers

An entry into the mail list servers market is Net-Shopper. Their product is closely related to e-mail products (EMWAC's e-mail server also provides mail list services).

Net-Shopper's interNeTlist is a list server contained within the SMTP and POST services supplied by NTMail. The SMTP server accepts messages and redirects them to the list server for processing. Once the list server has processed them it creates mail messages that are automatically treated as lower priority mail by the POST service.

SMTP/POP-3 Services

Though Microsoft Exchange Server offers many of the mail services that an organization needs, Microsoft Exchange Server doesn't support POP-3 protocol.

Since an ISP will have clients who are not using Microsoft Exchange for e-mail, it is necessary to have a POP-3 compatible e-mail server. Fortunately there are several choices for e-mail products for ISPs running under Windows NT 4 Server, such as NetManage's JetMail and EMWAC's Internet Mail Services.

NetManage's JetMail Server is an Internet standards-based electronic mail server for ISPs. Simple to set up and configure, JetMail is a quick and inexpensive e-mail server. JetMail is available for both Windows 95 and Windows NT platforms.

EMWAC offers e-mail servers for Windows NT 4 Server:

- Freeware EMWAC Internet Mail Services—Internet mail (SMTP/POP-3) is necessary for all ISPs. Using Exchange is possible only if the client users are all using Microsoft Exchange, something of which public ISPs cannot be assured.
- EMAIL—The EMWAC Internet Mail Services for Windows NT (known as "IMS") are a suite of server programs that allow you to use Windows NT as a mail server for Internet mail. The EMWAC IMS requires an NTFS partition and Windows NT 3.51 or higher. With IMS, your Windows NT machine can receive messages from the Internet, put them in individual users' incoming mail boxes, accept outgoing mail from users, and relay that mail to its destination anywhere on the Internet. It supports mail aliases and can also run (optionally moderated) mailing lists.

IMail Server for Windows NT is a high-performance SMTP/POP-3 e-mail server that manages your Internet and corporate intranet electronic mail efficiently and economically. Easy to administer through a simple, intuitive graphical user interface, it offers businesses an attractive alternative to more complex, higher-priced UNIX-based systems. Easy-to-use features improve productivity, and unlike other Internet mail products, IMail Server for Windows NT is nonproprietary.

The foundation for an integrated family of Internet server software products, IMail Server for Windows NT is available for a range of scalable, price/performance platforms that include Intel, DEC/Alpha, and PowerPC. It can be used with Ipswitch's IMail Client for Windows or any other POP-3 mail client—giving you complete flexibility in setting up a total mail solution that incorporates disparate mail clients.

Finger Services

Keep your fingers off of my computer. No, not that kind of finger! A finger server provides information about all users on the server or information about a specific user on the server.

EMWAC's Freeware Finger Server provides basic finger capabilities. Though Finger is not supported by all Internet sites, it can be a useful service. Since the Freeware Finger Server is easy to obtain, install, and configure, running a finger server is not difficult.

WAIS Servers

EMWAC's Freeware WAIS Server—A WAIS (Wide Area Information Server) allows users to query indexes of distributed databases and retrieve data. Windows NT's Resource Kit included a WAIS server, and when Microsoft releases the Resource Kit for Windows NT 4 Server, a WAIS server should be included.

EMWAC also offers the WAIS Toolkit based on freeWAIS 0.3—a WAIS toolkit to assist in configuring and setting up freeWAIS 0.3 (the Freeware WAIS Server).

Time & Scheduling Services

Extreme Software offers a product that can be used effectively by Windows NT 4 Server-based ISPs. This product, ntcrond, is a powerful replacement for the Windows NT AT command.

Extreme Software's Internet site is www.dfw.net/~gparsons.

The ntcrond command is a Windows NT service that emulates the UNIX crond command scheduling utility. UNIX's crond was developed by AT&T and Hewlett Packard for UNIX. With ntcrond, Windows NT users may schedule the execution of commands at specified dates and times.

Accounting & Billing

Not a Windows NT 4 Server issue, but critical to your success as an ISP is the ability to bill your client users promptly and accurately.

Windows NT 4 Server, in the event log, maintains logon information you can extract to provide information about usage by client users. Extracting this information might be difficult were it not for a product called Crystal Reports (Version 4.5 or later), which allows you to create reports based on the event log.

Creative usage of Crystal Reports can result in a system that actually prints out detailed invoices for your client users! Or Crystal Reports can simply summarize the data and write a report to the disk, which an accounting program can then use to generate invoices.

Client User Connectivity

Hardware is one of the more critical issues when working with PC-compatible microcomputers. The PC has always been limited on communications (IBM originally thought no one would ever need more than two serial ports), and if we are to use a Windows NT 4 Server PC-based system as an ISP, we must be able to connect modems, lots of modems, to the server.

I/O Boards

Question: How do I connect a hundred modems to Windows NT 4 Server? Answer: Digiboards—Lots of them!

Well, many of us would ask, "What's a Digiboard?"

Most microcomputers come equipped with two to four serial ports. For a single-user system, four serial ports is usually sufficient. However if you are running a PC-compatible system (with ISA, PCI, MC, or EISA bus configurations) you can add up to 255 serial ports to your server by using a product such as the Digiboard.

Digi's multi-serial port products are typically configured as either 4, 8, or 16 serial ports. You can set speeds from 50 bps to 56 Kbps, and many models contain internal buffering and communications management. The use of onboard processing allows these products to only minimally load the server. All I/O to the serial ports is done using drivers provided by Digi, providing a seamless interface with Windows NT 4 Server.

More information on Digi's products can be obtained from their Internet site at http://www.dgii.com.

Modems

In contrast to how few choices there are for I/O boards, there are many choices for modems. Some selections include rack mount modems, standard commercial modems such as the Practical Peripherals PM288MT modem (small, this modem can be stacked for good density); modems from virtually every modem manufacturer are basically acceptable.

Despite what we may think, higher-priced, commercial-quality modems may not necessarily be the best choice. Modem technology continues to change quickly, and modems must be replaced frequently not because they fail, but because they don't offer features demanded by users. Reliability is seldom a problem—even inexpensive modems, once working, seem to be as reliable as their more expensive cousins.

You must have a plan to test and ensure that modems are working correctly. Generally, a telephone hunt group (which allows client users to dial a single number, and be connected to any of a number of different phone lines) will start at a predefined line, and search in order until an unused line is found. This means that the first modems and lines see more usage than the last ones! One technique is to place the older, slower, modems on the least frequently used lines until they can be upgraded to higher speeds.

Index

A

Access Permissions dialog box 546
Access Through Share Permissions dialog box 500
access, IIS services 440, 447–450
Accessibility Options component 85
Accessories component 85
accessory programs 633–646
Account Operators, security group 548
account policy, User Manager for Domains program 564–567
accounts, system administrator 82–83
Active Leases dialog box 162
adapters
  mass storage 68–69
  SCSI 8, 225, 228
  supported types 68–69
  video 226
Add Computer To Domains dialog box 513–514
Add Port - Digital Network Port dialog box 519
Add Printer Wizard 516–533
  adding printers 516–524
  device settings 533
  port settings 517–520
  printer name/sharing options 521–523
  printer ports 529
  printer properties 524–533
  printer type selection 520–521
  scheduling printers 530–531
  security 532
  sharing 531
  test page printing 523–524
Add Reserved Clients dialog box 161
Add to Chart (Ctrl+I) keyboard shortcut 270
Add to Chart dialog box 270
address allocations, ISP 678
Address Book 29
Admin program (Microsoft SNA Server) 305–310
  administration functions 306–307
  connection administration 309
  groups administration 310
  LU pool administration 308
  server administration 309
  user administration 310
administration
  DNS (Domain Name Server) 19
  messages 19–20
  performance monitoring 20
  remote 41–42
Administrator Account window 82
administrator login ID 51
Administrators
  security group 548
  system 51
advance payments 670
Advanced IP Addressing dialog box 143
Agent program 681
Alerts on server dialog box 507
Alerts window (SMS) 329
alerts, audit 7
aliases, virtual directories (IIS) 437–438
anonymous connections, IIS 426–428
anonymous FTP sites, RFC1542 specifications 165
Apple Macintosh networks 185, 197–199
AppleTalk networks 9
applets
  Network 107–130, 139–152
  SNA Server 3270 310–311
  User Profiles System 554–556

applications
  backing up 581
  memory protection 7
  switching between 294
archival backups 578
ArcNet 259
ARPA-192.REV file, DNS Manager 171
Asynchronous Procedure Calls 10
AT&T WorldNet, Internet connections 675
ATRLS Ataman TCP Remote Logon Services program 682
attacks, internal/external 536–537
ATTRIB (DOS) command 625
audit alerts 7
audit policy, user/group security 567–569

B

B2 level security 16
backups, user lists 564
background information, installation 77–80
background writes 10
BackOffice 301–334
backup devices, SQL Enterprise Manager 391
backup hardware 584–587
  optical media 586–587
  tape technologies 584–586
Backup Information dialog box 592
backup media, physical security 579–580
Backup Operators, security group 548
backup/restore functions 14-15
backups
  application software 581
  archival 578
  bulk erasers 600
  complete 582–583
  data types 580–581
  erasing tapes 600
  frequency 578–579
  hardware 584–587
  incremental 581–582
  overview 577–578
  physical security 579–580
  prior to installation 51
  restoring (Windows NT Backup) 597–600
  retaining copies 579
  security 578
  strategies 578–583
  system 577-601
  types 578
  Windows NT Backup program 588–600
Bain, Steve 423, 476
Banyan VINES (Visual Networking System), configuration 8, 199–200
BDC (Backup Domain Controller) 80–82, 179
BDC (Backup Domain Controller) Server, MS Exchange installation 337–343
bindings, network 96–97
Books Online
  Microsoft Exchange Server 347–348
  Microsoft SQL Server 6.5 373, 401
boot diskettes 62
boot partitions 231
boot PROM (Programmable Read-Only Memory) 110
BOOT.INI file 59, 624–631
  adding operating systems 627–628
  attributes 625–626
  boot options 628–629
  DNS Manager 169
  dual boot systems 626
  troubleshooting 630–631
BOOTP (bootstrap protocol) 35
BOOTSEC.DOS file 626
Brannon, Charles 5
Browser object counters 272–273
Budnick, Larry 5
bulk erasers, backup tapes 600
buses, system 225

C

C2 level security 16
cables, twisted pair 258, 262–263
CACHE file, DNS Manager 170
Cache object counters 274–276
cache RAM, performance 224
Calculator program 634
Catapult server, IP Spoofing 678–680
CD Player program 648
CD-ROM
  I386 folder 53
  readme.txt file 43
CD-ROM drives 226–227
  letter assignments 238
  supported types 8
CDW (Writeable CD-ROM), backup hardware 586
certificates, SSL 481–486
Character Map program 635

characters, semicolon (;) 167
Chat program 636–637
CHDIR (DOS) 64
CHKDSK (DOS) command 242
classes, IP address 135–137
cleaning files 237
client.src folder 319
clients
Macintosh 197–199
remote booting 42–45
SMS (Microsoft Systems Management Server) 312–313, 319–321
Clipboard Viewer program 637
Clock program 638
coax (coaxial cable) 258, 262–263
Command Line Properties dialog box (SMS) 327
comments
IIS 428
semicolon (;) character, DNS server 167
common groups 44–45
Communications component 85
communications, UPS (un-interruptible power supply) 573
companies, resources 659–668
complete backups 582–583
components
installation 84–85
Microsoft Exchange 339–340
server 107–130
compression, files 245–248
Computer | Add to Domain command 513
Computer | Promote to Primary Domain Controller command 512
Computer | Properties (Server Manager) command 502
Computer | Remove from Domain command 513
Computer | Select Domain command 513
Computer | Send Message command 511
Computer | Services command 509
Computer | Shared Directories command 508
Config folder 605–607
Configure Port Usage dialog box 213, 539
connections
gateways 678–679
Internet 672–676
IP Spoofing 679–680
Microsoft SNA Server administration 309
PoP (Point of Presence) 673–675
Context key, Windows 95 compatible keyboards 25
Control Panel
features 32–33
IIS (Microsoft Internet Information Server) installation 418
Network applet 107–130, 139–152
Registry editing 610–611
CONVERT utility, non-destructive file format convert 243–245
counters
Browser object 272–273
Cache object 274–276
instance 268
Logical Disk object 276–278
Memory object 278–281
Paging File object 281
Performance Monitor 266–269
Physical Disk object 282–283
Process object 283–284
Processor object 284–285
Server object 286–289
System object 290–292
Thread object 292–293
Work Queues 289–290
CPU (Central Processing Unit), upgrading 224
CRC Errors 263
Create Scope dialog box 160
CTS (Clear-to-send) 573
current Windows NT installations screen 70
custom recipients, Microsoft Exchange Administrator 353

D

DAT (Digital Audio Tape), backup hardware 586
data types, Registry 618–620
database devices, SQL Enterprise Manager 389–390
databases
library option configurations (SQL) 380–381
master, Microsoft SQL Server 6.5 372
message storage 29
SQL Enterprise Manager 391–394
WINS 181–183
date, configuring 101
Date/Time Properties dialog box 101
DCD (Data-carrier-detect) 573
DCE (Distributed Computing Environment) 128
DCE-compatible RPC 9

DDK (Windows NT Server Device Driver Kit) 271
default.htm file, Web service 441–442
deinstal command 320
Deny Access On dialog box (IIS) 449
Describe Net Cards dialog box 257
Desktop 27–28
  IIS (Microsoft Internet Information Server)
    installation 417
devices
  backup 391
  database 389–390
  printer 533
  standard update 70–72
DHCP Manager
  adding/removing servers 159
  client address display 162
  client machine reserved scope 161
  IP address modifications 159
  main window 159
  scope activation 161
  scope deletion 161
  scope modification 161
  starting 158
DHCP (Dynamic Host Configuration Protocol)
  Relay Agent 35, 165–166
  configuration 165–166
  networks 9
  server, IP address 95
  TCP/IP Services configuration 149–150
DHCP Options: Default Values dialog box 164
DHCP Options: Global dialog box 164
DHCP Options: Scope dialog box 163
dial-up connections, Internet 672
Dial-Up Networking window 203
Digiboards, client user connectivity 685–686
DIR command (DOS) 64
directories (folders) 28
  See Also Folders
  account information (IIS) 438–439
  adding/deleting (IIS) 435–442
  home (IIS) 437
  IIS services 434–442
  installation selection 73–74
  Registry files 605
  temporary 66
  virtual 437–438
directory
  access, IIS 440
  caching 10
  hashing 10
Directory Replication on server dialog box 506
directory support 13
Disk Administrator 228–239
  boot partitions 231
  destructive convert 243–244
  drive error checking 238
  drive letter assignments 238
  FAT-NTFS conversions 243–245
  fault tolerance 232–237
  forcing changes 232
  formatting drives 237
  labeling drives 238
  logical drives 230–231
  mirror sets 235
  partitions 228–232
  saving/restoring configurations 231–232
  stripe sets 235–236
  tools 237–239
  viewing properties 239
  volume sets, creating/extending 230–231
Disk Administrator Format dialog box 244
disk I/O, performance 225
diskless workstations 42
  Remote Boot Service configuration 110–116
disks
  backup hardware 587
  boot 62
  ERD (Emergency Repair Disk) 103
  formatting 237
Display Properties dialog box 102
distribution lists, Microsoft Exchange Administrator 351–353
DLC (Data Link Control) protocol
  networks 9
  Remote Boot Service 111–112
DLT (Digital Linear Tape), backup hardware 585
DMA (Direct Memory Access) 225
DNS (Domain Name Server) 19, 35–37, 420, 677
  TCP/IP Services entries 145–147
  WINS integration 37
DNS Manager 168–175
  ARPA-192.REV file 171
  BOOT file 169
  CACHE file 170
  domain server records 174–175
  main window 172
  options 172–174
  PLACE.DOM file 170
DNS Preferences dialog box 174

DNS | Delete command 173
DNS | New Domain command 173
DNS | New Host command 173
DNS | New Record command 174
DNS | New Server command 173
DNS | New Zone command 173
DNS | Pause Zone command 173
DNS | Properties command 173
DNS | Update Server Data Files command 173
documents, default Web service 441–442
Domain Admins, security group 548
domain names, registering 676–677
domain servers, records 174–175
Domain Users, security group 548
domains
  IP Address 137
  Server Manager 513–514
downloading
  Internet Assistant 477
  Microsoft Internet Explorer 421
drive letters, assigning 238
drivers
  hardware 44
  printer 520
drives
  CD-ROM 226–227, 238
  compressing 247–248
  error checking 238
  formatting 237
  hard disk 227–228
  installation 72–73
  labeling 238
  letter assignments 238
  NTFS-formatted 58
  viewing properties 239
DTR (Data-terminal-ready) 573
dual-boot systems 58–59, 626–628
DUN (Dial-Up Networking) 45–46, 201–222
  configuration 201–222
  entry names 204–205
  entry properties editing 209–210
  New Phonebook Entry Wizard 204–210
  phone numbers 207–208
  RAS (Remote Access Service) 201, 203, 210–221
  RASADMIN program 220–221
  RASDIAL program 218–220
  server options 205–207
  TCP/IP configuration 140, 202–210
  Telephony Dialing Properties 208
dynamic cache 10

Edit Database Device dialog box (SQL Enterprise Manager) 390
Edit | Add to Chart command 270
8-MM tape, backup hardware 585
e-mail
  internal 28–29
  Internet 28–29
  Internet format addresses 429
  online information services 29
  servers 683
Emergency Repair Disk window 83
encryptions, RAS (Remote Access Service) 217–218, 542
Enterprise editions, Microsoft BackOffice 302
environmental security 575
ERD (emergency repair disk) 83–84, 103
error checking, Network Monitor 263–264
error logs, RAS (Remote Access Service) 543
ET (electronic funds transfer) 670
Ethernet 259
event viewing, remote 42
Events window (SMS) 332
events, displaying 332
EVENTVWR.EXE file 42
Exchange component 85
Execute Query dialog box (SMS) 323
EXHEALTH.PMW file 357
EXHIST.PMW file 357
EXLOAD.PMW file 361
EXQUEUE.PMW file 358
external attacks, system security 536–537
EXUSER.PMW file 360

FAT (File Allocation Table) 6, 11, 240
  NTFS conversions 243–245
  partition limitations 229, 241
FAT-16 file systems 11–12, 241
FAT-32 file systems 11–12, 241
fault tolerance 13–14, 232–237
  mirror sets 235
  RAID (Redundant Arrays of Inexpensive Disks) 232–234
  stripe sets 235–236
  stripe sets with parity 236–237
FDDI connections, Internet 672
FDISK program (DOS) 228

file caching 10
file extensions
  GTG 456
  PST 647
File Find and Search utility 31
file formats 240–248
  FAT (File Allocation Table) 240
  NTFS (NT File System) 240–248
file sharing 496–514
  Explorer management 496–502
  Server Manager 501–514
file systems 11–12
File | Execute Query (SMS) command 323
File | New Custom Recipient command 353
filenames, naming conventions 24–25
files (objects) 28
  accessing recently used 25
  ARPA-192.REV (DNS) 171
  BOOT (DNS) 169
  BOOT.INI 59, 624–631
  BOOTSEC.DOS 626
  CACHE (DNS) 170
  cleaning 237
  compressing 245–248
  Config folder 605–607
  copying installation 75–76
  default.htm 441–442
  DNS Server 167–168
  EVENTVWR.EXE 42
  EXHEALTH.PMW 357
  EXHIST.PMW 357
  EXLOAD.PMW 361
  EXQUEUE.PMW 358
  EXUSER.PMW 360
  finding 31
  IMCQUEUE.PMW 362
  IMCSTATS.PMW 362
  INI 604–605
  LMHOSTS 43–44
  logging to (IIS) 443–444
  long filename conventions 24–25
  Microsoft ODBC SQL Server Driver
    help 376
  PCL.SEP 526
  PLACE.DOM (DNS) 170
  PSCRIPT.SEP 526
  RDISK.EXE 103
  readme.txt 43
  readme.txt, Microsoft SQL Server 6.5 379
  Registry 605–607
  SQL Distributed Management Objects
    help 384–387
  SRVMGR.EXE 41–42
  SYSPRINT.SEP 526
  SYSTEM 231-232
  SYSTEM.DAT 607
  SYSTEM.INI 604
  tag 456–464
  TEMP.BAT 562–563
  USER.DAT 607
  USERLIST.DAT 563
  USMGR.EXE 42
  WIN.INI 604
  WINNT.EXE 53–54
  WINNT32.EXE 53–54
  workspace 266
Finger Server program 684
finger services 684
firewalls
  Internet 138
  intranet 5
  proxy servers 680
folders 28
  See also directories
  adding/deleting (IIS) 435–442
  compressing 246–247
  Config 605–607
  hives (Registry) 608–609
  IIS services 434–442
FORMAT (DOS) command 237
FormQuery, WWW Server (IIS) 472
4-MM tape, backup hardware 585
Frame Relay connections, Internet 672
Frames Dropped (Hardware) errors 263
Frames Dropped (No Buffers) errors 263
FreeCell program 652
FTP (File Transfer Protocol) service (IIS)
  464–466
  directory listing types 441
  directory properties 437
  exit message (IIS) 433
  maximum connections message 433
  messages, IIS 430–433
  welcome message (IIS) 432–433
ftproot folder (IIS) 435

G

games 652–655
Games component 85
Gateway Services for NetWare 187–190
Gateway Service for NetWare dialog box 189
gateway

- Internet 138
- connections 678–679
- intranet 5
- NetWare services 187–190

GDSSET program, creating/using tag files 457–460
Gopher service (IIS) 453–464
- anonymous connections (IIS) 426–428
- directory properties (IIS) 436
- GDSSET program 457–460
- Gopher+ selector strings 454–455
- GTG file extension 456
- manual links 454
- Microsoft Internet Explorer support 454
- Service Administrator (IIS) 428–429
- setup 455–464
- tag files 456–464
- text-oriented 453
- uses 454
- virtual directory aliases 438
- vs FTP service 454

Gopher sites 455
gophroot folder (IIS) 435
graphs, Performance Monitor 265–266
group security 547–548
groups
- common 44–45
- Microsoft SNA Server administration 310
- rights/privileges 557–561
- security 547–548
- security controls 556–570

GTG file extensions 456
Guestbook database, WWW Server (IIS) 472
Guests, security group 548

H

HAL (Hardware Abstraction Layer) 6
hard disks 227–228
- backup hardware 587
- creating/extending volume sets 230–231
- error checking 238
- examining on installation 74–75
- labeling 238
- letter assignments 238
- mirror sets 235
- partitions 228–232
- stripe sets 235–236
- stripe sets with parity 236–237
- viewing properties 239

hardware drivers, new features 44
Hardware Profiles 29
hardware requirements 6, 50
- Microsoft Exchange 336–337
- Microsoft Systems Management Server 313

hardware
- CD-ROM drives 226–227
- configuration 223–250
- CPU upgrades 224
- Disk Administrator 228–239
- disk I/O 225
- DOS-based initialization file non-support 8
- hard disks 227–228
- high-performance NICs (Network Interface Cards) 226
- ISDN lines 227
- mirror sets 235
- modems 227
- motherboard replacement 224
- RAID (Redundant Arrays of Inexpensive Disks) 232–234
- RAM upgrades 224
- SCSI adapters 225, 228
- system buses 225
- video cards 226

hard-wired networks, TCP/IP Services configuration 134
HCL (Hardware Compatibility List) 7, 47
help
- resources for program 659–668
- SQL Distributed Management Objects 384–387

HHLAPI, third-party software 9
histograms, Performance Monitor 265–269
hives (folders), Registry 608–609
host protocols 671
HPFS (High Performance File System) 11
HTML (HyperText Markup Language) 468, 475
- documents, WWW Server (IIS) sample sheets 474–475
- pages, creating 475–479

HyperTerminal program 638–640

I/O boards, client connections 685–686
IBM mainframe A/S400, Microsoft SNA Server 303–312
IDE CD-ROM drives 226–227
IDE hard drives 228

Identifier key (Registry) 608
IFS (Installable File Systems) 6
IIS (Microsoft Internet Information Server) 38–39, 415–452
  access setup 447–450
  Account Information controls 439
  adding/deleting service directories 435–442
  aliases, virtual directories 437–438
  anonymous connections 426–428
  beta versions 416
  CD-ROM installation 418
  comments 428
  configuration 420–421
  Connection Timeout control 425
  Control Panel installation 418
  desktop installation 417
  directory access 440
  directory account information 438–439
  directory browsing 442
  directory setup 434–442
  directory virtual server 439–450
  DNS (Domain Name Server) 420
  editing properties 441
  Except Those Listed Below access 448
  exit message (FTP) 433
  FTP configuration 423–449
  FTP messages 430–433
  FTP server 464–466
  Gopher configuration 423–449
  Gopher service 453–464
  Gopher's Service Administrator 428–429
  Granted Access/Denied Access 448
  hard drive storage requirements 419
  home directory 437
  installation 87–88, 417–421
  Internet Service Manager 422–423
  Limit Network Use by All Internet Services access 449–450
  log storage 420
  log to file 443–444
  log to SQL/ODBC Database 444–446
  logging 442–446
  Maximum Connections control 425
  Maximum Connections message (FTP) 433
  Microsoft Internet Information Server Manager 421–423
  overview 415–416
  performance 451
  reliability 450
  root directories 435
  server services 416
  service directory properties 436–439
  service setup 425–430
  setup program 418–421
  virtual directories 437–438
  Web servers configuration 423–449
  welcome message (FTP) 432–433
  Windows NT 4 Workstation functionality 421
  WWW password authentication 430
iisadmin folder (IIS) 435
Imaging program 640–641
IMail server for Windows NT 683
IMC (Internet Mail Connector), Microsoft Exchange monitoring 361–364
IMCQUEUE.PMW file 362
IMCSTATS.PMW file 362
Inbox Repair Tool program 647
incremental backups 581–582
INI files, vs Registry 604–605
installation 49–106
  adapters, supported types 68–69
  administrator account 82–83
  background information 77–80
  backups 51
  boot diskettes 62
  BOOT.INI file 59
  CD-ROM drive access 64
  clean 57–58
  components 84–85
  computer name 80
  copying files 75–76
  copying files to temporary directory 66
  current Windows NT installations screen 70
  directory selection 73–74
  dual-boot systems 58–59
  ERD (emergency repair disk) 83–84, 103
  first time network start up 97–100
  hard disk examination 74–75
  hardware requirements 50
  HCL (hardware compatibility list) 50
  IIS (Microsoft Internet Information Server) 87–88, 417–421
  installation drive selection 72–73
  licensing modes 79
  Microsoft Exchange 336–343
  Microsoft SNA Server 304–305
  Microsoft SQL Server 6.5 368–374
  MS-DOS/Windows 95 upgrade 58–60
  multiple 51
  network bindings 96–97
  network components 85–104
  Network Monitor Agent 253
  Network Monitor Tools 253

network options 86–89
network protocols/services 90–94
non-standard systems 71–72
options 52–54
overview 49–51
PnP (Plug-and-Play) PCI slot dependency 59–60
pre-installation checklist 63–64
product ID code 78
questions/answers 54–55
rebooting the system 75
scanning for mass storage 67–69
selecting type 69–70
server configuration 94–97
server type selection 80–82
Setup Program 54–57
SMS (Microsoft Systems Management Server) 313–318
SMS clients 319–321
standard devices update 70–72
supported platforms 53
system administrator tasks 76–85
TCP/IP properties 95–96
testing 104
time requirements 51
time zone settings 100–101
types 52–54, 69–70
video adapter 101–102
Windows 95 FAT-32/FAT-16 file system conversion 58
Windows 95 SMS client 320
Windows NT 3.5x upgrade 60–61
Windows NT 4 beta versions 61
instances, Performance Monitor counter 268
insurance 670
interface, Windows 95 emulation 24–28
internal attacks, system security 536–537
internal e-mail 28–29
Internet
AT&T WorldNet connections 675
connection techniques 134
connection window 88
connections 672–676
DNS (Domain Name Server) 420
e-mail 28–29
firewalls 138
gateway 138
Gopher sites 455
MCI Communications connections 674
multi-homed systems 675–676
node limitations 136–137
Pacific Bell connections 675
PoP (Point of Presence) connections 673–675
RAS/DUN (Remote Access Service/Dial-Up Networking) 134
server e-mail addresses 429
SprintLink connections 674
system security 538
TLC-HLC.internet connections 675
user-defined special groups 43–44
vs intranet 5
Internet Explorer 28
Internet Mail Services program 682–683
Internet Protocol, RIP (Routing Information Protocol) 153–156
Internet Service Manager 422–423
FTP Services Properties dialog box 424
Web Directory Properties dialog box 436
interNeTlist server 682
InterNIC (Internet Network Information Center) 36
domain name registering 676–677
intranet 38
firewalls 5
gateways 5
system security 538
TCP/IP protocol 5
vs Internet 5
IP Addresses
advanced addressing 143–144
allocating 678
classes 135–137
configuration 142–145
domain 137
Microsoft DHCP server 159–162
TCP/IP Services assignments 135–138
IP Spoofing 679–680
IPCs (Inter-Process Calls) 9–10
IPX protocol
RAS port configuration 216–217
system security 545
IPXROUTE utility 191–192
ISA bus, performance limitations 225
ISDN connections 87, 227, 672
ISP (Internet Service Provider) 669–686
account/billing 685
address allocations 678
advance payments 670
AT&T WorldNet connections 675
client user connectivity 685–686
connecting between 673–674
connecting to Internet 672
contract with clients 670
Digiboards 685–686

DNS (Domain Name Server) 677
domain names 676–677
electronic funds transfer (ET) 670
e-mail servers 683
ensuring prompt payment 670
finger services 684
firewalls 680
gateway connections 678–679
insurance 670
Internet connections 672–676
list servers 682
mail list servers 682
MCI Communications connections 674
modems 686
multi-homed systems 675–676
news server 681
Pacific Bell, Internet connections 675
PoP (Point of Presence) connections 672–675
protocols to offer to clients 671
proxy servers 680
reasons to begin 670
scheduling services 684
servers 681–685
services 671, 681–685
SMTP/POP-3 services 682–683
SprintLink connections 674
telephone hunt group 686
telnet servers 681–682
time services 684
TLC-HLC.internet connections 675
WAIS servers 684
working capital 670
ISQL/w utility, Microsoft SQL Server 6.5 374–375

J

JetMail program 682–683
jobs, displaying/creating 328–329
Jobs window (SMS) 328

K

key values, (Registry) 609
keyboards
Microsoft's Natural Keyboard 25–26
Windows 95 compatible 25
Windows key 25
KEYGEN.EXE program 481, 488–489
keys
Context 25
F5 (Refresh) 173
Identifier (Registry) 608
Registry 608, 622–624
Window-E 25–26
Windows 25

L

LAN (local area network) 4–5
Apple Macintosh Networks interaction 185, 197–199
Banyan VINES Networks interaction 186, 199–200
interactions 185–200
Novell's NetWare interaction 185–196
LAN Manager 2.x, server configuration 110
LFD (Lost Functionality Disorder) 389
libraries, database options (SQL) 380–381
Licensing Modes window 79
links, Gopher service (IIS) 454
list servers 682
LMHOSTS file 43–44
logging, IIS 442–446
Logical Disks object counters 276–278
logical drives, creating/extending 230–231
login IDs, administrator 51
logins
SQL Enterprise Manager 394–395
SQL Server Web Assistant 402
long filenames 24–25
LPC (Local Procedure Call) 9
LU pools, Microsoft SNA Server administration 308
LU Pools window 308

M

MacFile properties dialog box 198
Machine Groups window (SMS) 330
machine groups, displaying/creating 330
Macintosh clients, configuration 197–199
Macintosh file/print servers, configuration 197–199
mail list servers 682
mailboxes, Microsoft Exchange Administrator 349–351

management
remote server 41–42
remote user 42
Mansfield, Richard 5
Mappings | Backup Database command 183
Mappings | Initiate Scavenging command 182
Mappings | Restore Local Database command 183
Mappings | Show Database command 181
Mappings | Static Mappings command 182
mass storage
scanning for 67–69
supported adapters 68–69
master database, Microsoft SQL Server 6.5 372
MCI Communications, Internet connections 674
Media Player program 649
Memory object counters 278–281
memory, optimizing 109–110
message storage database 29
messages
administration 19–20
alert 329, 507
FTP (IIS) 430–433
Hierarchy Manager doesn't respond (SMS) 316
SQL Server 332–333
Microsoft BackOffice 301–334
Enterprise editions 302
IIS (Microsoft Internet Information Server) 415–452
license agreement 302
machine groups 330
Microsoft Exchange program 335–366
Microsoft SNA Server 303–312
Microsoft SQL Server 6.5 367–412
Microsoft Windows NT 3.51 302
SMS (Microsoft Systems Management Server) 312–333
version number issues 303
Microsoft Catapult 137–138
Microsoft DHCP (Dynamic Host Configuration Protocol) 158–164
Microsoft DHCP server 158–164
configuration 158–164
IP Addresses 159–162
options 163–165
Microsoft DHCP Server/Agent 132
Microsoft DNS (Domain Name Server) 132, 167–175
ARPA-192.REV file 171
BOOT file 169
CACHE file 170
configuration 167–175
DNS Manager 168–175
files 167–168
PLACE.DOM file 170
semicolon (;) character with comments 167
Microsoft Exchange
(IMC) Internet Mail Connector monitoring 361–364
Address Book 29
Administrator 339–340
Books Online 339–340, 347–348
components 339, 347–365
distribution CD-ROM 338
documentation 339–340
installation 336–343
installation types 338
license agreement 340
message storage database 29
Migration Wizard 355–356
monitors 356–361
new site creation 342
Optimizer 356
organization name 342
performance optimization 343–346
planning worksheets 340–341
processor support 338
Setup Editor 364–365
site name 342
system requirements 336–337
Microsoft Exchange Administrator
custom recipients 353
distribution lists 351–353
mailboxes 349–351
Microsoft Exchange Server 348–355
New Other menu options 354–355
Microsoft Exchange Client 28–29
Microsoft Exchange Server 28–29
Health 357
History 357–358
IMC Queues 362
IMC Statistics 362–363
IMC Traffic 363–364
Load 361
Queues 358–359
Users 360
Microsoft Explorer, file sharing 496–502
Microsoft FrontPage, creating/editing HTML documents 478–479
Microsoft Internet Assistant
creating/editing HTML documents 476–478
downloading 477

Microsoft Internet Explorer
  downloading 421
  Gopher service support 454
Microsoft Internet Information Server 2.0 dialog box 419
Microsoft Internet Information Server Manager 421–423
Microsoft KB (Knowledge Base) 611–612
Microsoft networks 8
Microsoft ODBC SQL Server Driver help file 376
Microsoft Paint 30
Microsoft SNA (Systems Network Architecture) Server 303–312
  3270 Applet 310–311
  Admin program 305–310
  administration functions 306–307
  communications 303–304
  connection administration 309
  groups administration 310
  IBM mainframe AS/400 303
  installation 304–305
  LU pool administration 308
  ODBC Administrator program 310
  overview 303–304
  Pack #1 312
  server administration 309
  terminal emulations 304
  Trace program 312
  user administration 310
Microsoft SNMP (Simple Network Management Protocol) 192–193
Microsoft SNMP Properties dialog box 194–196
Microsoft SQL Server 6.5 367–412
  administrator's user ID 373–374
  advanced options 382–383
  Books Online 373
  Client Configuration utility 379–383
  Distributed Management Objects help file 384–387
  Enterprise Manager 388–395
  installation 368–374
  installation path 372
  ISQL/w utility 374–375
  licensing mode 371–372
  master database 372
  MS Query 376–378
  network protocol configuration 381–382
  ODBC SQL Server Driver help file 376
  Performance Monitor 395–397
  readme.txt file 379
  Security Manager 398–400
  Server Books Online 401
  Server Web Assistant 401–407
  Service Manager 408–409
  setup options 370–371
  SQL Setup utility 410
  SQL Trace utility 410–411
  supported systems 368
Microsoft Systems Management Server, system requirements 313
Microsoft TCP/IP Properties window 96
Microsoft Windows Messaging System 28–29
Microsoft WINS (Windows Internet Name Service) 132
Microsoft WordPad 29–30
Microsoft's Natural Keyboard, Window-E key 25–26
Migration Wizard, Microsoft Exchange 355–356
Minesweeper program 653
mirror sets 235
modems 227, 686
  RAS (Remote Access Server) configuration 210–221
  Telephony Dialing Properties 208
motherboards, CPU upgrades 224
MPR (Multi-Protocol Routing) 40–41
MS Query 376–378
MS Query SQL dialog box 378
multi-homed systems, Internet 675–676
Multimedia component 85
multimedia tools 648–651
Mutexes 10

N

Name and Organization window 78
Named Pipes (client/server) 9
NET command 562
NET USE command 43
NET USERS>TEMP.BAT command 562
NetBEUI protocol, RAS port configuration 214–215
  IPX/SPX support 8–9
  system security 545
NetBIOS Configuration dialog box 129
NetBIOS interface, configuration 129–130
NetBios networks 9
NetManage IntraNet Forum Server program 681
Net-Shopper program 682
NetWare

configuration 185–196
gateway services 187–190
IPX/SPX support 8
IPXROUTE utility 191–192
RIP services 190–192
SAP (Service Advertising Protocol) 192–193
SNMP Services 193–196
Network Adapter selection window 89
Network applet
server component configuration 107–130
TCP/IP services configuration 139–152
Network Configuration dialog box 214, 540–541
Network Monitor 252–265
error checking 263–264
error rates 264
Ethernet 259
file Bytes Per Second 260
finding routers 254
identifying users 254
Network Utilization percentage 259
packet Frames Per Second 260
passwords 256–257
performance monitoring 259–265
speed enhancements 262–263
tools 254
transfer rates 260–261
Network Monitor Agent
configuration 256–258
installation 253
Network Monitor Driver 317
Network Monitor Tools, installation 253
Network Monitoring Password Change dialog box 257
Network Protocols selection window 90
Network Services window 91
networks
Apple Macintosh 185, 197–199
Banyan VINES 8, 186, 199–200
bindings 96–97
component installation 85–104
diskless workstations 42, 110–116
error checking 263–264
first time start up 97–100
hard-wired 134
intranet vs Internet 5
intranets 38
LAN (local area network) 4–5
Microsoft 8
mixed server/client 40
NetWare 8, 185–196
protocols 8–9
protocols/services installation 90–94
RAS/DUN TCP/IP connection 134
remote access 87
speed enhancements 262–263
system security 537
WAN (wide area network) 4–5
wired 87
New Phonebook Entry Wizard 204–210
editing entry properties 209–210
entry names 204–205
phone numbers 207–208
server options 205–207
New Remoteboot Workstation dialog box 123
New User dialog box 550
News Reader program 681
news server 681
newsgroups, news servers 681
NIC (Network Interface Card) 9, 41, 87, 110
adding to RPLCMD utility 125–126
high-performance 226
NNS USENET Network News Server program 681
non-standard systems, installation 71–72
NOS (Network Operating System) 5
Notepad program 641
Novell's NetWare networks 185–196
ntcrond program 684
NTFS (NT File System) 6, 11–12, 240–248
benefits 240–241
destructive convert 243–244
directory support 13
drive compression 247–248
FAT conversions 243–245
file compression 245–248
file sharing security 496
file system object rights 13
non-destructive convert 244–245
partition limitations 241
vs other formats 241–242
NTFS-based partitions 229
NTFS-formatted drives 58
Null UTP cable 264

O

Object Packager program 642
object/folder paradigm 28
objects 28, 269
ODBC Administrator program 310
OEM (Original Equipment Manufacturer) 6
Open Resources on server dialog box 505
operating systems, adding to BOOT.INI file 627–628

optical media, backup hardware 586–587
Optimizer, Microsoft Exchange 356
Options dialog box 66
Options | Chart command 265, 271
Options | Default command 164
Options | Global command 163
Options | Preferences command 183
Options | Scope command 163
Organization and Site Dialog Box (Exchange) 342
OS/2, HPFS (High Performance File System) 11
Other Network Monitor Installations dialog box 255
overlapped seeks 10

P

Pacific Bell, Internet connections 675
Packages window (SMS) 327
packages, displaying/creating 326–328
paged virtual memory 7
Paging File object counters 281
Paint program 643
Partition | Commit Changes Now command 232
Partition | Configuration command 231
Partition | Configuration | Restore command 231
Partition | Configuration | Save command 231
Partition | Configuration | Search command 232
Partition | Create command 229
Partition | Create Extended command 229
Partition | Create Volume Set command 230
Partition | Delete command 229
Partition | Extend Volume Set command 230
Partition | Mark, Active command 231
partitions 228–232
  boot 231
  creating/deleting 339
passwords 256–257
  authentication (IIS) 430
  restrictions 565–566
  SMS (Microsoft Systems Management Server) 315–316
PCI bus, performance 225
  PnP (Plug-and-Play) slot dependency 59–60
PCL.SEP file 526
PDC (Primary Domain Controller) 62, 80–82, 179, 512
  server, Microsoft Exchange installation 337–343
Per Seat licensing mode 78–79
Per Server licensing mode 78–79
performance
  features 10
  optimizing 109–110
Performance Monitor 265–293
  adding items to object counter list 270
  Browser object counters 272–273
  Cache object counters 274–276
  chart settings 266
  Committed Bytes in Use counter percentage 269
  configuration 269–271
  counter instance 268
  counters 266–269
  data viewing 265–266
  extending with DLL files 271
  graphs 265–266
  histograms 265–269
  Logical Disks object counters 276–278
  Memory object counters 278–281
  objects 269
  Paging File object counters 281
  Physical Disk object counters 282–283
  Process object counters 283–284
  Processor object counters 284–285
  Processor Time counter percentage 269
  Server object counters 286–289
  starting 265
  System object counters 290–292
  Thread object counters 292–293
  Total Processor Time counter percentage 267
  Work Queues object counters 289–290
  workspace file 266
performance monitoring 20, 251–298
  Network Monitor 252–265
  Performance Monitor 265–293
  SQL Performance Monitor 395–397
  Windows NT Task Manager 294–297
Performance Optimizer (Exchange) 343–346
Personal Computer Properties dialog box (SMS) 321
Pfaffenberger, Bryan 423, 476
Phone Dialer program 644
Physical Disk object counters 282–283

physical security 570–575
- environmental 575
- server locations 570–571
- UPS (un-interruptible power supply) 571–574

Pinball program 654
PKZIP program 587
PLACE.DOM file, DNS Manager 170
platforms, supported types 53
PnP (Plug-and-Play)
- non-support 7, 29
- PCI slot dependency 59–60

Policies | Account in User Manager command 564
Policies | Audit command 567
Policies | Trust Relationships command 569
Policies | User Rights command 557
PoP (Point of Presence) 672
POP (Post Office Protocol) 672
ports
- printer 517–520, 529
- RAS 212–213

Primary Site Configuration dialog box (SMS) 315
Print Operators, security group 548
print services 18
Printer Ports dialog box 519
Printer Properties dialog box 525
printer sharing 514–533
- Add Printer Wizard 516–533
- devices 533
- port settings 517–520
- ports 529
- properties 524–533
- scheduling 530–531
- security 532
- selecting type 520–521
- spooling 515
- test page printing 523–524

printers
- adding 516–524
- devices 533
- general properties 526–529
- non-supported 520
- port settings 517–520
- ports 529
- properties 524–533
- scheduling 530–531
- security 532
- selecting type 520–521
- separator pages 526
- test page printing 523–524

printing
- test page 523–524
- user lists 562–563

privileges, users 557–561
Process object counters 283–284
Processor object counters 284–285
product ID code, installation 78
profiles, user 552–556
Program Groups window (SMS) 331
program groups, displaying 331
program resources 659–668
programming, WWW Server (IIS) example 473–474
programs
- accessories 633–646
- Admin (Microsoft SNA Server) 305–310
- Agent 681
- ATRLS Ataman TCP Remote Logon Services 682
- Calculator 634
- CD Player 648
- Character Map 635
- Chat 636–637
- Clipboard Viewer 637
- Clock 638
- CONVERT utility 243–245
- FDISK (DOS) 228
- Finger Server 685
- FreeCell 652
- games 652–655
- GDSSET 457–460
- HyperTerminal 638–640
- Imaging 640–641
- Inbox Repair Tool 647
- Internet Mail Services 682–683
- IPXROUTE utility 191–192
- JetMail 682–683
- KEYGEN.EXE 481, 488–489
- Media Player 649
- Microsoft BackOffice 301–334
- Minesweeper 653
- multimedia tools 648–651
- NetManage IntraNet Forum Server 681
- Net-Shopper 682
- Network Monitor 253–265
- News Reader 681
- NNS USENET Network News Server 681
- Notepad 641
- ntcrond 684
- Object Packager 642
- ODBC Administrator 310
- Paint 643
- Phone Dialer 644

Pinball 654
PKZIP 587
RASADMIN 220–221
RASDIAL 218–220
RegEdit 605, 613–615
RegEdt32 607, 615–618
RPCLMD utility 124–127
SETKEY.EXE 481, 487
SNA Server Pack #1 312
SNA Server Setup 312
SNA Server Trace 312
Solitaire 655
Sound Recorder 650
Telnet 644–645
User Manager for Domains 556–570
Volume Control 651
WAIS Server 684
WinZip 587
WordPad 645–646
PROM (Programmable Read-Only Memory) 42
Properties for server dialog box 502
protocols
DLC (Data Link Control) 111–112
Internet Protocol 153–156
IPX 216–217
Microsoft SNMP (Simple Network Management Protocol) 192–193
Microsoft SQL Server 6.5 network 381–382
NetBEUI 214–215
offered by ISP 671
RAS network port 213–218
RIP (Routing Information Protocol) 153–156, 190–192
SAP (Service Advertising Protocol) 192–193
TCP/IP 5, 9, 215–216
TCP/IP (PPTP) 9
proxy servers 680
PSCRIPT.SEP file 526
PST file extension 647
publications
Ethernet Networking Questions and Answers 265
HCL (Hardware Compatibility List) 47
HTML Publishing With Internet Assistant 476
Looking Good Online 423, 476
Microsoft Windows NT 4 Workstation Desktop Companion 5
NT Web Server Book 5
Reseller Management 1
RFC 1034 35
RFC 1035 35
RFC 1542 35, 165
RFC 951 35
Ten Secrets for Web Success 423, 476

Queries window (SMS) 325
queries
ISQL/w 374–375
MS Query 376–378
results display 324
return as a hyperlink, WWW Server (IIS) 472
SQL Server Web Assistant 403
submitting 323–324
WWW Server (IIS) 472
questions, installation 54–55
queues, IMC (Internet Mail Connector) 362

RAID (Redundant Arrays of Inexpensive Disks) 13, 232–234
RAM (Random Access Memory)
cached/uncached performance 224
upgrading 224
RAS (Remote Access Server) 41, 45, 87
configuration 210–221
DUN (Dial-Up Networking) configuration 210–221
encryption settings 217–218
IPX protocol port configuration 216–217
multiple port server connections 218
NetBEUI protocol port configuration 214–215
port configurations 212–213
port network protocols 213–218
RASADMIN program 220–221
RASDIAL program 218–220
TCP/IP protocol port configuration 140, 215–216
RAS (Remote Access Service) 201, 203, 210–221
encryption settings 542
error log 543
IPX security configuration 545
security configuration 538–547
TCP/IP security configuration 542–545

RAS Server IPX Configuration dialog box 217
RAS Server NetBEUI configuration dialog box 215
RAS Server TCP/IP Configuration dialog box 216
RASADMIN program 220–221
RASDIAL program 218–220
RDISK.EXE file 103
read-ahead caching 10
readme.txt file 43, 379
recipients, custom 353
records, domain server 174–175
redundancy 13–14
Refresh (F5) keyboard shortcut 173
RegEdit program 605, 613–615
RegEdt32 program 607, 615–618
Registry 603–632
  Config folder 605–607
  Control Panel vs editor modifications 610–611
  data types 618–620
  editing 609–618
  file storage directory 605
  files 605–607
  hives = folders 608–609
  HKEY_CLASSES_ROOT key 622
  HKEY_CURRENT_CONFIG 624
  HKEY_CURRENT_USER key 622
  HKEY_LOCAL_MACHINE key 623
  HKEY_USERS key 624
  KB (Knowledge Base) 611–612
  key values 609
  keys 608, 622–624
  overview 603–604
  REG_BINARY data type 618
  REG_DWORD data type 619
  REG_EXPAND_SZ data type 619
  REG_FULL_RESOURCE_DESCRIPTOR_ data type 620
  REG_MULTI_SZ data type 620
  REG_NONE data type 621
  REG_SZ data type 619
  REG_UNKNOWN data type 621
  RegEdit program 613–615
  RegEdt32 program 615–618
  vs INI files 604–605
Remote Access Admin, security configuration 545–547
remote access networks 87
Remote Access Setup dialog box 212, 539
remote administration 41–42
Remote Boot Manager 114–116, 123–124
Remote Boot Service
  boot PROM (Programmable Read-Only Memory) 110
  configuration 110–116
  DLC (Data Link Control) protocol 111–112
  Remote Boot Manager 114–116, 123–124
  Windows 3.1x non-support 111
  Windows for Workgroups non-support 111
  Workstation client non-support 111
remote booting, Windows 95 clients 42–43
remote event viewing 42
remote server management 41–42
remote user management 42
Remoteboot Workstation Properties dialog box 119
replication partners 179–180
Replicator, security group 548
resources, 659–668
Restart Computer dialog box 104
restore functions 14-15
returnable memory 10
RFC (Request For Comments) 35
rights, users 557–561
RIP (Routing Information Protocol) 131, 153–156
  Internet Protocol configuration 153–156
  NetWare services 190–192
root directories, IIS 435
ROUTE command 152
routing, TCP/IP Services configuration 150–152
RPC (Remote Procedure Calls), configuration 127–128
RPC Configuration dialog box 128
RPLCMD utility 124–127
RUNSMS.BAT command 319
RUNSMS.CMD command 319

SampSite HTML 470–471
SAP (Service Advertising Protocol), NetWare configuration 192–193
scheduling services 684
scheduling, SQL Server Web Assistant 404–405
Scope | Active Leases command 162
Scope | Add Reservations command 161
Scope | Create command 159
Scope | Delete command 161
Scope | Properties command 161

scope, DHCP Manager modifications 161
screens
  current Windows NT installations 70
  splash 631
  Windows NT Server Setup 67
  Windows NT Server Setup default selections screen 71
  Windows NT Server Setup mass storage detection 68
scripts folder (IIS) 435
SCSI adapters 8, 225, 228
SCSI devices, tape backups 14
SCSI hard drives 227–228
searches
  file 31
  Unicode 31
secure server 15
security 15–17, 535–576
  account lockout 566–567
  account policy 564–567
  audit policy 567–569
  B2 level 16
  backup media 579–580
  C2 level 16
  directory structure 434
  encryption settings 542
  environmental 575
  firewalls 680
  group controls 556–570
  groups 547–548
  internal/external attacks 536–537
  Internet 538
  intranet 538
  IP Address 144–145
  NTFS file sharing 496
  password restrictions 565–566
  physical 570–575
  RAS (Remote Access Service) 538–547
  shared printers 532
  SQL Security Manager 398–400
  SSL 480–481
  system 535–547
  TCP/IP Services 144–145
  trust relationships 569–570
  UPS (un-interruptible power supply) 571–574
  user controls 556–570
  User Manager for Domains program 556–570
  USERLIST.DAT 563
  users 549–556
security auditing 17
security backups 578
Select Components window 84
Select Domain dialog box 514
Select Preferred Server for NetWare dialog box 188
Selecting Users | Permissions command 545
semaphores 9
Send Message dialog box 511
separator pages, printers 526
server components 107–130
  configuration 107–130
  NetBIOS interface configuration 129–130
  Remote Boot Service configuration 110–116
  RPC (Remote Procedure Calls) configuration 127–128
  server configuration 109–110
  workstation configuration 110, 116–123
Server dialog box 109
server management, remote 42
Server Manager 501–514
  alert management 506–507
  directory replication 506
  domains 513–514
  object management 505
  PDC (primary domain controllers) 512
  remote administration 502
  sending messages 511
  services management 509–510
  shared directory management 508–509
  shares management 504–505
  starting 501
  user management 503–504
  viewing server properties 502–503
  viewing/resetting server description 503
Server object counters 286–289
Server Operators, security group 548
Server Type window 81
Server Wizard, features 34
Server | Add WINS Server command 177
Server | Replication Partners command 179
Servers and Connections window 306, 309
servers 5
  adding to WINS Manager 177
  Catapult 678–679
  configuring 109–110
  DHCP 95
  DNS (Domain Name Server) 677
  e-mail 683
  e-mail addresses 429
  FTP (IIS) 464–466
  Gopher (IIS) 453–464
  IIS (Microsoft Internet Information Server) 38–39
  IMail Server for Windows NT 683

installation configuration 94–97
interNeTlist 682
LAN Manager 2.x 110
list 682
Macintosh file/print 197–199
mail net 682
memory optimization 109–110
Microsoft SNA Server administration 309
multiple port connections 218
news 681
performance monitoring 251–298
performance optimization 109–110
physical security 570–571
proxy 680
remote management 408–409
secure 15
SMS (Microsoft Systems Management) 312–333
supported types 91–93
telnet 581–682
viewing/resetting description 503
virtual (IIS) 439–440
WAIS Server 684
WWW (IIS) 467–492
Service on server dialog box 510
Services applet dialog box 155
Services on server dialog box 509
services
offered by ISP 671
supported types 91–93
SETKEY.EXE program 481, 487
Setup Program 54–57
options 56–57
WINNT.EXE file 54
WINNT32.EXE file 54
Setup Progress dialog box (SMS) 316
Setup Wizard
administrator account 82–83
background information 77–80
components installation 84–85
computer name 80
ERD (emergency repair disk) 83–84, 103
first time network start up 97–100
IIS (Microsoft Internet Information Server) 87–88
licensing modes 79
network bindings 96–97
network components installation 85–104
network options installation 86–89
network protocols/services installation 90–94
product ID code 78
server configuration 94–97
server type selection 80–82
TCP/IP properties 95–96
video adapter installation 101–102
Share Properties dialog box 509
Shared Directories on server dialog box 508
Shared Resources on server dialog box 504
sharing 495–534
sharing, printers 514–533
Show Bindings window 97
Simple TCP/IP Services, configuration 131, 156–157
Site Groups window (SMS) 331
site groups, displaying 330–331
Sites window (SMS) 326
SMS (Microsoft Systems Management Server) 252, 312–333
Administrator 322–333
client installation 319–321
client properties 321
client support 312–313
client.src folder 319
deinstal command 320
installation 313–318
Network Monitor Driver 317
passwords 315–316
pre-installation requirements 314
primary site configuration 315
Windows 95 client installation 320
SMS Administrator 322–333
alerts 329
default queries 324–325
events 332
jobs 328
packages 326–328
program groups 331
query results display 324
query submission 323–324
site groups 330–331
SMS hierarchy 325–326
SQL Server messages 332–333
SMTP/POP-3 services 682–683
SNA Server 3270 Applet 310–311
SNA Server Pack #1 program 312
SNA Server Setup program 312
SNA Server Trace program 312
SNMP (Simple Network Management Protocol), NetWare configuration 192–193
sockets 9
software, application backups 581
Solitaire program 655
Sound Recorder program 650
special groups, user-defined Internet 43–44
splash screen, customizing 631

split seeks 10
spooling, printers 515
SprintLink, Internet connections 674
SQL Client Configuration utility 379–383
SQL Client Configuration Utility Locate Libraries dialog box 380
SQL Distributed Management Objects help files 384–387
SQL Enterprise Manager 388–395
  backup devices 391
  context menus 389
  database devices 389–390
  databases 391–394
  logins 394–395
  starting services 389
SQL Performance Monitor 395–397
SQL Performance Monitor Add to Chart dialog box 397
SQL Security Manager 398–400
SQL Security Manager Account Detail dialog box 400
SQL Security Manager Configure dialog box 399
SQL Server Messages window (SMS) 333
SQL Server Web Assistant 401–407
SQL Server, message display 332–333
SQL Service Manager 408–409
SQL Trace utility 410–411
SQL/ODBC Database, logging to (IIS) 444–446
SRVMGR.EXE file 41–42
SSL (Secure Sockets Layer)
  certificates 481–486
  certifying authorities 481
  KEYGEN.EXE program 481, 488–489
  security 480–481
  SETKEY.EXE program 481, 487
  WWW Server (IIS) 479–489
standard devices, updating 70–72
Start menu 26–27
Start | Documents command 25
stripe sets 235–236
stripe sets with parity 236–237
SYSPRINT.SEP file 526
system administrator 51
  account 82–83
  components installation 84–85
  computer name 80
  ERD (emergency repair disk) 83–84, 103
  first time network start up 97–100
  IIS (Microsoft Internet Information Server) 87–88
  installation tasks 76–85
  installation testing 104
  IP address assignments 136–138
  licensing modes 79
  network bindings 96–97
  network components installation 85–104
  network options installation 86–89
  network protocols/services installation 90–94
  product ID code 78
  server configuration 94–97
  server type selection 80–82
  TCP/IP properties 95–96
  video adapter 101–102
system backups 577-602
system buses 225
SYSTEM file 231–232
System object counters 290–292
system security 535–547
  encryption settings 542
  internal attacks 536–537
  Internet 538
  intranet 538
  IPX security configuration 545
  NetBEUI security configuration 545
  networks 537
  overview 535–537
  RAS (Remote Access Service) 538–547
  Remote Access Admin 545–547
  TCP/IP configuration 542–545
  wireless networks 537
SYSTEM.DAT file 607
SYSTEM.INI file 604
systems
  dual-boot 58–59, 626–628
  non-standard 71–72
  operating 627–628
  rebooting on installation 75

T

T1 speed connections, Internet 672
T3 speed connections, Internet 672
tag files, Gopher service (IIS) 456–464
tape backup facility 14-15
tape technology, backup hardware 584–586
tapes, erasing 600
Task Manager 294–297
Taskbar 26
tasks, system administrator installation 76–85

TCP/IP (PPTP) protocol 9
TCP/IP (Transmission Control Protocol/ Internet Protocol) 9, 131
  DUN (Dial-Up Networking) configuration 202–210
  installation properties 95–96
  intranet 5
  RAS port configuration 215–216
  RAS security configuration 542–545
TCP/IP Properties dialog box 166
TCP/IP Security dialog box 145
TCP/IP Services 131–185
  advanced IP Addressing 143–144
  configuration 133–152
  DHCP relay 149–150
  DNS entries 145–147
  DUN (Dial-Up Networking) configuration 140
  hard-wired network configuration 134
  Internet connection techniques 134
  IP address assignments 135–138
  IP Address configuration 142–145
  IP address security 144–145
  RAS (Remote Access Server) configuration 140
  RAS/DUN TCP/IP configuration 134
  routing configuration 150–152
  Simple TCP/IP 156–157
  supported types 131–132
  Windows NT re-install procedure 141
  WINS configuration 147–149
telephone hunt group 686
Telephony Dialing Properties 208
Telnet program 644–645
telnet servers 681–682
TEMP.BAT file 562–563
temporary directory, copying files to 66
test page, printing 523–524
third-party software, B2 level security 16
Thomas, Andy 461
Thread object counters 292–293
time services 684
time zone settings 100–101
timers 10
TLC-HLC.internet, Internet connections 675
Token Ring 259
Tools | Change Format command 237
Tools | Check for Errors command 238
Tools | Format command 230
Tools | Performance Monitor command 254
Transport Library Interface 9
troubleshooting, BOOT.INI file 630–631
Trust Relationship dialog box 569
trust relationships, user/group security 569–570
twisted pair cables 258, 262–263

UNC (Unified Naming Convention), DNS support 37
Unicode 7, 31
upgrades, installation 52–53
UPS (uninterruptible power supply) 13, 571–574
user access 17–18
User Environment Profile dialog box 552
user ID, Microsoft SQL Server 6.5 administrator 372–374
user interface
  components 25–28
  Desktop 27–28
  long filenames 24–25
  object/folder paradigm 28
  recently used file access 25
  Start menu 26–27
  Taskbar 26
  Windows 95 compatible keyboards 25
  Windows 95 emulation 24–28
  Windows Explorer 25–26
user lists
  backing up 564
  printing 562–563
user management, remote 42
User Manager for Domains program 556–570
  account lockout 566–567
  account policy 564–567
  audit policy 567–569
  password restrictions 565–566
  printing user lists 562–563
  rights/privileges 557–561
  security controls 556–570
  trust relationships 569–570
  user list back up 564
User Profiles System applet 554–556
User Rights Policy dialog box 558
USER.DAT file 607
User | New Global Group command 547
User | New Local Group in User Manager for Domains command 547
User | New User command 549
user-defined Internet special groups 43–44

USERLIST.DAT file 563
Users Sessions on server dialog box 502
users
  account lockout 566–567
  adding new 549–551
  audit policy 567–569
  defining 549–551
  managing 503–504
  Microsoft SNA Server administration 310
  password restrictions 565–566
  printing lists 562–563
  profiles 552–556
  rights/privileges 557–561
  security 549–556
  security controls 556–570
  security group 548
  trust relationships 569–570
USMGR.EXE file 42
utilities
  CONVERT 243–245
  IPXROUTE 191–192
  ISQL/w 374–375
  RPCLMD 124–127
  SQL Client Configuration 379–383
  SQL Trace 410–411
UTP (Unshielded Twisted Pair) cable 258, 262–263

V

VeriSign, SSL certificate certifying authority 481–482
VESA/VLB bus, performance limitations 225
video adapters, installation 101–102
video cards 225
View | Clear Statistics command 181
View | Preferences command 173
View | Refresh command 173
View | Refresh Statistics command 181
views, remote event 42
virtual
  directories 437–438
  memory 10
  servers, IIS 439–440
Volume Control program 651
Volume Properties dialog box 239

W

WAIS Server program 684
WAN (Wide Area Network) 4–5
Web pages, SQL Server Web Assistant 401–407
Web sites
  Andy Thomas 461
  Digiboards 686
  Ethernet Networking Questions and Answers 265
  Extreme Software 684
  HCL (Hardware Compatibility List) 47
  hits 468
  Internet Assistant 477
  Internet Explorer 421
  InterNIC 36
  InterNIC 676–677
  Microsoft 7, 470, 476
  RFC 36
  setup 469
  VeriSign 482
WIN.INI file 604
Window-E key, Microsoft's Natural Keyboard 25–26
Windows 95
  BOOTSEC.DOS file 626
  clients, remote booting 42–43
  compatible keyboards 25
  FAT-32/FAT-16 file system conversion 58
  SMS (Microsoft Systems Management Server) client installation 320
  SYSTEM.DAT file 607
  USER.DAT file 607
  user interface 24–28
Windows Explorer 25–26, 245–248
Windows key, Windows 95 compatible keyboards 25
Windows NT
  history 2
  Server vs Workstation version 3
  splash screen customization 631
  TCP/IP re-install procedure 141
Windows NT 3.5x upgrade 60–61
Windows NT 4 Server
  application memory protection 7
  audit alerts 7

backup/restore features 14-15
beta versions upgrade 61
CD-ROM drive support 8
companion products 20–21
directory support 13
DOS-based initialization file non-support 8
FAT (File Allocation Table) support 6
fault tolerance/redundancy 13–14
file systems 11–12
hardware requirements 6
HCL (Hardware Compatibility List) 7
IFS (Installable File Systems) support 6
installation 49–106
IPCs (Inter-Process Calls) 9–10
new features 23–48
NIC (Network Interface Card) support 9
NTFS (NT File System) 6
paged virtual memory 7
performance features 10
performance monitoring 20
PnP (Plug-and-Play) non-support 7
print services 18
security auditing 17
security features 15–17
symmetric multiprocessing 6
Unicode support 7
user access 17–18
vs Workstation versions 3, 46–47
when to use 3–5

Windows NT 4 Workstation
IIS (Microsoft Internet Information Server) 421
vs Server version 46–47

Windows NT 4.0 Upgrade/Installation dialog box 65

Windows NT Backup 588–600
backup set information 594–595
copy backups 595
daily copy backups 595
differential backups 595
hardware installation 588–590
incremental backups 595
log information 596
normal backups 595
restoring 597–600
running backups 590–597
shortcomings 588
tape name options 593–594

Windows NT Server Device Driver Kit (DDK) 271

Windows NT Server Setup
default selections screen 71
mass storage detection screen 68
network access window 87
screen 67
welcome window 77
window 86

Windows NT Task Manager 294–297
performance listing 295–297
processes listing 295
switching between applications 294

windows
Administrator Account 82
Alerts (SMS) 329
DHCP Manager 159
Dial-Up Networking 203
DNS Manager 172
Emergency Repair Disk 83
Events (SMS) 332
Internet connection 88
Internet Service Manager 423
Jobs (SMS) 328
Licensing Modes 79
LU Pools 308
Machine Groups (SMS) 330
Microsoft TCP/IP Properties 96
Name and Organization 78
network adapter selection 89
Network Protocols selection 90
Network Services 91
Packages (SMS) 327
Program Groups (SMS) 331
Queries (SMS) 325
Select Components 84
Server Type 81
Servers and Connections 306, 309
Show Bindings 97
Site Groups (SMS) 331
Sites (SMS) 326
SQL Security Manager 398
SQL Server Messages (SMS) 333
SQL Server Web Assistant - File Options 405
SQL Server Web Assistant - Formatting 406
SQL Server Web Assistant - Login 402

SQL Server Web Assistant - Query 403
SQL Server Web Assistant - Scheduling 404
SQL Service Manager 408
Windows NT Server Setup network access 87
Windows NT Server Setup Wizard welcome 77
Windows NT Setup 86
WINS Manager 176
WINNT.EXE file 53–54
WINNT32.EXE file 53–54
WINS (Windows Internet Name Service) 36, 175–184
configuration 175–184
proxy server 680
TCP/IP Services configuration 147–149
WINS database 181–183
WINS Manager 175–184
accessing 175
adding servers 177
options 176–184
program window 176
replication partners 179–180
server configuration 178–184
WINS Manager Configuration dialog box 178
WINS Manager database display dialog box 181
WINS Manager Detailed Information dialog box 177
WINS Manager Preferences dialog box 183
WINS Manager Pull Partner Properties dialog box 180
WINS Manager Push Partner Properties dialog box 180
WINS Manager Replication Partners dialog box 179
WINS Manager Static Mappings dialog box 182
WINS servers
configuration 178–184
displaying information about 177
WinZip program 587
wired networks 87
wireless networks, system security 537
Wizards
Add Printer 516–533
Migration 355–356
New Phonebook Entry 204–210
Server 34
WordPad program 645–646
Work Queues object counters 289–290
working capital 670
worksheets, Microsoft Exchange installation planning 340–341
workspace file, Performance Monitor 266
Workstation
client Remote Boot Service non-support 111
configuring 110
workstations
automatic configuration 116–120
diskless 42, 110–116
manual configuration 120–123
WORM (Write Once, Read Many), backup hardware 586
WWW (World Wide Web) 467
WWW Server (IIS)
database examples 471–472
HTML Page creation 475–479
HTML sample sheets 474–475
long filename support 469
overview 468–469
programming examples 473–474
reliability 489–490
SampSite HTML 470–471
site setup 469
SSL (Secure Sockets Layer) 479–489
Web page samples 470
WWW service (IIS)
anonymous connections (IIS) 426–428
default document 441–442
directory browsing 442
directory properties 437
password authentication (IIS) 430
wwwroot folder (IIS) 435
WYSIWYG (What You See Is What You Get) 474

Macromedia Director 5 Power Toolkit

$49.95, 800 pages, illustrated, part #: 289-5

Macromedia Director 5 Power Toolkit views the industry's hottest multimedia authoring environment from the inside out. Features tools, tips and professional tricks for producing power-packed projects for CD-ROM and Internet distribution. Dozens of exercises detail the principles behind successful multimedia presentations and the steps to achieve professional results. The companion CD-ROM includes utilities, sample presentations, animations, scripts and files.

Shockwave!

$49.95, 400 pages, illustrated, part #: 441-3

Breathe new life into your web pages with Macromedia Shockwave. Ventana's *Shockwave!* teaches you how to enliven and animate your Web sites with online movies. Beginning with step-by-step exercises and examples, and ending with in-depth excursions into the use of Shockwave Lingo extensions, *Shockwave!* is a must-buy for both novices and experienced Director developers. Plus, tap into current Macromedia resources on the Internet with Ventana's *Online Companion*. The companion CD-ROM includes the Shockwave player plug-in, sample Director movies and tutorials, and much more!

$49.99, 700 pages, illustrated, part #: 463-4

Master the Lingo of Macromedia Director's scripting language for adding interactivity to presentations. Covers beginning scripts to advanced techniques, including creating movies for the Web and problem solving. The companion CD-ROM features demo movies of all scripts in the book, plus numerous examples, a searchable database of problems and solutions, and much more!

Web Favorites

Voodoo Windows 95

$24.95, 504 pages, illustrated, part #: 145-7

Users will need voodoo to make the move to Windows 95! Nelson is back with more secrets, shortcuts and spells than ever. Scores of tips—many never before published—on installing, customizing, editing, printing, virtual memory, Internet connections and much more. Organized by task for easy reference. The companion disk contains shareware utilities, fonts and magic!

The Windows 95 Book

$39.95, 1232 pages, illustrated, part #: 154-6

The anxiously awaited revamp of Windows means new working styles for PC users. This new handbook offers an insider's look at the all-new interface–arming users with tips and techniques for file management, desktop design, optimizing and more. A must-have for a prosperous '95! The companion CD-ROM features tutorials, demos, previous and online help plus utilities, screensavers, wallpaper and sounds.

Windows 95 Power Toolkit

$49.95, 744 pages, illustrated, part #: 319-0

If Windows 95 includes everything but the kitchen sink, get ready to get your hands wet! Maximize the customizing capabilities of Windows 95 with ready-to-use tools, applications and tutorials, including a guide to VBA. CD-ROM: the complete toolkit, plus additional graphics, sounds and applications.Online Companion: updated versions of software, hyper-linked listings and links to helpful resources on the Internet.

All technical support for this product is available from Ventana.
The technical support office is open from 8:00 A.M. to 6:00 P.M. (EST) Monday through Friday and can be reached via the following methods:

World Wide Web: http://www.netscapepress.com/support

E–mail: help@vmedia.com

Phone: (919) 544-9404 extension 81

FAX: (919) 544-9472

America Online: keyword **Ventana**